D1131430

OUTLAW TERRITORY™

VOLUME 1

Image Comics
Berkeley, California
2009

MICHAEL WOODS
Editor

GREG RUTH
Cover Art

THOMAS MAUER
Book Design

Outlaw Territory Presented by
RIOT CAFÉ

Image Comics, Inc.

Robert Kirkman - *Chief Operating Officer*
Erik Larsen - *Chief Financial Officer*
Todd McFarlane - *President*
Marc Silvestri - *Chief Executive Officer*
Jim Valentino - *Vice-President*

ericstephenson - *Publisher*
Joe Keatinge - *PR & Marketing Coordinator*
Branwyn Bigglestone - *Accounts Manager*
Sarah deLaine - *Administrative Assistant*
Tyler Shainline - *Traffic Manager*
Allen Hui - *Production Manager*
Drew Gill - *Production Artist*
Jonathan Chan - *Production Artist*
Monica Howard - *Production Artist*

www.imagecomics.com

International Rights Representative:

Christine Jensen (christine@gfloystudio.com)

OUTLAW TERRITORY, VOL. 1
ISBN: 978-1-60706-004-8
First Printing

Published by Image Comics, Inc. Office of publication:
2134 Allston Way, 2nd Floor, Berkeley, CA 94704. Copyright © 2009
Michael Woods. OUTLAW TERRITORY™ and its logo are trademarks
of Michael Woods. All stories and character likenesses are trademarks
of their respective creators, unless otherwise noted.

PRINTED IN SOUTH KOREA

006
DANIEL 5:27

Story as told in written word and drawn pictures by **Moritat**

Claim of ownership by copyright to Justin Norman.

013
BALLAD OF A BAD MAN

Story as told in written word by **Joe Kelly**

Story as illustrated in pencil, ink and color by **Max Fiumara**

Story as lettered by **Thomas Mauer**

Claim of ownership by copyright to Joe Kelly & Max Fiumara.

021
SUNDOWN

Story as told in written word by **Joshua Ortega**

Story as illustrated in pencil and ink by **Trevor Goring**

Pictures put to color by **Dean White**

Story as lettered by **Thomas Mauer**

Claim of ownership by copyright to Joshua Ortega & Trevor Goring.

029
DISPATCH

Story as told in written word by **Shay**

Story as illustrated in pencil and ink by **Dean Kotz**

Pictures put to color by **Ramiro Díaz Legaspe**

Story as lettered by **Thomas Mauer**

Claim of ownership by copyright to Chas Shay & Dean Kotz.

037
AMERICAN DREAM

Story as told in written word by **Jose L. Torres**

Story as illustrated in pencil, ink and color by **Jorge Molina Manzanero**

Story as lettered by **Thomas Mauer**

Claim of ownership by copyright to Jose L. Torres & Jorge Molina Manzanero.

045
THE FIRST CAR IN MEXICO

Story as told in written word by **Ivan Brandon**

Story as illustrated in pencil and ink by **Andy Macdonald**

Pictures put to color by **Daniel Heard**

Story as lettered by **Kristyn Ferretti**

Claim of ownership by copyright to Ivan Brandon & Andy Macdonald.

051
THE MOST CIVILIZED ESTABLISHMENT FROM OCEAN TO OCEAN

Story as told in written word by **James Patrick**

Story as illustrated in pencil and ink by **Khoi Pham**

Pictures put to color by **Jeremy Colwell**

Story as lettered by **Thomas Mauer**

Claim of ownership by copyright to James Patrick & Khoi Pham.

059
AHIGA

Story as told in written word by **Christian Beranek**

Story as illustrated in pencil, ink and color by **Koray Kuranel**

Story as lettered by **Thomas Mauer**

Claim of ownership by copyright to Christian Beranek & Koray Kuranel.

067
INCIDENT OVER THIRTY-SIX DAYS IN THE COLORADO ROCKIES

Story as told in written word by **Joshua Hale Fialkov**

Story as illustrated in pencil, ink and color by **Christie Tseng**

Story as lettered by **Thomas Mauer**

Claim of ownership by copyright to Joshua Hale Fialkov & Christie Tseng.

075
RIO CHINO

Story as told in written word by **Greg Pak**

Story as illustrated in pencil, ink and color by **Ian Kim**

Story as lettered by **Thomas Mauer**

Claim of ownership by copyright to Pak Man Productions.

163

THEM WHAT COMES

Story as told in written word and drawn pictures by **mpMann**

Story as lettered by **Thomas Mauer**

Claim of ownership by copyright to mpMann.

171

CRAFTSMANSHIP

Story as told in written word by **Frank Beaton**

Story as illustrated in pencil, ink and color by **Melika Acar**

Story as lettered by **Thomas Mauer**

Claim of ownership by copyright to Frank Beaton & Melike Acar.

179

WE NEVER SLEEP

Story as told in written word by **Nemo Woodbrine**

Story as illustrated in pencil, ink and color by **Yeray Gil Hernandez**

Story as lettered by **Thomas Mauer**

Claim of ownership by copyright to Nemo Woodbrine & Yeray Gil Hernandez.

185

THE BALLAD OF SID GRENADINE

Story as told in written word by **Josh Wagner**

Story as illustrated in pencil, ink and color by **Joiton**

Story as lettered by **Thomas Mauer**

Claim of ownership by copyright to Josh Wagner & Joiton.

191

THE MORE THINGS CHANGE

Story as told in written word by **Skipper Martin**

Story as illustrated in pencil and ink by **Christopher Provencher**

Pictures put to color by **Ellen Everett**

Story as lettered by **Thomas Mauer**

Claim of ownership by copyright to Skipper Martin & Christopher Provencher.

199

WORKING ON CHRISTMAS

Story as told in written word by **Steve Orlando**

Story as illustrated in pencil and ink by **Tyler Niccum**

Pictures put to color by **Matt Razzano**

Story as lettered by **Thomas Mauer**

Claim of ownership by copyright to Steve Orlando & Tyler Niccum.

209

HELL HATH NO FURY

Story as told in written word by **Noble Larimer**

Story as illustrated in pencil and ink by **Jason Cheeseman-Meyer**

Pictures put to color by **John Forcucci**

Story as lettered by **Thomas Mauer**

Claim of ownership by copyright to Noble Larimer & Jason Cheeseman-Meyer.

217

WE MEET AT TWELVE

Story as told in written word by **P.J. Kryfko**

Story as illustrated in pencil and ink by **William Simpson**

Pictures put to color by **Mark Murphy**

Story as lettered by **Thomas Mauer**

Claim of ownership by copyright to P.J. Kryfko & William Simpson.

225

ASS MEAT

Story as told in written word and drawn pictures by **Simon Fraser**

Story as lettered by **Thomas Mauer**

Claim of ownership by copyright to Simon Fraser.

230

MEMORIES

Story as told in written word by **Michael Woods**

Story as illustrated in pencil, ink and color by **Chad Sell**

Story as lettered by **Thomas Mauer**

Claim of ownership by copyright to Michael Woods & Chad Sell.

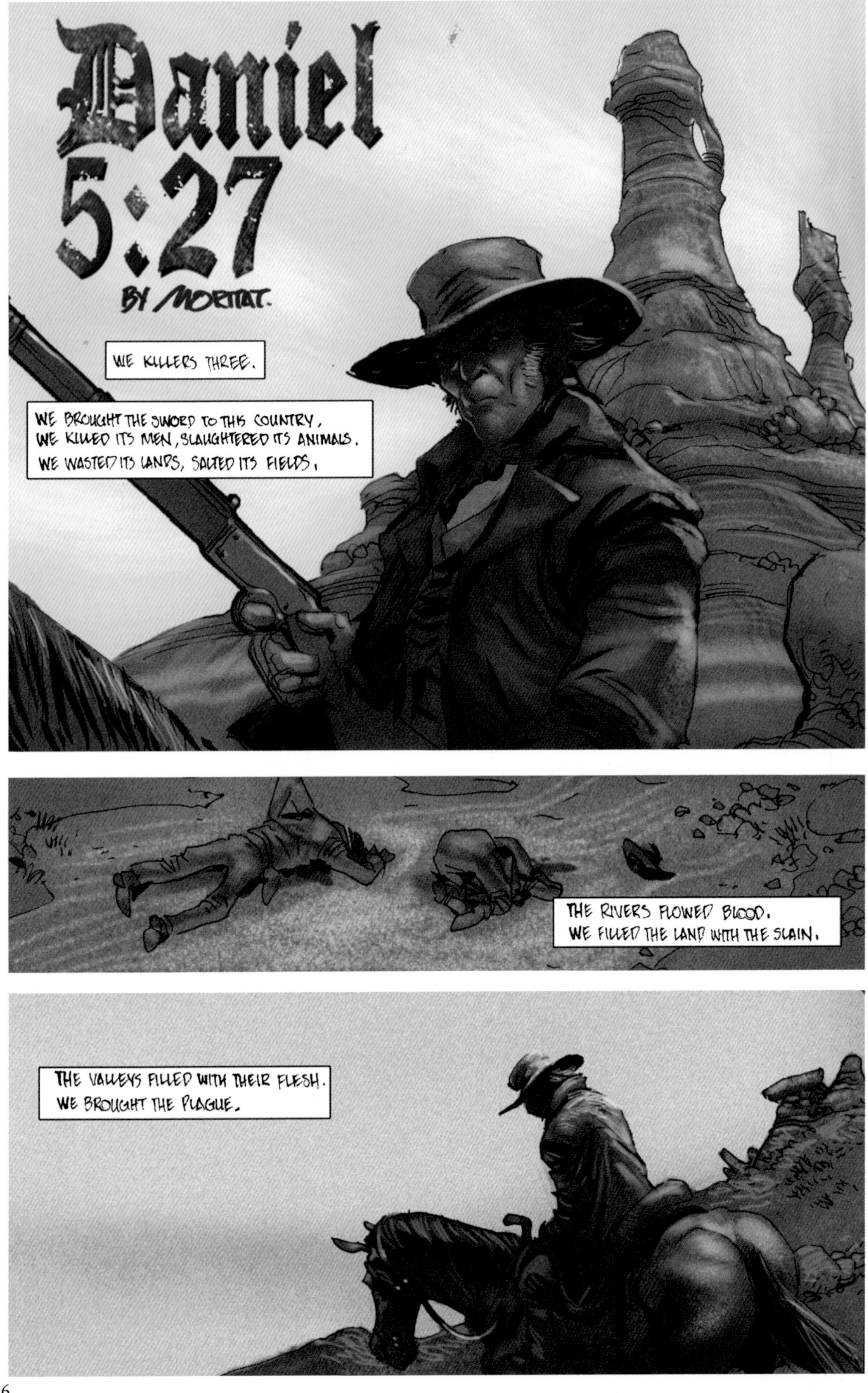
Daniel 5:27
BY MORITAT.
WE KILLERS THREE.
WE BROUGHT THE SWORD TO THIS COUNTRY, WE KILLED ITS MEN, SLAUGHTERED ITS ANIMALS. WE WASTED ITS LANDS, SALTED ITS FIELDS,
THE RIVERS FLOWED BLOOD. WE FILLED THE LAND WITH THE SLAIN.
THE VALLEYS FILLED WITH THEIR FLESH. WE BROUGHT THE PLAGUE.

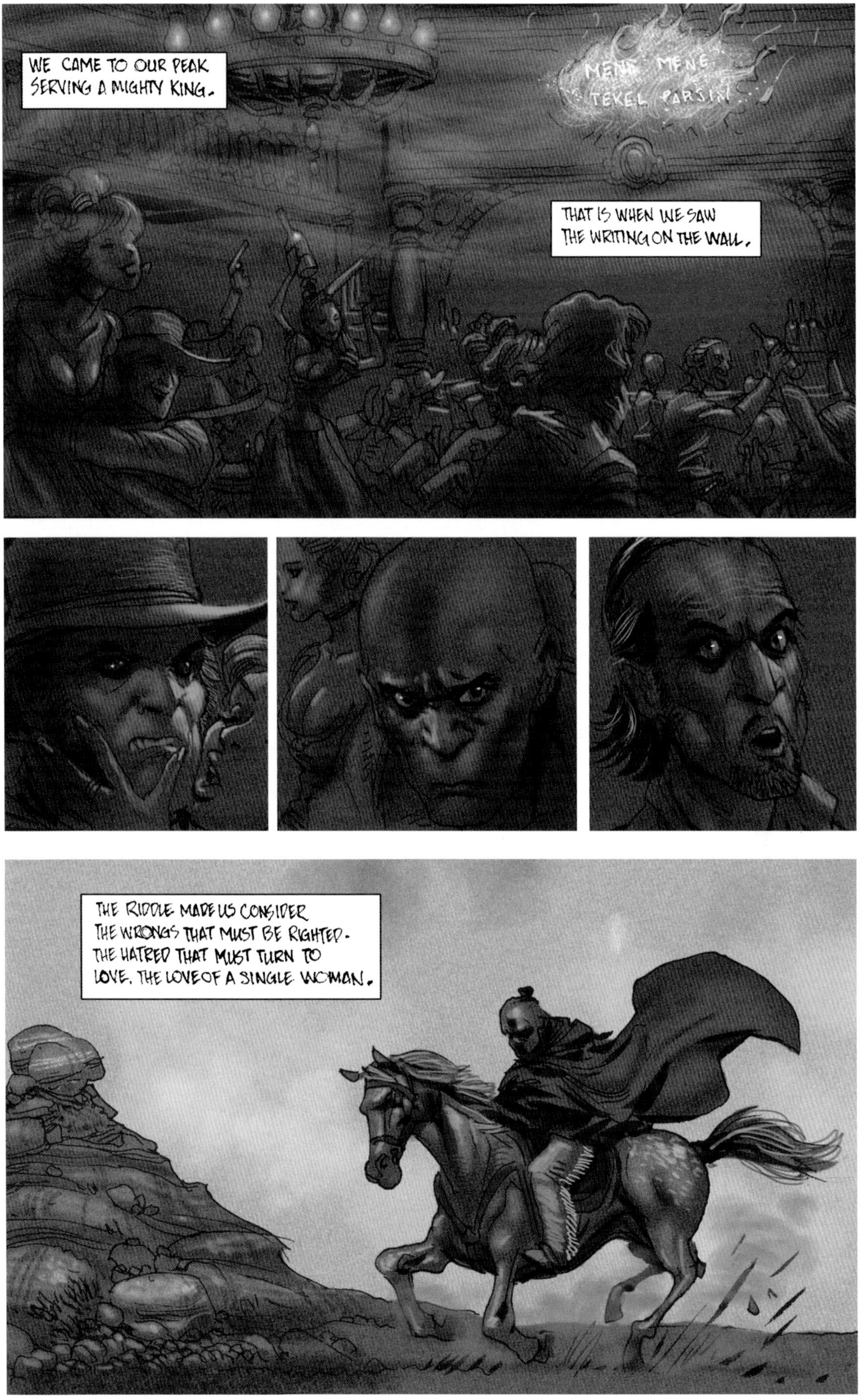
WE CAME TO OUR PEAK SERVING A MIGHTY KING.
MENE MENE TEKEL PARSIN
THAT IS WHEN WE SAW THE WRITING ON THE WALL.
THE RIDDLE MADE US CONSIDER THE WRONGS THAT MUST BE RIGHTED. THE HATRED THAT MUST TURN TO LOVE. THE LOVE OF A SINGLE WOMAN.

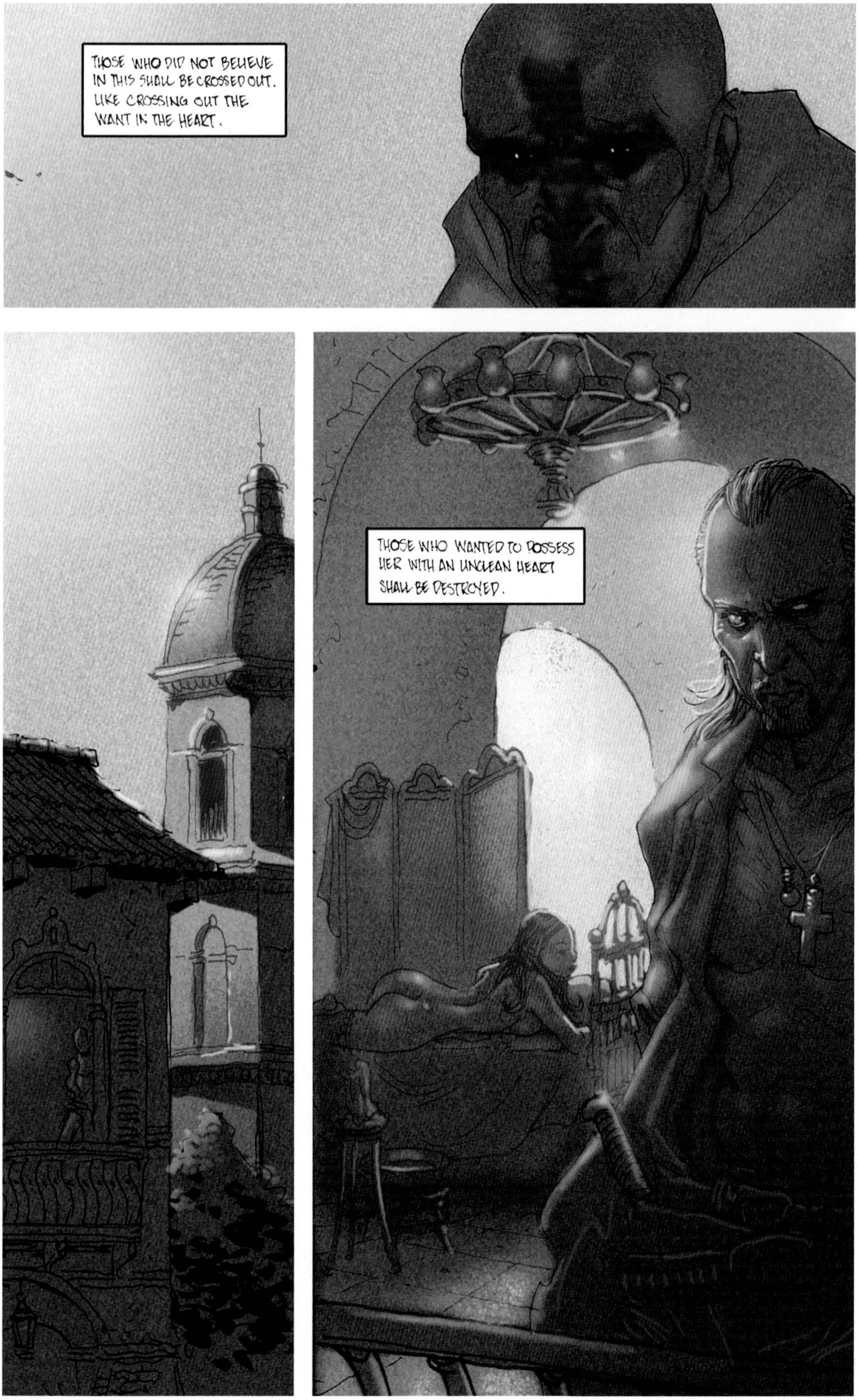
THOSE WHO DID NOT BELIEVE IN THIS SHALL BE CROSSED OUT. LIKE CROSSING OUT THE WANT IN THE HEART.
THOSE WHO WANTED TO POSSESS HER WITH AN UNCLEAN HEART SHALL BE DESTROYED.

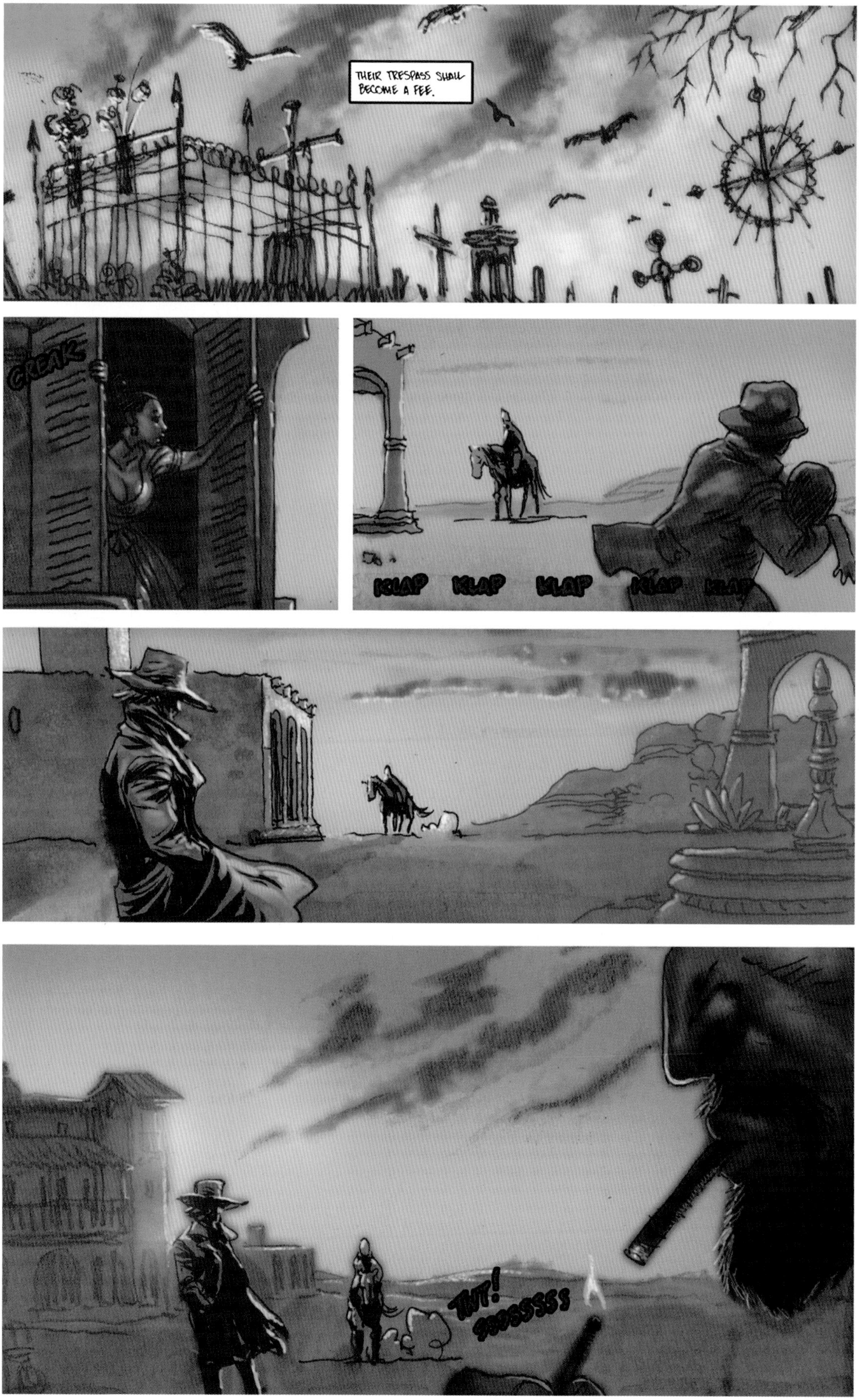
THEIR TRESPASS SHALL BECOME A FEE.
CREAK
KLAP
KLAP
KLAP
KLAP
TNT!

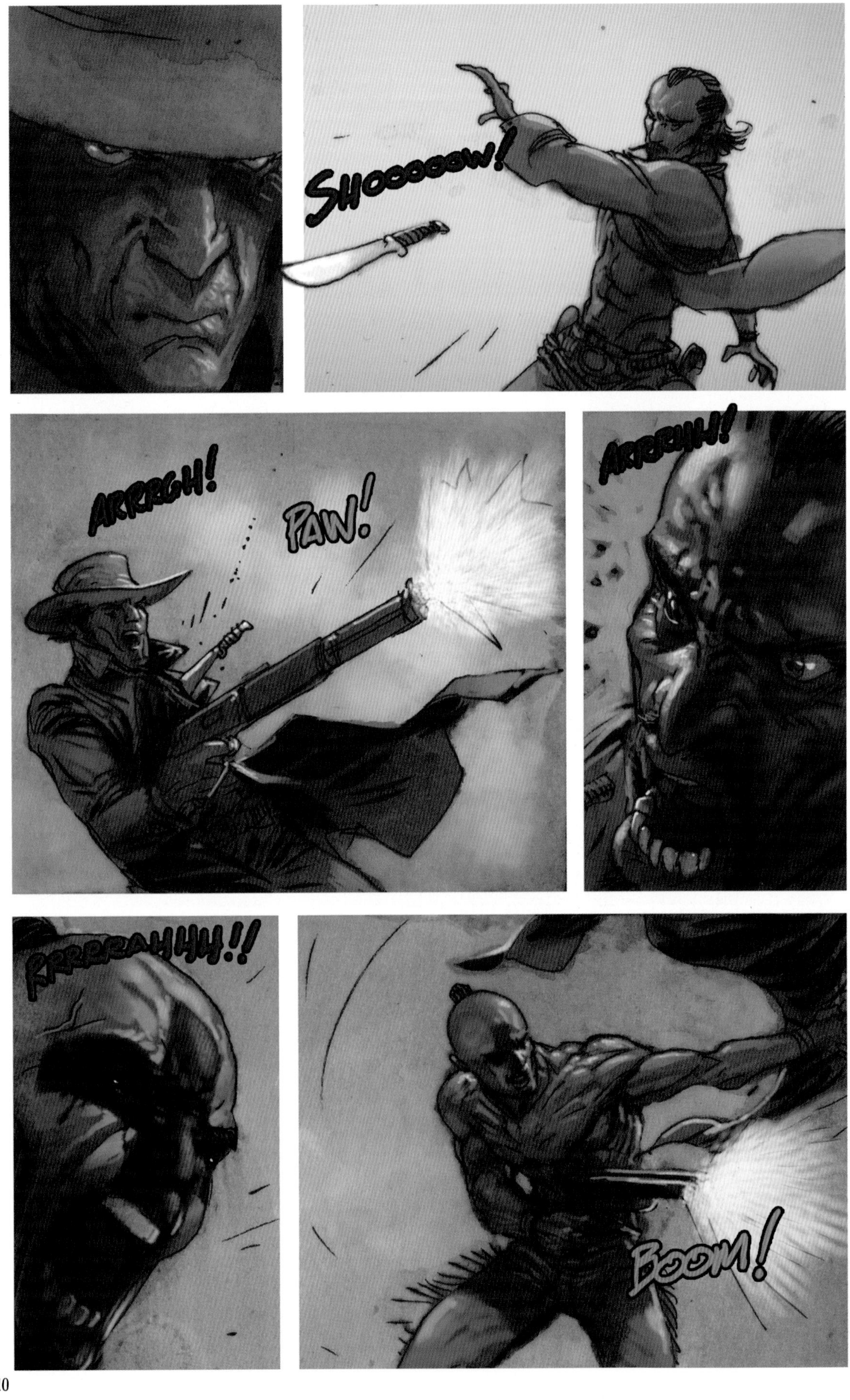
SHOOOOOW!
ARRRGH!
PAW!
ARRRGHH!
RRRRRAHHH!!
BOOM!

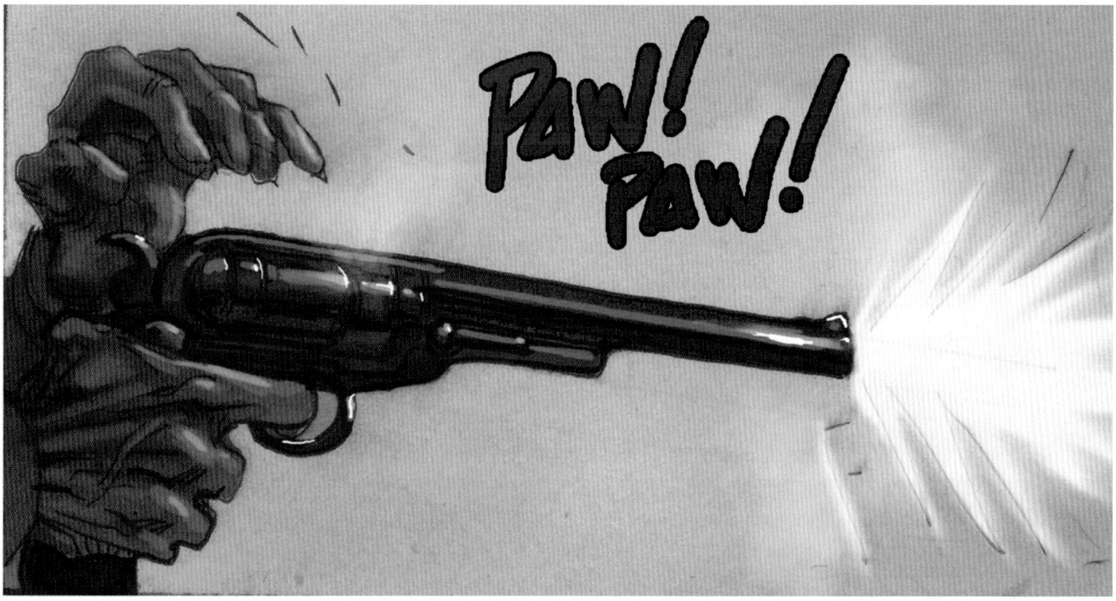
PAW! PAW!

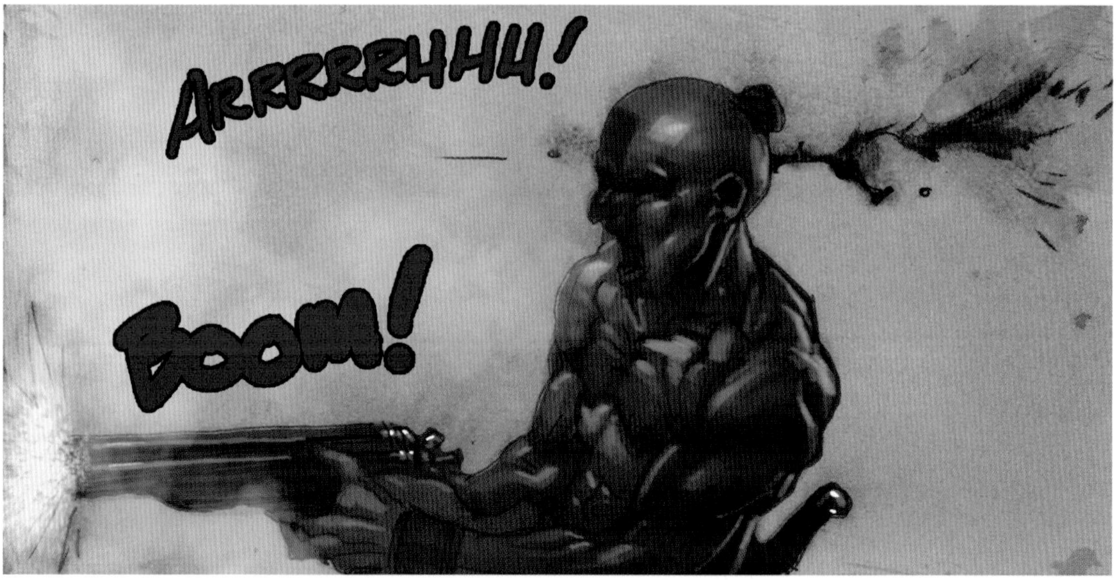
ARRRRHHH!
BOOM!

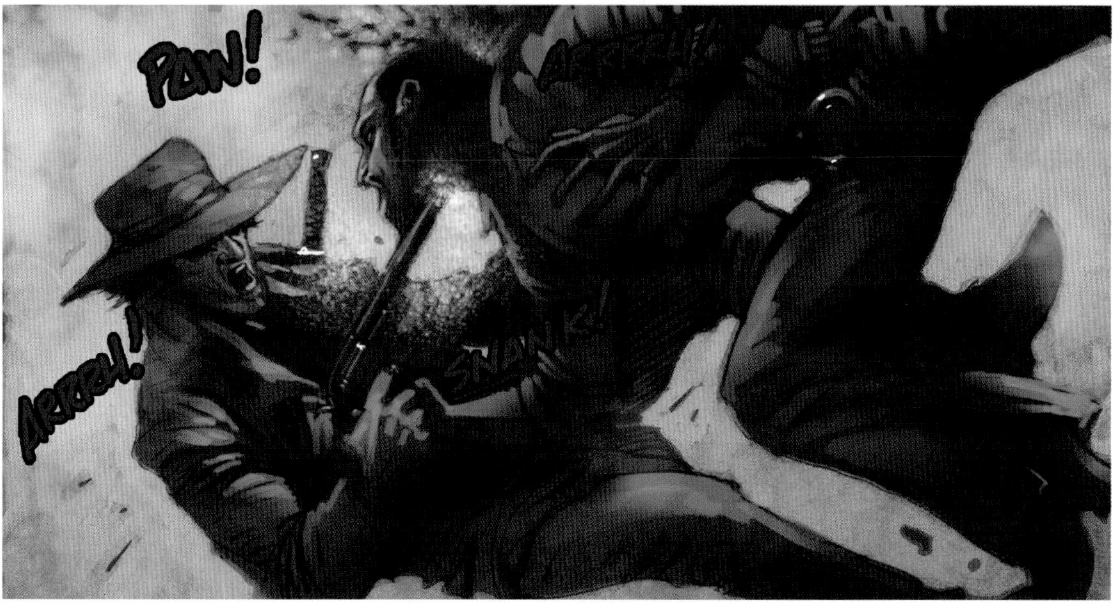
PAW!
ARRRH!

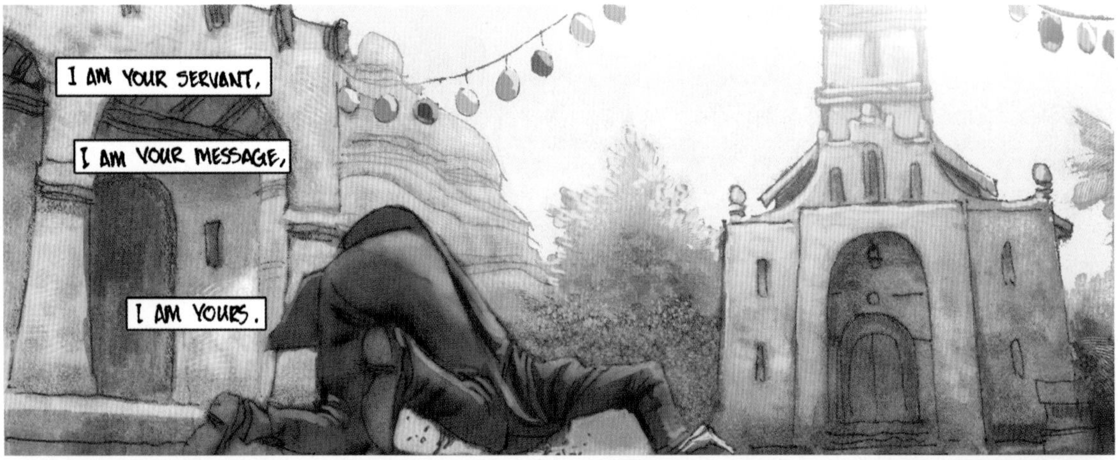
I AM YOUR SERVANT,
I AM YOUR MESSAGE,
I AM YOURS.

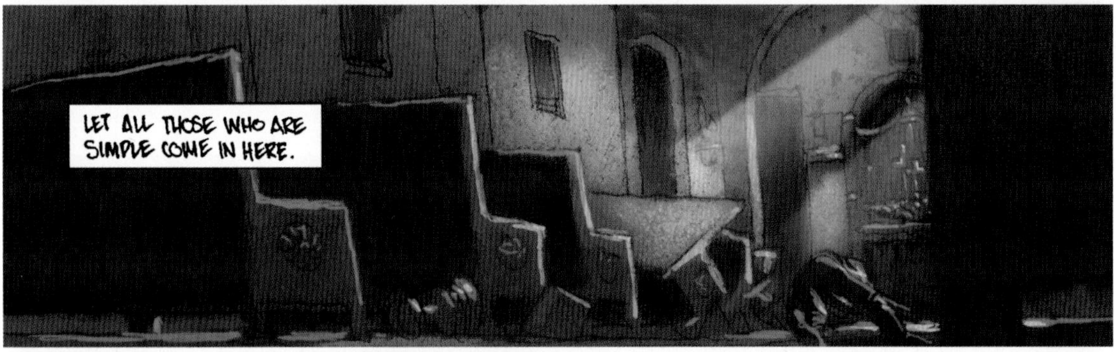
LET ALL THOSE WHO ARE SIMPLE COME IN HERE.

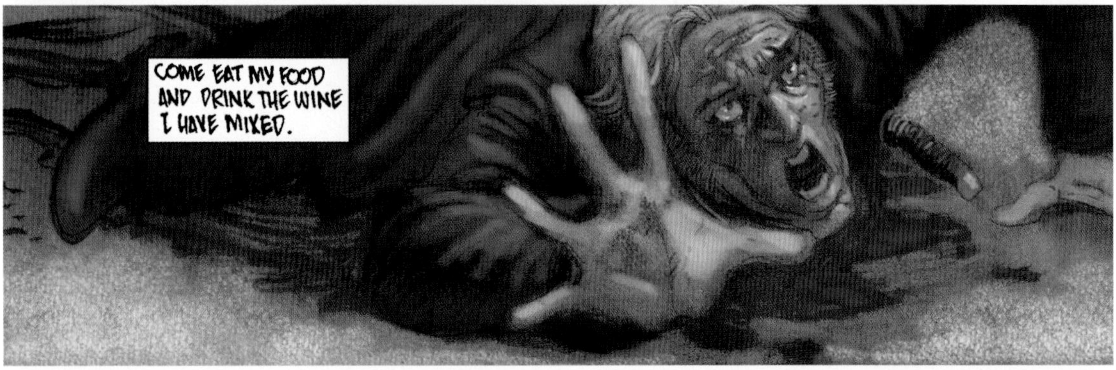
COME EAT MY FOOD AND DRINK THE WINE I HAVE MIXED.

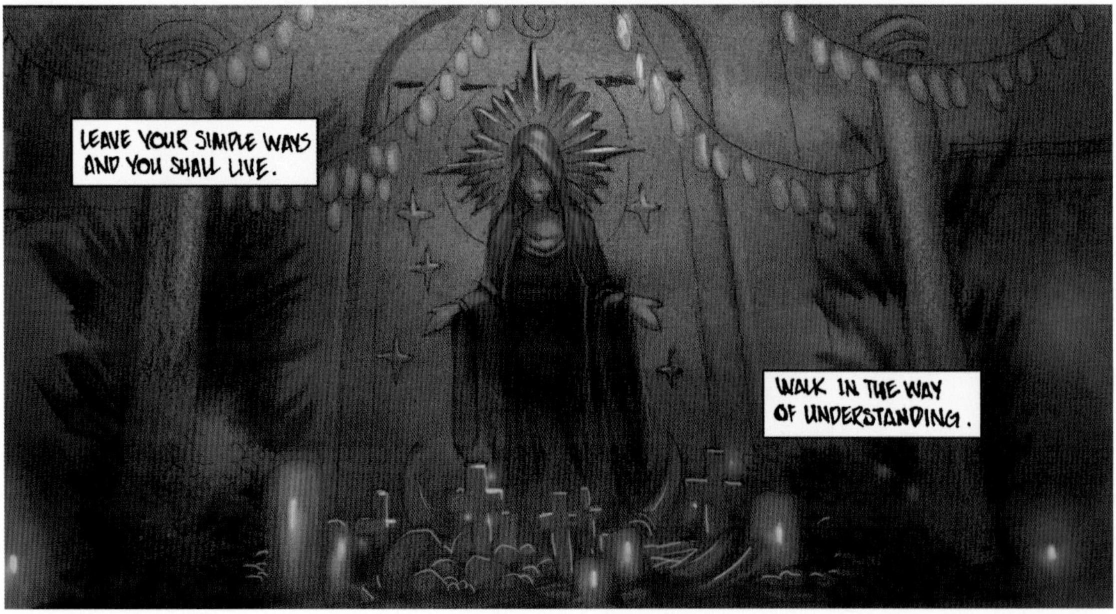
LEAVE YOUR SIMPLE WAYS AND YOU SHALL LIVE.
WALK IN THE WAY OF UNDERSTANDING.

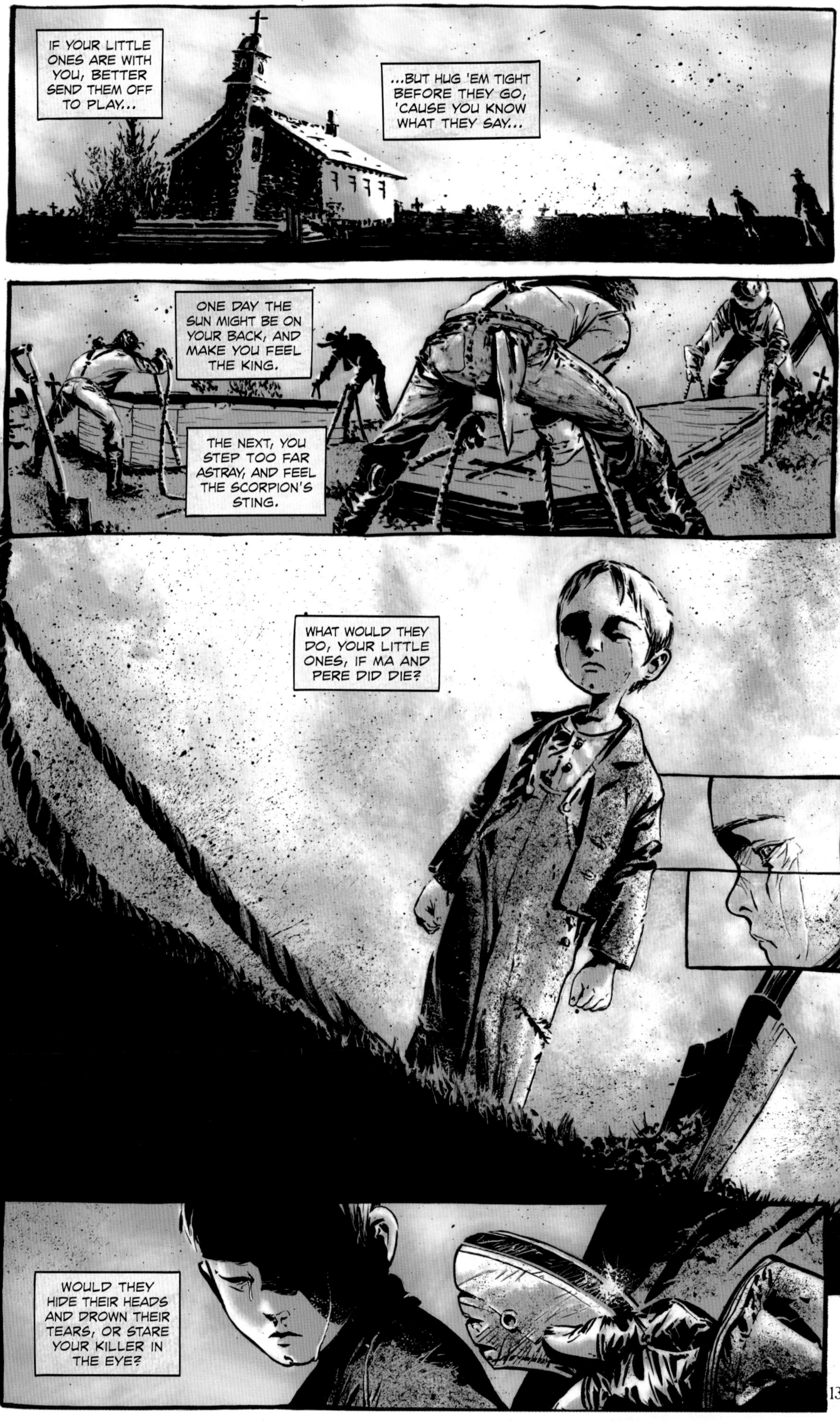

IF YOUR LITTLE ONES ARE WITH YOU, BETTER SEND THEM OFF TO PLAY...
...BUT HUG 'EM TIGHT BEFORE THEY GO, 'CAUSE YOU KNOW WHAT THEY SAY...
ONE DAY THE SUN MIGHT BE ON YOUR BACK, AND MAKE YOU FEEL THE KING.
THE NEXT, YOU STEP TOO FAR ASTRAY, AND FEEL THE SCORPION'S STING.
WHAT WOULD THEY DO, YOUR LITTLE ONES, IF MA AND PERE DID DIE?
WOULD THEY HIDE THEIR HEADS AND DROWN THEIR TEARS, OR STARE YOUR KILLER IN THE EYE?

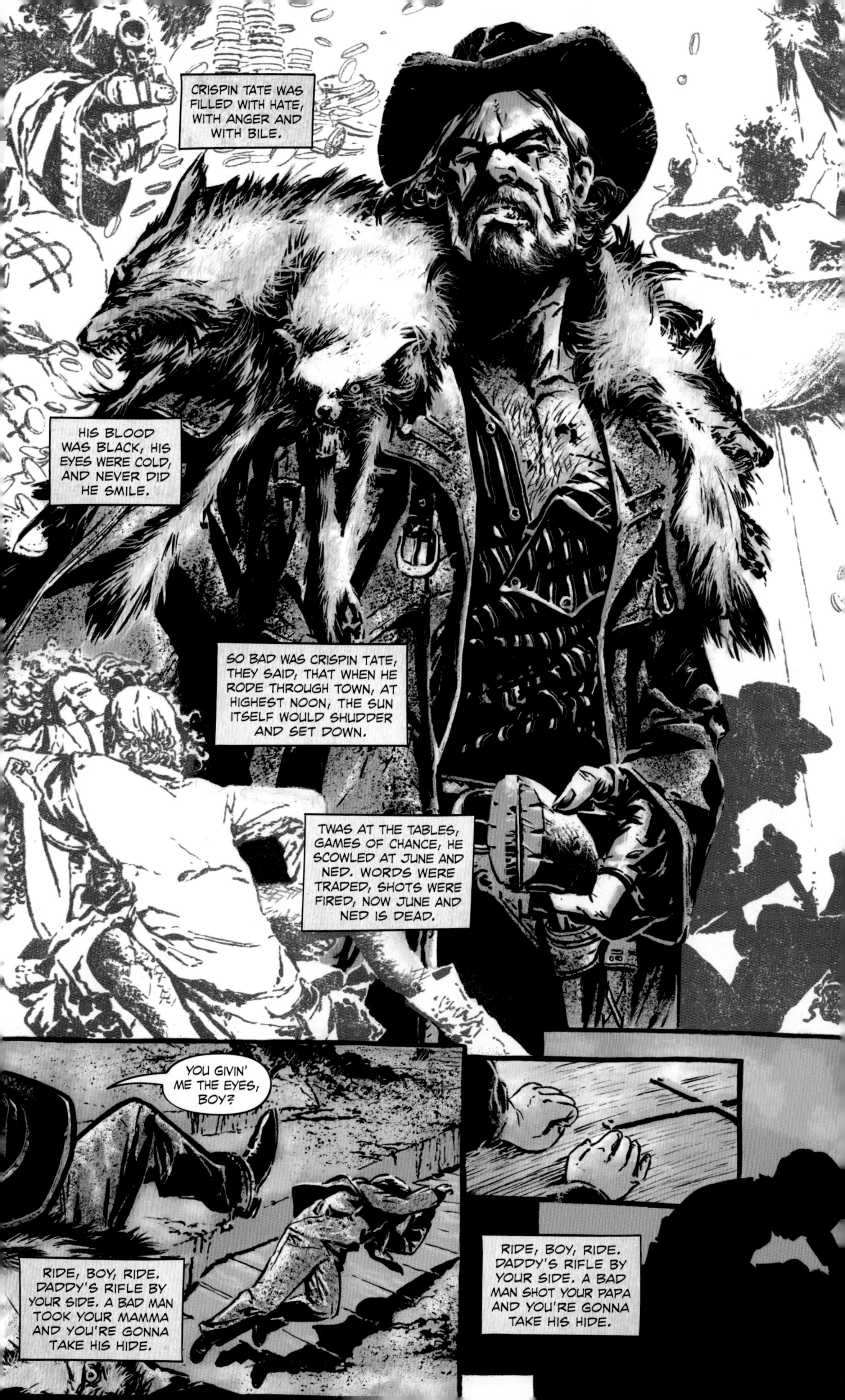
CRISPIN TATE WAS FILLED WITH HATE, WITH ANGER AND WITH BILE.
HIS BLOOD WAS BLACK, HIS EYES WERE COLD, AND NEVER DID HE SMILE.
SO BAD WAS CRISPIN TATE, THEY SAID, THAT WHEN HE RODE THROUGH TOWN, AT HIGHEST NOON, THE SUN ITSELF WOULD SHUDDER AND SET DOWN.
TWAS AT THE TABLES, GAMES OF CHANCE, HE SCOWLED AT JUNE AND NED. WORDS WERE TRADED, SHOTS WERE FIRED, NOW JUNE AND NED IS DEAD.
YOU GIVIN' ME THE EYES, BOY?
RIDE, BOY, RIDE. DADDY'S RIFLE BY YOUR SIDE. A BAD MAN TOOK YOUR MAMMA AND YOU'RE GONNA TAKE HIS HIDE.
RIDE, BOY, RIDE. DADDY'S RIFLE BY YOUR SIDE. A BAD MAN SHOT YOUR PAPA AND YOU'RE GONNA TAKE HIS HIDE.

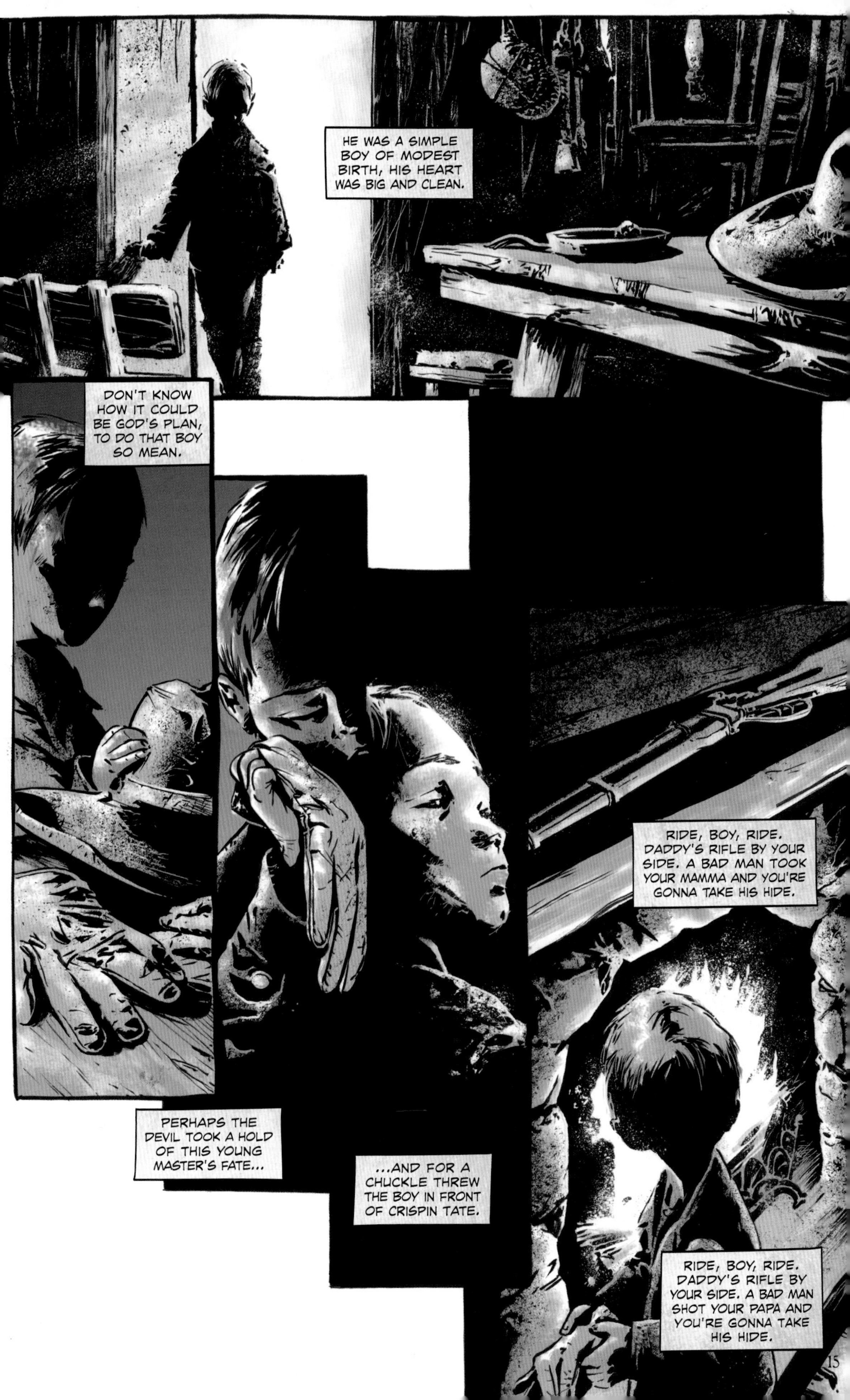
HE WAS A SIMPLE BOY OF MODEST BIRTH, HIS HEART WAS BIG AND CLEAN.
DON'T KNOW HOW IT COULD BE GOD'S PLAN, TO DO THAT BOY SO MEAN.
RIDE, BOY, RIDE. DADDY'S RIFLE BY YOUR SIDE. A BAD MAN TOOK YOUR MAMMA AND YOU'RE GONNA TAKE HIS HIDE.
PERHAPS THE DEVIL TOOK A HOLD OF THIS YOUNG MASTER'S FATE...
...AND FOR A CHUCKLE THREW THE BOY IN FRONT OF CRISPIN TATE.
RIDE, BOY, RIDE. DADDY'S RIFLE BY YOUR SIDE. A BAD MAN SHOT YOUR PAPA AND YOU'RE GONNA TAKE HIS HIDE.

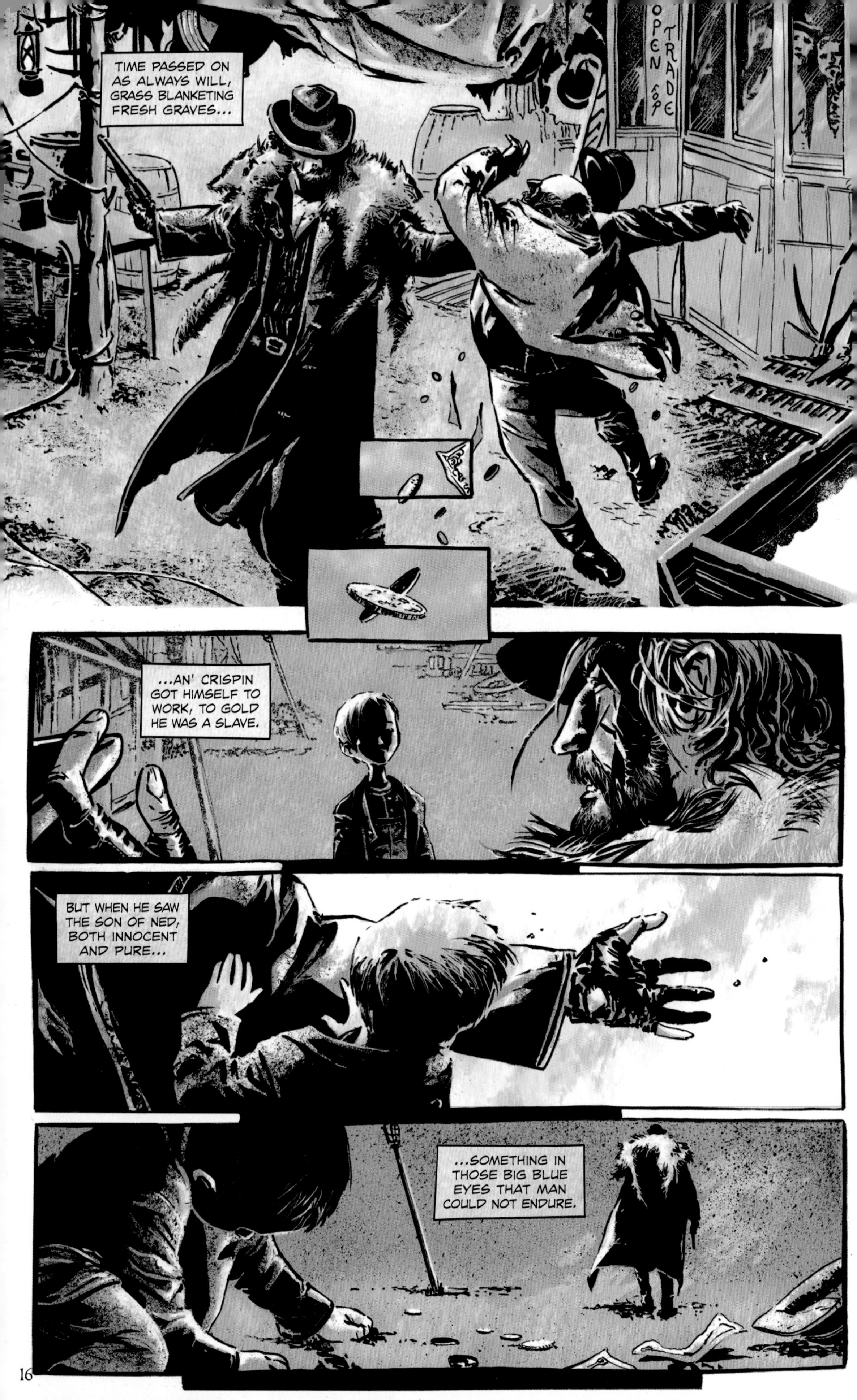
TIME PASSED ON AS ALWAYS WILL, GRASS BLANKETING FRESH GRAVES...
OPEN FOR TRADE
...AN' CRISPIN GOT HIMSELF TO WORK; TO GOLD HE WAS A SLAVE.
BUT WHEN HE SAW THE SON OF NED, BOTH INNOCENT AND PURE...
...SOMETHING IN THOSE BIG BLUE EYES THAT MAN COULD NOT ENDURE.

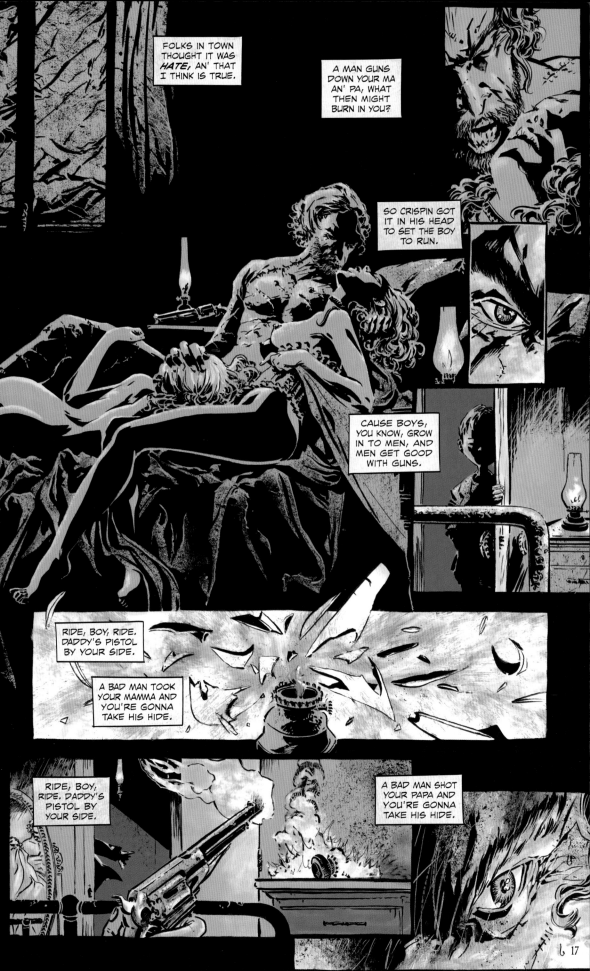

FOLKS IN TOWN THOUGHT IT WAS *HATE*, AN' THAT I THINK IS TRUE.

A MAN GUNS DOWN YOUR MA AN' PA, WHAT THEN MIGHT BURN IN YOU?

SO CRISPIN GOT IT IN HIS HEAD TO SET THE BOY TO RUN.

CAUSE BOYS, YOU KNOW, GROW IN TO MEN, AND MEN GET GOOD WITH GUNS.

RIDE, BOY, RIDE. DADDY'S PISTOL BY YOUR SIDE.

A BAD MAN TOOK YOUR MAMMA AND YOU'RE GONNA TAKE HIS HIDE.

RIDE, BOY, RIDE. DADDY'S PISTOL BY YOUR SIDE.

A BAD MAN SHOT YOUR PAPA AND YOU'RE GONNA TAKE HIS HIDE.

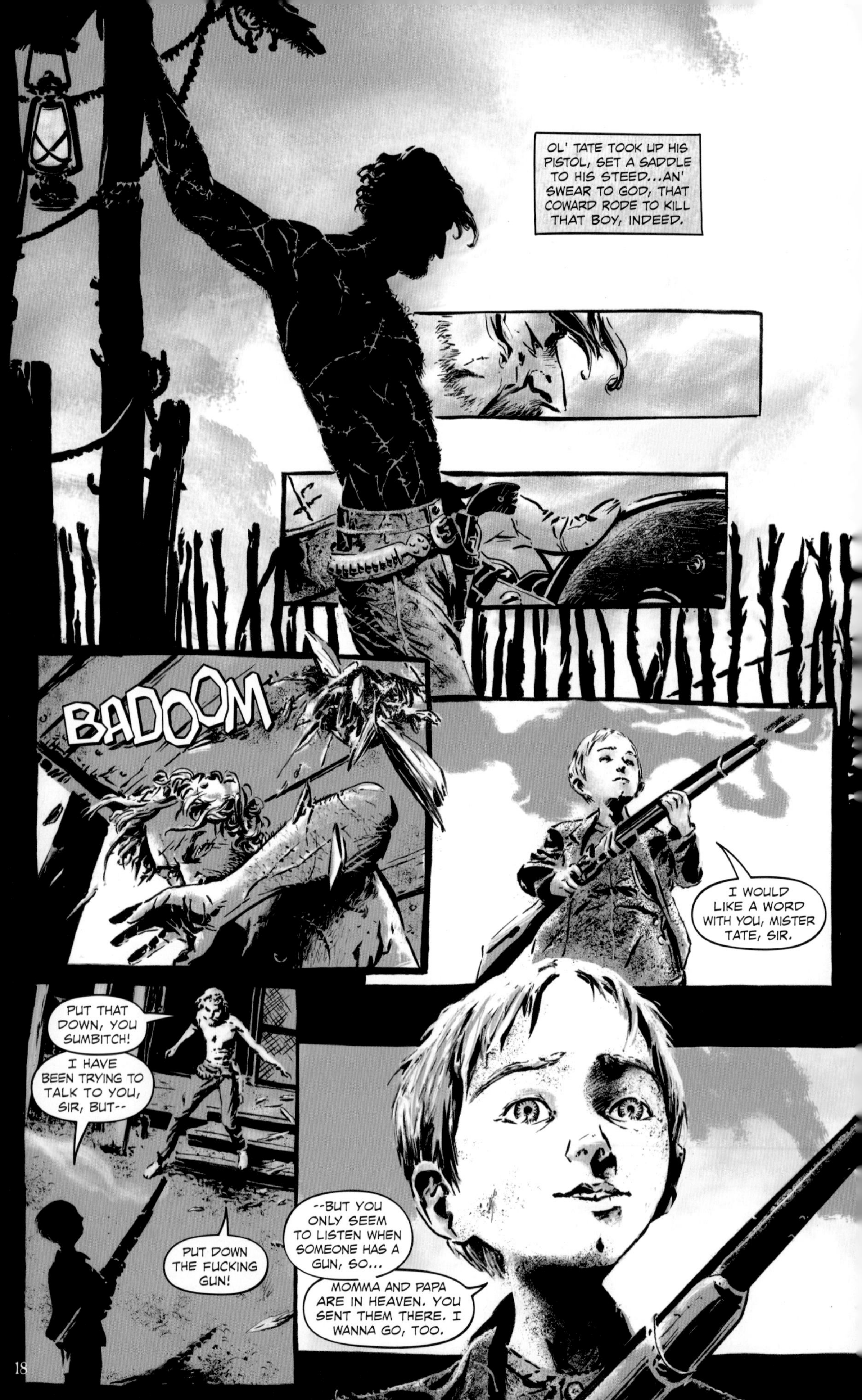
OL' TATE TOOK UP HIS PISTOL, SET A SADDLE TO HIS STEED...AN' SWEAR TO GOD, THAT COWARD RODE TO KILL THAT BOY, INDEED.
BADOOM
I WOULD LIKE A WORD WITH YOU, MISTER TATE, SIR.
PUT THAT DOWN, YOU SUMBITCH!
I HAVE BEEN TRYING TO TALK TO YOU, SIR, BUT--
PUT DOWN THE FUCKING GUN!
--BUT YOU ONLY SEEM TO LISTEN WHEN SOMEONE HAS A GUN, SO...
MOMMA AND PAPA ARE IN HEAVEN. YOU SENT THEM THERE. I WANNA GO, TOO.

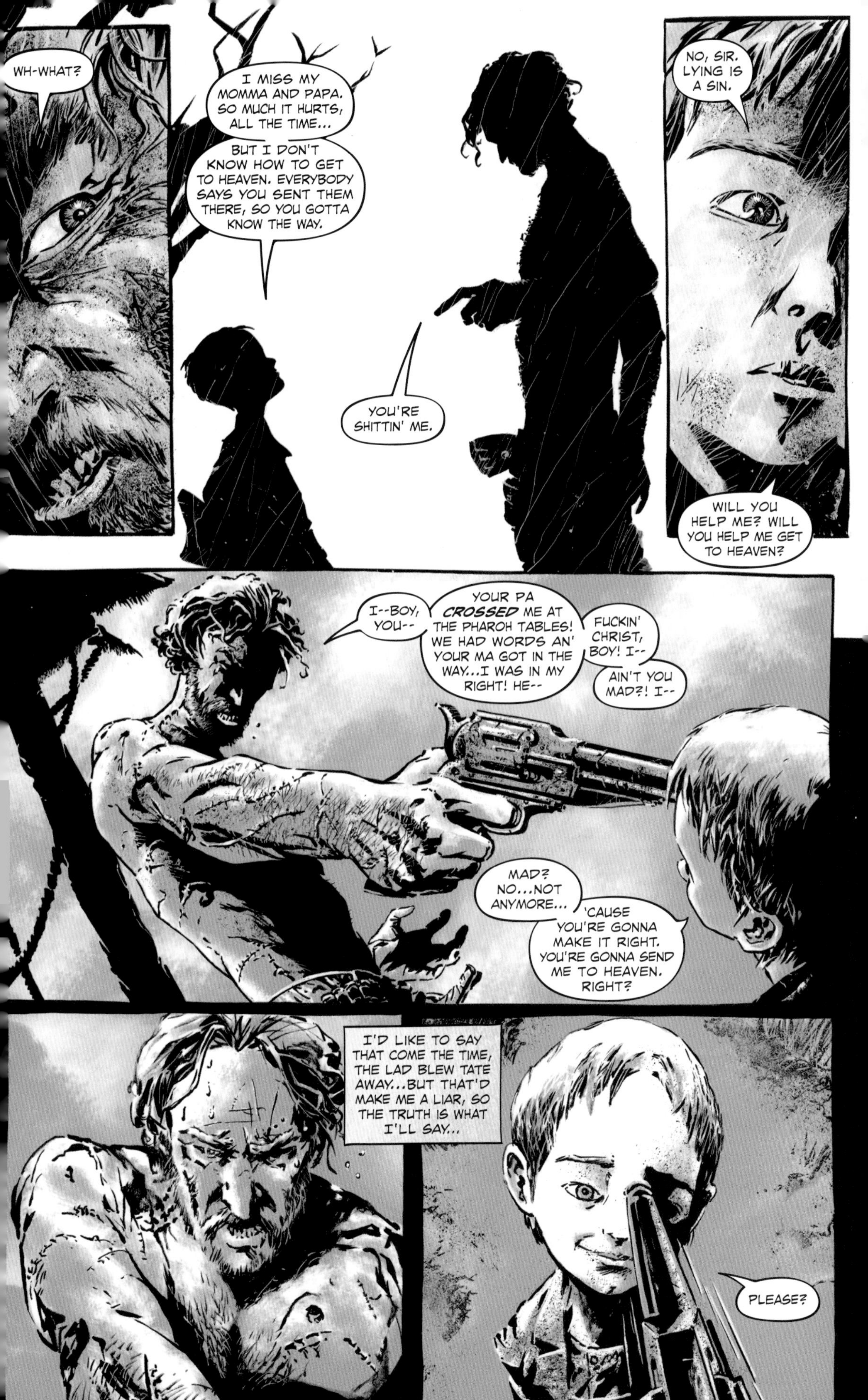
WH-WHAT?
I MISS MY MOMMA AND PAPA. SO MUCH IT HURTS, ALL THE TIME...
BUT I DON'T KNOW HOW TO GET TO HEAVEN. EVERYBODY SAYS YOU SENT THEM THERE, SO YOU GOTTA KNOW THE WAY.
YOU'RE SHITTIN' ME.
NO, SIR. LYING IS A SIN.
WILL YOU HELP ME? WILL YOU HELP ME GET TO HEAVEN?
I--BOY, YOU--
YOUR PA CROSSED ME AT THE PHAROH TABLES! WE HAD WORDS AN' YOUR MA GOT IN THE WAY...I WAS IN MY RIGHT! HE--
FUCKIN' CHRIST, BOY! I--
AIN'T YOU MAD?! I--
MAD? NO...NOT ANYMORE...
'CAUSE YOU'RE GONNA MAKE IT RIGHT. YOU'RE GONNA SEND ME TO HEAVEN. RIGHT?
I'D LIKE TO SAY THAT COME THE TIME, THE LAD BLEW TATE AWAY...BUT THAT'D MAKE ME A LIAR, SO THE TRUTH IS WHAT I'LL SAY...
PLEASE?

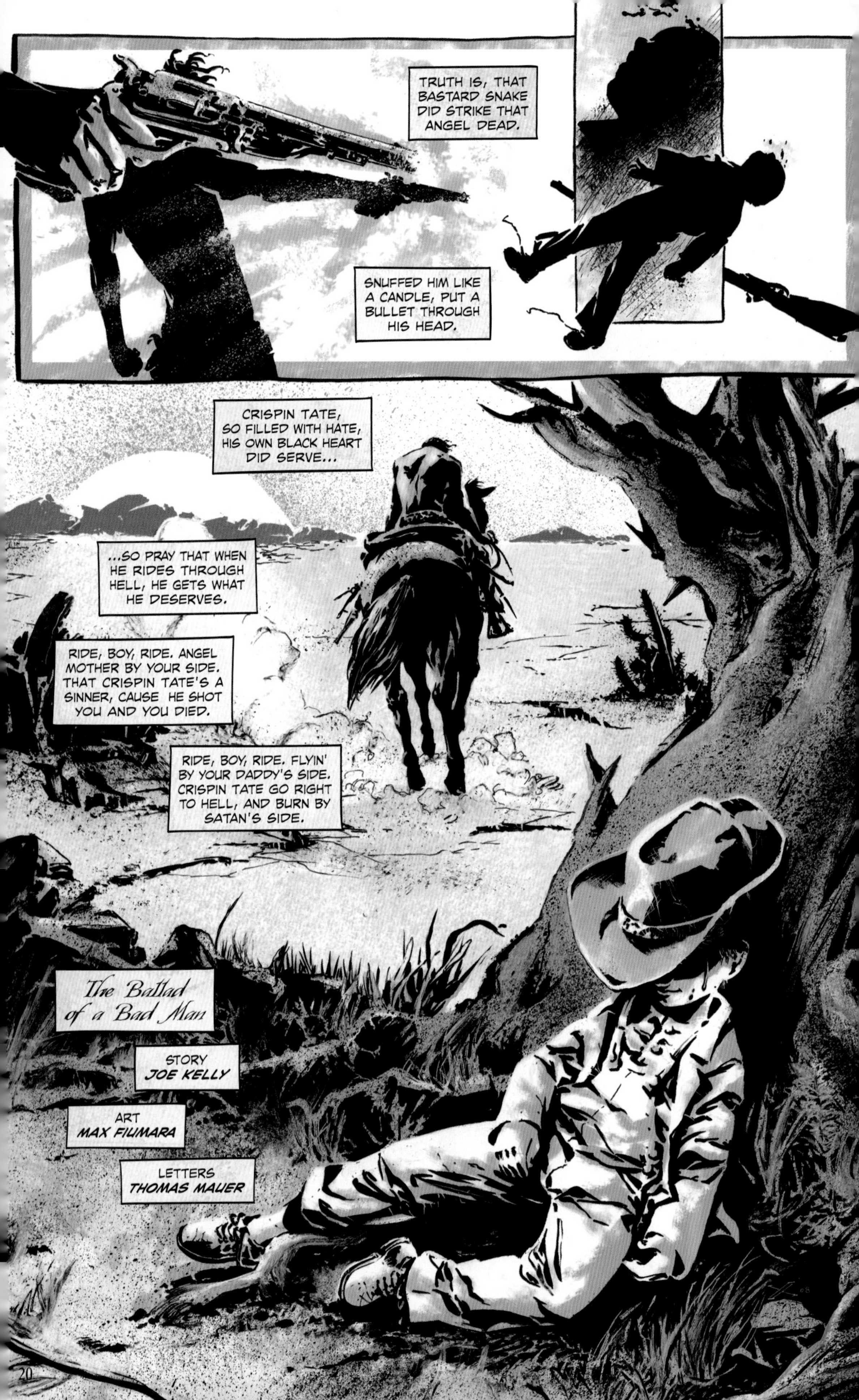
TRUTH IS, THAT BASTARD SNAKE DID STRIKE THAT ANGEL DEAD.
SNUFFED HIM LIKE A CANDLE, PUT A BULLET THROUGH HIS HEAD.
CRISPIN TATE, SO FILLED WITH HATE, HIS OWN BLACK HEART DID SERVE...
...SO PRAY THAT WHEN HE RIDES THROUGH HELL, HE GETS WHAT HE DESERVES.
RIDE, BOY, RIDE. ANGEL MOTHER BY YOUR SIDE. THAT CRISPIN TATE'S A SINNER, CAUSE HE SHOT YOU AND YOU DIED.
RIDE, BOY, RIDE. FLYIN' BY YOUR DADDY'S SIDE. CRISPIN TATE GO RIGHT TO HELL, AND BURN BY SATAN'S SIDE.
The Ballad of a Bad Man
STORY JOE KELLY
ART MAX FIUMARA
LETTERS THOMAS MAUER

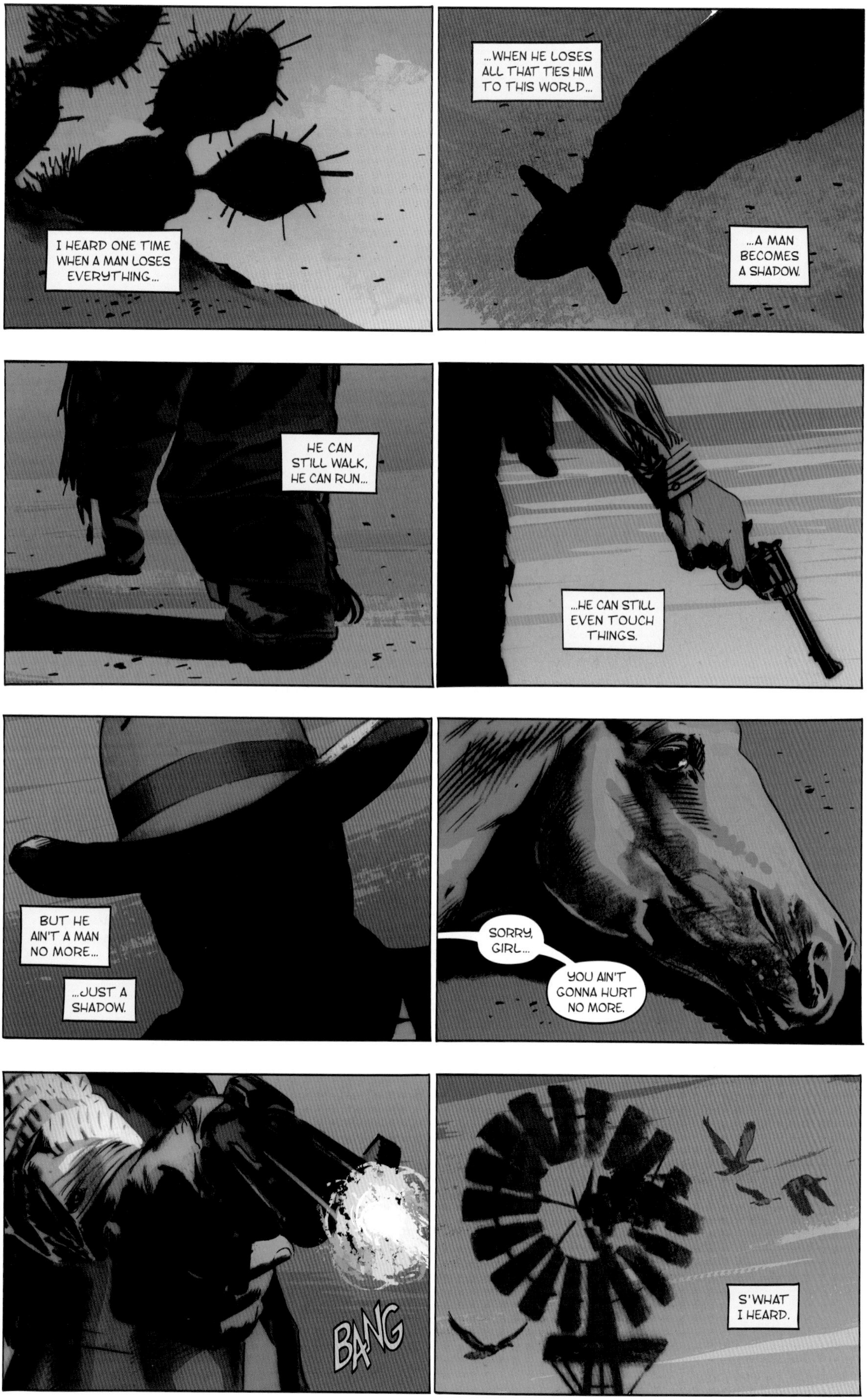
I HEARD ONE TIME WHEN A MAN LOSES EVERYTHING...
...WHEN HE LOSES ALL THAT TIES HIM TO THIS WORLD...
...A MAN BECOMES A SHADOW.
HE CAN STILL WALK, HE CAN RUN...
...HE CAN STILL EVEN TOUCH THINGS.
BUT HE AIN'T A MAN NO MORE...
...JUST A SHADOW.
SORRY, GIRL...
YOU AIN'T GONNA HURT NO MORE.
BANG
S'WHAT I HEARD.

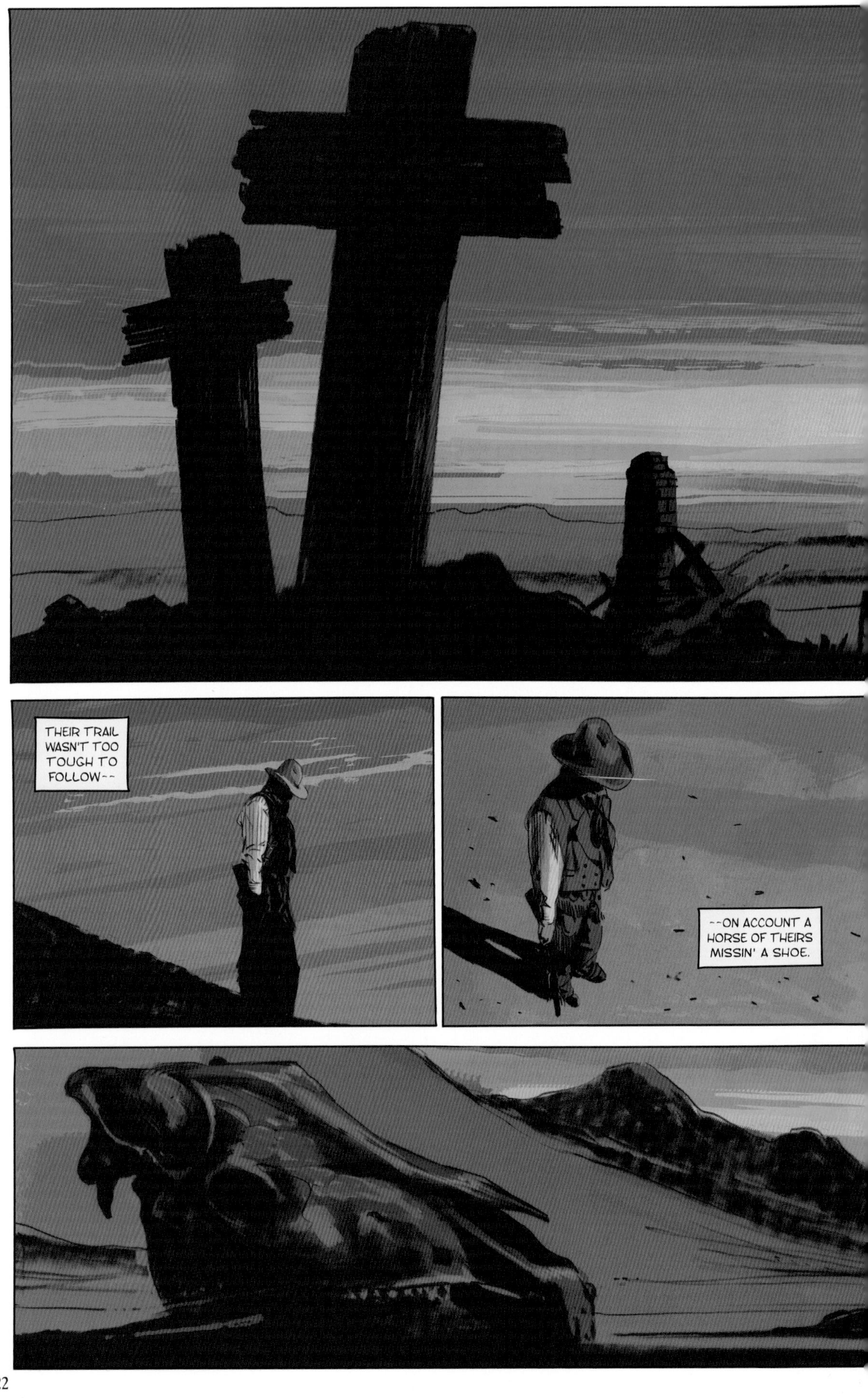
THEIR TRAIL WASN'T TOO TOUGH TO FOLLOW--
--ON ACCOUNT A HORSE OF THEIRS MISSIN' A SHOE.

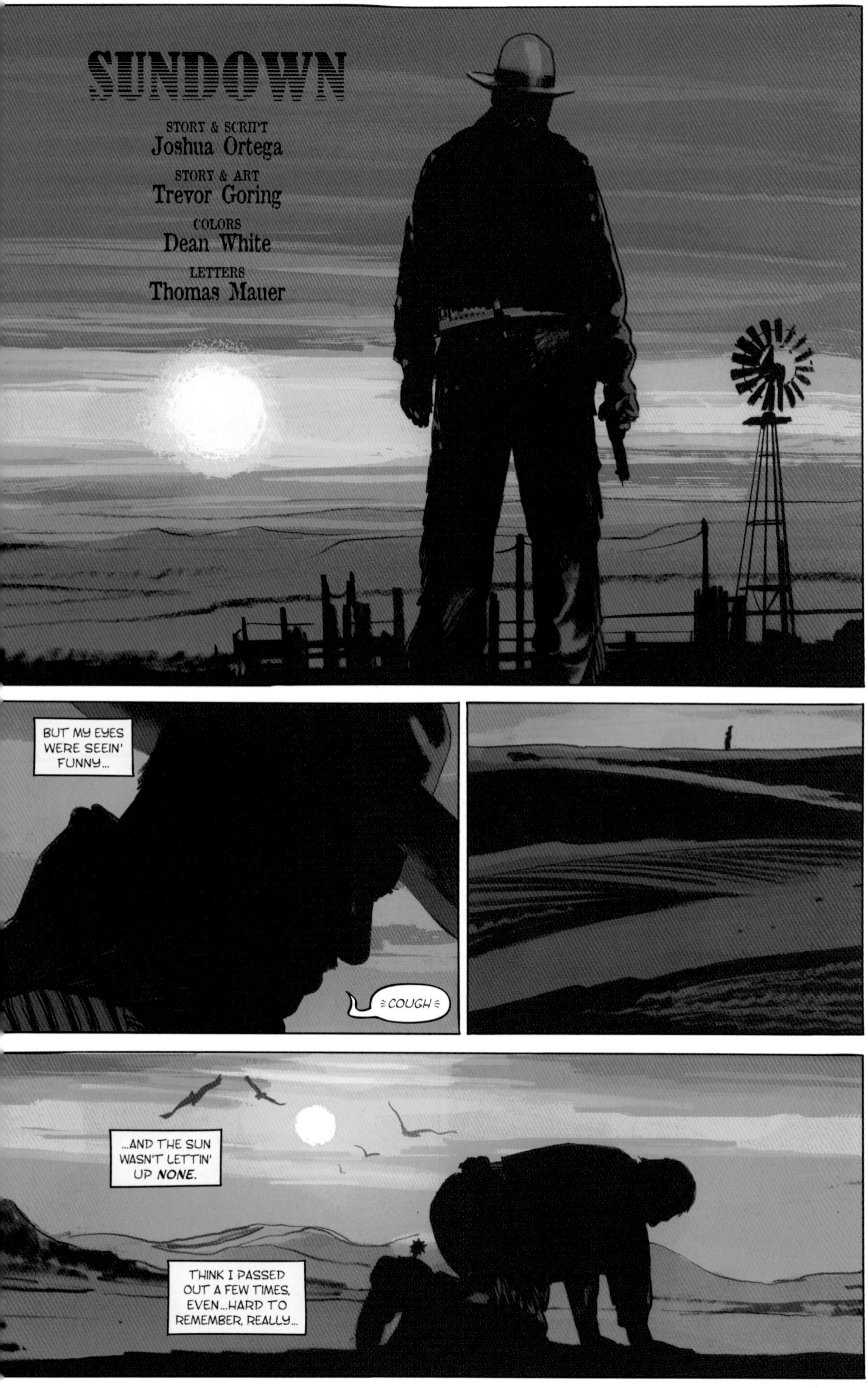
SUNDOWN
STORY & SCRIPT
Joshua Ortega
STORY & ART
Trevor Goring
COLORS
Dean White
LETTERS
Thomas Mauer
BUT MY EYES WERE SEEIN' FUNNY...
COUGH
...AND THE SUN WASN'T LETTIN' UP NONE.
THINK I PASSED OUT A FEW TIMES, EVEN...HARD TO REMEMBER, REALLY...

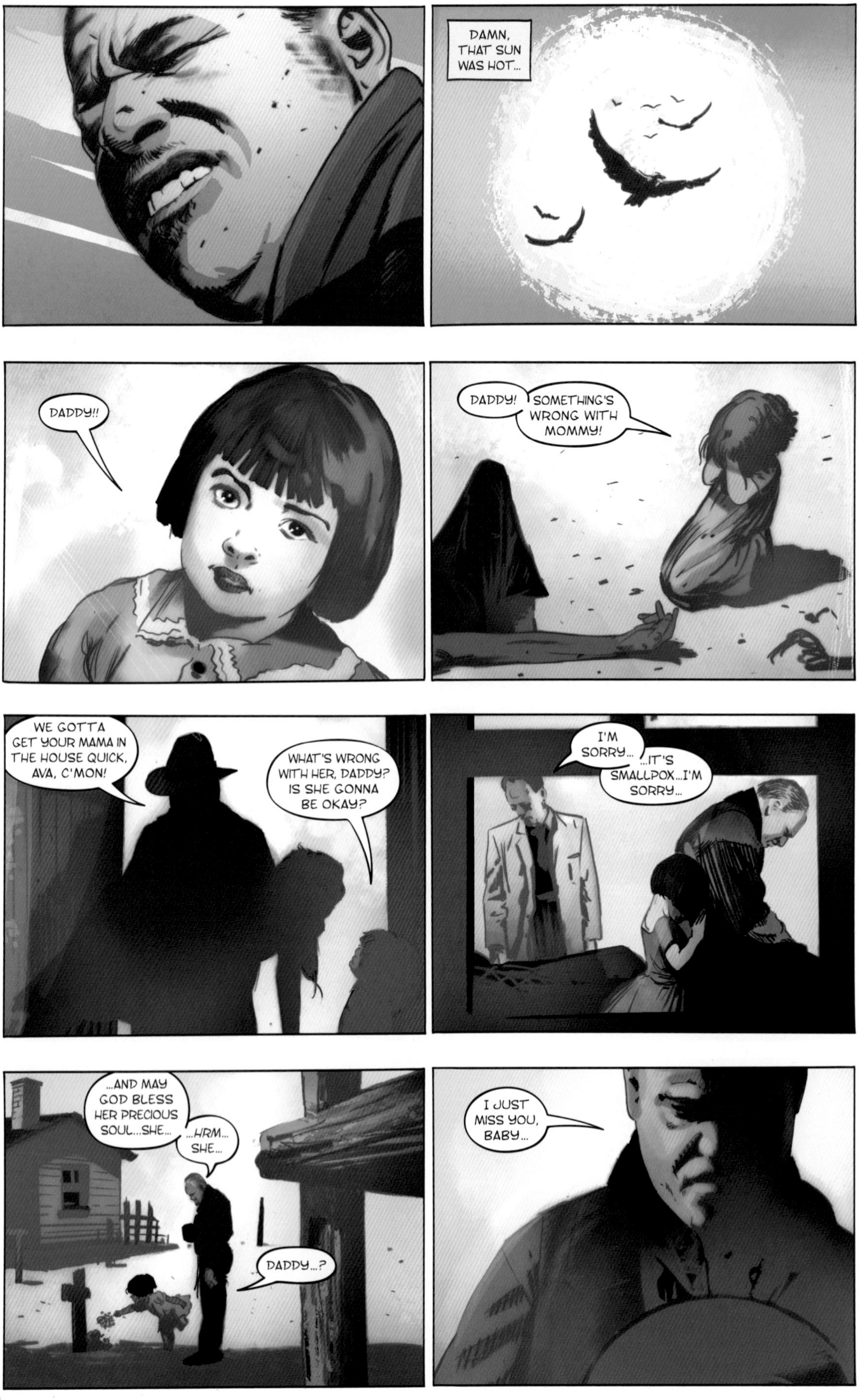
DAMN, THAT SUN WAS HOT...
DADDY!!
DADDY!
SOMETHING'S WRONG WITH MOMMY!
WE GOTTA GET YOUR MAMA IN THE HOUSE QUICK, AVA, C'MON!
WHAT'S WRONG WITH HER, DADDY? IS SHE GONNA BE OKAY?
I'M SORRY...
...IT'S SMALLPOX...I'M SORRY...
...AND MAY GOD BLESS HER PRECIOUS SOUL...SHE...
...HRM... SHE...
DADDY...?
I JUST MISS YOU, BABY...

...DADDY MISSES BOTH OF YOU SO MUCH.

MY PA USED TO TELL ME TO BE THANKFUL FOR THE SIMPLE THINGS...

..AND I GUESS AT THAT MOMENT, I WAS GRATEFUL THAT A SHADOW COULD STILL FETCH A DRINK...

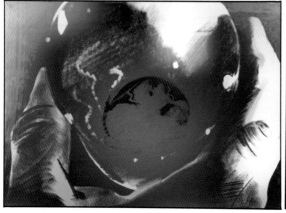

RAAAHEEEEE

GINGER?

GINGER!!

25

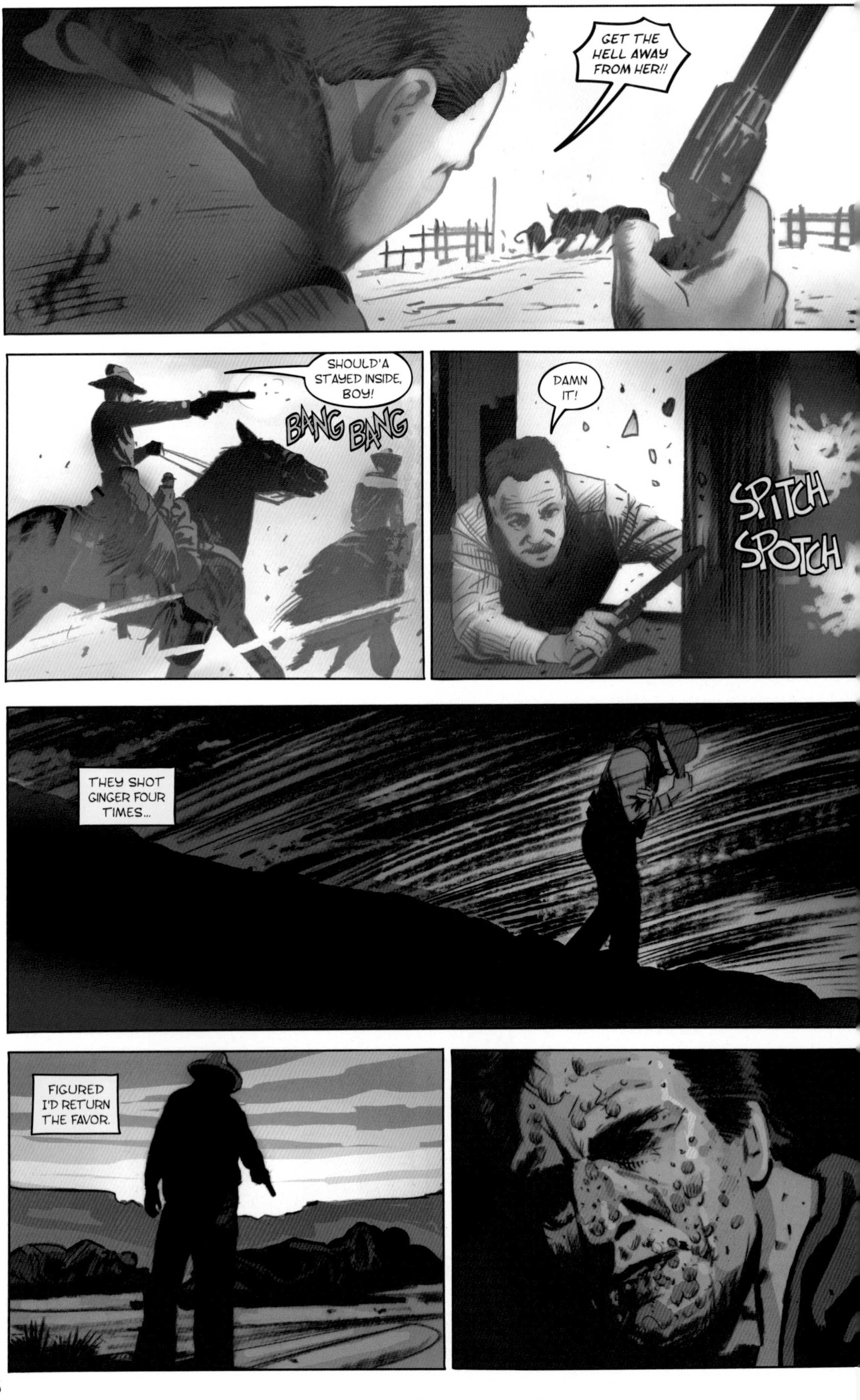

GET THE HELL AWAY FROM HER!!
SHOULD'A STAYED INSIDE, BOY!
BANG BANG
DAMN IT!
SPITCH SPOTCH
THEY SHOT GINGER FOUR TIMES...
FIGURED I'D RETURN THE FAVOR.

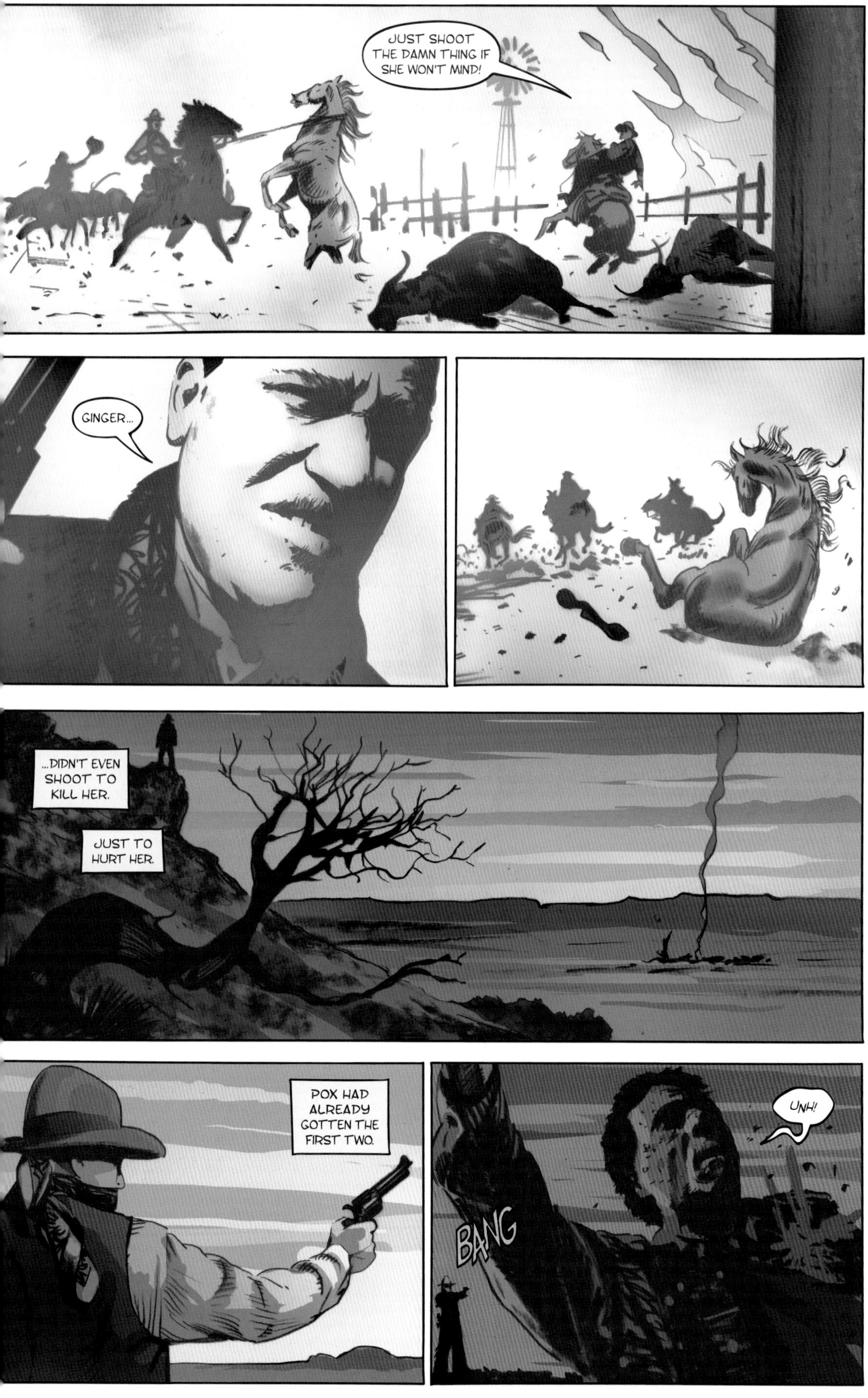
JUST SHOOT THE DAMN THING IF SHE WON'T MIND!
GINGER...
...DIDN'T EVEN SHOOT TO KILL HER.
JUST TO HURT HER.
POX HAD ALREADY GOTTEN THE FIRST TWO.
UNH!
BANG

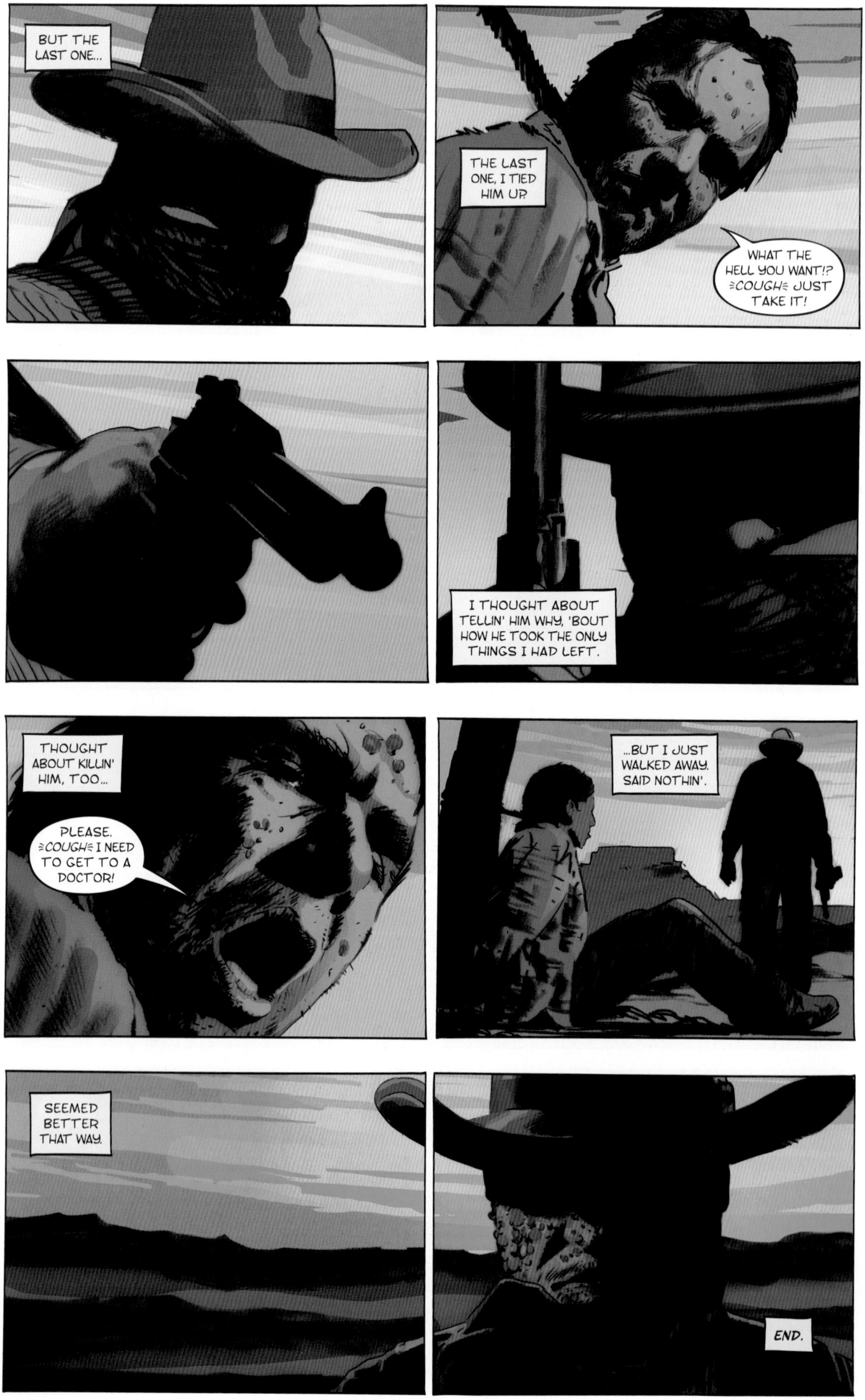

BUT THE LAST ONE...
THE LAST ONE, I TIED HIM UP.
WHAT THE HELL YOU WANT!? ≈COUGH≈ JUST TAKE IT!
I THOUGHT ABOUT TELLIN' HIM WHY, 'BOUT HOW HE TOOK THE ONLY THINGS I HAD LEFT.
THOUGHT ABOUT KILLIN' HIM, TOO...
PLEASE. ≈COUGH≈ I NEED TO GET TO A DOCTOR!
...BUT I JUST WALKED AWAY. SAID NOTHIN'.
SEEMED BETTER THAT WAY.
END.

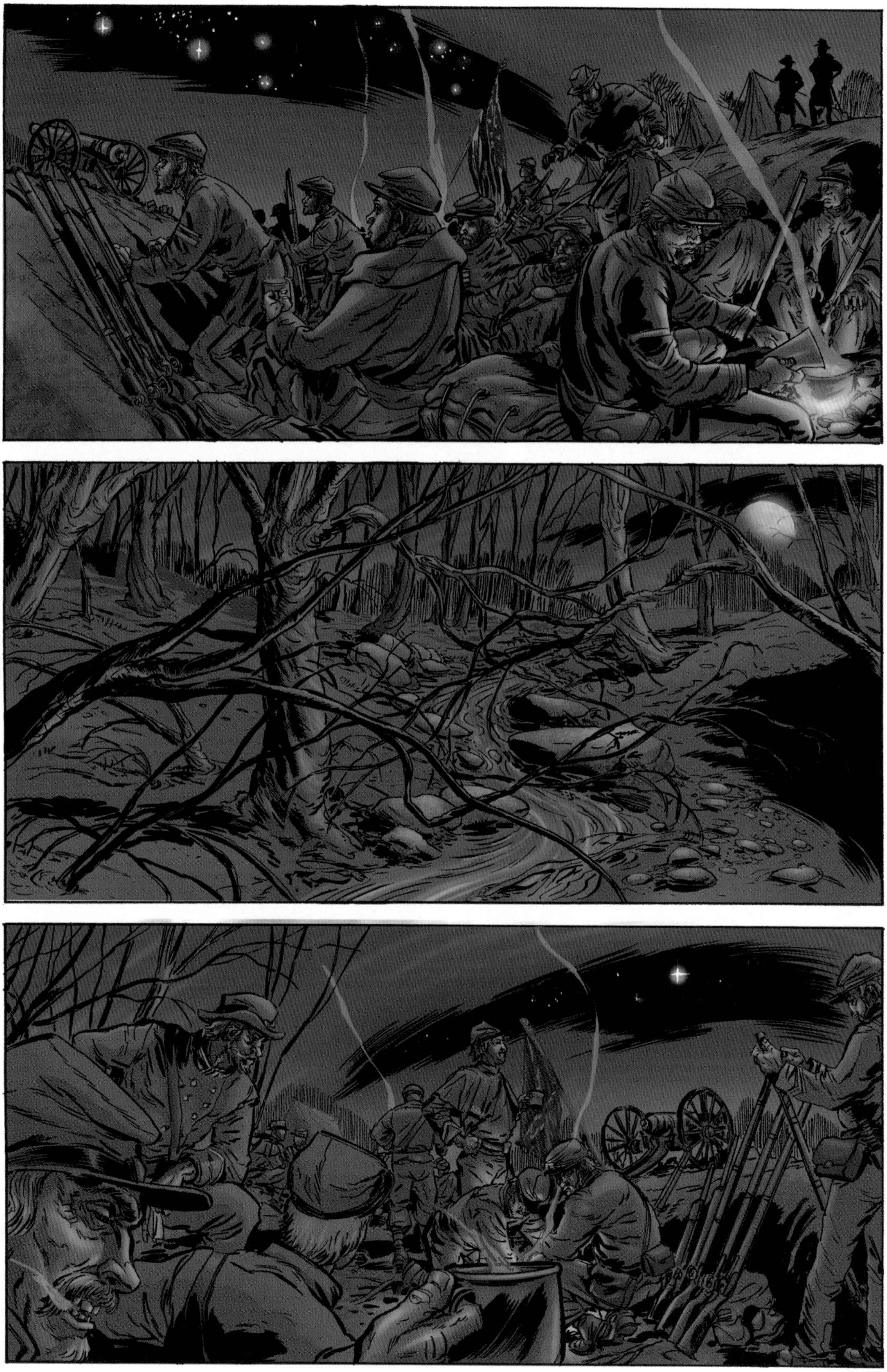

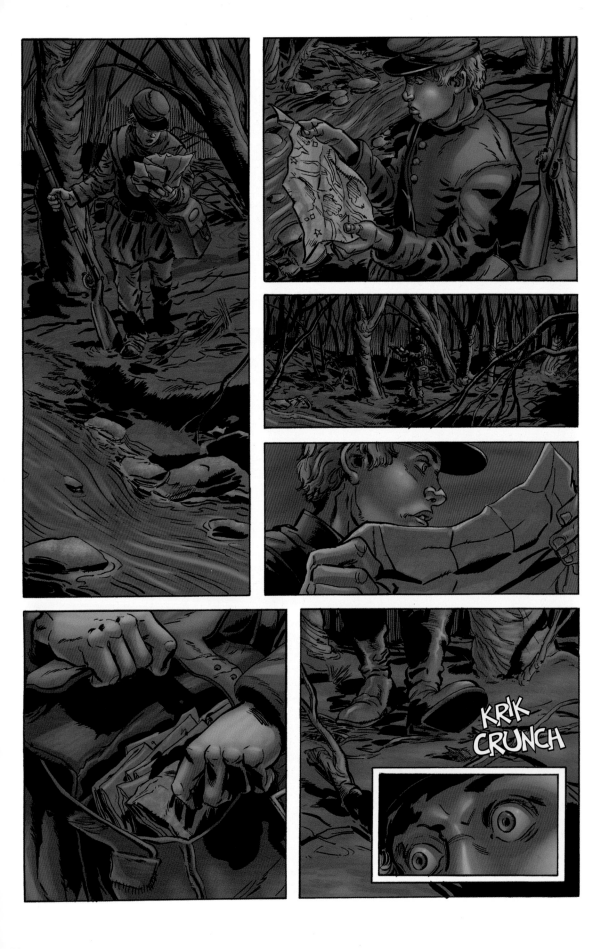

KRIK
CRUNCH

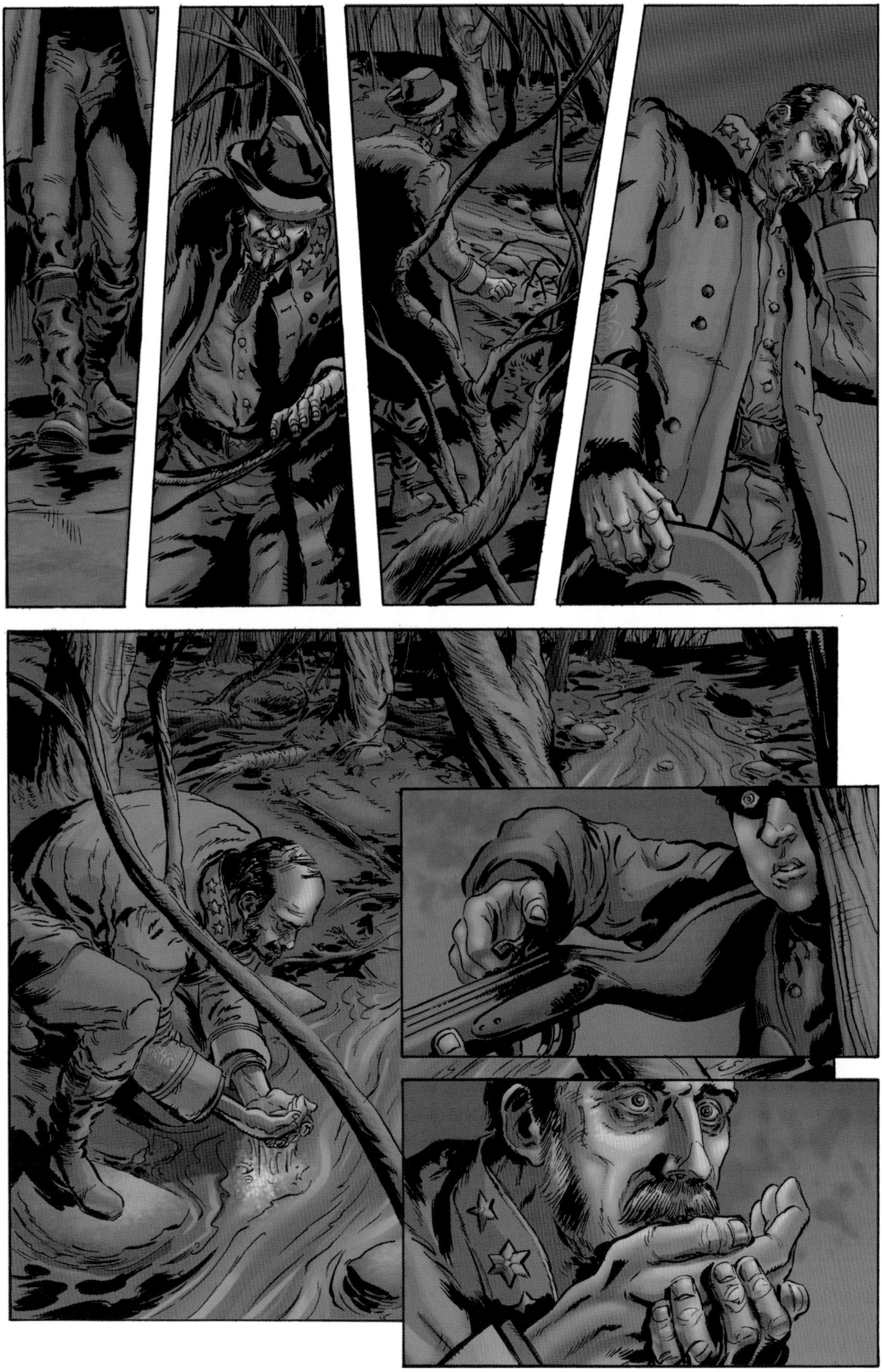

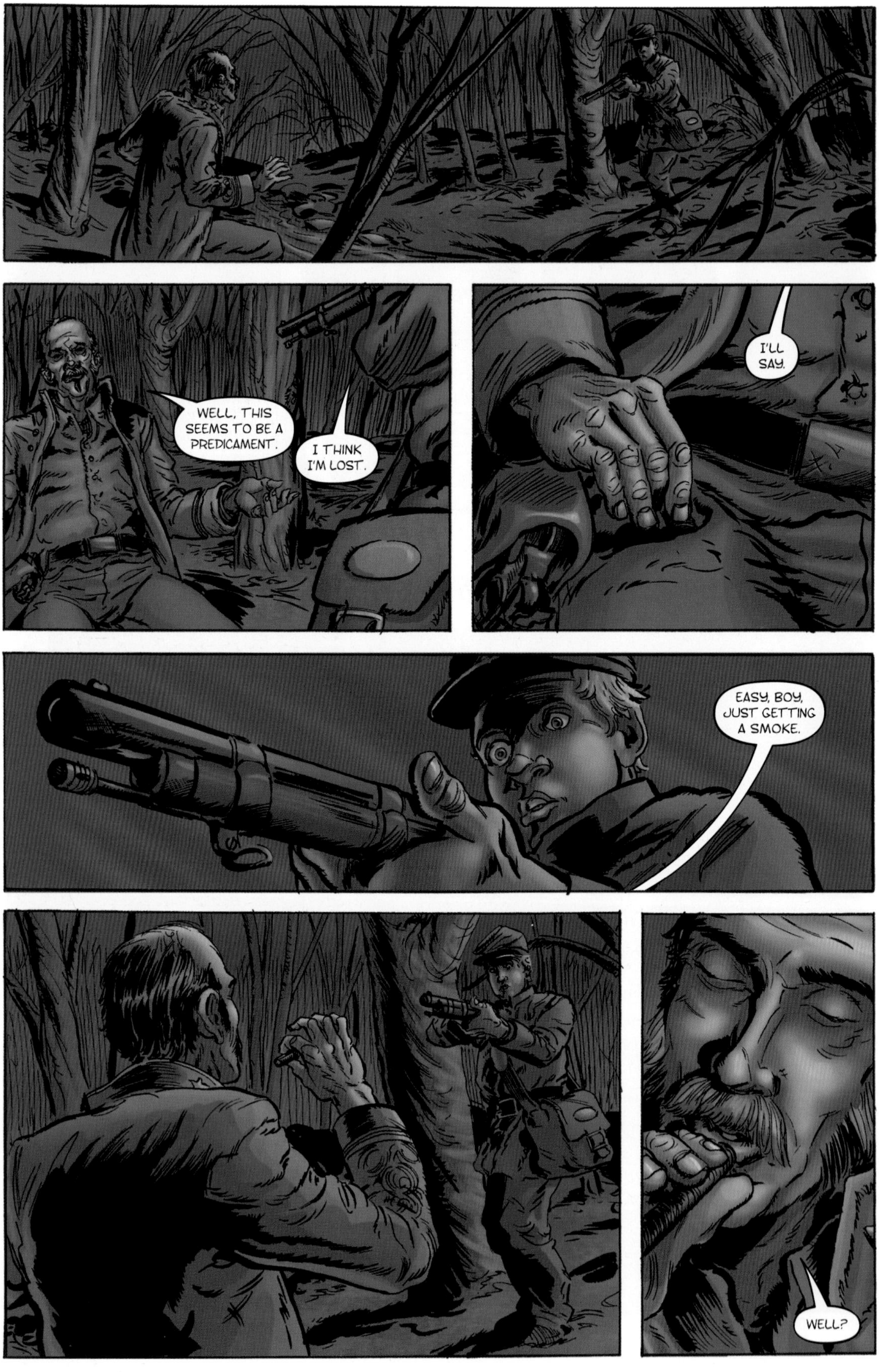
WELL, THIS SEEMS TO BE A PREDICAMENT.
I THINK I'M LOST.
I'LL SAY.
EASY, BOY, JUST GETTING A SMOKE.
WELL?

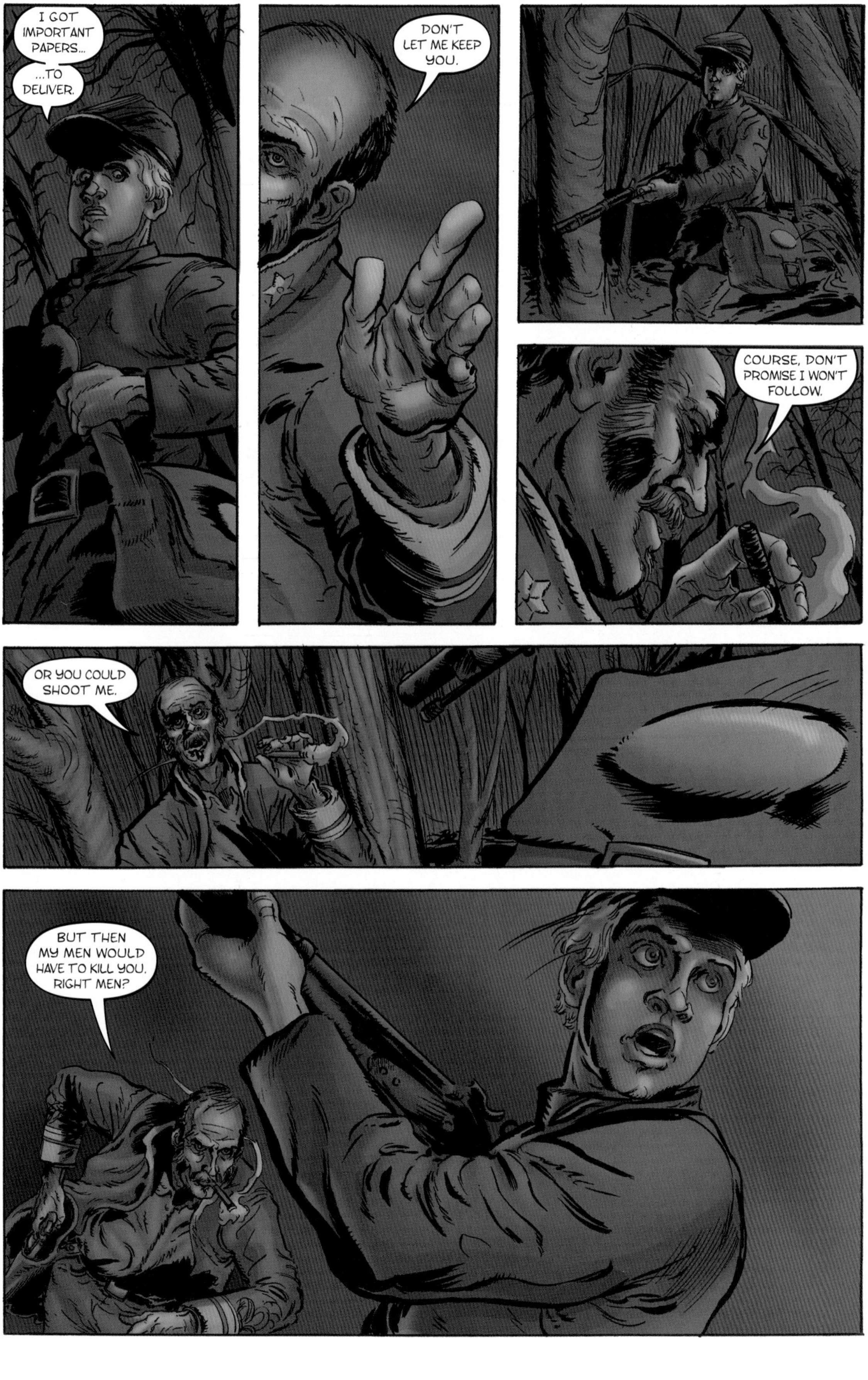
I GOT IMPORTANT PAPERS...
...TO DELIVER.
DON'T LET ME KEEP YOU.
COURSE, DON'T PROMISE I WON'T FOLLOW.
OR YOU COULD SHOOT ME.
BUT THEN MY MEN WOULD HAVE TO KILL YOU. RIGHT MEN?

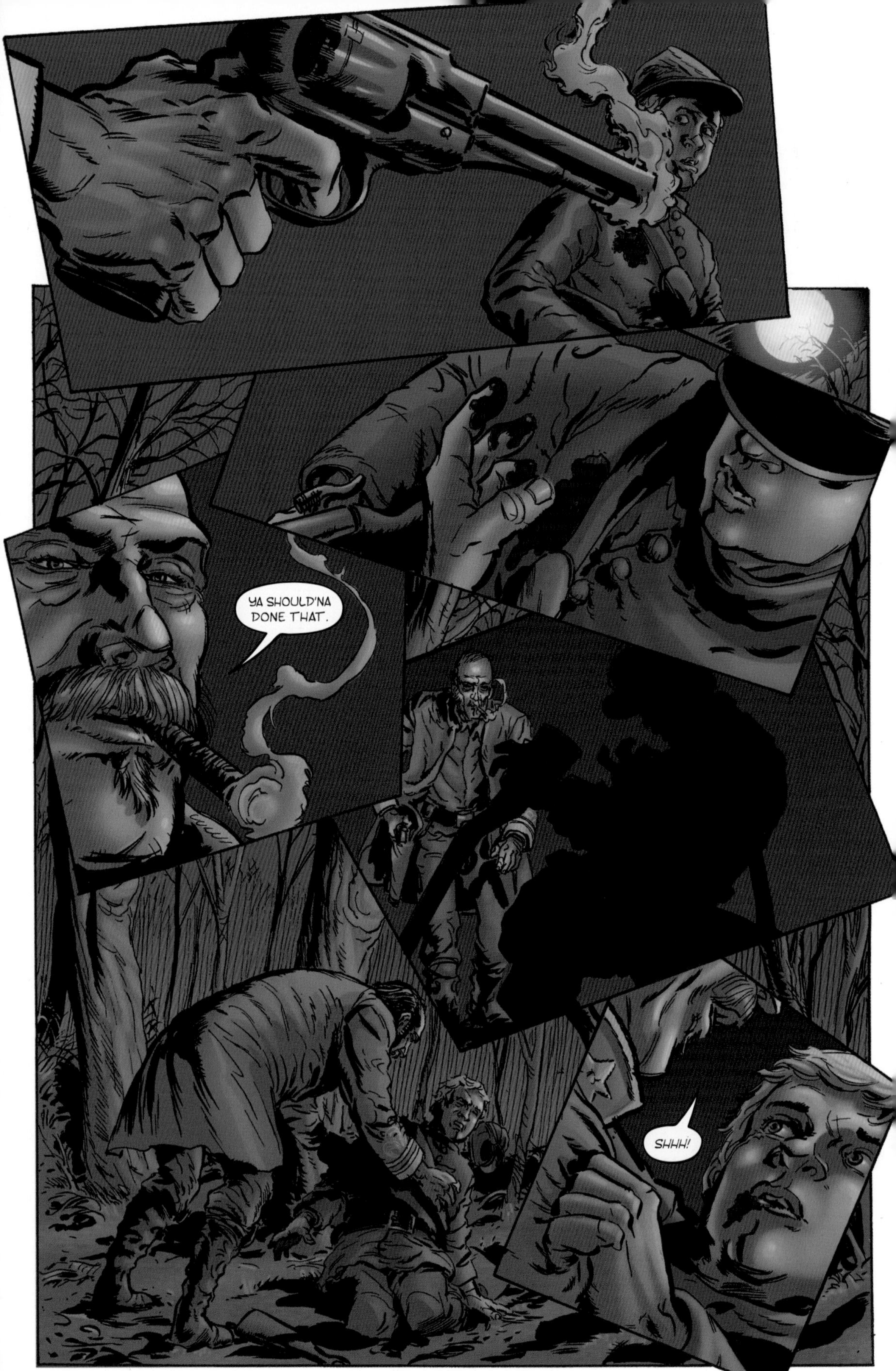
YA SHOULD'NA DONE THAT.
SHHH!

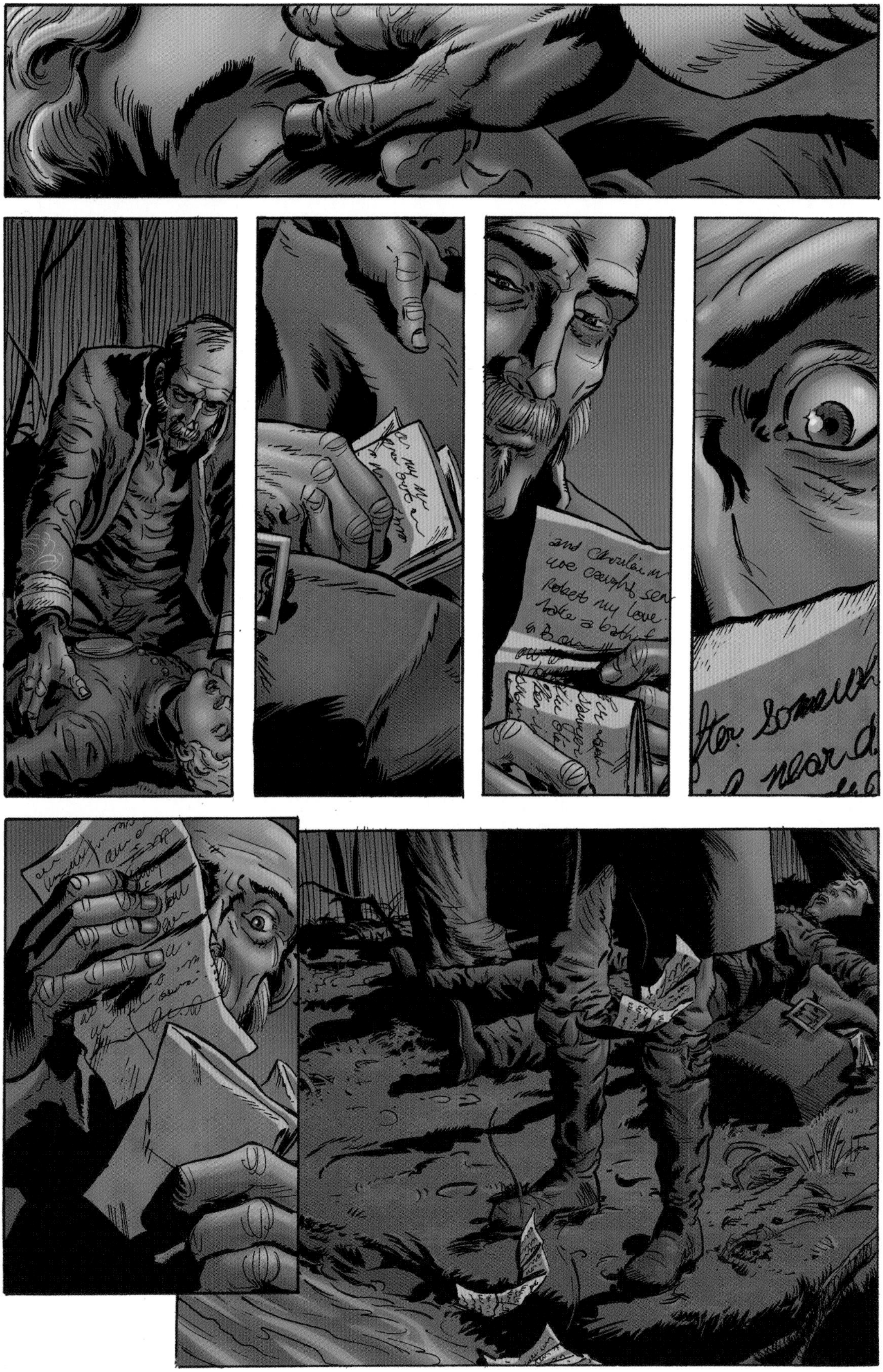

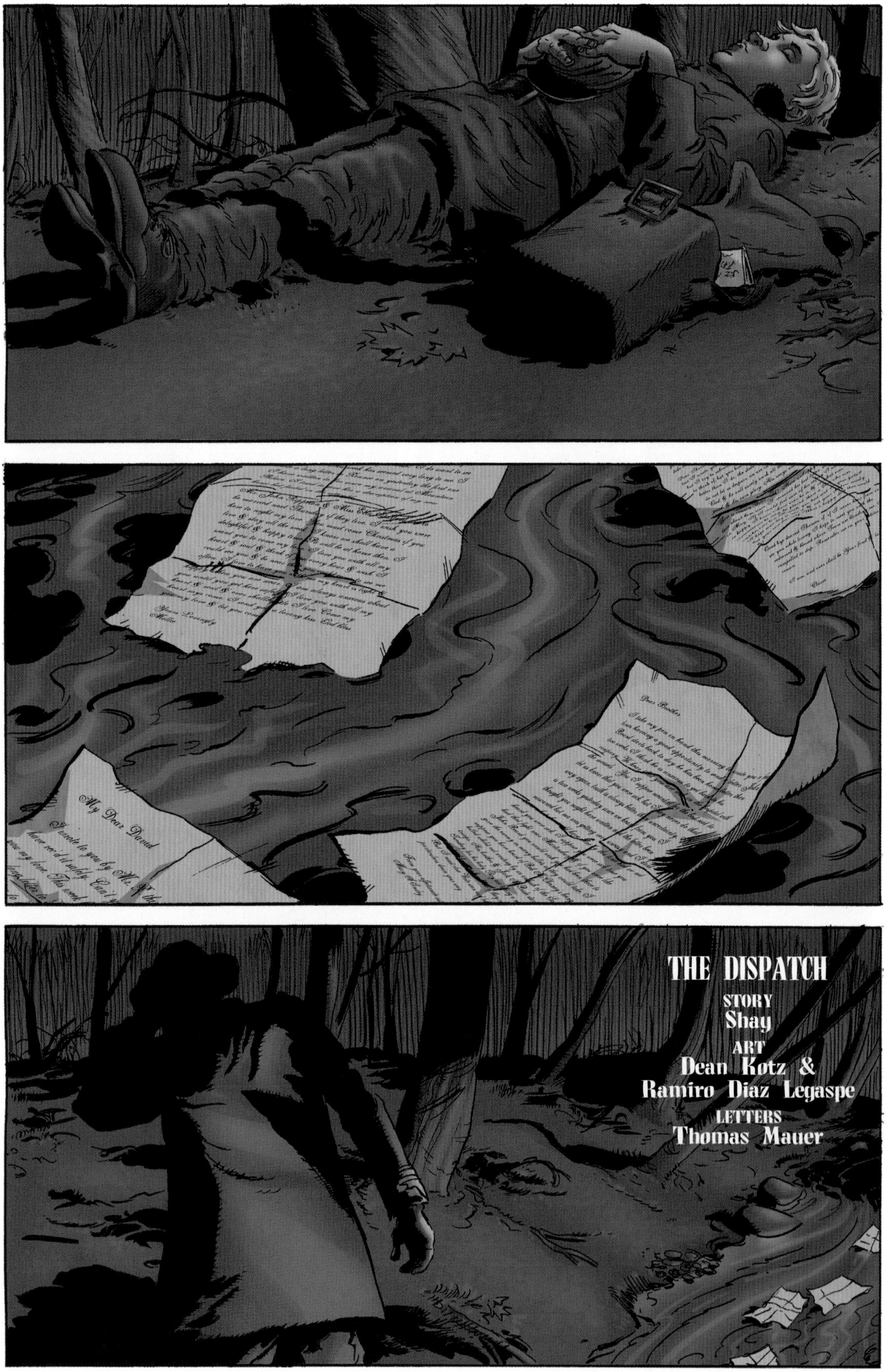
My Dear David
THE DISPATCH
STORY
Shay
ART
Dean Kotz &
Ramiro Diaz Legaspe
LETTERS
Thomas Mauer

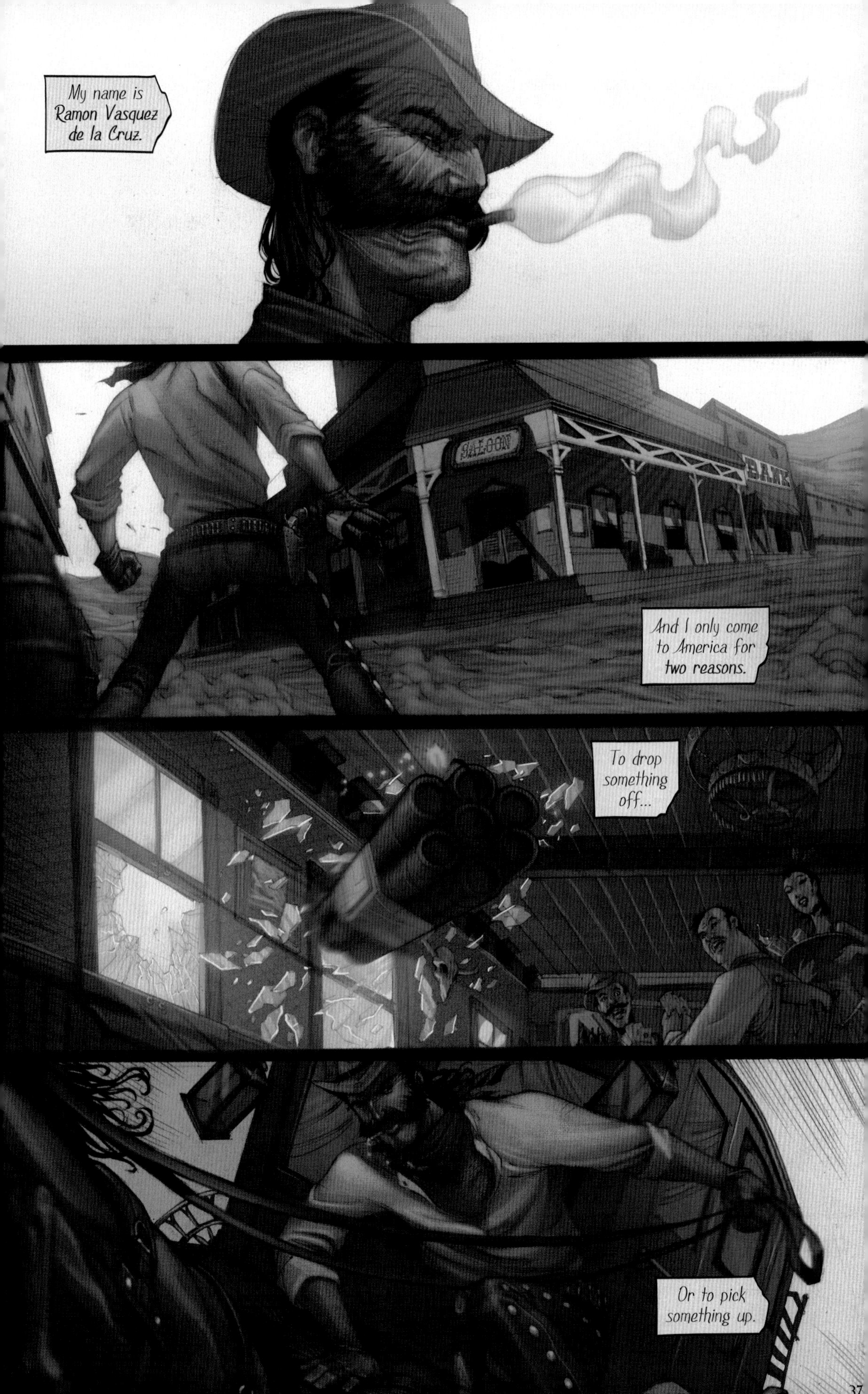
My name is Ramon Vasquez de la Cruz.
SALOON
BANK
And I only come to America for two reasons.
To drop something off...
Or to pick something up.

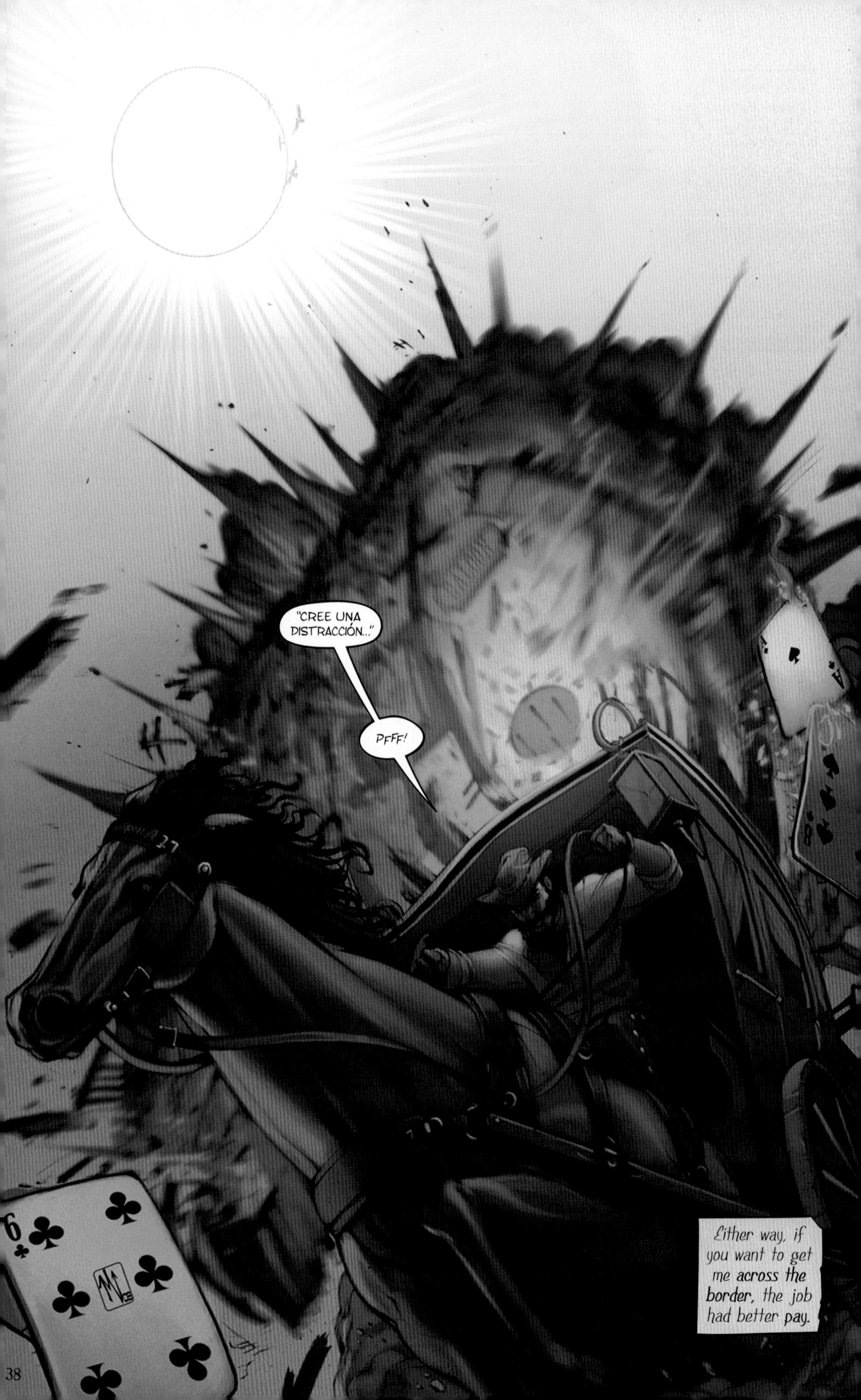
"CREE UNA DISTRACCIÓN..."
PFFF!
Either way, if you want to get me across the border, the job had better pay.

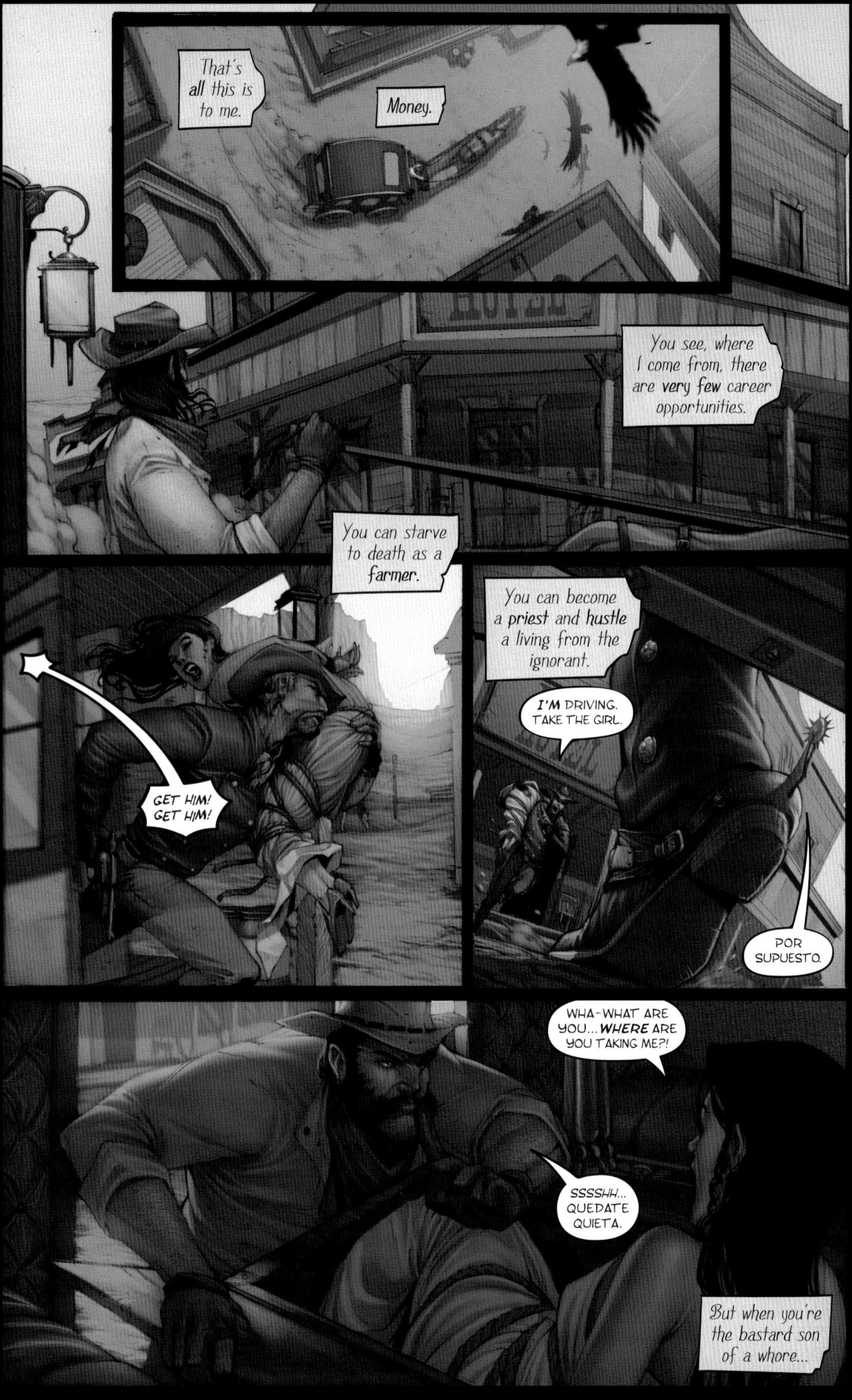

That's all this is to me.
Money.
You see, where I come from, there are very few career opportunities.
You can starve to death as a farmer.
GET HIM! GET HIM!
You can become a priest and hustle a living from the ignorant.
I'M DRIVING. TAKE THE GIRL.
POR SUPUESTO.
WHA-WHAT ARE YOU... WHERE ARE YOU TAKING ME?!
SSSSHH... QUEDATE QUIETA.
But when you're the bastard son of a whore...

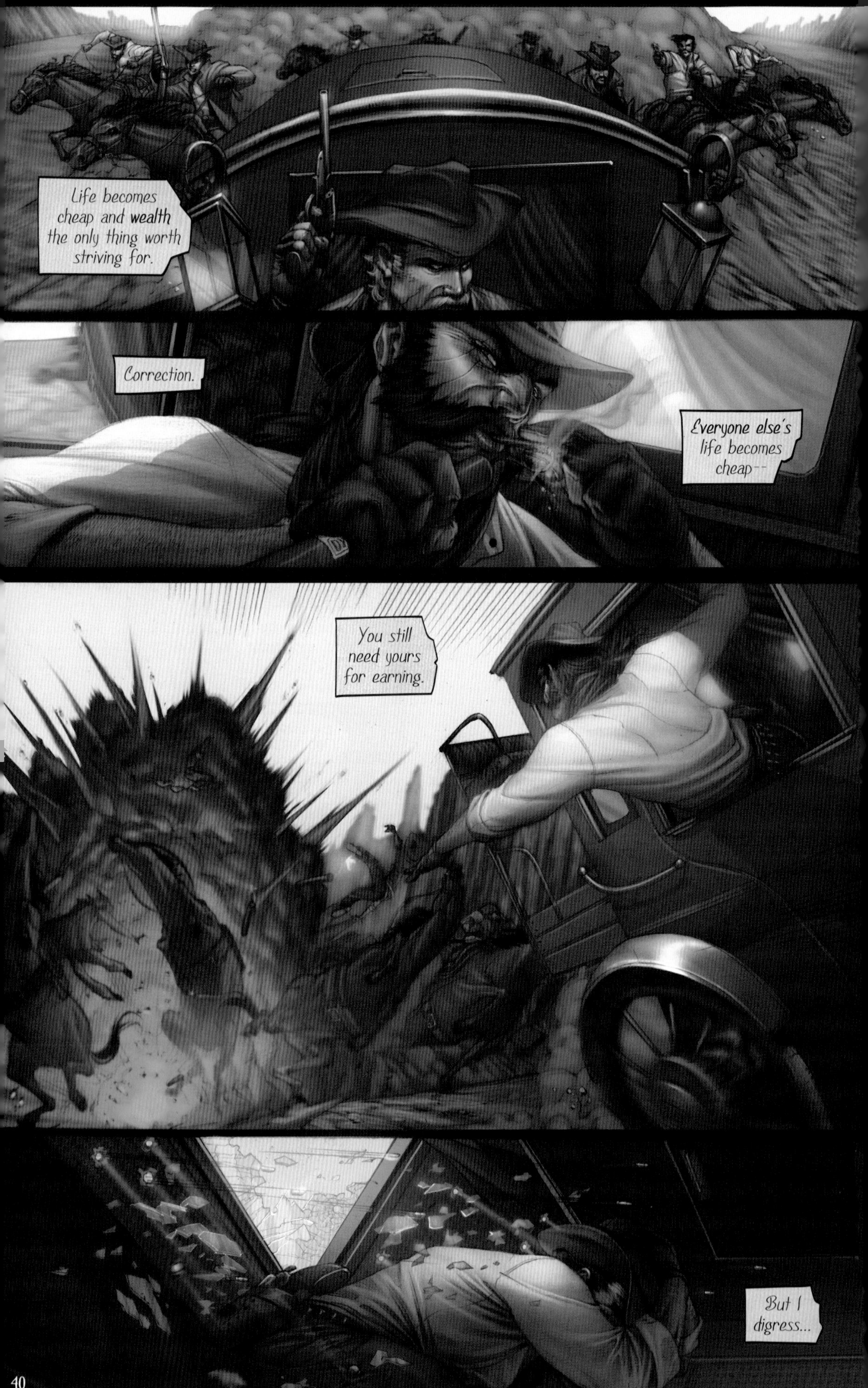
Life becomes cheap and wealth the only thing worth striving for.
Correction.
Everyone else's life becomes cheap--
You still need yours for earning.
But I digress...

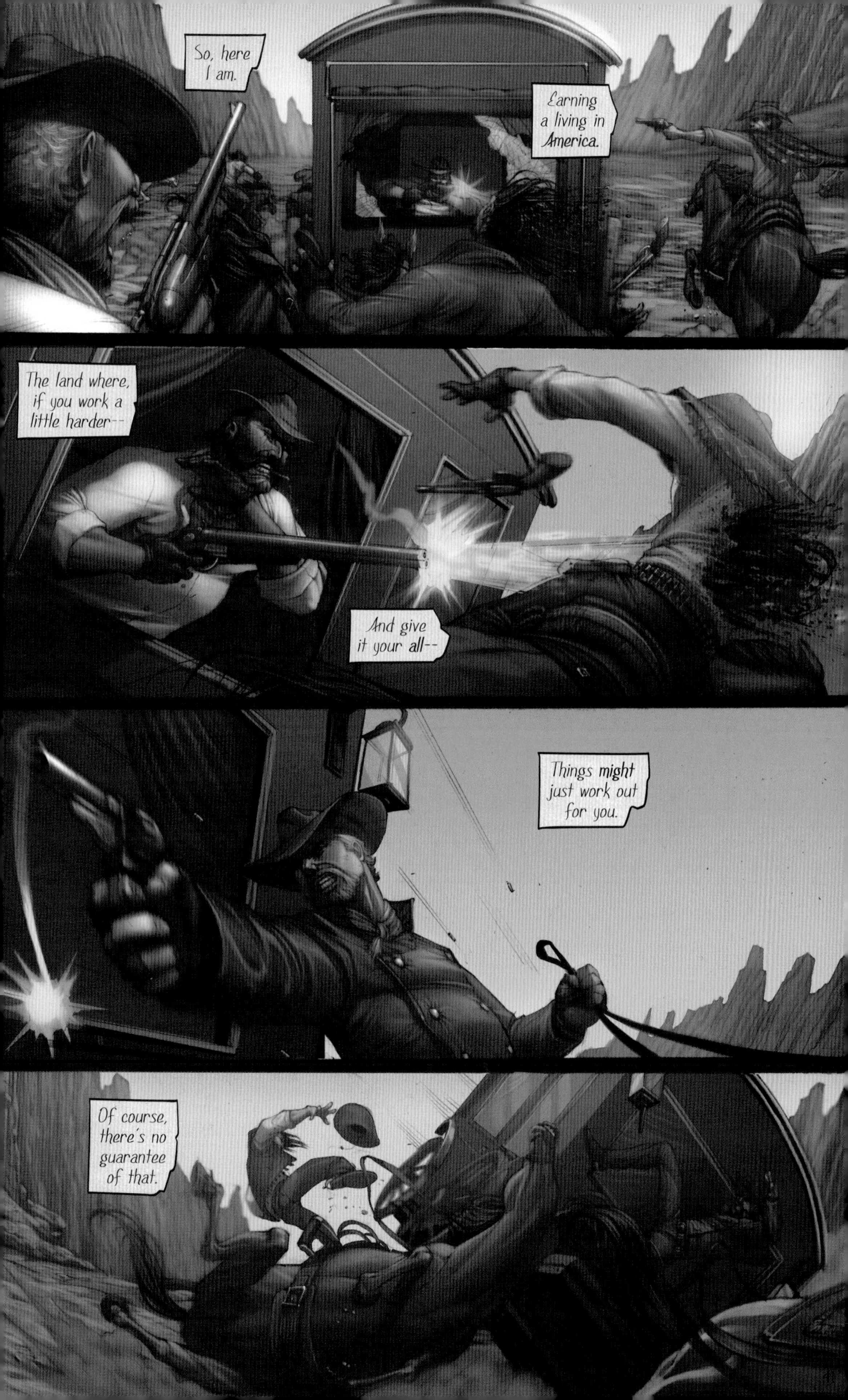
So, here I am.
Earning a living in America.
The land where, if you work a little harder--
And give it your all--
Things might just work out for you.
Of course, there's no guarantee of that.

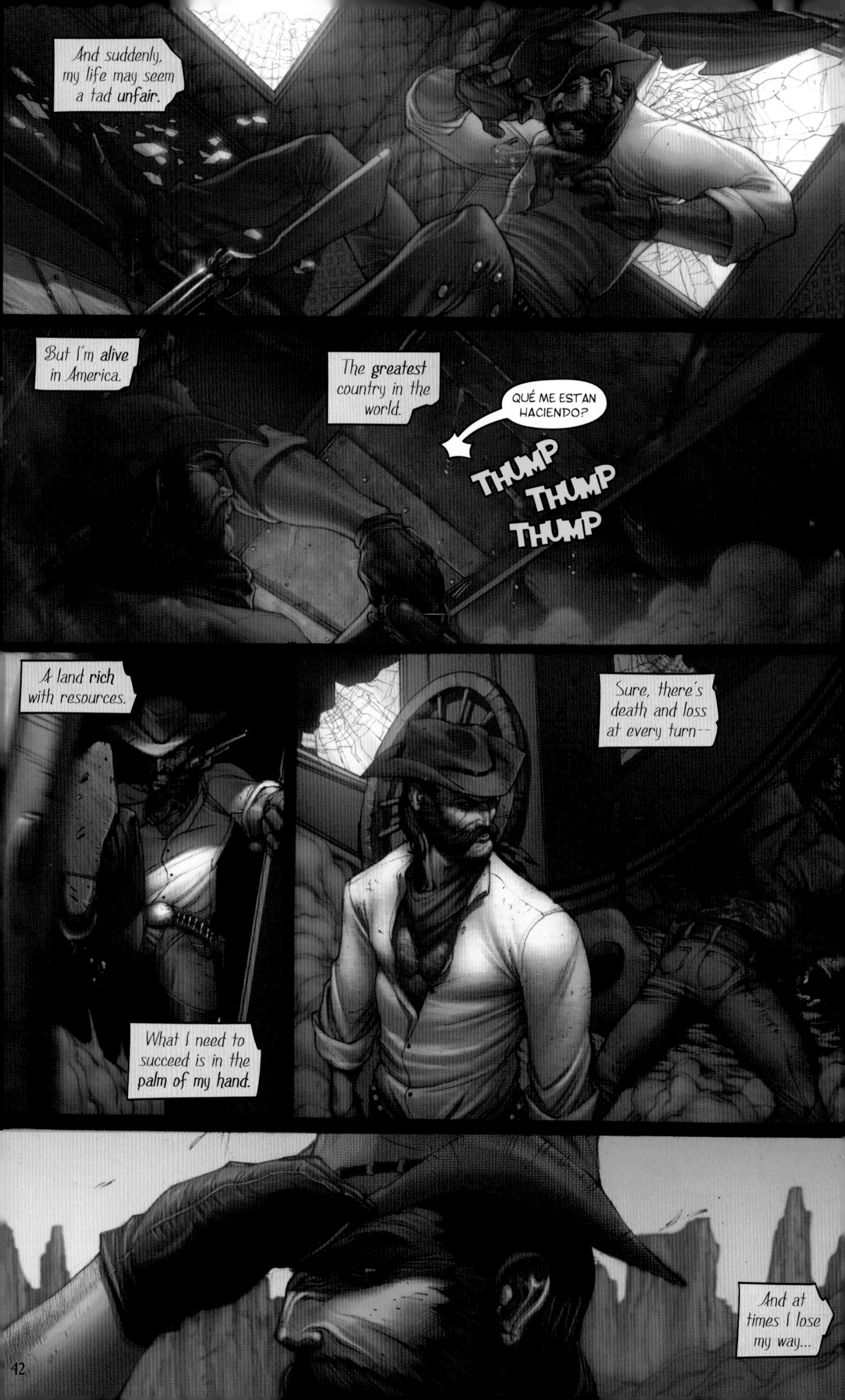

And suddenly, my life may seem a tad unfair.
But I'm alive in America.
The greatest country in the world.
QUÉ ME ESTAN HACIENDO?
THUMP
THUMP
THUMP
A land rich with resources.
What I need to succeed is in the palm of my hand.
Sure, there's death and loss at every turn--
And at times I lose my way...

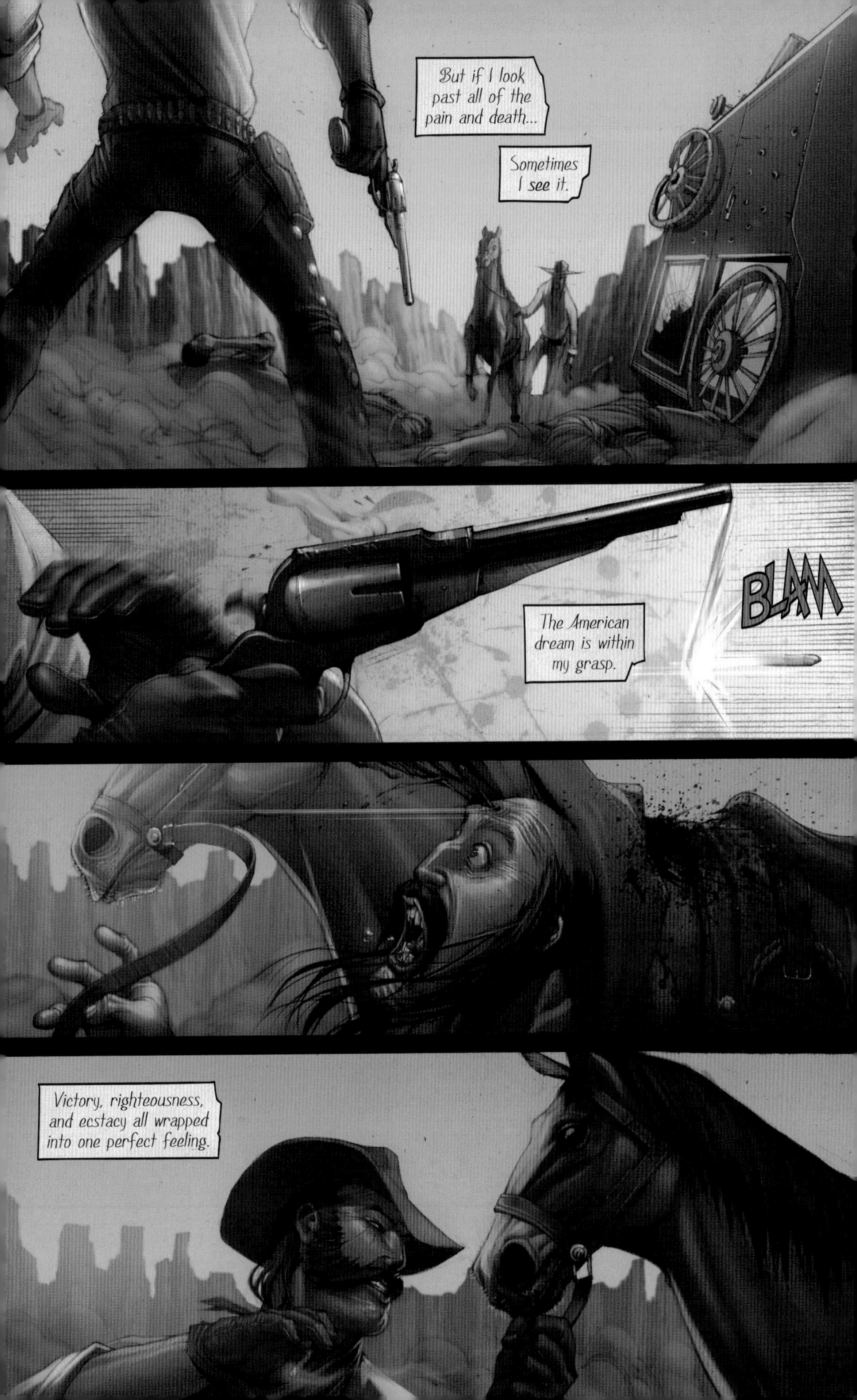

But if I look past all of the pain and death...
Sometimes I see it.
BLAM
The American dream is within my grasp.
Victory, righteousness, and ecstacy all wrapped into one perfect feeling.

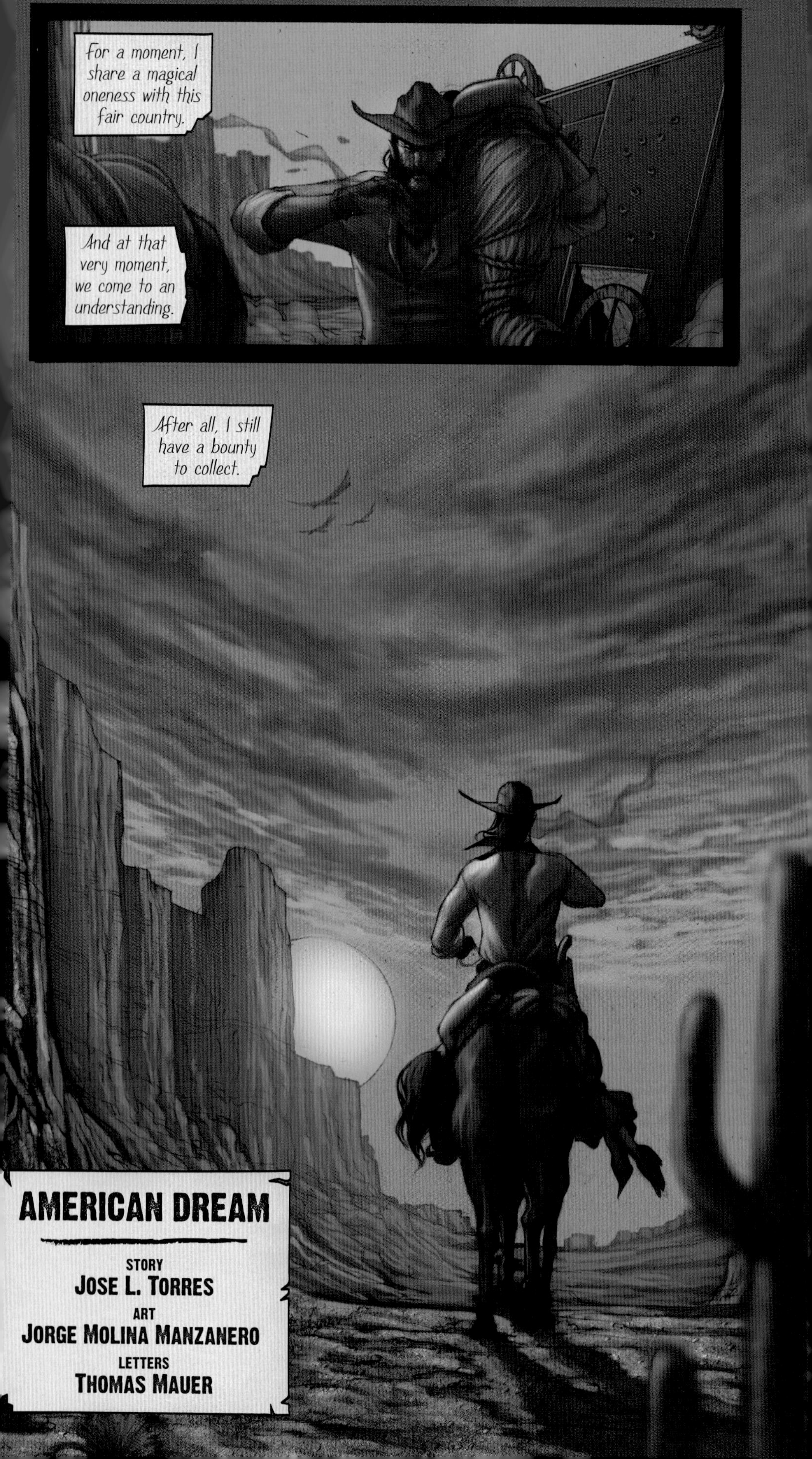
For a moment, I share a magical oneness with this fair country.
And at that very moment, we come to an understanding.
After all, I still have a bounty to collect.
AMERICAN DREAM
STORY
JOSE L. TORRES
ART
JORGE MOLINA MANZANERO
LETTERS
THOMAS MAUER

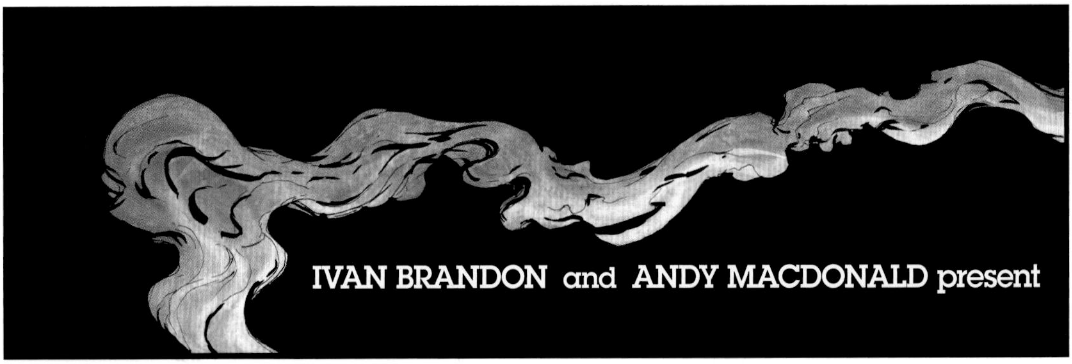
IVAN BRANDON and ANDY MACDONALD present

THE FIRST THING I SAW WAS HIS CAR.

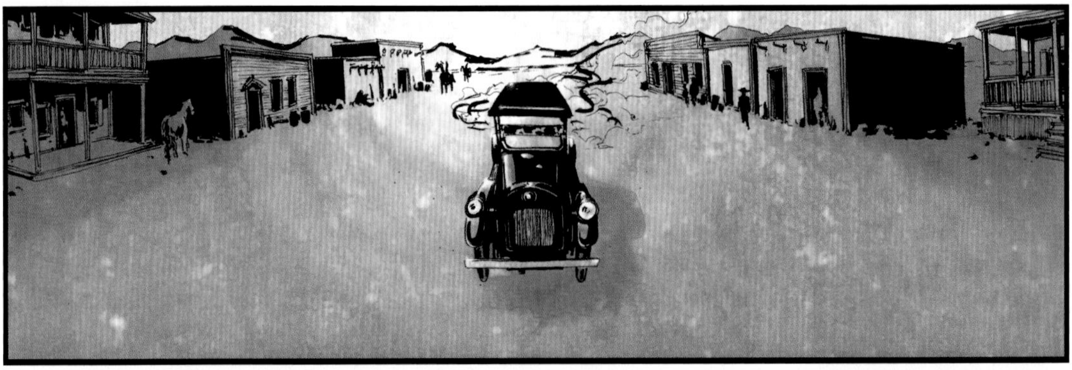

the FIRST CAR in MEXICO or the END of PANCHO VILLA

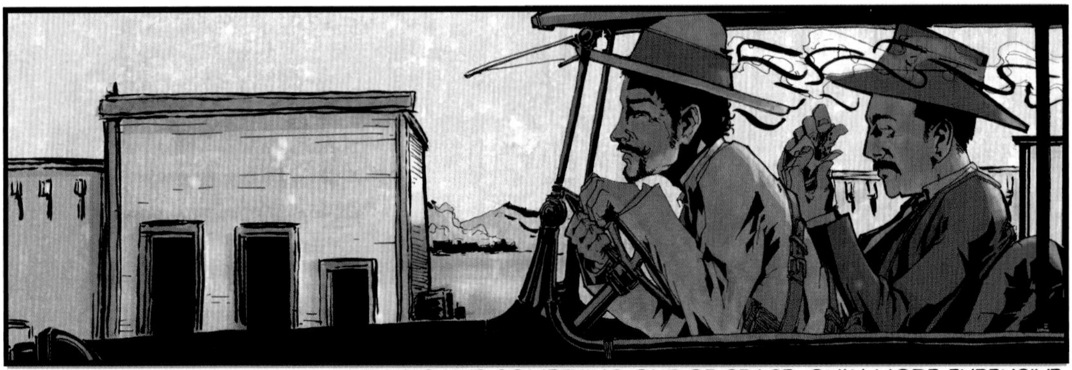

IT WAS LIKE SOMETHING OUT OF SPACE, ONLY MORE EXPENSIVE.

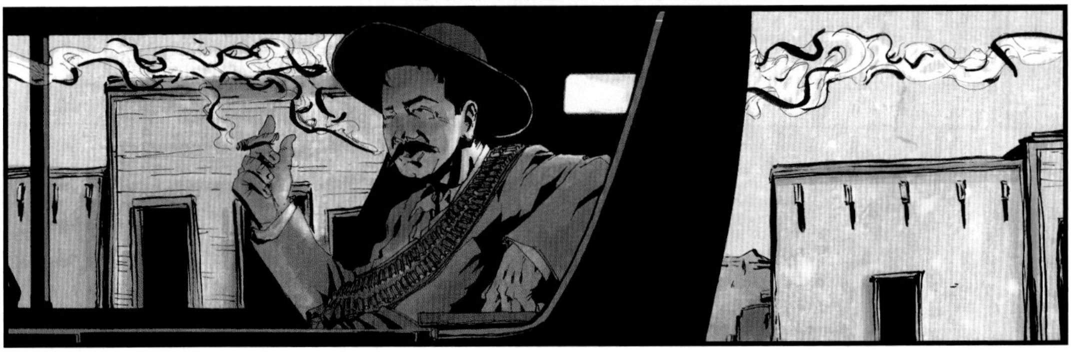

IT WAS SHINY AND LOUD AND I REMEMBER I ASKED
IF I'D GET TO TRY AND DRIVE IT WHEN ALL THIS WAS DONE.

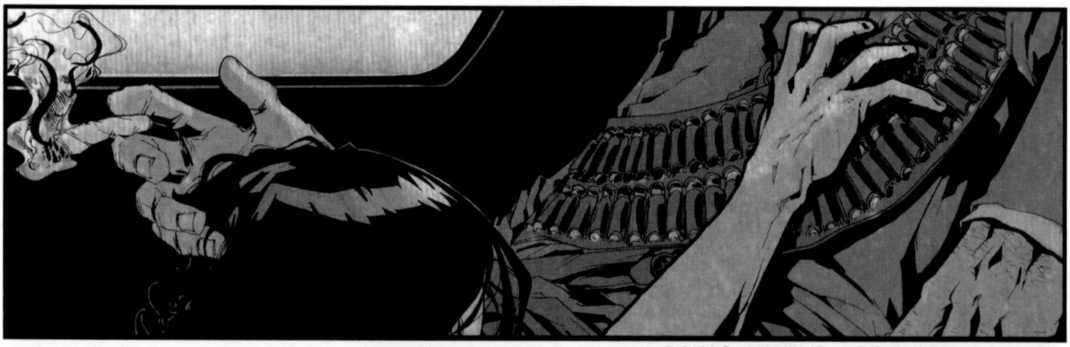

I WAS ALWAYS GOOD FOR A LAUGH.

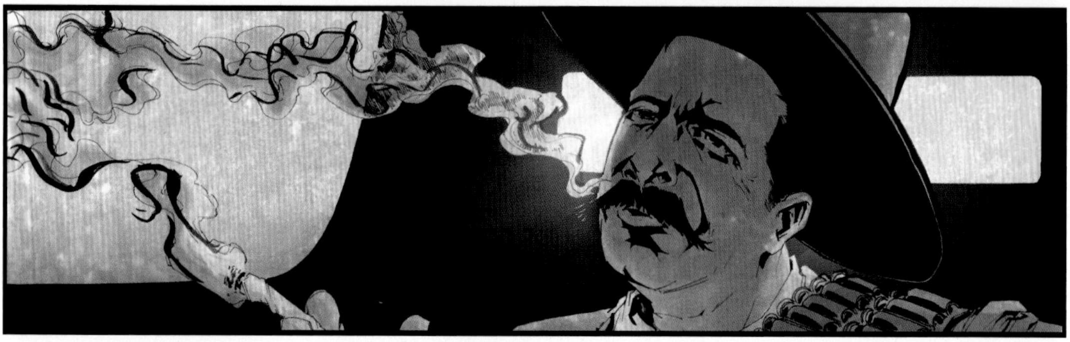

THEY CALLED ME 'PAYASITO': CLOWN.

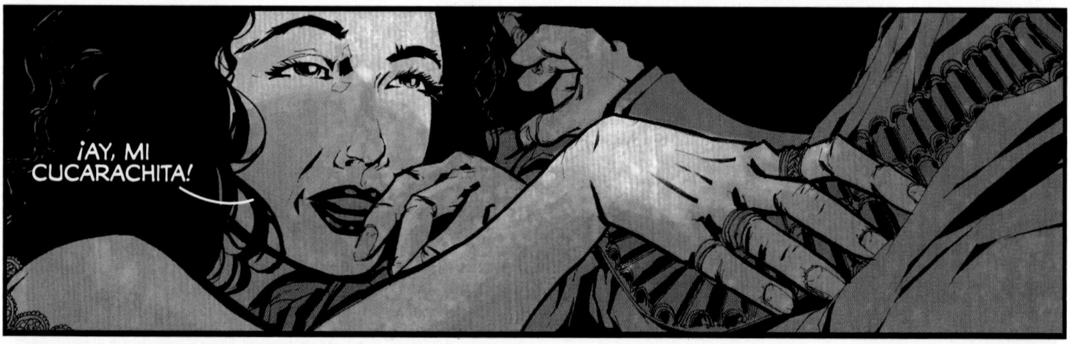
¡AY, MI CUCARACHITA!

CAUSE I WAS ALWAYS FUNNY BY WAY OF BEING A DUMB KID.

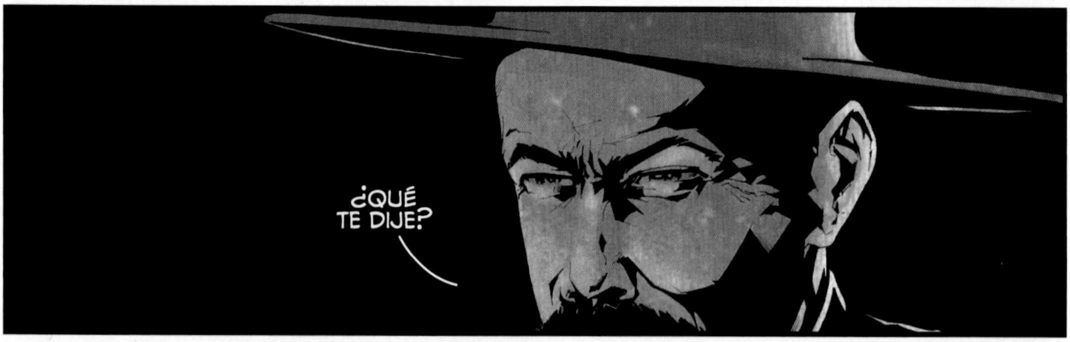
¿QUÉ TE DIJE?

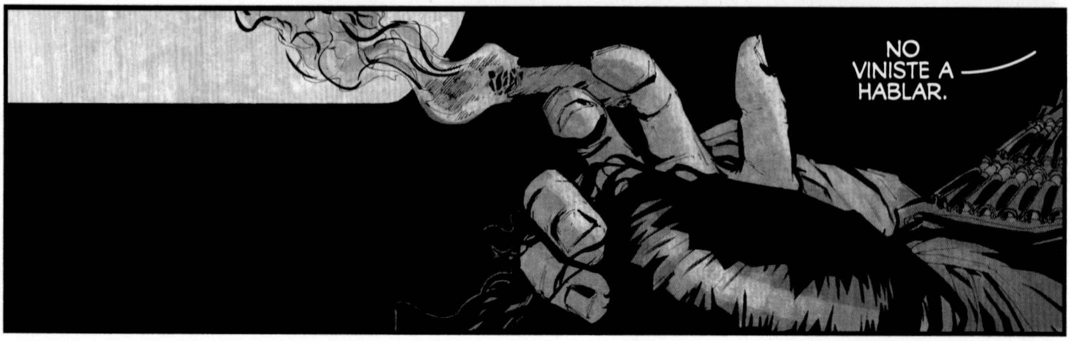
NO VINISTE A HABLAR.

BUT THE REAL FUNNY THING ON MY MIND, WAITING ON THEM TO PASS
WAS HOW I'D NEVER KILLED.

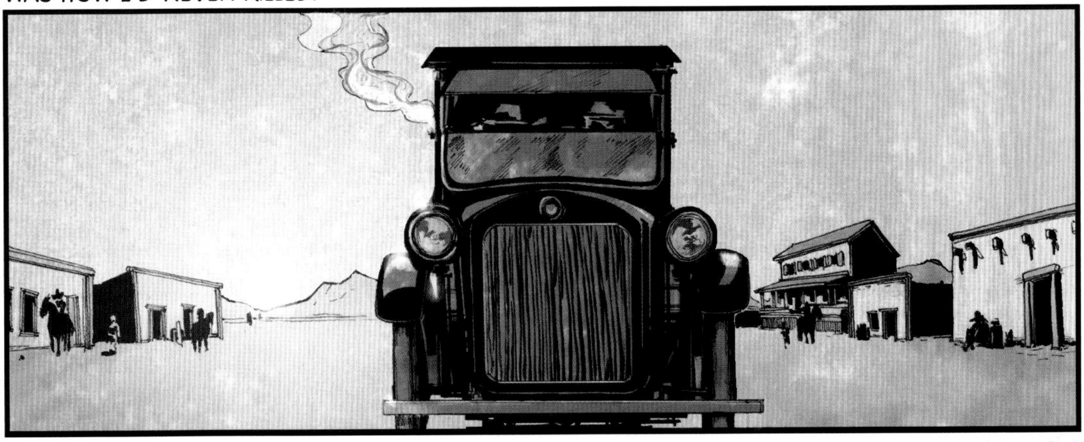

NOT THAT ANYONE KNEW.

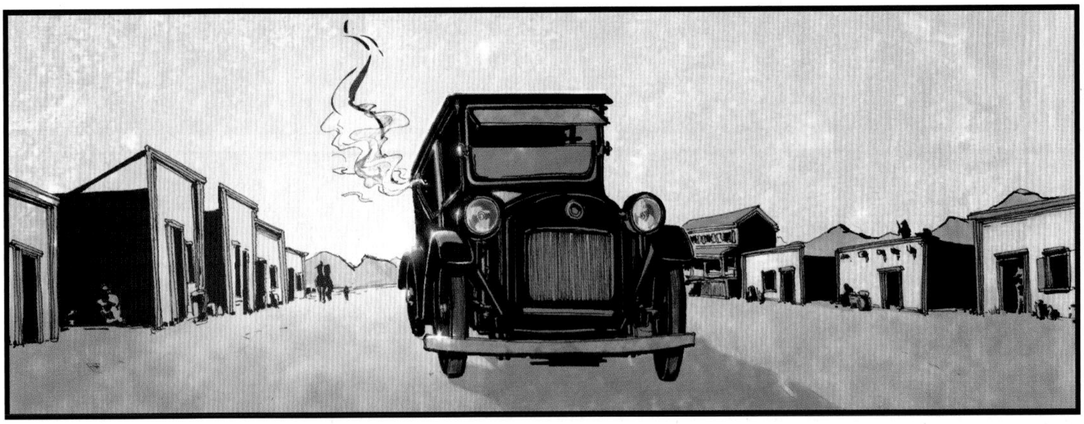

I WAS GOOD SHOOTING TARGETS, AND EVERYONE FIGURED I'D DRAWN SOME BLOOD ON THE WAY.

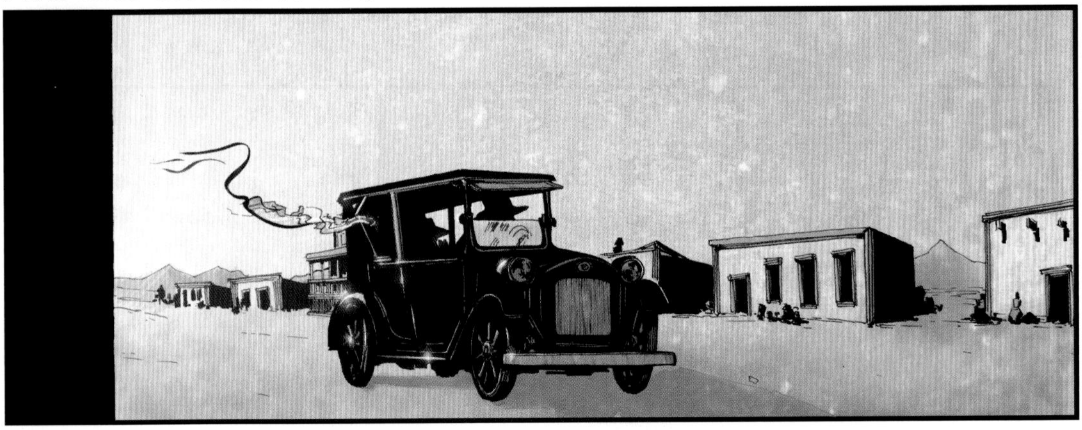

BUT I'D NEVER SCRATCHED THE SURFACE.

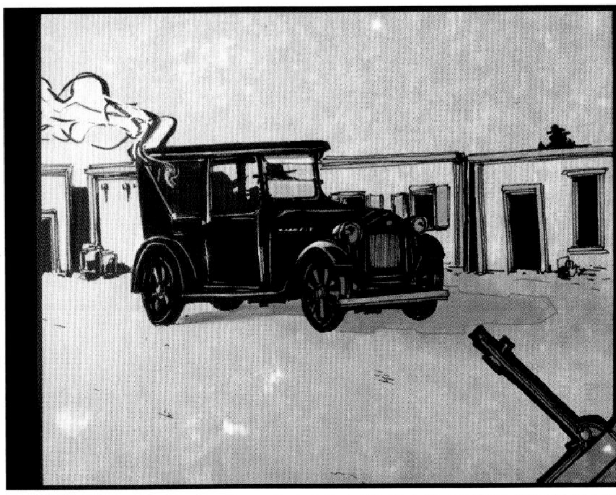

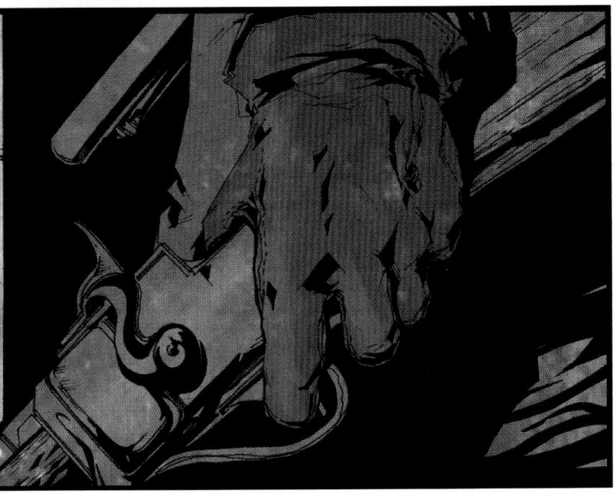

SO THE FIRST MAN I SHOT WAS UNTOUCHABLE UP TO THE MINUTE I FIRED AT HIS HEAD.

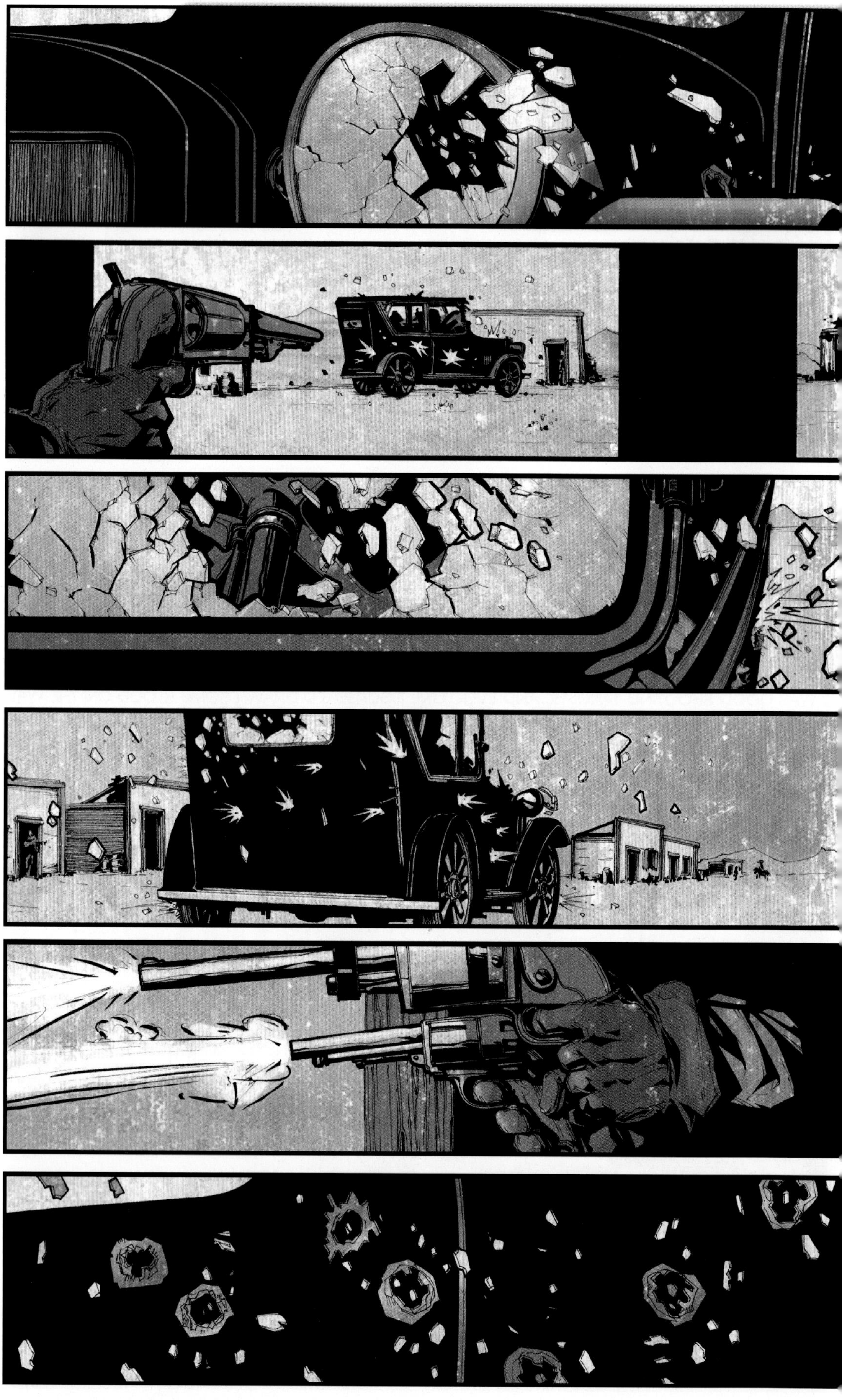

WE WEREN'T NONE OF US THE FIRST TO TRY.

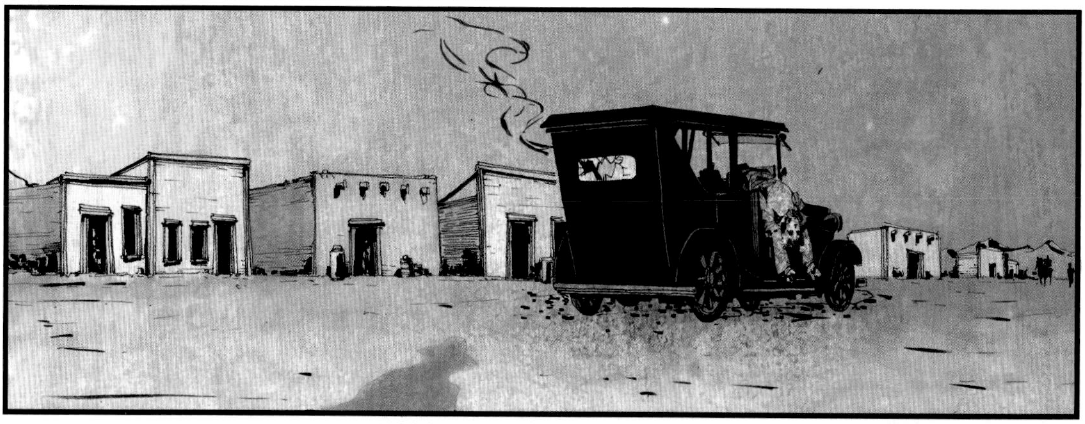

HOW IT HAPPENED, HE DIDN'T BELIEVE IT ANYMORE THAN I DID.

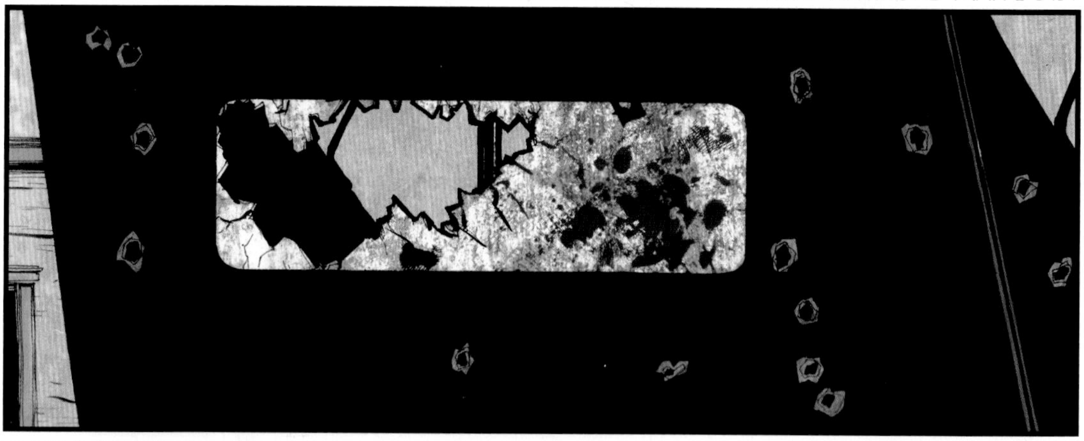

HE WAS STARING AT ME...

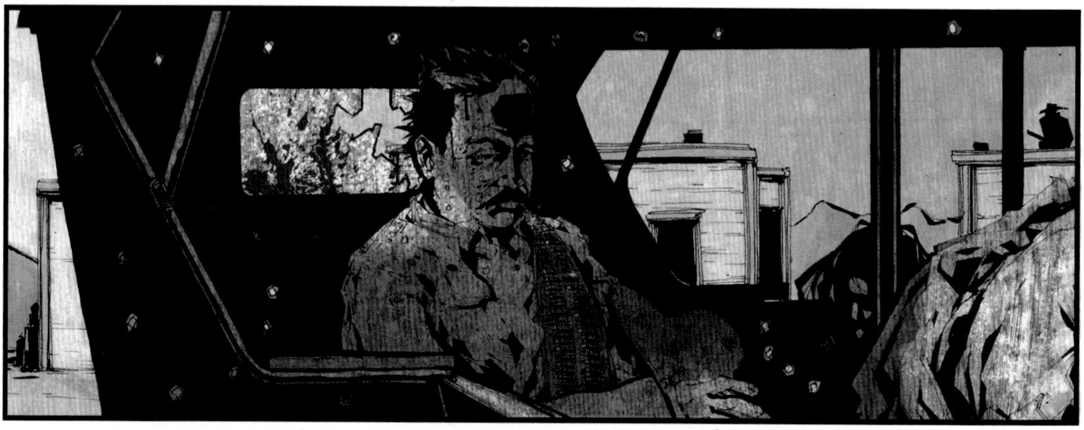

COVERED IN BLOOD AND COUGHING FROM ALL THE SMOKE.

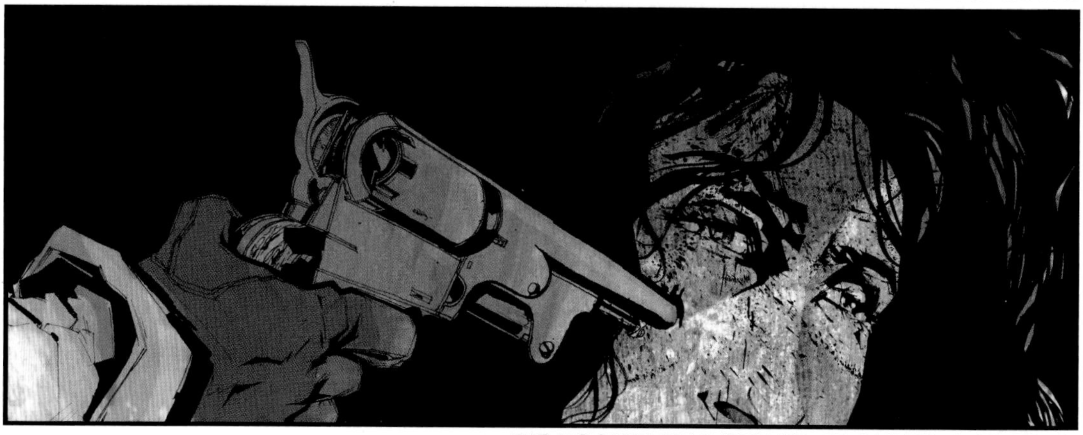

THE HOOKER WAS STONED OR MAYBE JUST GONE.

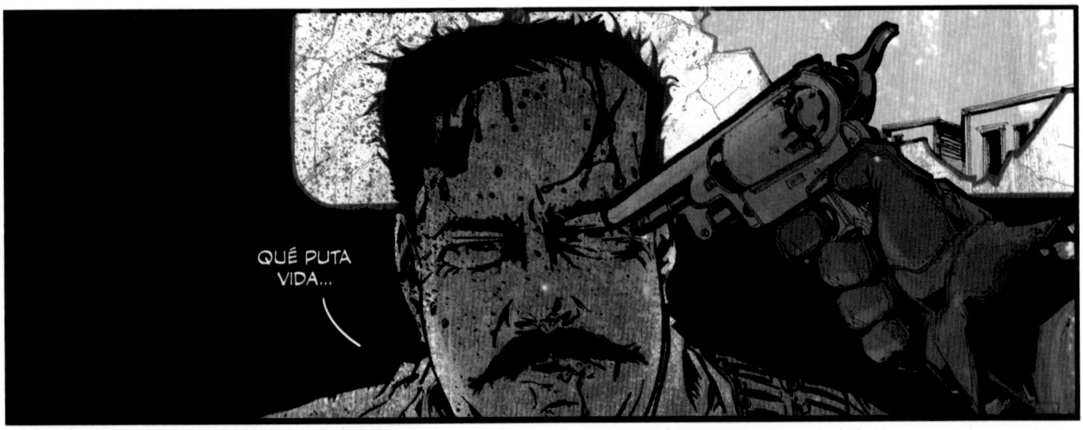
QUÉ PUTA VIDA...

AND EVEN AS I PULLED THE TRIGGER...

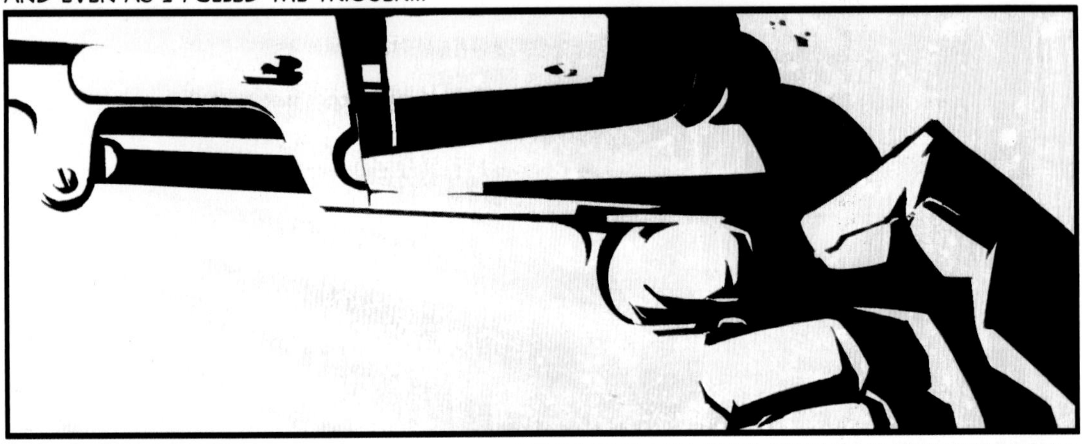

... I THOUGHT FOR SURE IT WAS ME THAT WAS DEAD.

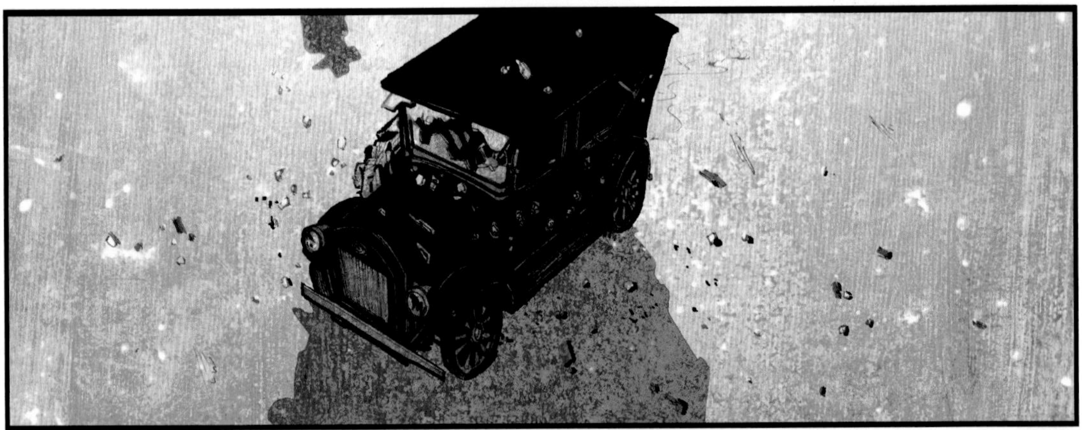

END.

"...ya con esta me despido,
por la Rosa de Castilla:

*¡aquí termina el corrido
del General Francisco Villa!"*

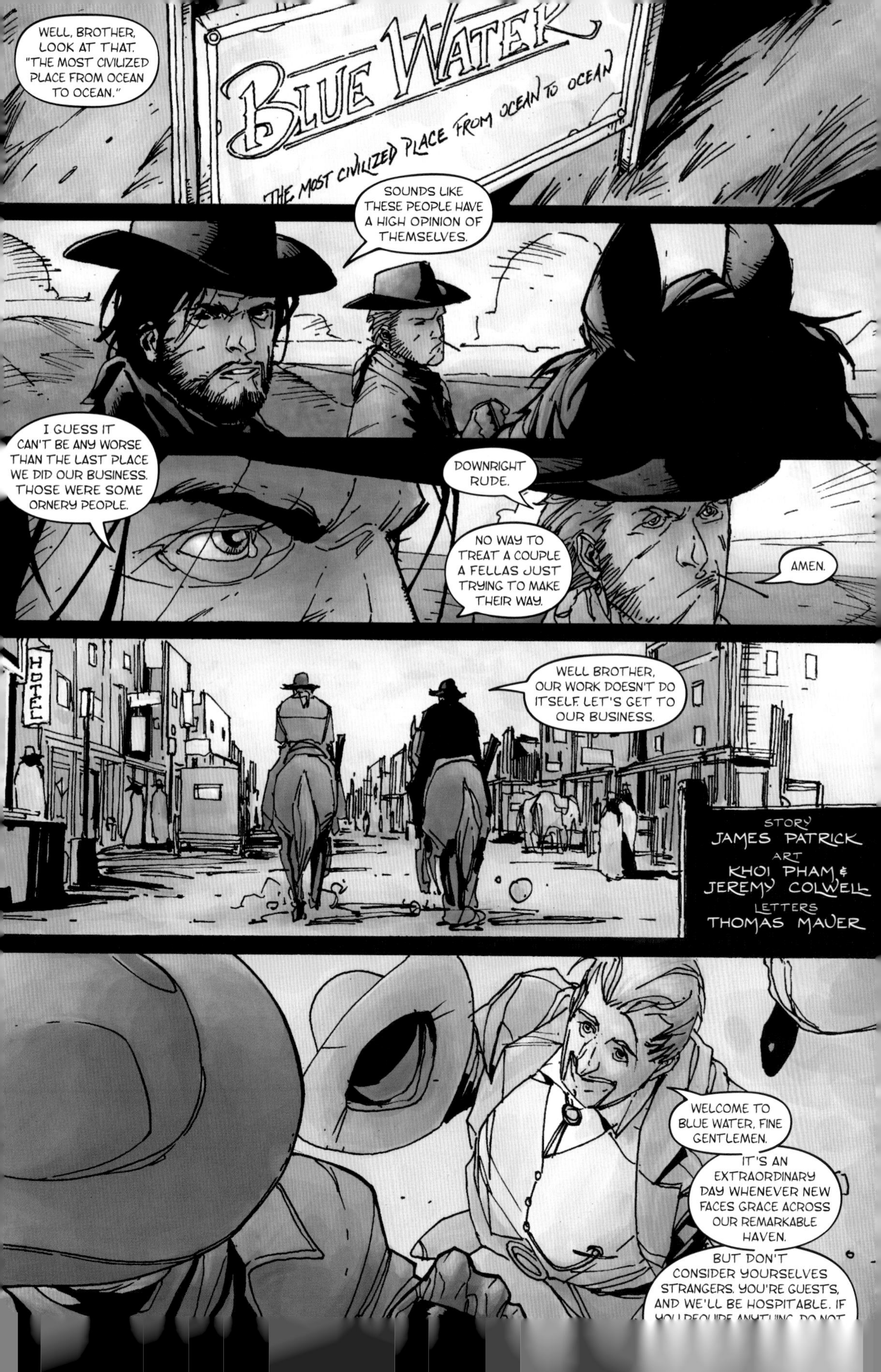
BLUE WATER
THE MOST CIVILIZED PLACE FROM OCEAN TO OCEAN
WELL, BROTHER, LOOK AT THAT. "THE MOST CIVILIZED PLACE FROM OCEAN TO OCEAN."
SOUNDS LIKE THESE PEOPLE HAVE A HIGH OPINION OF THEMSELVES.
I GUESS IT CAN'T BE ANY WORSE THAN THE LAST PLACE WE DID OUR BUSINESS. THOSE WERE SOME ORNERY PEOPLE.
DOWNRIGHT RUDE.
NO WAY TO TREAT A COUPLE A FELLAS JUST TRYING TO MAKE THEIR WAY.
AMEN.
HOTEL
WELL BROTHER, OUR WORK DOESN'T DO ITSELF. LET'S GET TO OUR BUSINESS.
STORY JAMES PATRICK
ART KHOI PHAM & JEREMY COLWELL
LETTERS THOMAS MAUER
WELCOME TO BLUE WATER, FINE GENTLEMEN.
IT'S AN EXTRAORDINARY DAY WHENEVER NEW FACES GRACE ACROSS OUR REMARKABLE HAVEN.
BUT DON'T CONSIDER YOURSELVES STRANGERS. YOU'RE GUESTS, AND WE'LL BE HOSPITABLE. IF

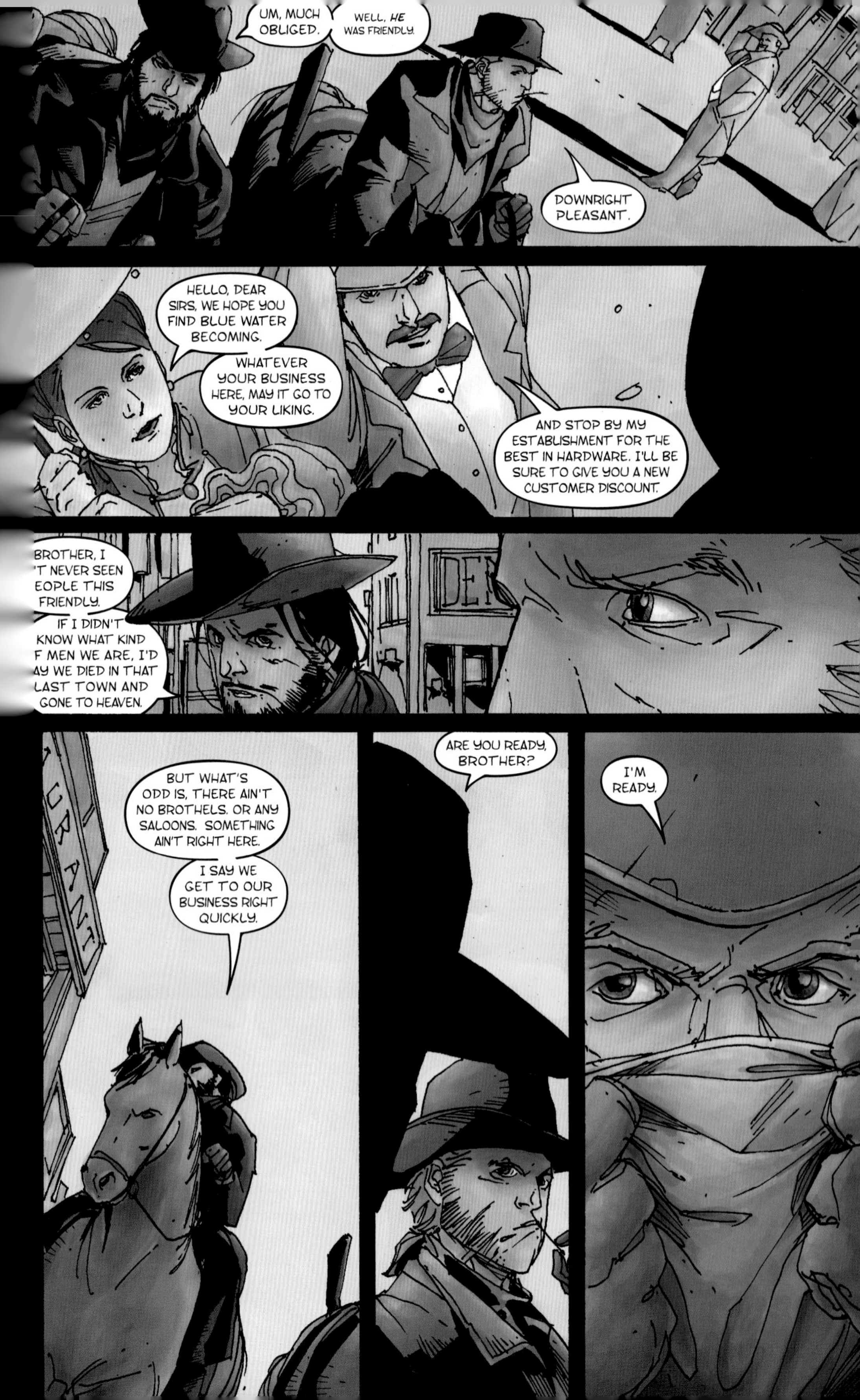
UM, MUCH OBLIGED.
WELL, HE WAS FRIENDLY.
DOWNRIGHT PLEASANT.
HELLO, DEAR SIRS, WE HOPE YOU FIND BLUE WATER BECOMING.
WHATEVER YOUR BUSINESS HERE, MAY IT GO TO YOUR LIKING.
AND STOP BY MY ESTABLISHMENT FOR THE BEST IN HARDWARE. I'LL BE SURE TO GIVE YOU A NEW CUSTOMER DISCOUNT.
BROTHER, I 'T NEVER SEEN EOPLE THIS FRIENDLY.
IF I DIDN'T KNOW WHAT KIND F MEN WE ARE, I'D AY WE DIED IN THAT LAST TOWN AND GONE TO HEAVEN.
BUT WHAT'S ODD IS, THERE AIN'T NO BROTHELS. OR ANY SALOONS. SOMETHING AIN'T RIGHT HERE.
I SAY WE GET TO OUR BUSINESS RIGHT QUICKLY.
ARE YOU READY, BROTHER?
I'M READY.

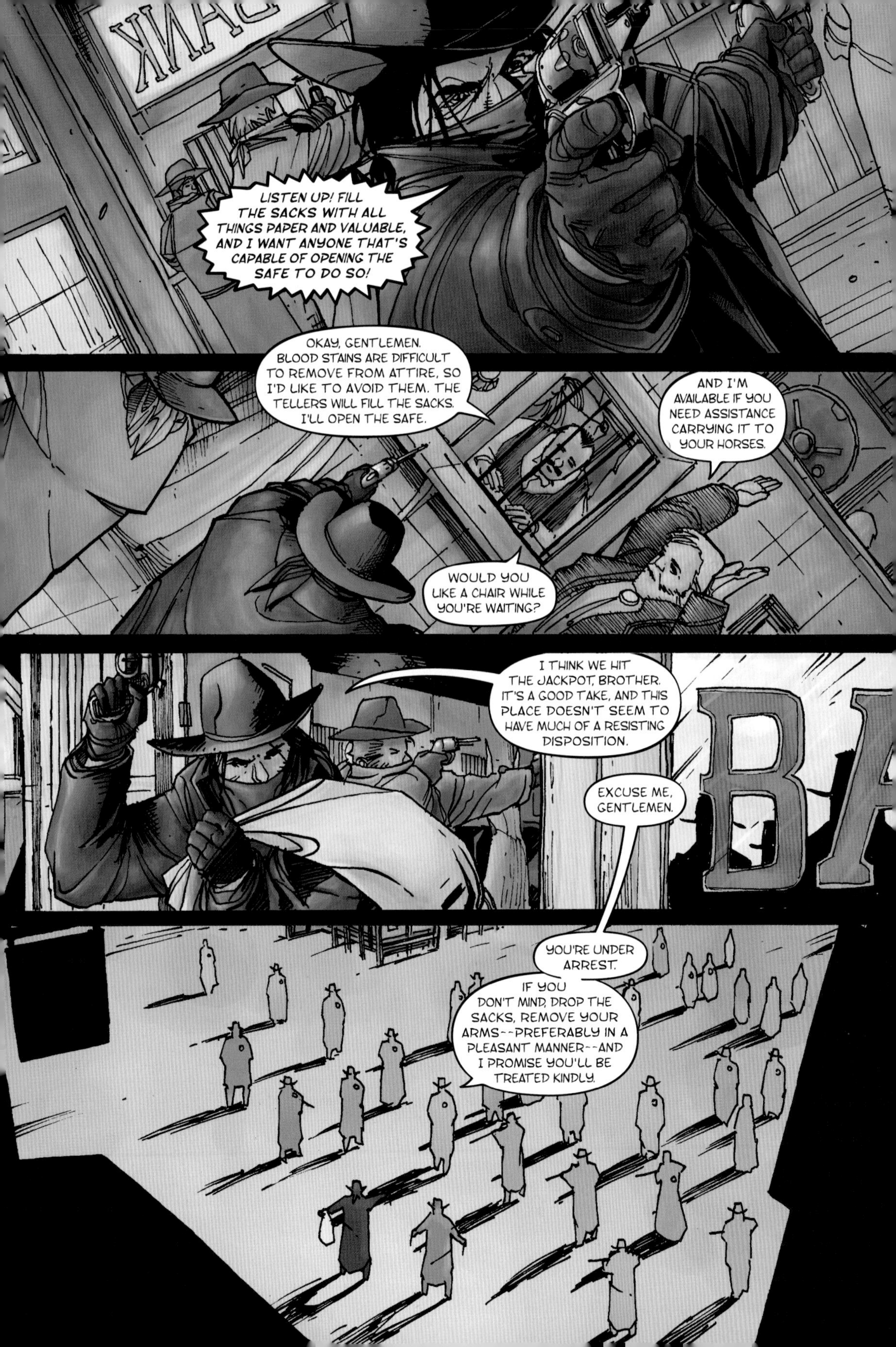
BANK
LISTEN UP! FILL THE SACKS WITH ALL THINGS PAPER AND VALUABLE, AND I WANT ANYONE THAT'S CAPABLE OF OPENING THE SAFE TO DO SO!
OKAY, GENTLEMEN. BLOOD STAINS ARE DIFFICULT TO REMOVE FROM ATTIRE, SO I'D LIKE TO AVOID THEM. THE TELLERS WILL FILL THE SACKS. I'LL OPEN THE SAFE.
AND I'M AVAILABLE IF YOU NEED ASSISTANCE CARRYING IT TO YOUR HORSES.
WOULD YOU LIKE A CHAIR WHILE YOU'RE WAITING?
I THINK WE HIT THE JACKPOT, BROTHER. IT'S A GOOD TAKE, AND THIS PLACE DOESN'T SEEM TO HAVE MUCH OF A RESISTING DISPOSITION.
EXCUSE ME, GENTLEMEN.
YOU'RE UNDER ARREST.
IF YOU DON'T MIND, DROP THE SACKS, REMOVE YOUR ARMS--PREFERABLY IN A PLEASANT MANNER--AND I PROMISE YOU'LL BE TREATED KINDLY.

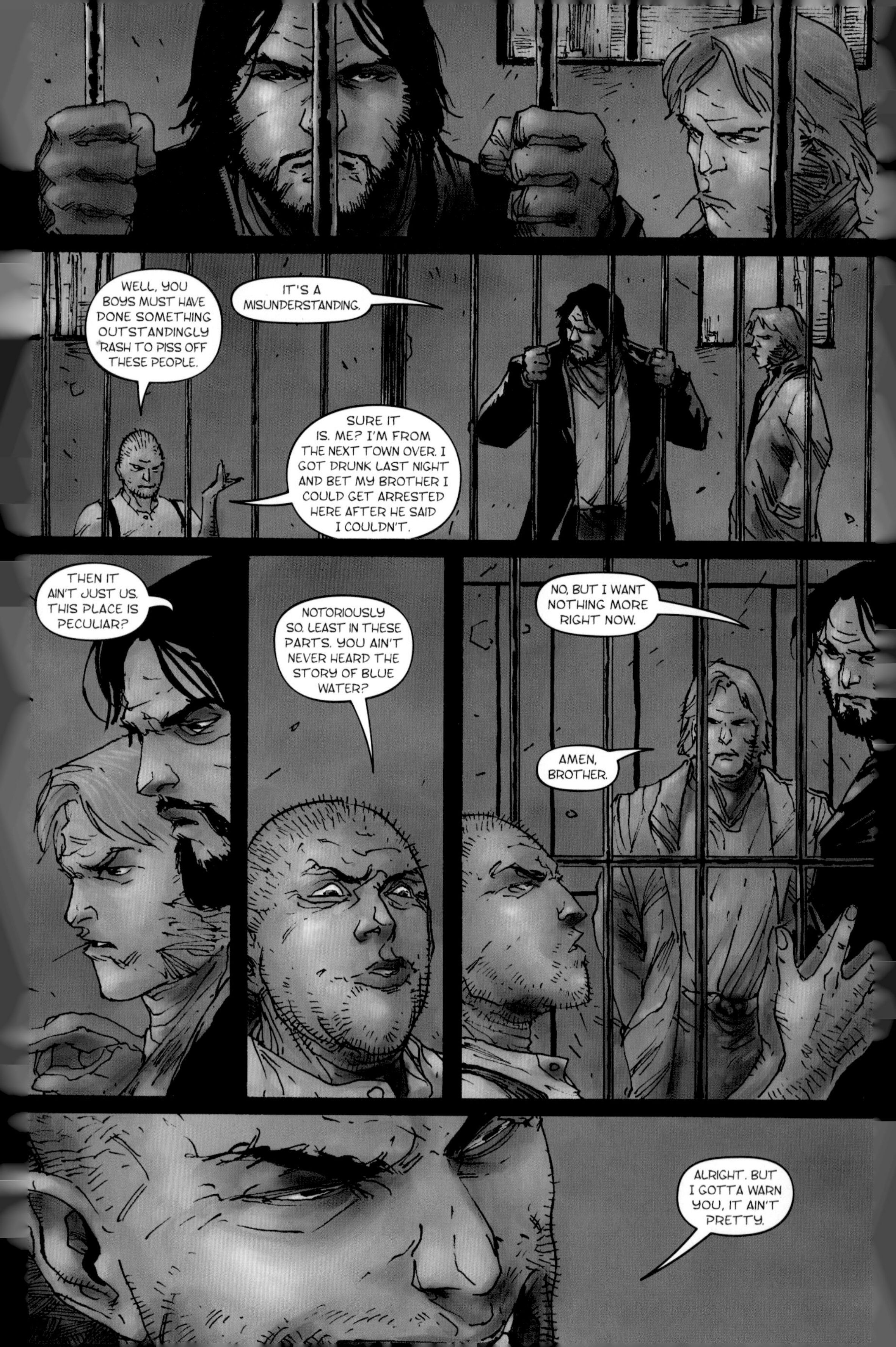
WELL, YOU BOYS MUST HAVE DONE SOMETHING OUTSTANDINGLY RASH TO PISS OFF THESE PEOPLE.
IT'S A MISUNDERSTANDING.
SURE IT IS. ME? I'M FROM THE NEXT TOWN OVER. I GOT DRUNK LAST NIGHT AND BET MY BROTHER I COULD GET ARRESTED HERE AFTER HE SAID I COULDN'T.
THEN IT AIN'T JUST US. THIS PLACE IS PECULIAR?
NOTORIOUSLY SO. LEAST IN THESE PARTS. YOU AIN'T NEVER HEARD THE STORY OF BLUE WATER?
NO, BUT I WANT NOTHING MORE RIGHT NOW.
AMEN, BROTHER.
ALRIGHT. BUT I GOTTA WARN YOU, IT AIN'T PRETTY.

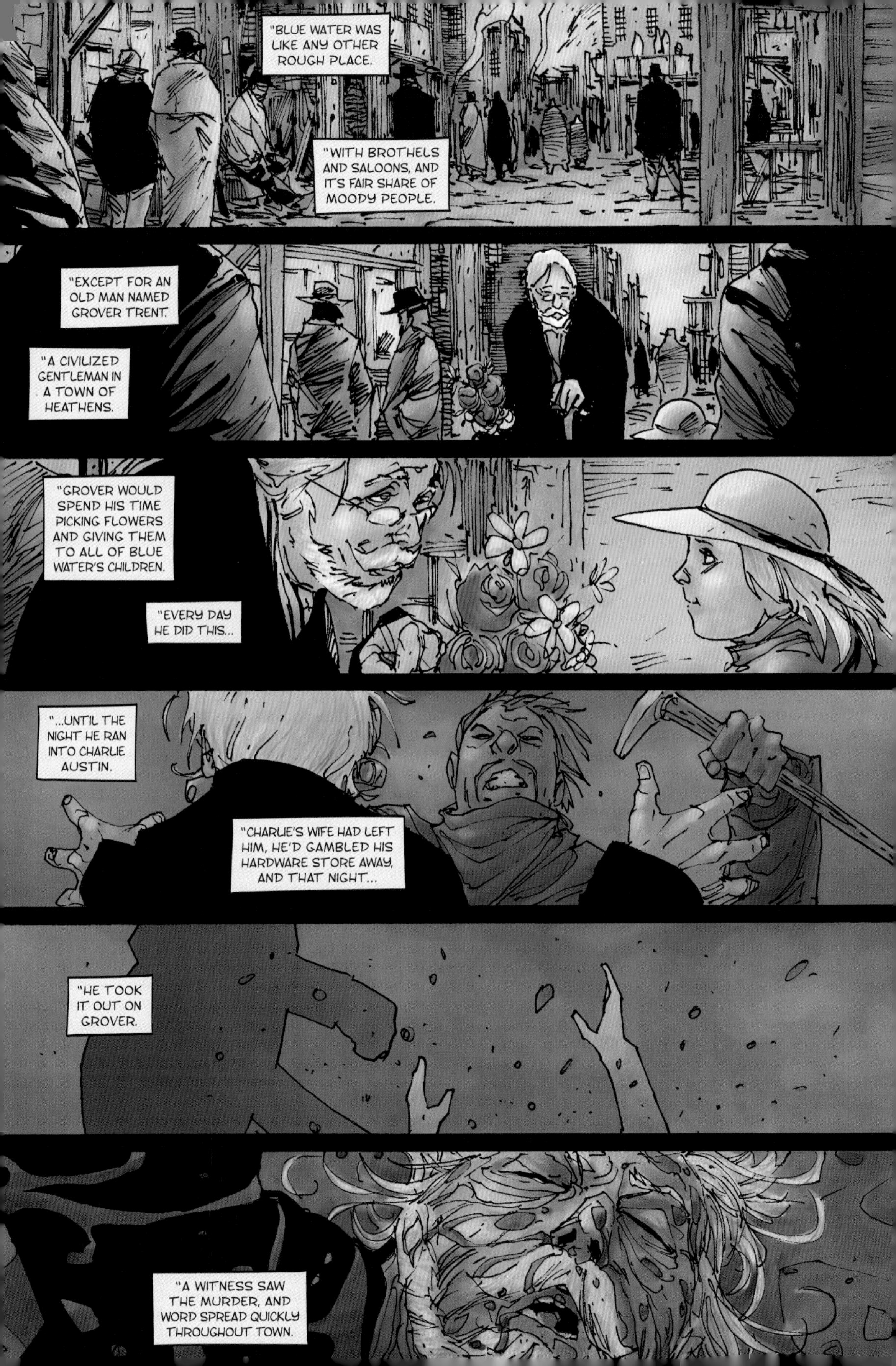
"BLUE WATER WAS LIKE ANY OTHER ROUGH PLACE.
"WITH BROTHELS AND SALOONS, AND IT'S FAIR SHARE OF MOODY PEOPLE.
"EXCEPT FOR AN OLD MAN NAMED GROVER TRENT.
"A CIVILIZED GENTLEMAN IN A TOWN OF HEATHENS.
"GROVER WOULD SPEND HIS TIME PICKING FLOWERS AND GIVING THEM TO ALL OF BLUE WATER'S CHILDREN.
"EVERY DAY HE DID THIS...
"...UNTIL THE NIGHT HE RAN INTO CHARLIE AUSTIN.
"CHARLIE'S WIFE HAD LEFT HIM, HE'D GAMBLED HIS HARDWARE STORE AWAY, AND THAT NIGHT...
"HE TOOK IT OUT ON GROVER.
"A WITNESS SAW THE MURDER, AND WORD SPREAD QUICKLY THROUGHOUT TOWN.

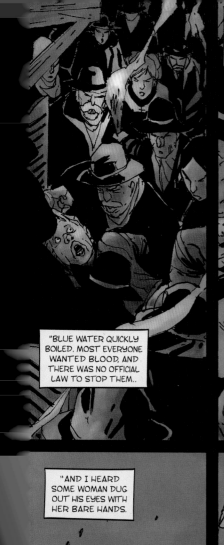

"BLUE WATER QUICKLY BOILED. MOST EVERYONE WANTED BLOOD, AND THERE WAS NO OFFICIAL LAW TO STOP THEM.."

"MAYBE IF IT HAPPENED AGAIN, THE PEOPLE OF BLUE WATER WOULD ACT DIFFERENTLY. MAYBE NOT.

"ALL I CAN SAY IS, THINGS GOT UGLY.

"I HEARD ONE MAN TOOK A ROCK AND STARTED BASHING AT CHARLIE'S SKULL WHILE THE OTHERS HELD HIM DOWN.

"AND I HEARD SOME WOMAN DUG OUT HIS EYES WITH HER BARE HANDS.

"I GUESS HE WAS STILL ALIVE WHEN THE REST OF THE TOWN TORE HIM APART.

" NOW, AT SOME POINT, THEY REALIZED WHAT THEY'D DONE, AND WERE HORRIFIED WITH THEMSELVES.

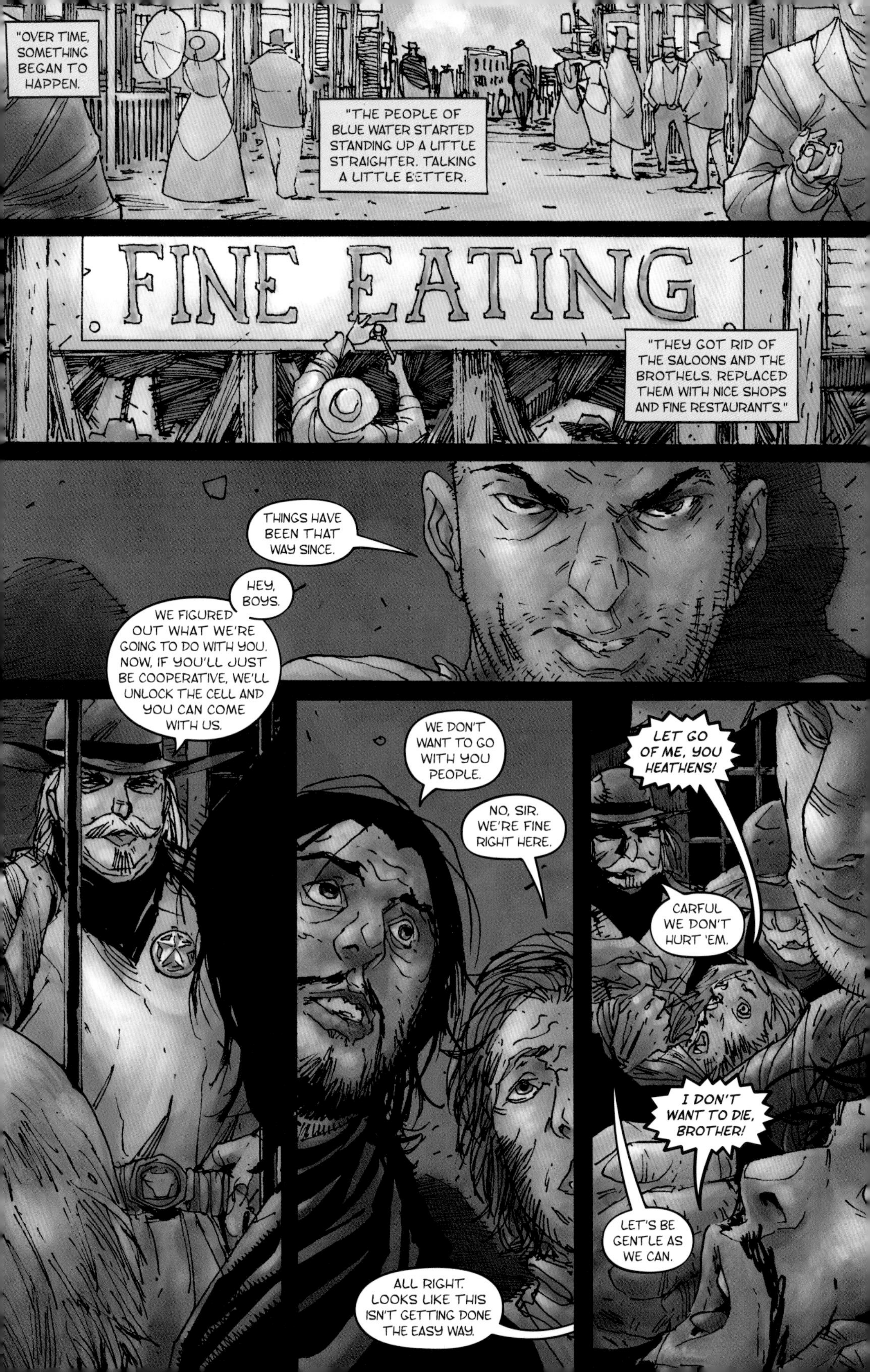
"OVER TIME, SOMETHING BEGAN TO HAPPEN.
"THE PEOPLE OF BLUE WATER STARTED STANDING UP A LITTLE STRAIGHTER. TALKING A LITTLE BETTER.
FINE EATING
"THEY GOT RID OF THE SALOONS AND THE BROTHELS. REPLACED THEM WITH NICE SHOPS AND FINE RESTAURANTS."
THINGS HAVE BEEN THAT WAY SINCE.
HEY, BOYS.
WE FIGURED OUT WHAT WE'RE GOING TO DO WITH YOU. NOW, IF YOU'LL JUST BE COOPERATIVE, WE'LL UNLOCK THE CELL AND YOU CAN COME WITH US.
WE DON'T WANT TO GO WITH YOU PEOPLE.
NO, SIR. WE'RE FINE RIGHT HERE.
ALL RIGHT. LOOKS LIKE THIS ISN'T GETTING DONE THE EASY WAY.
LET GO OF ME, YOU HEATHENS!
CARFUL WE DON'T HURT 'EM.
I DON'T WANT TO DIE, BROTHER!
LET'S BE GENTLE AS WE CAN.

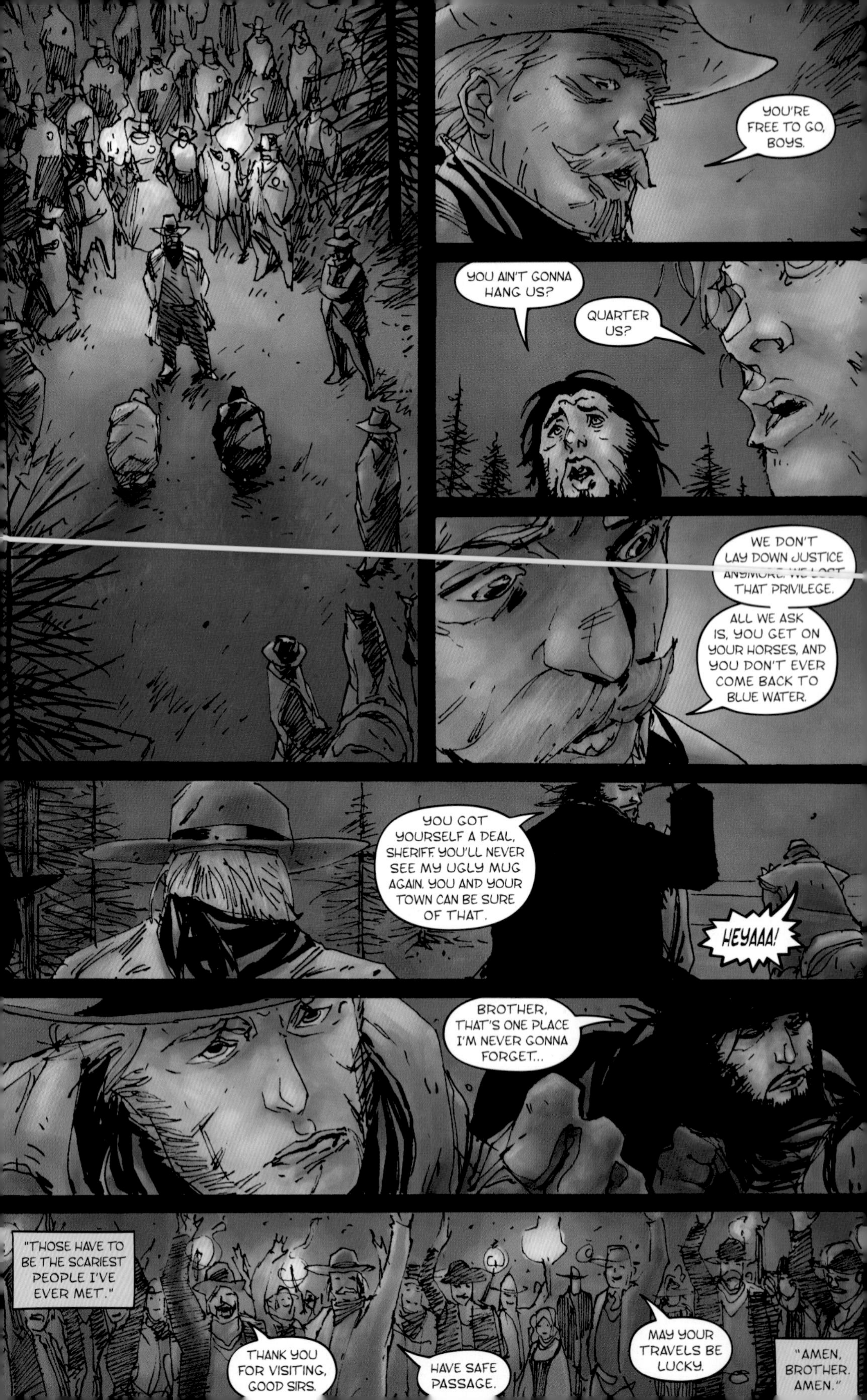
YOU'RE FREE TO GO, BOYS.
YOU AIN'T GONNA HANG US?
QUARTER US?
WE DON'T LAY DOWN JUSTICE ANYMORE. WE LOST THAT PRIVILEGE.
ALL WE ASK IS, YOU GET ON YOUR HORSES, AND YOU DON'T EVER COME BACK TO BLUE WATER.
YOU GOT YOURSELF A DEAL, SHERIFF. YOU'LL NEVER SEE MY UGLY MUG AGAIN. YOU AND YOUR TOWN CAN BE SURE OF THAT.
HEYAAA!
BROTHER, THAT'S ONE PLACE I'M NEVER GONNA FORGET...
"THOSE HAVE TO BE THE SCARIEST PEOPLE I'VE EVER MET."
THANK YOU FOR VISITING, GOOD SIRS.
HAVE SAFE PASSAGE.
MAY YOUR TRAVELS BE LUCKY.
"AMEN, BROTHER. AMEN."

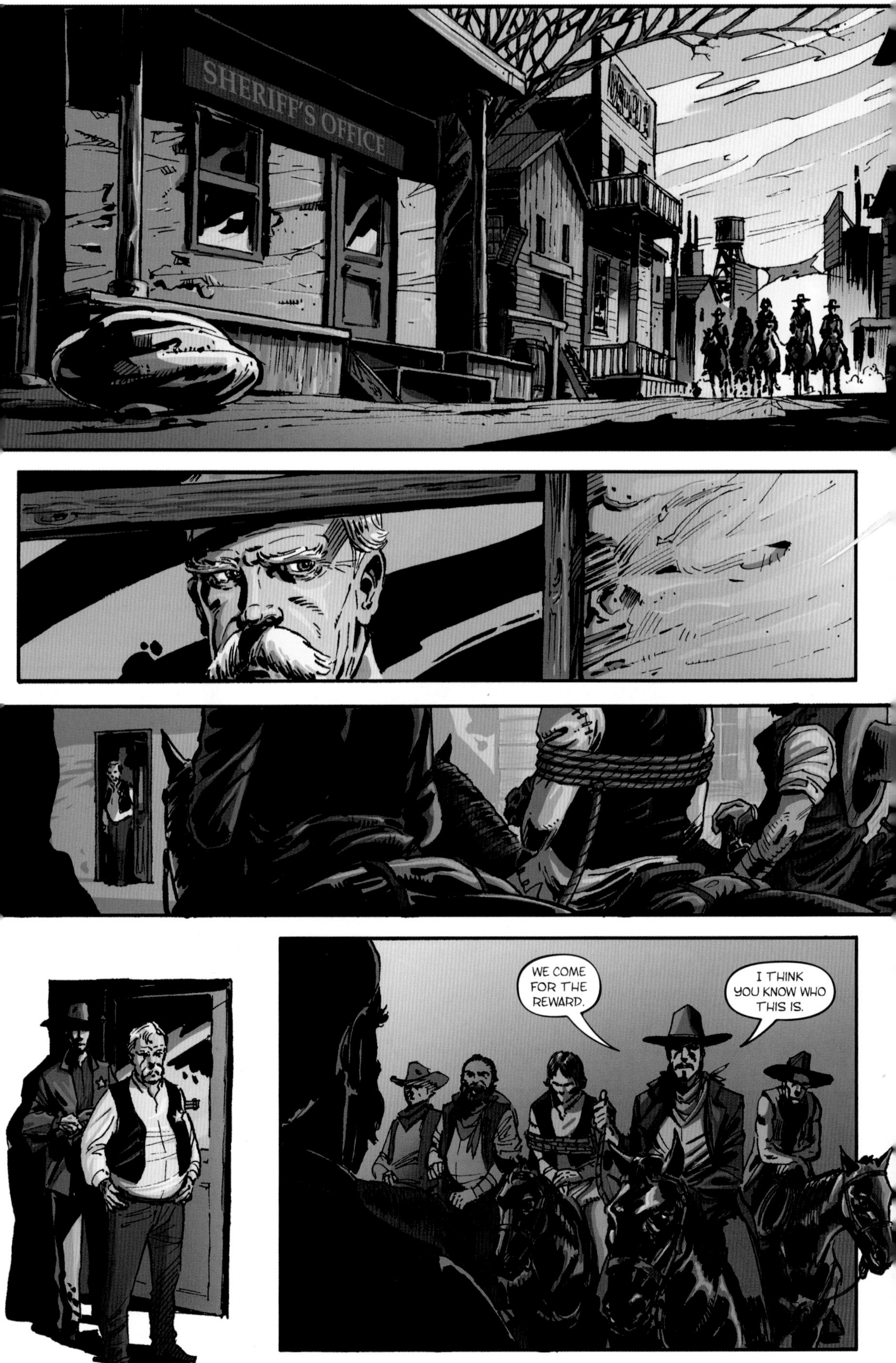
SHERIFF'S OFFICE
WE COME FOR THE REWARD.
I THINK YOU KNOW WHO THIS IS.

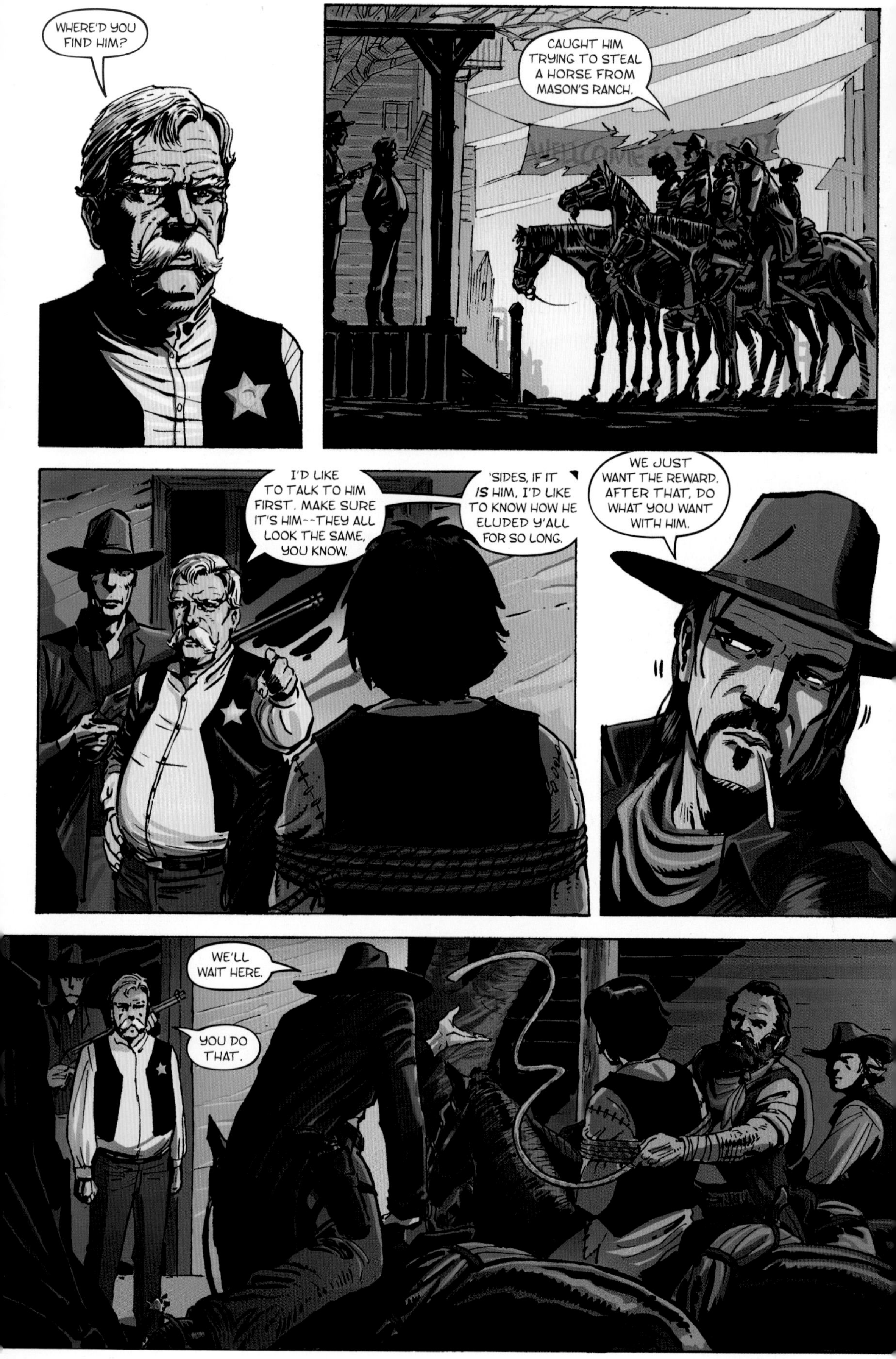
WHERE'D YOU FIND HIM?
CAUGHT HIM TRYING TO STEAL A HORSE FROM MASON'S RANCH.
I'D LIKE TO TALK TO HIM FIRST. MAKE SURE IT'S HIM--THEY ALL LOOK THE SAME, YOU KNOW.
'SIDES, IF IT *IS* HIM, I'D LIKE TO KNOW HOW HE ELUDED Y'ALL FOR SO LONG.
WE JUST WANT THE REWARD. AFTER THAT, DO WHAT YOU WANT WITH HIM.
WE'LL WAIT HERE.
YOU DO THAT.

WE'LL TAKE HIM FROM HERE.

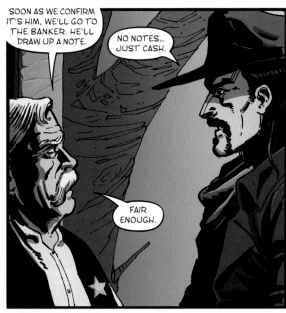

SOON AS WE CONFIRM IT'S HIM, WE'LL GO TO THE BANKER. HE'LL DRAW UP A NOTE.

NO NOTES... JUST CASH.

FAIR ENOUGH.

SO YOU'RE AHIGA.

YOU'RE WORTH QUITE A BIT...MORE SO ALIVE THAN DEAD. YOU'RE LUCKY TO BE SO FAMOUS. MOST TIMES, WE JUST SHOOT YOU BASTARDS ON PRINCIPLE ALONE.

CARE FOR SOME WATER?

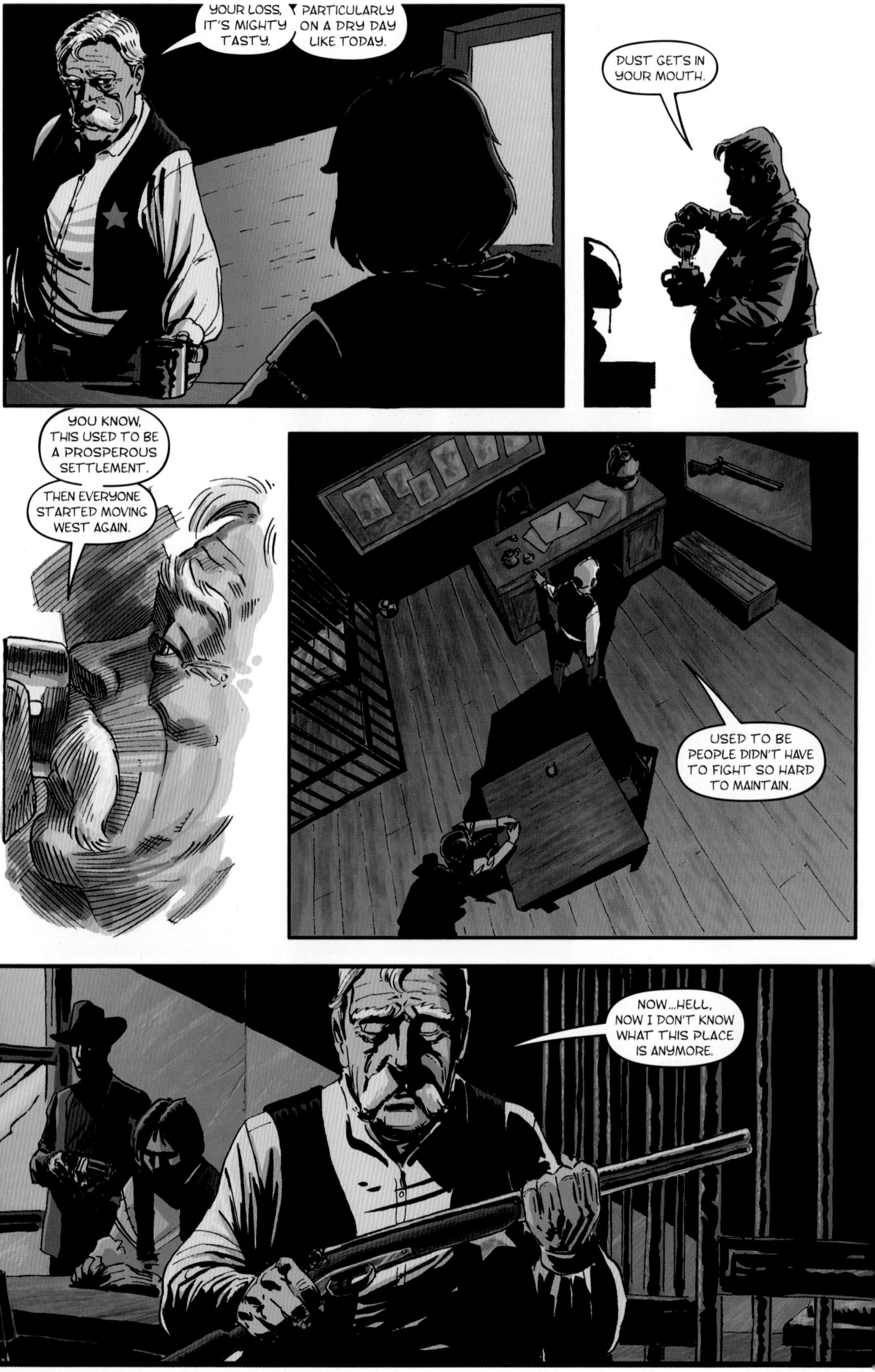
YOUR LOSS, IT'S MIGHTY TASTY.
PARTICULARLY ON A DRY DAY LIKE TODAY.
DUST GETS IN YOUR MOUTH.
YOU KNOW, THIS USED TO BE A PROSPEROUS SETTLEMENT.
THEN EVERYONE STARTED MOVING WEST AGAIN.
USED TO BE PEOPLE DIDN'T HAVE TO FIGHT SO HARD TO MAINTAIN.
NOW...HELL, NOW I DON'T KNOW WHAT THIS PLACE IS ANYMORE.

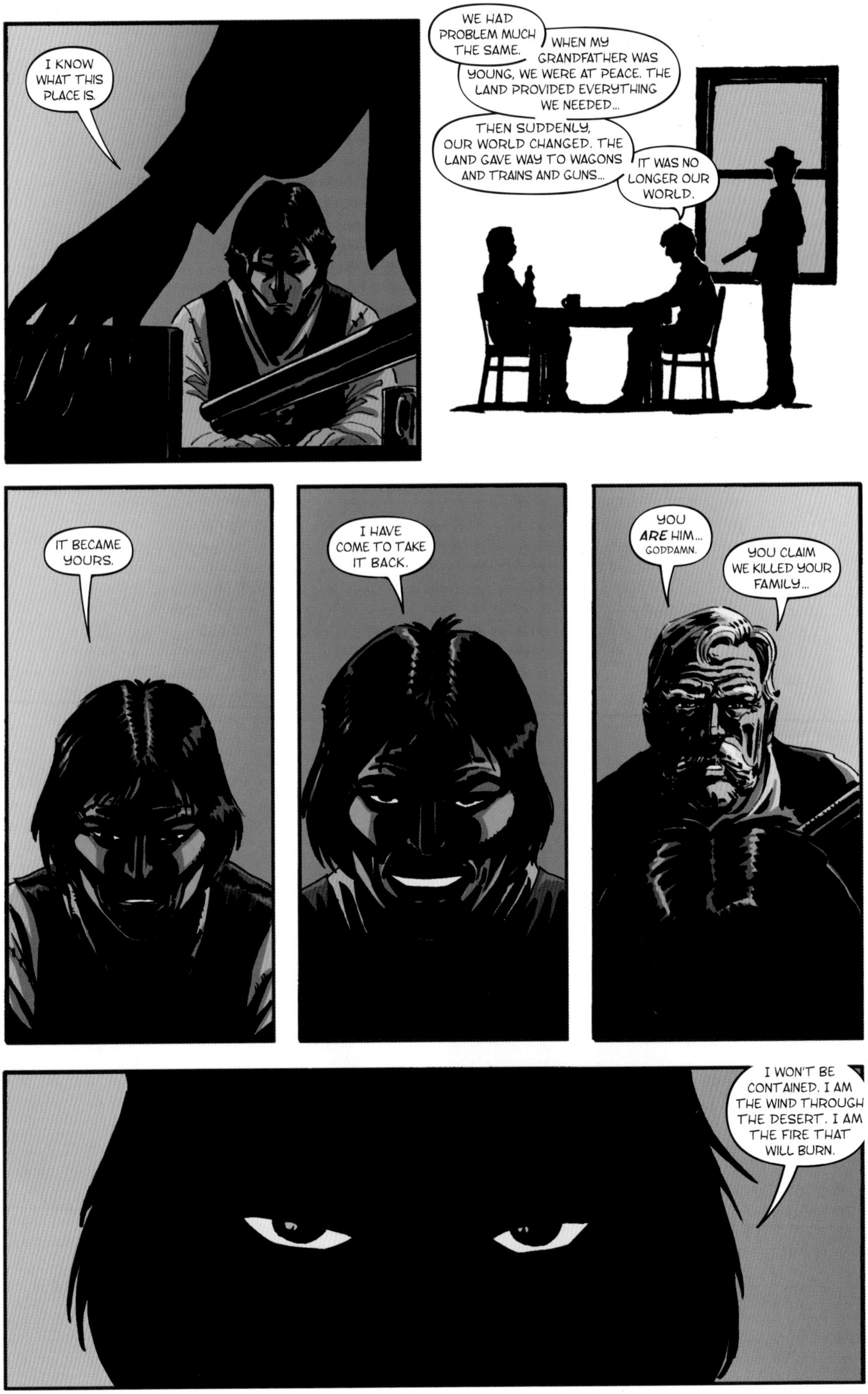

I KNOW WHAT THIS PLACE IS.
WE HAD PROBLEM MUCH THE SAME.
WHEN MY GRANDFATHER WAS YOUNG, WE WERE AT PEACE. THE LAND PROVIDED EVERYTHING WE NEEDED...
THEN SUDDENLY, OUR WORLD CHANGED. THE LAND GAVE WAY TO WAGONS AND TRAINS AND GUNS...
IT WAS NO LONGER OUR WORLD.
IT BECAME YOURS.
I HAVE COME TO TAKE IT BACK.
YOU **ARE** HIM... GODDAMN.
YOU CLAIM WE KILLED YOUR FAMILY...
I WON'T BE CONTAINED. I AM THE WIND THROUGH THE DESERT. I AM THE FIRE THAT WILL BURN.

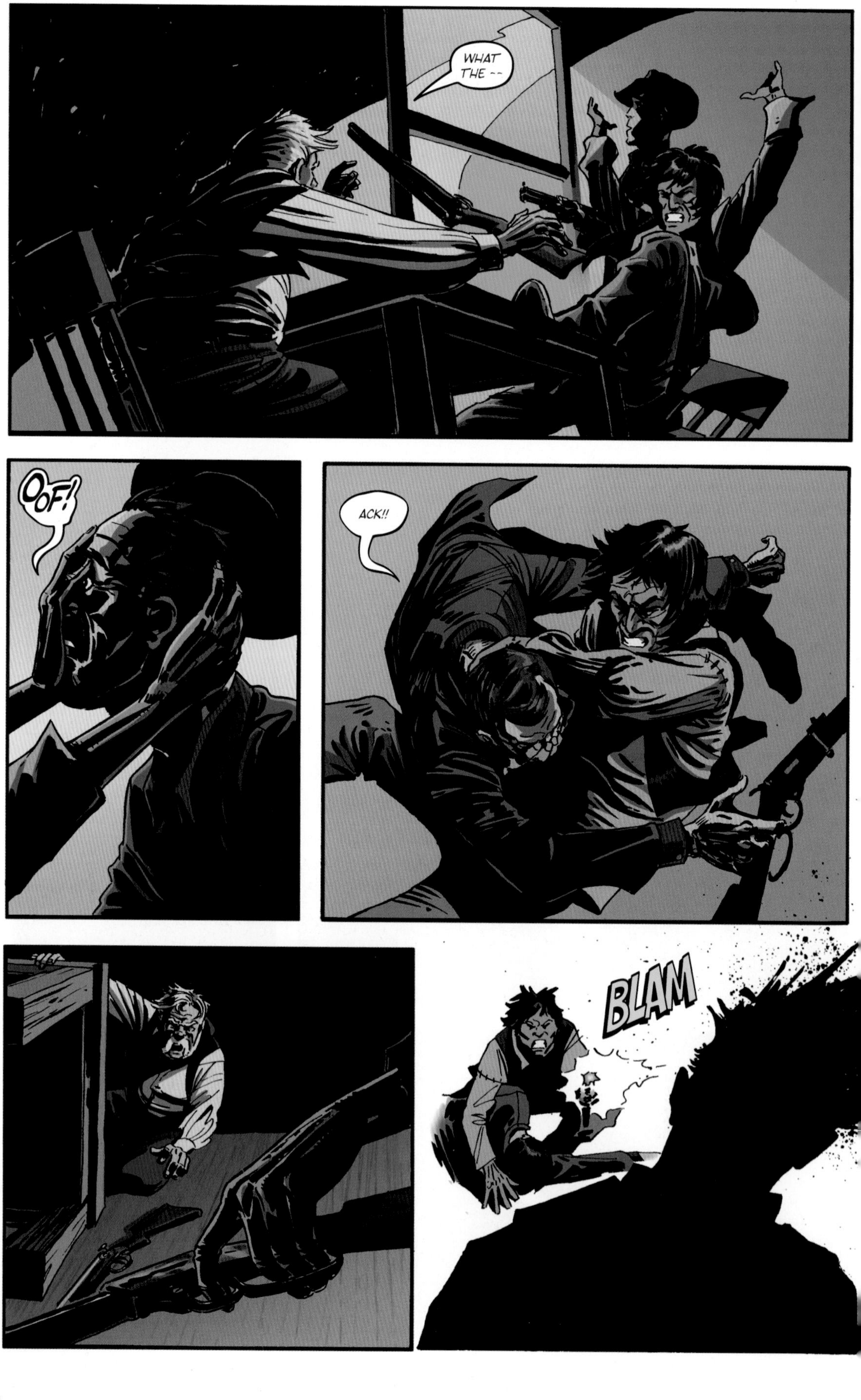
WHAT THE --
OOF!
ACK!!
BLAM

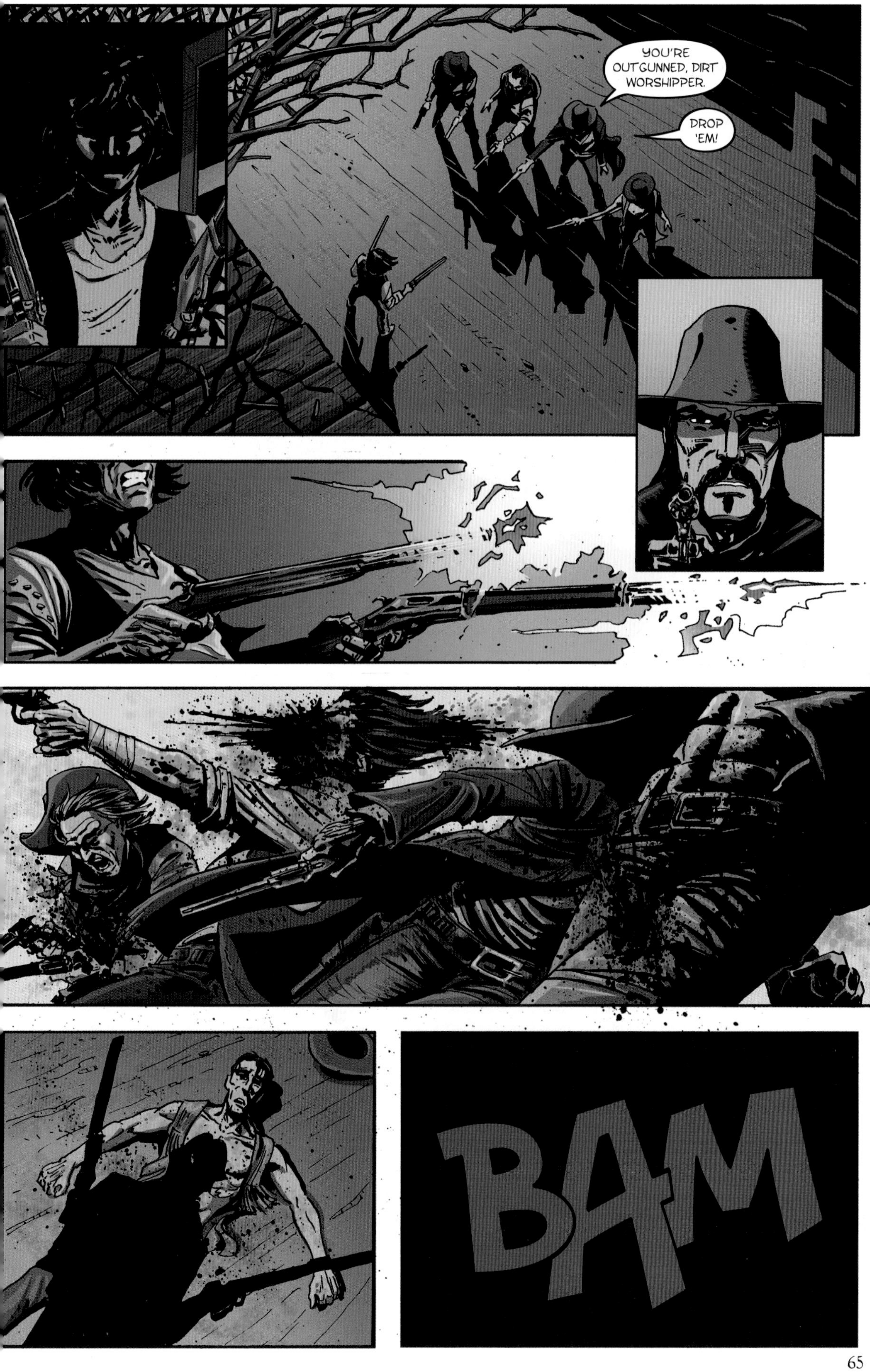

YOU'RE OUTGUNNED, DIRT WORSHIPPER.
DROP 'EM!
BAM

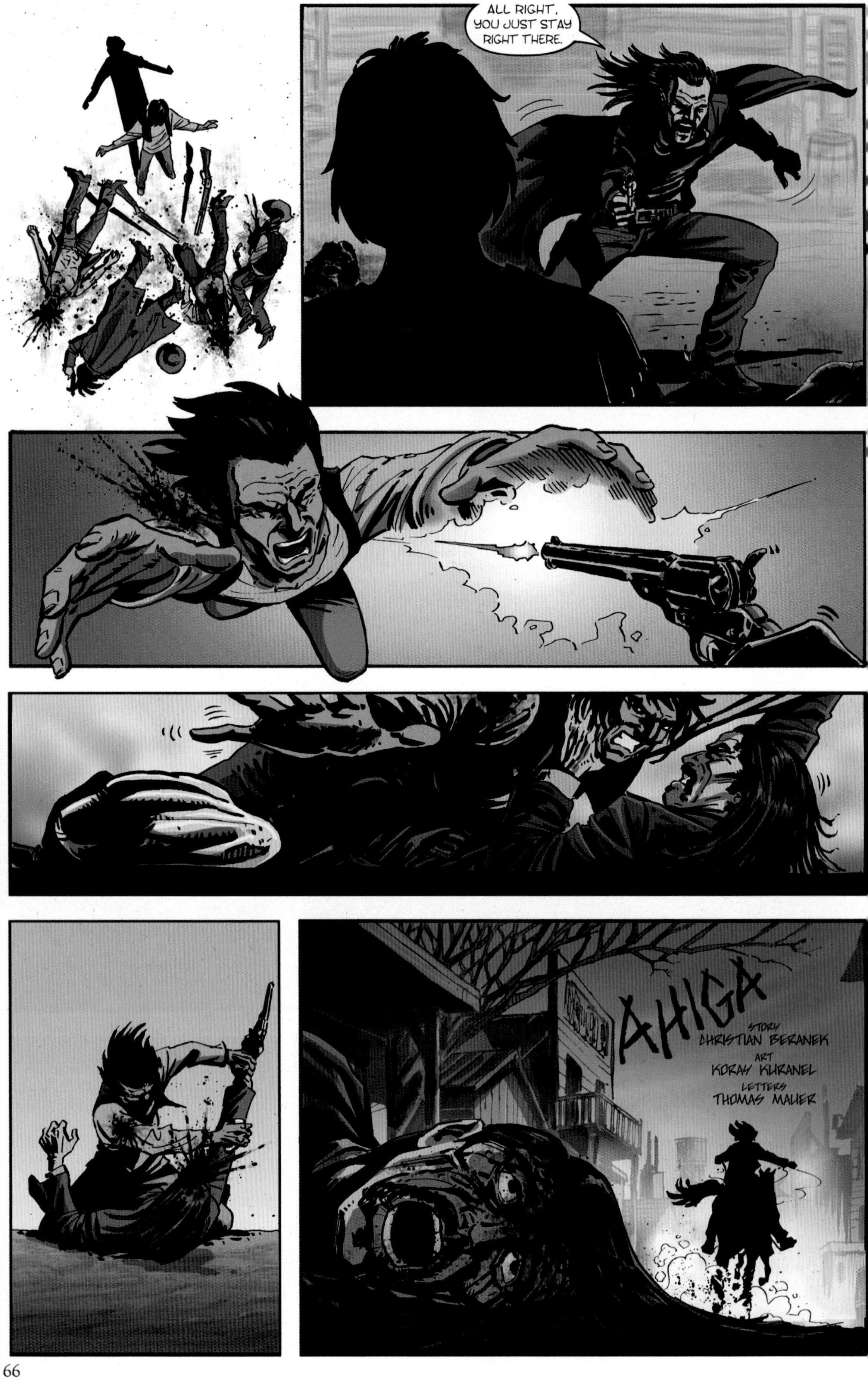
ALL RIGHT, YOU JUST STAY RIGHT THERE.
AHIGA
STORY
CHRISTIAN BERANEK
ART
KORAY KURANEL
LETTERS
THOMAS MAUER

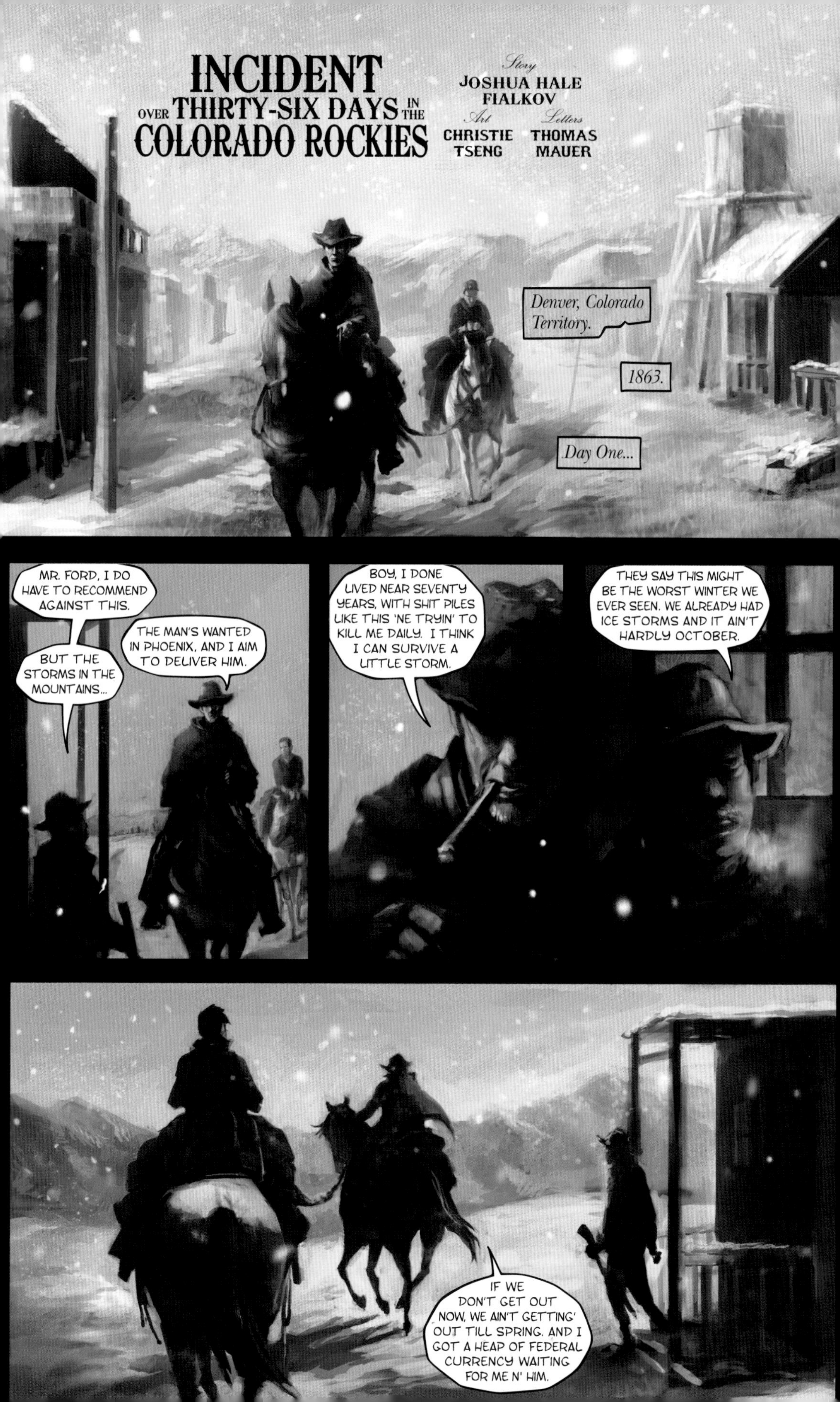
INCIDENT OVER THIRTY-SIX DAYS IN THE COLORADO ROCKIES
Story JOSHUA HALE FIALKOV
Art CHRISTIE TSENG
Letters THOMAS MAUER
Denver, Colorado Territory.
1863.
Day One...
MR. FORD, I DO HAVE TO RECOMMEND AGAINST THIS.
BUT THE STORMS IN THE MOUNTAINS...
THE MAN'S WANTED IN PHOENIX, AND I AIM TO DELIVER HIM.
BOY, I DONE LIVED NEAR SEVENTY YEARS, WITH SHIT PILES LIKE THIS 'NE TRYIN' TO KILL ME DAILY. I THINK I CAN SURVIVE A LITTLE STORM.
THEY SAY THIS MIGHT BE THE WORST WINTER WE EVER SEEN. WE ALREADY HAD ICE STORMS AND IT AIN'T HARDLY OCTOBER.
IF WE DON'T GET OUT NOW, WE AIN'T GETTING' OUT TILL SPRING. AND I GOT A HEAP OF FEDERAL CURRENCY WAITING FOR ME N' HIM.

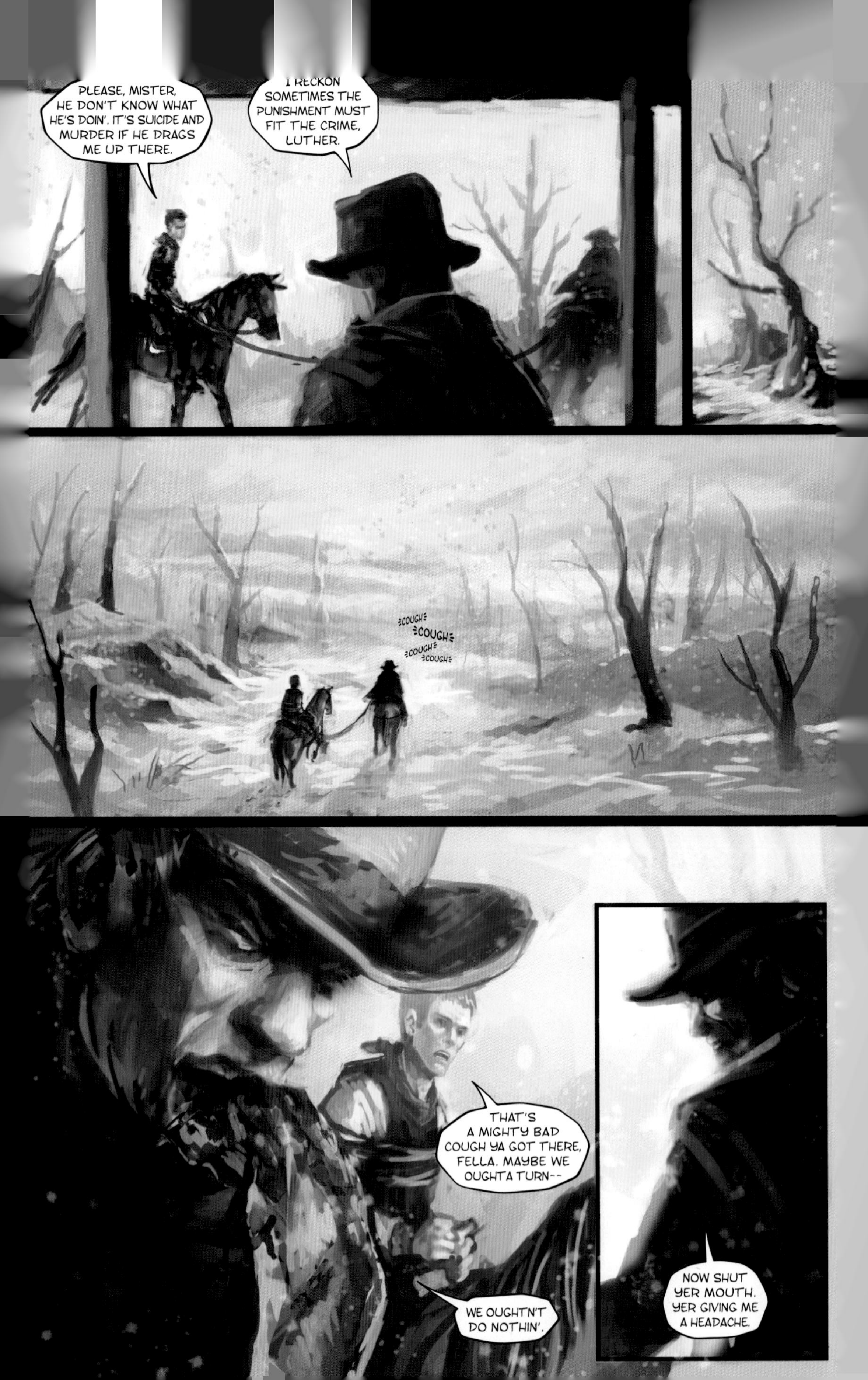
PLEASE, MISTER, HE DON'T KNOW WHAT HE'S DOIN'. IT'S SUICIDE AND MURDER IF HE DRAGS ME UP THERE.
I RECKON SOMETIMES THE PUNISHMENT MUST FIT THE CRIME, LUTHER.
COUGH
COUGH
COUGH
COUGH
THAT'S A MIGHTY BAD COUGH YA GOT THERE, FELLA. MAYBE WE OUGHTA TURN--
WE OUGHT'N'T DO NOTHIN'.
NOW SHUT YER MOUTH. YER GIVING ME A HEADACHE.

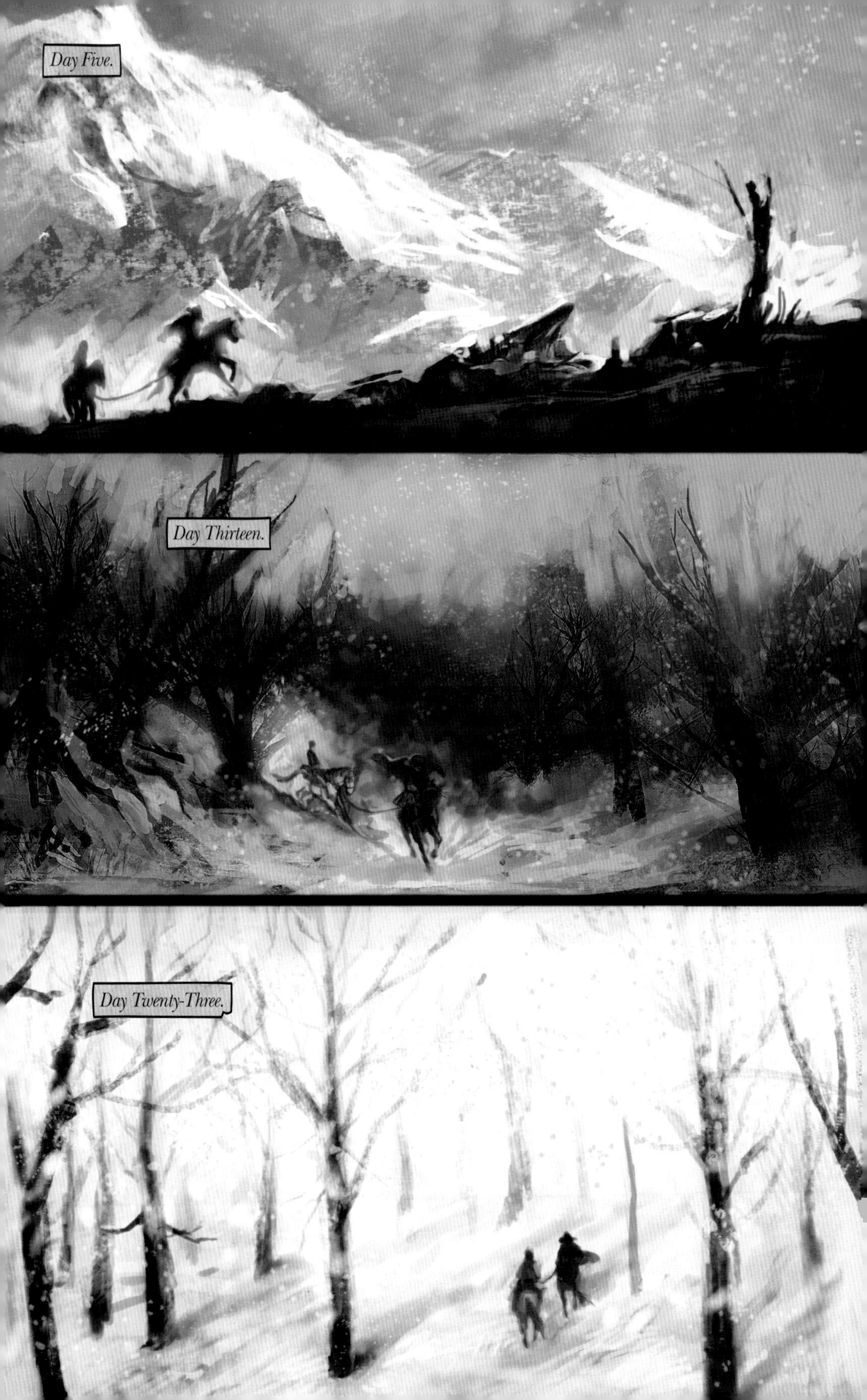
Day Five.
Day Thirteen.
Day Twenty-Three.

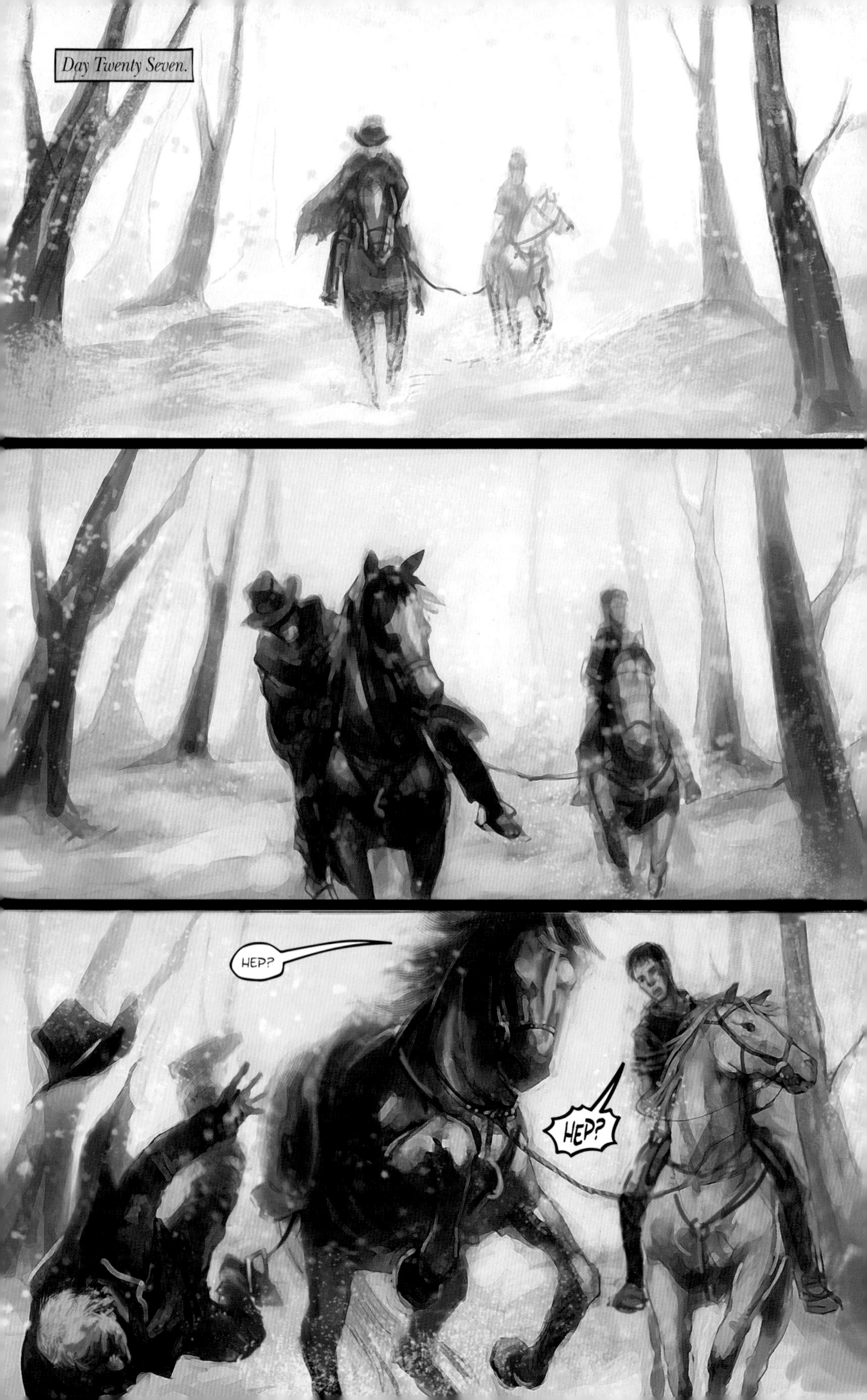
Day Twenty Seven.
HEP?
HEP?

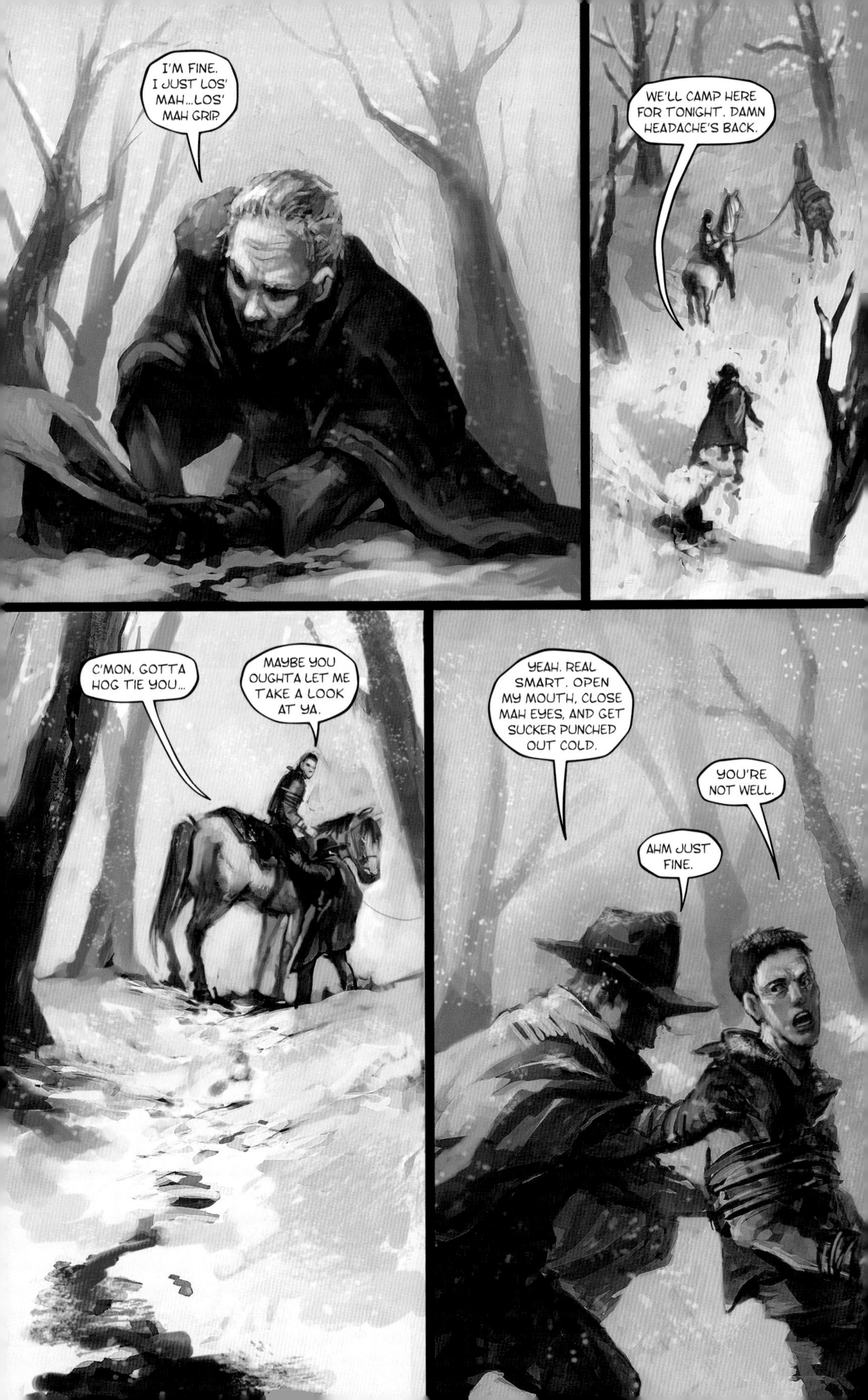
I'M FINE. I JUST LOS' MAH...LOS' MAH GRIP.
WE'LL CAMP HERE FOR TONIGHT. DAMN HEADACHE'S BACK.
C'MON. GOTTA HOG TIE YOU...
MAYBE YOU OUGHTA LET ME TAKE A LOOK AT YA.
YEAH. REAL SMART. OPEN MY MOUTH, CLOSE MAH EYES, AND GET SUCKER PUNCHED OUT COLD.
YOU'RE NOT WELL.
AHM JUST FINE.

LOOK, HEP.

I GET IT, YOU'RE DOING A JOB. TAKIN' ME IN FOR A MOST HEINOUS CRIME WHICH I DID INDEED COMMIT. BUT FACT IS, NEITHER OF US WANTS TO DIE OUT HERE, AND AT LEAST I GOT A FIGHTING CHANCE BACK IN ARIZONA.

YOU'RE SICK, PARD; YOU AIN'T GONNA MAKE IT, AND IF YOU LEAVE ME TIED UP LIKE THIS, I AIN'T GETTIN' NOWHERE NEITHER. I GIVE YOU MY WORD I WON'T TURN ON YA, OR KILL YA, OR WHAT NOT YOU MIGHT BE THINKIN'. I JUST DON'T WANT TO FREEZE TO DEATH, NOR STARVE TO DEATH NEITHER.

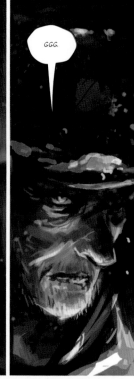

GGG.

THEN JUST KILL ME NOW. YOU CAN DRAG MY CARCASS BACK, YOU DON'T NEED ME ALIVE TO COLLECT THE REWARD. HEP, I MEAN IT. I'M SCARED TO DIE OUT HERE. I'D RATHER JUST GET A BULLET BEHIND THE EAR.

GGAH.

HEP?

HEP? YOU-YOU OKAY?
STOP FOOLIN' NOW. GET ON UP.
HEP!
HEP, YOU COW SHIT OLD TURD, GET THE FUCK UP AND UNTIE ME!
NOW! STOP MESSING AROUND AND UNTIE ME!
NOOOOOOOOOOOOOO!

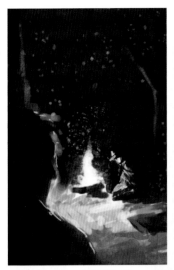

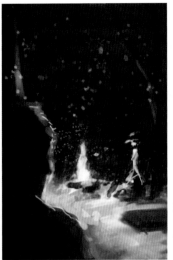

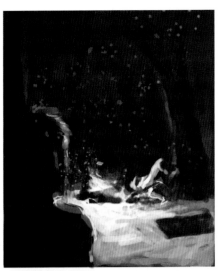

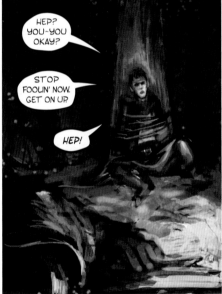

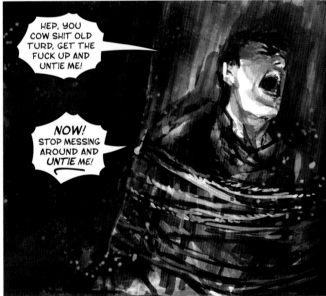

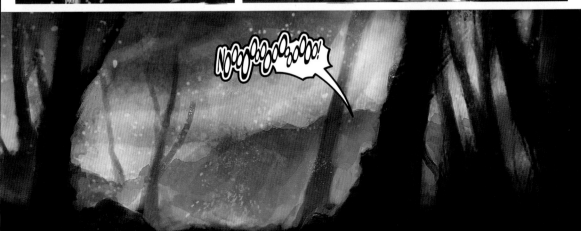

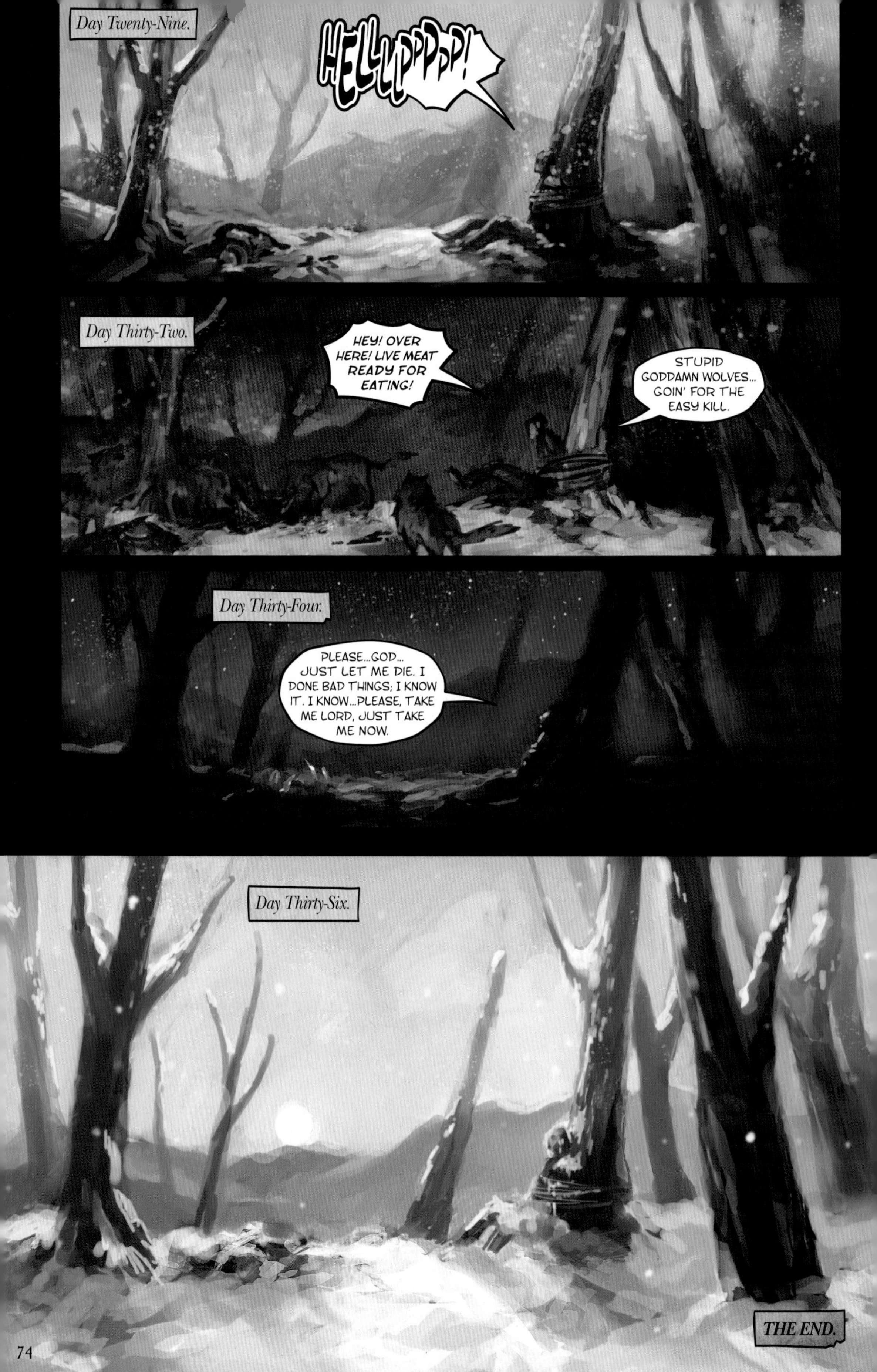
Day Twenty-Nine.
HELLLLPPPPP!
Day Thirty-Two.
HEY! OVER HERE! LIVE MEAT READY FOR EATING!
STUPID GODDAMN WOLVES... GOIN' FOR THE EASY KILL.
Day Thirty-Four.
PLEASE...GOD... JUST LET ME DIE. I DONE BAD THINGS; I KNOW IT. I KNOW...PLEASE, TAKE ME LORD, JUST TAKE ME NOW.
Day Thirty-Six.
THE END.

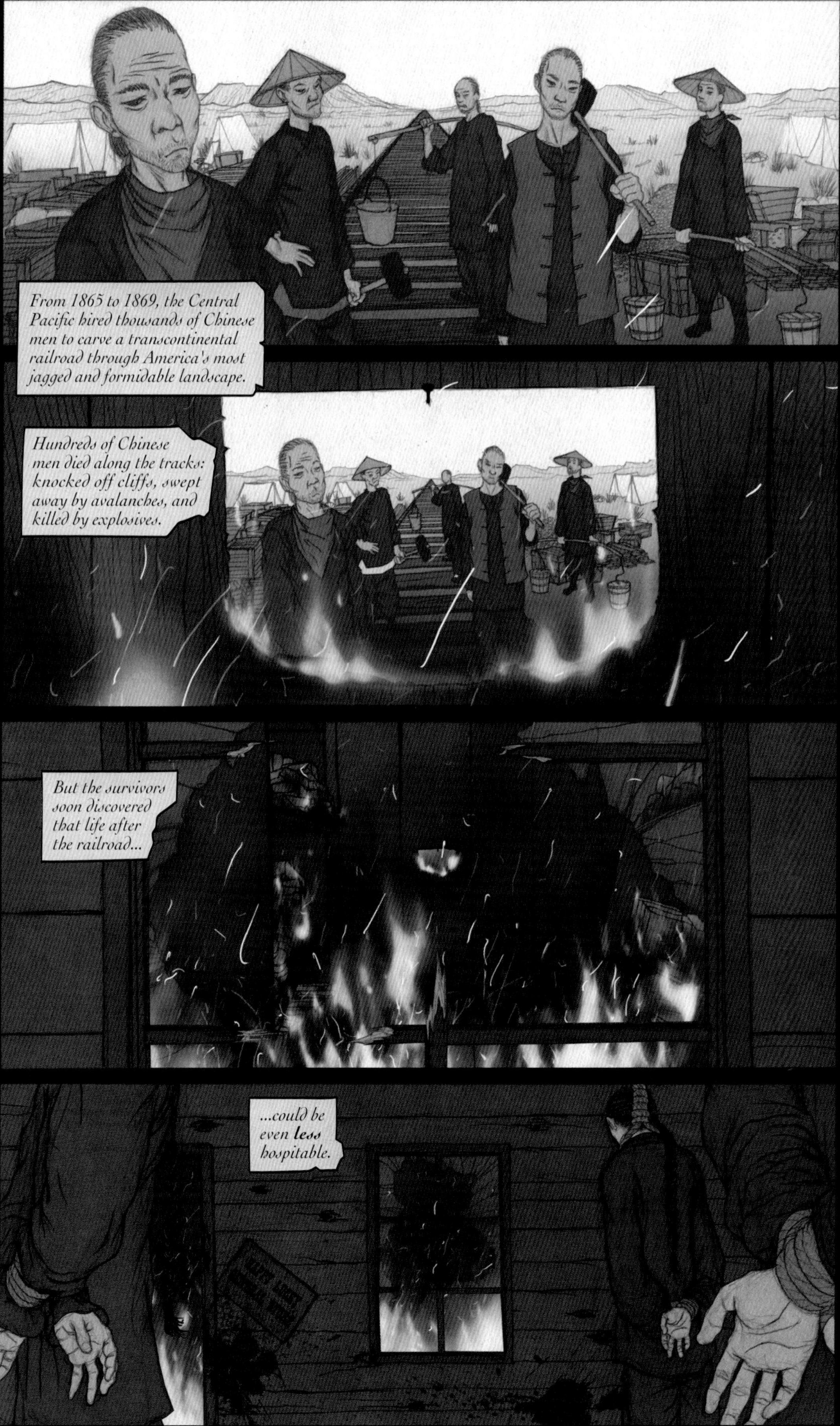
From 1865 to 1869, the Central Pacific hired thousands of Chinese men to carve a transcontinental railroad through America's most jagged and formidable landscape.
Hundreds of Chinese men died along the tracks: knocked off cliffs, swept away by avalanches, and killed by explosives.
But the survivors soon discovered that life after the railroad...
...could be even **less** hospitable.

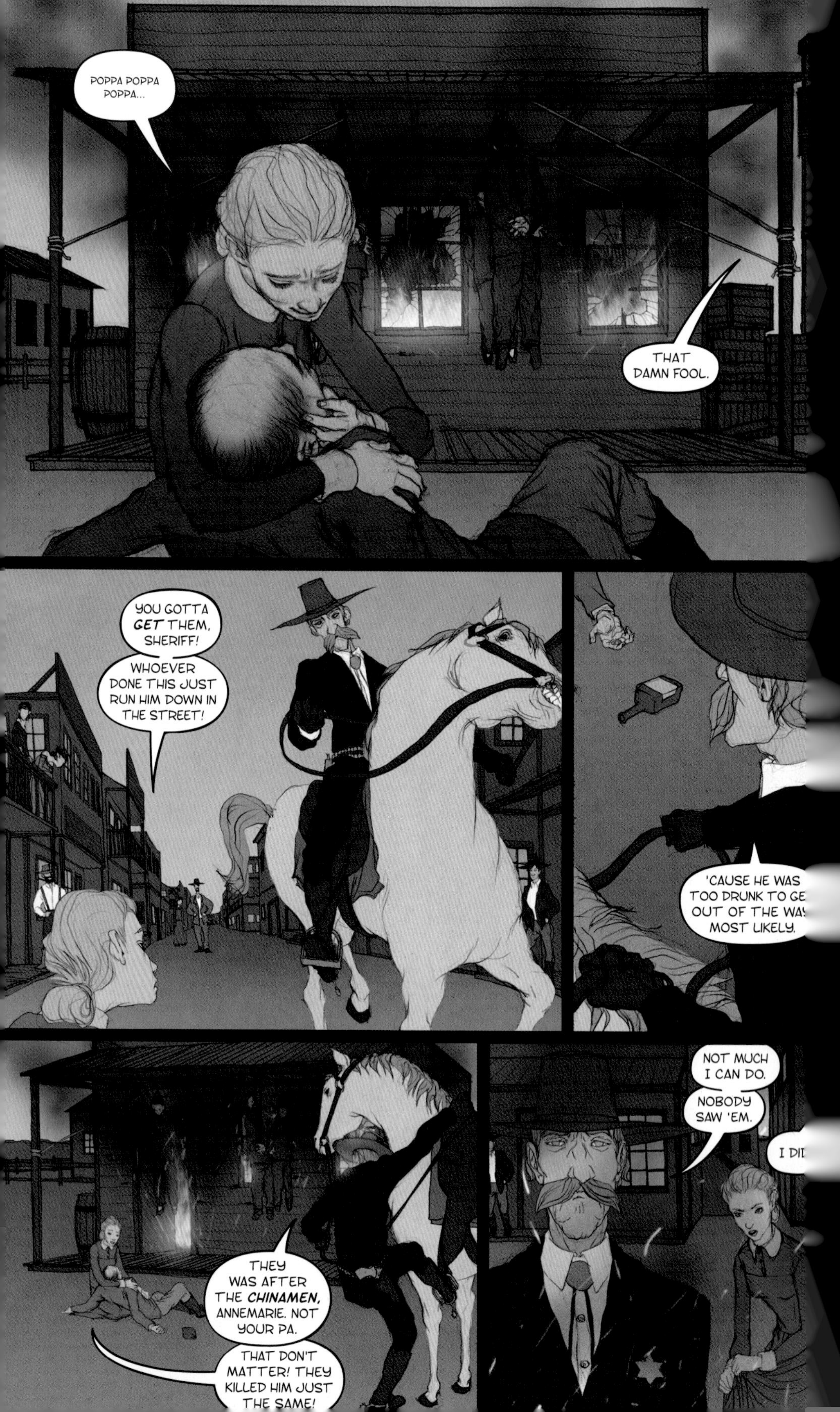
POPPA POPPA POPPA...
THAT DAMN FOOL.
YOU GOTTA GET THEM, SHERIFF!
WHOEVER DONE THIS JUST RUN HIM DOWN IN THE STREET!
'CAUSE HE WAS TOO DRUNK TO GE OUT OF THE WA MOST LIKELY.
THEY WAS AFTER THE CHINAMEN, ANNEMARIE. NOT YOUR PA.
THAT DON'T MATTER! THEY KILLED HIM JUST THE SAME!
NOT MUCH I CAN DO.
NOBODY SAW 'EM.
I DI

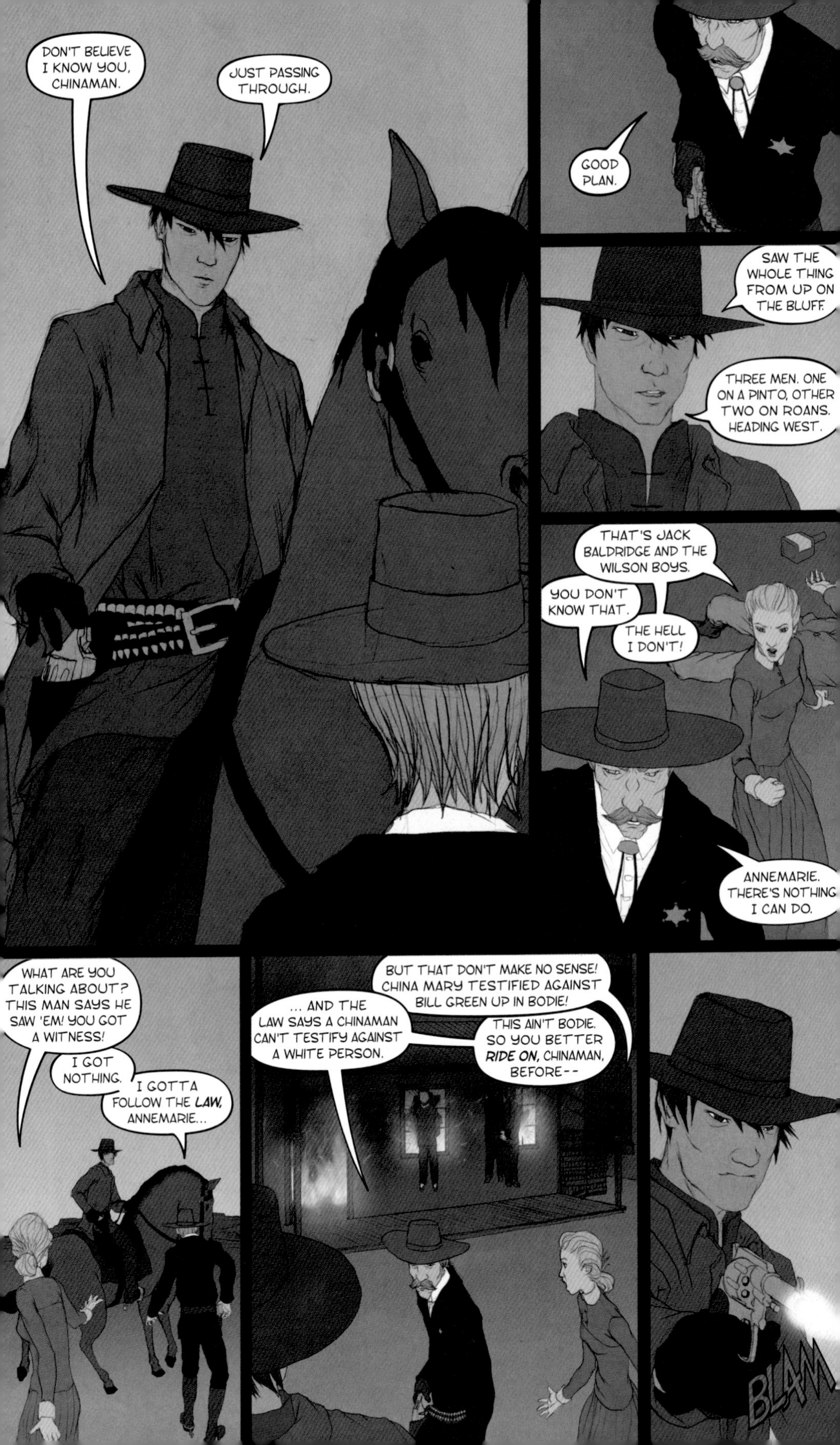
DON'T BELIEVE I KNOW YOU, CHINAMAN.
JUST PASSING THROUGH.
GOOD PLAN.
SAW THE WHOLE THING FROM UP ON THE BLUFF.
THREE MEN. ONE ON A PINTO, OTHER TWO ON ROANS. HEADING WEST.
THAT'S JACK BALDRIDGE AND THE WILSON BOYS.
YOU DON'T KNOW THAT.
THE HELL I DON'T!
ANNEMARIE. THERE'S NOTHING I CAN DO.
WHAT ARE YOU TALKING ABOUT? THIS MAN SAYS HE SAW 'EM! YOU GOT A WITNESS!
I GOT NOTHING.
I GOTTA FOLLOW THE *LAW,* ANNEMARIE...
... AND THE LAW SAYS A CHINAMAN CAN'T TESTIFY AGAINST A WHITE PERSON.
BUT THAT DON'T MAKE NO SENSE! CHINA MARY TESTIFIED AGAINST BILL GREEN UP IN BODIE!
THIS AIN'T BODIE. SO YOU BETTER *RIDE ON,* CHINAMAN, BEFORE--
BLAM

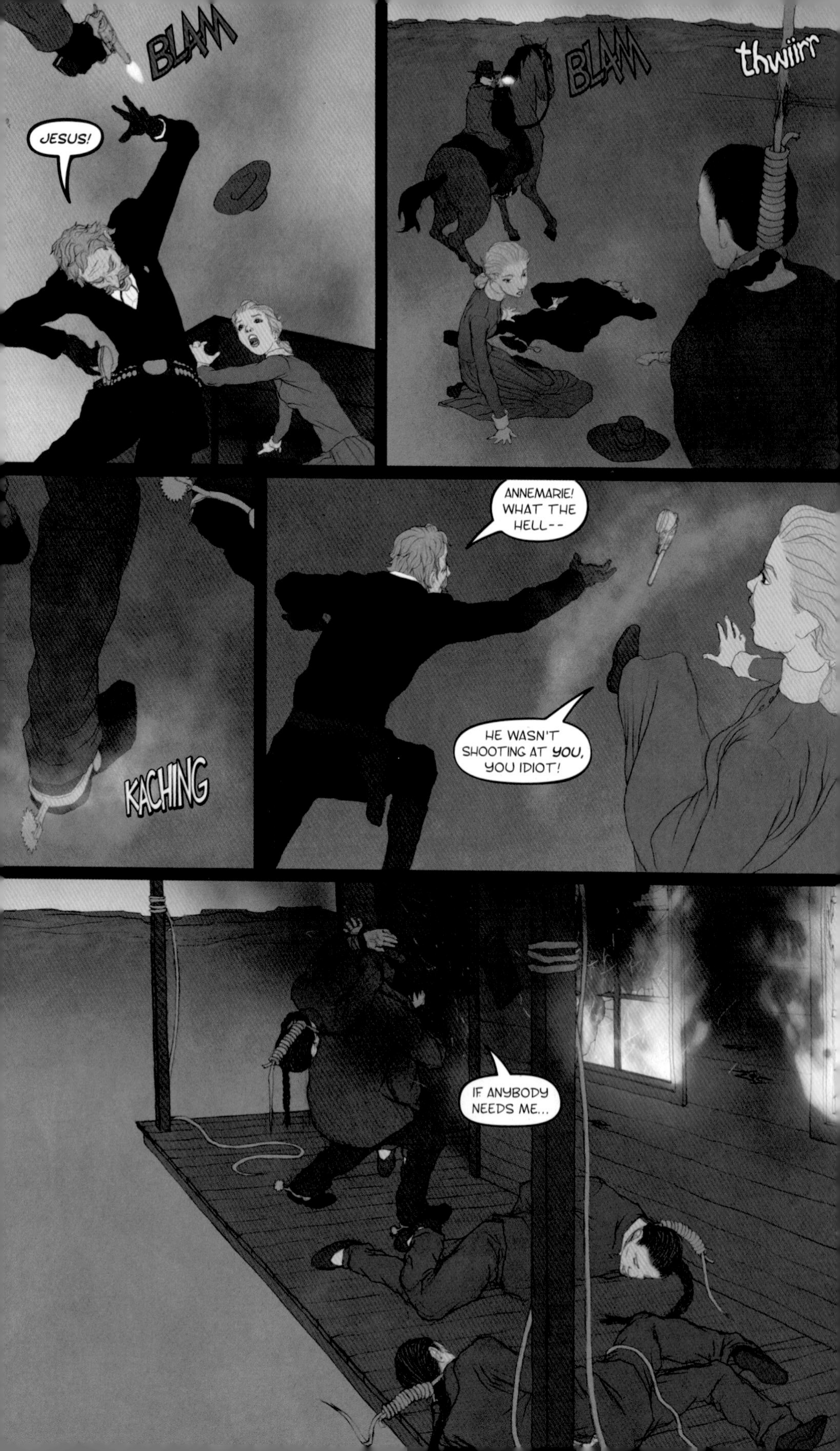
BLAM
JESUS!
BLAM
thwiirr
KACHING
ANNEMARIE! WHAT THE HELL--
HE WASN'T SHOOTING AT YOU, YOU IDIOT!
IF ANYBODY NEEDS ME...

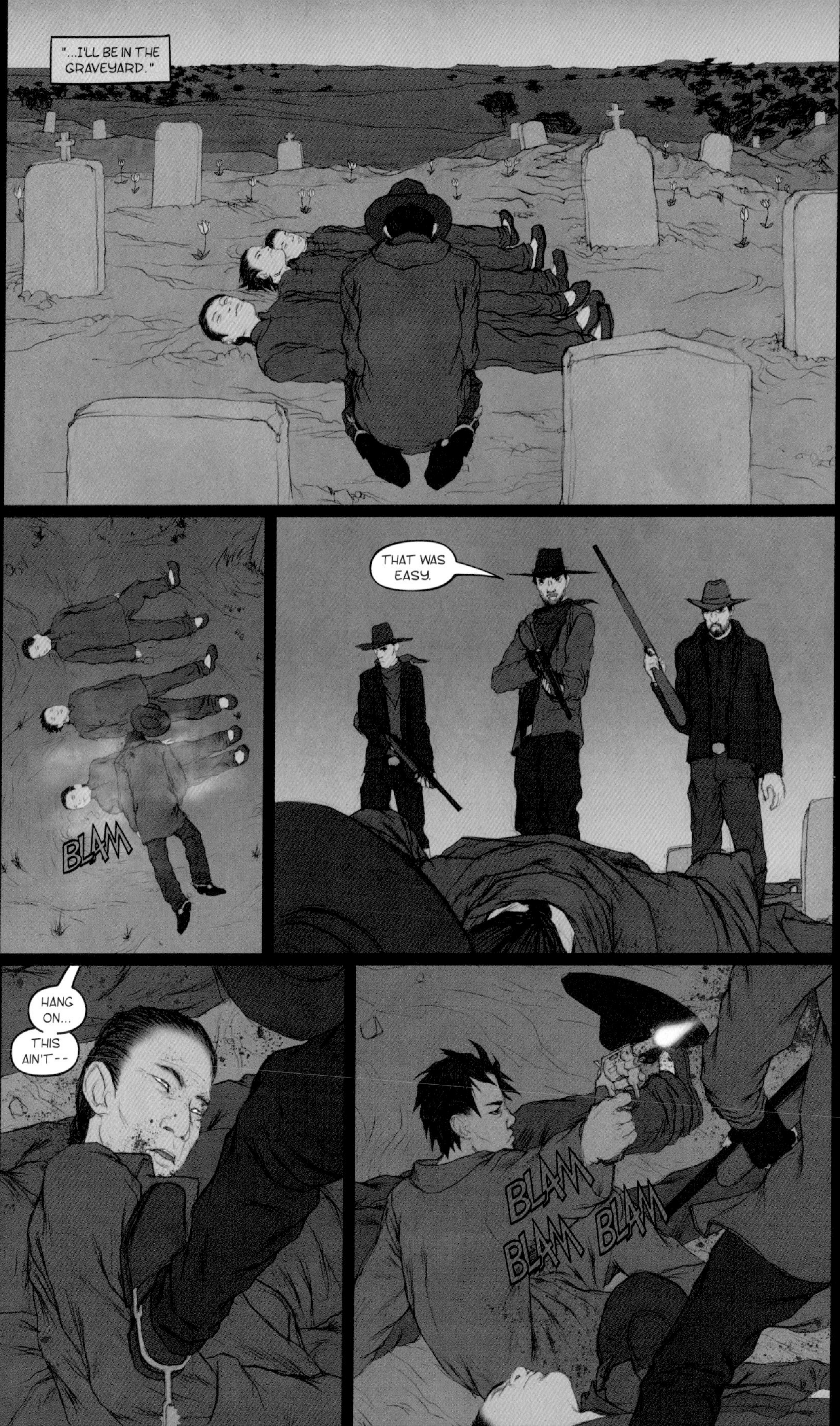
"...I'LL BE IN THE GRAVEYARD."
BLAM
THAT WAS EASY.
HANG ON... THIS AIN'T--
BLAM
BLAM BLAM

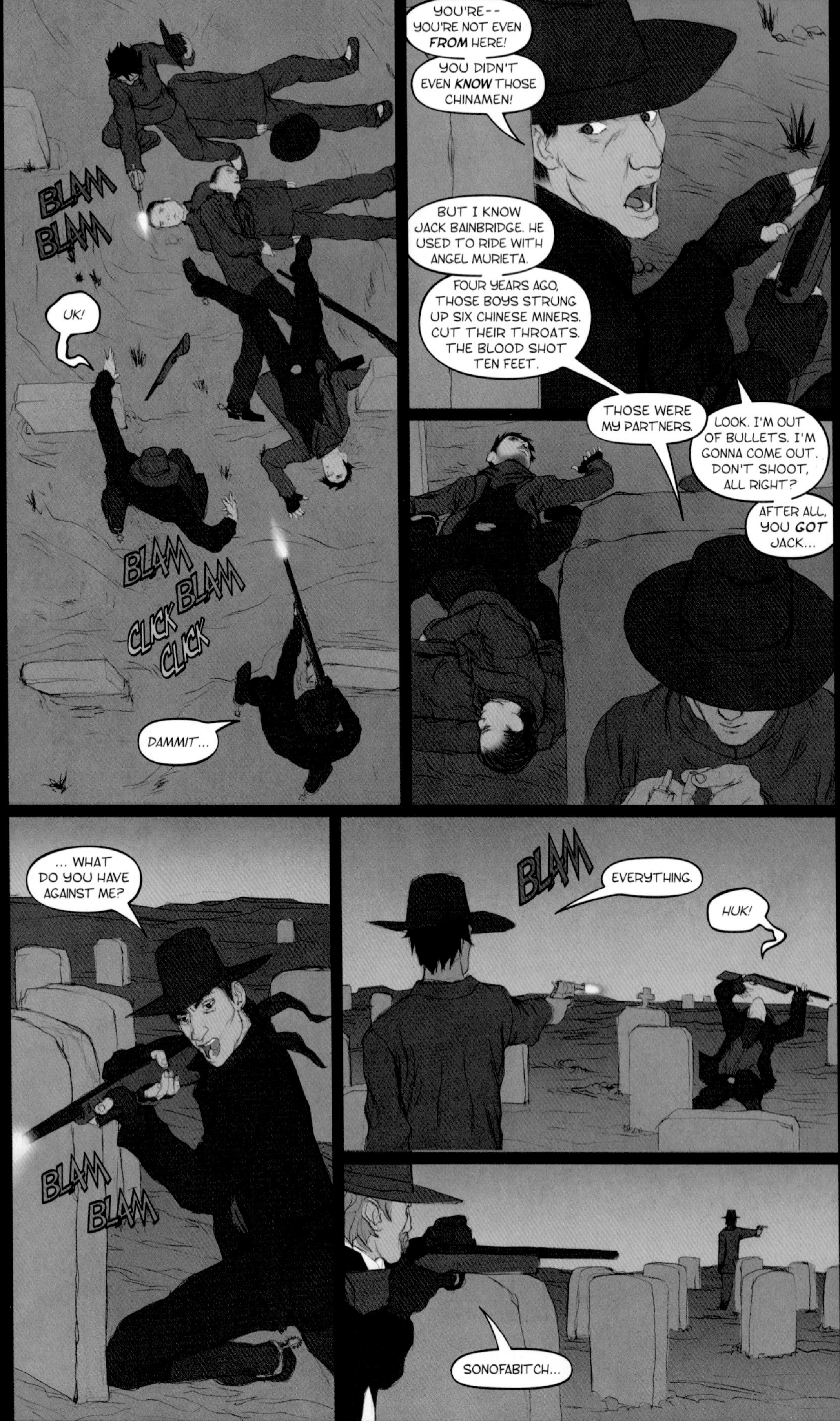
BLAM
BLAM
UK!
BLAM
CLICK BLAM
CLICK
DAMMIT...
YOU'RE-- YOU'RE NOT EVEN FROM HERE!
YOU DIDN'T EVEN KNOW THOSE CHINAMEN!
BUT I KNOW JACK BAINBRIDGE. HE USED TO RIDE WITH ANGEL MURIETA.
FOUR YEARS AGO, THOSE BOYS STRUNG UP SIX CHINESE MINERS. CUT THEIR THROATS. THE BLOOD SHOT TEN FEET.
THOSE WERE MY PARTNERS.
LOOK. I'M OUT OF BULLETS. I'M GONNA COME OUT. DON'T SHOOT, ALL RIGHT?
AFTER ALL, YOU GOT JACK...
... WHAT DO YOU HAVE AGAINST ME?
BLAM
BLAM
BLAM
EVERYTHING.
HUK!
SONOFABITCH...

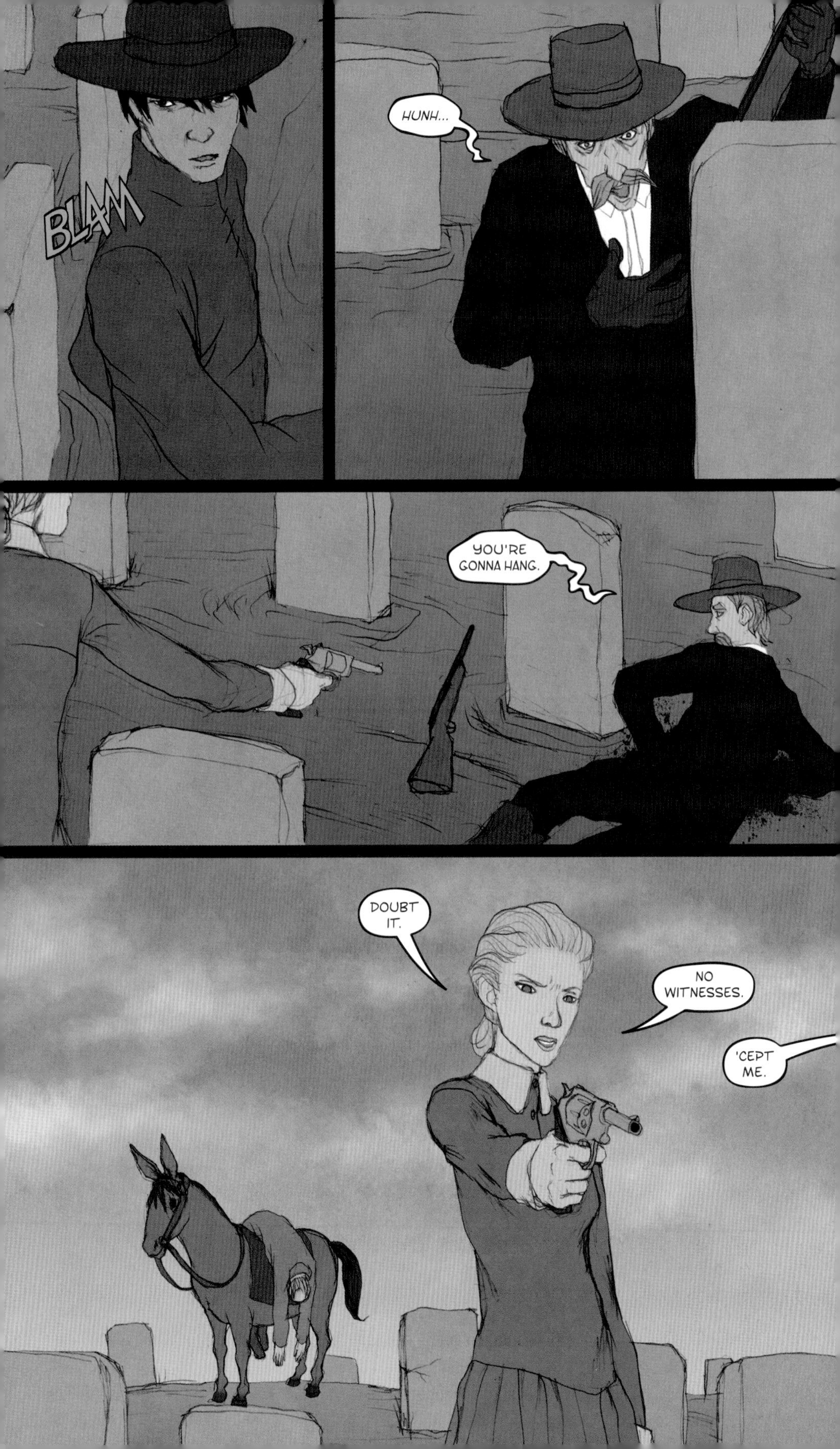
BLAM
HUNH...
YOU'RE GONNA HANG.
DOUBT IT.
NO WITNESSES.
'CEPT ME.

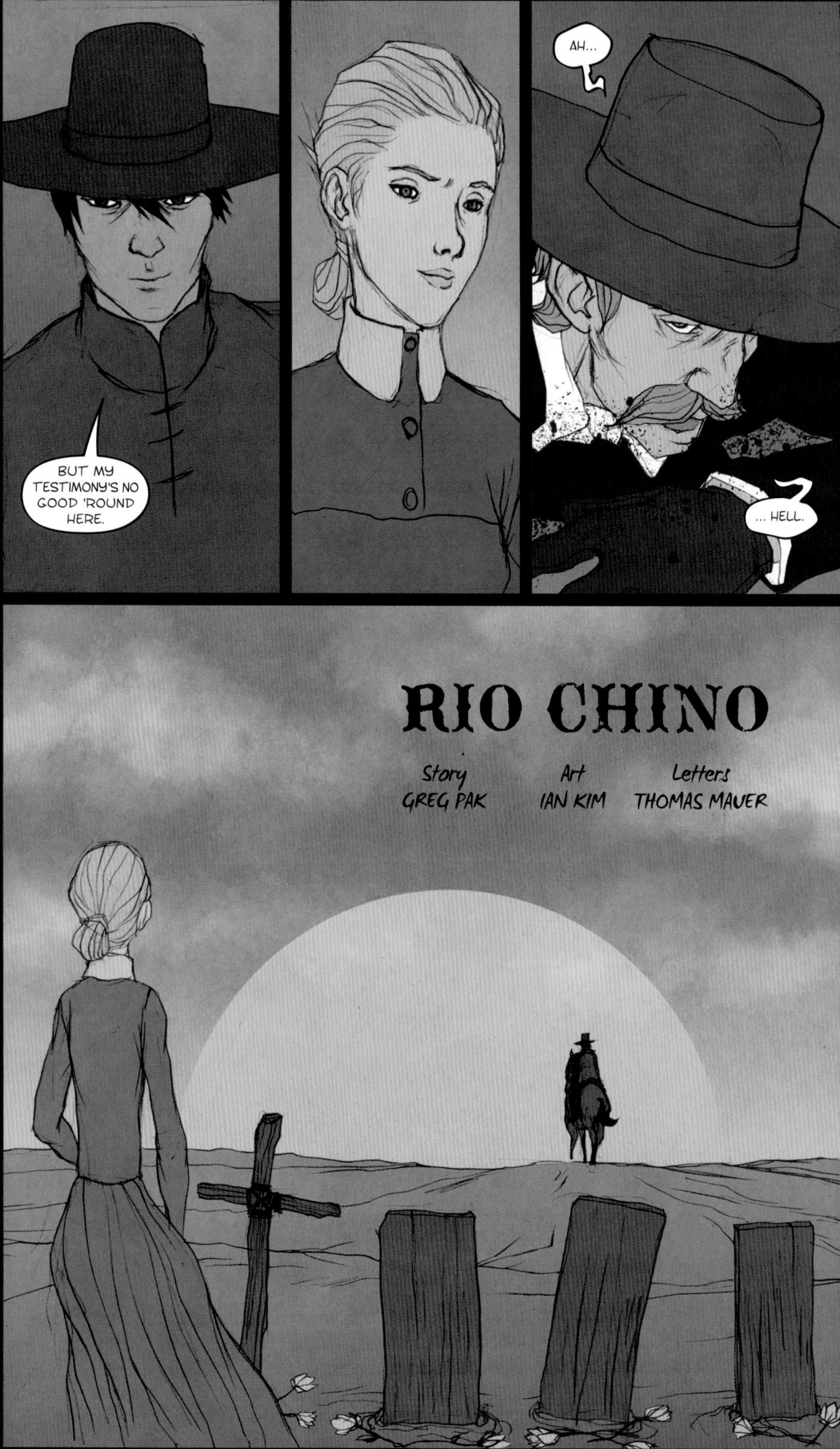
BUT MY TESTIMONY'S NO GOOD 'ROUND HERE.
AH...
... HELL.
RIO CHINO
Story GREG PAK
Art IAN KIM
Letters THOMAS MAUER

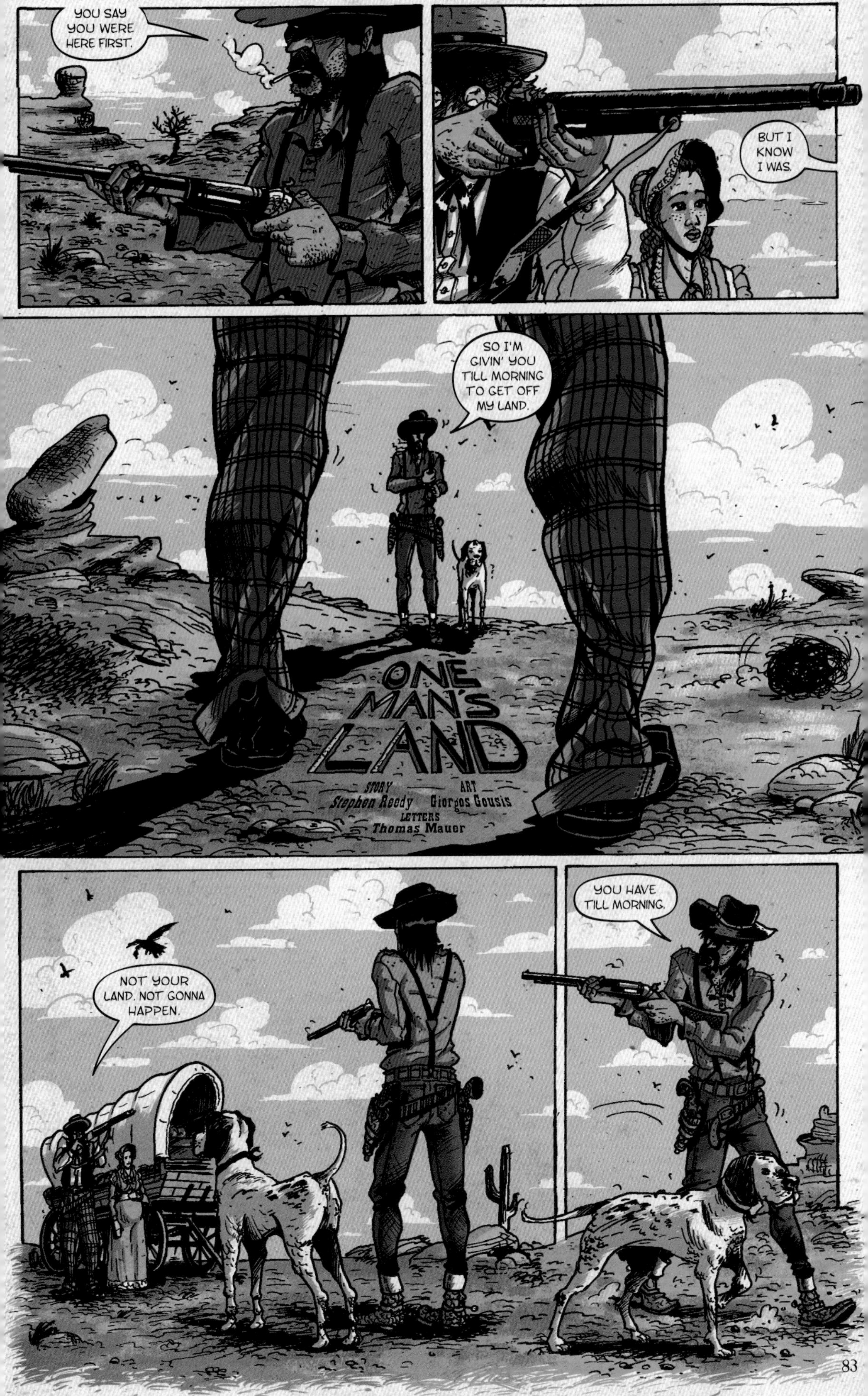

YOU SAY YOU WERE HERE FIRST.
BUT I KNOW I WAS.
SO I'M GIVIN' YOU TILL MORNING TO GET OFF MY LAND.
ONE MAN'S LAND
STORY Stephen Reedy
ART Giorgos Gousis
LETTERS Thomas Mauer
NOT YOUR LAND. NOT GONNA HAPPEN.
YOU HAVE TILL MORNING.

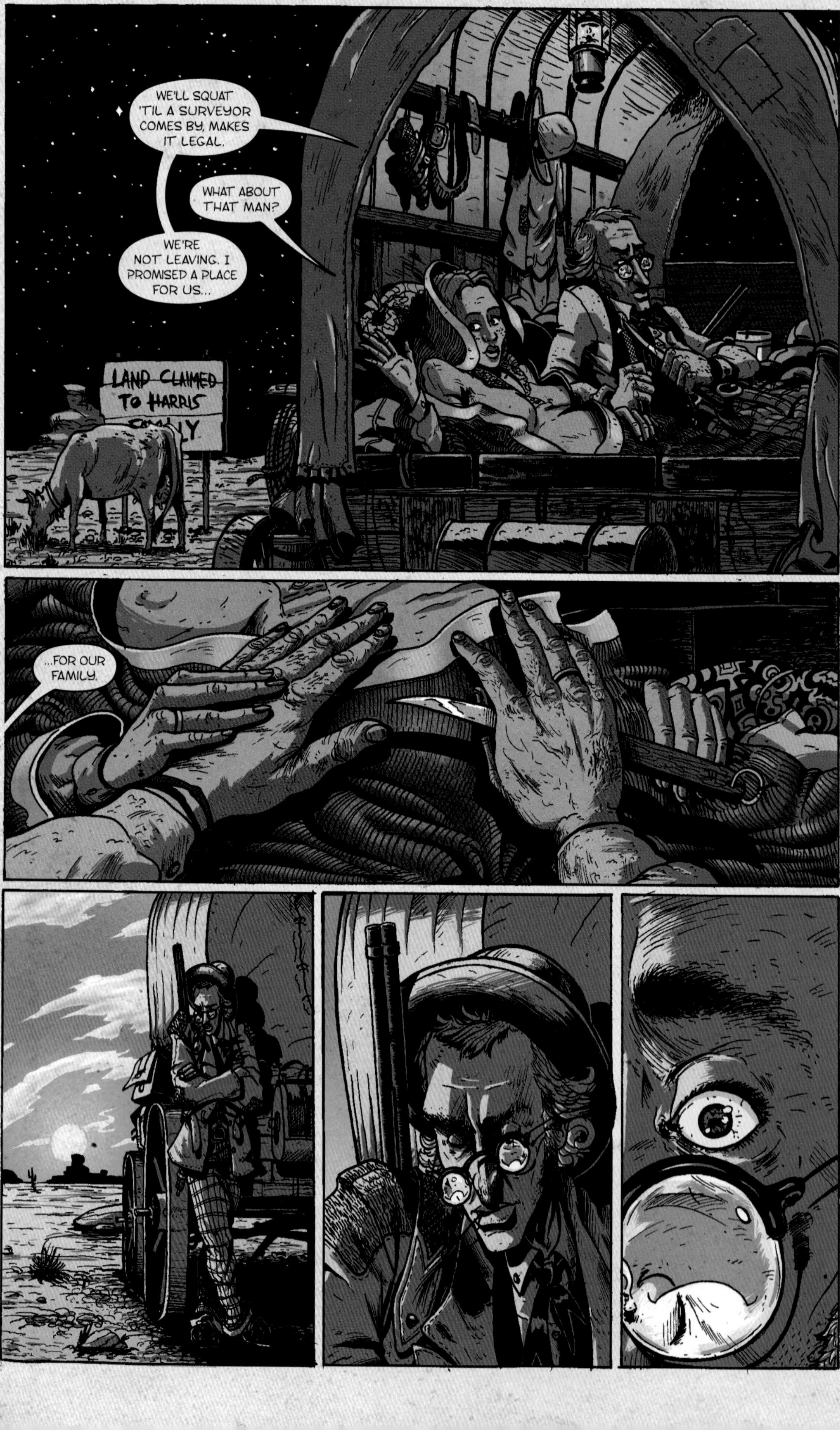

WE'LL SQUAT 'TIL A SURVEYOR COMES BY, MAKES IT LEGAL.
WHAT ABOUT THAT MAN?
WE'RE NOT LEAVING. I PROMISED A PLACE FOR US...
LAND CLAIMED TO HARRIS
...FOR OUR FAMILY.

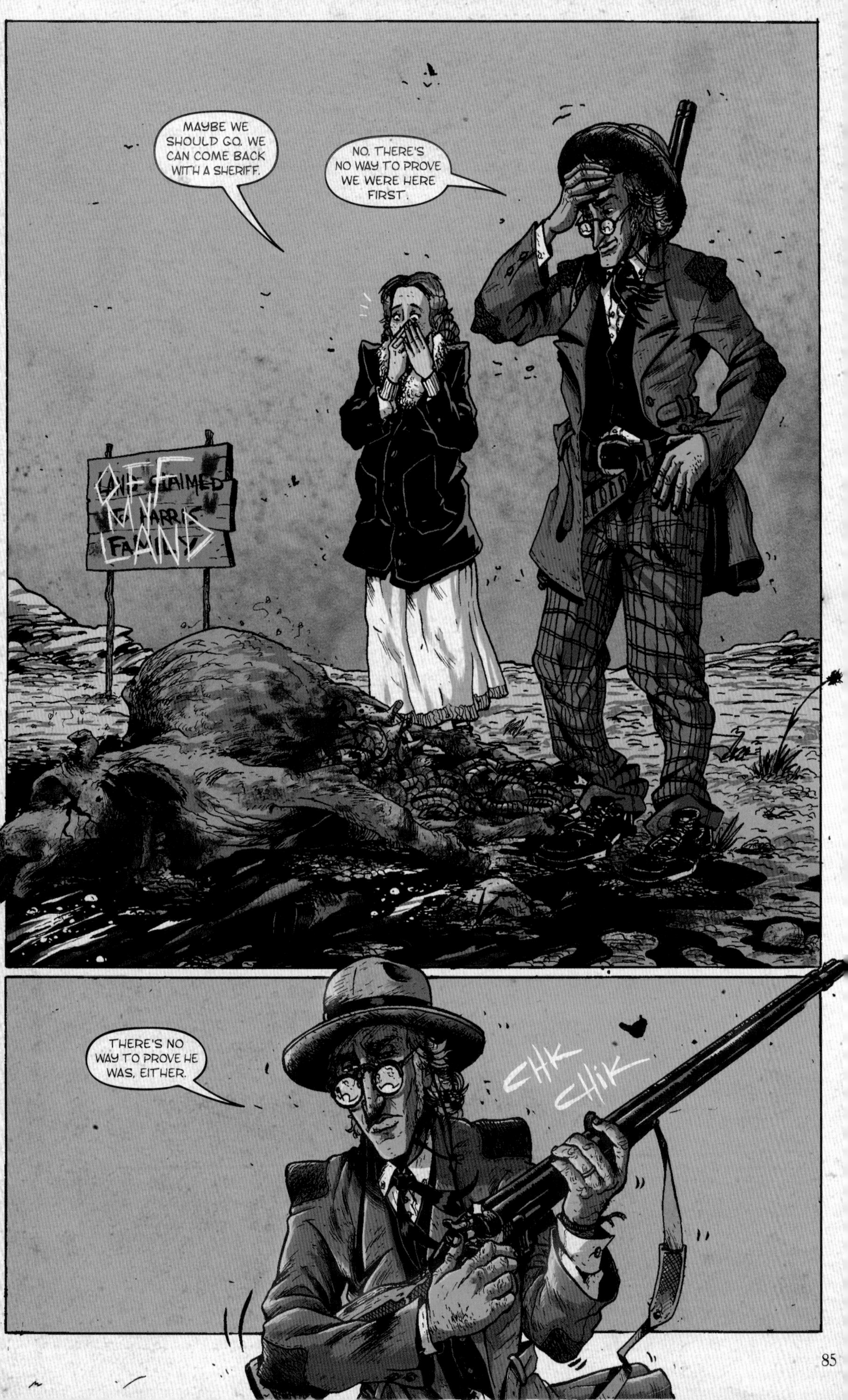
MAYBE WE SHOULD GO. WE CAN COME BACK WITH A SHERIFF.
NO. THERE'S NO WAY TO PROVE WE WERE HERE FIRST.
OFF MY LAND
THERE'S NO WAY TO PROVE HE WAS, EITHER.
CHK CHIK

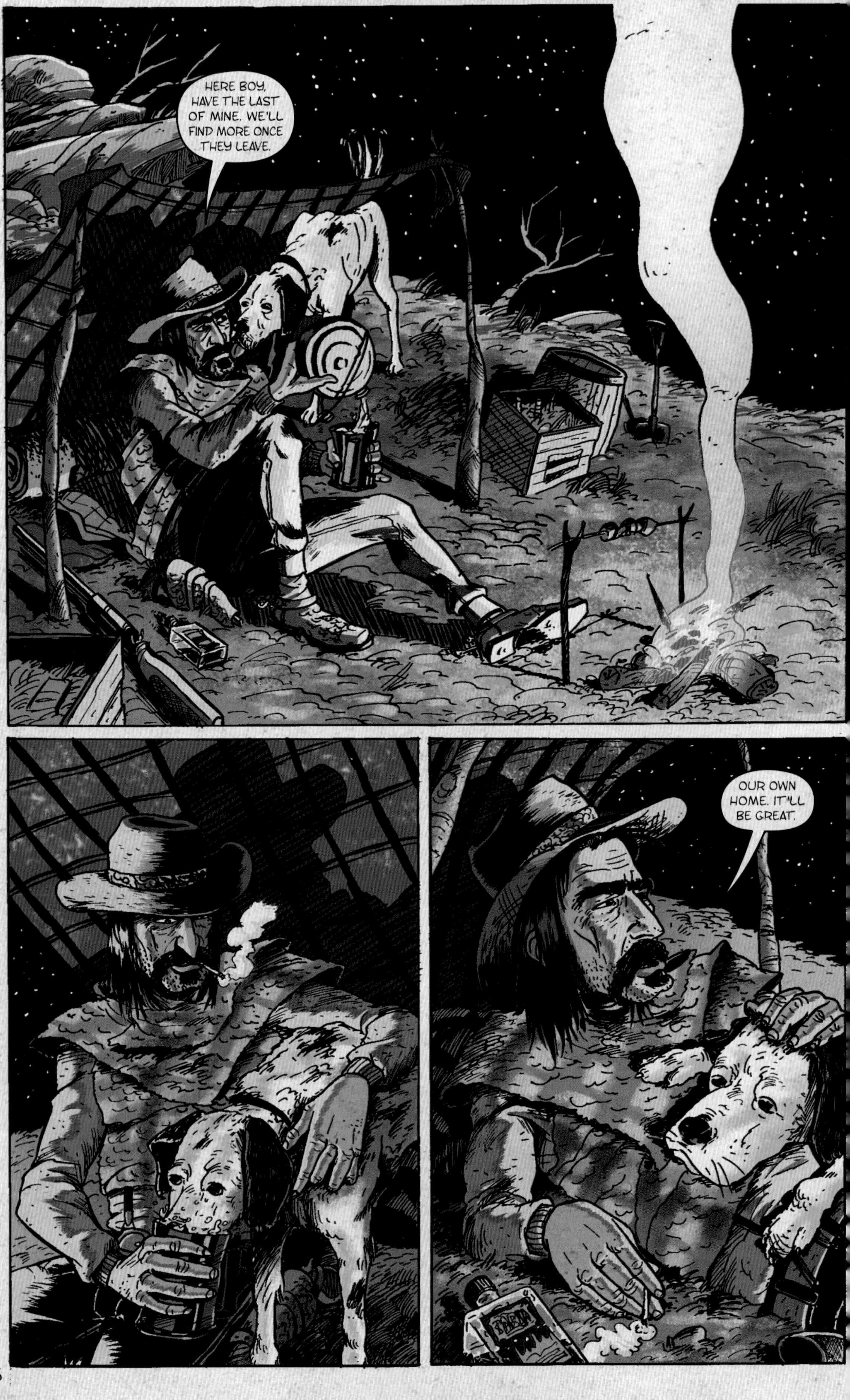
HERE BOY, HAVE THE LAST OF MINE. WE'LL FIND MORE ONCE THEY LEAVE.
OUR OWN HOME. IT'LL BE GREAT.

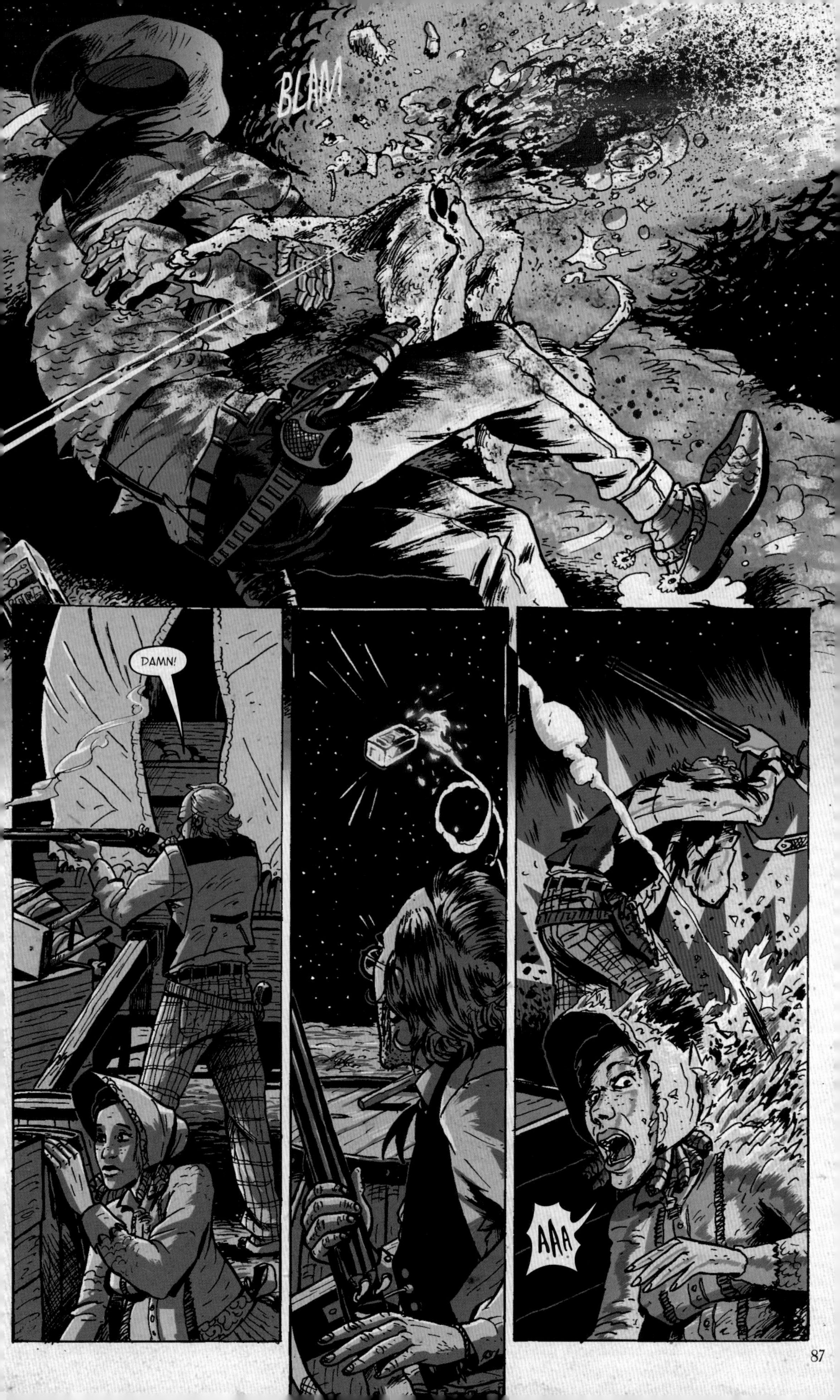
BLAM
DAMN!
AAA

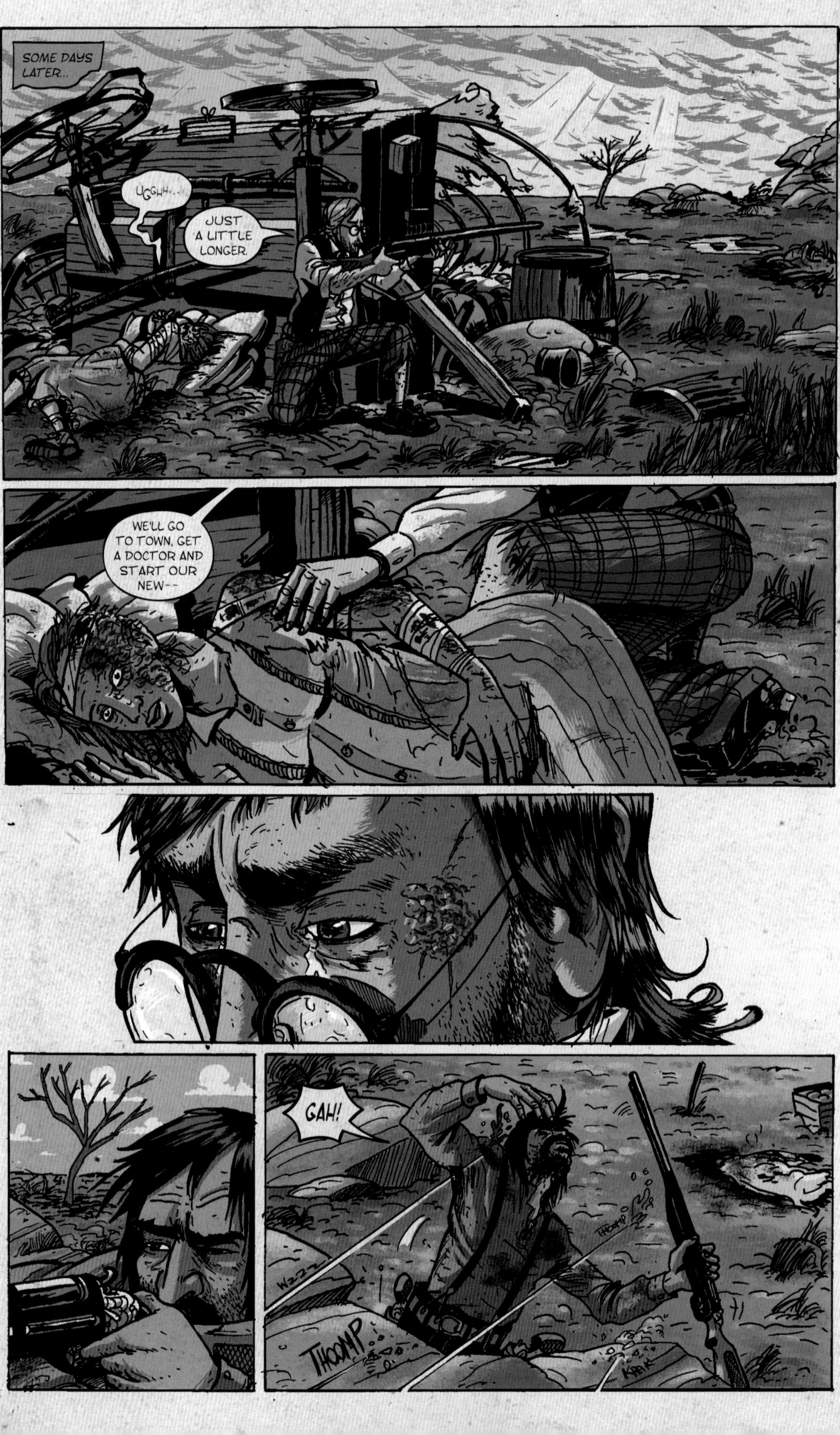
SOME DAYS LATER...
UGGHH...
JUST A LITTLE LONGER.
WE'LL GO TO TOWN, GET A DOCTOR AND START OUR NEW--
GAH!
THOOMP
THOOMP
KRAK

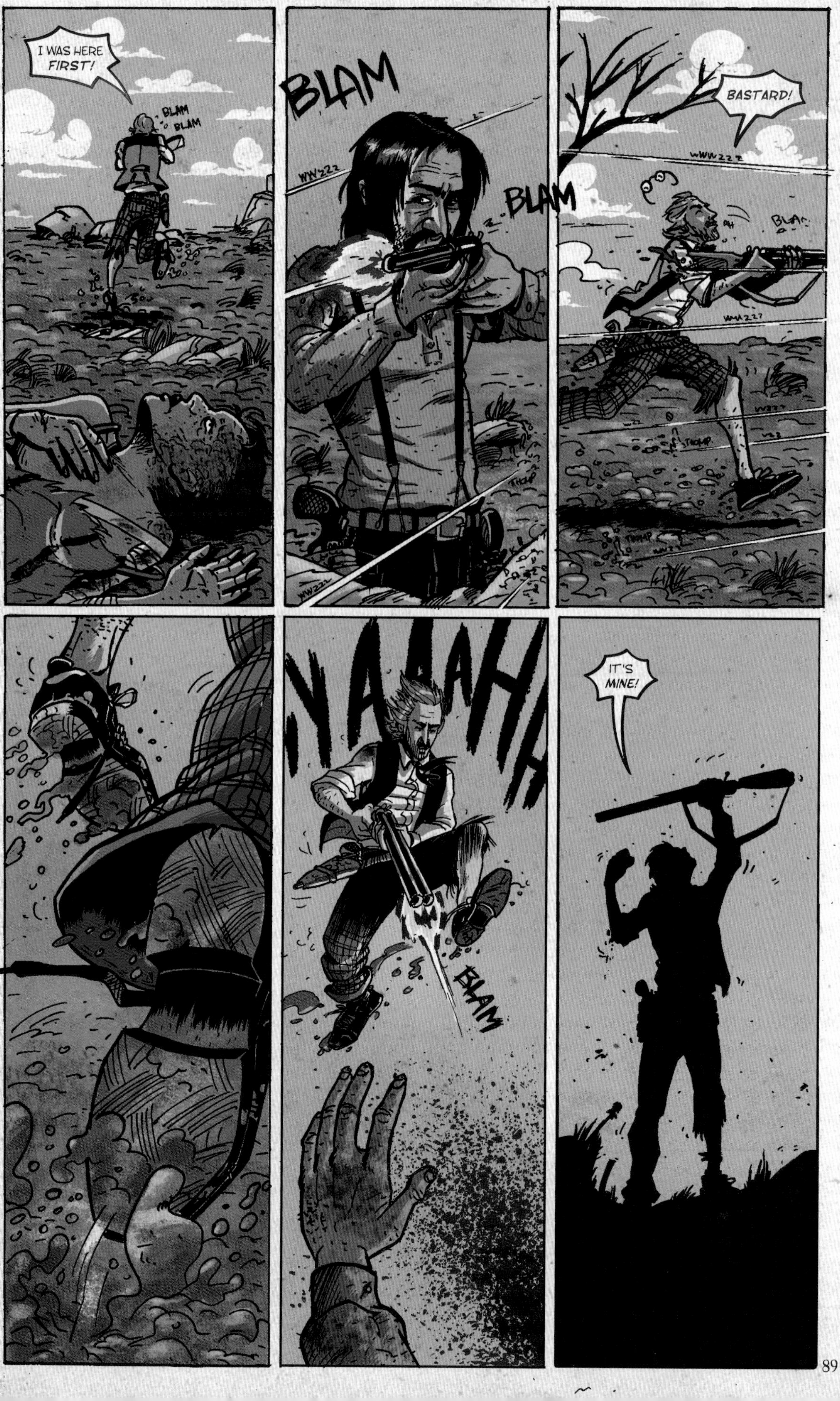
I WAS HERE FIRST!
BLAM
BLAM
BLAM
BLAM
BASTARD!
YAAAHH
BLAM
IT'S MINE!

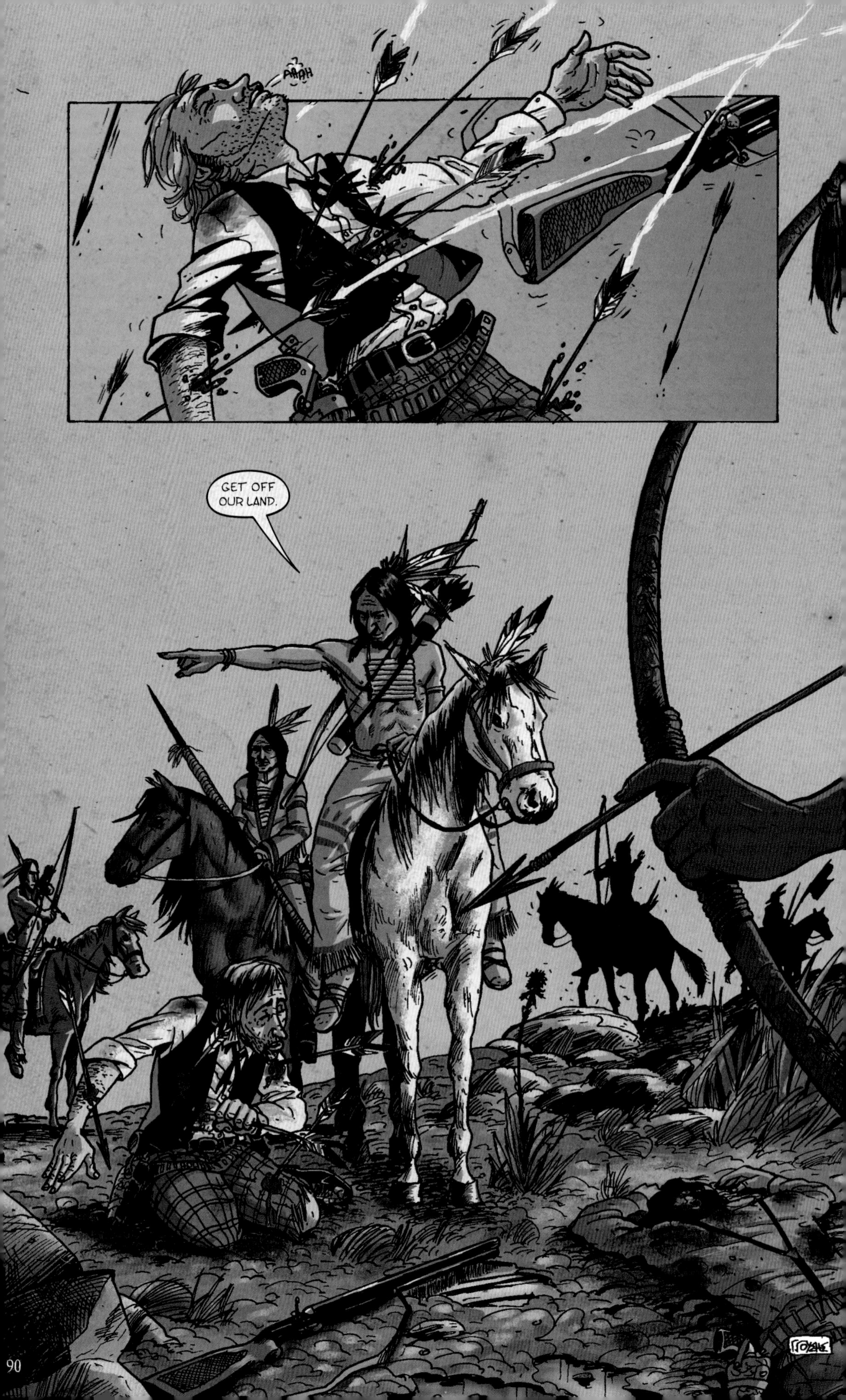
AHHH
GET OFF OUR LAND.

The Bounty Killers

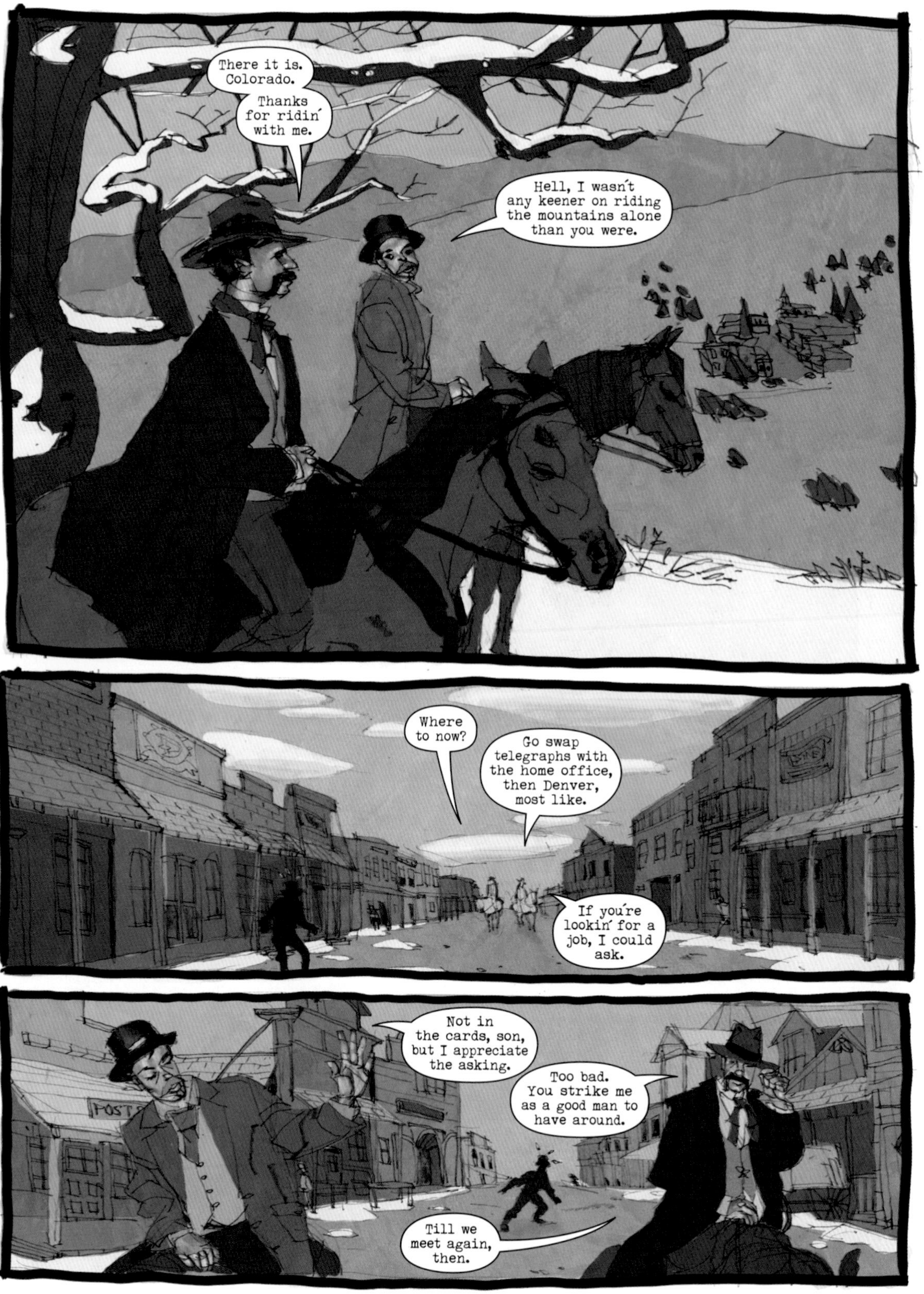

There it is. Colorado.
Thanks for ridin´ with me.
Hell, I wasn´t any keener on riding the mountains alone than you were.
Where to now?
Go swap telegraphs with the home office, then Denver, most like.
If you´re lookin´ for a job, I could ask.
Not in the cards, son, but I appreciate the asking.
Too bad. You strike me as a good man to have around.
Till we meet again, then.

Story
Steve Grant

Art
Shannon Eric Denton & John Cboins

Letters
Thomas Mauer

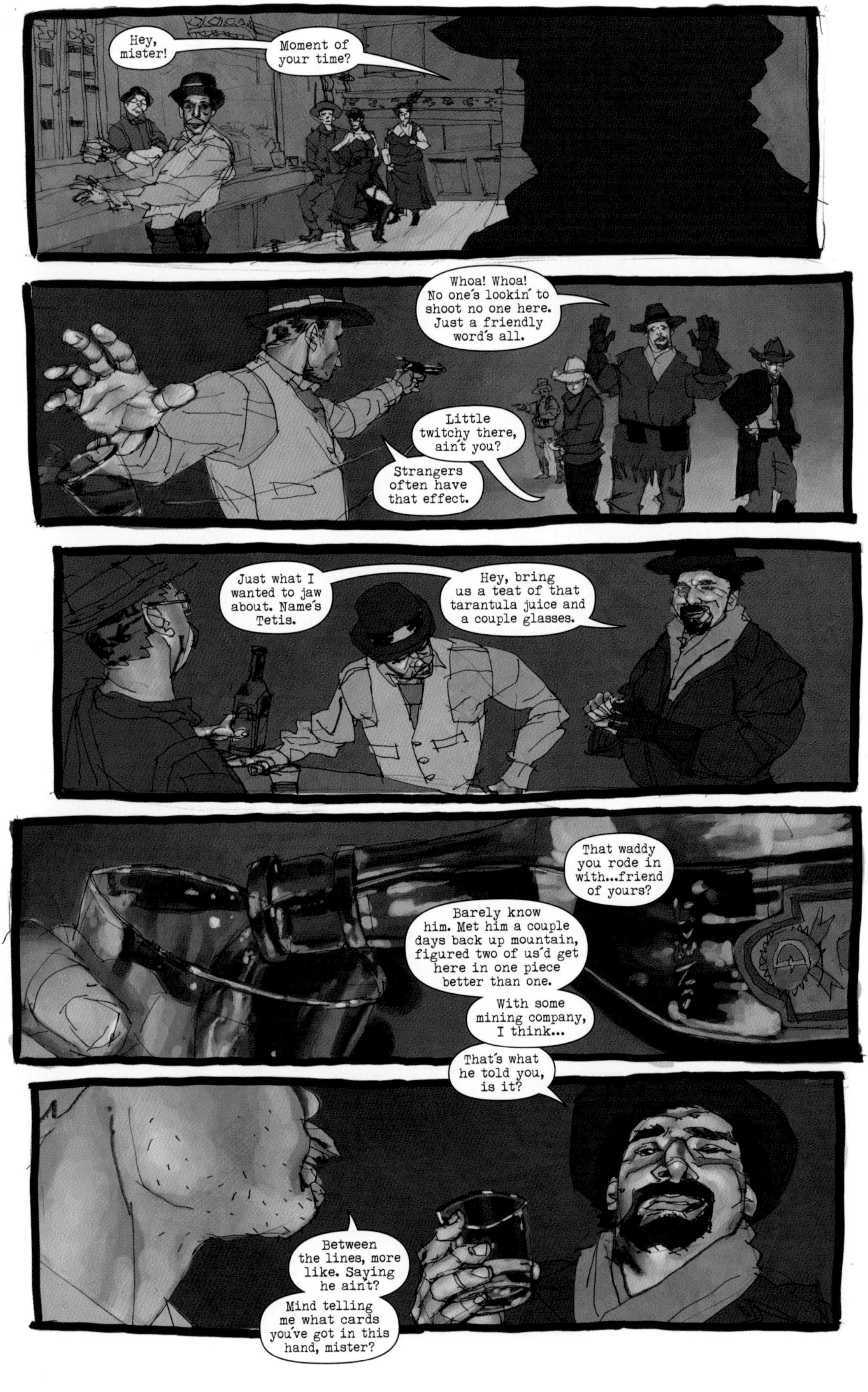
Hey, mister!
Moment of your time?
Whoa! Whoa! No one's lookin' to shoot no one here. Just a friendly word's all.
Little twitchy there, ain't you?
Strangers often have that effect.
Just what I wanted to jaw about. Name's Tetis.
Hey, bring us a teat of that tarantula juice and a couple glasses.
That waddy you rode in with...friend of yours?
Barely know him. Met him a couple days back up mountain, figured two of us'd get here in one piece better than one.
With some mining company, I think...
That's what he told you, is it?
Between the lines, more like. Saying he ain't?
Mind telling me what cards you've got in this hand, mister?

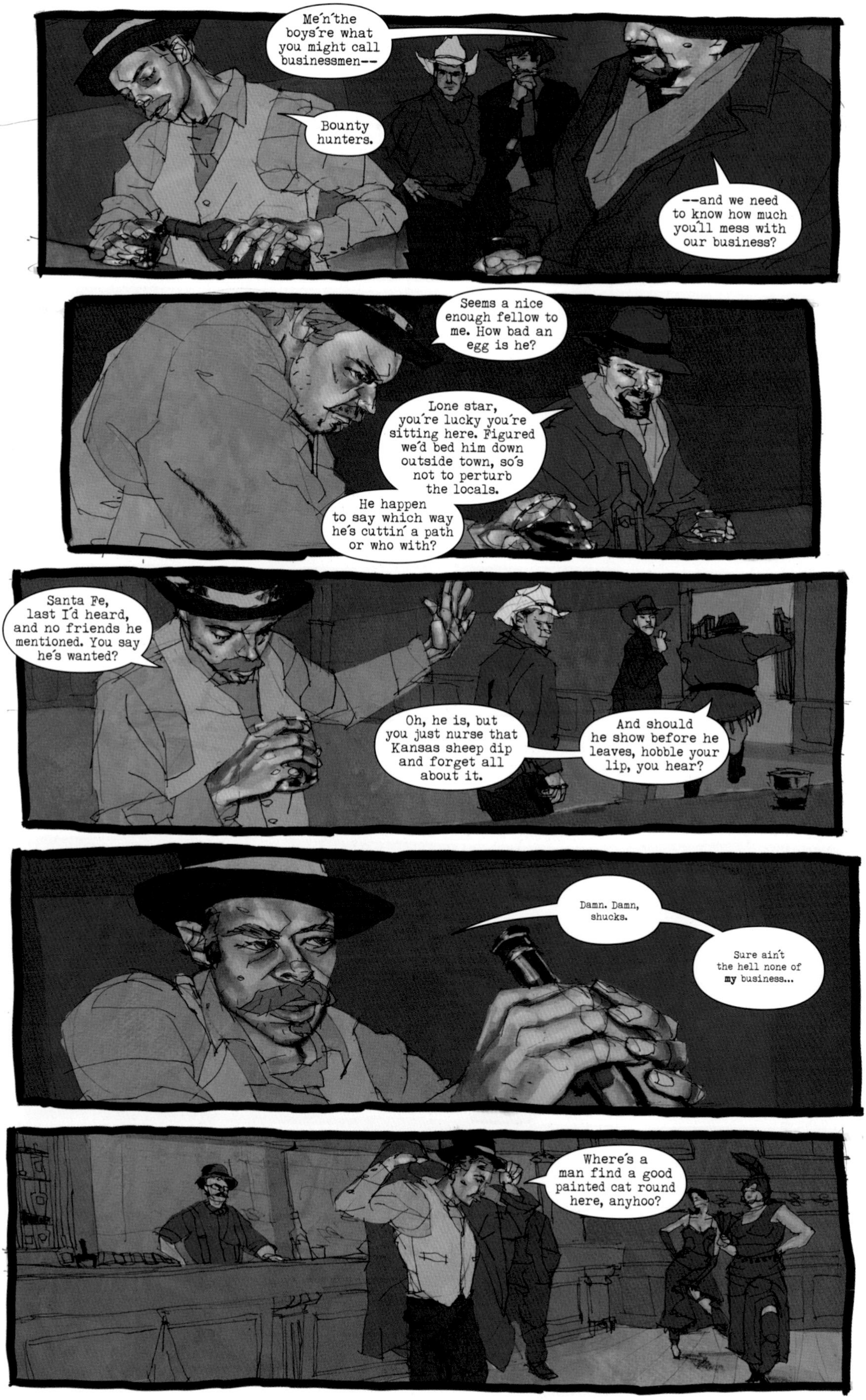
Me'n'the boys're what you might call businessmen--
Bounty hunters.
--and we need to know how much you'll mess with our business?
Seems a nice enough fellow to me. How bad an egg is he?
Lone star, you're lucky you're sitting here. Figured we'd bed him down outside town, so's not to perturb the locals.
He happen to say which way he's cuttin' a path or who with?
Santa Fe, last I'd heard, and no friends he mentioned. You say he's wanted?
Oh, he is, but you just nurse that Kansas sheep dip and forget all about it.
And should he show before he leaves, hobble your lip, you hear?
Damn. Damn, shucks.
Sure ain't the hell none of **my** business...
Where's a man find a good painted cat round here, anyhoo?

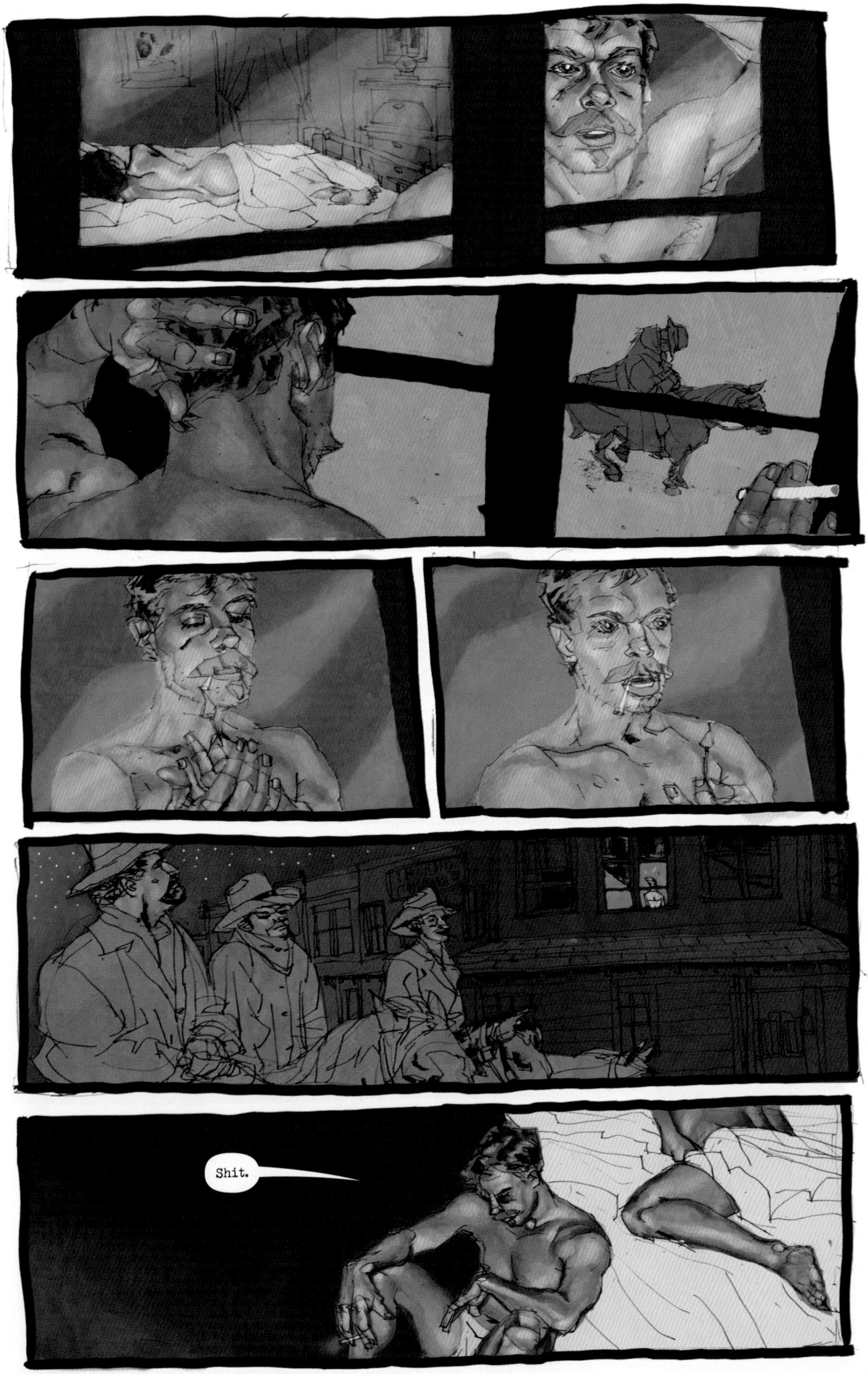
Shit.

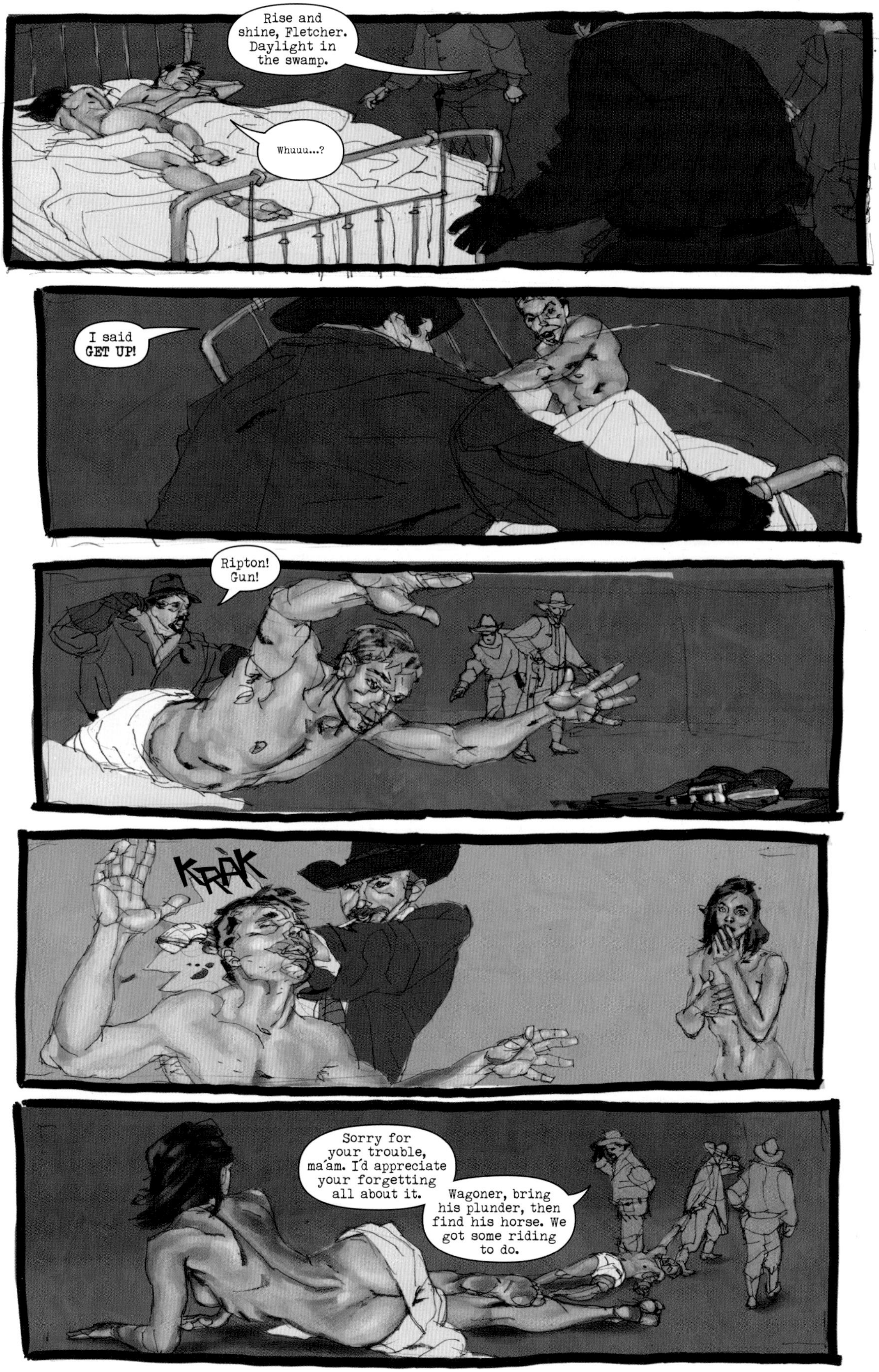

Rise and shine, Fletcher. Daylight in the swamp.
Whuuu...?
I said GET UP!
Ripton! Gun!
KRAK
Sorry for your trouble, ma'am. I'd appreciate your forgetting all about it.
Wagoner, bring his plunder, then find his horse. We got some riding to do.

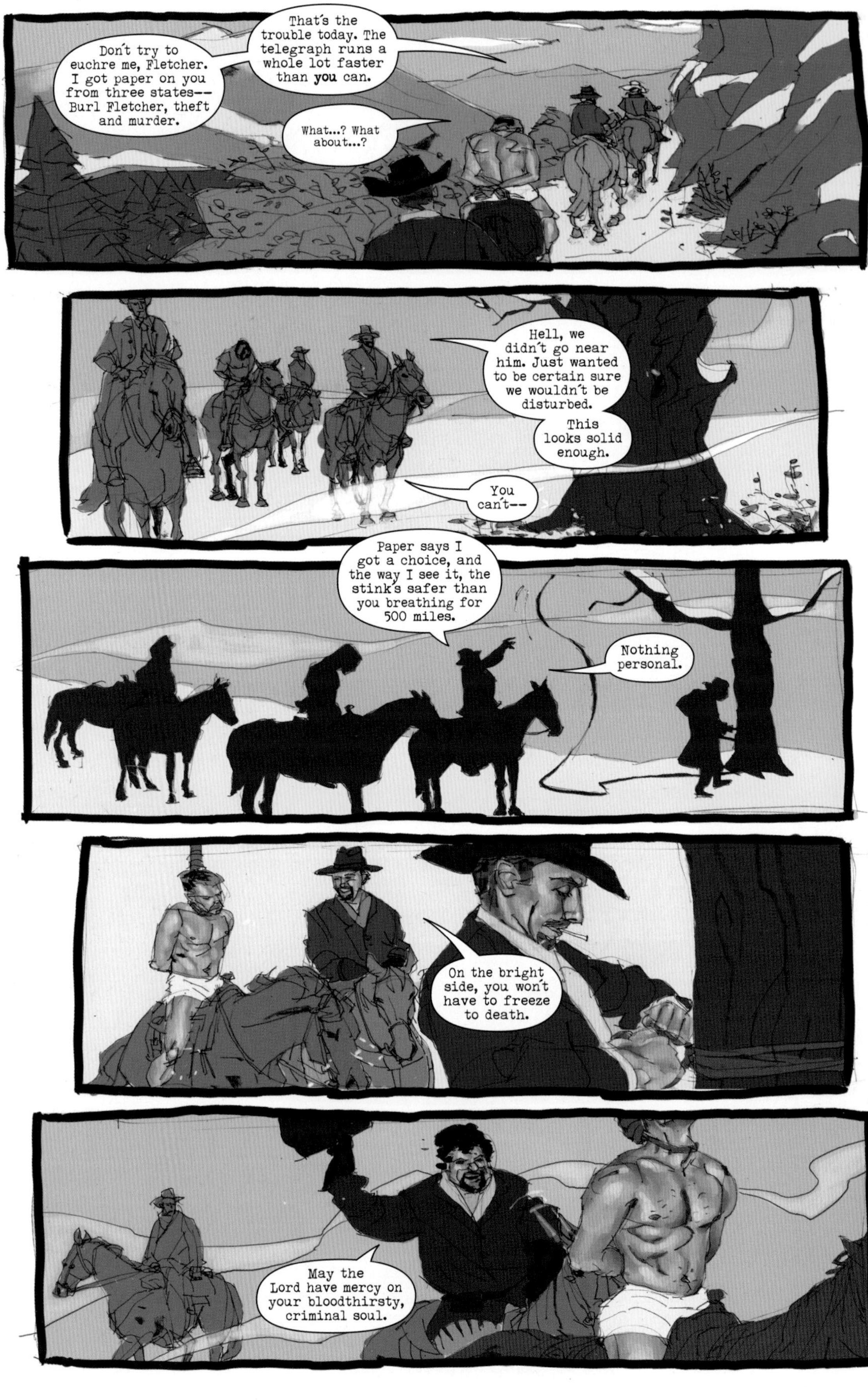
Don't try to euchre me, Fletcher. I got paper on you from three states-- Burl Fletcher, theft and murder.
That's the trouble today. The telegraph runs a whole lot faster than **you** can.
What...? What about...?
Hell, we didn't go near him. Just wanted to be certain sure we wouldn't be disturbed.
This looks solid enough.
You can't--
Paper says I got a choice, and the way I see it, the stink's safer than you breathing for 500 miles.
Nothing personal.
On the bright side, you won't have to freeze to death.
May the Lord have mercy on your bloodthirsty, criminal soul.

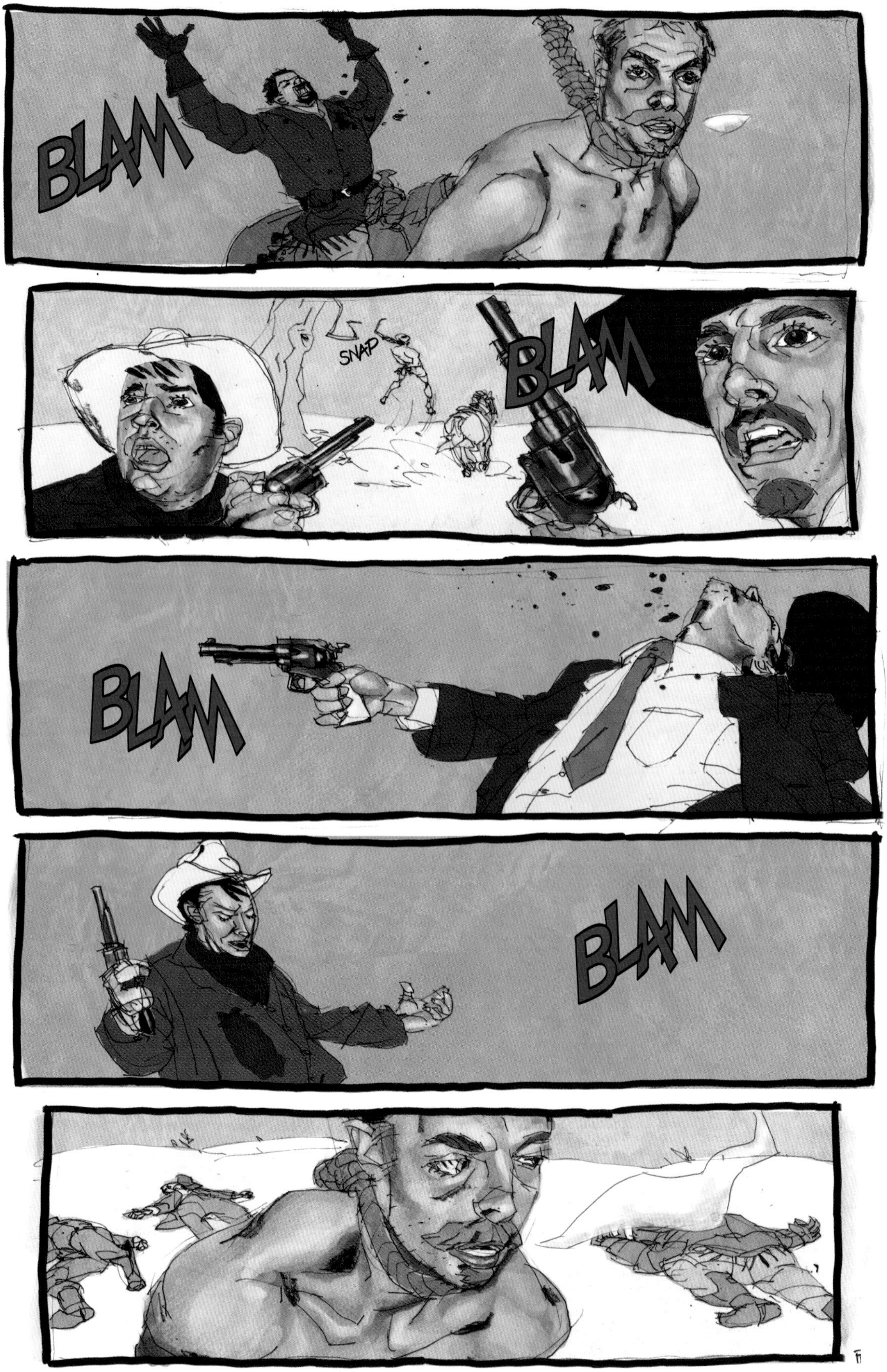
BLAM
SNAP
BLAM
BLAM
BLAM

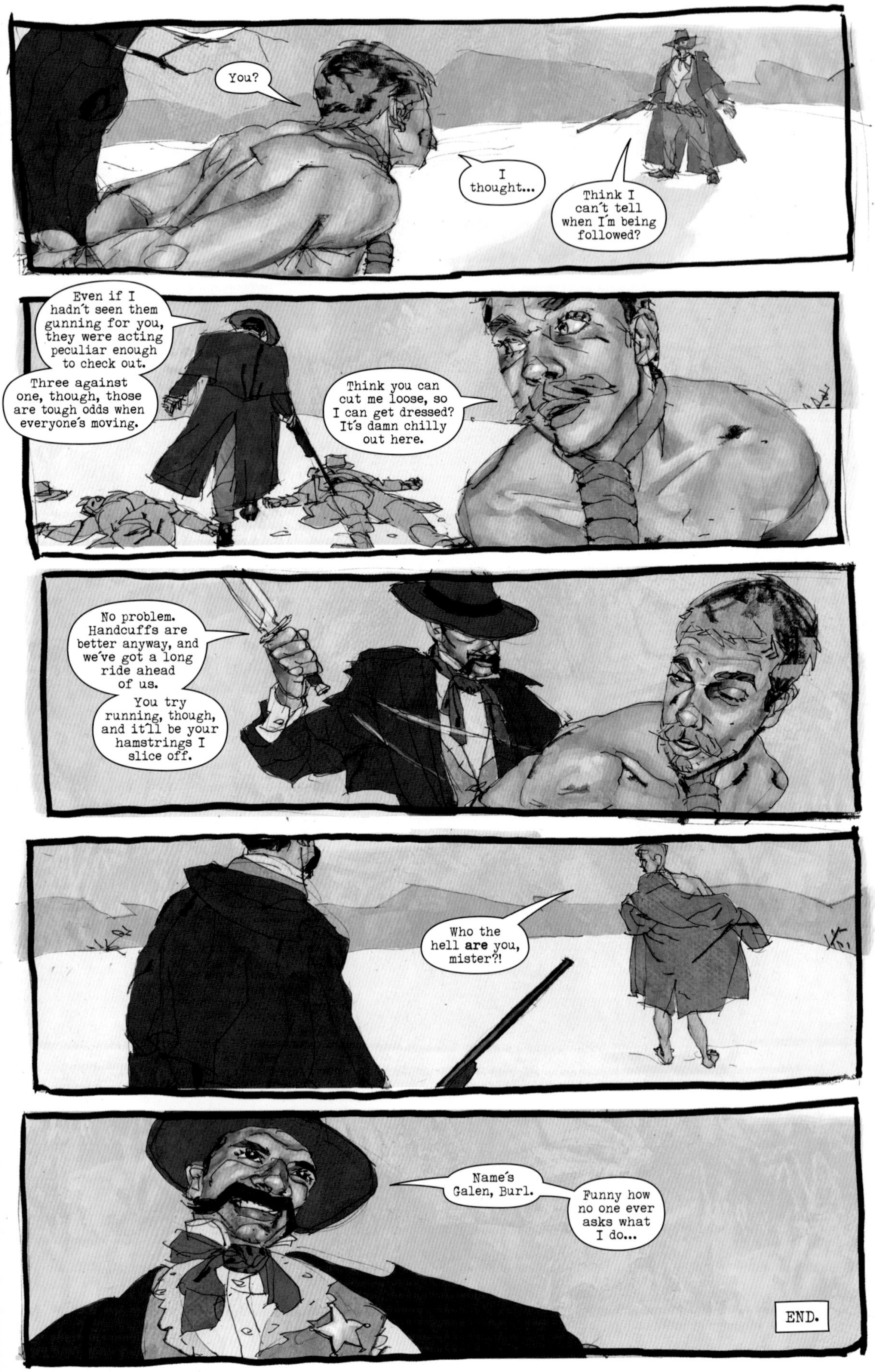
You?
I thought...
Think I can't tell when I'm being followed?
Even if I hadn't seen them gunning for you, they were acting peculiar enough to check out.
Three against one, though, those are tough odds when everyone's moving.
Think you can cut me loose, so I can get dressed? It's damn chilly out here.
No problem. Handcuffs are better anyway, and we've got a long ride ahead of us.
You try running, though, and it'll be your hamstrings I slice off.
Who the hell **are** you, mister?!
Name's Galen, Burl.
Funny how no one ever asks what I do...
END.

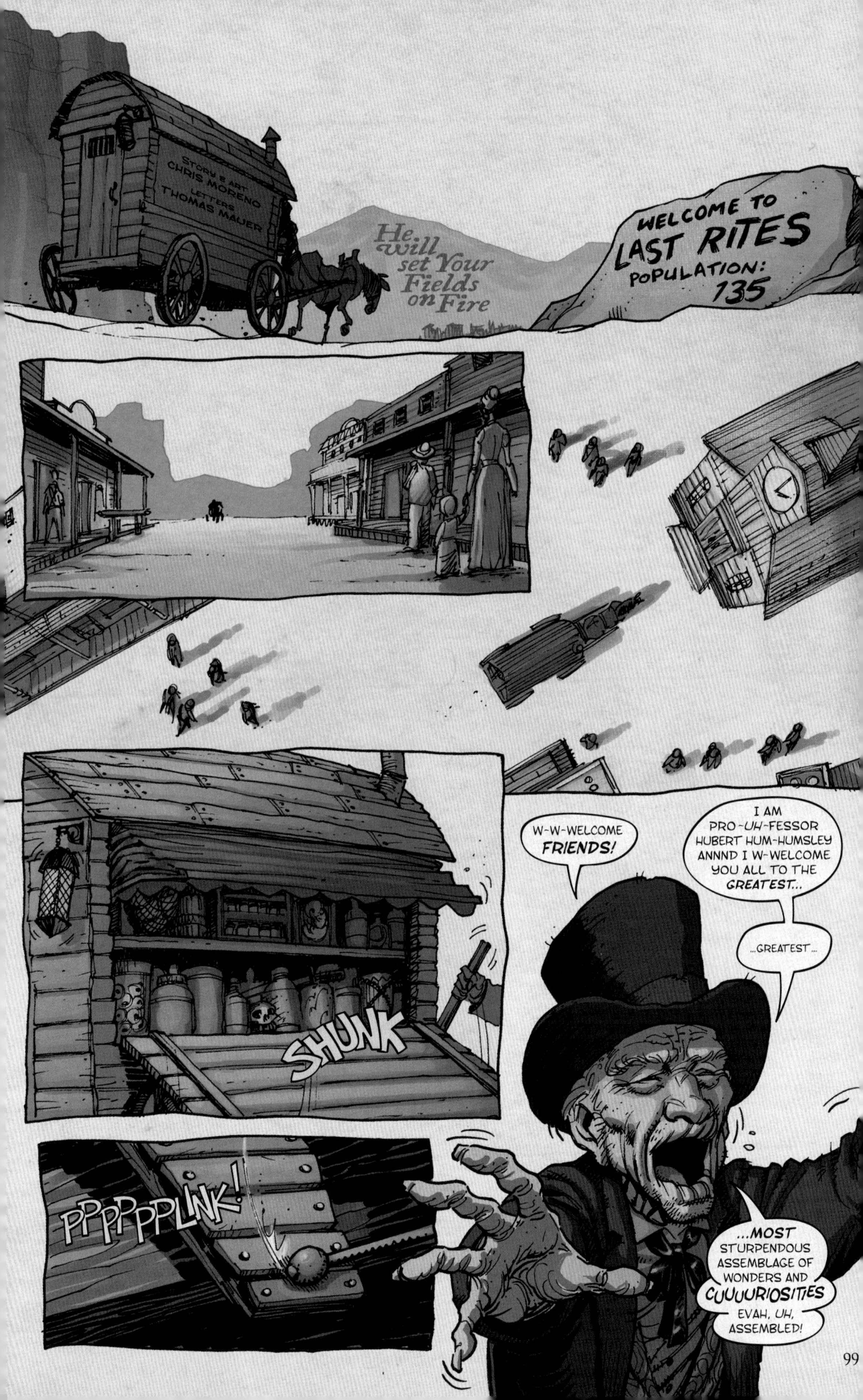
Story & Art
Chris Moreno
Letters
Thomas Mauer
He will set Your Fields on Fire
WELCOME TO
LAST RITES
POPULATION:
135
SHUNK
PPPPPPLINK!
W-W-WELCOME FRIENDS!
I AM PRO-UH-FESSOR HUBERT HUM-HUMSLEY ANNND I W-WELCOME YOU ALL TO THE GREATEST...
...GREATEST...
...MOST STURPENDOUS ASSEMBLAGE OF WONDERS AND CUUUURIOSITIES EVAH, UH, ASSEMBLED!

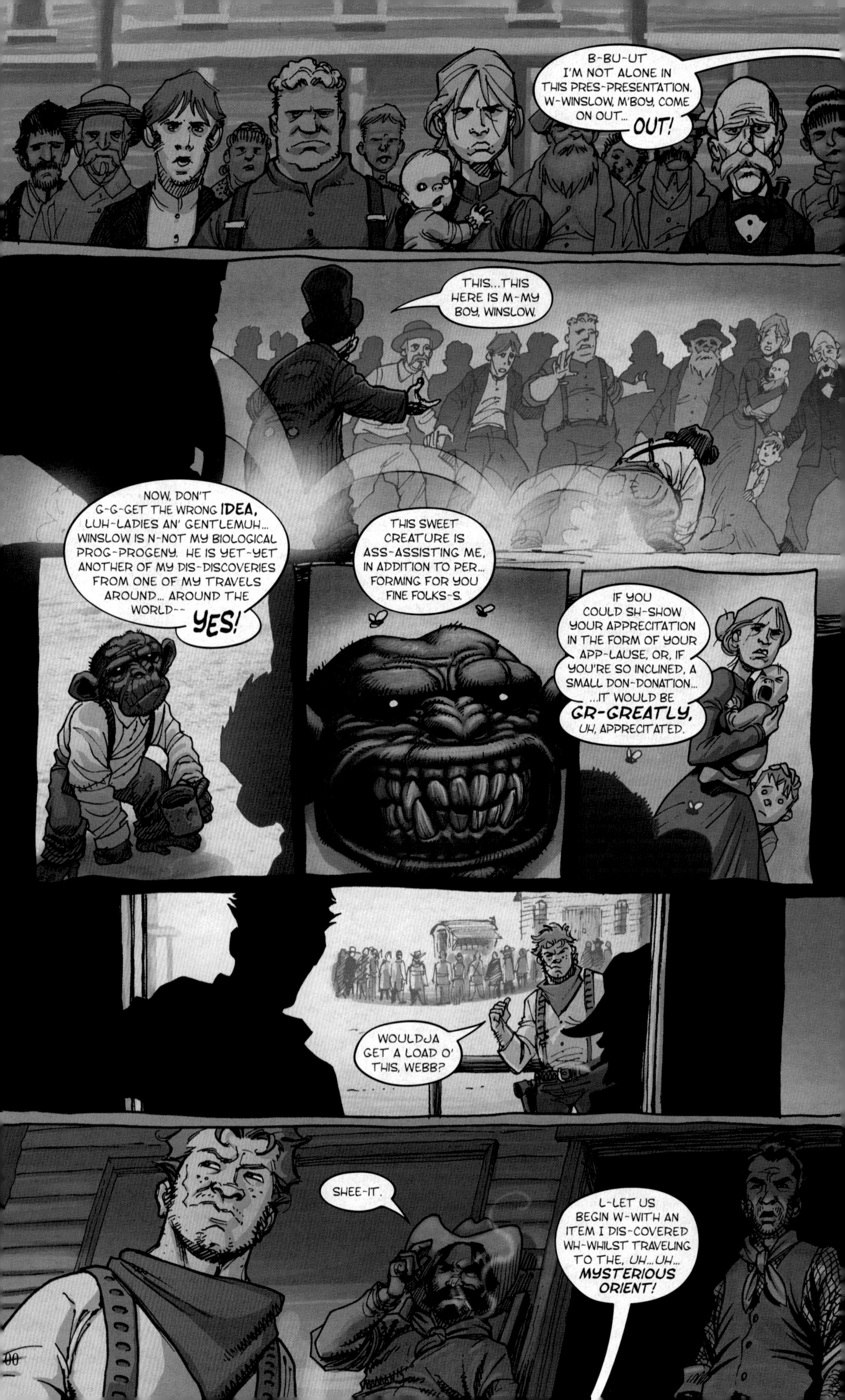
B-BU-UT I'M NOT ALONE IN THIS PRES-PRESENTATION. W-WINSLOW, M'BOY, COME ON OUT... OUT!
THIS...THIS HERE IS M-MY BOY, WINSLOW.
NOW, DON'T G-G-GET THE WRONG IDEA, LUH-LADIES AN' GENTLEMUH... WINSLOW IS N-NOT MY BIOLOGICAL PROG-PROGENY. HE IS YET-YET ANOTHER OF MY DIS-DISCOVERIES FROM ONE OF MY TRAVELS AROUND... AROUND THE WORLD-- YES!
THIS SWEET CREATURE IS ASS-ASSISTING ME, IN ADDITION TO PER... FORMING FOR YOU FINE FOLKS-S.
IF YOU COULD SH-SHOW YOUR APPRECITATION IN THE FORM OF YOUR APP-LAUSE, OR, IF YOU'RE SO INCLINED, A SMALL DON-DONATION... ...IT WOULD BE GR-GREATLY, UH, APPRECITATED.
WOULDJA GET A LOAD O' THIS, WEBB?
SHEE-IT.
L-LET US BEGIN W-WITH AN ITEM I DIS-COVERED WH-WHILST TRAVELING TO THE, UH...UH... MYSTERIOUS ORIENT!

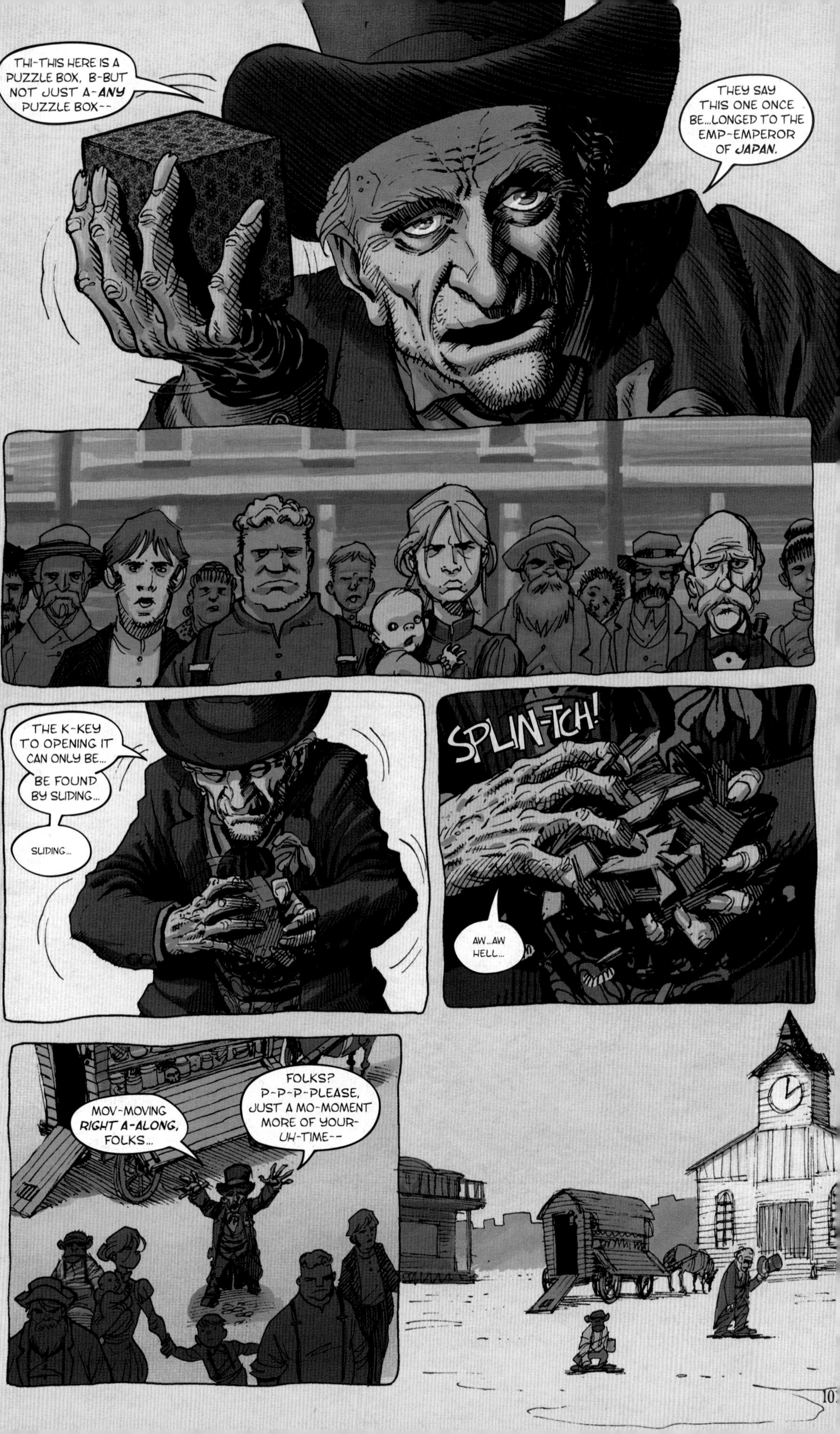
THI-THIS HERE IS A PUZZLE BOX, B-BUT NOT JUST A-ANY PUZZLE BOX--
THEY SAY THIS ONE ONCE BE...LONGED TO THE EMP-EMPEROR OF JAPAN.
THE K-KEY TO OPENING IT CAN ONLY BE...
BE FOUND BY SLIDING...
SLIDING...
SPLIN-TCH!
AW...AW HELL...
MOV-MOVING RIGHT A-ALONG, FOLKS...
FOLKS? P-P-P-PLEASE, JUST A MO-MOMENT MORE OF YOUR-UH-TIME--

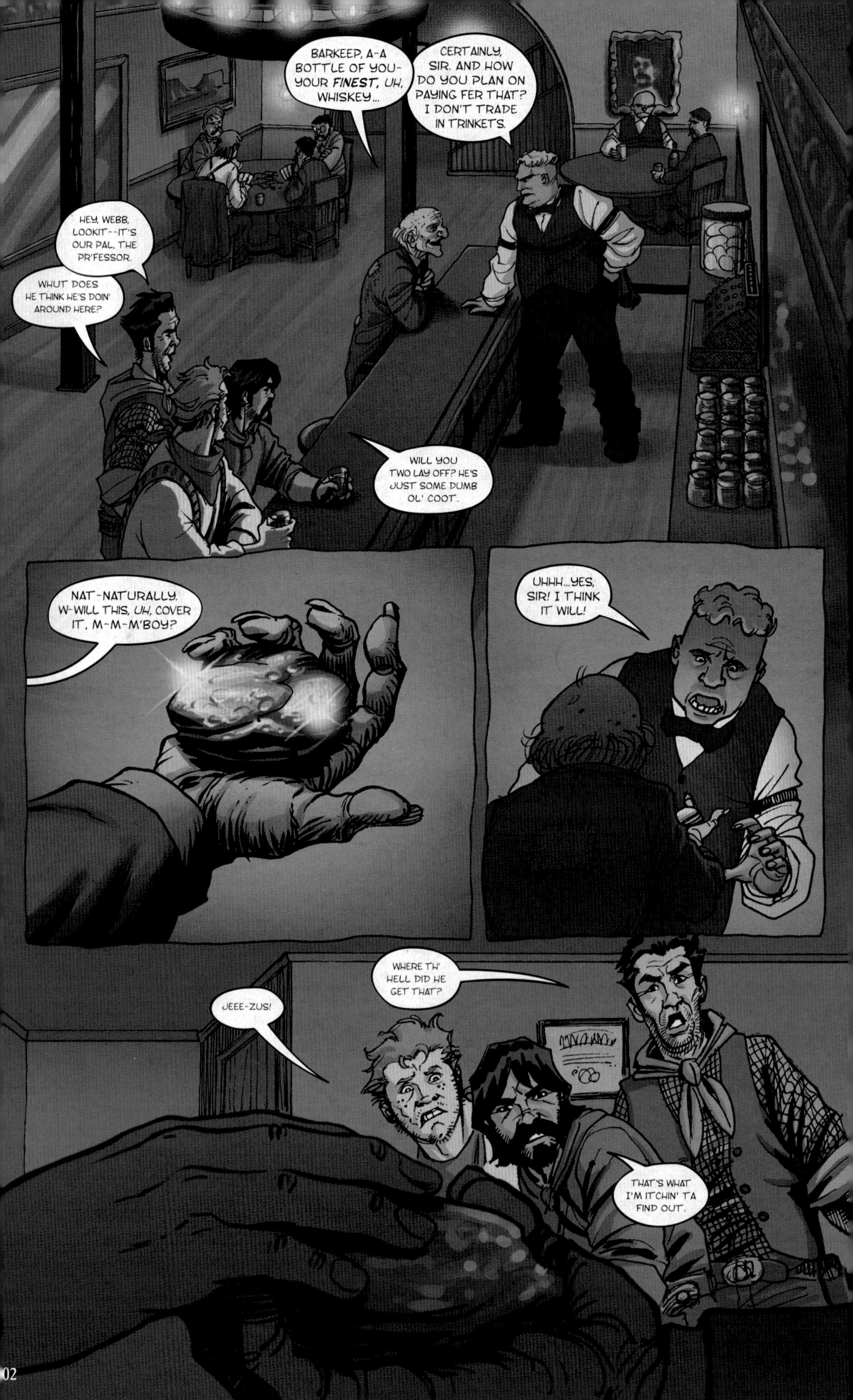
BARKEEP, A-A BOTTLE OF YOU- YOUR FINEST, UH, WHISKEY...
CERTAINLY, SIR. AND HOW DO YOU PLAN ON PAYING FER THAT? I DON'T TRADE IN TRINKETS.
HEY, WEBB, LOOKIT--IT'S OUR PAL, THE PR'FESSOR.
WHUT DOES HE THINK HE'S DOIN' AROUND HERE?
WILL YOU TWO LAY OFF? HE'S JUST SOME DUMB OL' COOT.
NAT-NATURALLY. W-WILL THIS, UH, COVER IT, M-M-M'BOY?
UHHH...YES, SIR! I THINK IT WILL!
JEEE-ZUS!
WHERE TH' HELL DID HE GET THAT?
THAT'S WHAT I'M ITCHIN' TA FIND OUT.

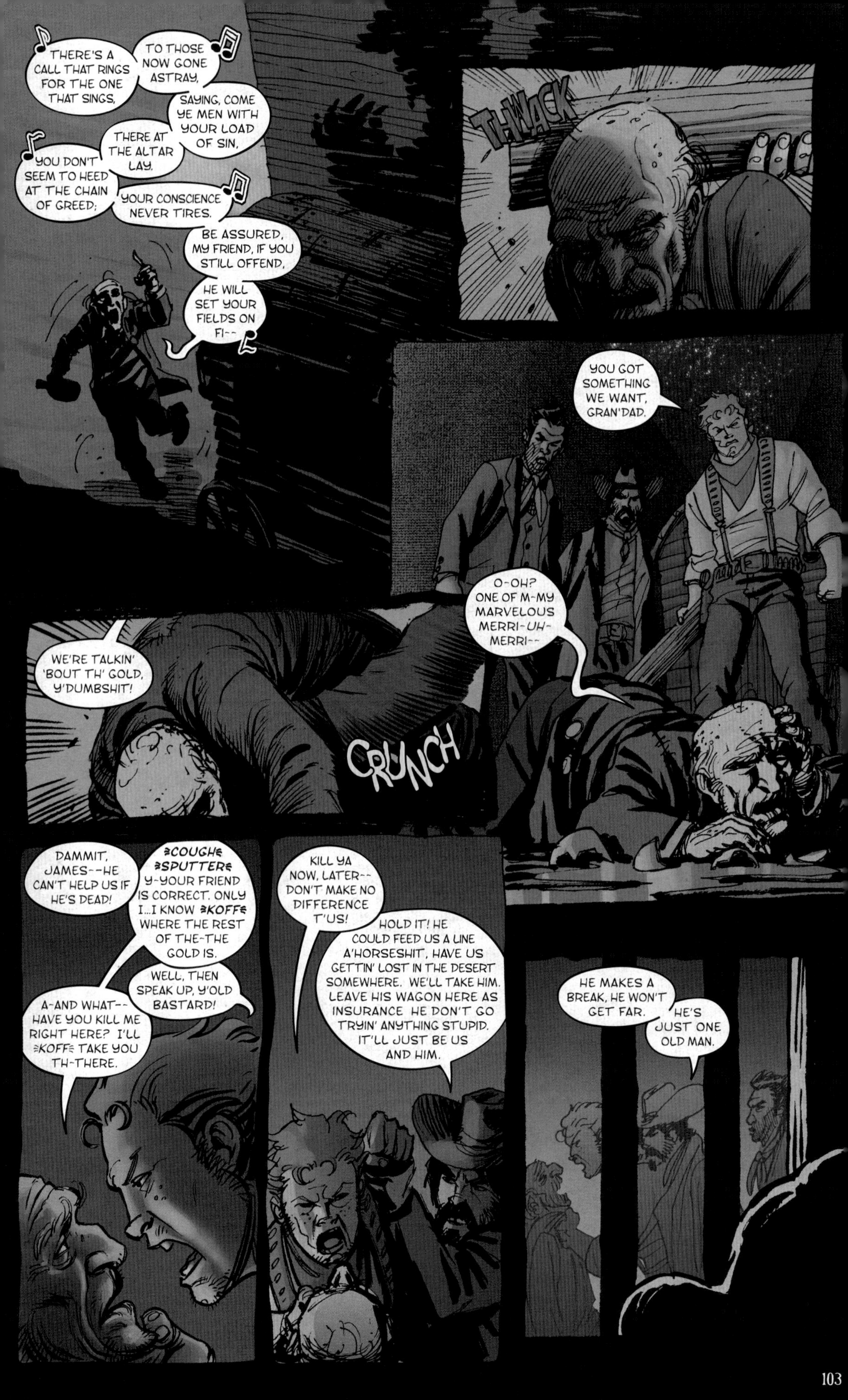
THERE'S A CALL THAT RINGS FOR THE ONE THAT SINGS,
TO THOSE NOW GONE ASTRAY,
SAYING, COME YE MEN WITH YOUR LOAD OF SIN,
THERE AT THE ALTAR LAY.
YOU DON'T SEEM TO HEED AT THE CHAIN OF GREED;
YOUR CONSCIENCE NEVER TIRES.
BE ASSURED, MY FRIEND, IF YOU STILL OFFEND,
HE WILL SET YOUR FIELDS ON FI--
THWACK
YOU GOT SOMETHING WE WANT, GRAN'DAD.
O-OH? ONE OF M-MY MARVELOUS MERRI-UH-MERRI--
WE'RE TALKIN' 'BOUT TH' GOLD, Y'DUMBSHIT!
CRUNCH
DAMMIT, JAMES--HE CAN'T HELP US IF HE'S DEAD!
COUGH SPUTTER Y-YOUR FRIEND IS CORRECT. ONLY I...I KNOW KOFF WHERE THE REST OF THE-THE GOLD IS.
WELL, THEN SPEAK UP, Y'OLD BASTARD!
A-AND WHAT--HAVE YOU KILL ME RIGHT HERE? I'LL KOFF TAKE YOU TH-THERE.
KILL YA NOW, LATER--DON'T MAKE NO DIFFERENCE T'US!
HOLD IT! HE COULD FEED US A LINE A'HORSESHIT, HAVE US GETTIN' LOST IN THE DESERT SOMEWHERE. WE'LL TAKE HIM. LEAVE HIS WAGON HERE AS INSURANCE HE DON'T GO TRYIN' ANYTHING STUPID. IT'LL JUST BE US AND HIM.
HE MAKES A BREAK, HE WON'T GET FAR.
HE'S JUST ONE OLD MAN.

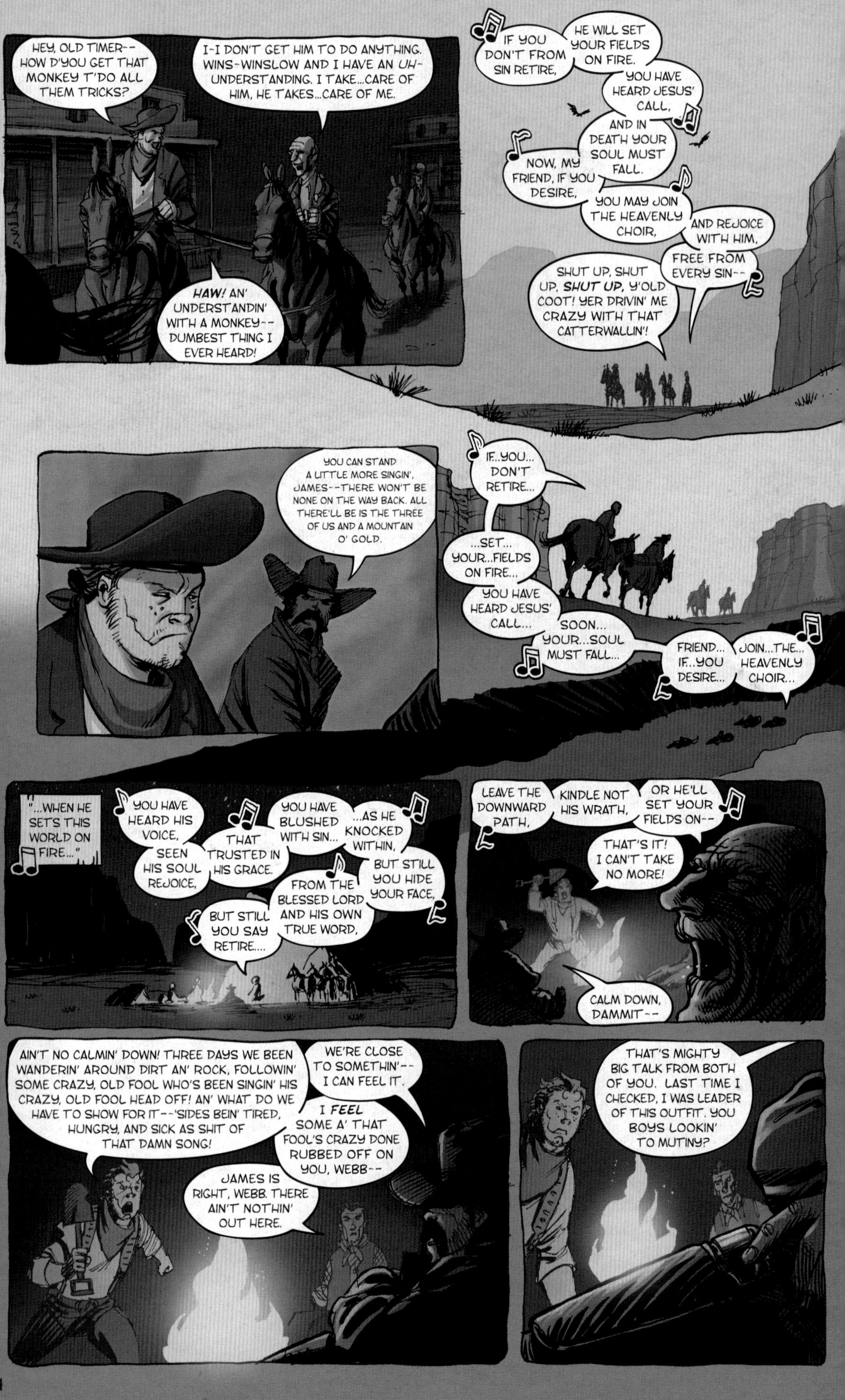
HEY, OLD TIMER-- HOW D'YOU GET THAT MONKEY T'DO ALL THEM TRICKS?
I-I DON'T GET HIM TO DO ANYTHING. WINS-WINSLOW AND I HAVE AN UH- UNDERSTANDING. I TAKE...CARE OF HIM, HE TAKES...CARE OF ME.
HAW! AN' UNDERSTANDIN' WITH A MONKEY-- DUMBEST THING I EVER HEARD!
IF YOU DON'T FROM SIN RETIRE,
HE WILL SET YOUR FIELDS ON FIRE.
YOU HAVE HEARD JESUS' CALL,
AND IN DEATH YOUR SOUL MUST FALL.
NOW, MY FRIEND, IF YOU DESIRE,
YOU MAY JOIN THE HEAVENLY CHOIR,
AND REJOICE WITH HIM,
FREE FROM EVERY SIN--
SHUT UP, SHUT UP, SHUT UP, Y'OLD COOT! YER DRIVIN' ME CRAZY WITH THAT CATTERWALLIN'!
YOU CAN STAND A LITTLE MORE SINGIN', JAMES--THERE WON'T BE NONE ON THE WAY BACK. ALL THERE'LL BE IS THE THREE OF US AND A MOUNTAIN O' GOLD.
IF...YOU... DON'T RETIRE...
...SET... YOUR...FIELDS ON FIRE...
YOU HAVE HEARD JESUS' CALL...
SOON... YOUR...SOUL MUST FALL...
FRIEND... IF...YOU DESIRE...
JOIN...THE... HEAVENLY CHOIR...
"...WHEN HE SETS THIS WORLD ON FIRE..."
YOU HAVE HEARD HIS VOICE,
SEEN HIS SOUL REJOICE,
THAT TRUSTED IN HIS GRACE.
YOU HAVE BLUSHED WITH SIN...
...AS HE KNOCKED WITHIN,
BUT STILL YOU HIDE YOUR FACE,
FROM THE BLESSED LORD AND HIS OWN TRUE WORD,
BUT STILL YOU SAY RETIRE....
LEAVE THE DOWNWARD PATH,
KINDLE NOT HIS WRATH,
OR HE'LL SET YOUR FIELDS ON--
THAT'S IT! I CAN'T TAKE NO MORE!
CALM DOWN, DAMMIT--
AIN'T NO CALMIN' DOWN! THREE DAYS WE BEEN WANDERIN' AROUND DIRT AN' ROCK, FOLLOWIN' SOME CRAZY, OLD FOOL WHO'S BEEN SINGIN' HIS CRAZY, OLD FOOL HEAD OFF! AN' WHAT DO WE HAVE TO SHOW FOR IT--'SIDES BEIN' TIRED, HUNGRY, AND SICK AS SHIT OF THAT DAMN SONG!
WE'RE CLOSE TO SOMETHIN'-- I CAN FEEL IT.
I FEEL SOME A' THAT FOOL'S CRAZY DONE RUBBED OFF ON YOU, WEBB--
JAMES IS RIGHT, WEBB. THERE AIN'T NOTHIN' OUT HERE.
THAT'S MIGHTY BIG TALK FROM BOTH OF YOU. LAST TIME I CHECKED, I WAS LEADER OF THIS OUTFIT. YOU BOYS LOOKIN' TO MUTINY?

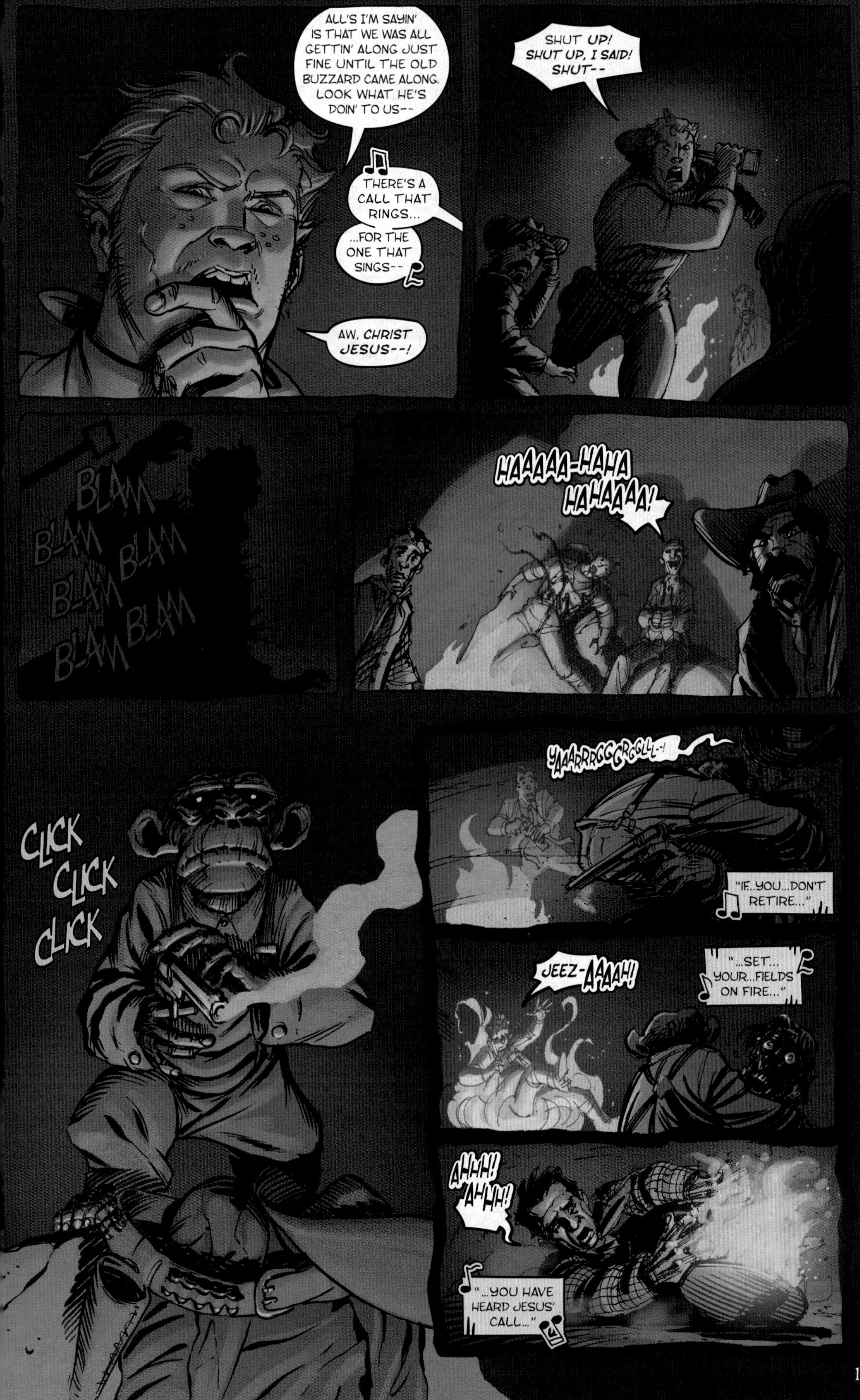
ALL'S I'M SAYIN' IS THAT WE WAS ALL GETTIN' ALONG JUST FINE UNTIL THE OLD BUZZARD CAME ALONG. LOOK WHAT HE'S DOIN' TO US--
THERE'S A CALL THAT RINGS...
...FOR THE ONE THAT SINGS--
AW, CHRIST JESUS--!
SHUT UP! SHUT UP, I SAID! SHUT--
BLAM BLAM BLAM BLAM BLAM BLAM BLAM
HAAAAA-HAHA HAHAAAA!
CLICK CLICK CLICK
YAAARRGGGRGGLL--!
"IF...YOU...DON'T RETIRE..."
JEEZ-AAAAH!
"...SET... YOUR...FIELDS ON FIRE..."
AHHH! AHHH!
"...YOU HAVE HEARD JESUS' CALL..."

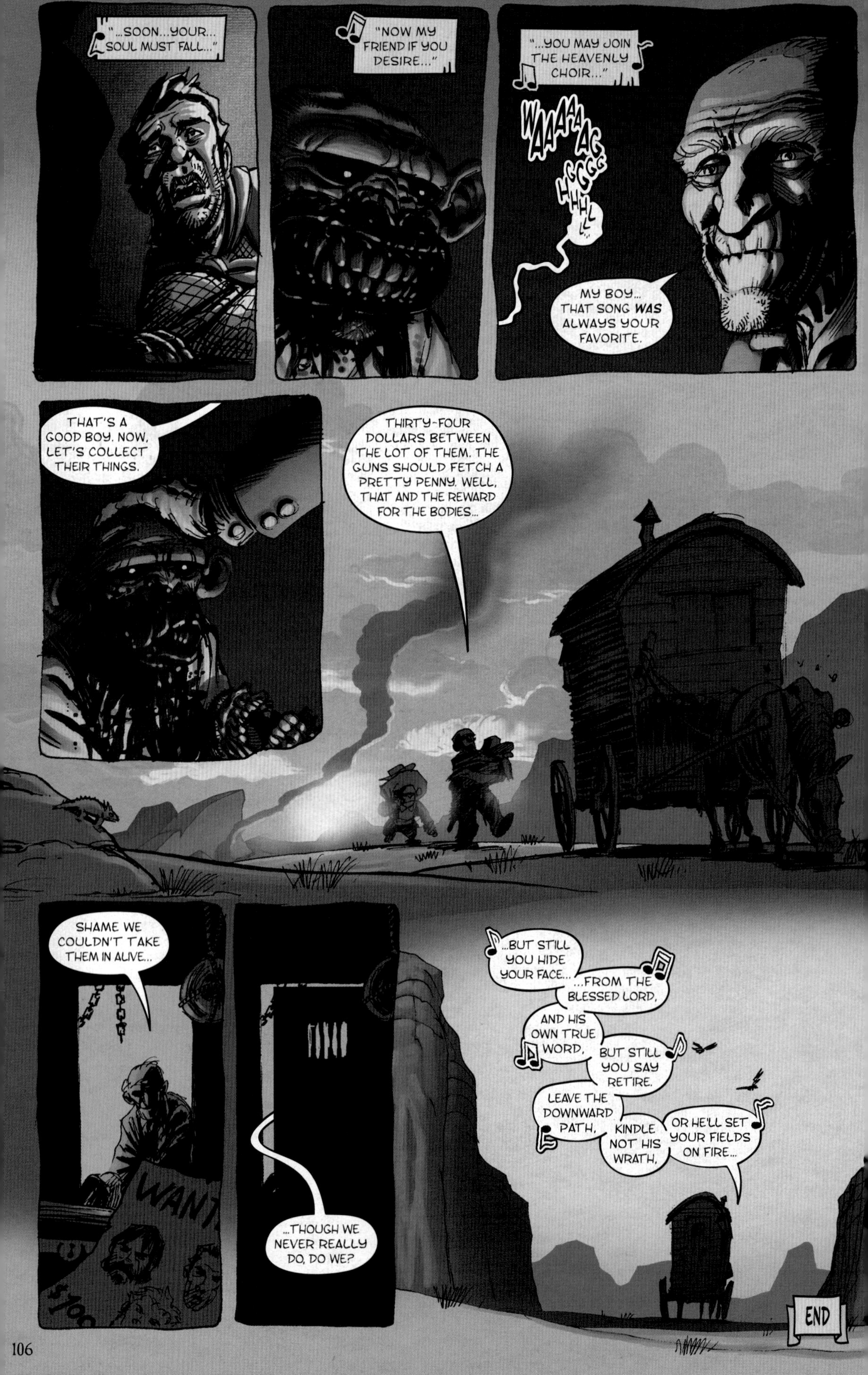
"...SOON...YOUR... SOUL MUST FALL..."
"NOW MY FRIEND IF YOU DESIRE..."
"...YOU MAY JOIN THE HEAVENLY CHOIR..."
WAAAAAAGGGGGHHHLLL
MY BOY... THAT SONG **WAS** ALWAYS YOUR FAVORITE.
THAT'S A GOOD BOY. NOW, LET'S COLLECT THEIR THINGS.
THIRTY-FOUR DOLLARS BETWEEN THE LOT OF THEM. THE GUNS SHOULD FETCH A PRETTY PENNY. WELL, THAT AND THE REWARD FOR THE BODIES...
SHAME WE COULDN'T TAKE THEM IN ALIVE...
WANT
...THOUGH WE NEVER REALLY DO, DO WE?
...BUT STILL YOU HIDE YOUR FACE...
...FROM THE BLESSED LORD,
AND HIS OWN TRUE WORD,
BUT STILL YOU SAY RETIRE.
LEAVE THE DOWNWARD PATH,
KINDLE NOT HIS WRATH,
OR HE'LL SET YOUR FIELDS ON FIRE...
END

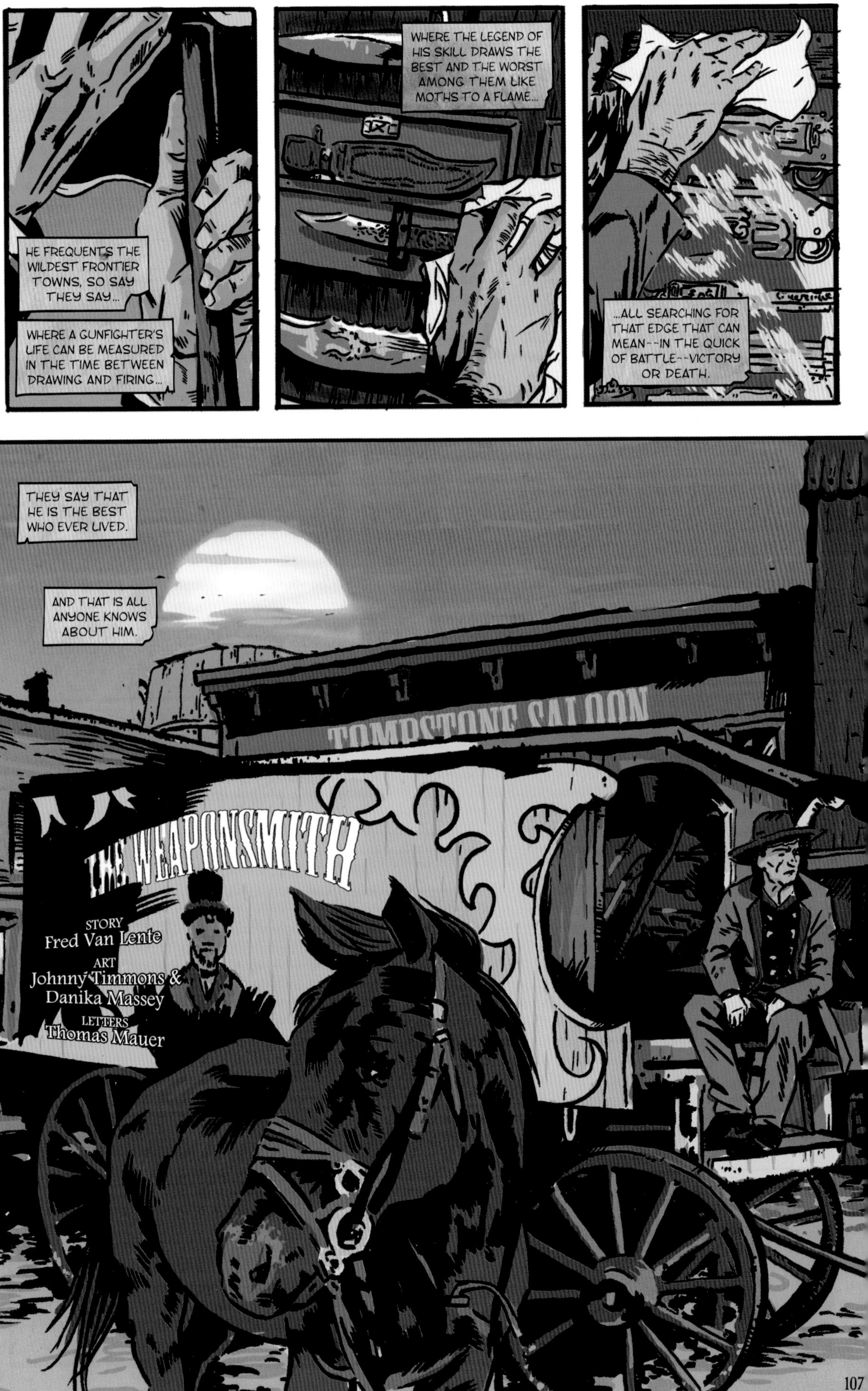
HE FREQUENTS THE WILDEST FRONTIER TOWNS, SO SAY THEY SAY...
WHERE A GUNFIGHTER'S LIFE CAN BE MEASURED IN THE TIME BETWEEN DRAWING AND FIRING...
WHERE THE LEGEND OF HIS SKILL DRAWS THE BEST AND THE WORST AMONG THEM LIKE MOTHS TO A FLAME...
...ALL SEARCHING FOR THAT EDGE THAT CAN MEAN--IN THE QUICK OF BATTLE--VICTORY OR DEATH.
THEY SAY THAT HE IS THE BEST WHO EVER LIVED.
AND THAT IS ALL ANYONE KNOWS ABOUT HIM.
TOMBSTONE SALOON
THE WEAPONSMITH
STORY
Fred Van Lente
ART
Johnny Timmons &
Danika Massey
LETTERS
Thomas Mauer

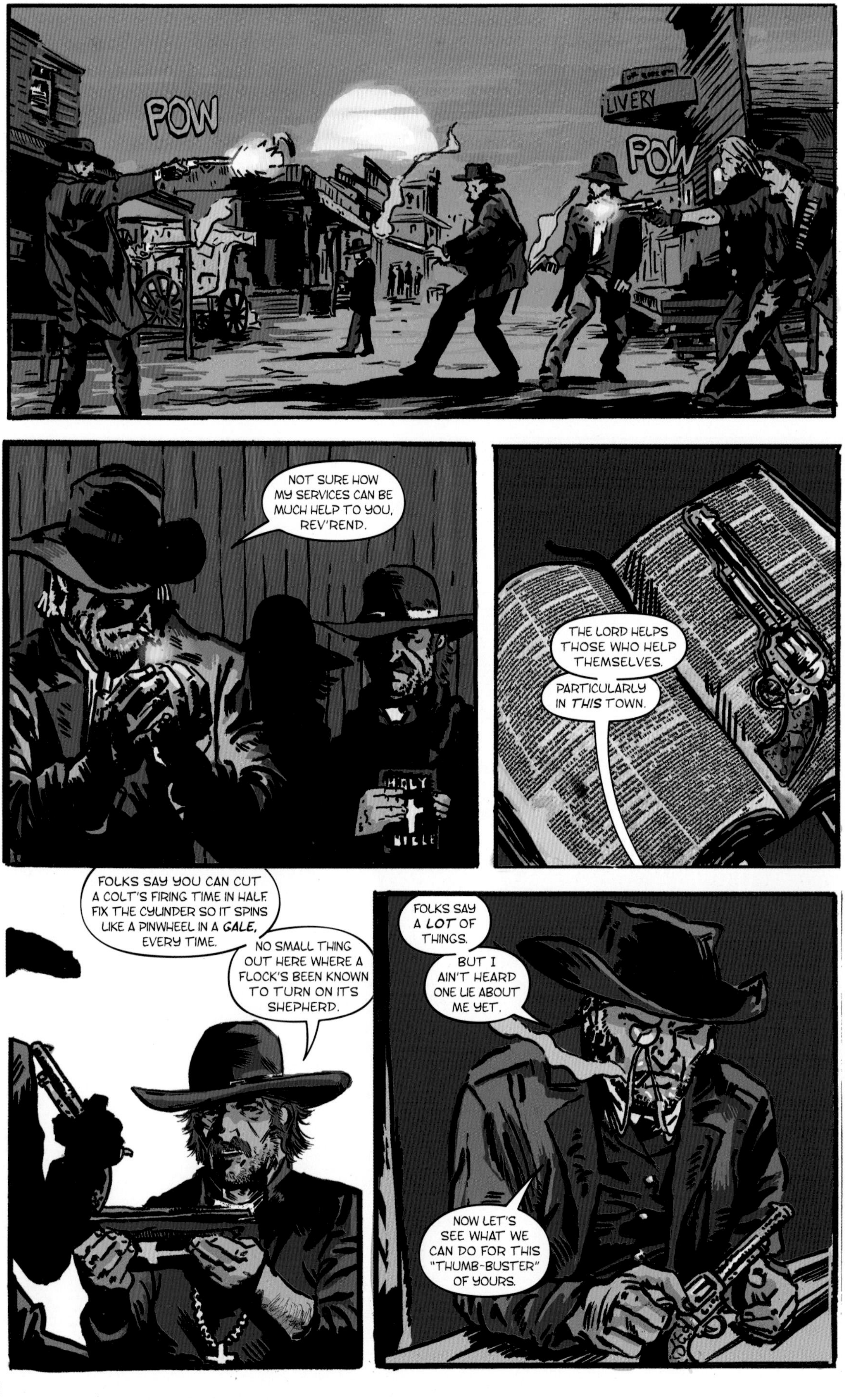
POW
LIVERY
POW
NOT SURE HOW MY SERVICES CAN BE MUCH HELP TO YOU, REV'REND.
HOLY BIBLE
THE LORD HELPS THOSE WHO HELP THEMSELVES.
PARTICULARLY IN *THIS* TOWN.
FOLKS SAY YOU CAN CUT A COLT'S FIRING TIME IN HALF. FIX THE CYLINDER SO IT SPINS LIKE A PINWHEEL IN A *GALE,* EVERY TIME.
NO SMALL THING OUT HERE WHERE A FLOCK'S BEEN KNOWN TO TURN ON IT'S SHEPHERD.
FOLKS SAY A *LOT* OF THINGS.
BUT I AIN'T HEARD ONE LIE ABOUT ME YET.
NOW LET'S SEE WHAT WE CAN DO FOR THIS "THUMB-BUSTER" OF YOURS.

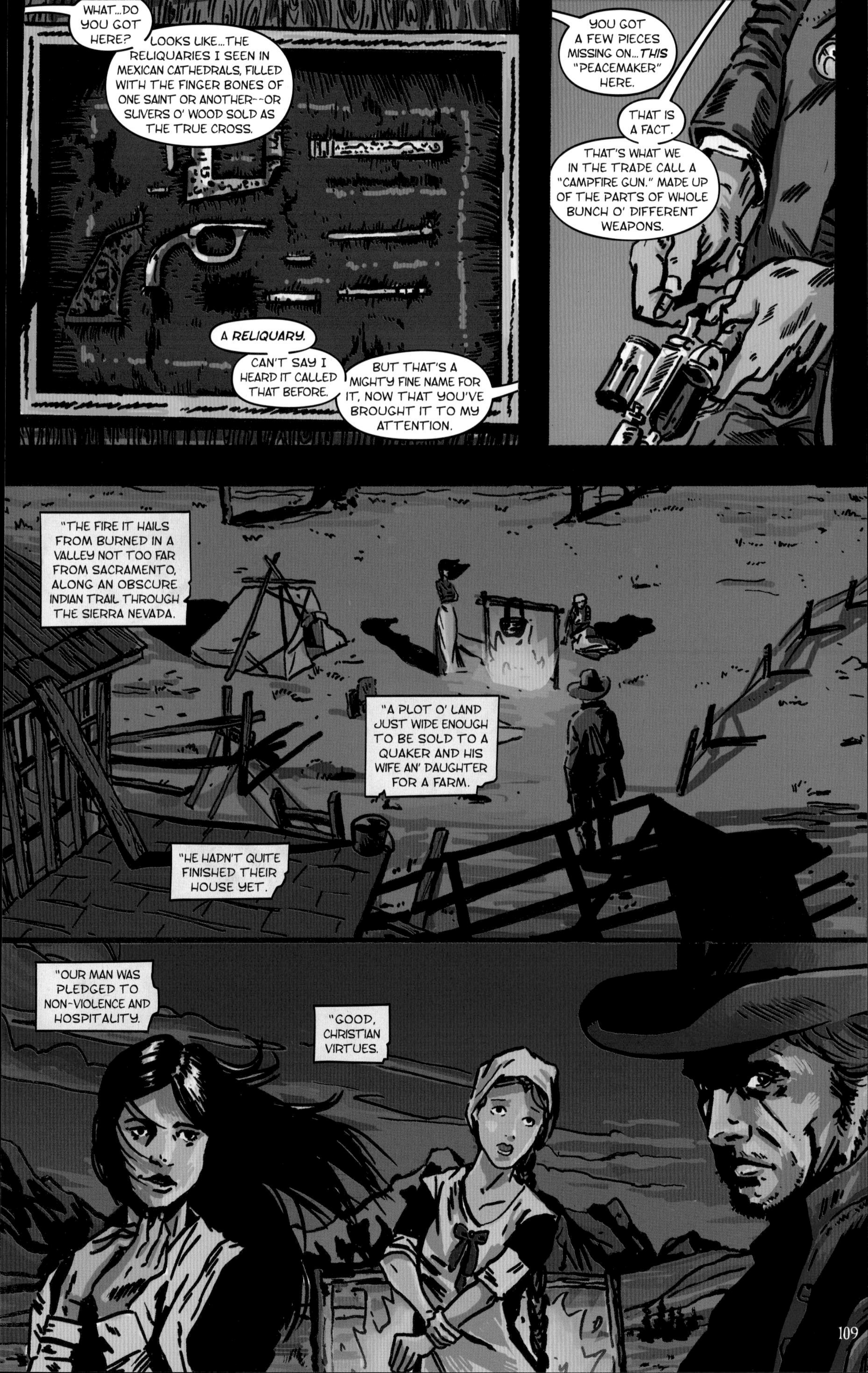
WHAT...DO YOU GOT HERE?
LOOKS LIKE...THE RELIQUARIES I SEEN IN MEXICAN CATHEDRALS, FILLED WITH THE FINGER BONES OF ONE SAINT OR ANOTHER--OR SLIVERS O' WOOD SOLD AS THE TRUE CROSS.
A RELIQUARY.
CAN'T SAY I HEARD IT CALLED THAT BEFORE.
BUT THAT'S A MIGHTY FINE NAME FOR IT, NOW THAT YOU'VE BROUGHT IT TO MY ATTENTION.
YOU GOT A FEW PIECES MISSING ON...THIS "PEACEMAKER" HERE.
THAT IS A FACT.
THAT'S WHAT WE IN THE TRADE CALL A "CAMPFIRE GUN." MADE UP OF THE PARTS OF WHOLE BUNCH O' DIFFERENT WEAPONS.
"THE FIRE IT HAILS FROM BURNED IN A VALLEY NOT TOO FAR FROM SACRAMENTO, ALONG AN OBSCURE INDIAN TRAIL THROUGH THE SIERRA NEVADA.
"A PLOT O' LAND JUST WIDE ENOUGH TO BE SOLD TO A QUAKER AND HIS WIFE AN' DAUGHTER FOR A FARM.
"HE HADN'T QUITE FINISHED THEIR HOUSE YET.
"OUR MAN WAS PLEDGED TO NON-VIOLENCE AND HOSPITALITY.
"GOOD, CHRISTIAN VIRTUES.

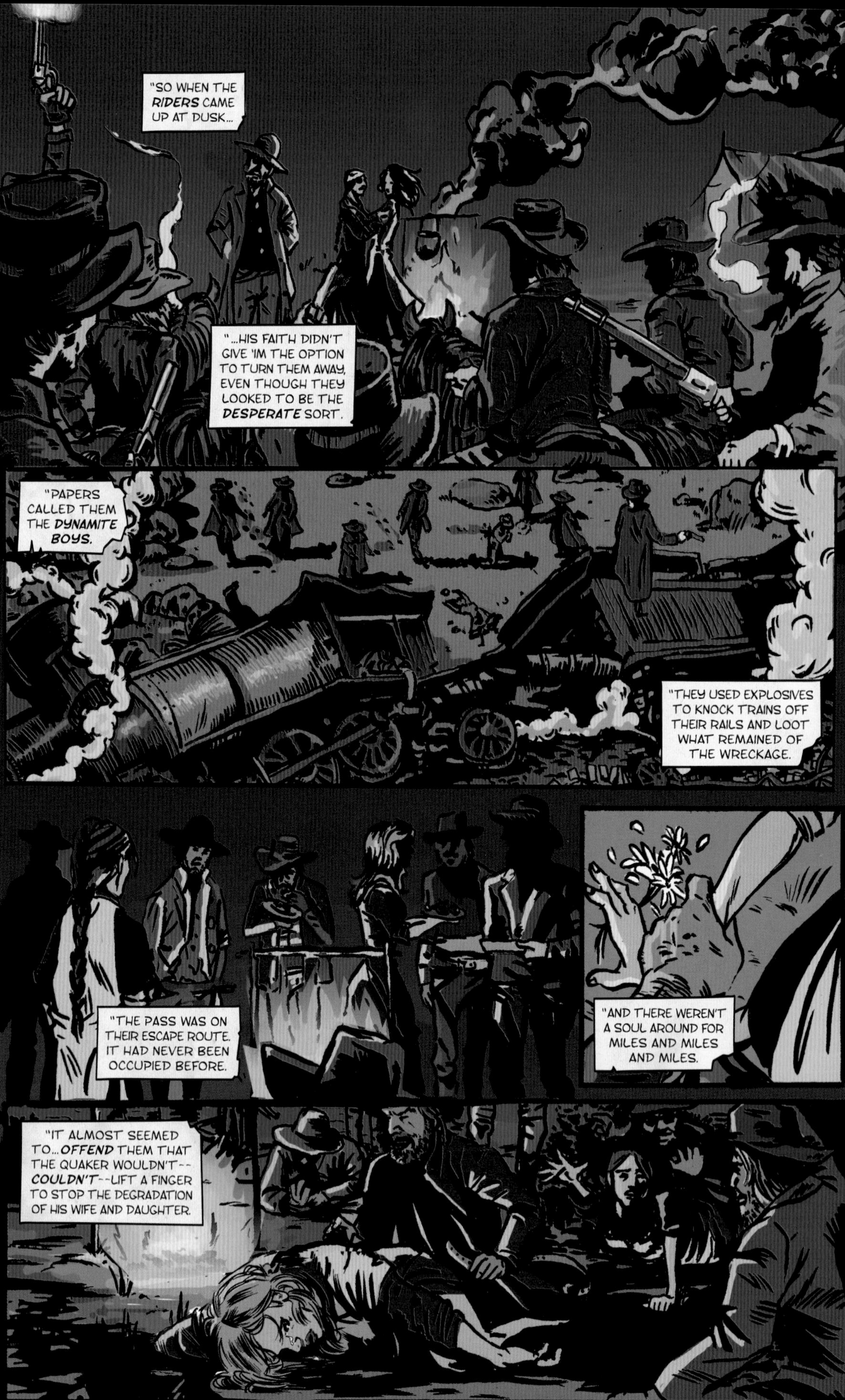
"SO WHEN THE RIDERS CAME UP AT DUSK...
"...HIS FAITH DIDN'T GIVE 'IM THE OPTION TO TURN THEM AWAY, EVEN THOUGH THEY LOOKED TO BE THE DESPERATE SORT.
"PAPERS CALLED THEM THE DYNAMITE BOYS.
"THEY USED EXPLOSIVES TO KNOCK TRAINS OFF THEIR RAILS AND LOOT WHAT REMAINED OF THE WRECKAGE.
"THE PASS WAS ON THEIR ESCAPE ROUTE. IT HAD NEVER BEEN OCCUPIED BEFORE.
"AND THERE WEREN'T A SOUL AROUND FOR MILES AND MILES AND MILES.
"IT ALMOST SEEMED TO... OFFEND THEM THAT THE QUAKER WOULDN'T--COULDN'T--LIFT A FINGER TO STOP THE DEGRADATION OF HIS WIFE AND DAUGHTER.

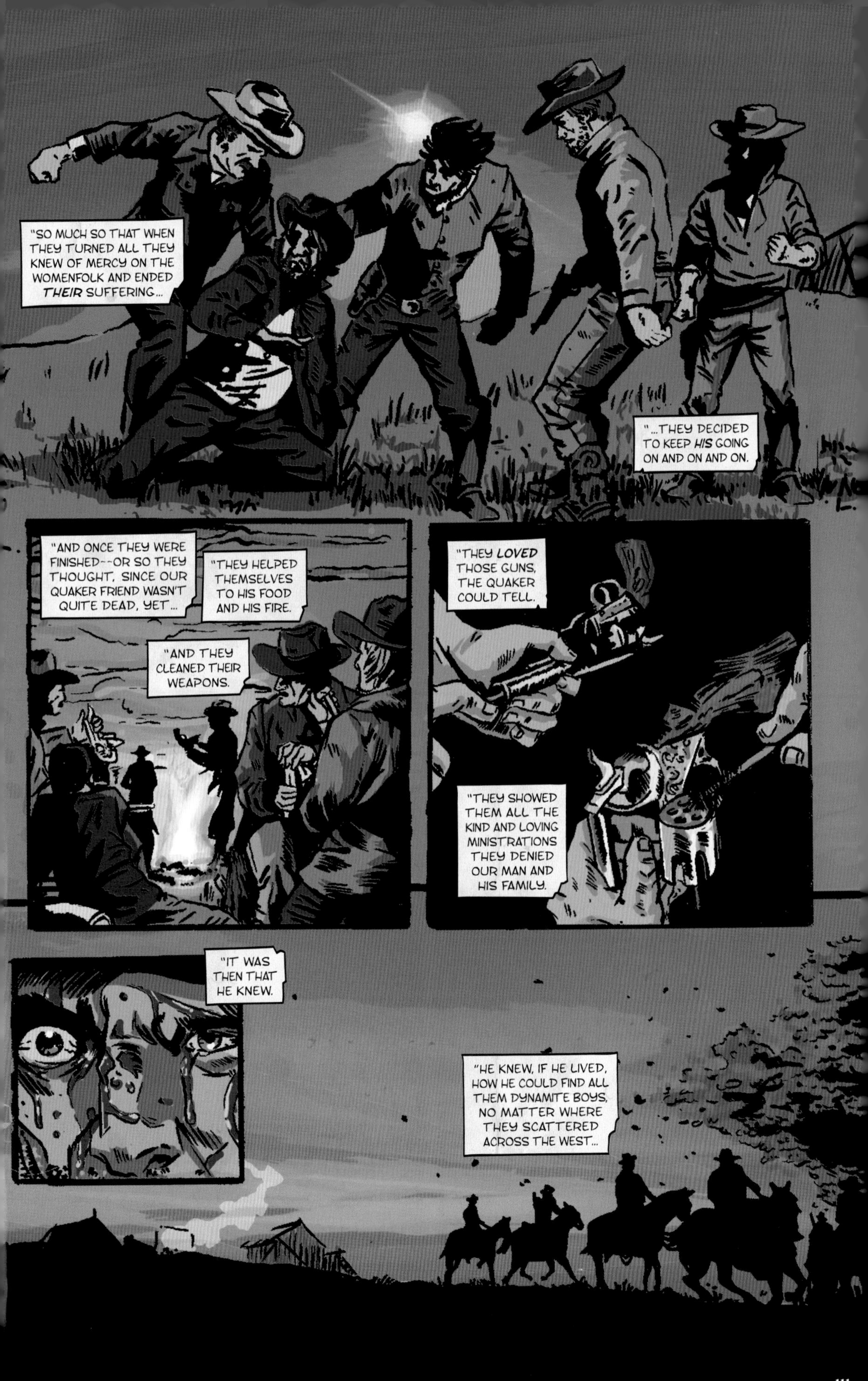
"SO MUCH SO THAT WHEN THEY TURNED ALL THEY KNEW OF MERCY ON THE WOMENFOLK AND ENDED ***THEIR*** SUFFERING...
"...THEY DECIDED TO KEEP ***HIS*** GOING ON AND ON AND ON.
"AND ONCE THEY WERE FINISHED--OR SO THEY THOUGHT, SINCE OUR QUAKER FRIEND WASN'T QUITE DEAD, YET...
"THEY HELPED THEMSELVES TO HIS FOOD AND HIS FIRE.
"AND THEY CLEANED THEIR WEAPONS.
"THEY ***LOVED*** THOSE GUNS, THE QUAKER COULD TELL.
"THEY SHOWED THEM ALL THE KIND AND LOVING MINISTRATIONS THEY DENIED OUR MAN AND HIS FAMILY.
"IT WAS THEN THAT HE KNEW.
"HE KNEW, IF HE LIVED, HOW HE COULD FIND ALL THEM DYNAMITE BOYS, NO MATTER WHERE THEY SCATTERED ACROSS THE WEST...

...OR, MORE PRECISELY... ...HOW TO GET THEM--AND THOSE GUNS THEY LOVED SO VERY MUCH-- --TO COME TO HIM.

BUT...I RECKON...YOU FIGURED *THAT* PART OUT ALREADY, AIN'T YOU...

..."REVEREND?"

HOW CAN YOU BE HIM? YOU DON'T LOOK ANYTHING *LIKE* HIM.

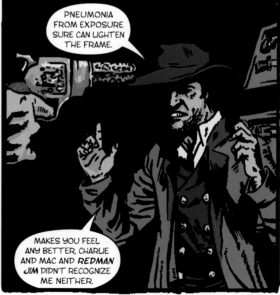

PNEUMONIA FROM EXPOSURE SURE CAN LIGHTEN THE FRAME.

MAKES YOU FEEL ANY BETTER, CHARLIE AND MAC AND *REDMAN JIM* DIDN'T RECOGNIZE ME NEITHER.

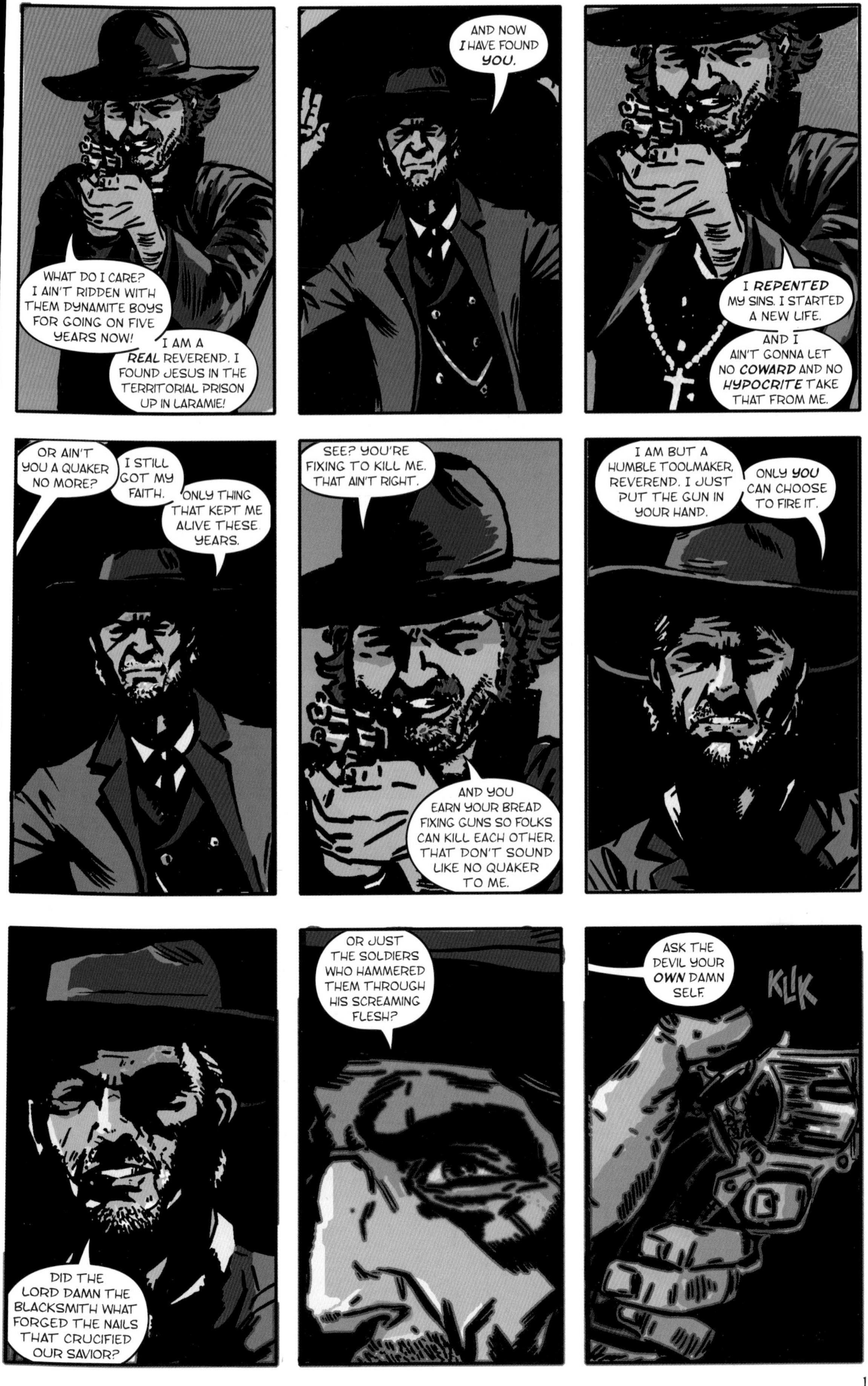
WHAT DO I CARE? I AIN'T RIDDEN WITH THEM DYNAMITE BOYS FOR GOING ON FIVE YEARS NOW!
I AM A REAL REVEREND. I FOUND JESUS IN THE TERRITORIAL PRISON UP IN LARAMIE!
AND NOW I HAVE FOUND YOU.
I REPENTED MY SINS. I STARTED A NEW LIFE.
AND I AIN'T GONNA LET NO COWARD AND NO HYPOCRITE TAKE THAT FROM ME.
OR AIN'T YOU A QUAKER NO MORE?
I STILL GOT MY FAITH.
ONLY THING THAT KEPT ME ALIVE THESE YEARS.
SEE? YOU'RE FIXING TO KILL ME. THAT AIN'T RIGHT.
AND YOU EARN YOUR BREAD FIXING GUNS SO FOLKS CAN KILL EACH OTHER. THAT DON'T SOUND LIKE NO QUAKER TO ME.
I AM BUT A HUMBLE TOOLMAKER, REVEREND. I JUST PUT THE GUN IN YOUR HAND.
ONLY YOU CAN CHOOSE TO FIRE IT.
DID THE LORD DAMN THE BLACKSMITH WHAT FORGED THE NAILS THAT CRUCIFIED OUR SAVIOR?
OR JUST THE SOLDIERS WHO HAMMERED THEM THROUGH HIS SCREAMING FLESH?
ASK THE DEVIL YOUR OWN DAMN SELF.
KLIK

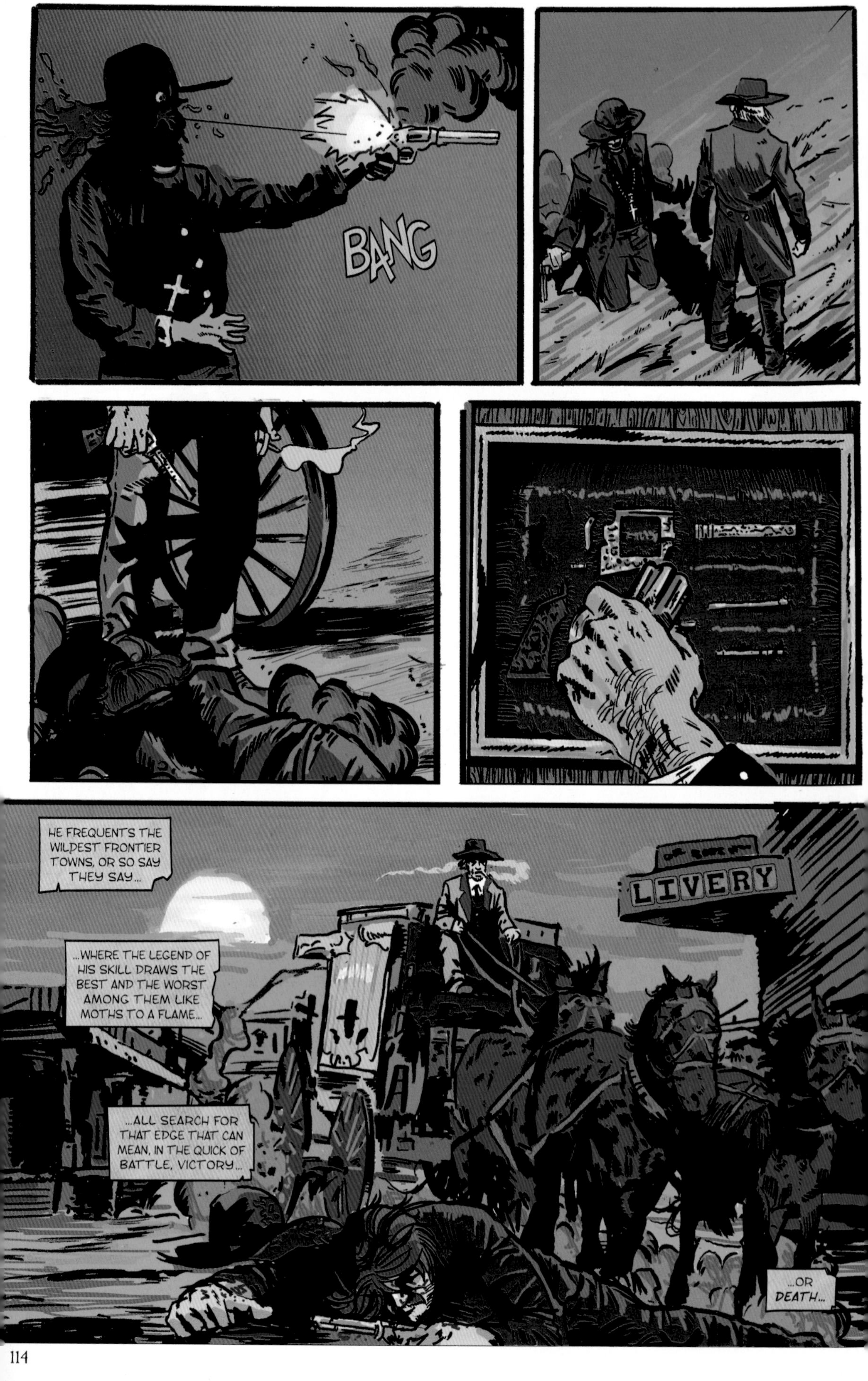
BANG
HE FREQUENTS THE WILDEST FRONTIER TOWNS, OR SO SAY THEY SAY...
LIVERY
...WHERE THE LEGEND OF HIS SKILL DRAWS THE BEST AND THE WORST AMONG THEM LIKE MOTHS TO A FLAME...
...ALL SEARCH FOR THAT EDGE THAT CAN MEAN, IN THE QUICK OF BATTLE, VICTORY...
...OR DEATH...

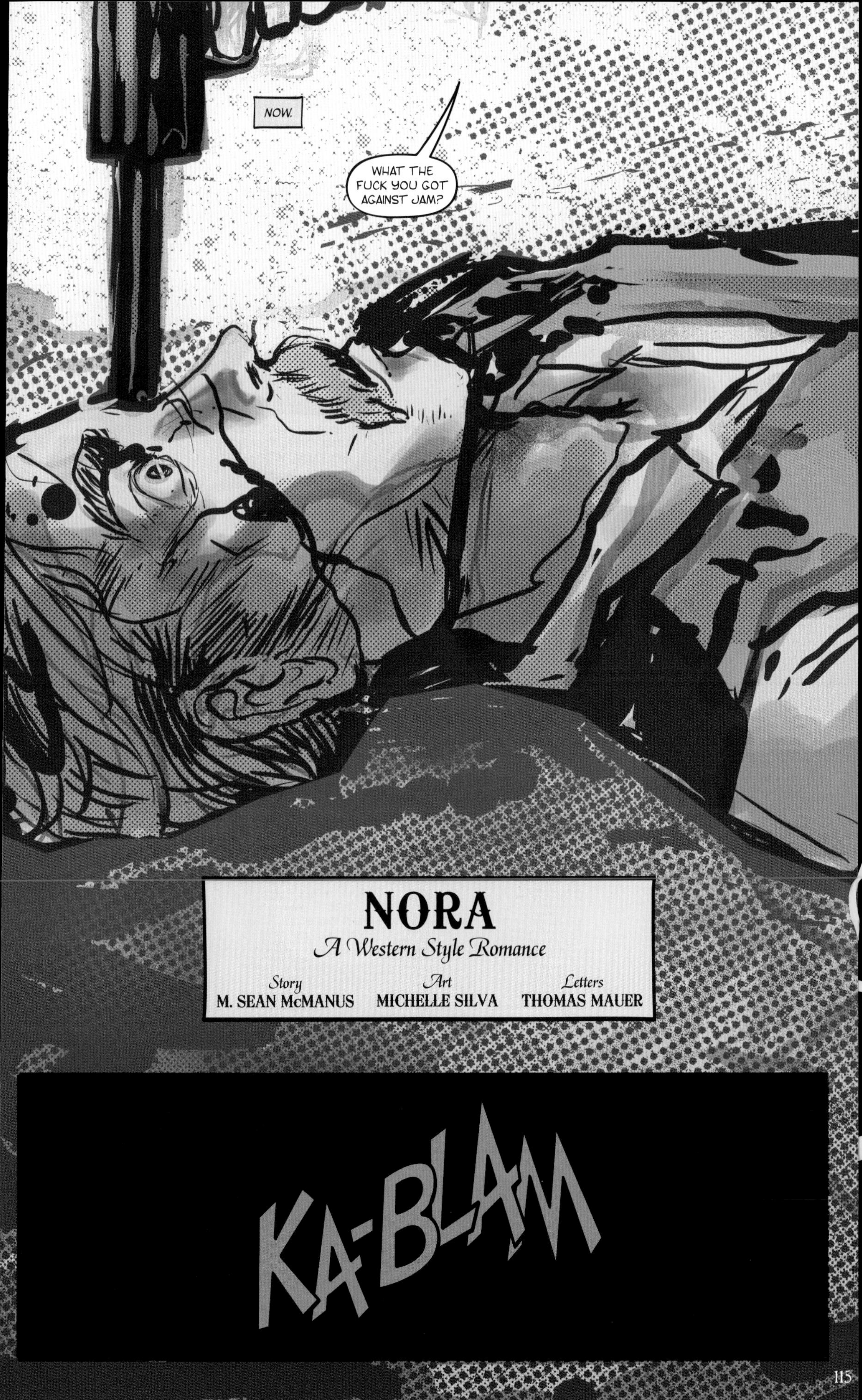
NOW.
WHAT THE FUCK YOU GOT AGAINST JAM?
NORA
A Western Style Romance
Story
M. SEAN McMANUS
Art
MICHELLE SILVA
Letters
THOMAS MAUER
KA-BLAM

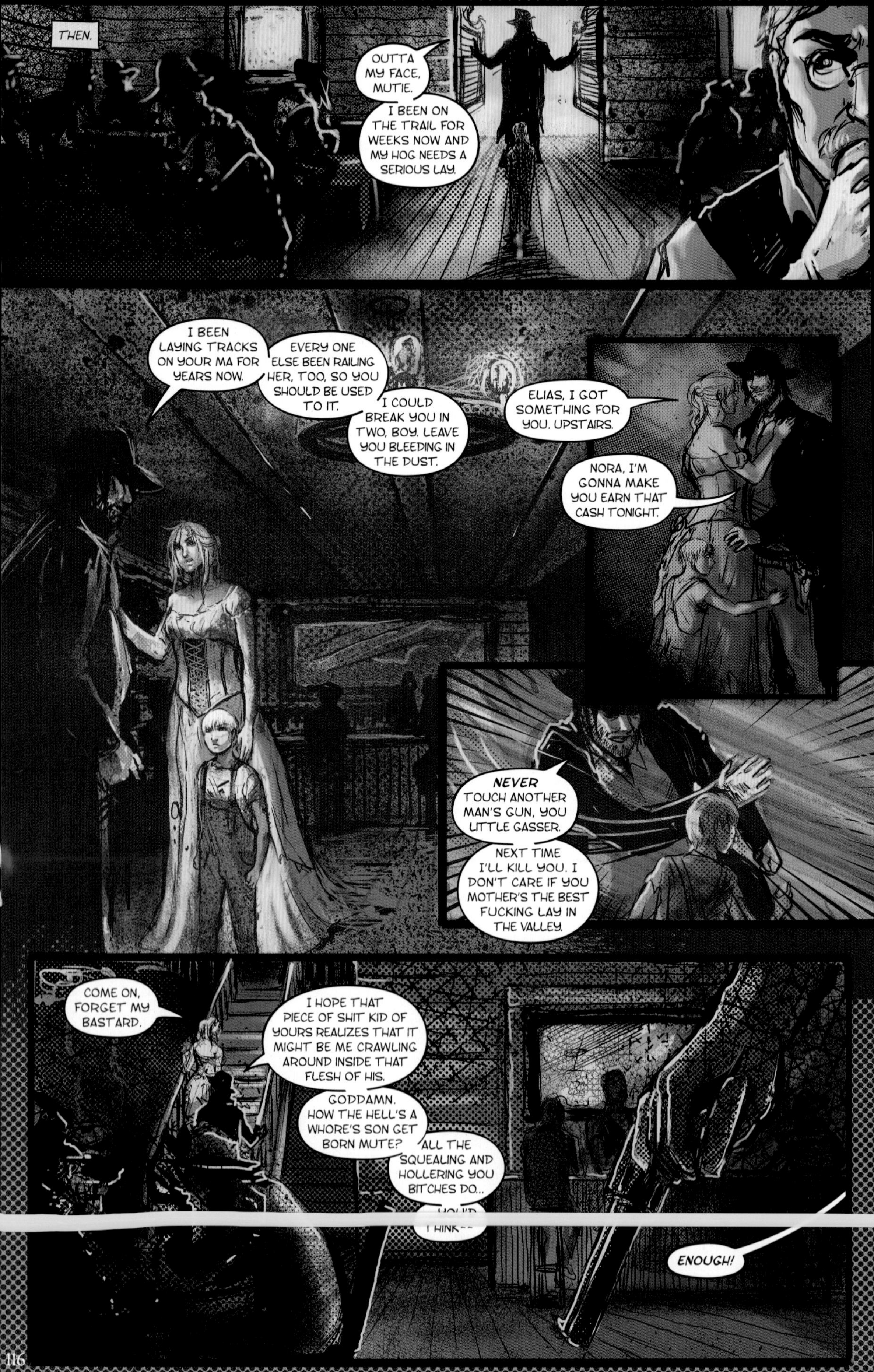
THEN.
OUTTA MY FACE, MUTIE.
I BEEN ON THE TRAIL FOR WEEKS NOW AND MY HOG NEEDS A SERIOUS LAY.
I BEEN LAYING TRACKS ON YOUR MA FOR YEARS NOW.
EVERY ONE ELSE BEEN RAILING HER, TOO, SO YOU SHOULD BE USED TO IT.
I COULD BREAK YOU IN TWO, BOY. LEAVE YOU BLEEDING IN THE DUST.
ELIAS, I GOT SOMETHING FOR YOU. UPSTAIRS.
NORA, I'M GONNA MAKE YOU EARN THAT CASH TONIGHT.
NEVER TOUCH ANOTHER MAN'S GUN, YOU LITTLE GASSER.
NEXT TIME I'LL KILL YOU. I DON'T CARE IF YOU MOTHER'S THE BEST FUCKING LAY IN THE VALLEY.
COME ON, FORGET MY BASTARD.
I HOPE THAT PIECE OF SHIT KID OF YOURS REALIZES THAT IT MIGHT BE ME CRAWLING AROUND INSIDE THAT FLESH OF HIS.
GODDAMN. HOW THE HELL'S A WHORE'S SON GET BORN MUTE?
ALL THE SQUEALING AND HOLLERING YOU BITCHES DO...
YOU'D THINK--
ENOUGH!

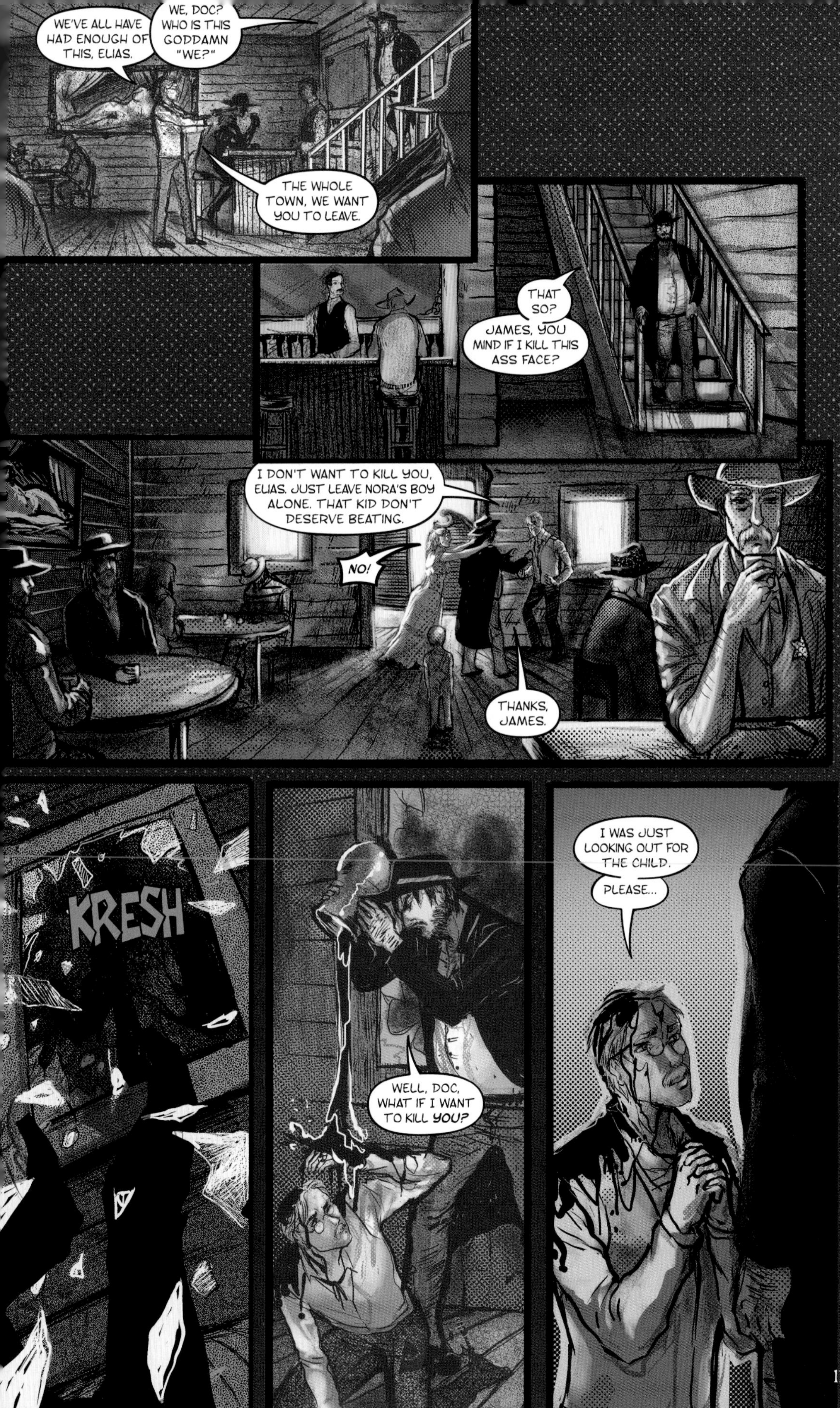

WE'VE ALL HAVE HAD ENOUGH OF THIS, ELIAS.
WE, DOC? WHO IS THIS GODDAMN "WE?"
THE WHOLE TOWN, WE WANT YOU TO LEAVE.
THAT SO? JAMES, YOU MIND IF I KILL THIS ASS FACE?
I DON'T WANT TO KILL YOU, ELIAS. JUST LEAVE NORA'S BOY ALONE. THAT KID DON'T DESERVE BEATING.
NO!
THANKS, JAMES.
KRESH
WELL, DOC, WHAT IF I WANT TO KILL YOU?
I WAS JUST LOOKING OUT FOR THE CHILD.
PLEASE...

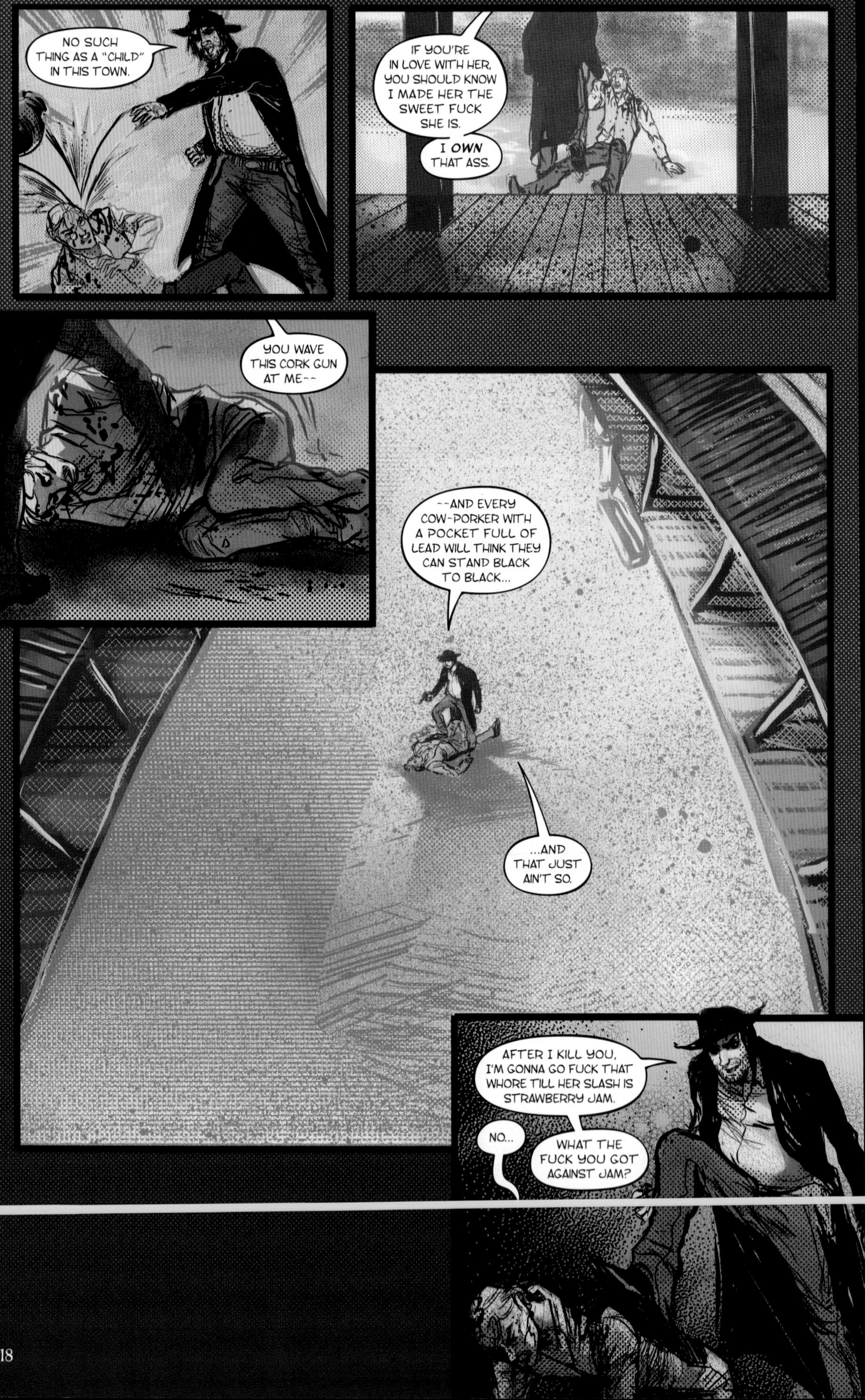
NO SUCH THING AS A "CHILD" IN THIS TOWN.
IF YOU'RE IN LOVE WITH HER, YOU SHOULD KNOW I MADE HER THE SWEET FUCK SHE IS.
I *OWN* THAT ASS.
YOU WAVE THIS CORK GUN AT ME--
--AND EVERY COW-PORKER WITH A POCKET FULL OF LEAD WILL THINK THEY CAN STAND BLACK TO BLACK...
...AND THAT JUST AIN'T SO.
AFTER I KILL YOU, I'M GONNA GO FUCK THAT WHORE TILL HER SLASH IS STRAWBERRY JAM.
NO...
WHAT THE FUCK YOU GOT AGAINST JAM?

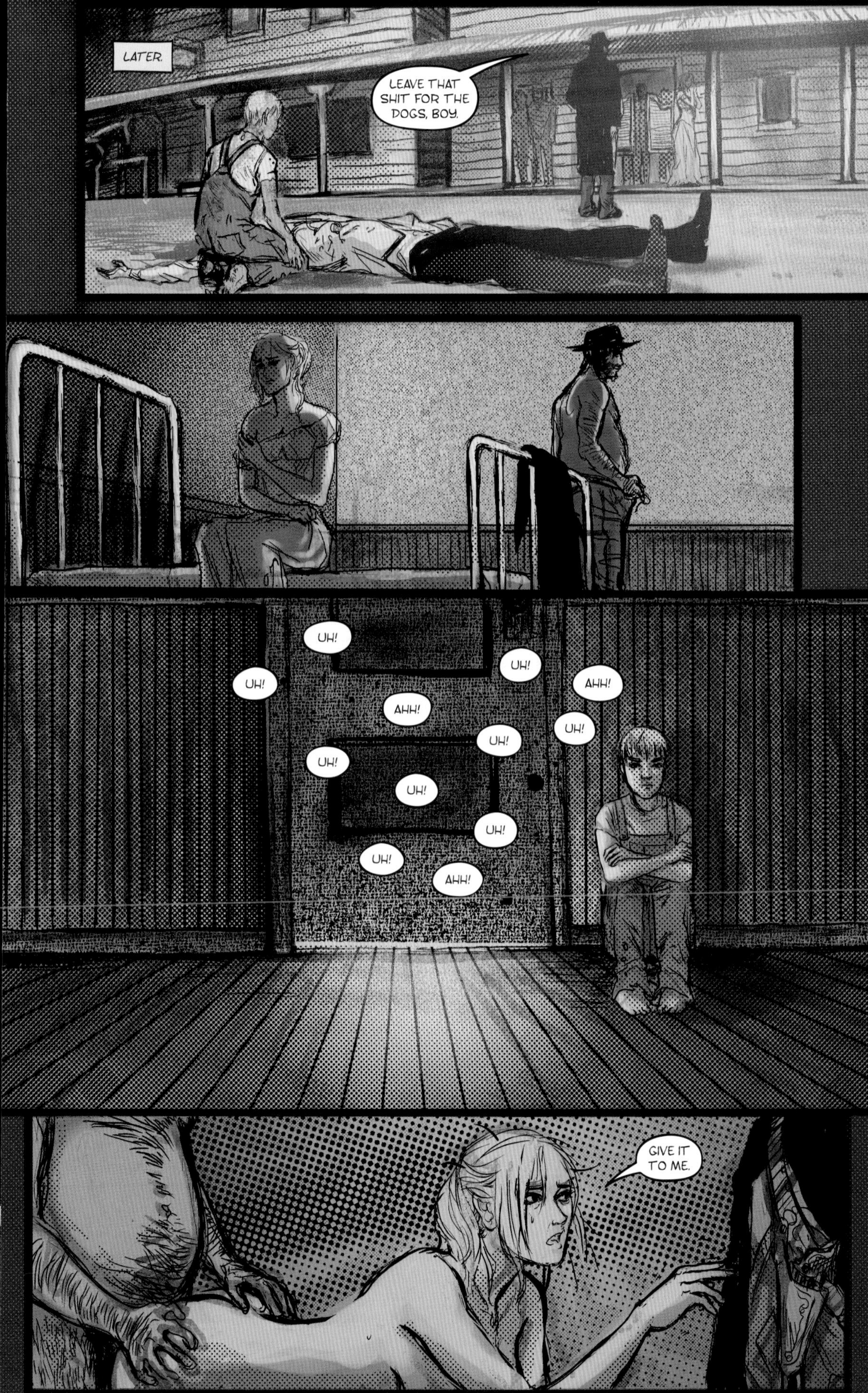
LATER.
LEAVE THAT SHIT FOR THE DOGS, BOY.
UH!
UH!
UH!
AHH!
AHH!
UH!
UH!
UH!
UH!
UH!
UH!
AHH!
GIVE IT TO ME.

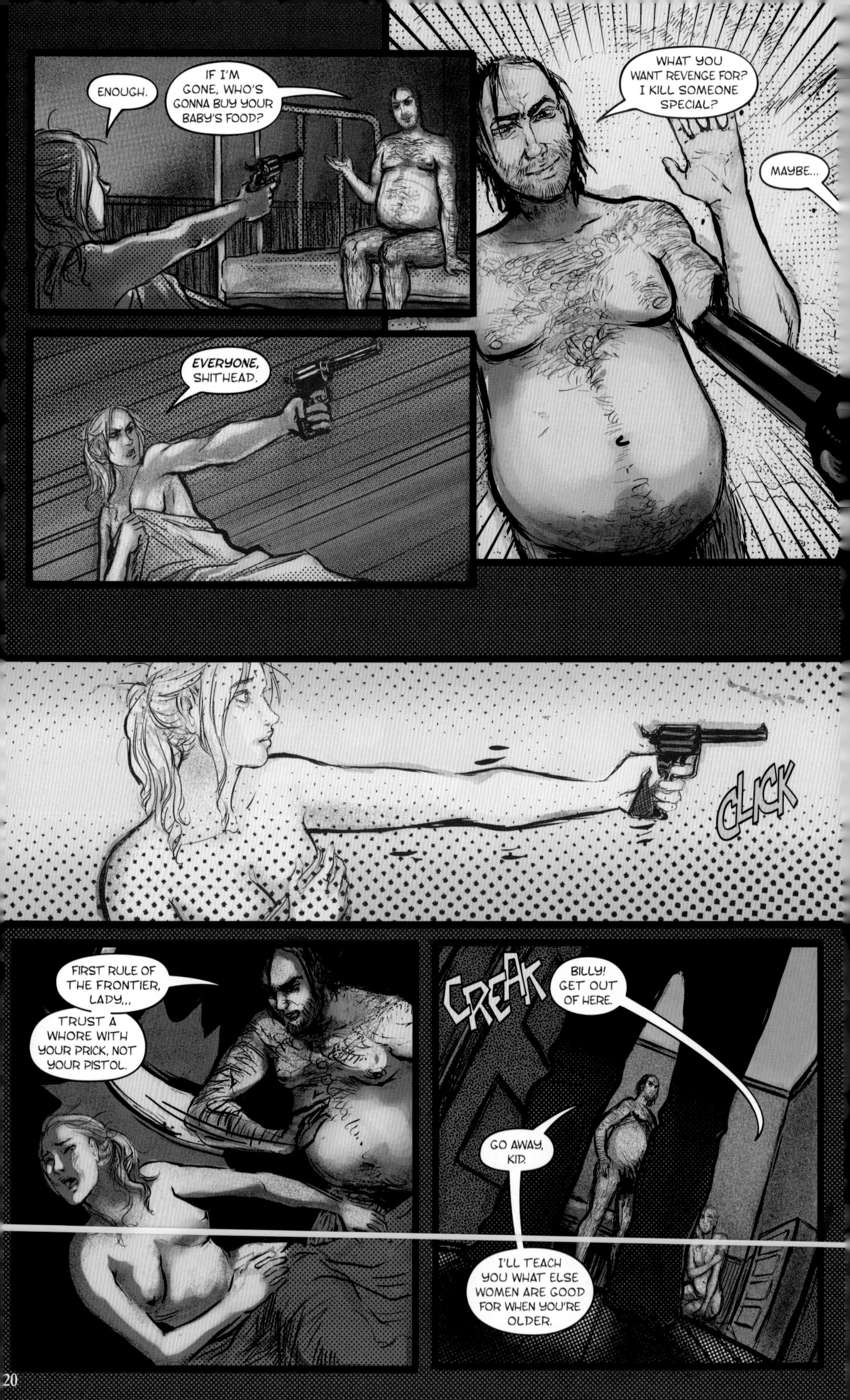

ENOUGH.
IF I'M GONE, WHO'S GONNA BUY YOUR BABY'S FOOD?
WHAT YOU WANT REVENGE FOR? I KILL SOMEONE SPECIAL?
MAYBE...
EVERYONE, SHITHEAD.
CLICK
FIRST RULE OF THE FRONTIER, LADY,,,
TRUST A WHORE WITH YOUR PRICK, NOT YOUR PISTOL.
CREAK
BILLY! GET OUT OF HERE.
GO AWAY, KID.
I'LL TEACH YOU WHAT ELSE WOMEN ARE GOOD FOR WHEN YOU'RE OLDER.

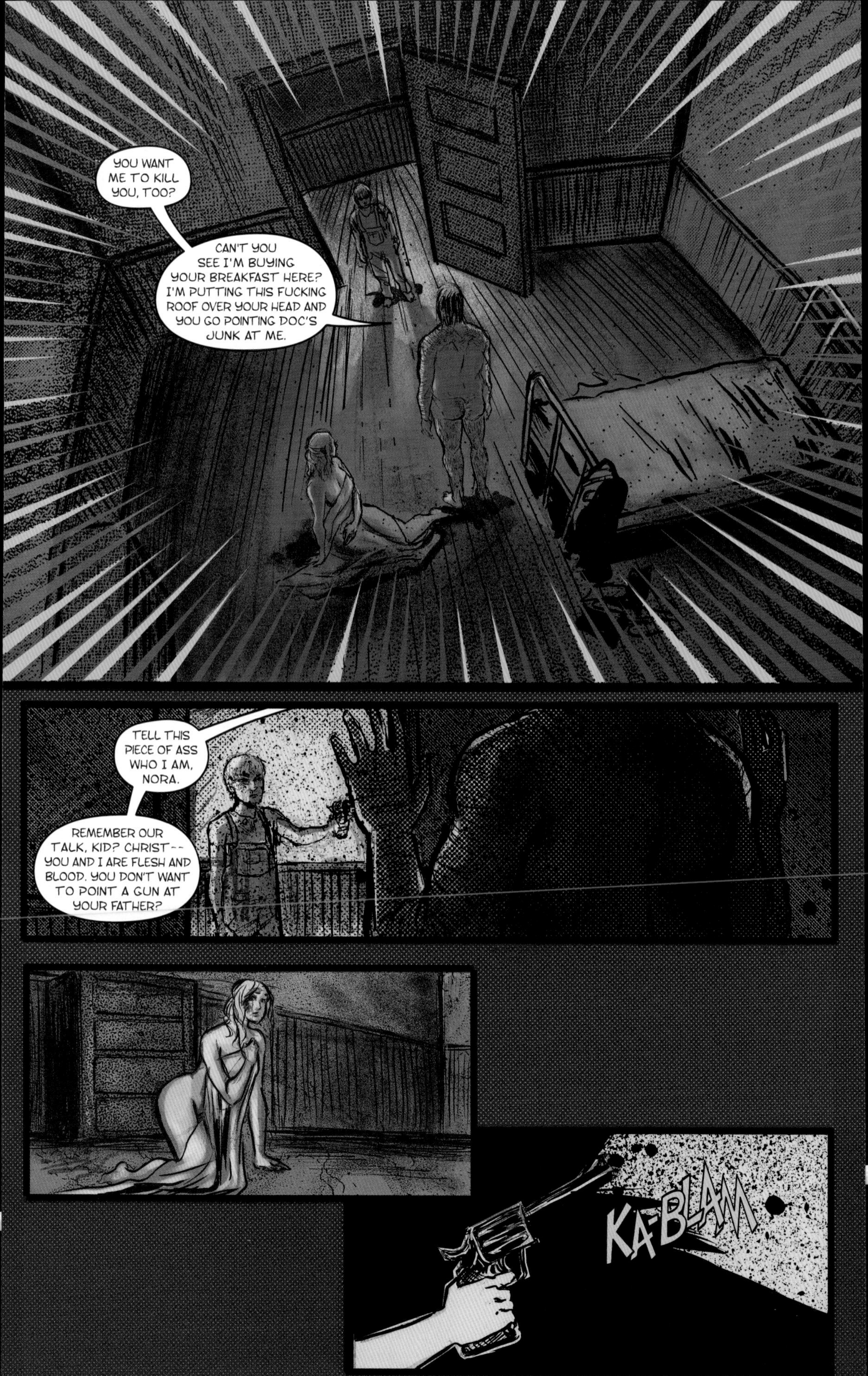
YOU WANT ME TO KILL YOU, TOO?
CAN'T YOU SEE I'M BUYING YOUR BREAKFAST HERE? I'M PUTTING THIS FUCKING ROOF OVER YOUR HEAD AND YOU GO POINTING DOC'S JUNK AT ME.
TELL THIS PIECE OF ASS WHO I AM, NORA.
REMEMBER OUR TALK, KID? CHRIST-- YOU AND I ARE FLESH AND BLOOD. YOU DON'T WANT TO POINT A GUN AT YOUR FATHER?
KA-BLAM

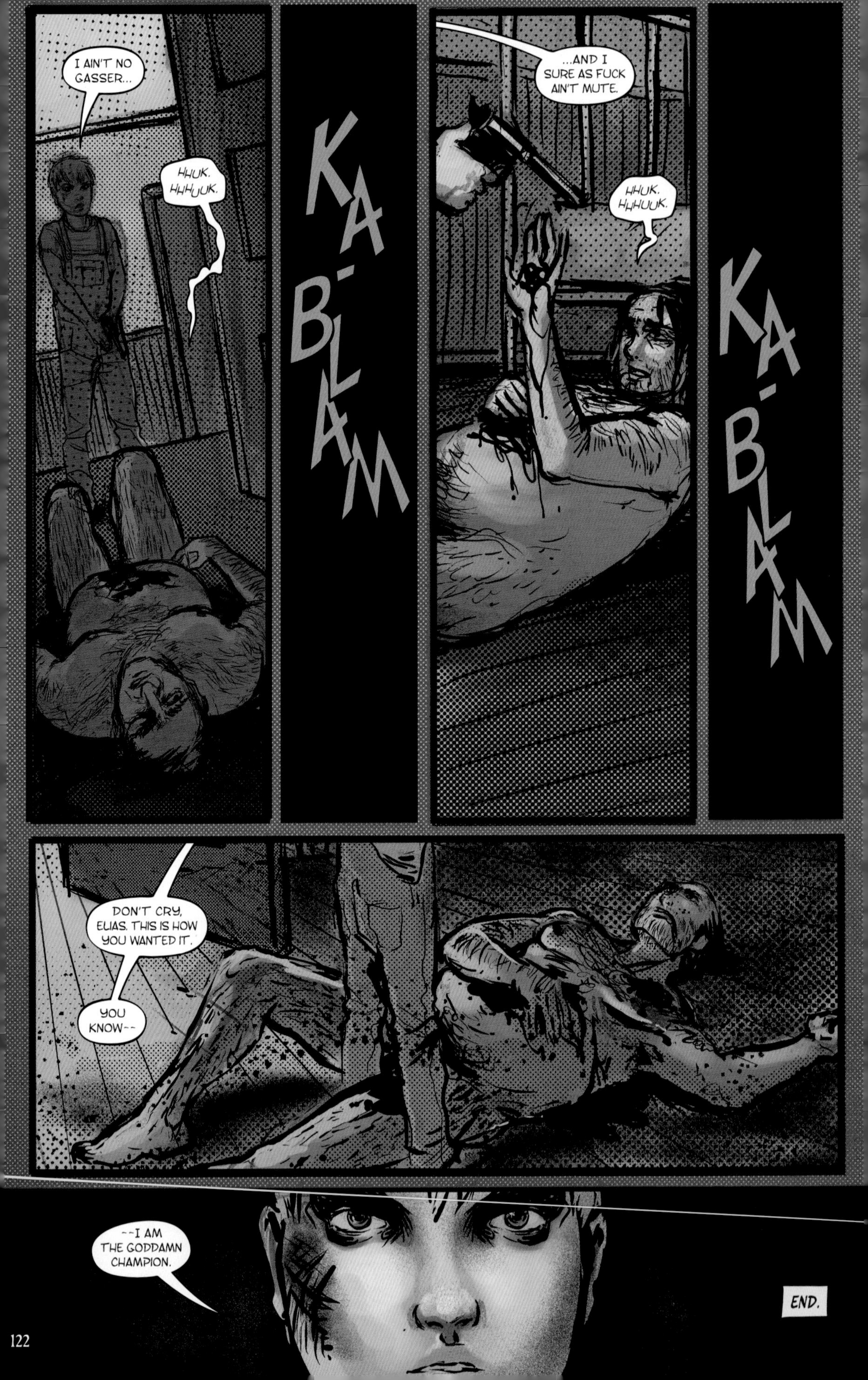
I AIN'T NO GASSER...
HHUK. HHHUUK.
KA-BLAM
...AND I SURE AS FUCK AIN'T MUTE.
HHUK. HHHUUK.
KA-BLAM
DON'T CRY, ELIAS. THIS IS HOW YOU WANTED IT.
YOU KNOW--
--I AM THE GODDAMN CHAMPION.
END.

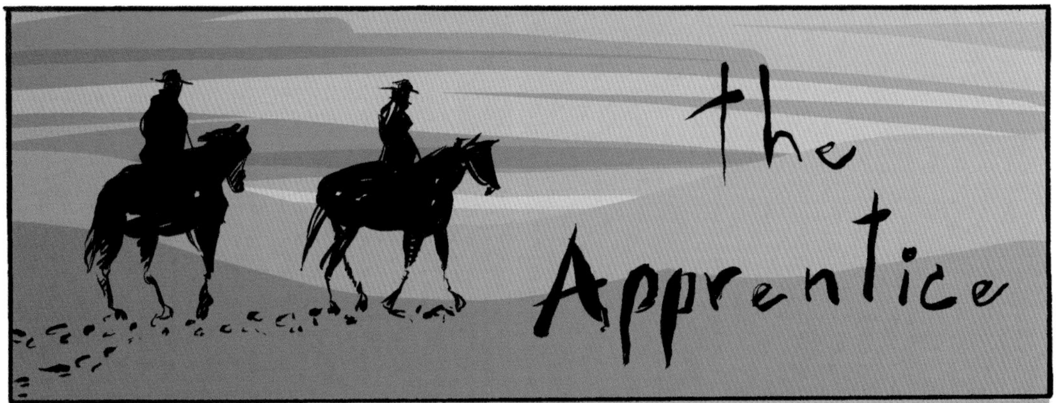
the Apprentice

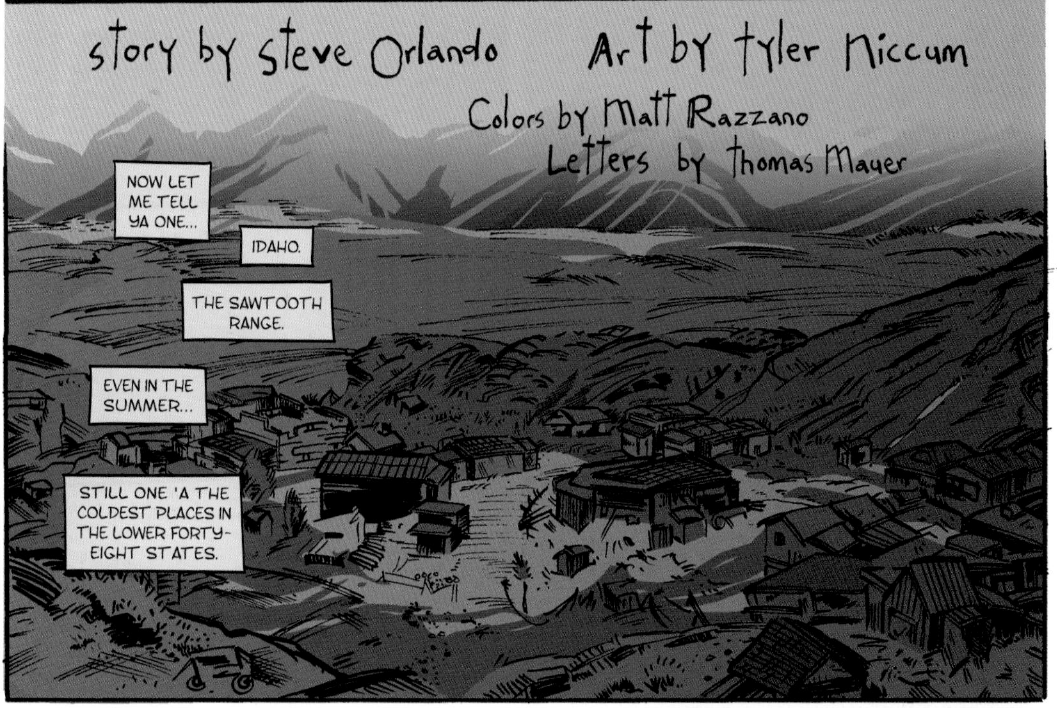
story by steve Orlando
Art by tyler Niccum
Colors by Matt Razzano
Letters by thomas Mauer
NOW LET ME TELL YA ONE...
IDAHO.
THE SAWTOOTH RANGE.
EVEN IN THE SUMMER...
STILL ONE 'A THE COLDEST PLACES IN THE LOWER FORTY-EIGHT STATES.

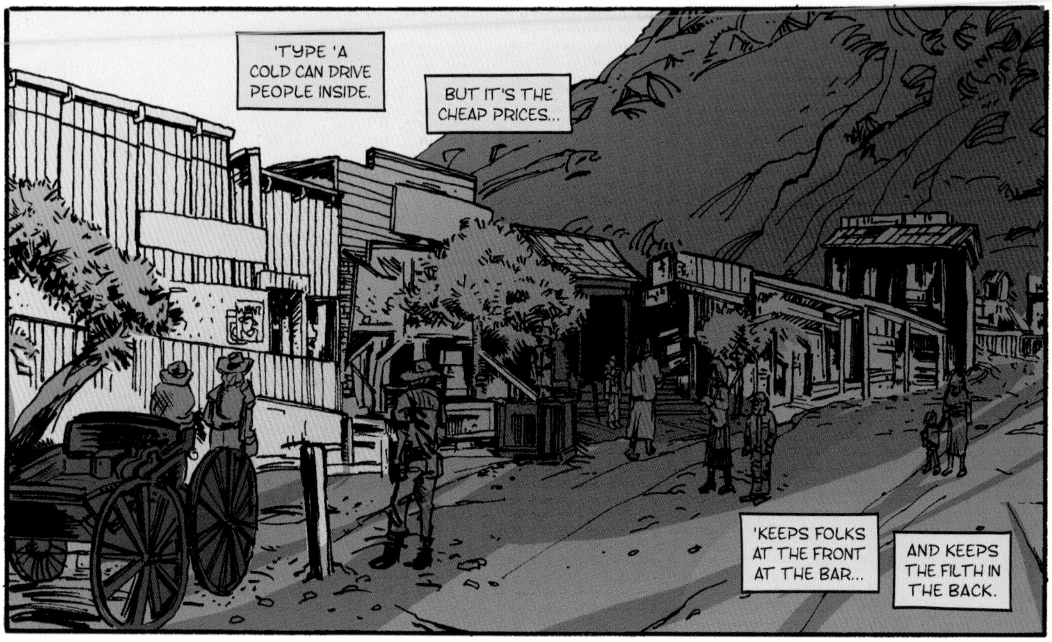
'TYPE 'A COLD CAN DRIVE PEOPLE INSIDE.
BUT IT'S THE CHEAP PRICES...
'KEEPS FOLKS AT THE FRONT AT THE BAR...
AND KEEPS THE FILTH IN THE BACK.

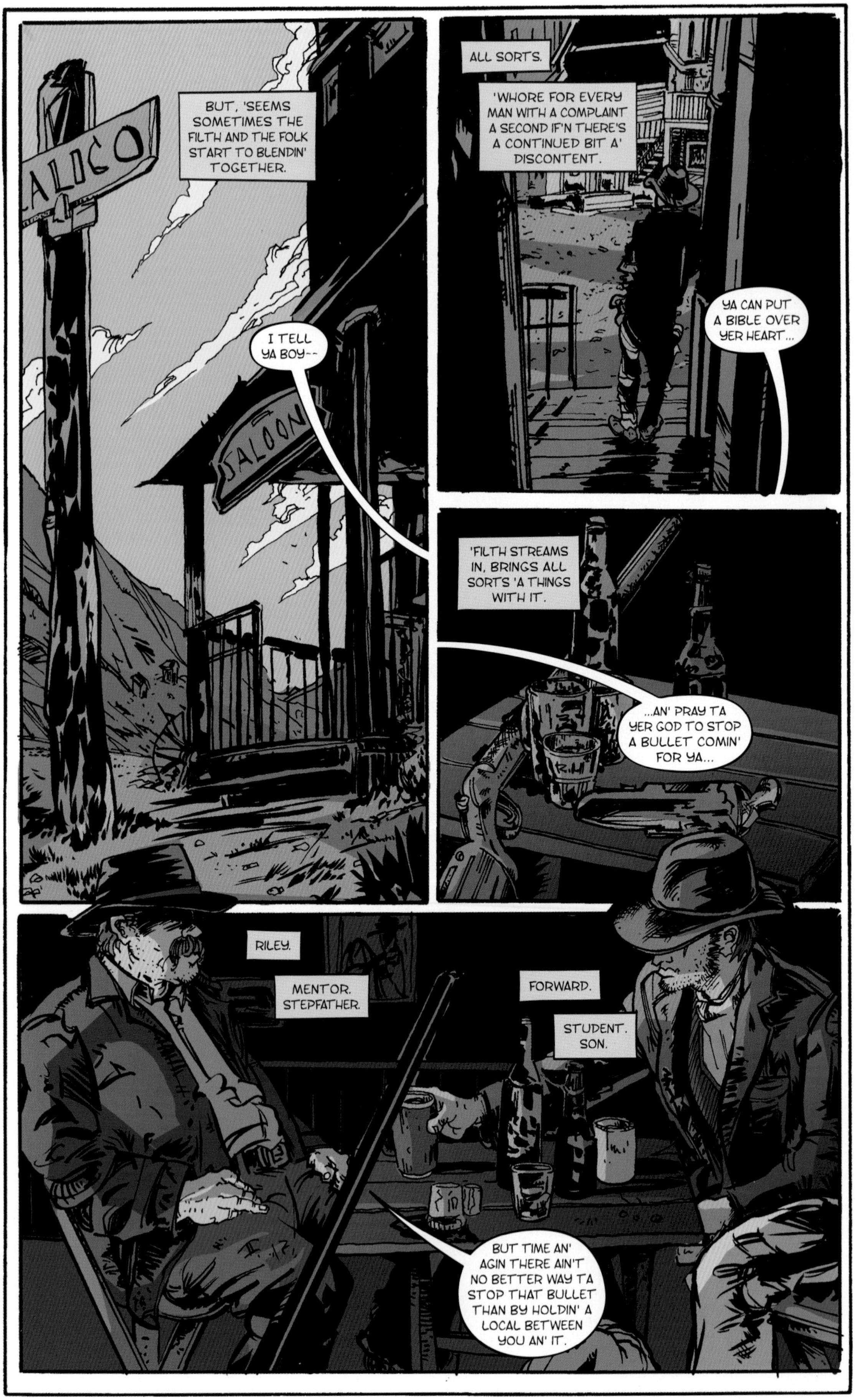
BUT, 'SEEMS SOMETIMES THE FILTH AND THE FOLK START TO BLENDIN' TOGETHER.
ALOCO
SALOON
I TELL YA BOY--
ALL SORTS.
'WHORE FOR EVERY MAN WITH A COMPLAINT A SECOND IF'N THERE'S A CONTINUED BIT A' DISCONTENT.
YA CAN PUT A BIBLE OVER YER HEART...
'FILTH STREAMS IN, BRINGS ALL SORTS 'A THINGS WITH IT.
...AN' PRAY TA YER GOD TO STOP A BULLET COMIN' FOR YA...
RILEY.
MENTOR. STEPFATHER.
FORWARD.
STUDENT. SON.
BUT TIME AN' AGIN THERE AIN'T NO BETTER WAY TA STOP THAT BULLET THAN BY HOLDIN' A LOCAL BETWEEN YOU AN' IT.

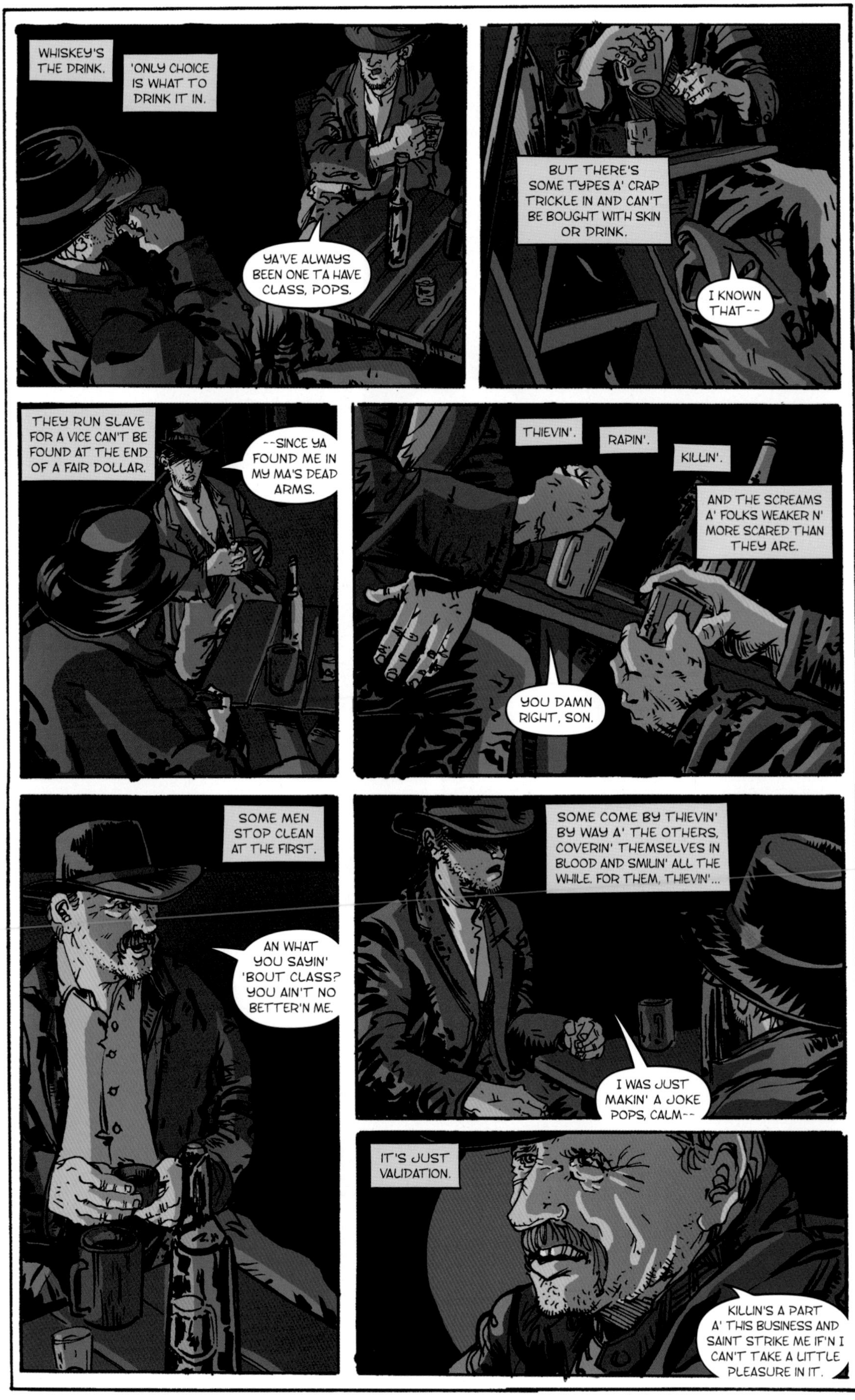

WHISKEY'S THE DRINK.
'ONLY CHOICE IS WHAT TO DRINK IT IN.
YA'VE ALWAYS BEEN ONE TA HAVE CLASS, POPS.
BUT THERE'S SOME TYPES A' CRAP TRICKLE IN AND CAN'T BE BOUGHT WITH SKIN OR DRINK.
I KNOWN THAT--
THEY RUN SLAVE FOR A VICE CAN'T BE FOUND AT THE END OF A FAIR DOLLAR.
--SINCE YA FOUND ME IN MY MA'S DEAD ARMS.
THIEVIN'.
RAPIN'.
KILLIN'.
AND THE SCREAMS A' FOLKS WEAKER N' MORE SCARED THAN THEY ARE.
YOU DAMN RIGHT, SON.
SOME MEN STOP CLEAN AT THE FIRST.
AN WHAT YOU SAYIN' 'BOUT CLASS? YOU AIN'T NO BETTER'N ME.
SOME COME BY THIEVIN' BY WAY A' THE OTHERS, COVERIN' THEMSELVES IN BLOOD AND SMILIN' ALL THE WHILE. FOR THEM, THIEVIN'...
I WAS JUST MAKIN' A JOKE POPS, CALM--
IT'S JUST VALIDATION.
KILLIN'S A PART A' THIS BUSINESS AND SAINT STRIKE ME IF'N I CAN'T TAKE A LITTLE PLEASURE IN IT.

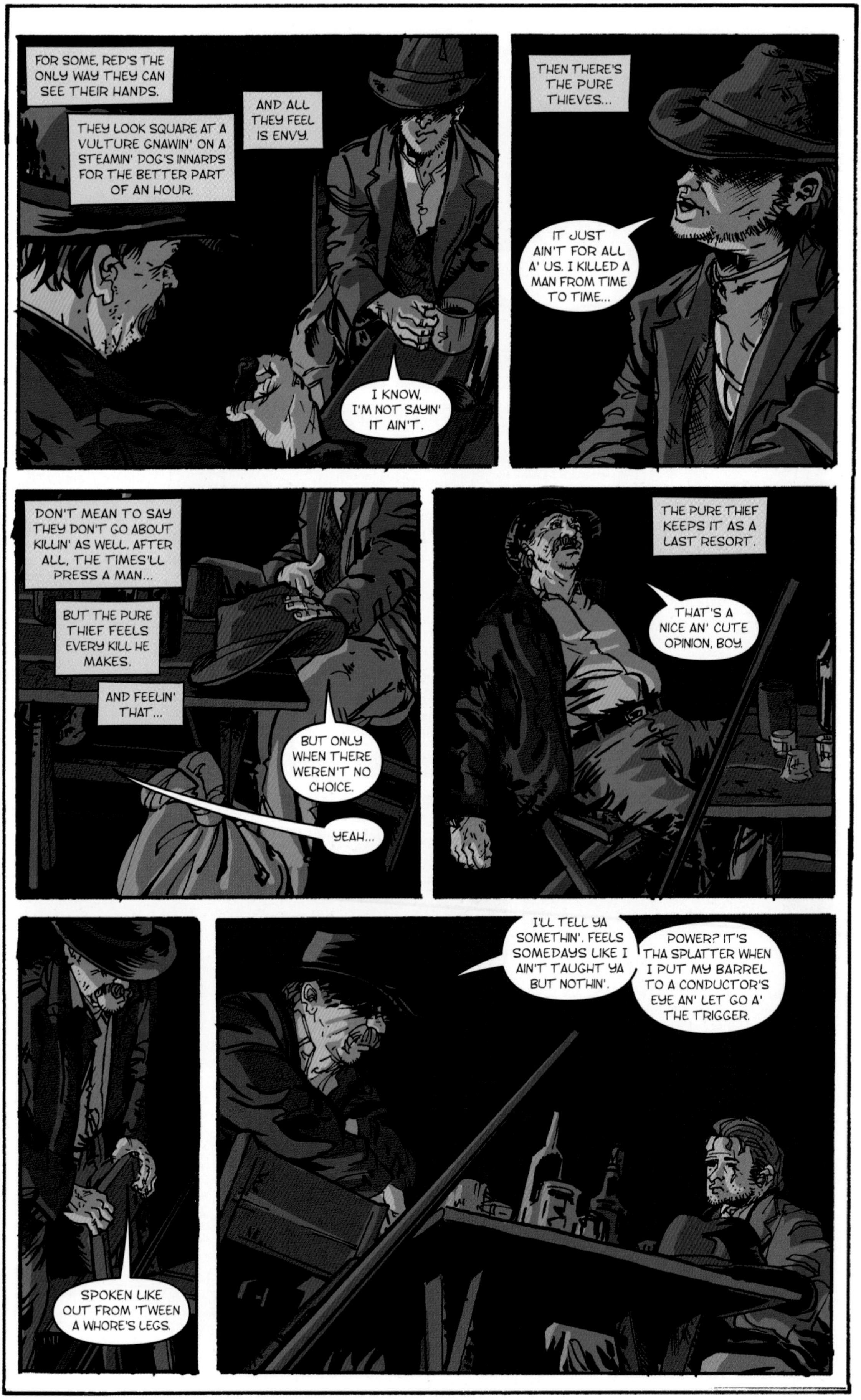

FOR SOME, RED'S THE ONLY WAY THEY CAN SEE THEIR HANDS.
THEY LOOK SQUARE AT A VULTURE GNAWIN' ON A STEAMIN' DOG'S INNARDS FOR THE BETTER PART OF AN HOUR.
AND ALL THEY FEEL IS ENVY.
I KNOW, I'M NOT SAYIN' IT AIN'T.
THEN THERE'S THE PURE THIEVES...
IT JUST AIN'T FOR ALL A' US. I KILLED A MAN FROM TIME TO TIME...
DON'T MEAN TO SAY THEY DON'T GO ABOUT KILLIN' AS WELL. AFTER ALL, THE TIMES'LL PRESS A MAN...
BUT THE PURE THIEF FEELS EVERY KILL HE MAKES.
AND FEELIN' THAT...
BUT ONLY WHEN THERE WEREN'T NO CHOICE.
YEAH...
THE PURE THIEF KEEPS IT AS A LAST RESORT.
THAT'S A NICE AN' CUTE OPINION, BOY.
SPOKEN LIKE OUT FROM 'TWEEN A WHORE'S LEGS.
I'LL TELL YA SOMETHIN'. FEELS SOMEDAYS LIKE I AIN'T TAUGHT YA BUT NOTHIN'.
POWER? IT'S THA SPLATTER WHEN I PUT MY BARREL TO A CONDUCTOR'S EYE AN' LET GO A' THE TRIGGER.

RILEY AND FORWARD'VE BEEN SPLITTING THE DIFFERENCE BETWEEN THE TWO...

BUT I--

NOPE.

BEEN POOLIN' THEIR EFFORTS--FORWARD'S WIT, RILEY'S EXPERIENCE...

YA ALWAYS BEEN A' THAT OPINION ON THA MATTER. IT'S YOURS AN' I RESPECT THAT.

BUT FACT REMAINS YER WRONG.

...SINCE BEFORE FORWARD FIRST KNEW WHAT A KNIFE WAS FOR OR WHERE IT GOES.

SCREAMS.

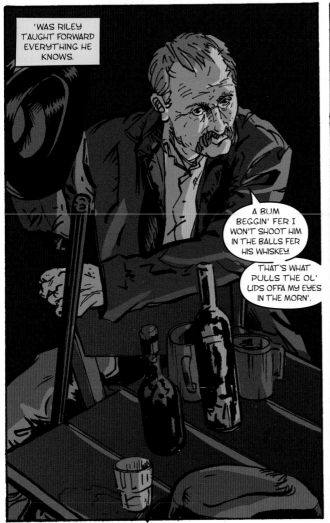

'WAS RILEY TAUGHT FORWARD EVERYTHING HE KNOWS.

A BUM BEGGIN' FER I WON'T SHOOT HIM IN THE BALLS FER HIS WHISKEY.

THAT'S WHAT PULLS THE OL' LIDS OFFA MY EYES IN THE MORN'.

'WAS RILEY TOOK AN ORPHAN AND GAVE HIM A TRADE.

YA ROUGH 'EM UP.

YA TAKE THE MONEY.

YA SET 'EM UP, BUT YA WON'T KNOCK 'EM DOWN. AN' THAT SISSY WAY 'BOUT WORK'S WHY YER STILL JUS' MY PARTNER.

SON 'R NOT.

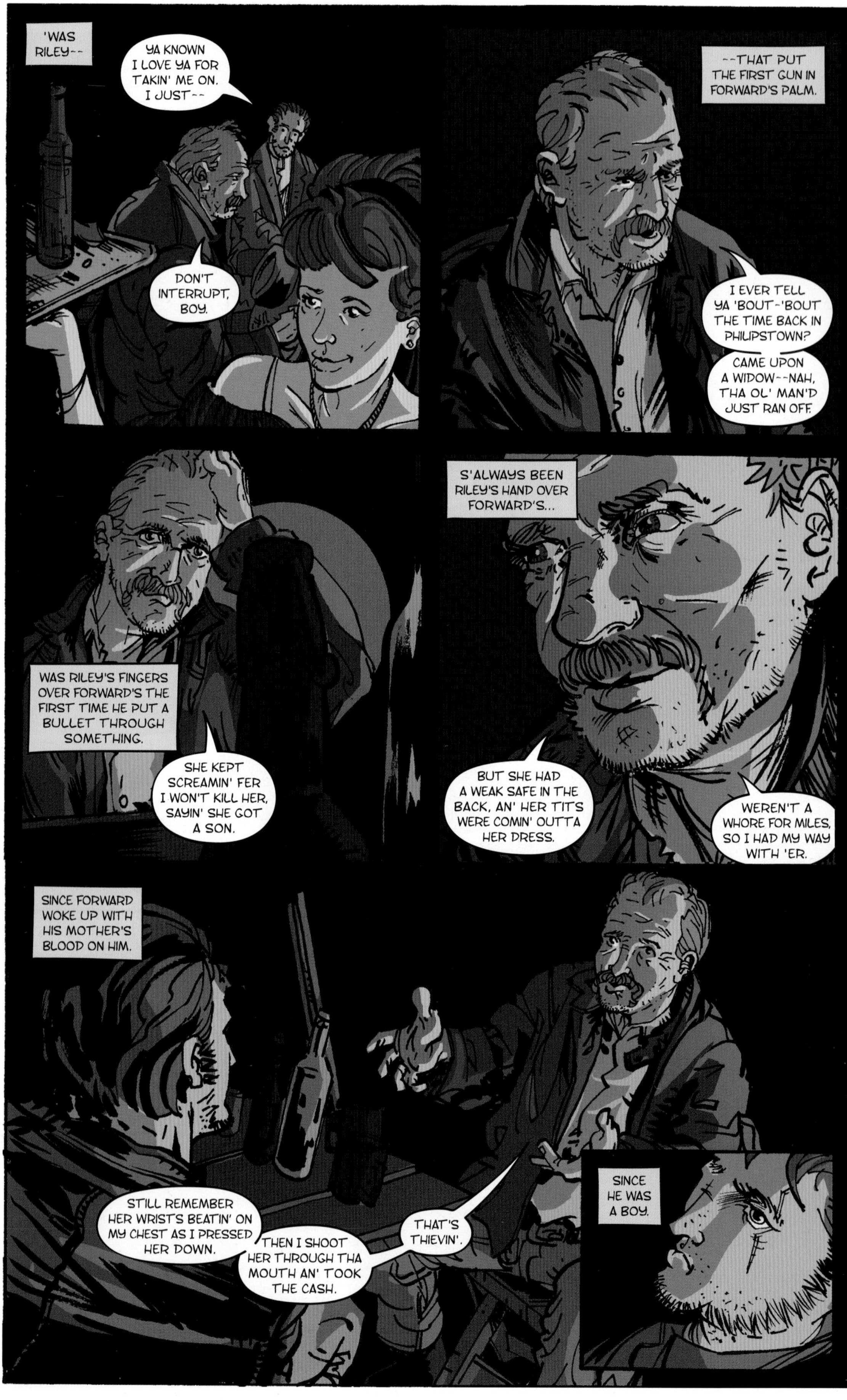
'WAS RILEY--
YA KNOWN I LOVE YA FOR TAKIN' ME ON. I JUST--
DON'T INTERRUPT, BOY.
--THAT PUT THE FIRST GUN IN FORWARD'S PALM.
I EVER TELL YA 'BOUT-'BOUT THE TIME BACK IN PHILIPSTOWN?
CAME UPON A WIDOW--NAH, THA OL' MAN'D JUST RAN OFF.
WAS RILEY'S FINGERS OVER FORWARD'S THE FIRST TIME HE PUT A BULLET THROUGH SOMETHING.
SHE KEPT SCREAMIN' FER I WON'T KILL HER, SAYIN' SHE GOT A SON.
S'ALWAYS BEEN RILEY'S HAND OVER FORWARD'S...
BUT SHE HAD A WEAK SAFE IN THE BACK, AN' HER TITS WERE COMIN' OUTTA HER DRESS.
WEREN'T A WHORE FOR MILES, SO I HAD MY WAY WITH 'ER.
SINCE FORWARD WOKE UP WITH HIS MOTHER'S BLOOD ON HIM.
STILL REMEMBER HER WRISTS BEATIN' ON MY CHEST AS I PRESSED HER DOWN.
THEN I SHOOT HER THROUGH THA MOUTH AN' TOOK THE CASH.
THAT'S THIEVIN'.
SINCE HE WAS A BOY.

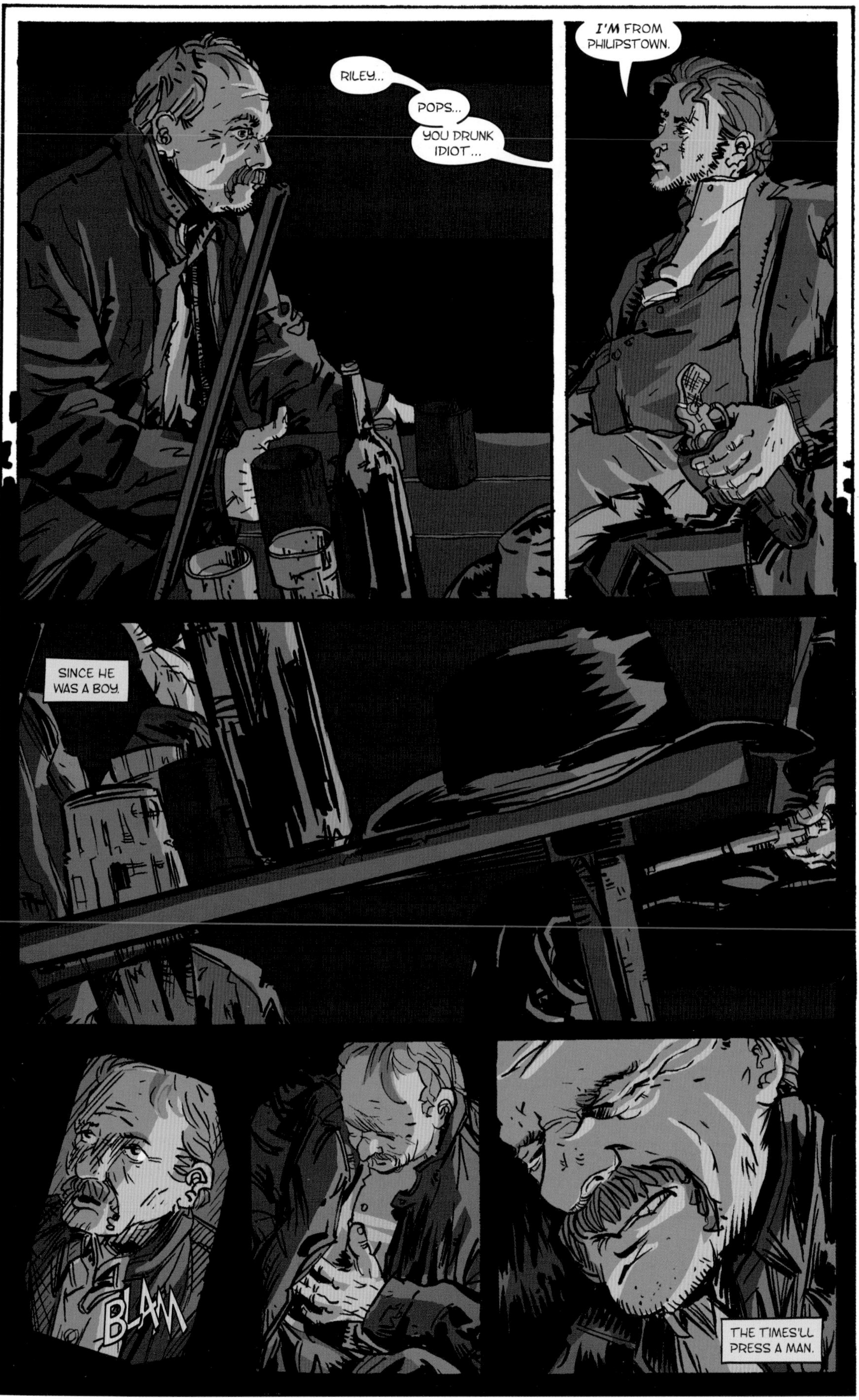
RILEY...
POPS...
YOU DRUNK IDIOT...
I'M FROM PHILIPSTOWN.
SINCE HE WAS A BOY.
BLAM
THE TIMES'LL PRESS A MAN.

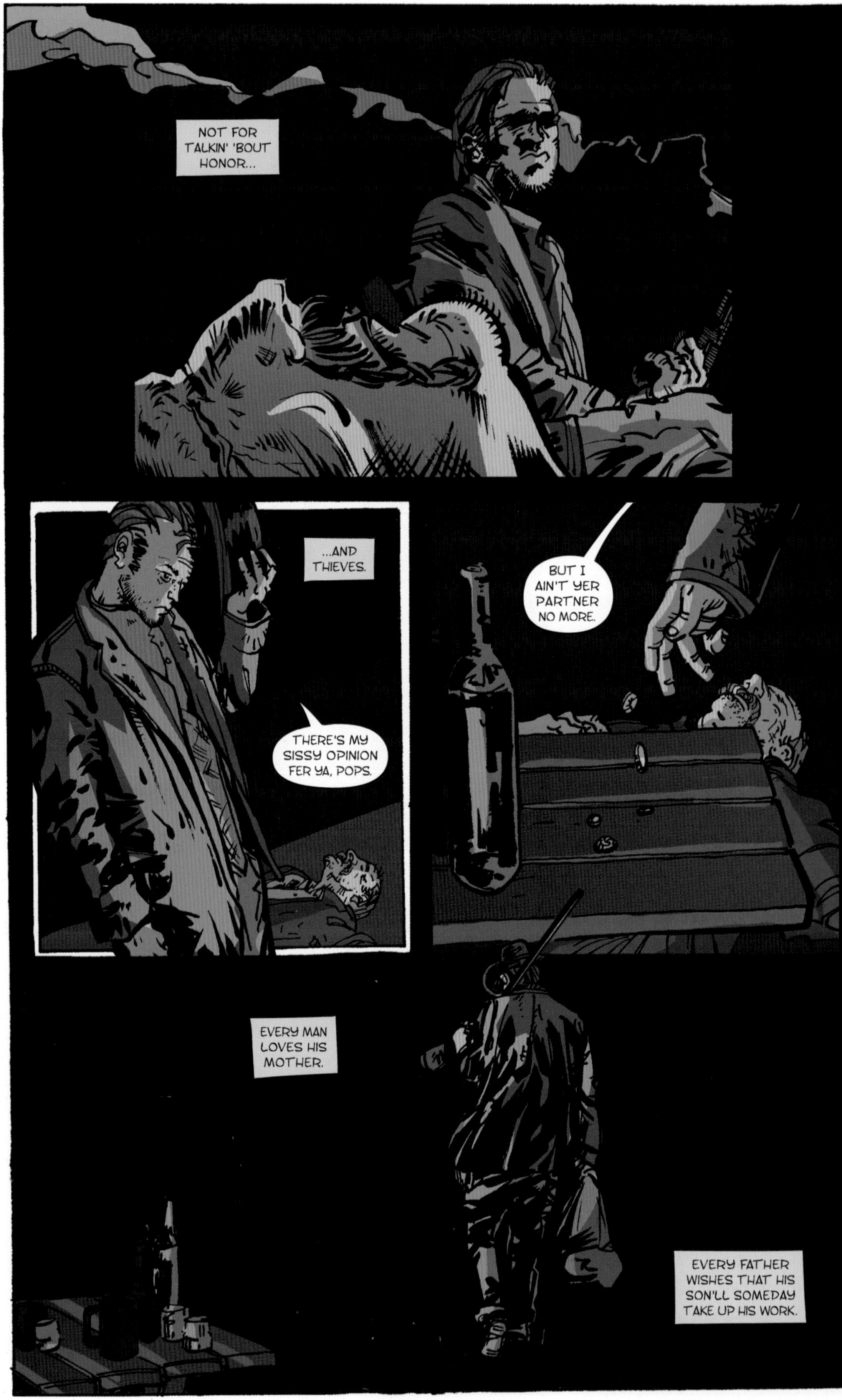

NOT FOR TALKIN' 'BOUT HONOR...
...AND THIEVES.
THERE'S MY SISSY OPINION FER YA, POPS.
BUT I AIN'T YER PARTNER NO MORE.
EVERY MAN LOVES HIS MOTHER.
EVERY FATHER WISHES THAT HIS SON'LL SOMEDAY TAKE UP HIS WORK.

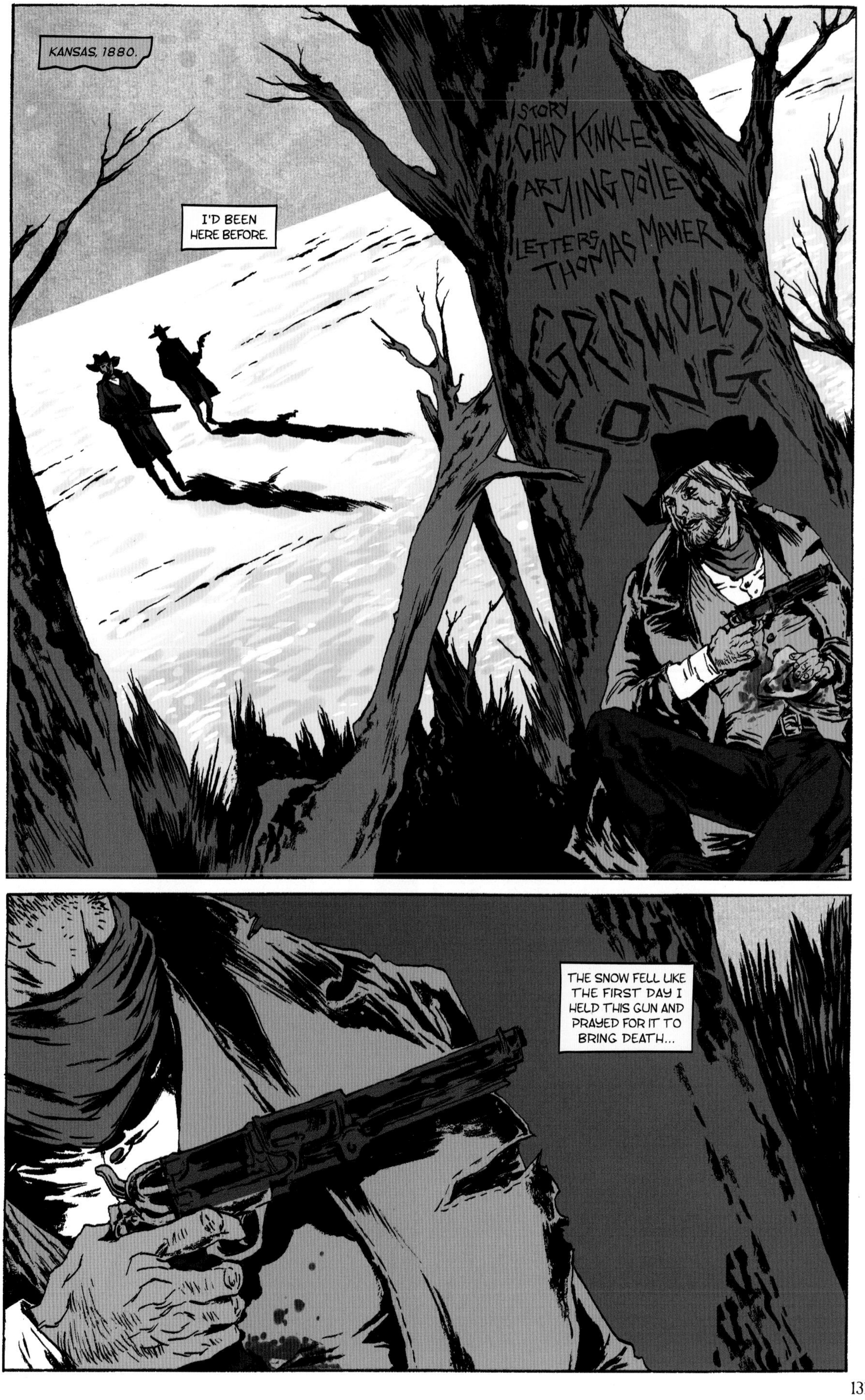
KANSAS, 1880.
STORY CHAD KINKLE
ART MING DOYLE
LETTERS THOMAS MAUER
GRISWOLD'S SONG
I'D BEEN HERE BEFORE.
THE SNOW FELL LIKE THE FIRST DAY I HELD THIS GUN AND PRAYED FOR IT TO BRING DEATH...

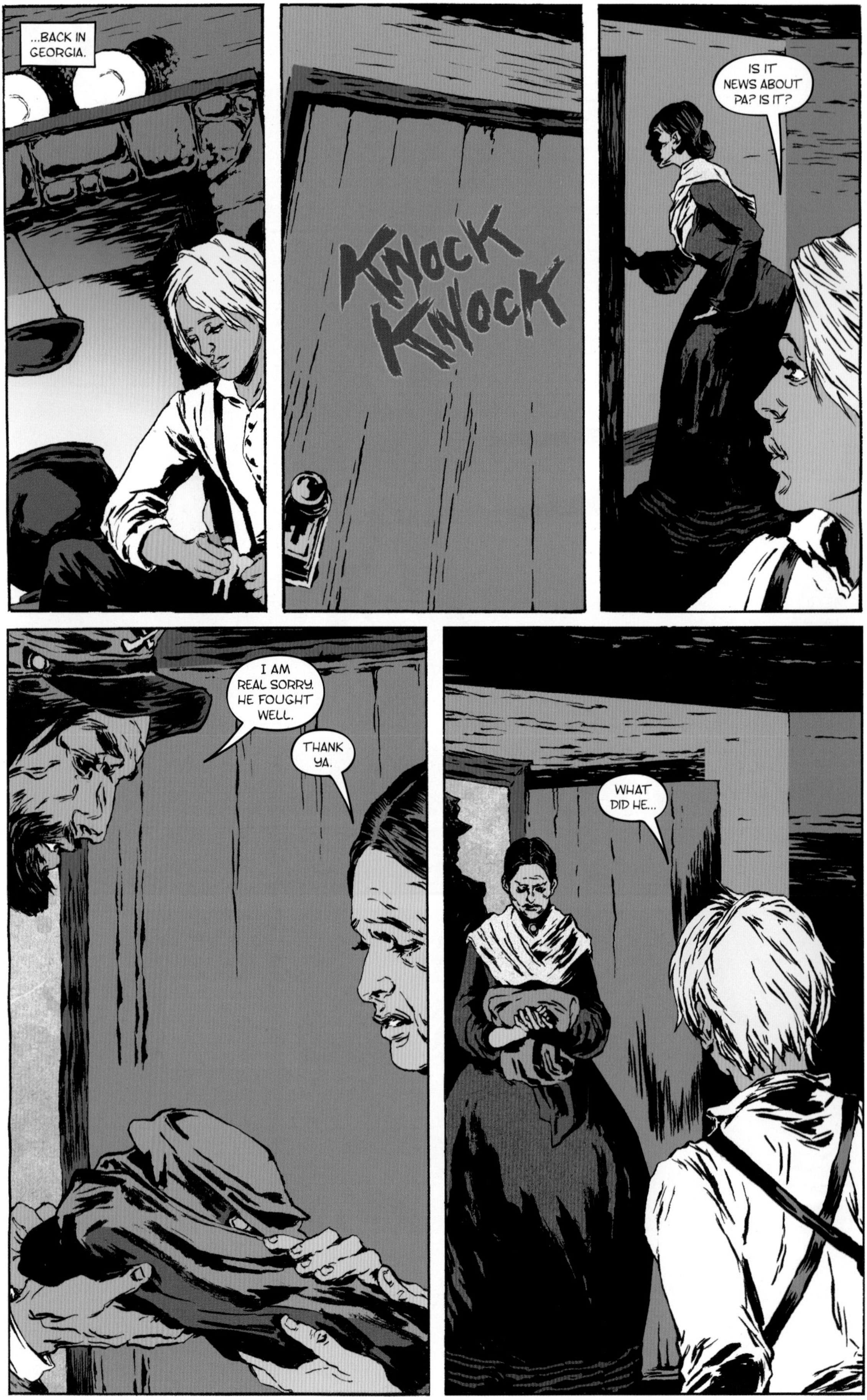
...BACK IN GEORGIA.
KNOCK KNOCK
IS IT NEWS ABOUT PA? IS IT?
I AM REAL SORRY. HE FOUGHT WELL.
THANK YA.
WHAT DID HE...

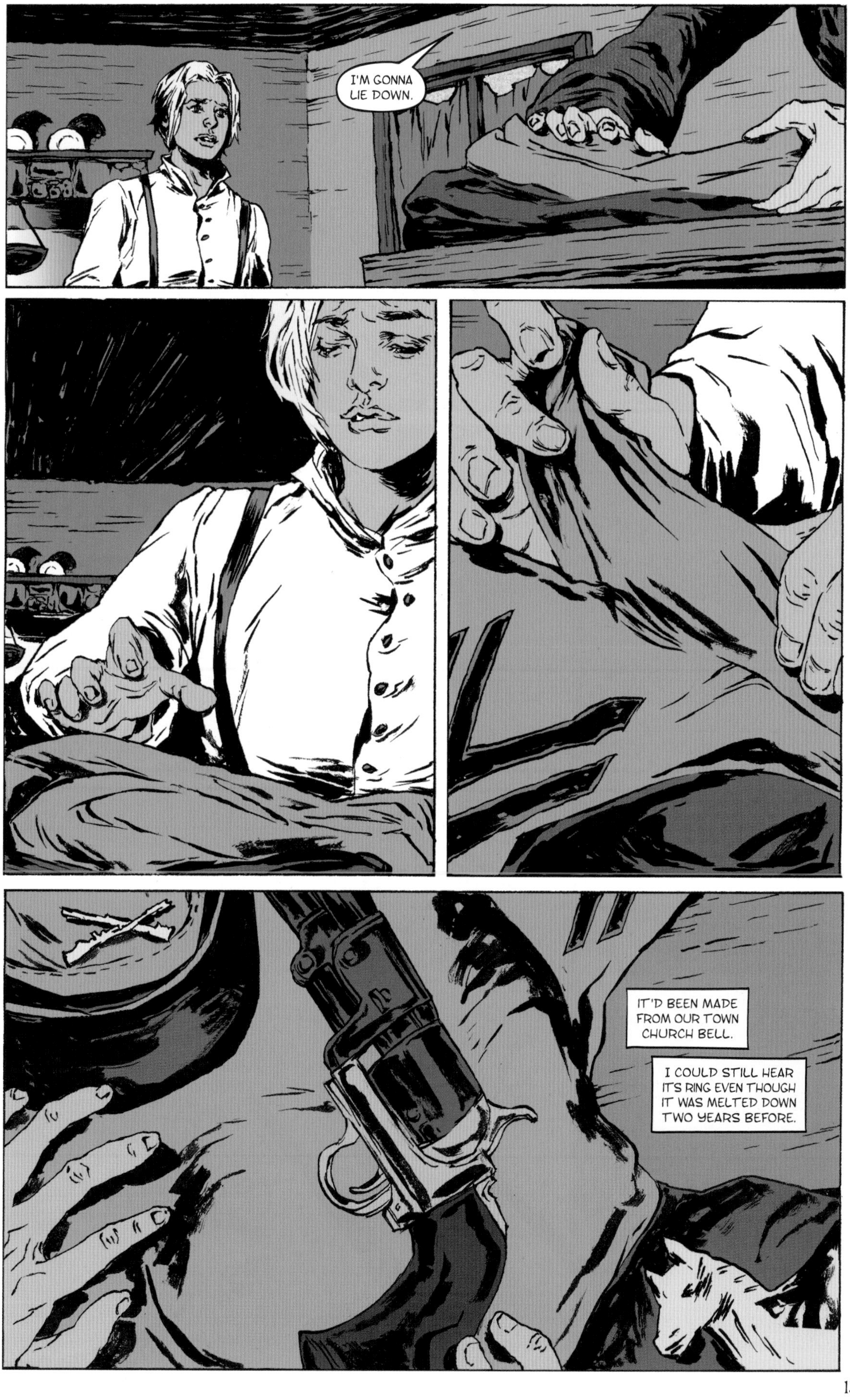
I'M GONNA LIE DOWN.
IT'D BEEN MADE FROM OUR TOWN CHURCH BELL.
I COULD STILL HEAR ITS RING EVEN THOUGH IT WAS MELTED DOWN TWO YEARS BEFORE.

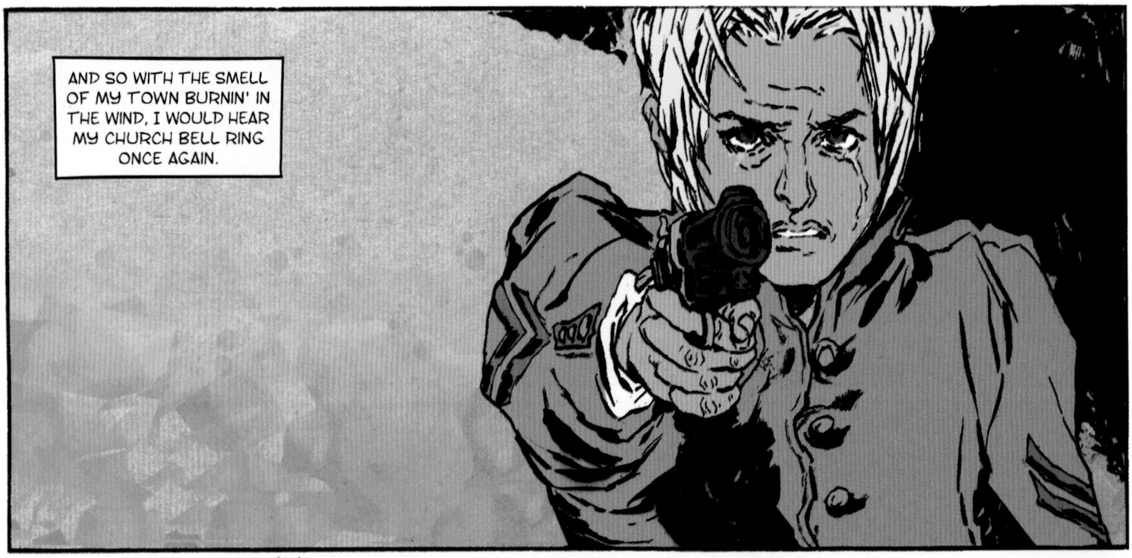
AND SO WITH THE SMELL OF MY TOWN BURNIN' IN THE WIND, I WOULD HEAR MY CHURCH BELL RING ONCE AGAIN.

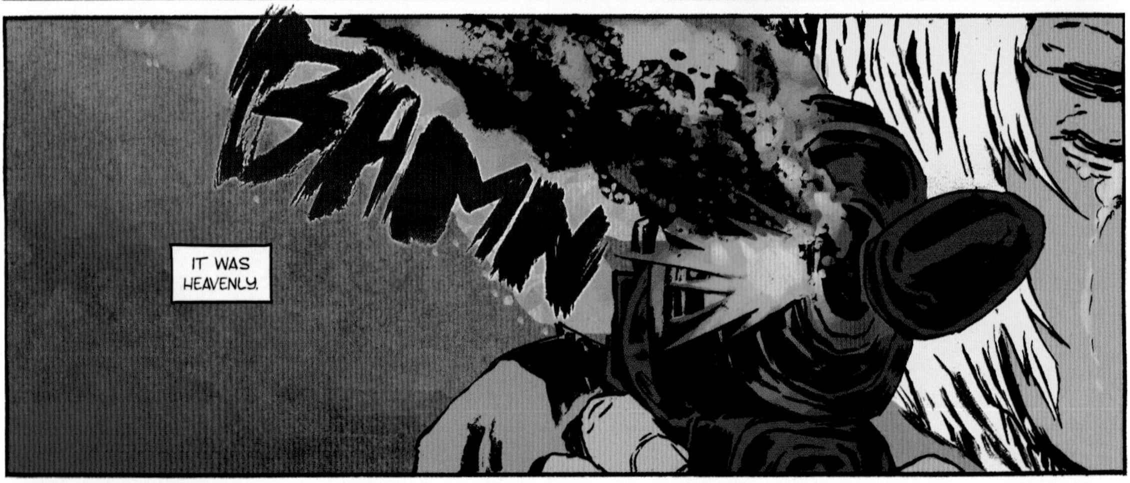
BAMM
IT WAS HEAVENLY.

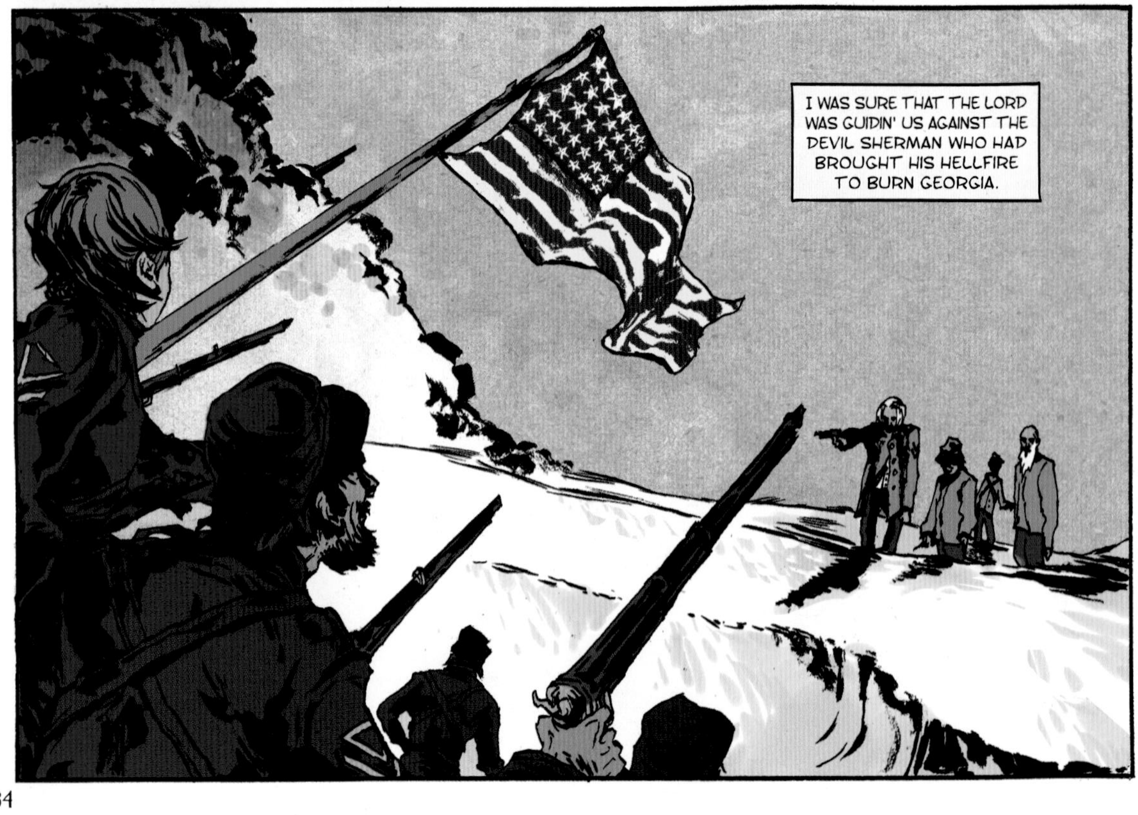
I WAS SURE THAT THE LORD WAS GUIDIN' US AGAINST THE DEVIL SHERMAN WHO HAD BROUGHT HIS HELLFIRE TO BURN GEORGIA.

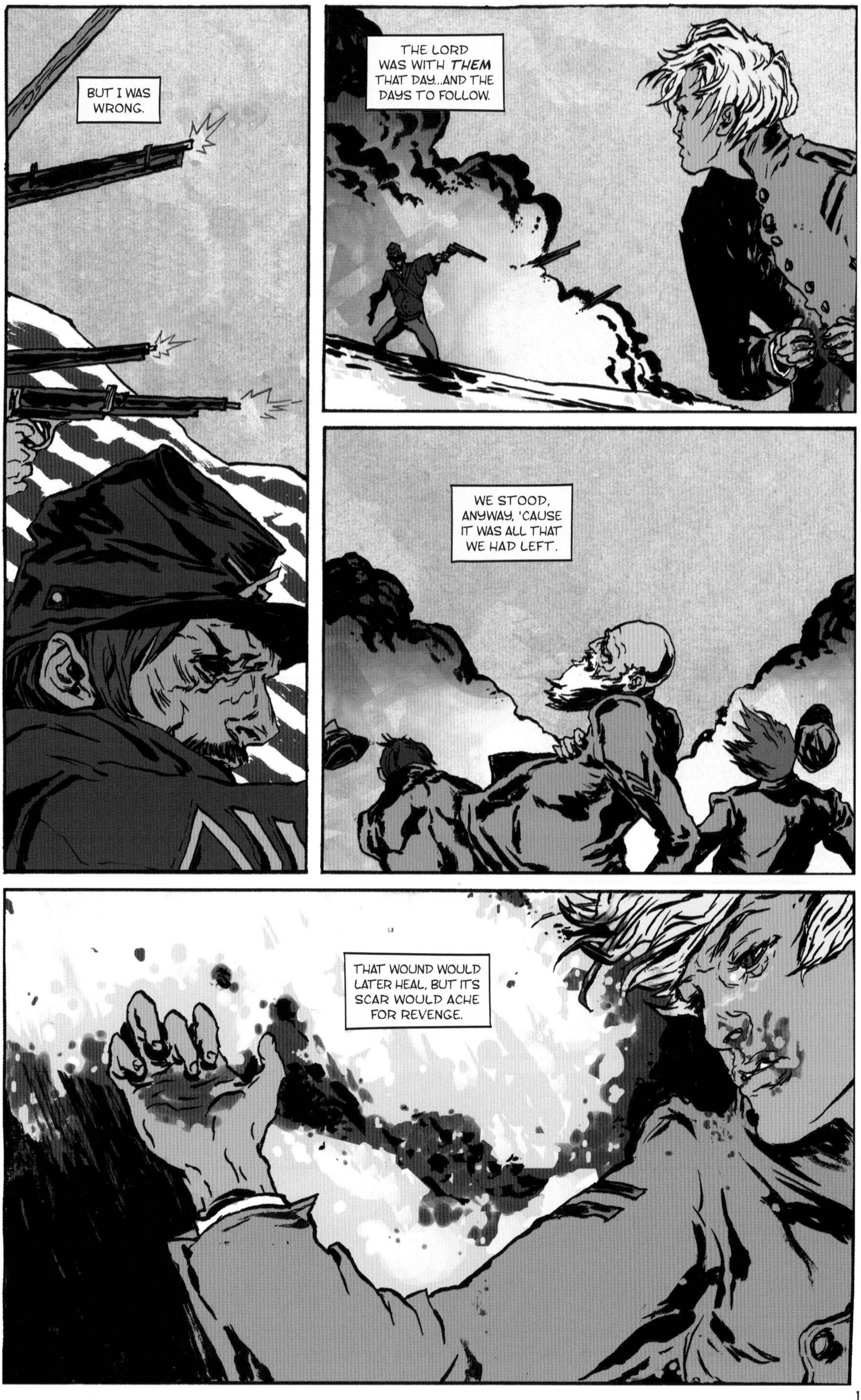
BUT I WAS WRONG.
THE LORD WAS WITH *THEM* THAT DAY...AND THE DAYS TO FOLLOW.
WE STOOD, ANYWAY, 'CAUSE IT WAS ALL THAT WE HAD LEFT.
THAT WOUND WOULD LATER HEAL, BUT ITS SCAR WOULD ACHE FOR REVENGE.

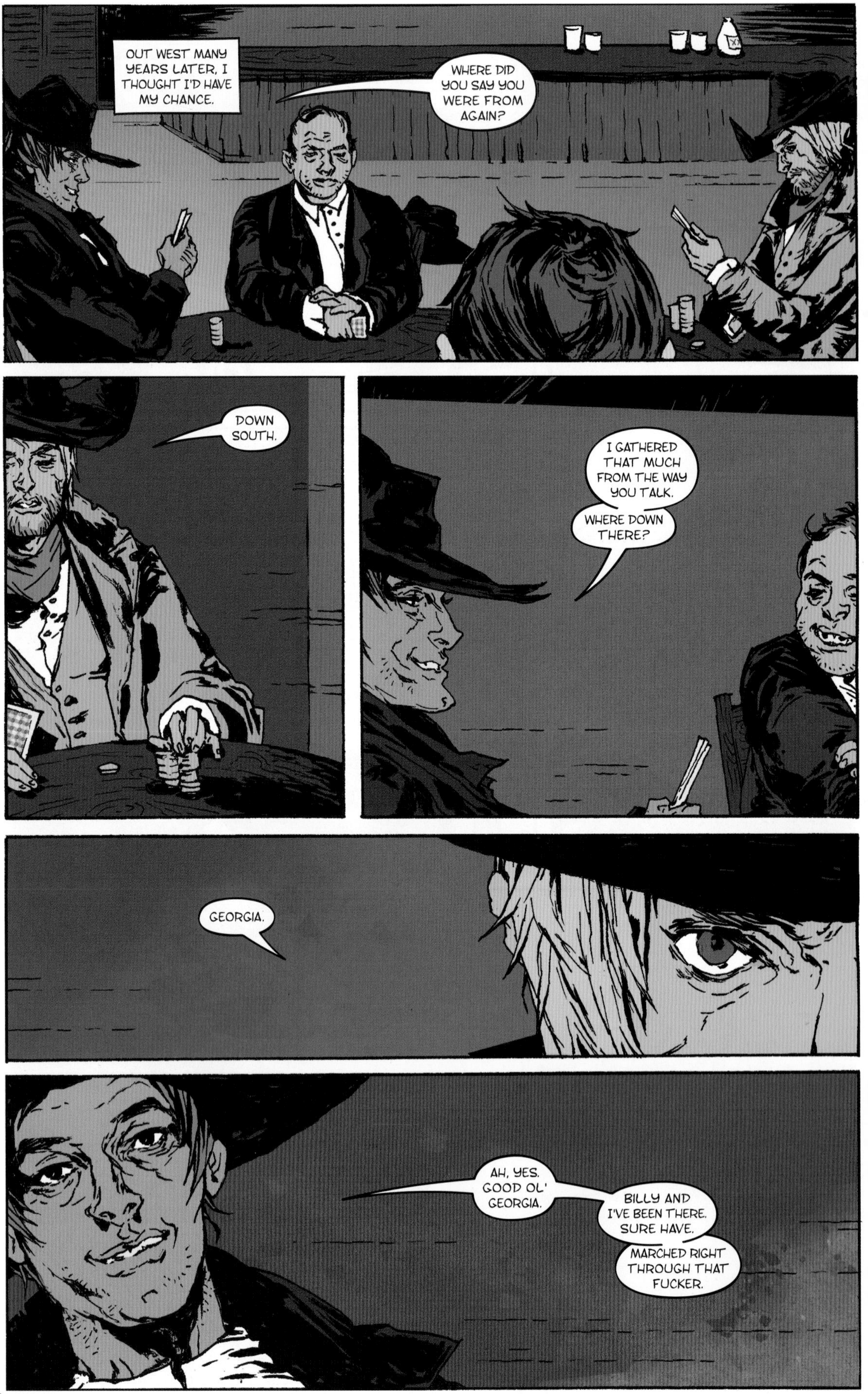
OUT WEST MANY YEARS LATER, I THOUGHT I'D HAVE MY CHANCE.
WHERE DID YOU SAY YOU WERE FROM AGAIN?
DOWN SOUTH.
I GATHERED THAT MUCH FROM THE WAY YOU TALK.
WHERE DOWN THERE?
GEORGIA.
AH, YES. GOOD OL' GEORGIA.
BILLY AND I'VE BEEN THERE. SURE HAVE.
MARCHED RIGHT THROUGH THAT FUCKER.

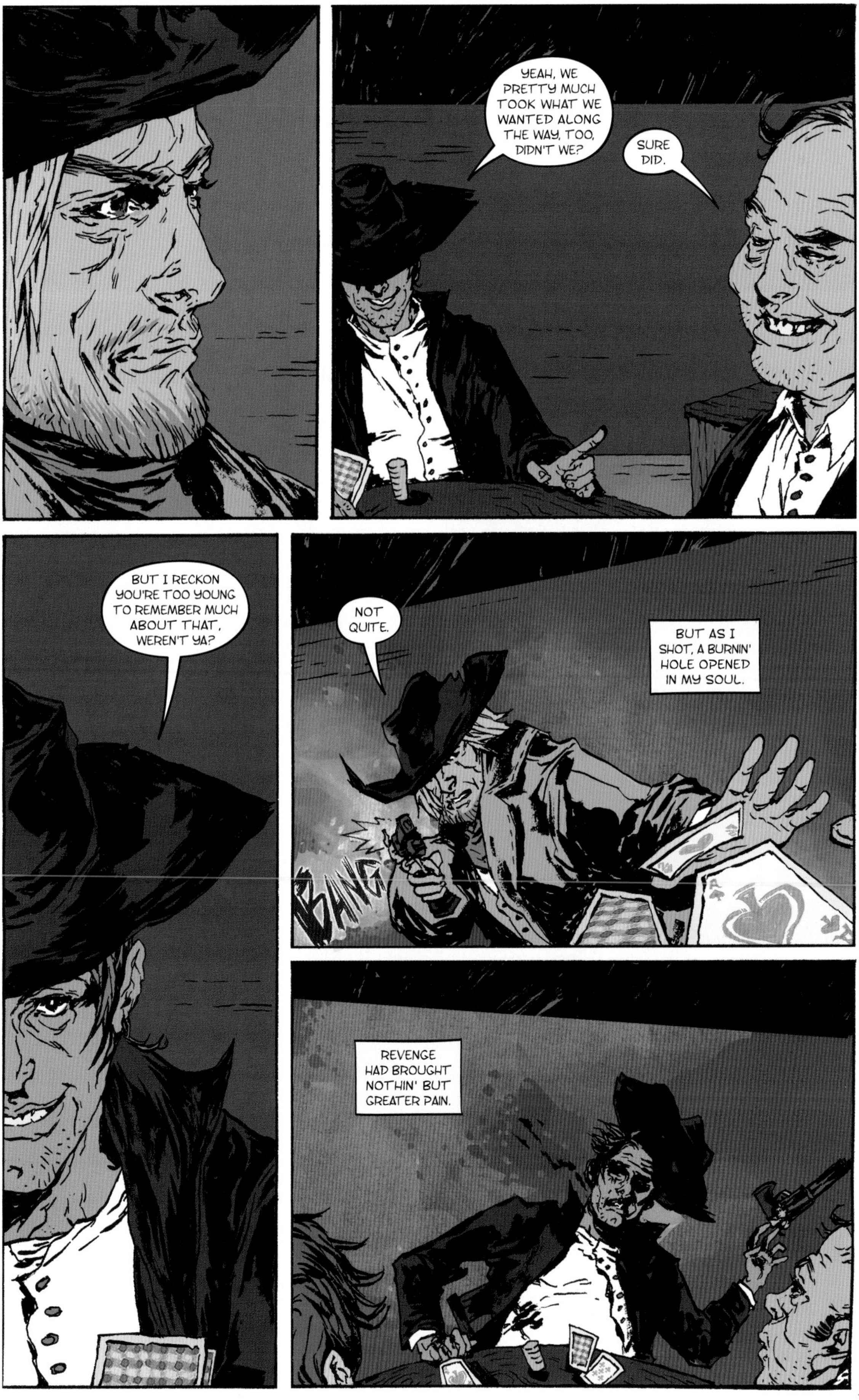

YEAH, WE PRETTY MUCH TOOK WHAT WE WANTED ALONG THE WAY, TOO, DIDN'T WE?
SURE DID.
BUT I RECKON YOU'RE TOO YOUNG TO REMEMBER MUCH ABOUT THAT, WEREN'T YA?
NOT QUITE.
BUT AS I SHOT, A BURNIN' HOLE OPENED IN MY SOUL.
BANG
REVENGE HAD BROUGHT NOTHIN' BUT GREATER PAIN.

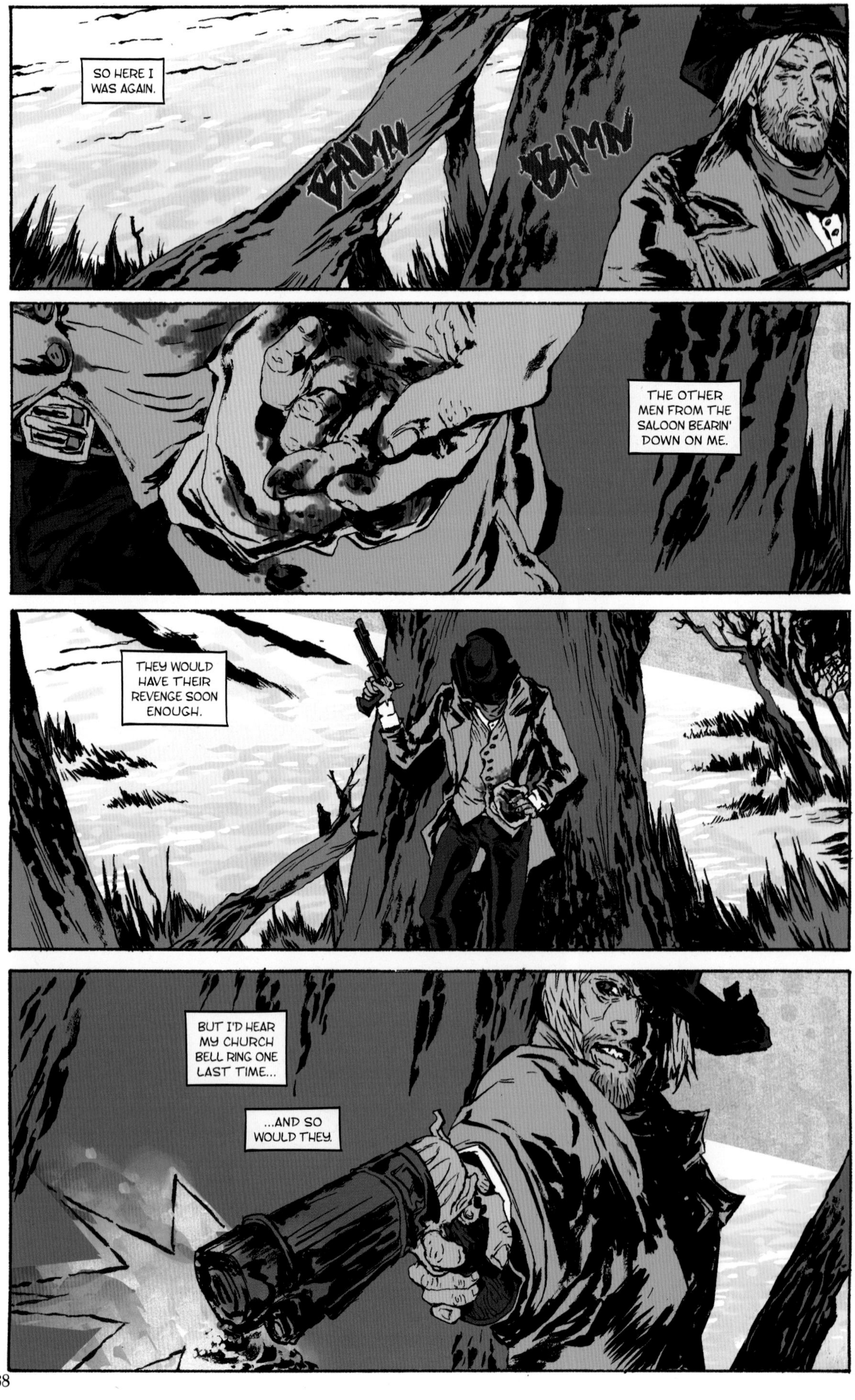

SO HERE I WAS AGAIN.
BAMN
BAMN
THE OTHER MEN FROM THE SALOON BEARIN' DOWN ON ME.
THEY WOULD HAVE THEIR REVENGE SOON ENOUGH.
BUT I'D HEAR MY CHURCH BELL RING ONE LAST TIME...
...AND SO WOULD THEY.

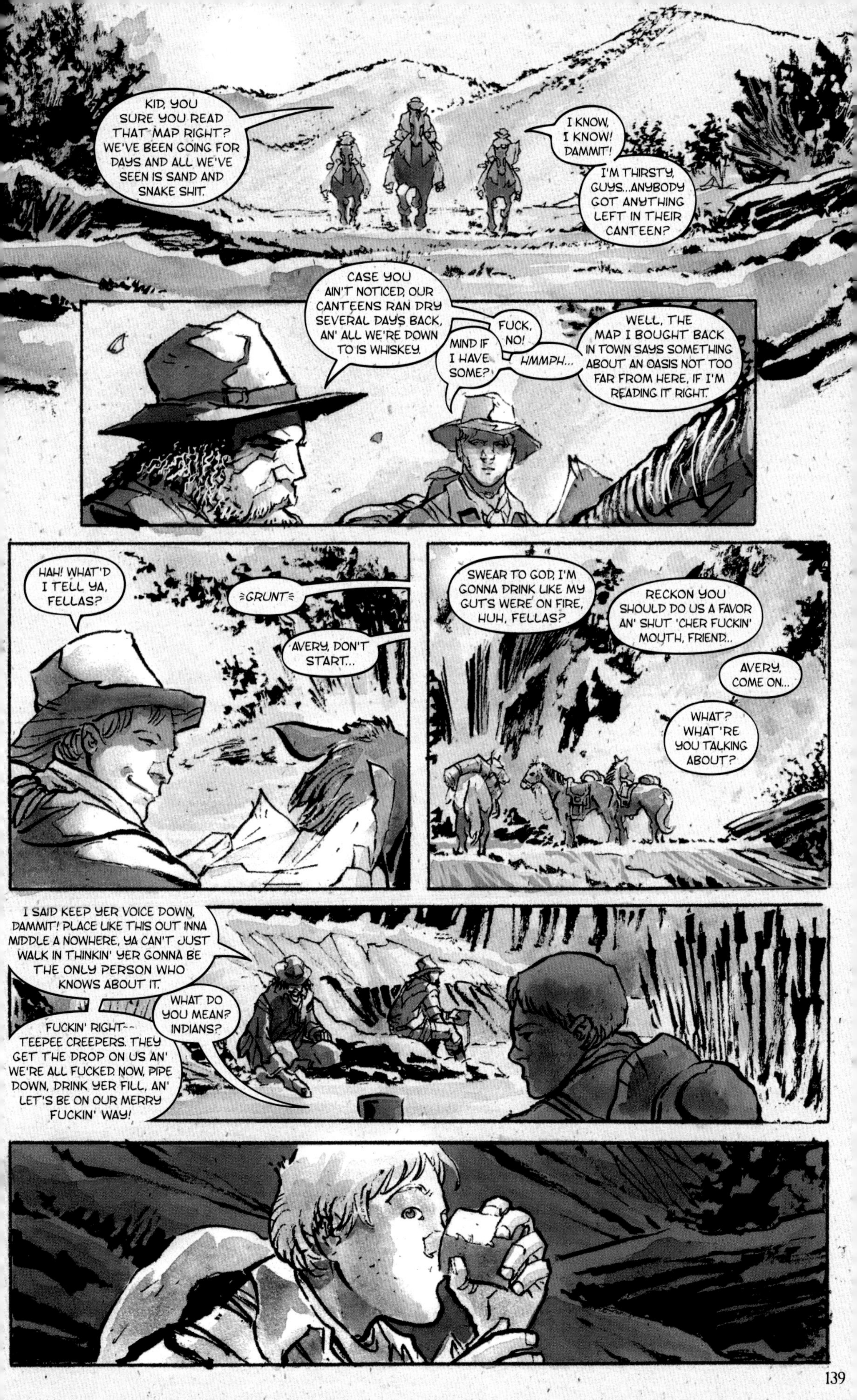
KID, YOU SURE YOU READ THAT MAP RIGHT? WE'VE BEEN GOING FOR DAYS AND ALL WE'VE SEEN IS SAND AND SNAKE SHIT.
I KNOW, I KNOW! DAMMIT!
I'M THIRSTY, GUYS...ANYBODY GOT ANYTHING LEFT IN THEIR CANTEEN?
CASE YOU AIN'T NOTICED, OUR CANTEENS RAN DRY SEVERAL DAYS BACK, AN' ALL WE'RE DOWN TO IS WHISKEY.
MIND IF I HAVE SOME?
FUCK, NO!
HMMPH...
WELL, THE MAP I BOUGHT BACK IN TOWN SAYS SOMETHING ABOUT AN OASIS NOT TOO FAR FROM HERE, IF I'M READING IT RIGHT.
HAH! WHAT'D I TELL YA, FELLAS?
GRUNT
AVERY, DON'T START...
SWEAR TO GOD, I'M GONNA DRINK LIKE MY GUTS WERE ON FIRE, HUH, FELLAS?
RECKON YOU SHOULD DO US A FAVOR AN' SHUT 'CHER FUCKIN' MOUTH, FRIEND...
AVERY, COME ON...
WHAT? WHAT'RE YOU TALKING ABOUT?
I SAID KEEP YER VOICE DOWN, DAMMIT! PLACE LIKE THIS OUT INNA MIDDLE A NOWHERE, YA CAN'T JUST WALK IN THINKIN' YER GONNA BE THE ONLY PERSON WHO KNOWS ABOUT IT.
WHAT DO YOU MEAN? INDIANS?
FUCKIN' RIGHT-- TEEPEE CREEPERS. THEY GET THE DROP ON US AN' WE'RE ALL FUCKED. NOW, PIPE DOWN, DRINK YER FILL, AN' LET'S BE ON OUR MERRY FUCKIN' WAY!

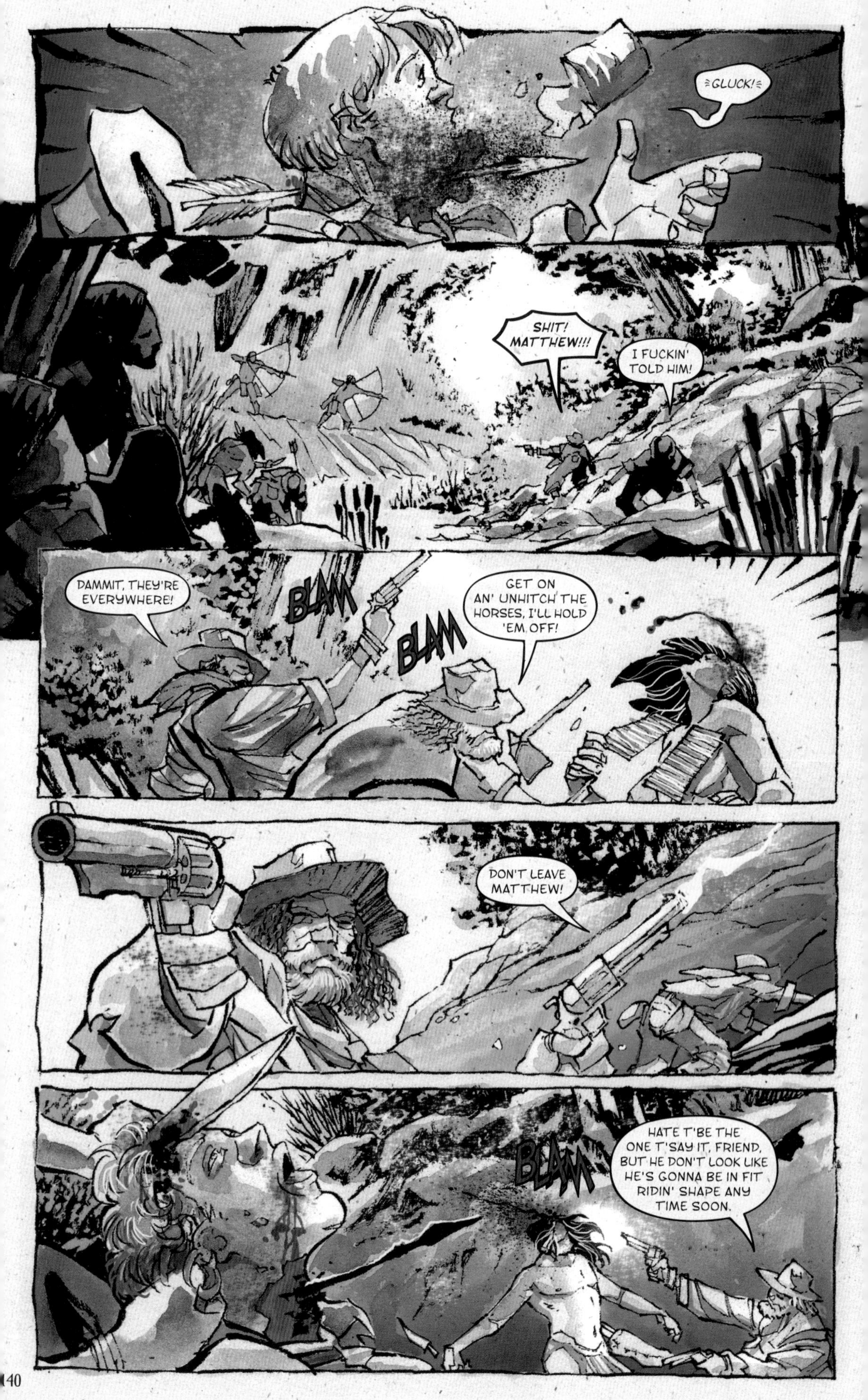
GLUCK!
SHIT! MATTHEW!!!
I FUCKIN' TOLD HIM!
DAMMIT, THEY'RE EVERYWHERE!
BLAM
BLAM
GET ON AN' UNHITCH THE HORSES, I'LL HOLD 'EM OFF!
DON'T LEAVE MATTHEW!
BLAM
HATE T'BE THE ONE T'SAY IT, FRIEND, BUT HE DON'T LOOK LIKE HE'S GONNA BE IN FIT RIDIN' SHAPE ANY TIME SOON.

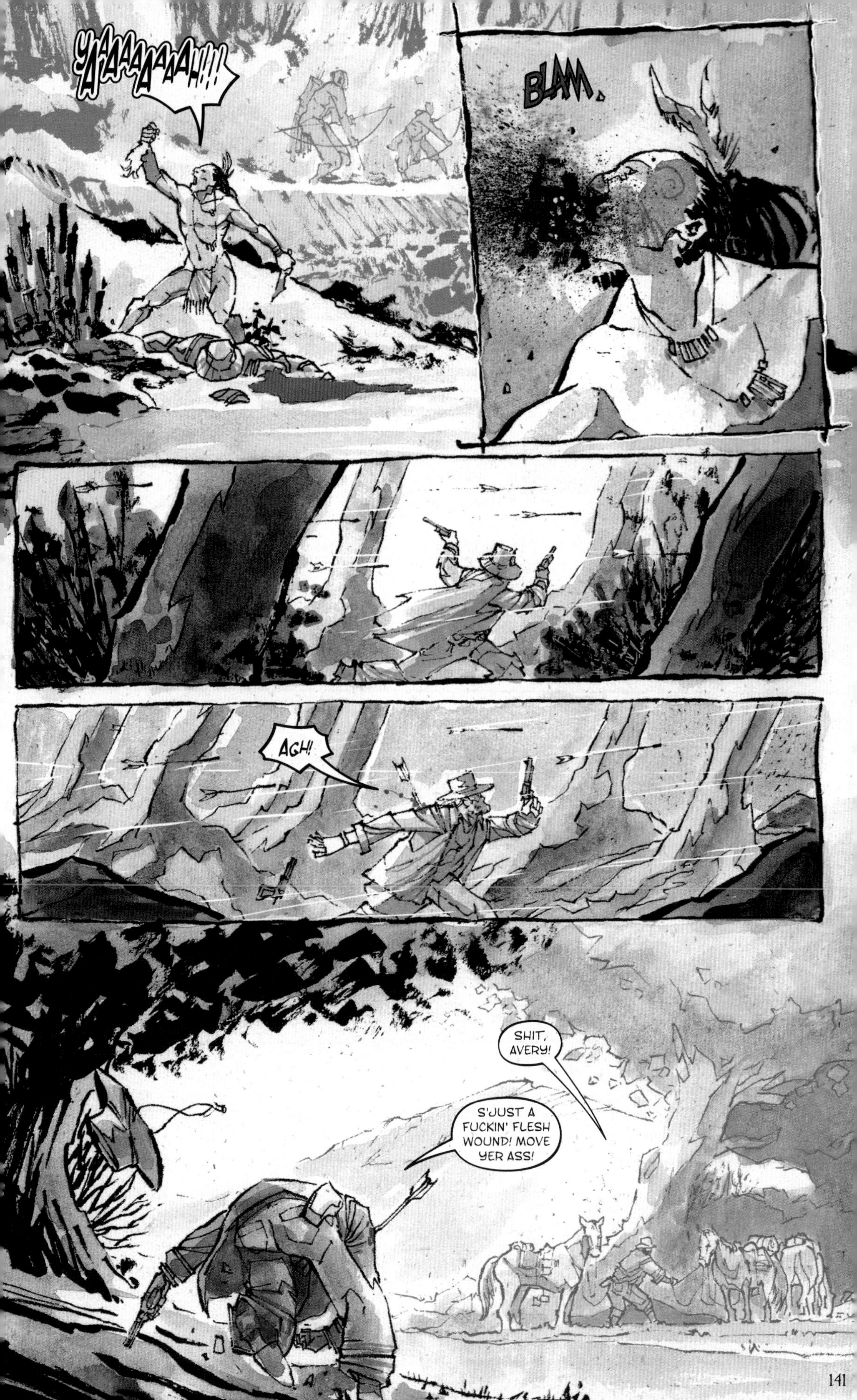
YAAAAAAAAH!!!
BLAM
AGH!
SHIT, AVERY!
S'JUST A FUCKIN' FLESH WOUND! MOVE YER ASS!

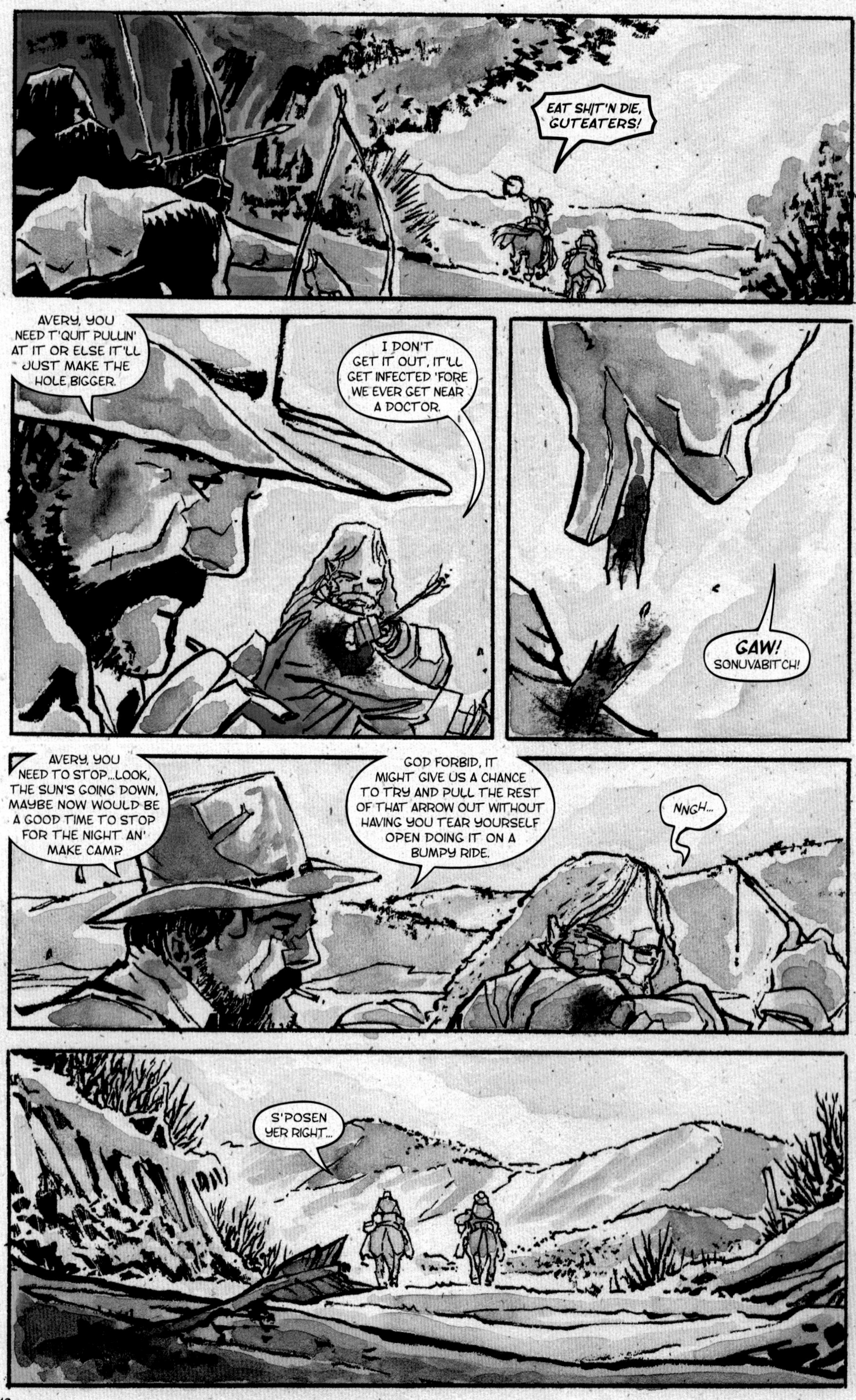
EAT SHIT'N DIE, GUTEATERS!
AVERY, YOU NEED T'QUIT PULLIN' AT IT OR ELSE IT'LL JUST MAKE THE HOLE BIGGER.
I DON'T GET IT OUT, IT'LL GET INFECTED 'FORE WE EVER GET NEAR A DOCTOR.
GAW! SONUVABITCH!
AVERY, YOU NEED TO STOP...LOOK, THE SUN'S GOING DOWN, MAYBE NOW WOULD BE A GOOD TIME TO STOP FOR THE NIGHT AN' MAKE CAMP?
GOD FORBID, IT MIGHT GIVE US A CHANCE TO TRY AND PULL THE REST OF THAT ARROW OUT WITHOUT HAVING YOU TEAR YOURSELF OPEN DOING IT ON A BUMPY RIDE.
NNGH...
S'POSEN YER RIGHT...

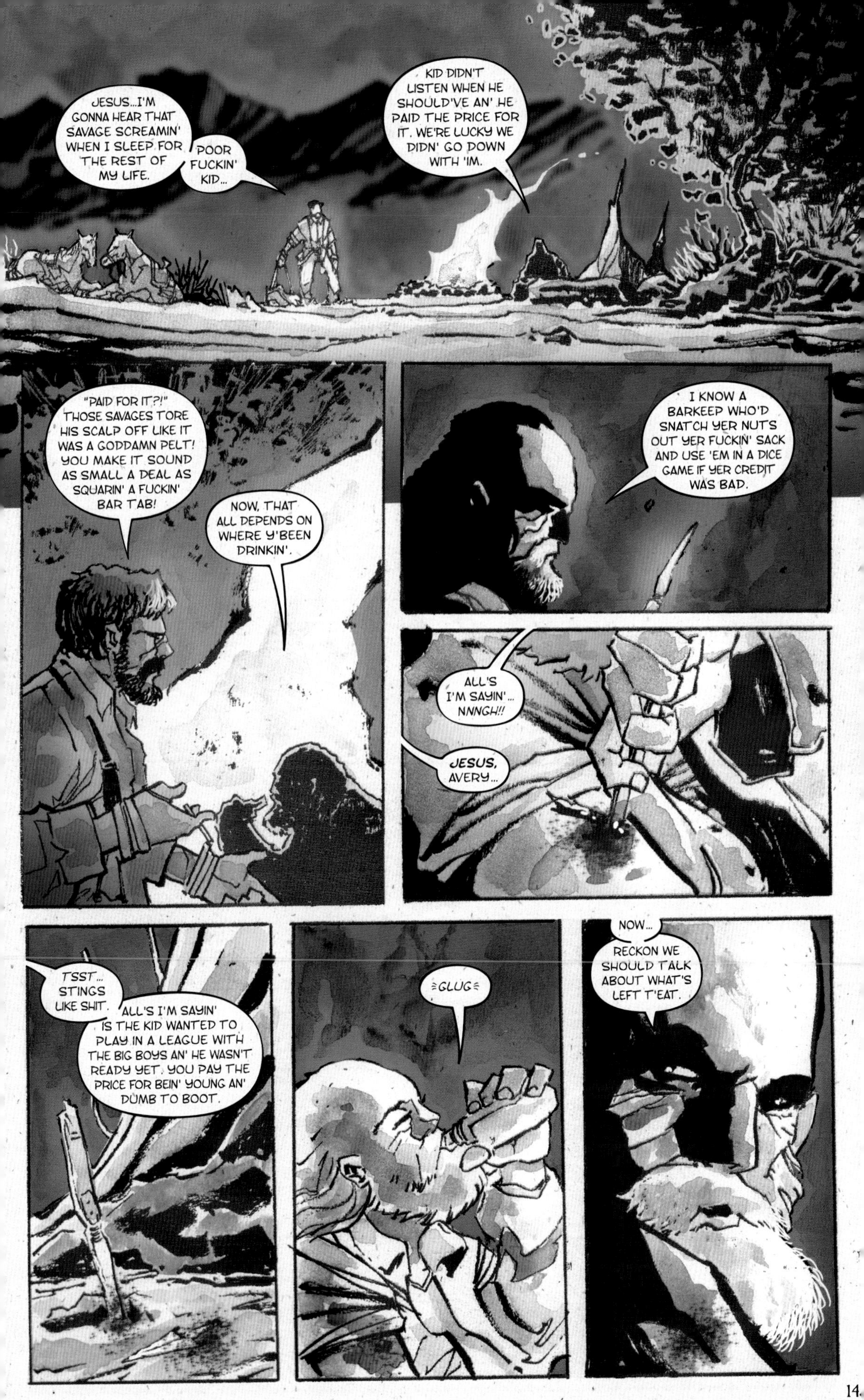
JESUS...I'M GONNA HEAR THAT SAVAGE SCREAMIN' WHEN I SLEEP FOR THE REST OF MY LIFE.
POOR FUCKIN' KID...
KID DIDN'T LISTEN WHEN HE SHOULD'VE AN' HE PAID THE PRICE FOR IT. WE'RE LUCKY WE DIDN' GO DOWN WITH 'IM.
"PAID FOR IT?!" THOSE SAVAGES TORE HIS SCALP OFF LIKE IT WAS A GODDAMN PELT! YOU MAKE IT SOUND AS SMALL A DEAL AS SQUARIN' A FUCKIN' BAR TAB!
NOW, THAT ALL DEPENDS ON WHERE Y'BEEN DRINKIN'.
I KNOW A BARKEEP WHO'D SNATCH YER NUTS OUT YER FUCKIN' SACK AND USE 'EM IN A DICE GAME IF YER CREDIT WAS BAD.
ALL'S I'M SAYIN'... NNNGH!!
JESUS, AVERY...
TSST... STINGS LIKE SHIT.
ALL'S I'M SAYIN' IS THE KID WANTED TO PLAY IN A LEAGUE WITH THE BIG BOYS AN' HE WASN'T READY YET. YOU PAY THE PRICE FOR BEIN' YOUNG AN' DUMB TO BOOT.
GLUG
NOW...
RECKON WE SHOULD TALK ABOUT WHAT'S LEFT T'EAT.

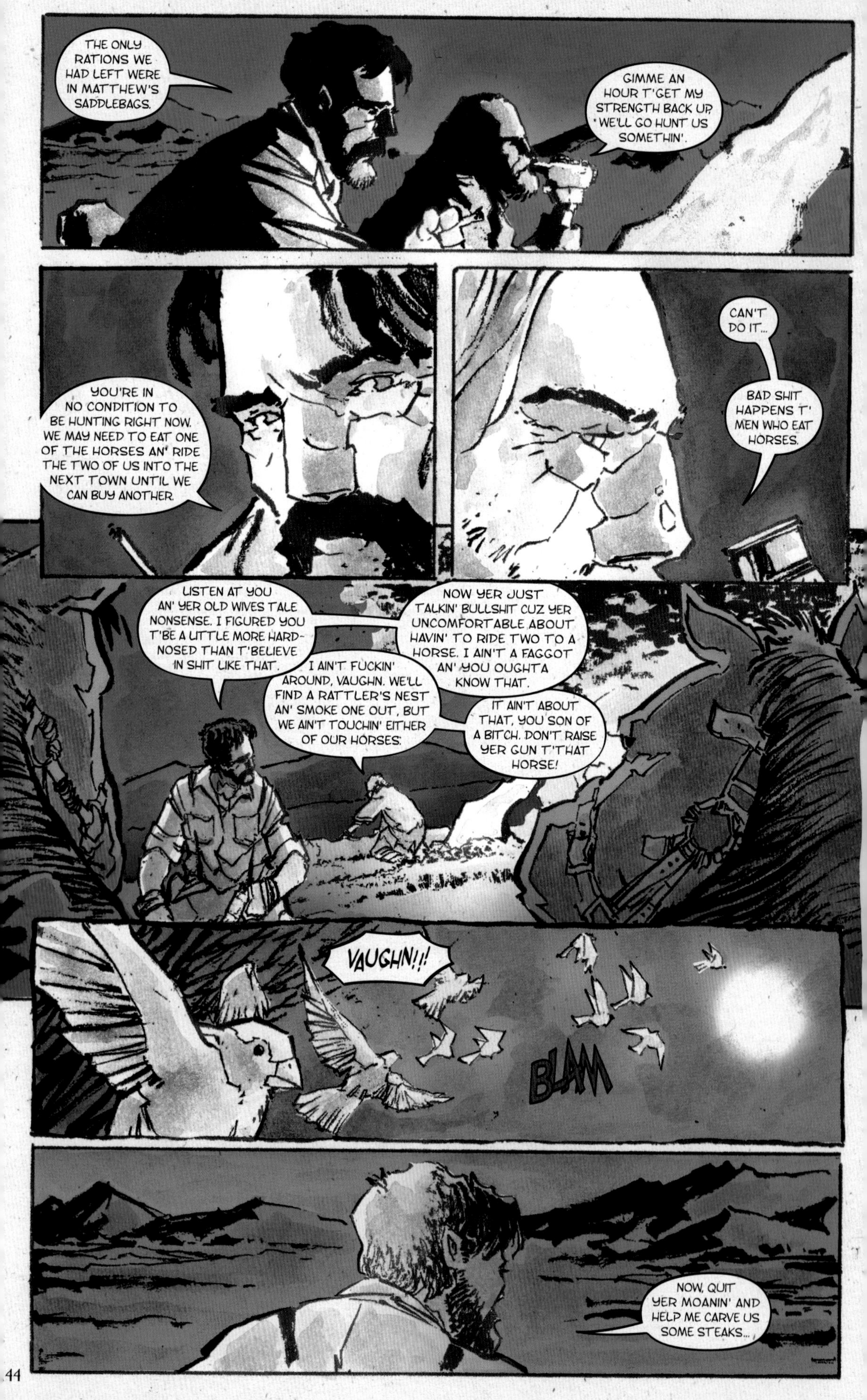
THE ONLY RATIONS WE HAD LEFT WERE IN MATTHEW'S SADDLEBAGS.
GIMME AN HOUR T'GET MY STRENGTH BACK UP, 'WE'LL GO HUNT US SOMETHIN'.
YOU'RE IN NO CONDITION TO BE HUNTING RIGHT NOW. WE MAY NEED TO EAT ONE OF THE HORSES AN' RIDE THE TWO OF US INTO THE NEXT TOWN UNTIL WE CAN BUY ANOTHER.
CAN'T DO IT...
BAD SHIT HAPPENS T' MEN WHO EAT HORSES.
LISTEN AT YOU AN' YER OLD WIVES TALE NONSENSE. I FIGURED YOU T'BE A LITTLE MORE HARD-NOSED THAN T'BELIEVE IN SHIT LIKE THAT.
I AIN'T FUCKIN' AROUND, VAUGHN. WE'LL FIND A RATTLER'S NEST AN' SMOKE ONE OUT, BUT WE AIN'T TOUCHIN' EITHER OF OUR HORSES.
NOW YER JUST TALKIN' BULLSHIT CUZ YER UNCOMFORTABLE ABOUT HAVIN' TO RIDE TWO TO A HORSE. I AIN'T A FAGGOT AN' YOU OUGHTA KNOW THAT.
IT AIN'T ABOUT THAT, YOU SON OF A BITCH. DON'T RAISE YER GUN T'THAT HORSE!
VAUGHN!!!
BLAM
NOW, QUIT YER MOANIN' AND HELP ME CARVE US SOME STEAKS...

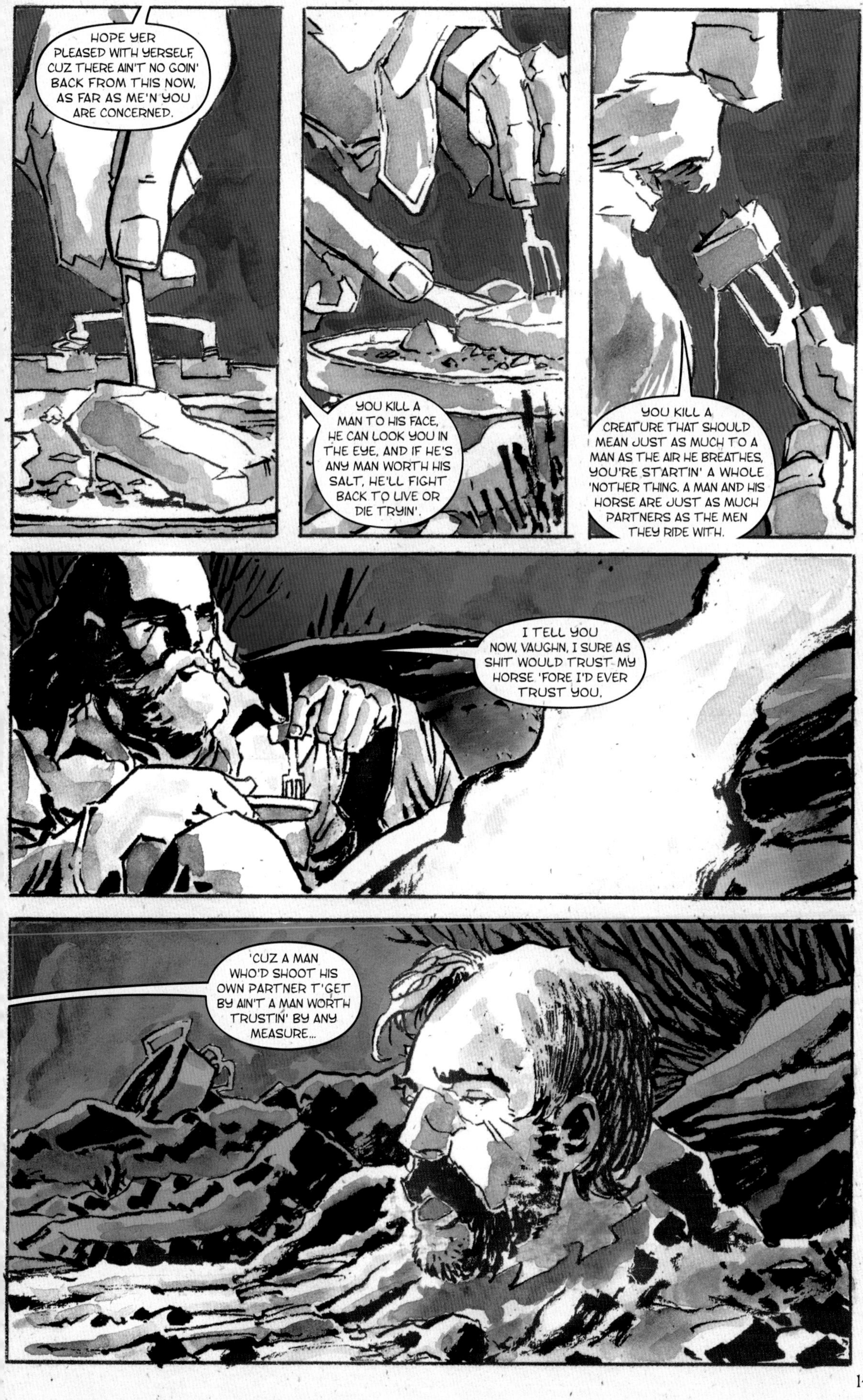
HOPE YER PLEASED WITH YERSELF, CUZ THERE AIN'T NO GOIN' BACK FROM THIS NOW, AS FAR AS ME'N YOU ARE CONCERNED.
YOU KILL A MAN TO HIS FACE, HE CAN LOOK YOU IN THE EYE, AND IF HE'S ANY MAN WORTH HIS SALT, HE'LL FIGHT BACK TO LIVE OR DIE TRYIN'.
YOU KILL A CREATURE THAT SHOULD MEAN JUST AS MUCH TO A MAN AS THE AIR HE BREATHES, YOU'RE STARTIN' A WHOLE 'NOTHER THING. A MAN AND HIS HORSE ARE JUST AS MUCH PARTNERS AS THE MEN THEY RIDE WITH.
I TELL YOU NOW, VAUGHN, I SURE AS SHIT WOULD TRUST MY HORSE 'FORE I'D EVER TRUST YOU.
'CUZ A MAN WHO'D SHOOT HIS OWN PARTNER T'GET BY AIN'T A MAN WORTH TRUSTIN' BY ANY MEASURE...

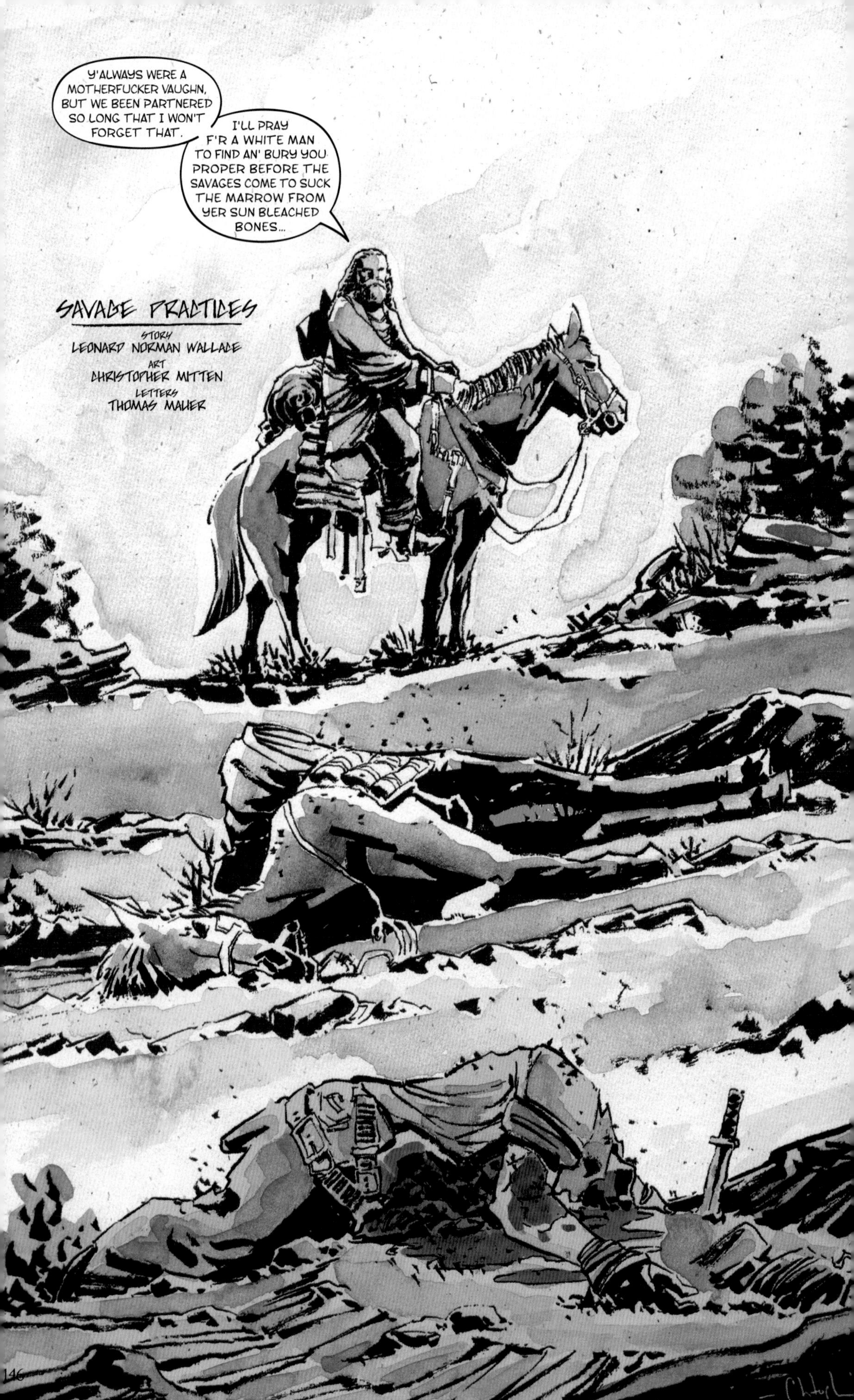
Y'ALWAYS WERE A MOTHERFUCKER VAUGHN, BUT WE BEEN PARTNERED SO LONG THAT I WON'T FORGET THAT.
I'LL PRAY F'R A WHITE MAN TO FIND AN' BURY YOU PROPER BEFORE THE SAVAGES COME TO SUCK THE MARROW FROM YER SUN BLEACHED BONES...
SAVAGE PRACTICES
STORY
LEONARD NORMAN WALLACE
ART
CHRISTOPHER MITTEN
LETTERS
THOMAS MAUER

For Old Times' Sake

Pat Loika story
art Jose Holder & Garry Henderson
Thomas Mauer letters

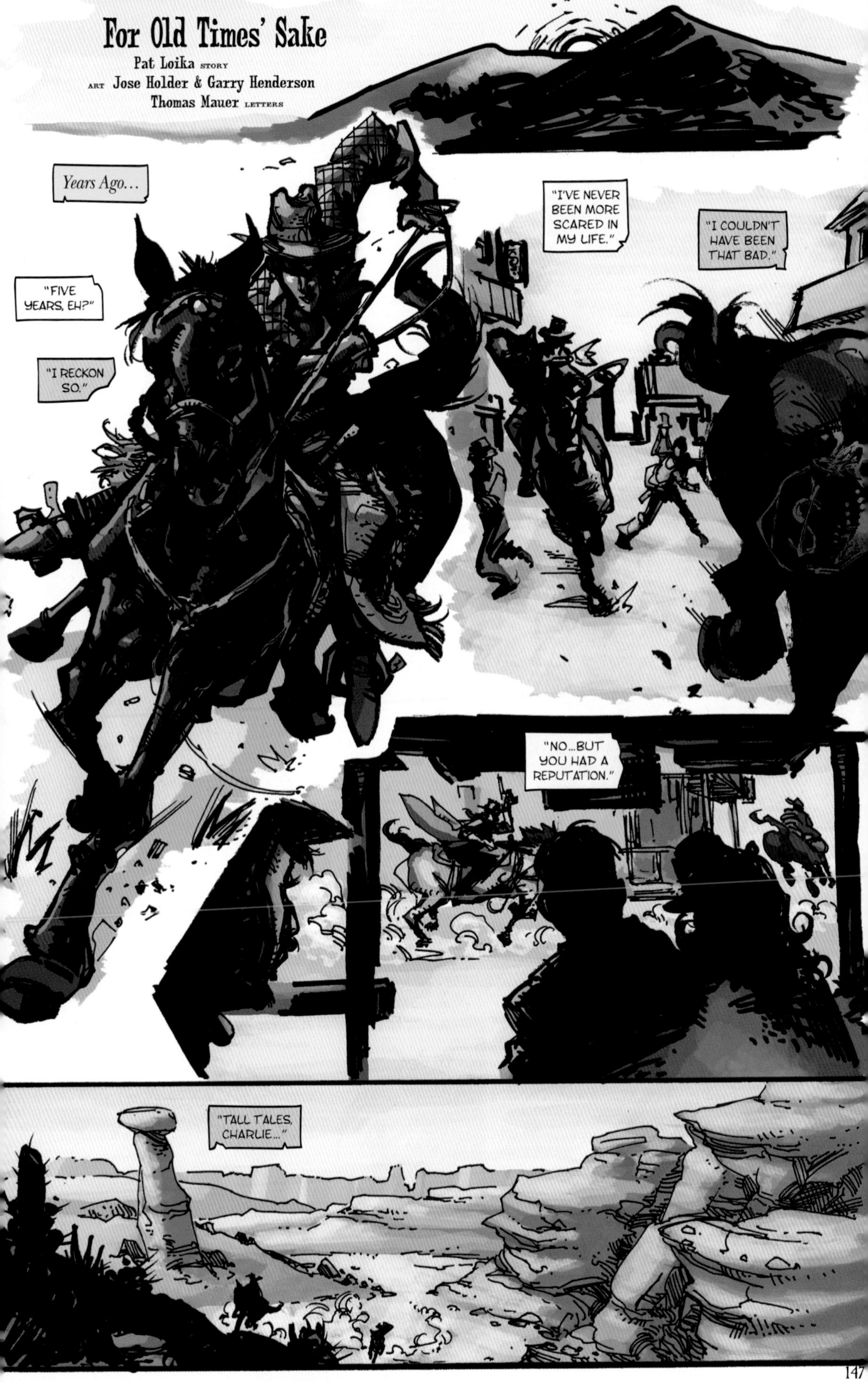

Years Ago…
"FIVE YEARS, EH?"
"I RECKON SO."
"I'VE NEVER BEEN MORE SCARED IN MY LIFE."
"I COULDN'T HAVE BEEN THAT BAD."
"NO…BUT YOU HAD A REPUTATION."
"TALL TALES, CHARLIE…"

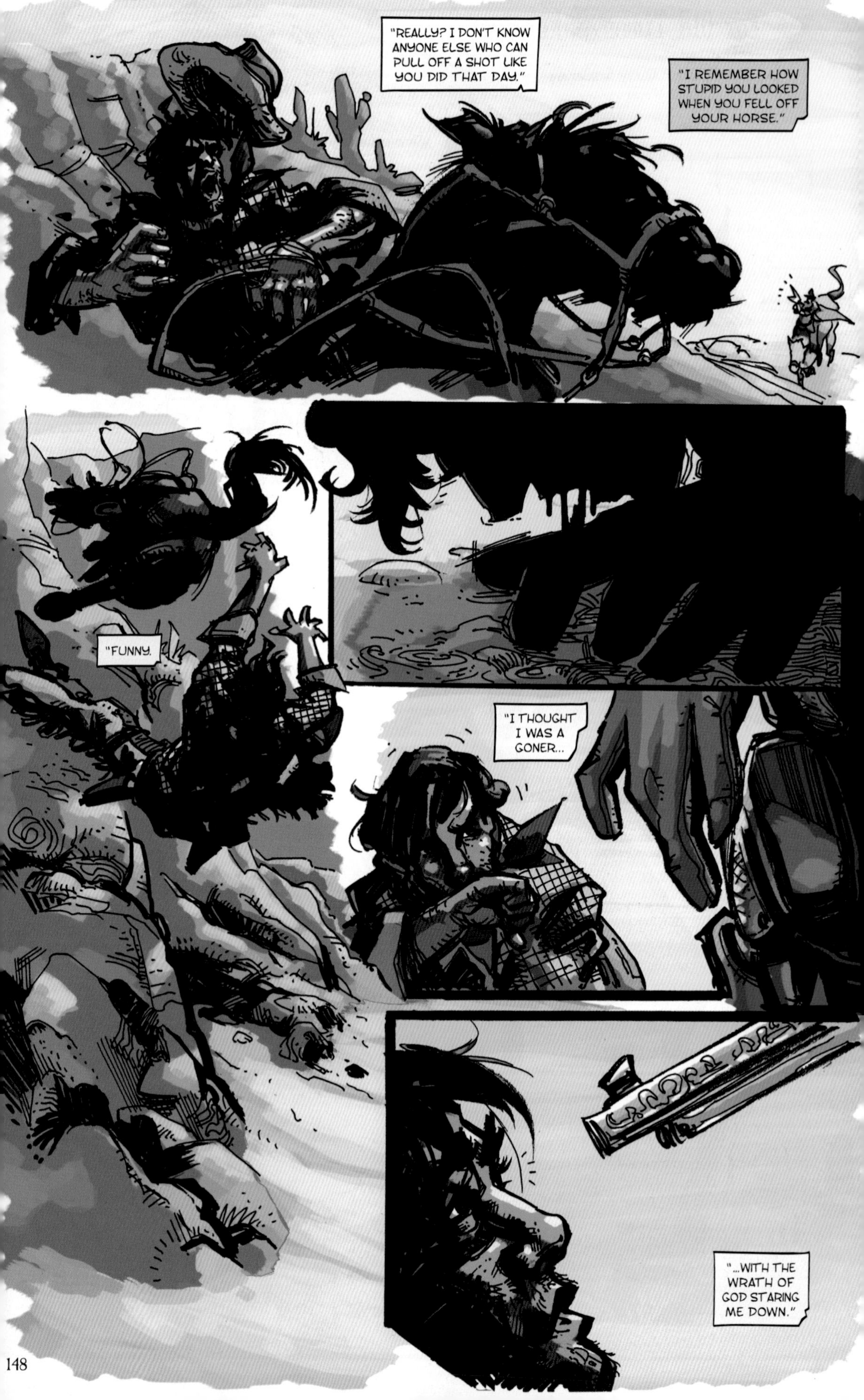
"REALLY? I DON'T KNOW ANYONE ELSE WHO CAN PULL OFF A SHOT LIKE YOU DID THAT DAY."
"I REMEMBER HOW STUPID YOU LOOKED WHEN YOU FELL OFF YOUR HORSE."
"FUNNY.
"I THOUGHT I WAS A GONER...
"...WITH THE WRATH OF GOD STARING ME DOWN."

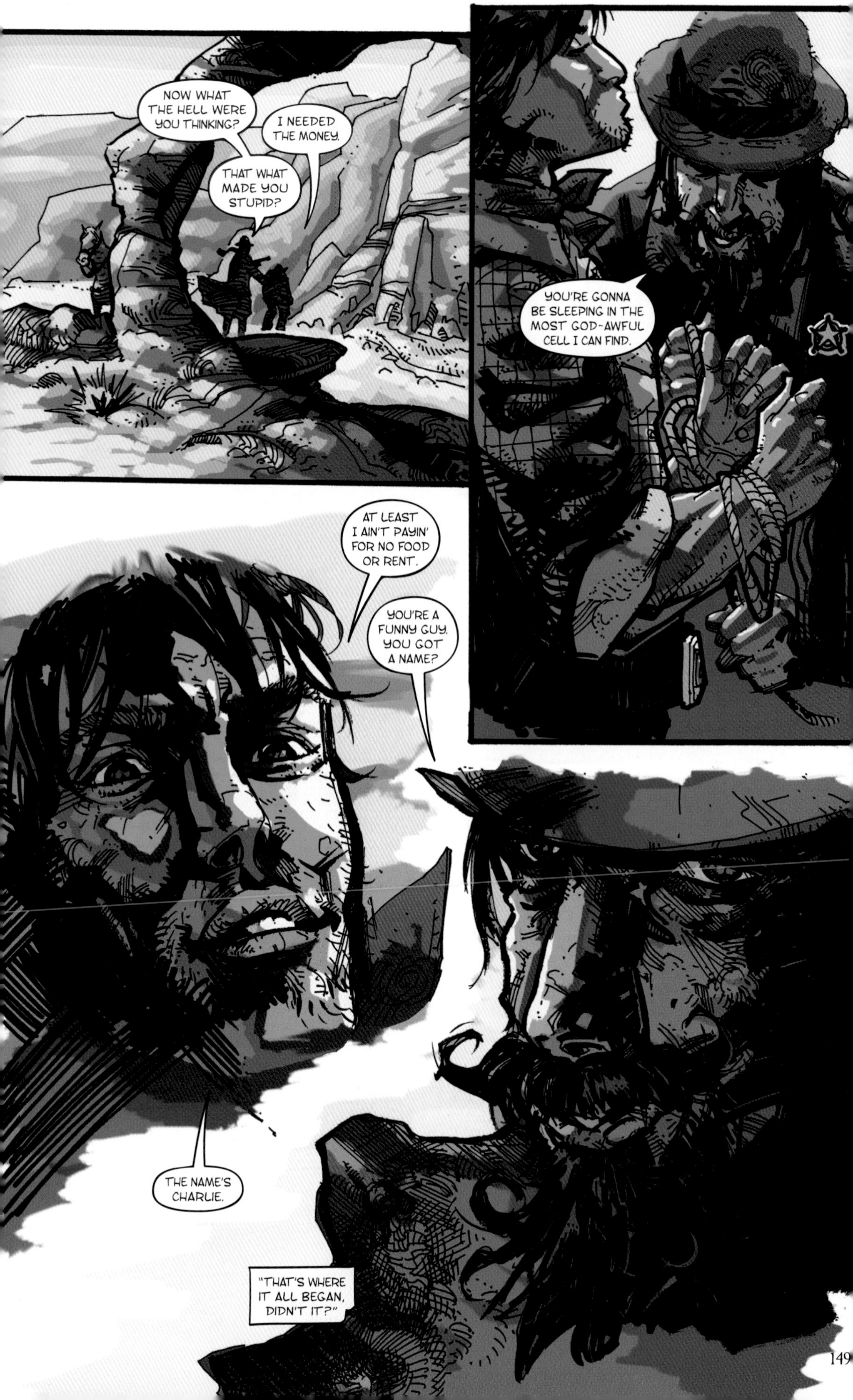
NOW WHAT THE HELL WERE YOU THINKING?
I NEEDED THE MONEY.
THAT WHAT MADE YOU STUPID?
YOU'RE GONNA BE SLEEPING IN THE MOST GOD-AWFUL CELL I CAN FIND.
AT LEAST I AIN'T PAYIN' FOR NO FOOD OR RENT.
YOU'RE A FUNNY GUY. YOU GOT A NAME?
THE NAME'S CHARLIE.
"THAT'S WHERE IT ALL BEGAN, DIDN'T IT?"

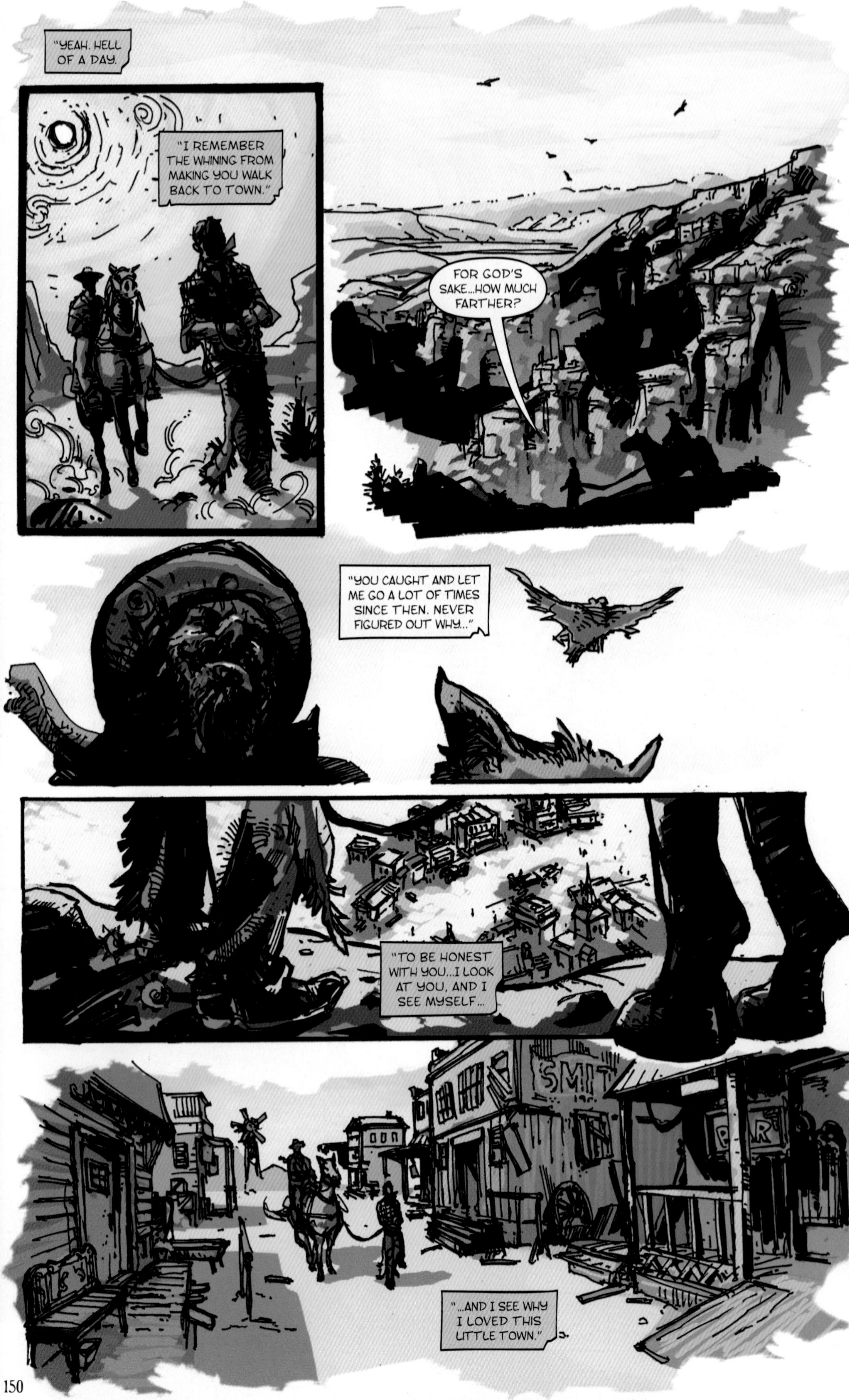
"YEAH. HELL OF A DAY.
"I REMEMBER THE WHINING FROM MAKING YOU WALK BACK TO TOWN."
FOR GOD'S SAKE...HOW MUCH FARTHER?
"YOU CAUGHT AND LET ME GO A LOT OF TIMES SINCE THEN. NEVER FIGURED OUT WHY..."
"TO BE HONEST WITH YOU...I LOOK AT YOU, AND I SEE MYSELF...
SMIT
BAR
"...AND I SEE WHY I LOVED THIS LITTLE TOWN."

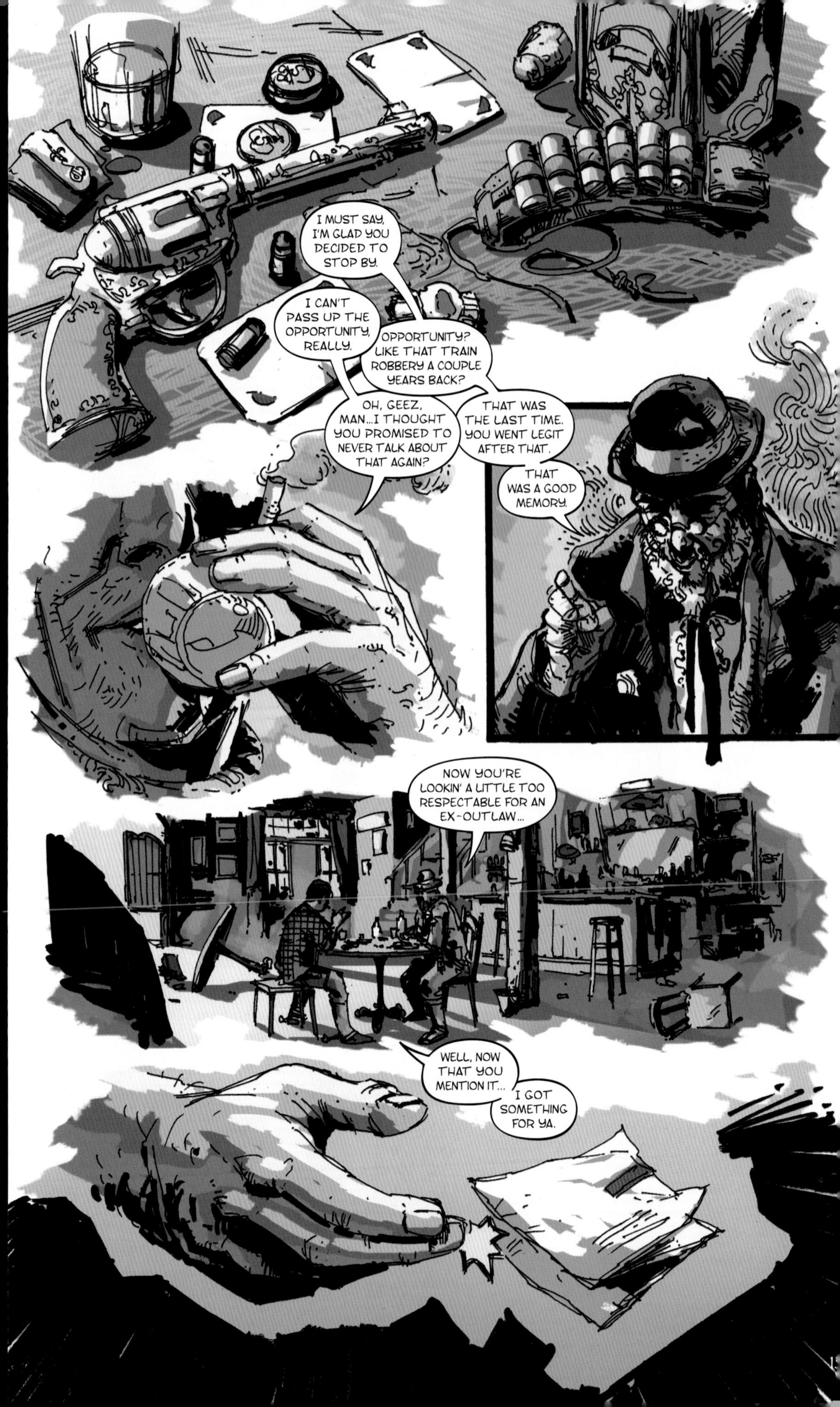

I MUST SAY, I'M GLAD YOU DECIDED TO STOP BY.
I CAN'T PASS UP THE OPPORTUNITY, REALLY.
OPPORTUNITY? LIKE THAT TRAIN ROBBERY A COUPLE YEARS BACK?
OH, GEEZ, MAN...I THOUGHT YOU PROMISED TO NEVER TALK ABOUT THAT AGAIN?
THAT WAS THE LAST TIME. YOU WENT LEGIT AFTER THAT.
THAT WAS A GOOD MEMORY.
NOW YOU'RE LOOKIN' A LITTLE TOO RESPECTABLE FOR AN EX-OUTLAW...
WELL, NOW THAT YOU MENTION IT...
I GOT SOMETHING FOR YA.

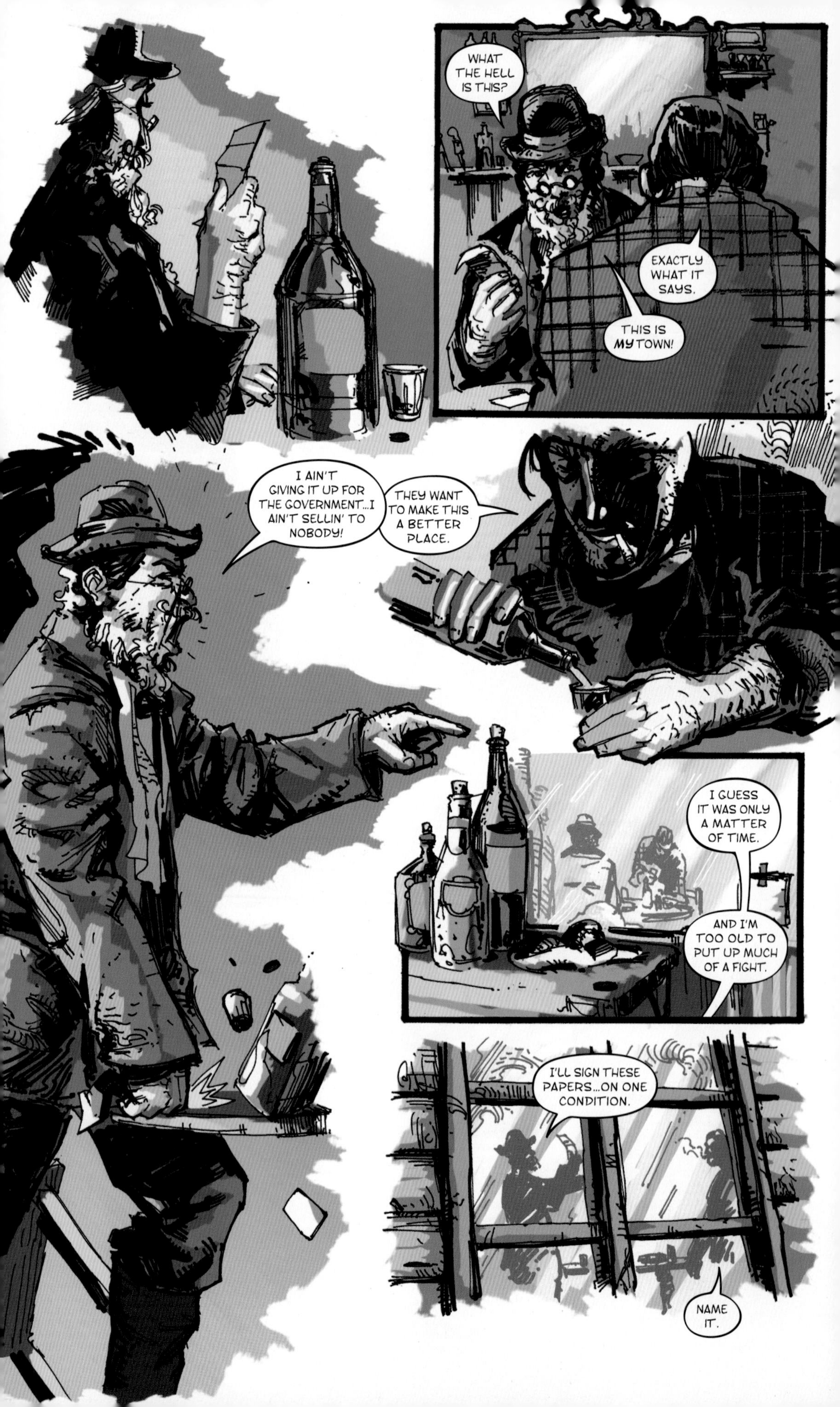
WHAT THE HELL IS THIS?
EXACTLY WHAT IT SAYS.
THIS IS **MY** TOWN!
THEY WANT TO MAKE THIS A BETTER PLACE.
I AIN'T GIVING IT UP FOR THE GOVERNMENT...I AIN'T SELLIN' TO NOBODY!
I GUESS IT WAS ONLY A MATTER OF TIME.
AND I'M TOO OLD TO PUT UP MUCH OF A FIGHT.
I'LL SIGN THESE PAPERS...ON ONE CONDITION.
NAME IT.

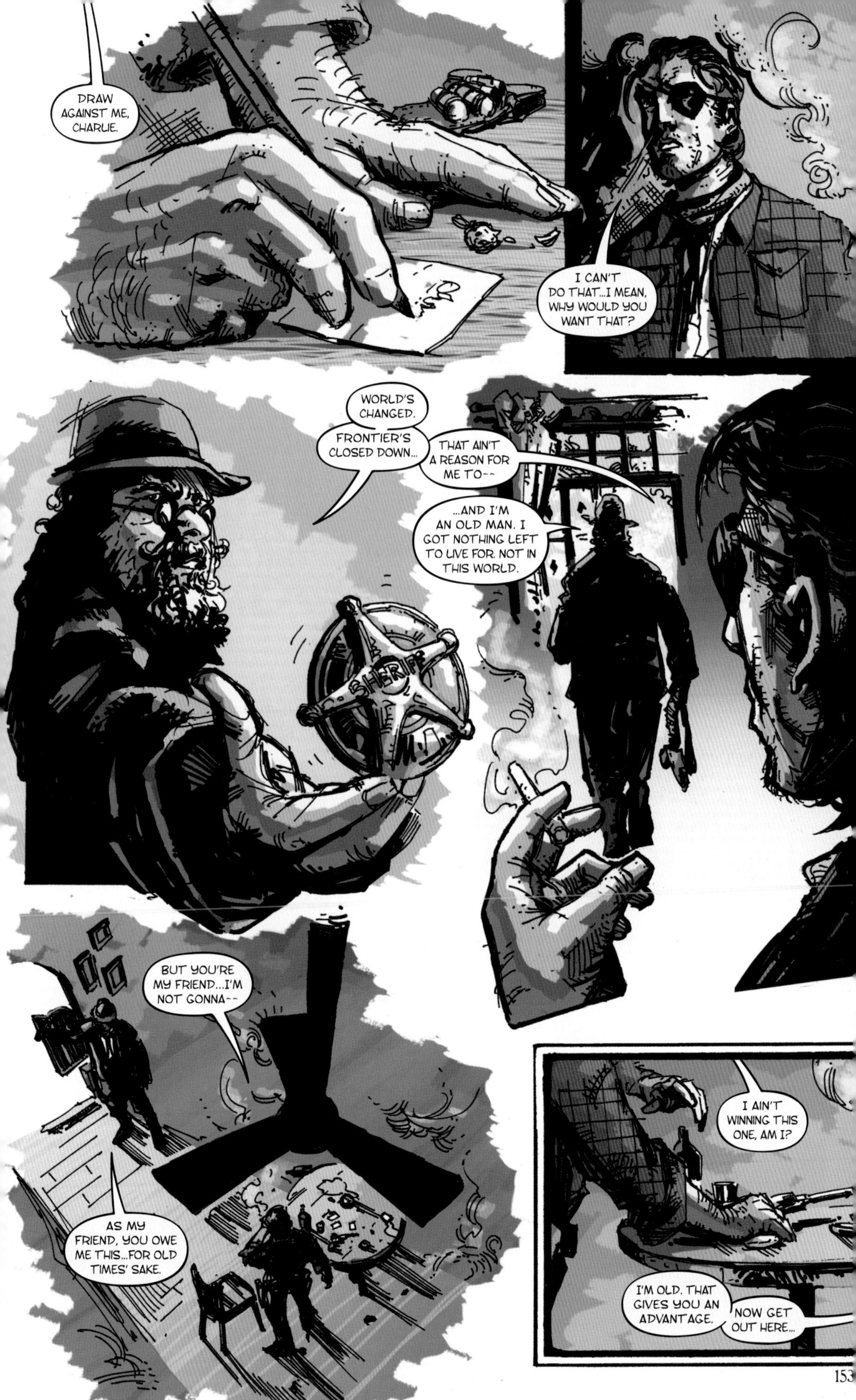
DRAW AGAINST ME, CHARLIE.
I CAN'T DO THAT...I MEAN, WHY WOULD YOU WANT THAT?
WORLD'S CHANGED.
FRONTIER'S CLOSED DOWN...
THAT AIN'T A REASON FOR ME TO--
...AND I'M AN OLD MAN. I GOT NOTHING LEFT TO LIVE FOR. NOT IN THIS WORLD.
SHERIFF
BUT YOU'RE MY FRIEND...I'M NOT GONNA--
AS MY FRIEND, YOU OWE ME THIS...FOR OLD TIMES' SAKE.
I AIN'T WINNING THIS ONE, AM I?
I'M OLD. THAT GIVES YOU AN ADVANTAGE.
NOW GET OUT HERE...

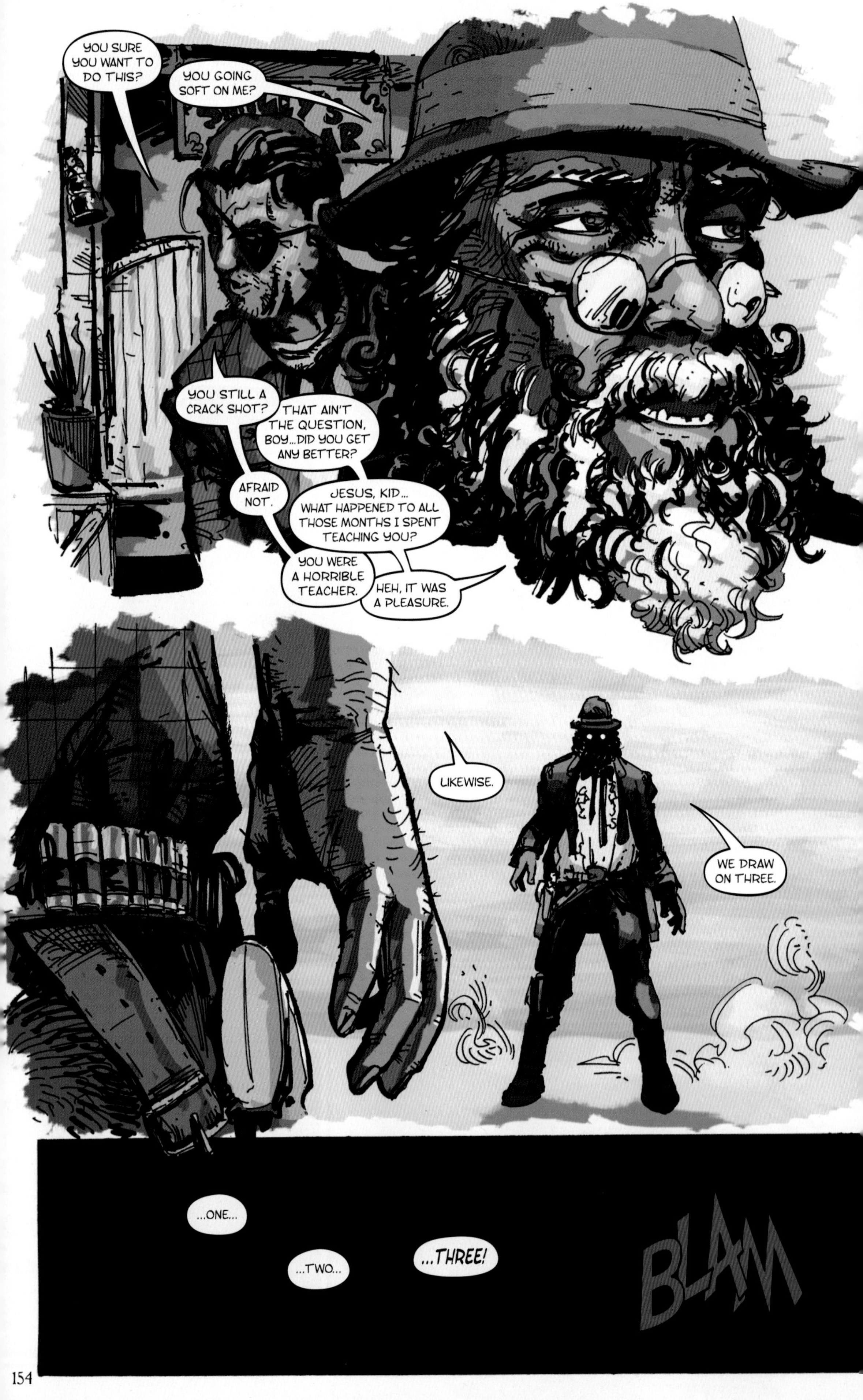

YOU SURE YOU WANT TO DO THIS?
YOU GOING SOFT ON ME?
YOU STILL A CRACK SHOT?
THAT AIN'T THE QUESTION, BOY...DID YOU GET ANY BETTER?
AFRAID NOT.
JESUS, KID... WHAT HAPPENED TO ALL THOSE MONTHS I SPENT TEACHING YOU?
YOU WERE A HORRIBLE TEACHER.
HEH, IT WAS A PLEASURE.
LIKEWISE.
WE DRAW ON THREE.
...ONE...
...TWO...
...THREE!
BLAM

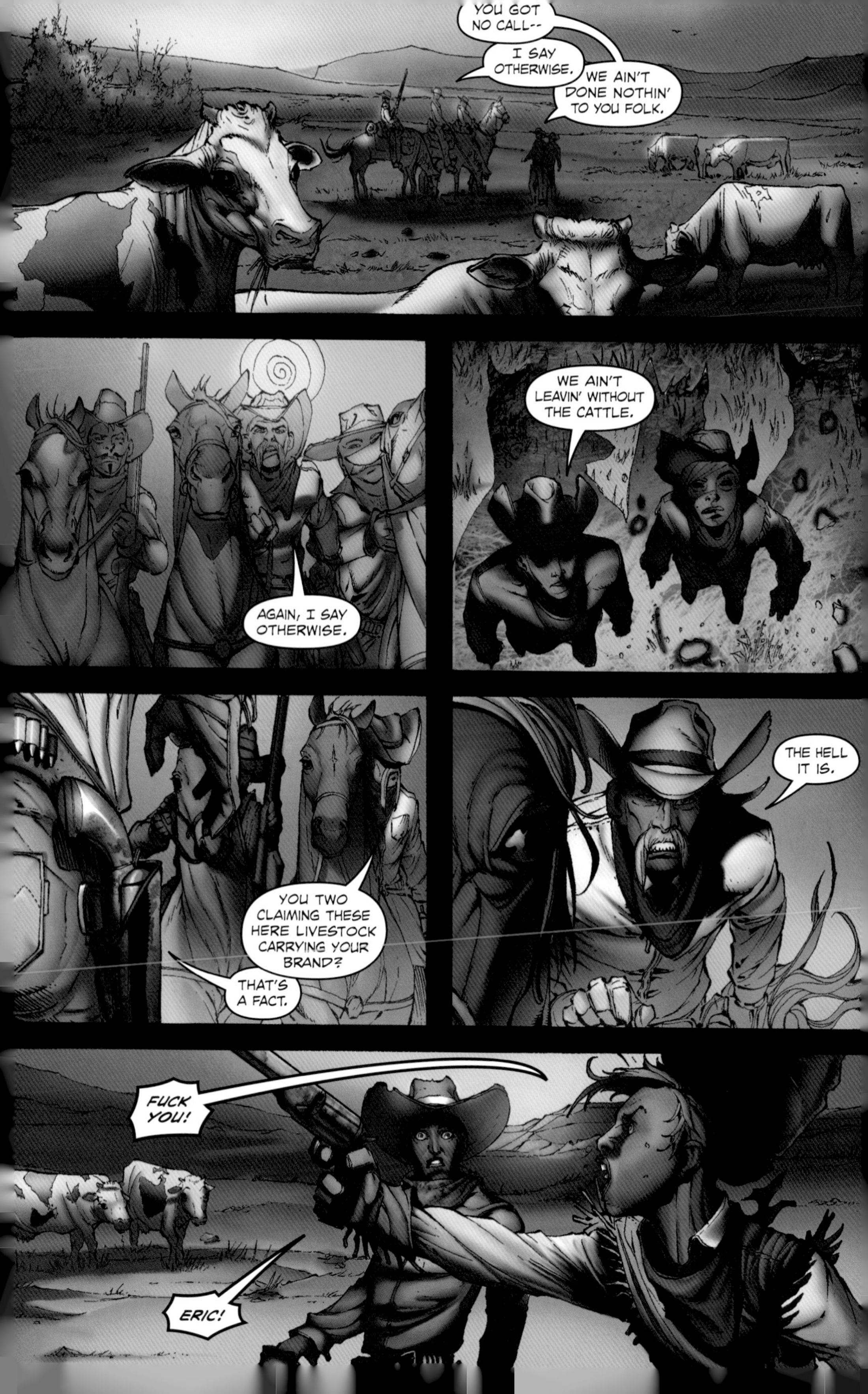
YOU GOT NO CALL--
I SAY OTHERWISE.
WE AIN'T DONE NOTHIN' TO YOU FOLK.
AGAIN, I SAY OTHERWISE.
WE AIN'T LEAVIN' WITHOUT THE CATTLE.
YOU TWO CLAIMING THESE HERE LIVESTOCK CARRYING YOUR BRAND?
THAT'S A FACT.
THE HELL IT IS.
FUCK YOU!
ERIC!

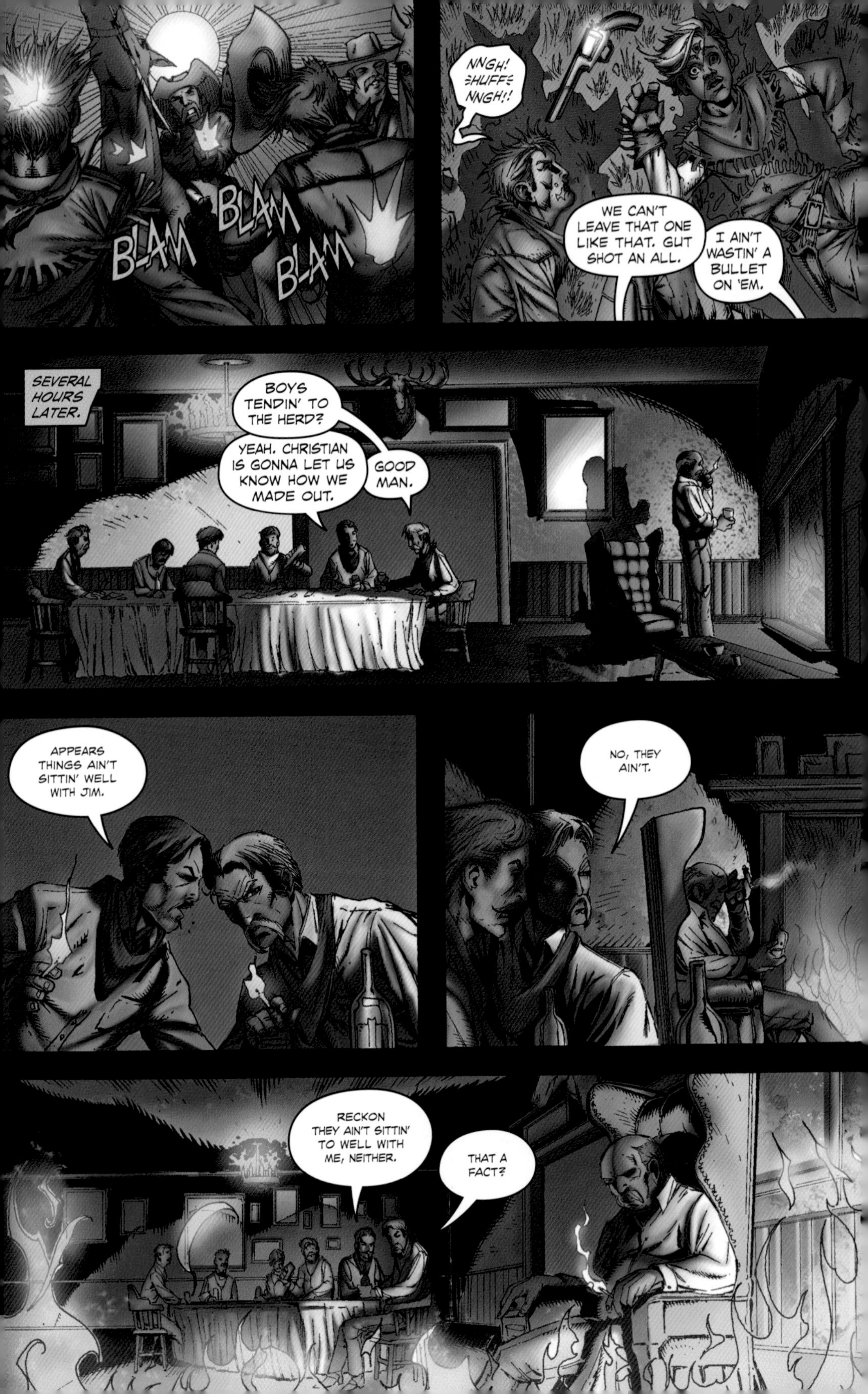
BLAM
BLAM
BLAM
NNGH! SHUFF! NNGH!!
WE CAN'T LEAVE THAT ONE LIKE THAT. GUT SHOT AN ALL.
I AIN'T WASTIN' A BULLET ON 'EM.
SEVERAL HOURS LATER.
BOYS TENDIN' TO THE HERD?
YEAH. CHRISTIAN IS GONNA LET US KNOW HOW WE MADE OUT.
GOOD MAN.
APPEARS THINGS AIN'T SITTIN' WELL WITH JIM.
NO, THEY AIN'T.
RECKON THEY AIN'T SITTIN' TO WELL WITH ME, NEITHER.
THAT A FACT?

WELL, SHUT THE FUCK UP ABOUT IT.

IT AIN'T YOURS TO CARRY.

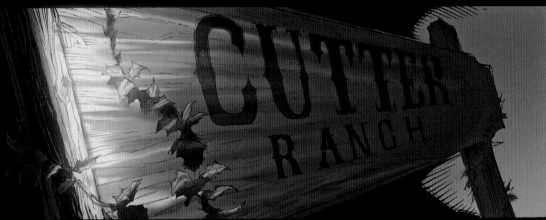

NNNNFUCK!

≥HUFF!≤
≥HUFF!≤

goddamnit...

"HEY, JIM."
JIM.
HUH?
OH. HEY, JACK.
SOMETHIN' ON YER MIND?
YOU KNOW WHAT'S ON MY MIND.
YEAH. RECKON I DO.
HOW WE GONNA MAKE IT RIGHT?

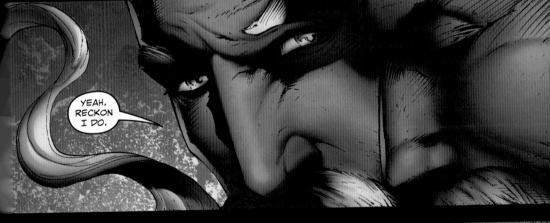

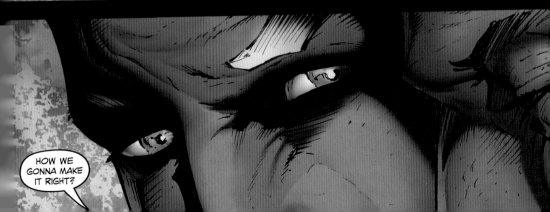

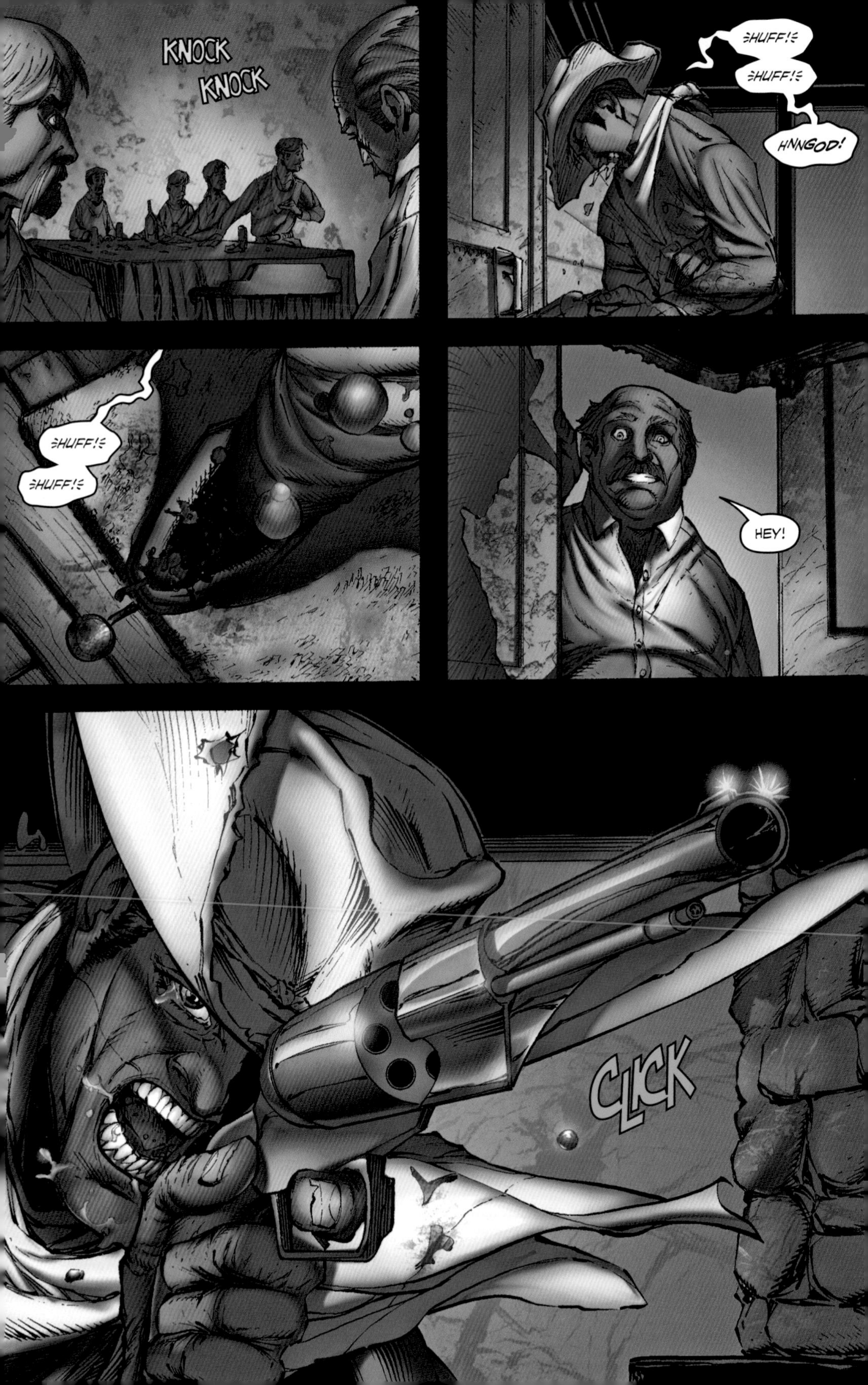
KNOCK
KNOCK
HUFF!
HUFF!
HNNGOD!
HUFF!
HUFF!
HEY!
CLICK

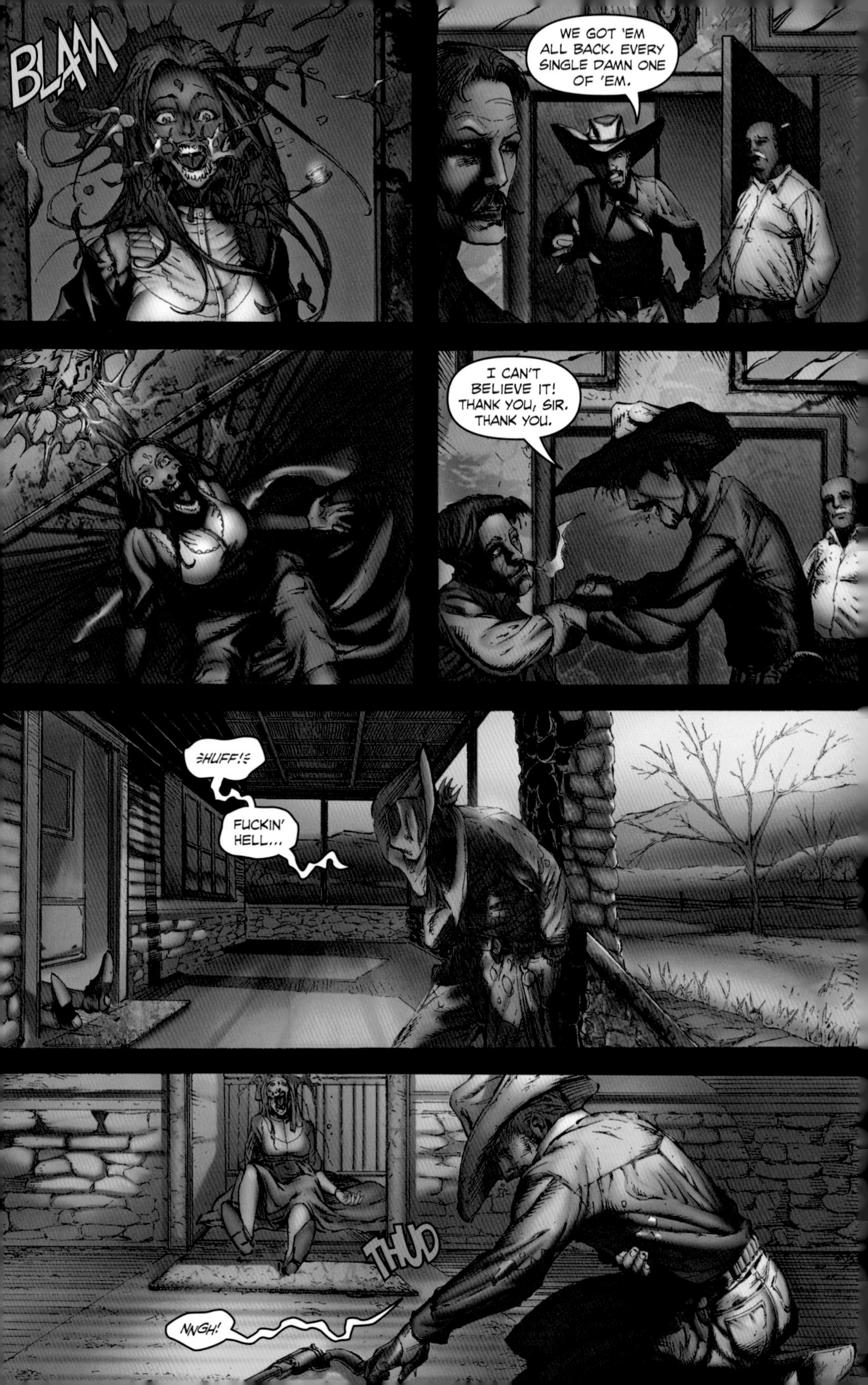
BLAM
WE GOT 'EM ALL BACK. EVERY SINGLE DAMN ONE OF 'EM.
I CAN'T BELIEVE IT! THANK YOU, SIR. THANK YOU.
HUFF!
FUCKIN' HELL...
THUD
NNGH!

Y'ALL FETCH A GLASS AN POUR IT TALL.

"I'M NOT MUCH FOR SPEAKING."

THUNK

OOPH!

NOT WITHOUT A FEW IN ME, ANYHOW. BUT I'M FIXIN' TO TRY.

"WE HAD OUR SHARE OF HARD TIMES."

CLOSE... NNGH... 'NUFF...

"THE WORST OF IT COMIN' MORE RECENT."

BUT WE'VE BEEN BLESSED TO HAVE ONE MAN TO HELP US THROUGH IT ALL.

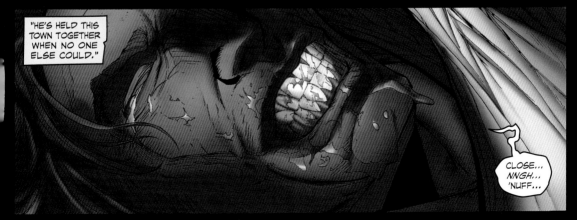

"HE'S HELD THIS TOWN TOGETHER WHEN NO ONE ELSE COULD."

CLOSE... NNGH... 'NUFF...

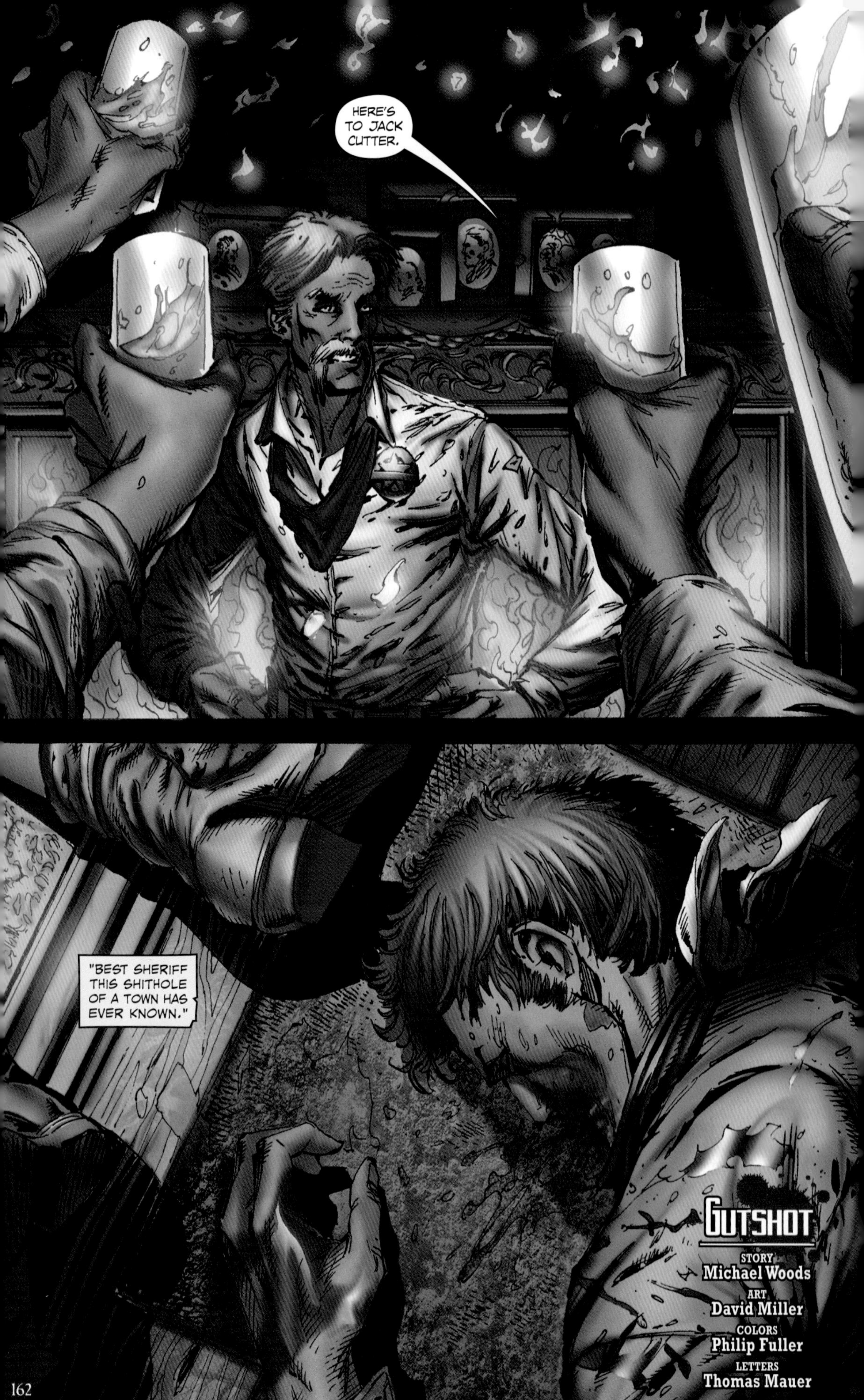
HERE'S TO JACK CUTTER.
"BEST SHERIFF THIS SHITHOLE OF A TOWN HAS EVER KNOWN."
GUTSHOT
STORY
Michael Woods
ART
David Miller
COLORS
Philip Fuller
LETTERS
Thomas Mauer

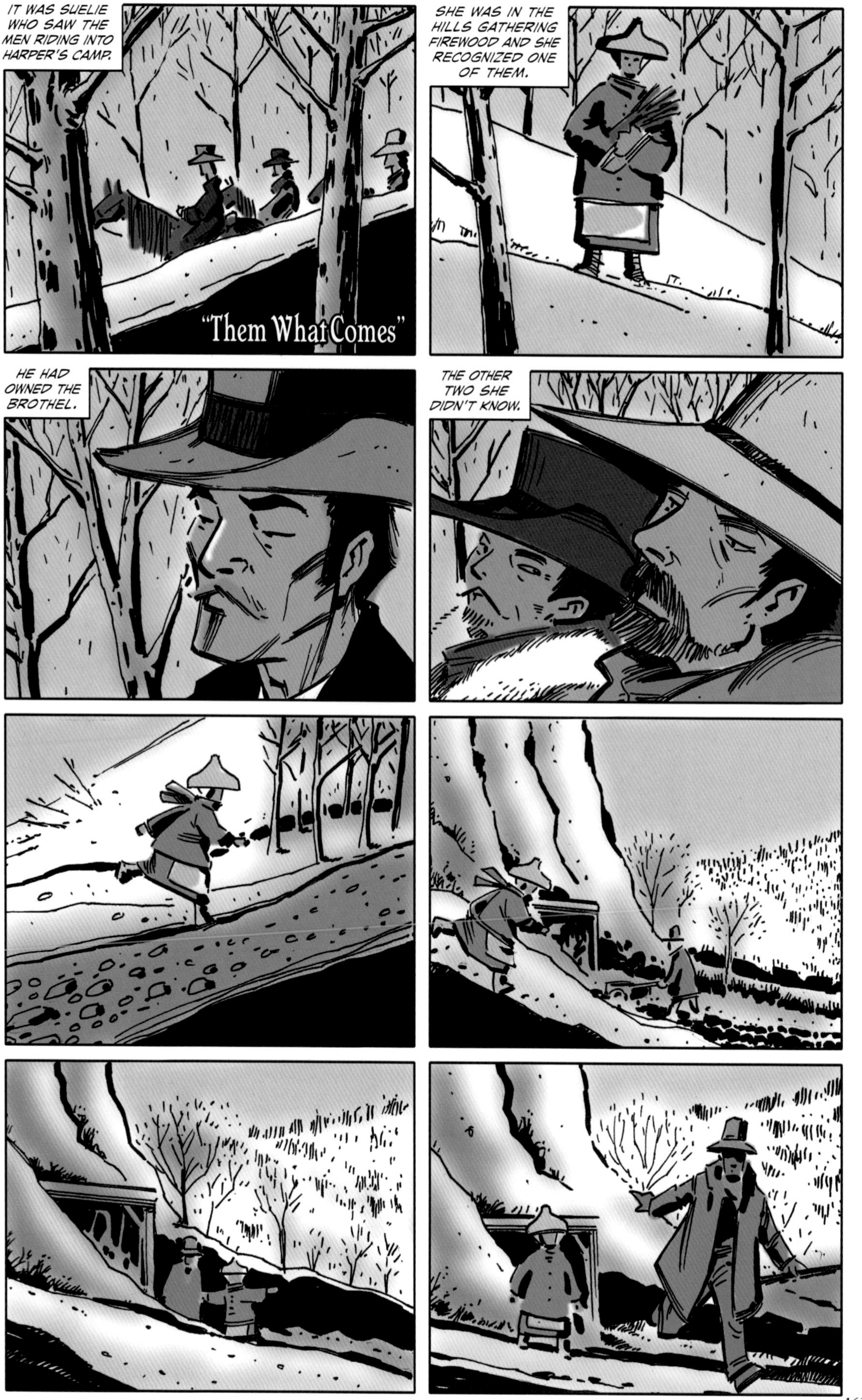
IT WAS SUELIE WHO SAW THE MEN RIDING INTO HARPER'S CAMP.
"Them What Comes"
SHE WAS IN THE HILLS GATHERING FIREWOOD AND SHE RECOGNIZED ONE OF THEM.
HE HAD OWNED THE BROTHEL.
THE OTHER TWO SHE DIDN'T KNOW.

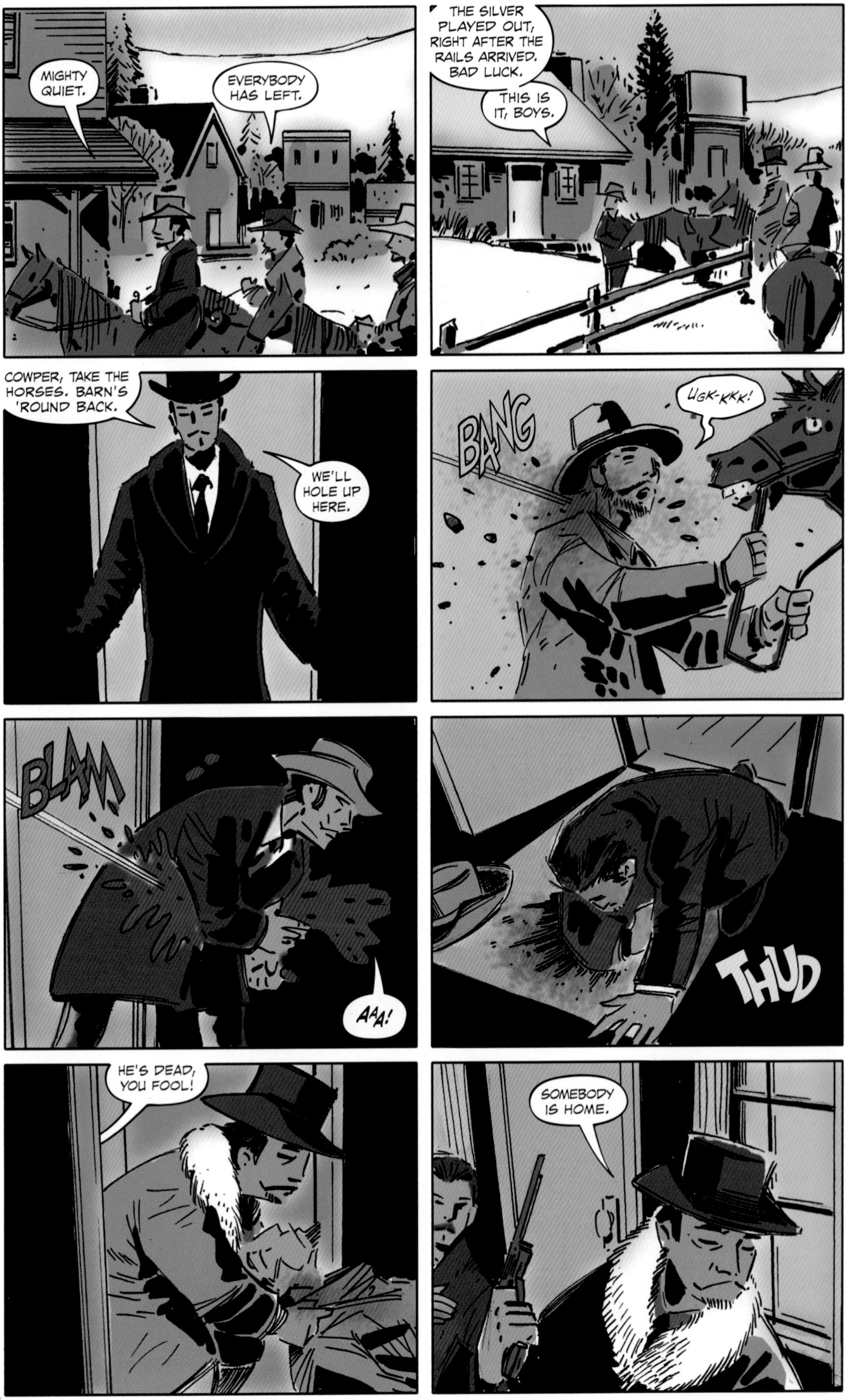
MIGHTY QUIET.
EVERYBODY HAS LEFT.
THE SILVER PLAYED OUT, RIGHT AFTER THE RAILS ARRIVED. BAD LUCK.
THIS IS IT, BOYS.
COWPER, TAKE THE HORSES. BARN'S 'ROUND BACK.
WE'LL HOLE UP HERE.
BANG
UGK-KKK!
BLAM
AAA!
THUD
HE'S DEAD, YOU FOOL!
SOMEBODY IS HOME.

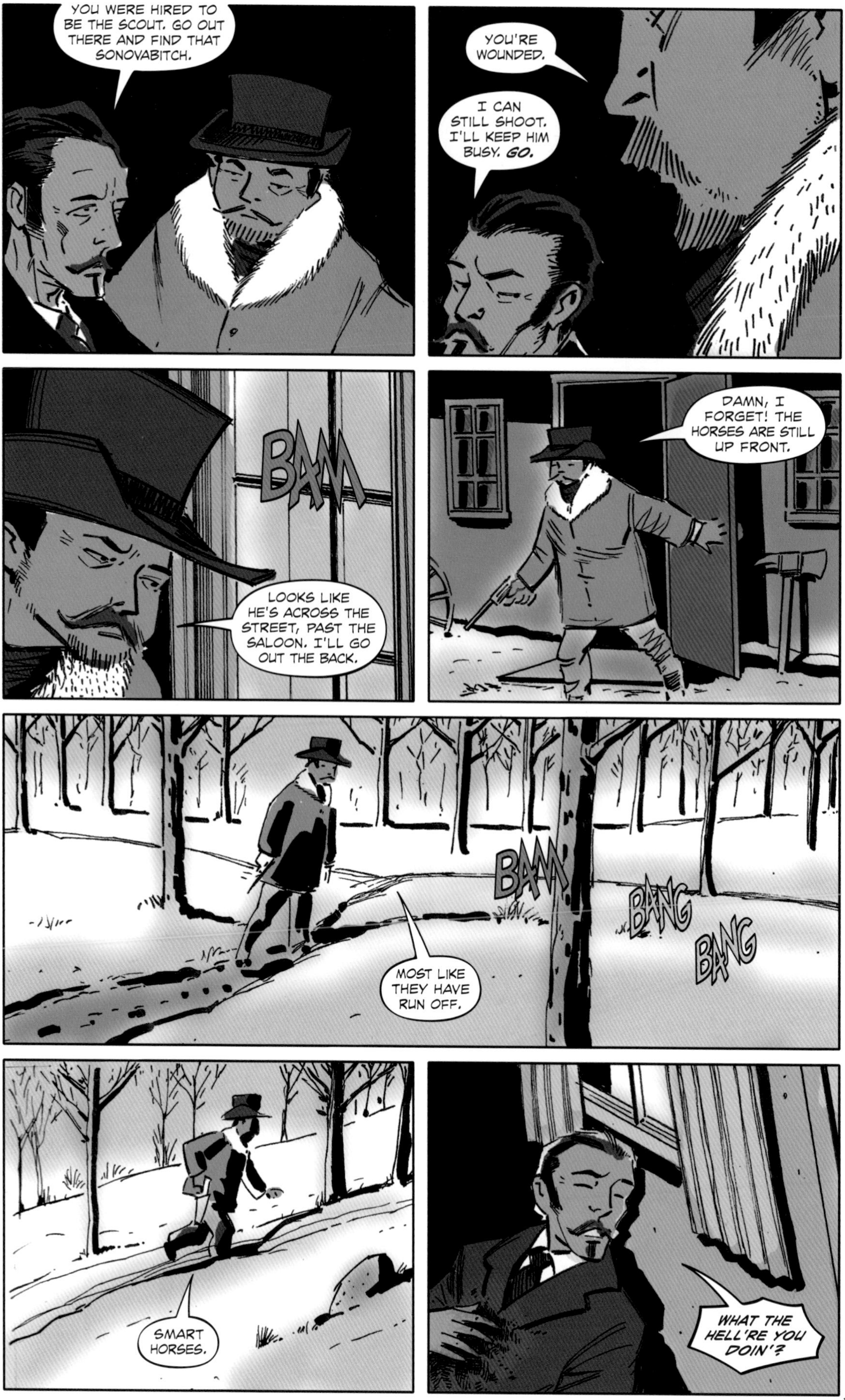
YOU WERE HIRED TO BE THE SCOUT. GO OUT THERE AND FIND THAT SONOVABITCH.
YOU'RE WOUNDED.
I CAN STILL SHOOT. I'LL KEEP HIM BUSY. GO.
BAM
LOOKS LIKE HE'S ACROSS THE STREET, PAST THE SALOON. I'LL GO OUT THE BACK.
DAMN, I FORGET! THE HORSES ARE STILL UP FRONT.
BAM
BANG
BANG
MOST LIKE THEY HAVE RUN OFF.
SMART HORSES.
WHAT THE HELL'RE YOU DOIN'?

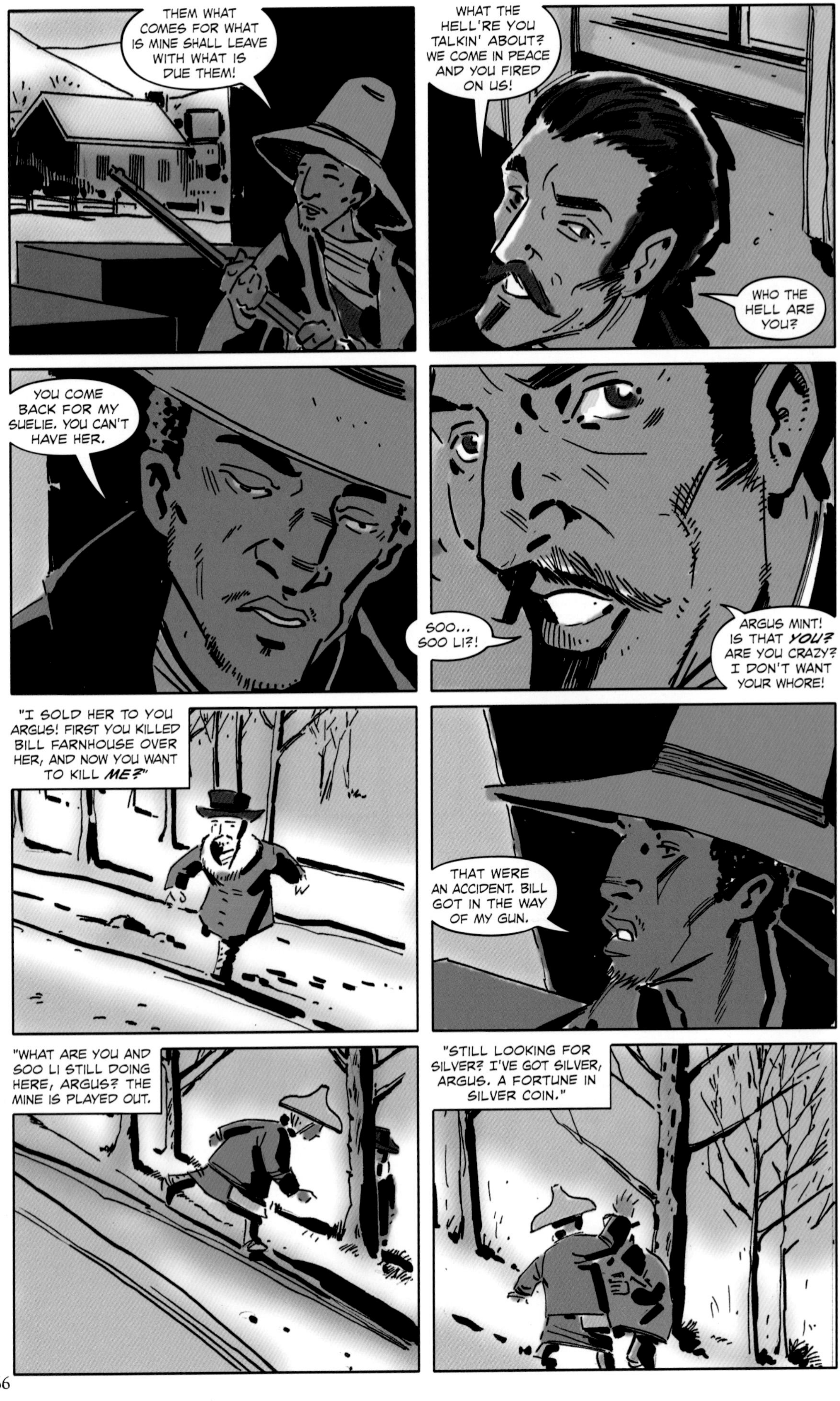
THEM WHAT COMES FOR WHAT IS MINE SHALL LEAVE WITH WHAT IS DUE THEM!
WHAT THE HELL'RE YOU TALKIN' ABOUT? WE COME IN PEACE AND YOU FIRED ON US!
WHO THE HELL ARE YOU?
YOU COME BACK FOR MY SUELIE. YOU CAN'T HAVE HER.
SOO... SOO LI?!
ARGUS MINT! IS THAT *YOU?* ARE YOU CRAZY? I DON'T WANT YOUR WHORE!
"I SOLD HER TO YOU ARGUS! FIRST YOU KILLED BILL FARNHOUSE OVER HER, AND NOW YOU WANT TO KILL *ME?*"
THAT WERE AN ACCIDENT. BILL GOT IN THE WAY OF MY GUN.
"WHAT ARE YOU AND SOO LI STILL DOING HERE, ARGUS? THE MINE IS PLAYED OUT.
"STILL LOOKING FOR SILVER? I'VE GOT SILVER, ARGUS. A FORTUNE IN SILVER COIN."

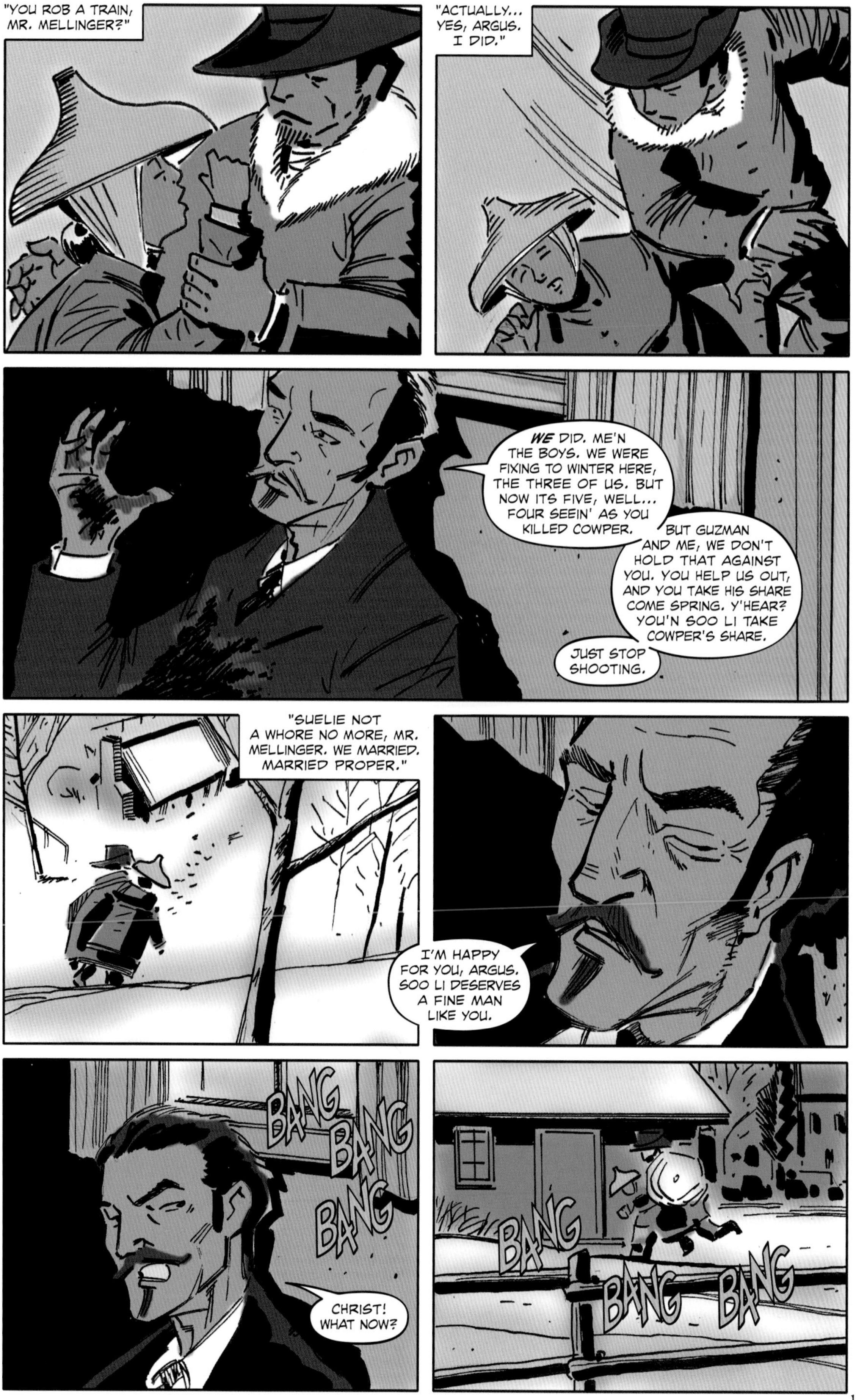
"YOU ROB A TRAIN, MR. MELLINGER?"
"ACTUALLY... YES, ARGUS. I DID."
WE DID. ME'N THE BOYS. WE WERE FIXING TO WINTER HERE, THE THREE OF US. BUT NOW ITS FIVE, WELL... FOUR SEEIN' AS YOU KILLED COWPER.
BUT GUZMAN AND ME, WE DON'T HOLD THAT AGAINST YOU. YOU HELP US OUT, AND YOU TAKE HIS SHARE COME SPRING. Y'HEAR? YOU'N SOO LI TAKE COWPER'S SHARE.
JUST STOP SHOOTING.
"SUELIE NOT A WHORE NO MORE, MR. MELLINGER. WE MARRIED. MARRIED PROPER."
I'M HAPPY FOR YOU, ARGUS. SOO LI DESERVES A FINE MAN LIKE YOU.
BANG
BANG
BANG
CHRIST! WHAT NOW?
BANG
BANG
BANG

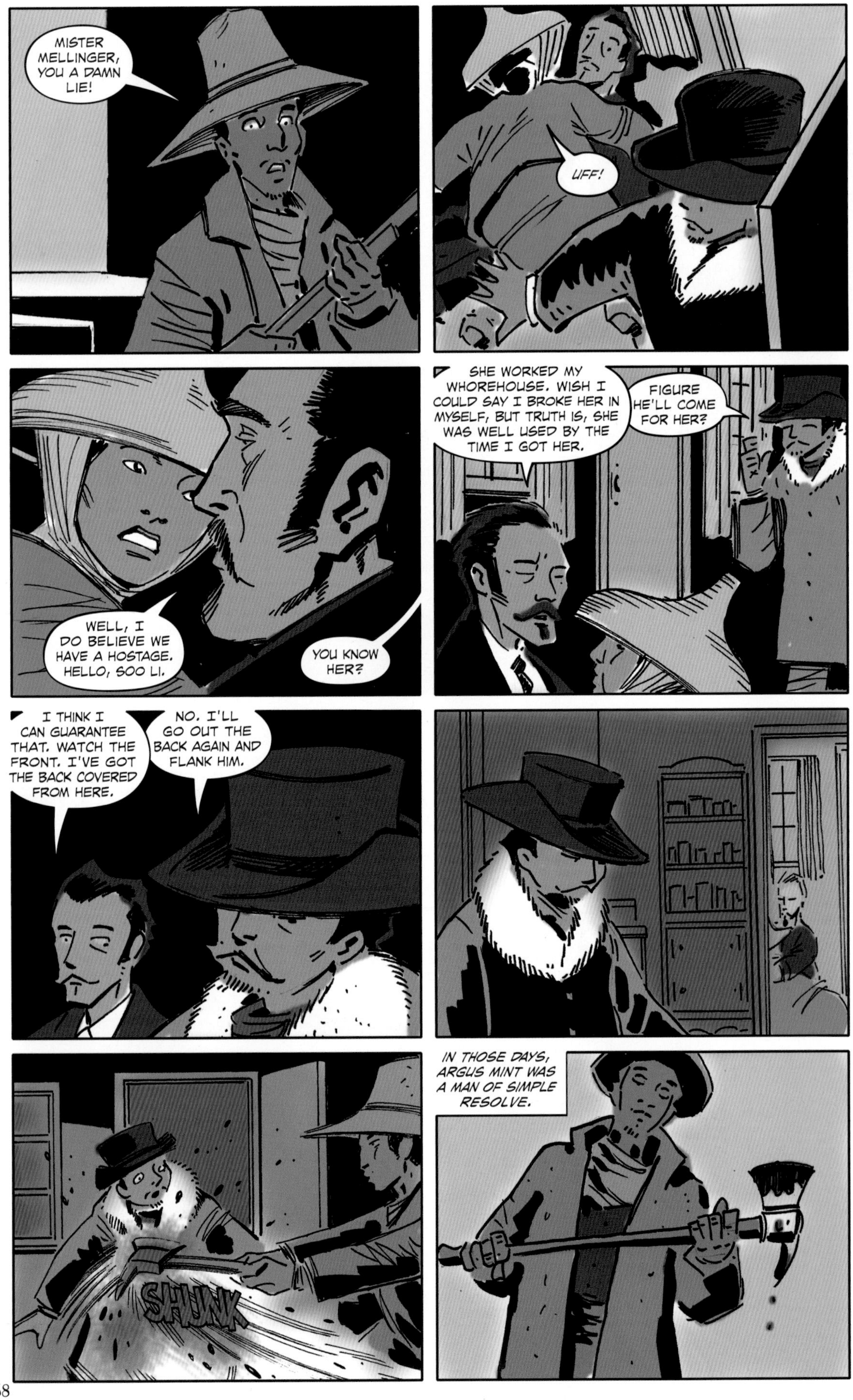
MISTER MELLINGER, YOU A DAMN LIE!
UFF!
WELL, I DO BELIEVE WE HAVE A HOSTAGE. HELLO, SOO LI.
YOU KNOW HER?
SHE WORKED MY WHOREHOUSE. WISH I COULD SAY I BROKE HER IN MYSELF, BUT TRUTH IS, SHE WAS WELL USED BY THE TIME I GOT HER.
FIGURE HE'LL COME FOR HER?
I THINK I CAN GUARANTEE THAT. WATCH THE FRONT. I'VE GOT THE BACK COVERED FROM HERE.
NO. I'LL GO OUT THE BACK AGAIN AND FLANK HIM.
SHUNK
IN THOSE DAYS, ARGUS MINT WAS A MAN OF SIMPLE RESOLVE.

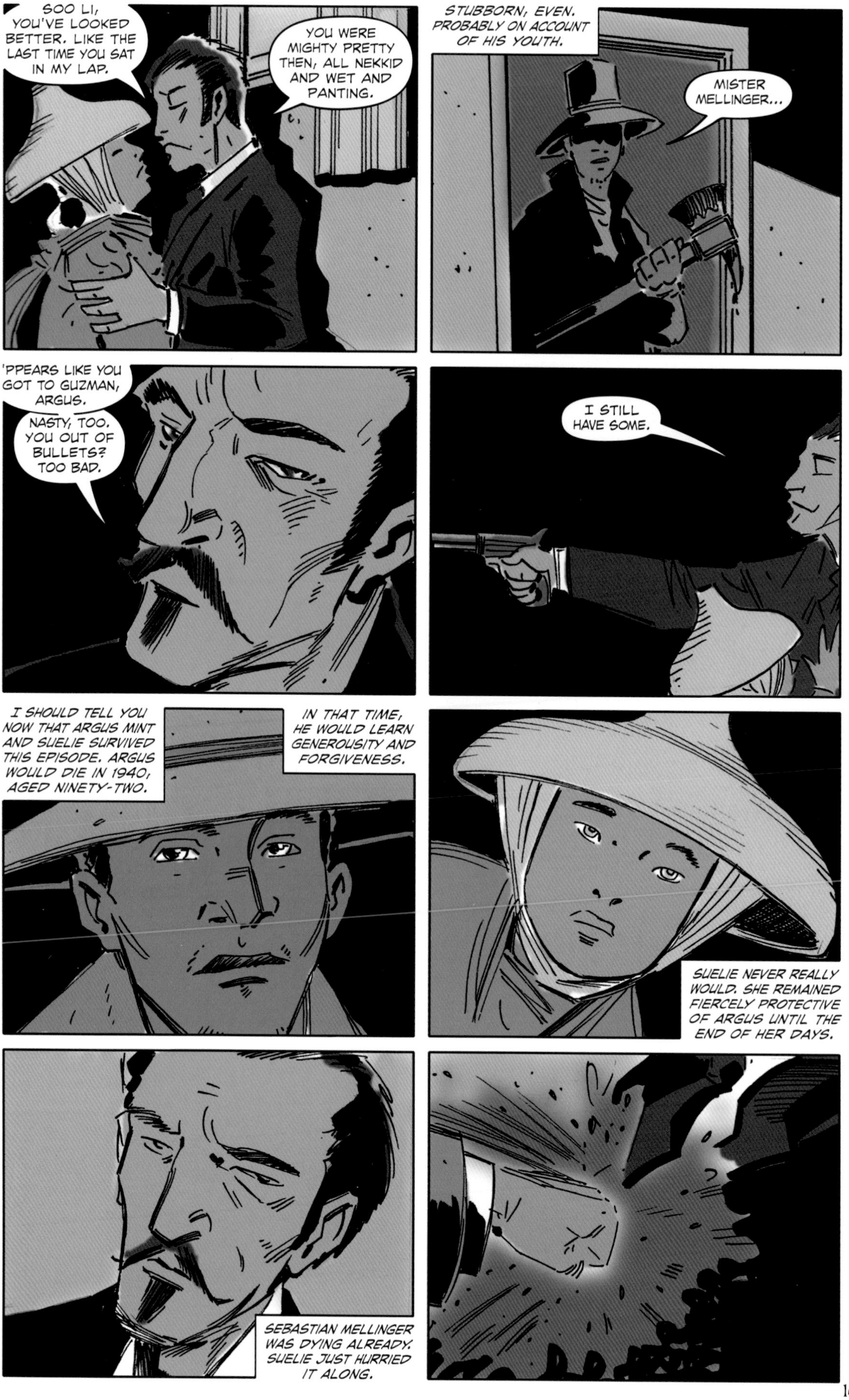
SOO LI, YOU'VE LOOKED BETTER. LIKE THE LAST TIME YOU SAT IN MY LAP.
YOU WERE MIGHTY PRETTY THEN, ALL NEKKID AND WET AND PANTING.
STUBBORN, EVEN. PROBABLY ON ACCOUNT OF HIS YOUTH.
MISTER MELLINGER...
'PPEARS LIKE YOU GOT TO GUZMAN, ARGUS.
NASTY, TOO. YOU OUT OF BULLETS? TOO BAD.
I STILL HAVE SOME.
I SHOULD TELL YOU NOW THAT ARGUS MINT AND SUELIE SURVIVED THIS EPISODE. ARGUS WOULD DIE IN 1940, AGED NINETY-TWO.
IN THAT TIME, HE WOULD LEARN GENEROUSITY AND FORGIVENESS.
SUELIE NEVER REALLY WOULD. SHE REMAINED FIERCELY PROTECTIVE OF ARGUS UNTIL THE END OF HER DAYS.
SEBASTIAN MELLINGER WAS DYING ALREADY. SUELIE JUST HURRIED IT ALONG.

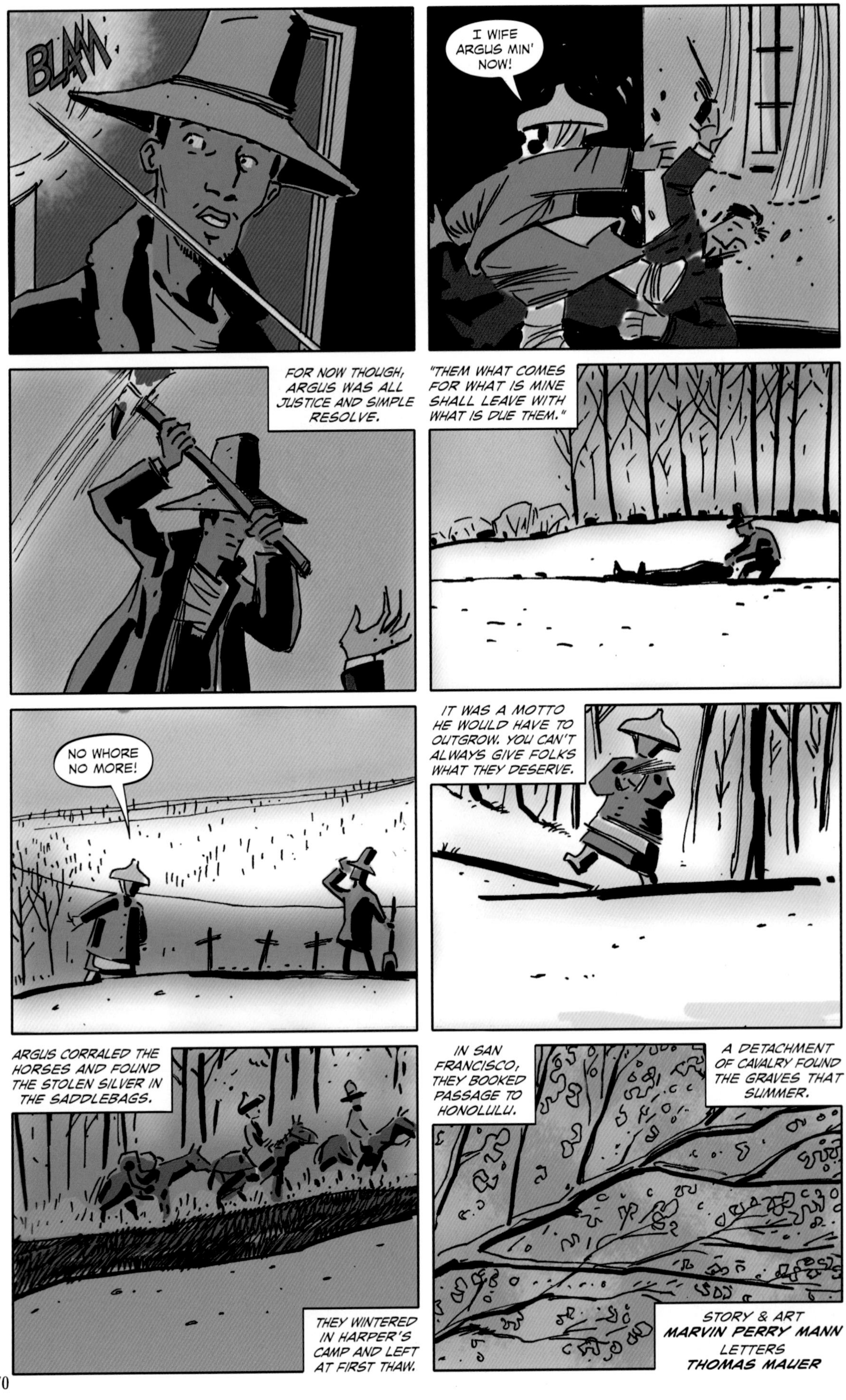
BLAM
I WIFE ARGUS MIN' NOW!
FOR NOW THOUGH, ARGUS WAS ALL JUSTICE AND SIMPLE RESOLVE.
"THEM WHAT COMES FOR WHAT IS MINE SHALL LEAVE WITH WHAT IS DUE THEM."
NO WHORE NO MORE!
IT WAS A MOTTO HE WOULD HAVE TO OUTGROW. YOU CAN'T ALWAYS GIVE FOLKS WHAT THEY DESERVE.
ARGUS CORRALED THE HORSES AND FOUND THE STOLEN SILVER IN THE SADDLEBAGS.
THEY WINTERED IN HARPER'S CAMP AND LEFT AT FIRST THAW.
IN SAN FRANCISCO, THEY BOOKED PASSAGE TO HONOLULU.
A DETACHMENT OF CAVALRY FOUND THE GRAVES THAT SUMMER.
STORY & ART
MARVIN PERRY MANN
LETTERS
THOMAS MAUER

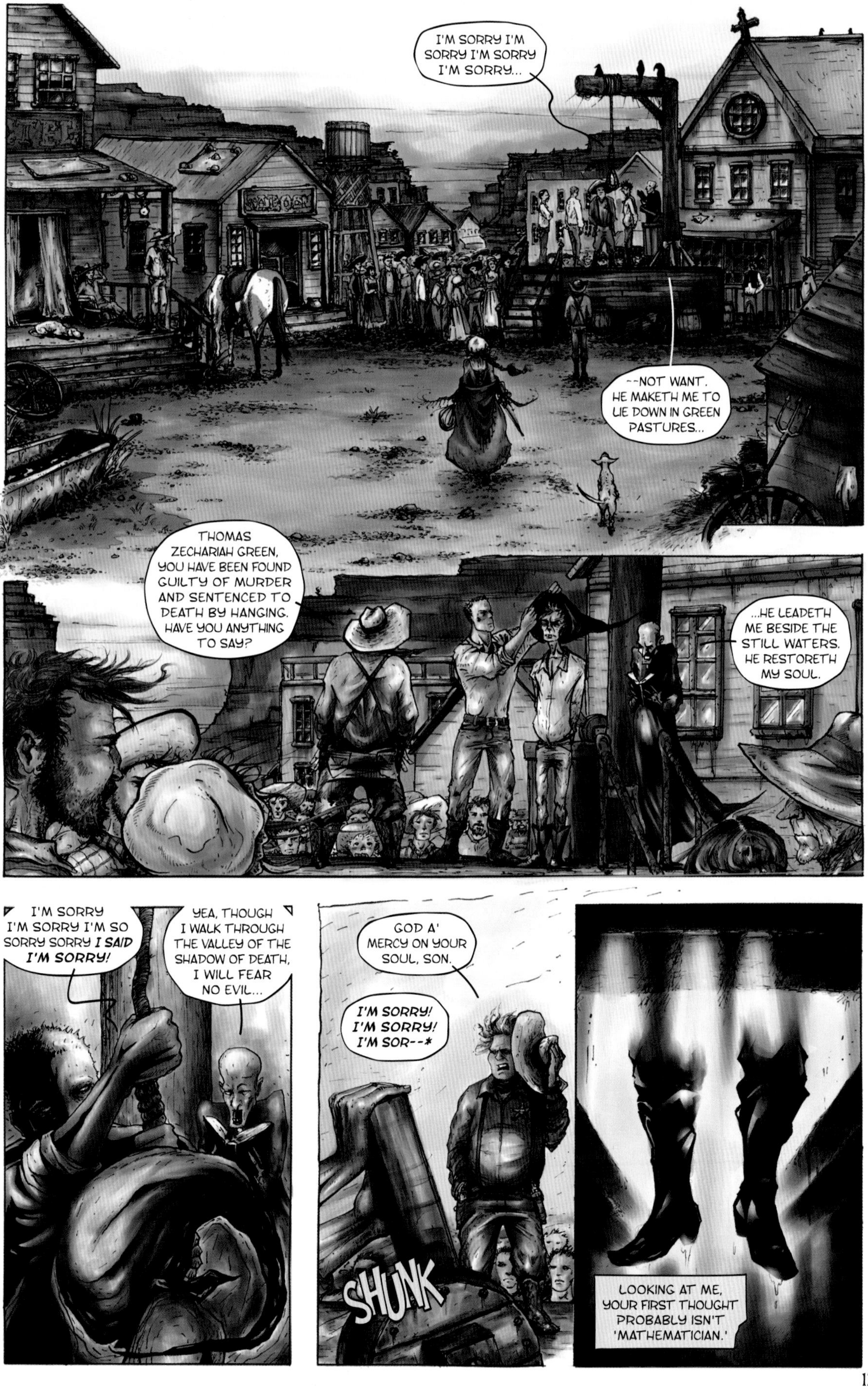

I'M SORRY I'M SORRY I'M SORRY I'M SORRY...
--NOT WANT. HE MAKETH ME TO LIE DOWN IN GREEN PASTURES...
THOMAS ZECHARIAH GREEN, YOU HAVE BEEN FOUND GUILTY OF MURDER AND SENTENCED TO DEATH BY HANGING. HAVE YOU ANYTHING TO SAY?
...HE LEADETH ME BESIDE THE STILL WATERS. HE RESTORETH MY SOUL.
I'M SORRY I'M SORRY I'M SO SORRY SORRY *I SAID I'M SORRY!*
YEA, THOUGH I WALK THROUGH THE VALLEY OF THE SHADOW OF DEATH, I WILL FEAR NO EVIL...
GOD A' MERCY ON YOUR SOUL, SON.
*I'M SORRY! I'M SORRY! I'M SOR--**
SHUNK
LOOKING AT ME, YOUR FIRST THOUGHT PROBABLY ISN'T 'MATHEMATICIAN.'

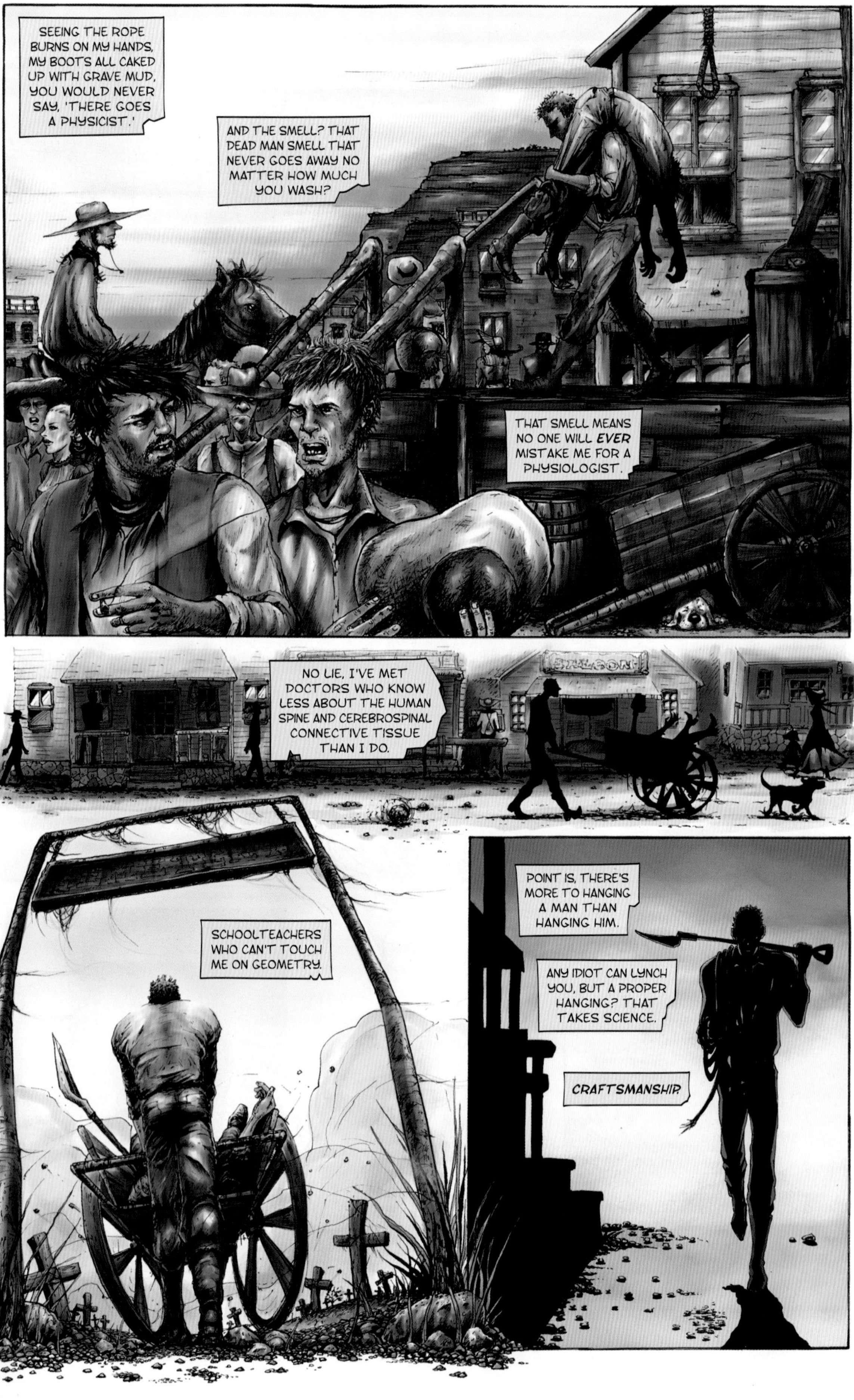
SEEING THE ROPE BURNS ON MY HANDS, MY BOOTS ALL CAKED UP WITH GRAVE MUD, YOU WOULD NEVER SAY, 'THERE GOES A PHYSICIST.'
AND THE SMELL? THAT DEAD MAN SMELL THAT NEVER GOES AWAY NO MATTER HOW MUCH YOU WASH?
THAT SMELL MEANS NO ONE WILL *EVER* MISTAKE ME FOR A PHYSIOLOGIST.
NO LIE, I'VE MET DOCTORS WHO KNOW LESS ABOUT THE HUMAN SPINE AND CEREBROSPINAL CONNECTIVE TISSUE THAN I DO.
SCHOOLTEACHERS WHO CAN'T TOUCH ME ON GEOMETRY.
POINT IS, THERE'S MORE TO HANGING A MAN THAN HANGING HIM.
ANY IDIOT CAN LYNCH YOU, BUT A PROPER HANGING? THAT TAKES SCIENCE.
CRAFTSMANSHIP.

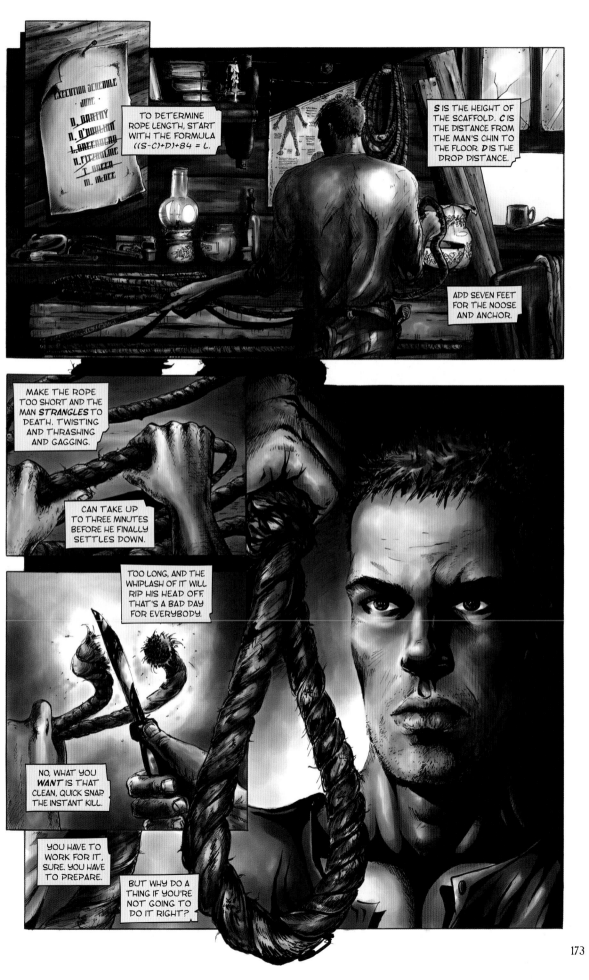

EXECUTION SCHEDULE
JUNE
D. BARTHY
R. O'DONOHUE
L. GREENBERG
M. FITZHOLME
T. GREER
M. McGEE

TO DETERMINE ROPE LENGTH, START WITH THE FORMULA $((S-C)+D)+84 = L.$

S IS THE HEIGHT OF THE SCAFFOLD. C IS THE DISTANCE FROM THE MAN'S CHIN TO THE FLOOR. D IS THE DROP DISTANCE.

ADD SEVEN FEET FOR THE NOOSE AND ANCHOR.

MAKE THE ROPE TOO SHORT AND THE MAN STRANGLES TO DEATH. TWISTING AND THRASHING AND GAGGING.

CAN TAKE UP TO THREE MINUTES BEFORE HE FINALLY SETTLES DOWN.

TOO LONG, AND THE WHIPLASH OF IT WILL RIP HIS HEAD OFF. THAT'S A BAD DAY FOR EVERYBODY.

NO, WHAT YOU WANT IS THAT CLEAN, QUICK SNAP. THE INSTANT KILL.

YOU HAVE TO WORK FOR IT, SURE. YOU HAVE TO PREPARE.

BUT WHY DO A THING IF YOU'RE NOT GOING TO DO IT RIGHT?

173

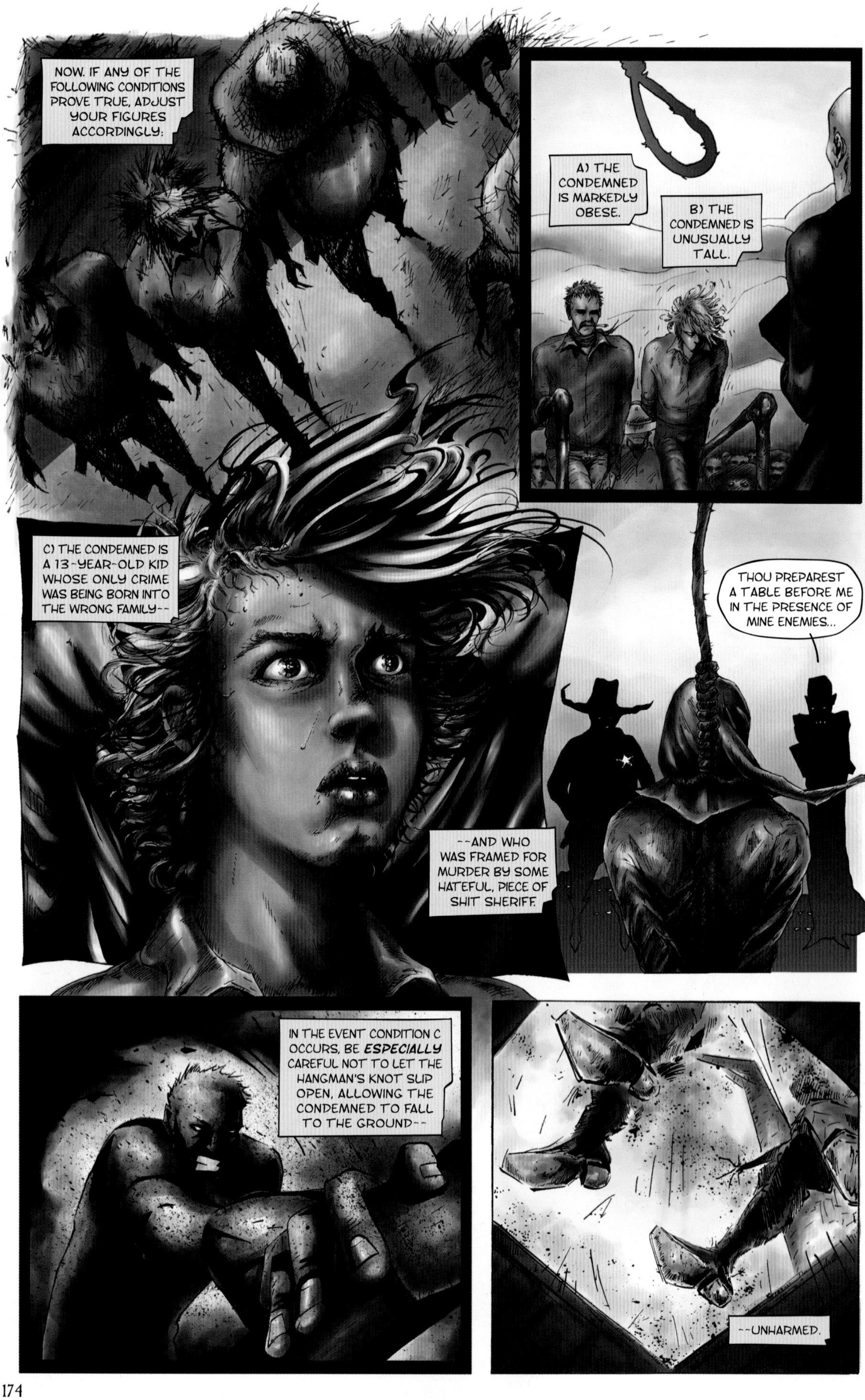
NOW. IF ANY OF THE FOLLOWING CONDITIONS PROVE TRUE, ADJUST YOUR FIGURES ACCORDINGLY:
A) THE CONDEMNED IS MARKEDLY OBESE.
B) THE CONDEMNED IS UNUSUALLY TALL.
C) THE CONDEMNED IS A 13-YEAR-OLD KID WHOSE ONLY CRIME WAS BEING BORN INTO THE WRONG FAMILY--
--AND WHO WAS FRAMED FOR MURDER BY SOME HATEFUL, PIECE OF SHIT SHERIFF.
THOU PREPAREST A TABLE BEFORE ME IN THE PRESENCE OF MINE ENEMIES...
IN THE EVENT CONDITION C OCCURS, BE ESPECIALLY CAREFUL NOT TO LET THE HANGMAN'S KNOT SLIP OPEN, ALLOWING THE CONDEMNED TO FALL TO THE GROUND--
--UNHARMED.

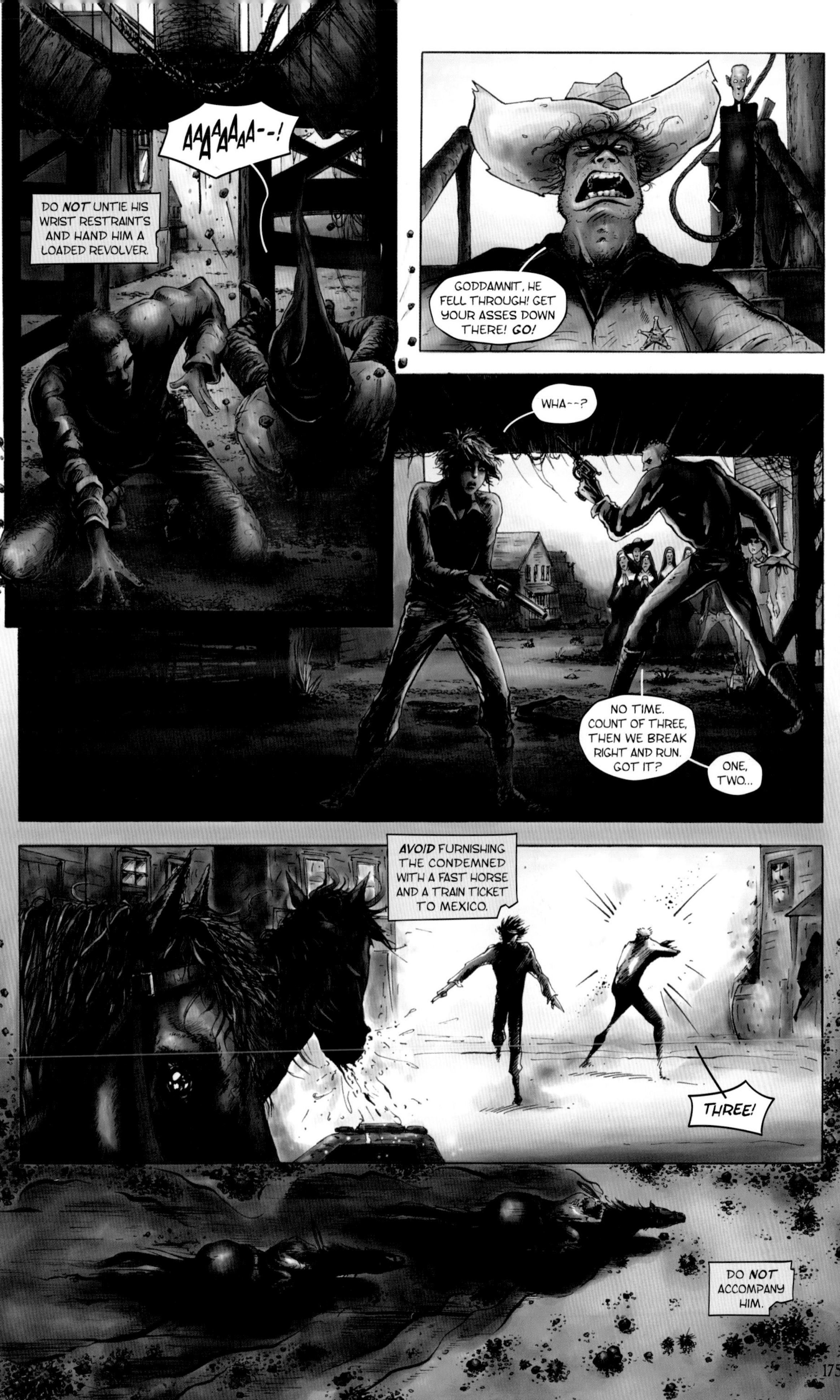
AAAAAAA--!
DO NOT UNTIE HIS WRIST RESTRAINTS AND HAND HIM A LOADED REVOLVER.
GODDAMNIT, HE FELL THROUGH! GET YOUR ASSES DOWN THERE! GO!
WHA--?
NO TIME. COUNT OF THREE, THEN WE BREAK RIGHT AND RUN. GOT IT?
ONE, TWO...
AVOID FURNISHING THE CONDEMNED WITH A FAST HORSE AND A TRAIN TICKET TO MEXICO.
THREE!
DO NOT ACCOMPANY HIM.

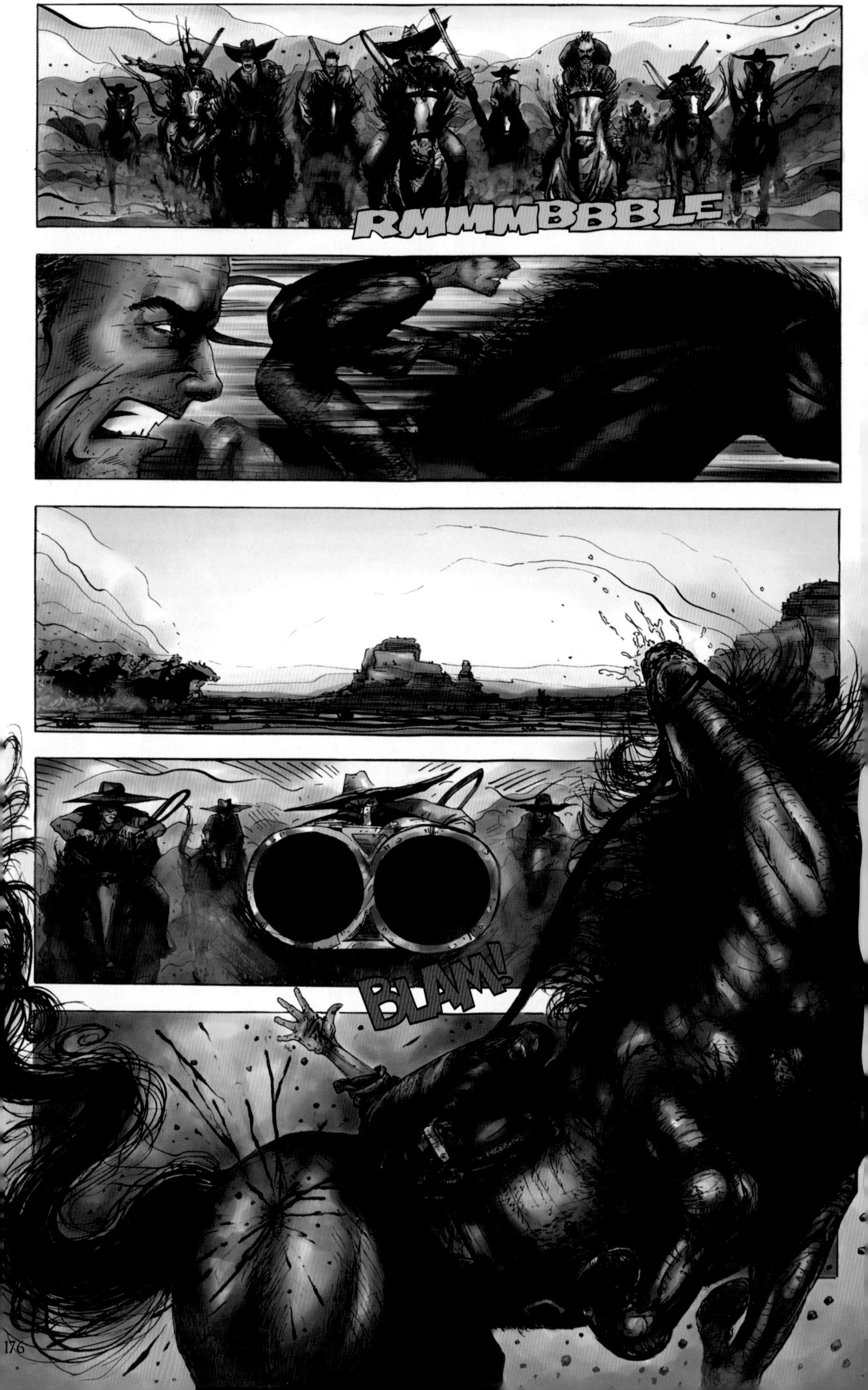
RMMMBBBLE
BLAM!

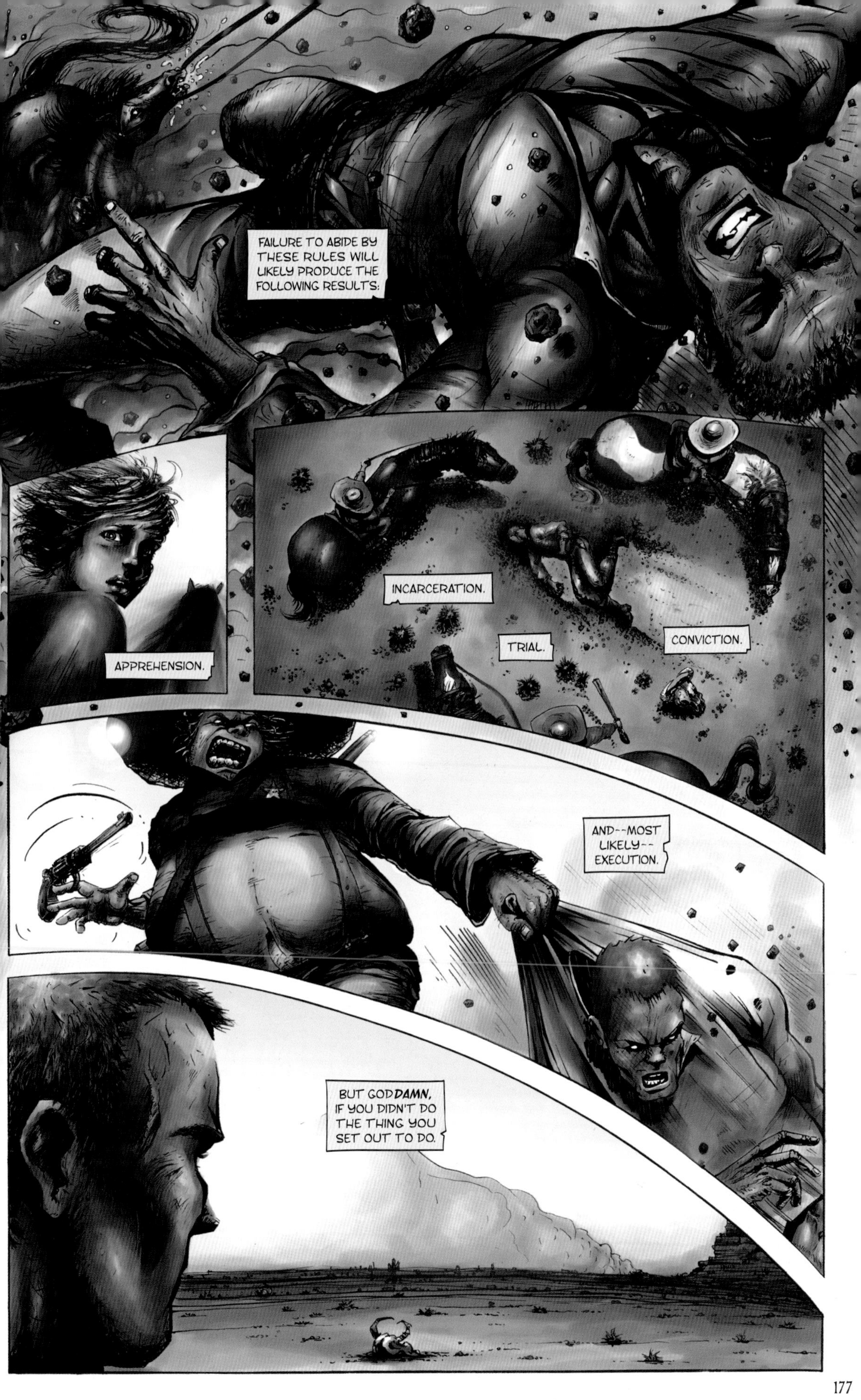
FAILURE TO ABIDE BY THESE RULES WILL LIKELY PRODUCE THE FOLLOWING RESULTS:
APPREHENSION.
INCARCERATION.
TRIAL.
CONVICTION.
AND--MOST LIKELY--EXECUTION.
BUT GOD**DAMN,** IF YOU DIDN'T DO THE THING YOU SET OUT TO DO.

SO HERE I AM.

THE NEW KID, THE *CITY* KID--HE WON'T SHOW ME HIS CALCULATIONS.

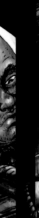

HE DOESN'T BELIEVE ME THAT I'M TRYING TO HELP.

I TELL HIM THE ROPE HE'S USING IS TOO THIN. HE JUST LAUGHS AND SAYS, *'SURE, BOSS. WHATEVER YOU SAY, BOSS.'*

OW--!

I MAY BE MAKING MY OWN ASSUMPTIONS HERE, BUT I DON'T THINK HE UNDERSTANDS HOW INVOLVED THIS WORK IS. HOW EXACTING.

MOREOVER, I DON'T BELIEVE HE GIVES A SHIT.

AND THAT'S A DAMN SHAME.

AFTER ALL, IF A MAN'S GOT NO PRIDE IN HIS WORK, WHAT HAS HE GOT?

CRAFTSMANSHIP

STORY Frank Beaton   *ART* Melike Acar   *LETTERS* Thomas Mauer

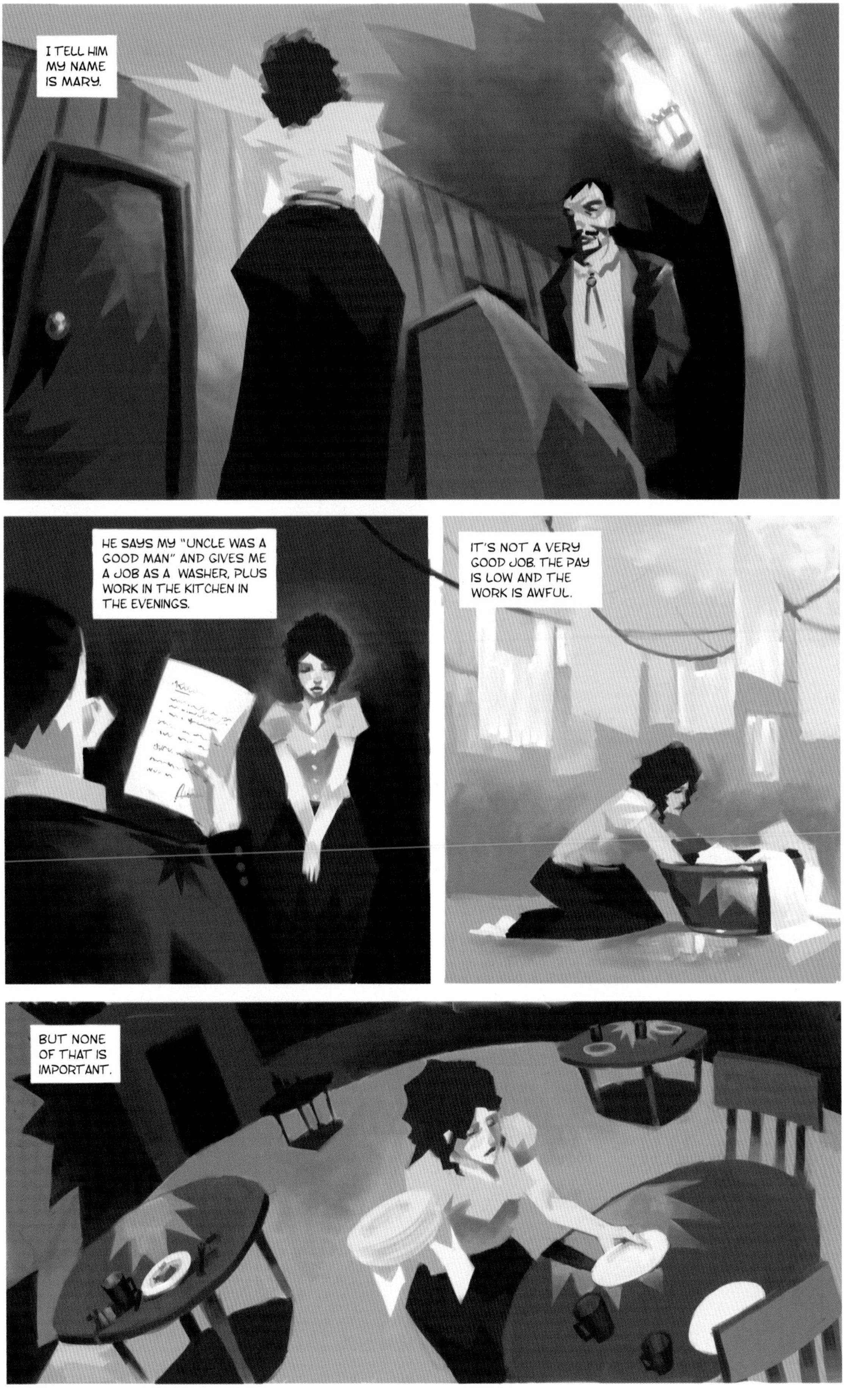
I TELL HIM MY NAME IS MARY.
HE SAYS MY "UNCLE WAS A GOOD MAN" AND GIVES ME A JOB AS A WASHER, PLUS WORK IN THE KITCHEN IN THE EVENINGS.
IT'S NOT A VERY GOOD JOB. THE PAY IS LOW AND THE WORK IS AWFUL.
BUT NONE OF THAT IS IMPORTANT.

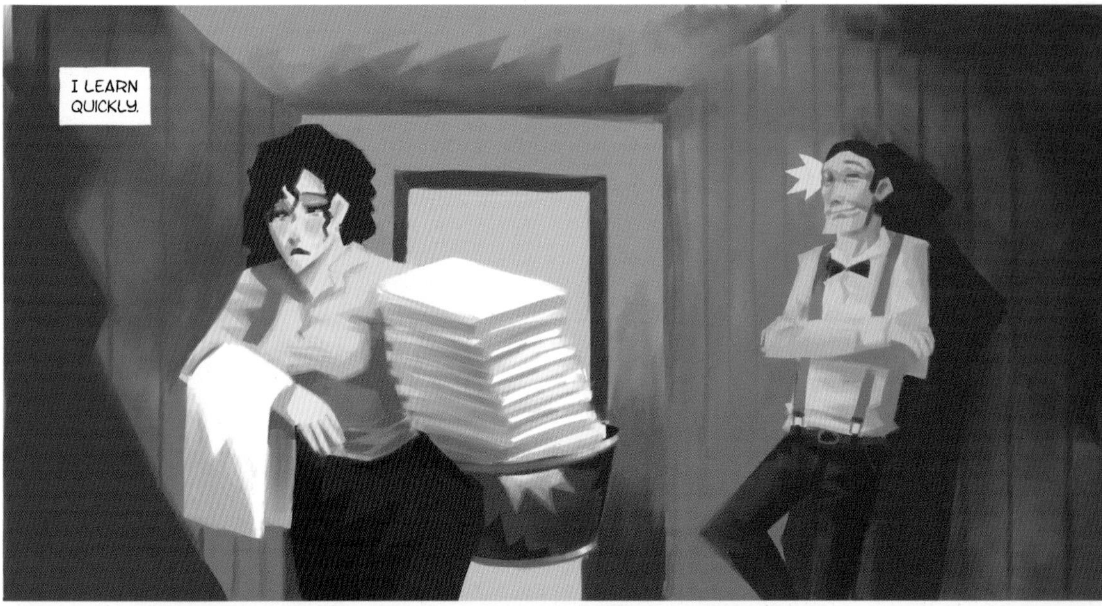
I LEARN QUICKLY.

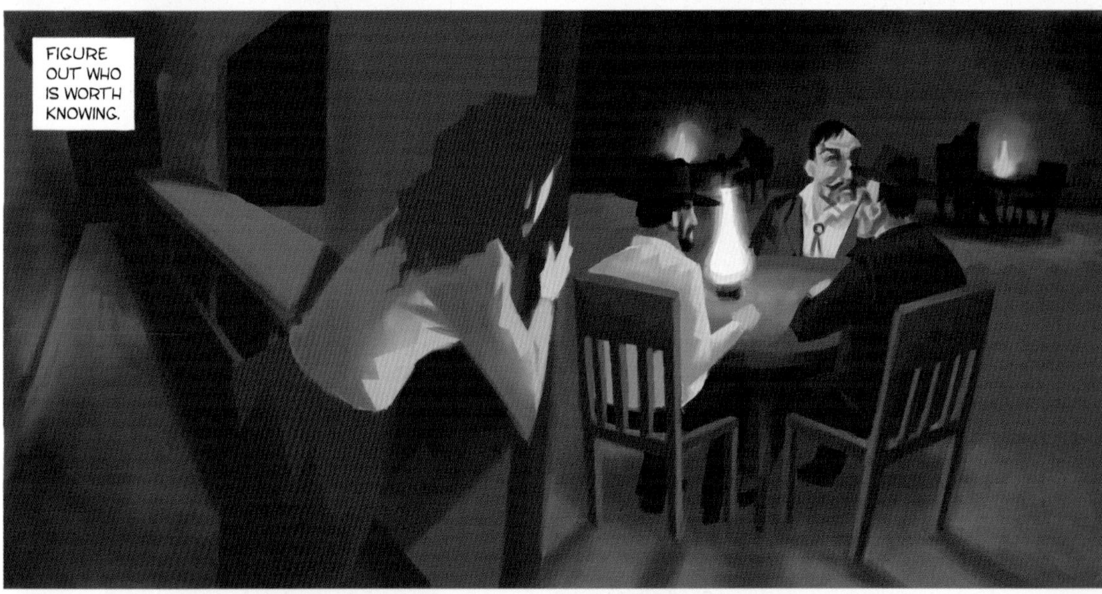
FIGURE OUT WHO IS WORTH KNOWING.

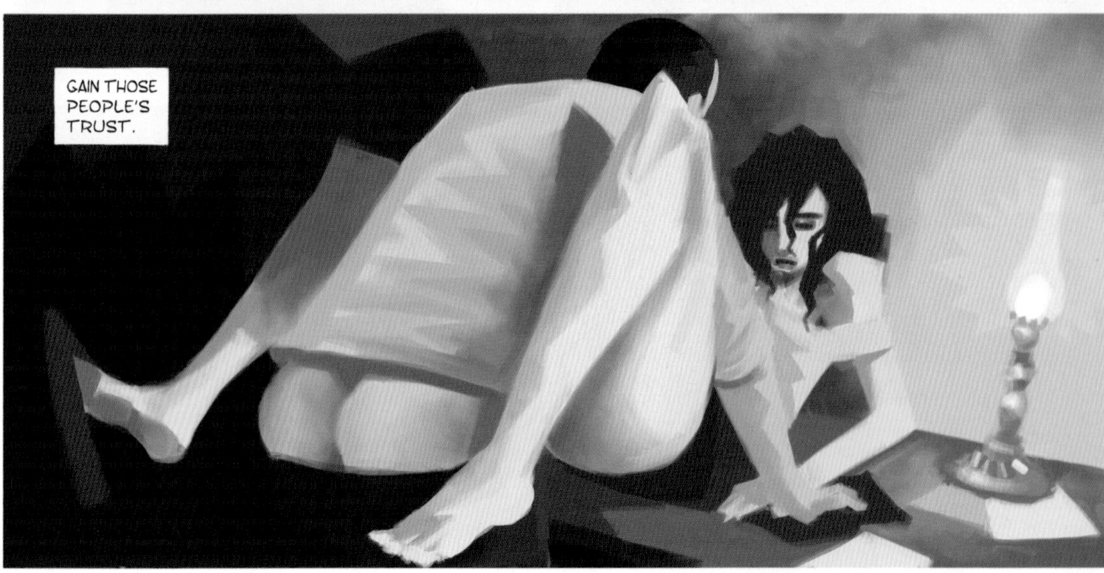
GAIN THOSE PEOPLE'S TRUST.

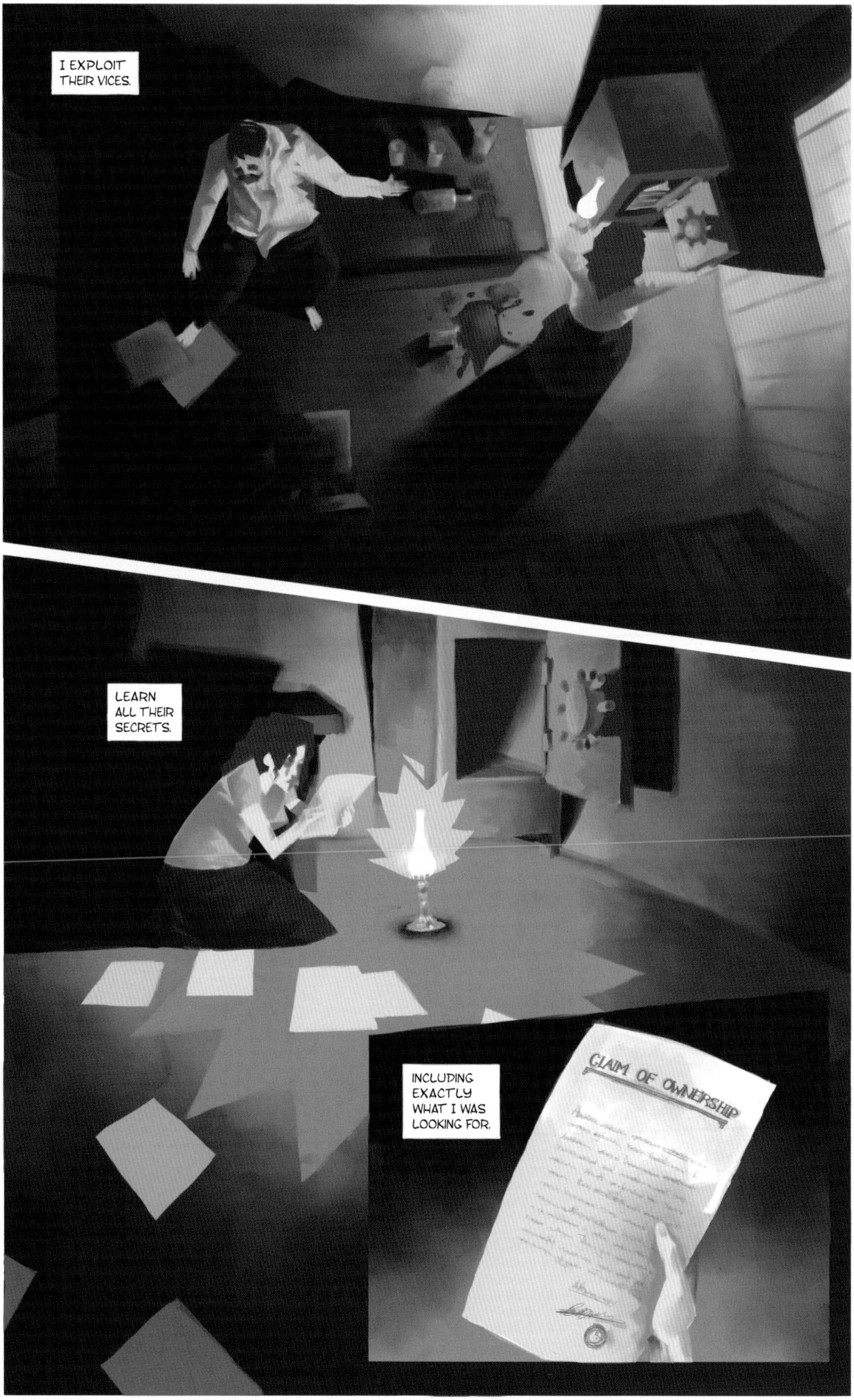
I EXPLOIT THEIR VICES.
LEARN ALL THEIR SECRETS.
INCLUDING EXACTLY WHAT I WAS LOOKING FOR.
CLAIM OF OWNERSHIP

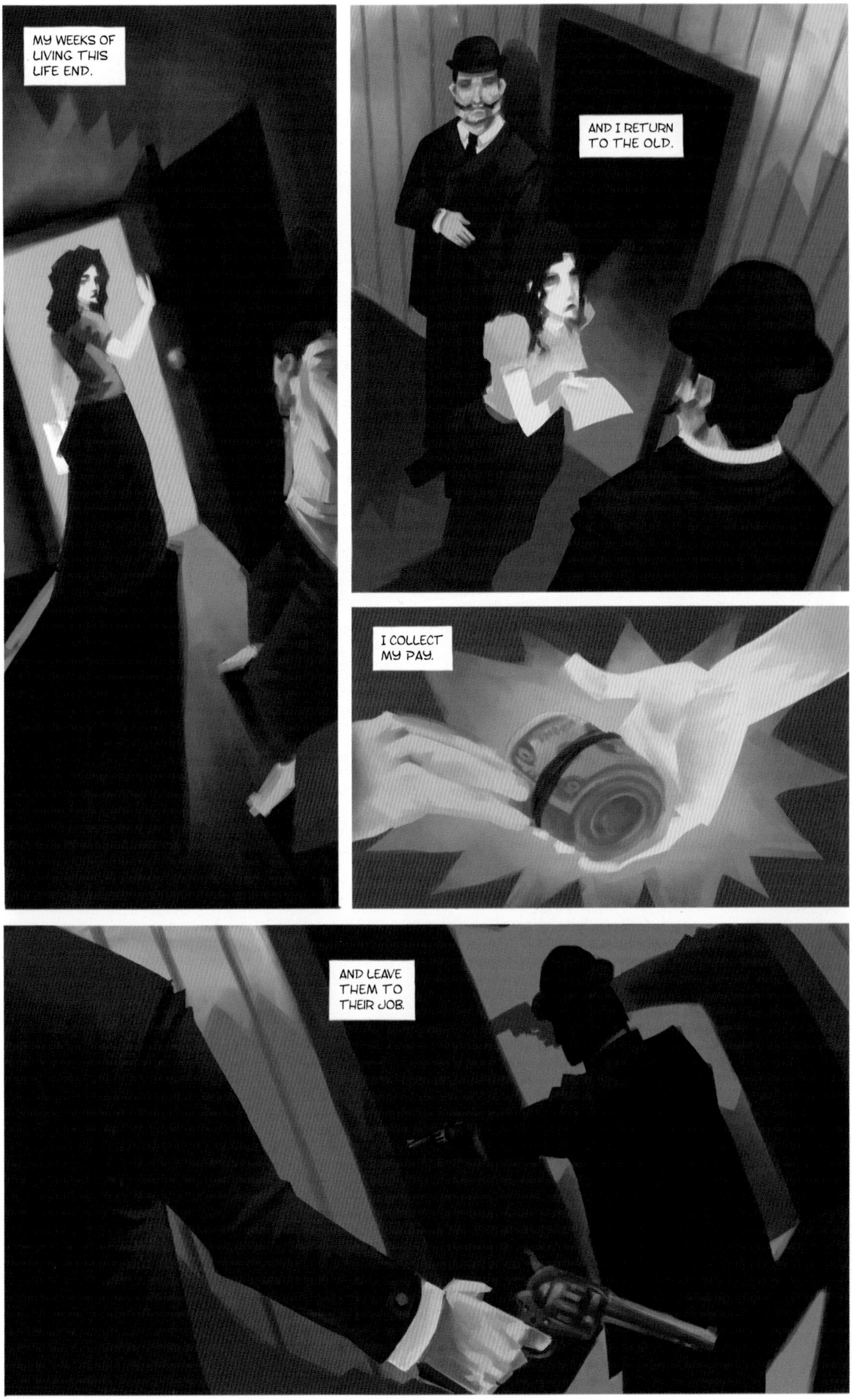
MY WEEKS OF LIVING THIS LIFE END.
AND I RETURN TO THE OLD.
I COLLECT MY PAY.
AND LEAVE THEM TO THEIR JOB.

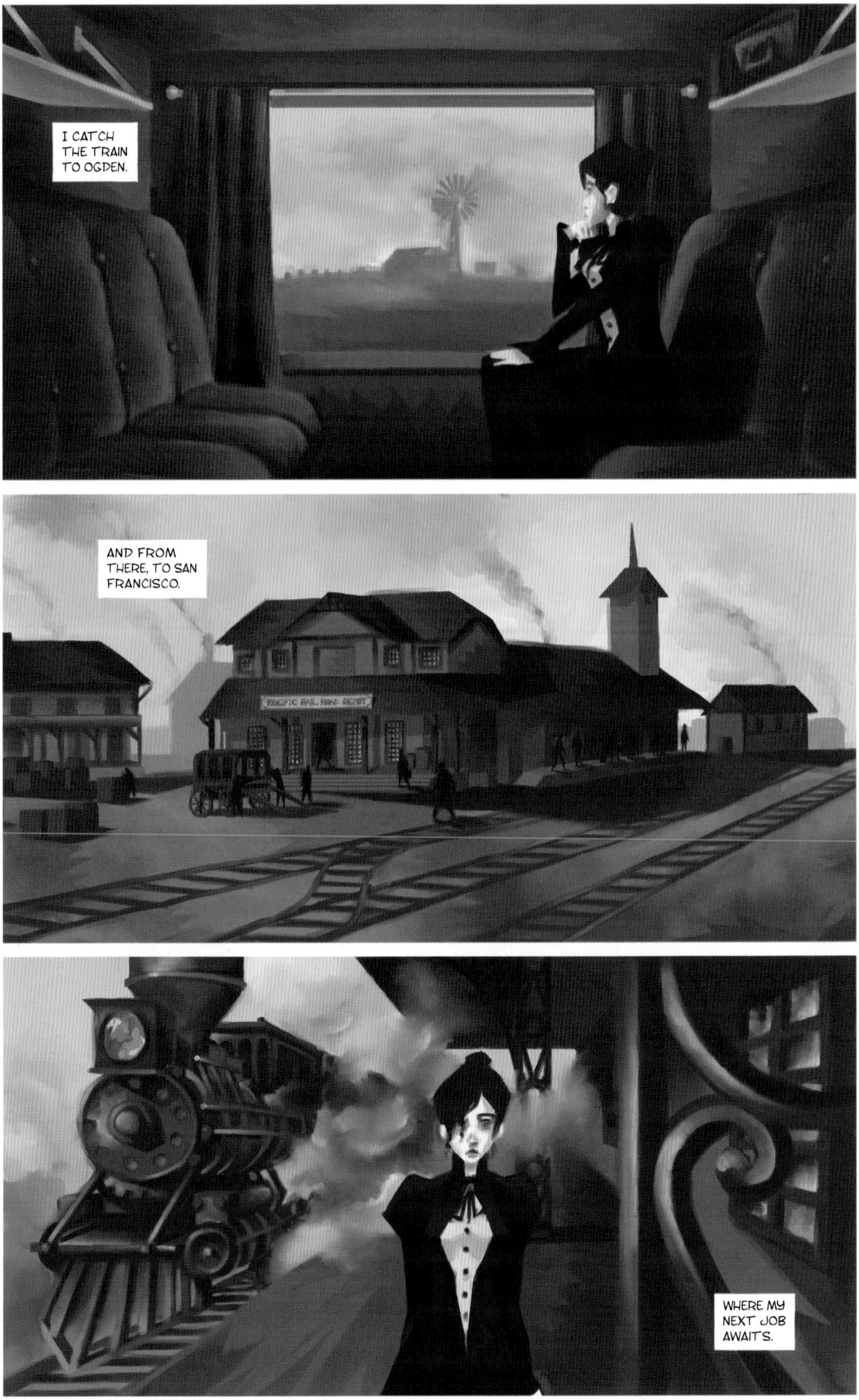
I CATCH THE TRAIN TO OGDEN.
AND FROM THERE, TO SAN FRANCISCO.
PACIFIC RAIL ROAD DEPOT
WHERE MY NEXT JOB AWAITS.

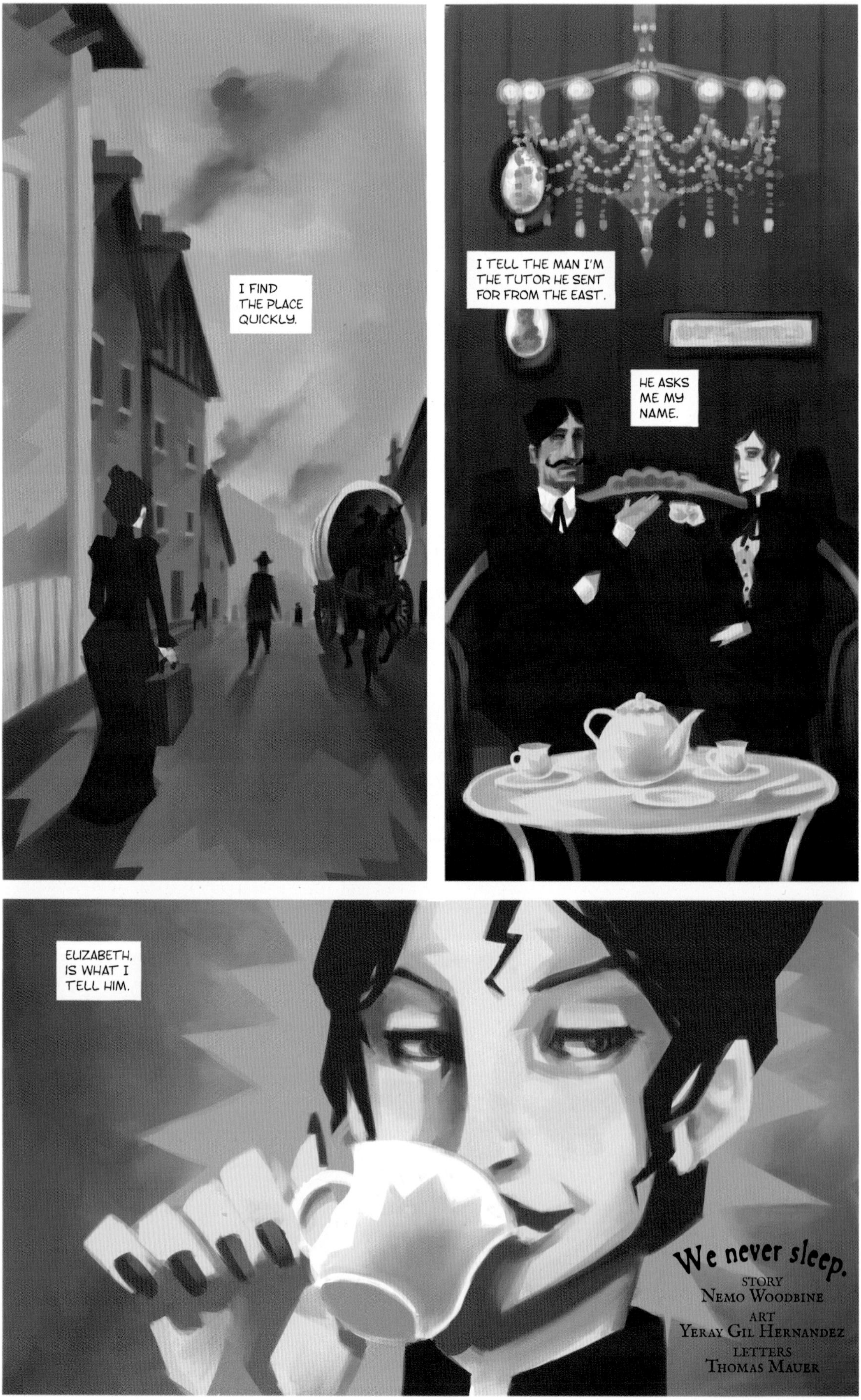

I FIND THE PLACE QUICKLY.
I TELL THE MAN I'M THE TUTOR HE SENT FOR FROM THE EAST.
HE ASKS ME MY NAME.
ELIZABETH, IS WHAT I TELL HIM.
We never sleep.
STORY
NEMO WOODBINE
ART
YERAY GIL HERNANDEZ
LETTERS
THOMAS MAUER

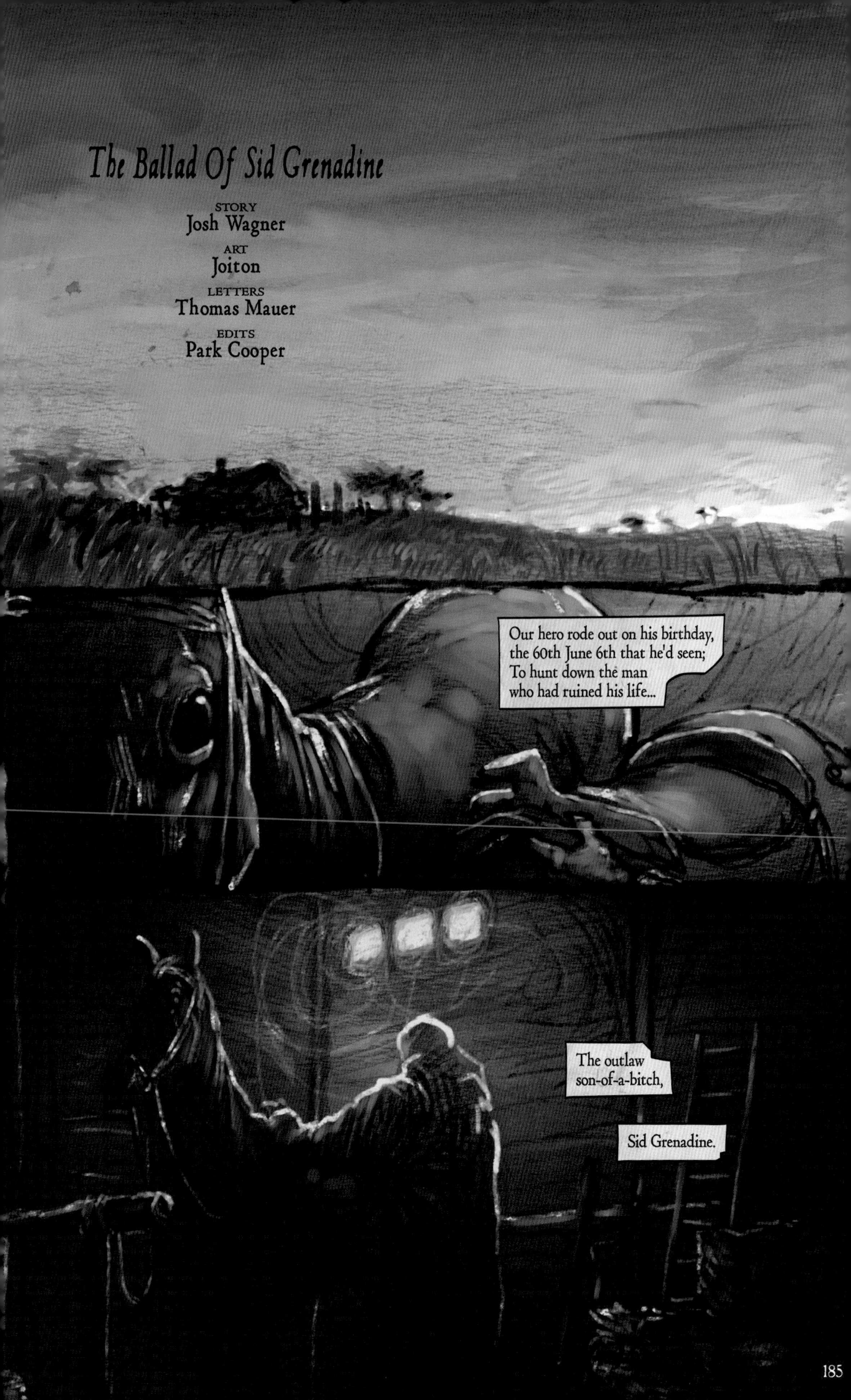
The Ballad Of Sid Grenadine
STORY
Josh Wagner
ART
Joiton
LETTERS
Thomas Mauer
EDITS
Park Cooper
Our hero rode out on his birthday, the 60th June 6th that he'd seen; To hunt down the man who had ruined his life...
The outlaw son-of-a-bitch,
Sid Grenadine.

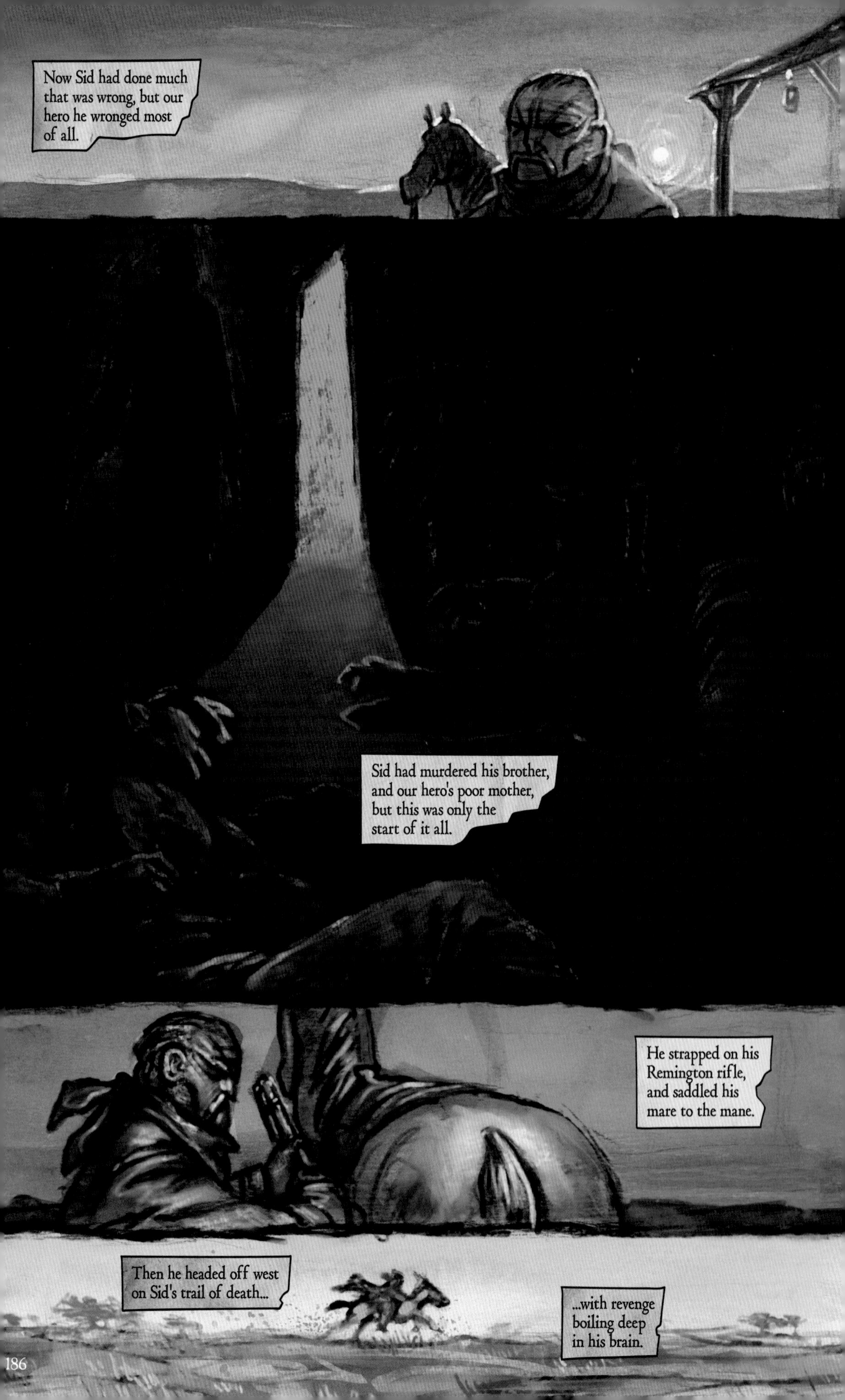
Now Sid had done much that was wrong, but our hero he wronged most of all.
Sid had murdered his brother, and our hero's poor mother, but this was only the start of it all.
He strapped on his Remington rifle, and saddled his mare to the mane.
Then he headed off west on Sid's trail of death...
...with revenge boiling deep in his brain.

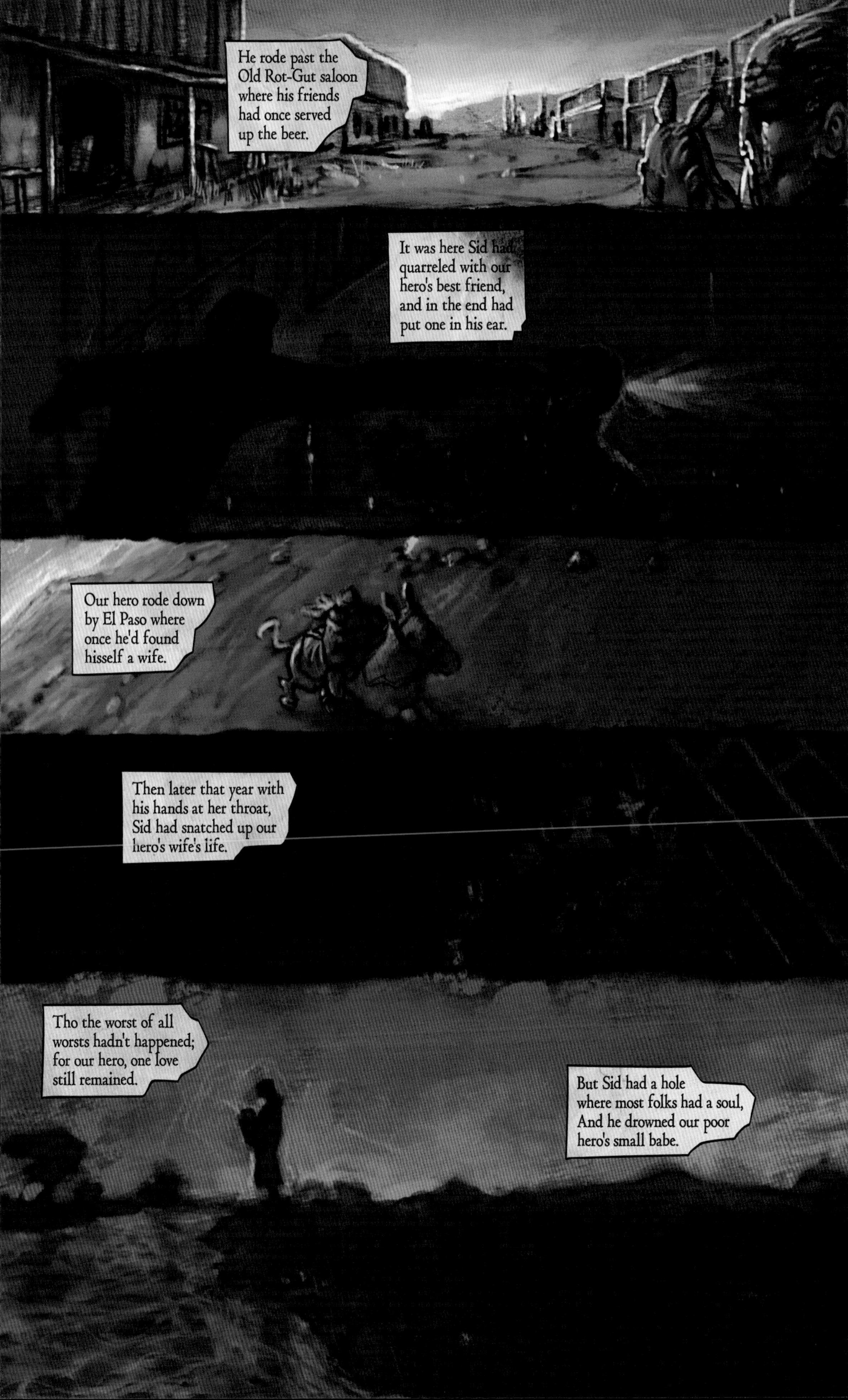
He rode past the Old Rot-Gut saloon where his friends had once served up the beer.
It was here Sid had quarreled with our hero's best friend, and in the end had put one in his ear.
Our hero rode down by El Paso where once he'd found hisself a wife.
Then later that year with his hands at her throat, Sid had snatched up our hero's wife's life.
Tho the worst of all worsts hadn't happened; for our hero, one love still remained.
But Sid had a hole where most folks had a soul, And he drowned our poor hero's small babe.

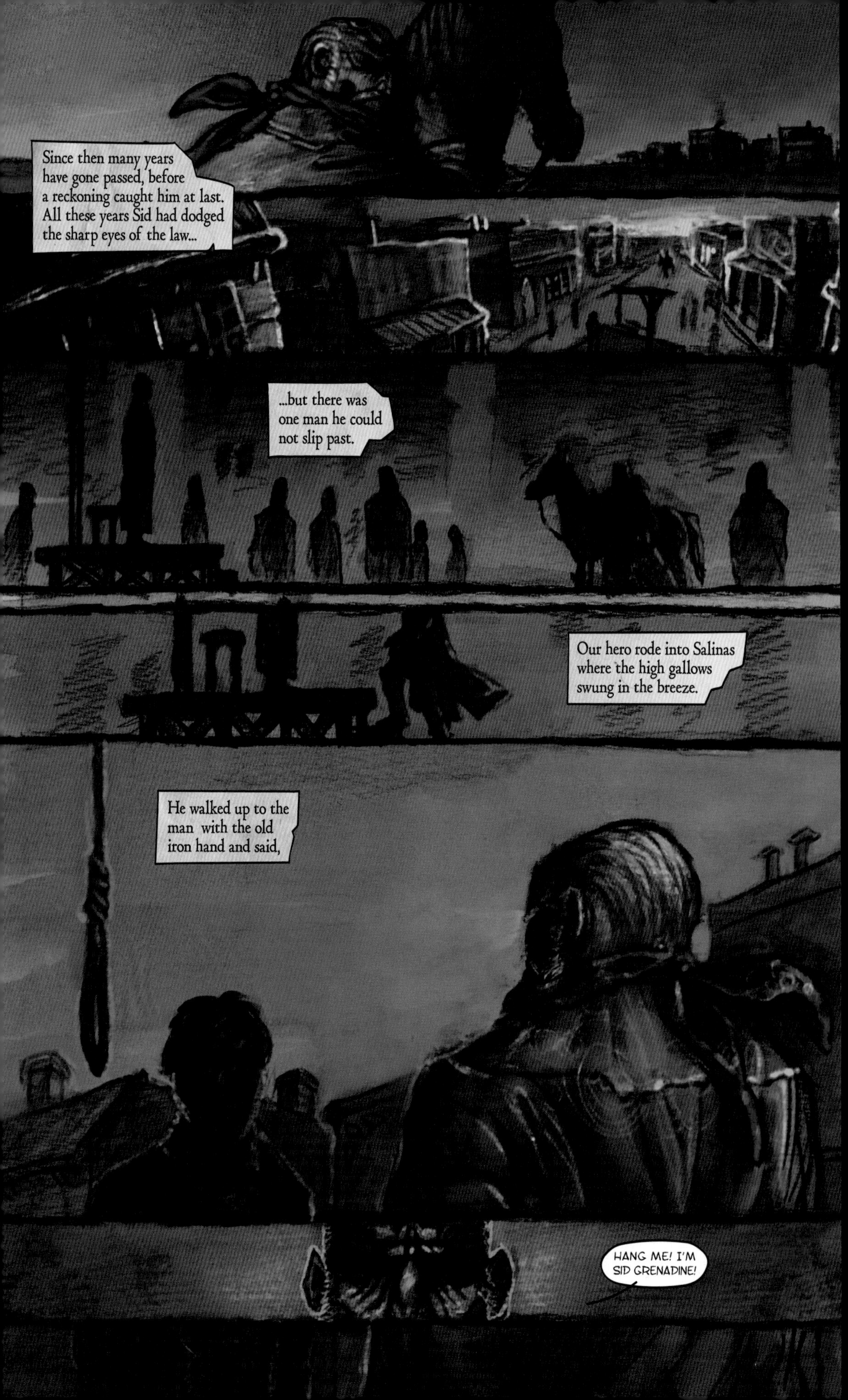
Since then many years have gone passed, before a reckoning caught him at last. All these years Sid had dodged the sharp eyes of the law...
...but there was one man he could not slip past.
Our hero rode into Salinas where the high gallows swung in the breeze.
He walked up to the man with the old iron hand and said,
HANG ME! I'M SID GRENADINE!

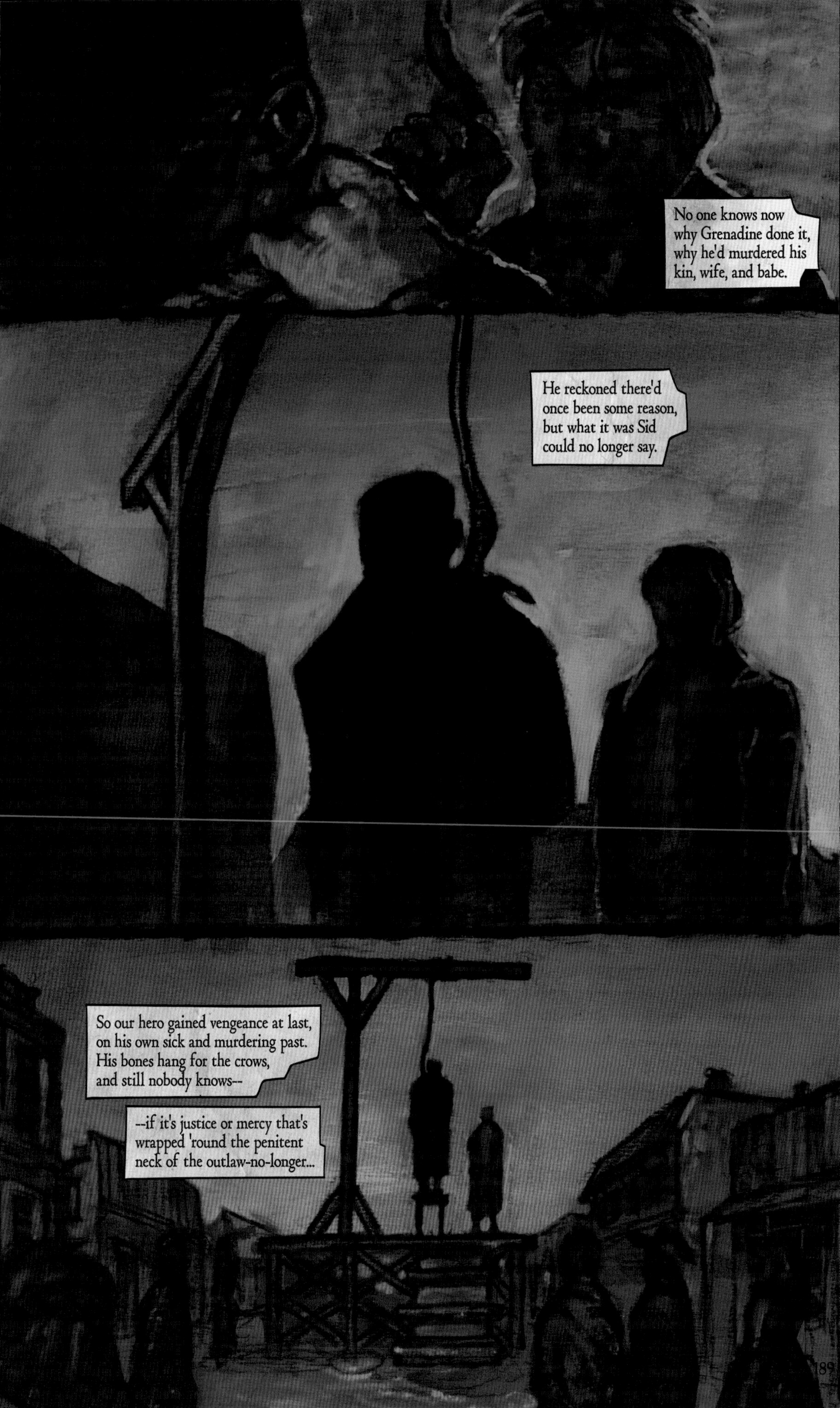
No one knows now why Grenadine done it, why he'd murdered his kin, wife, and babe.
He reckoned there'd once been some reason, but what it was Sid could no longer say.
So our hero gained vengeance at last, on his own sick and murdering past. His bones hang for the crows, and still nobody knows--
--if it's justice or mercy that's wrapped 'round the penitent neck of the outlaw-no-longer...

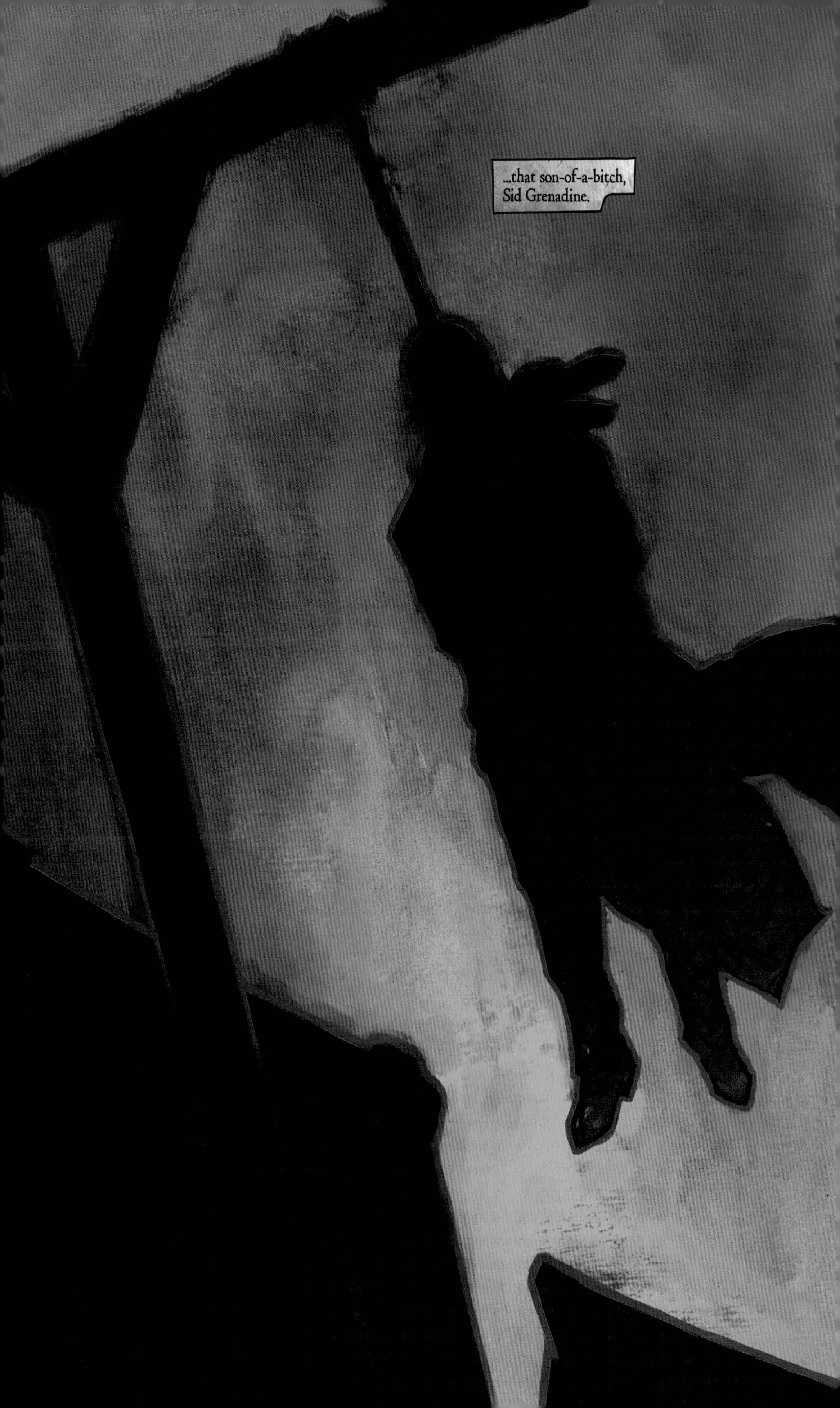
...that son-of-a-bitch, Sid Grenadine.

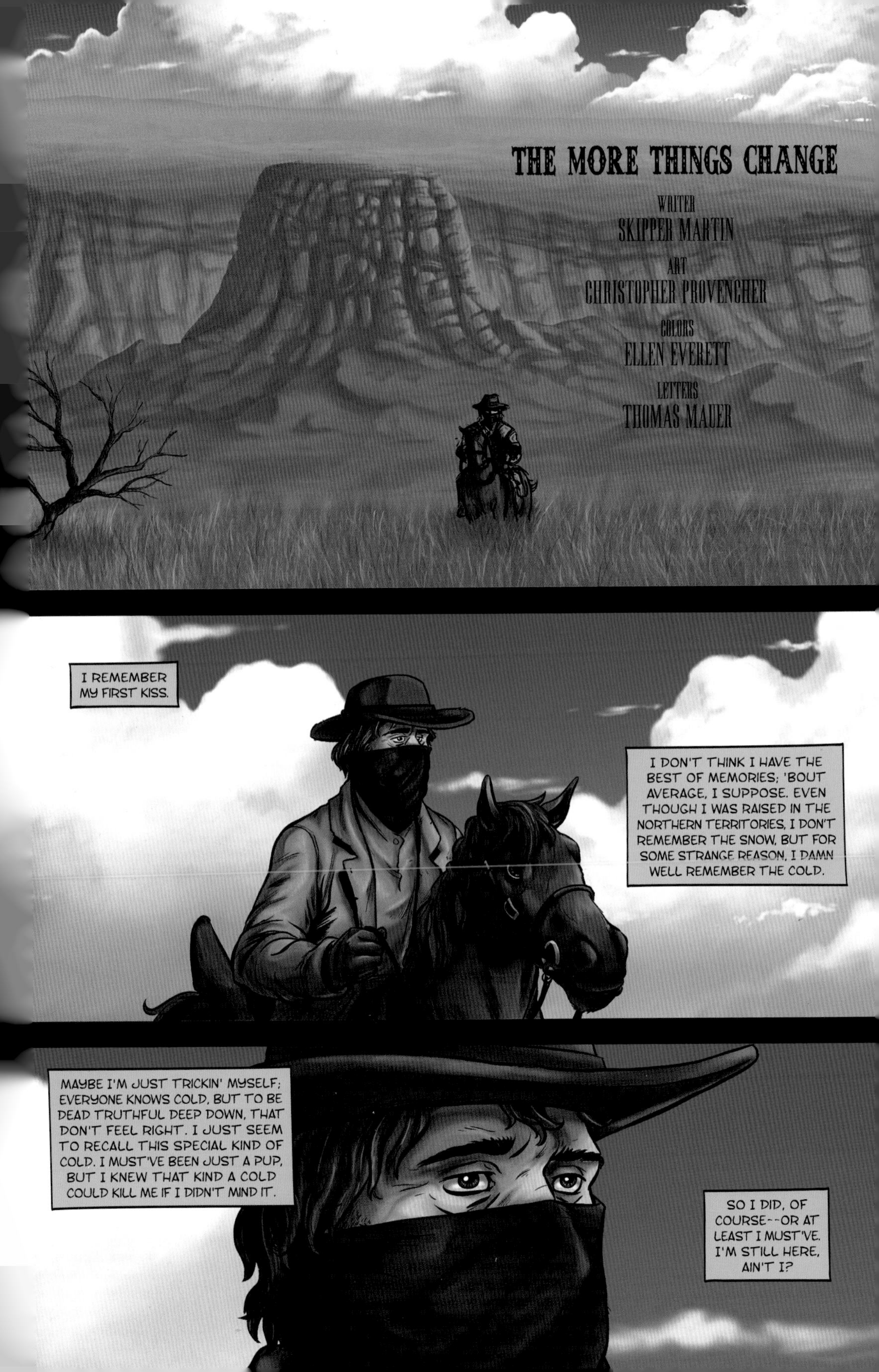
THE MORE THINGS CHANGE
WRITER
SKIPPER MARTIN
ART
CHRISTOPHER PROVENCHER
COLORS
ELLEN EVERETT
LETTERS
THOMAS MAUER
I REMEMBER MY FIRST KISS.
I DON'T THINK I HAVE THE BEST OF MEMORIES; 'BOUT AVERAGE, I SUPPOSE. EVEN THOUGH I WAS RAISED IN THE NORTHERN TERRITORIES, I DON'T REMEMBER THE SNOW, BUT FOR SOME STRANGE REASON, I DAMN WELL REMEMBER THE COLD.
MAYBE I'M JUST TRICKIN' MYSELF; EVERYONE KNOWS COLD, BUT TO BE DEAD TRUTHFUL DEEP DOWN, THAT DON'T FEEL RIGHT. I JUST SEEM TO RECALL THIS SPECIAL KIND OF COLD. I MUST'VE BEEN JUST A PUP, BUT I KNEW THAT KIND A COLD COULD KILL ME IF I DIDN'T MIND IT.
SO I DID, OF COURSE--OR AT LEAST I MUST'VE. I'M STILL HERE, AIN'T I?

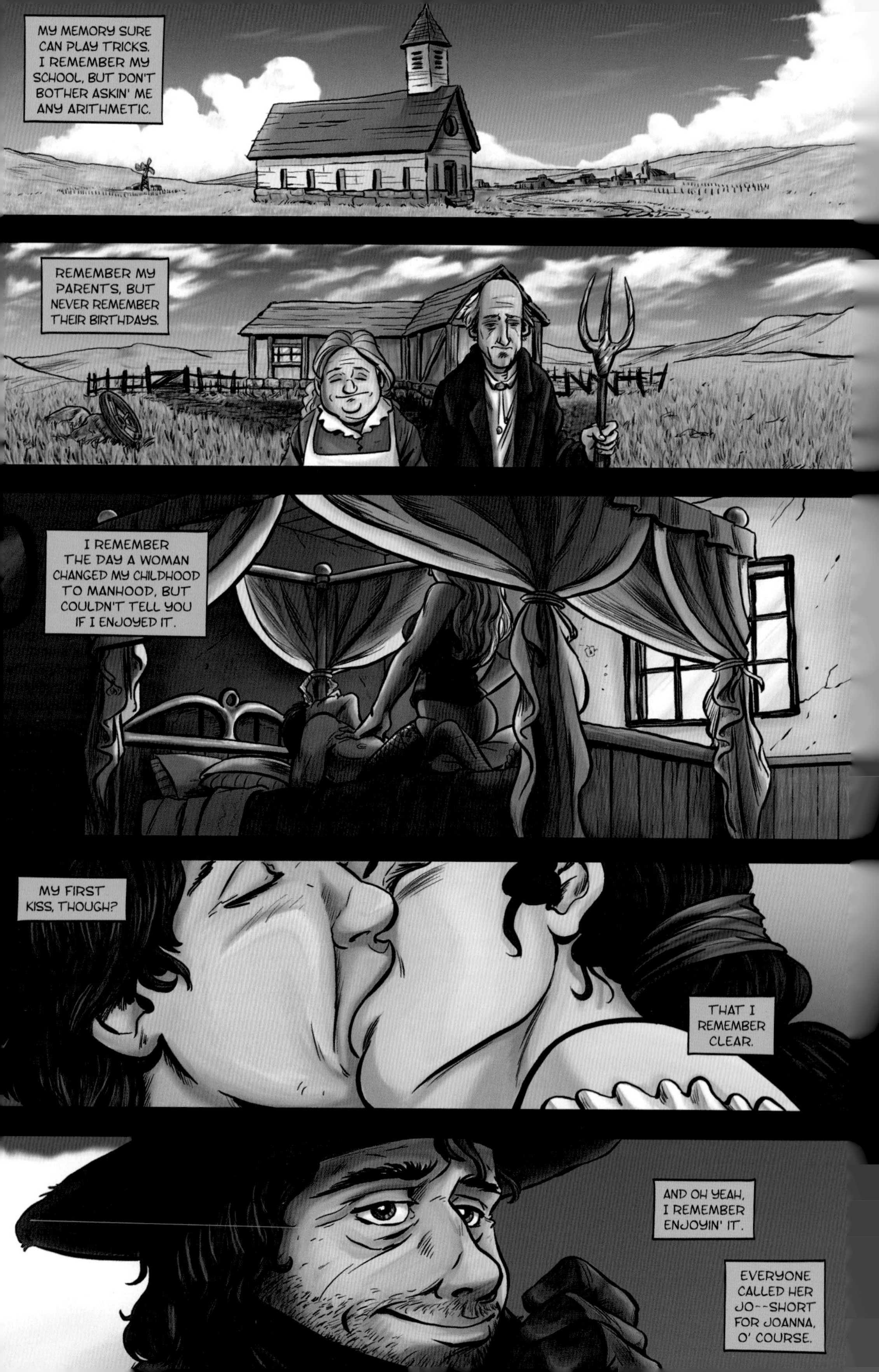
MY MEMORY SURE CAN PLAY TRICKS. I REMEMBER MY SCHOOL, BUT DON'T BOTHER ASKIN' ME ANY ARITHMETIC.
REMEMBER MY PARENTS, BUT NEVER REMEMBER THEIR BIRTHDAYS.
I REMEMBER THE DAY A WOMAN CHANGED MY CHILDHOOD TO MANHOOD, BUT COULDN'T TELL YOU IF I ENJOYED IT.
MY FIRST KISS, THOUGH?
THAT I REMEMBER CLEAR.
AND OH YEAH, I REMEMBER ENJOYIN' IT.
EVERYONE CALLED HER JO--SHORT FOR JOANNA, O' COURSE.

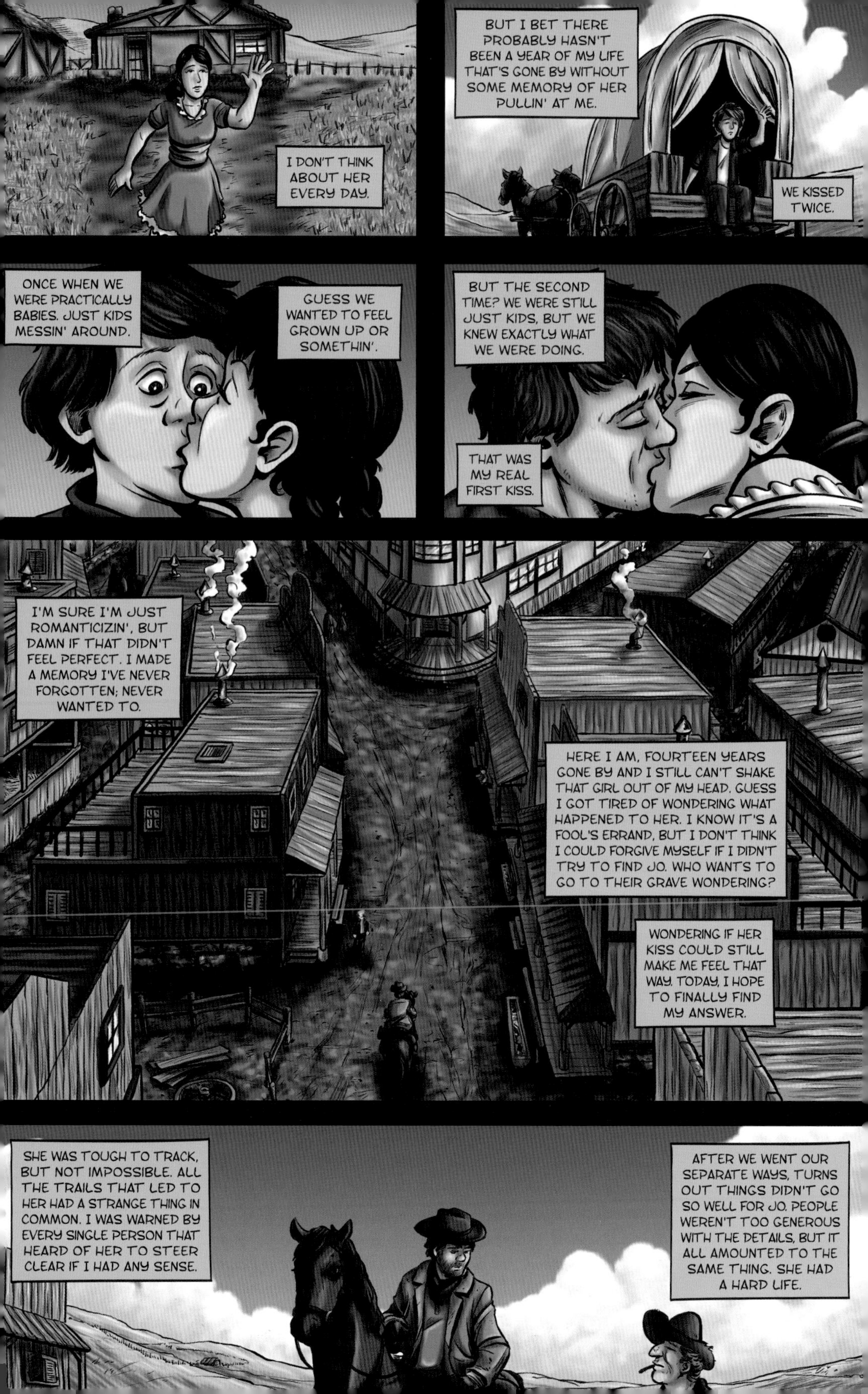
I DON'T THINK ABOUT HER EVERY DAY.
BUT I BET THERE PROBABLY HASN'T BEEN A YEAR OF MY LIFE THAT'S GONE BY WITHOUT SOME MEMORY OF HER PULLIN' AT ME.
WE KISSED TWICE.
ONCE WHEN WE WERE PRACTICALLY BABIES. JUST KIDS MESSIN' AROUND.
GUESS WE WANTED TO FEEL GROWN UP OR SOMETHIN'.
BUT THE SECOND TIME? WE WERE STILL JUST KIDS, BUT WE KNEW EXACTLY WHAT WE WERE DOING.
THAT WAS MY REAL FIRST KISS.
I'M SURE I'M JUST ROMANTICIZIN', BUT DAMN IF THAT DIDN'T FEEL PERFECT. I MADE A MEMORY I'VE NEVER FORGOTTEN; NEVER WANTED TO.
HERE I AM, FOURTEEN YEARS GONE BY AND I STILL CAN'T SHAKE THAT GIRL OUT OF MY HEAD. GUESS I GOT TIRED OF WONDERING WHAT HAPPENED TO HER. I KNOW IT'S A FOOL'S ERRAND, BUT I DON'T THINK I COULD FORGIVE MYSELF IF I DIDN'T TRY TO FIND JO. WHO WANTS TO GO TO THEIR GRAVE WONDERING?
WONDERING IF HER KISS COULD STILL MAKE ME FEEL THAT WAY. TODAY, I HOPE TO FINALLY FIND MY ANSWER.
SHE WAS TOUGH TO TRACK, BUT NOT IMPOSSIBLE. ALL THE TRAILS THAT LED TO HER HAD A STRANGE THING IN COMMON. I WAS WARNED BY EVERY SINGLE PERSON THAT HEARD OF HER TO STEER CLEAR IF I HAD ANY SENSE.
AFTER WE WENT OUR SEPARATE WAYS, TURNS OUT THINGS DIDN'T GO SO WELL FOR JO. PEOPLE WEREN'T TOO GENEROUS WITH THE DETAILS, BUT IT ALL AMOUNTED TO THE SAME THING. SHE HAD A HARD LIFE.

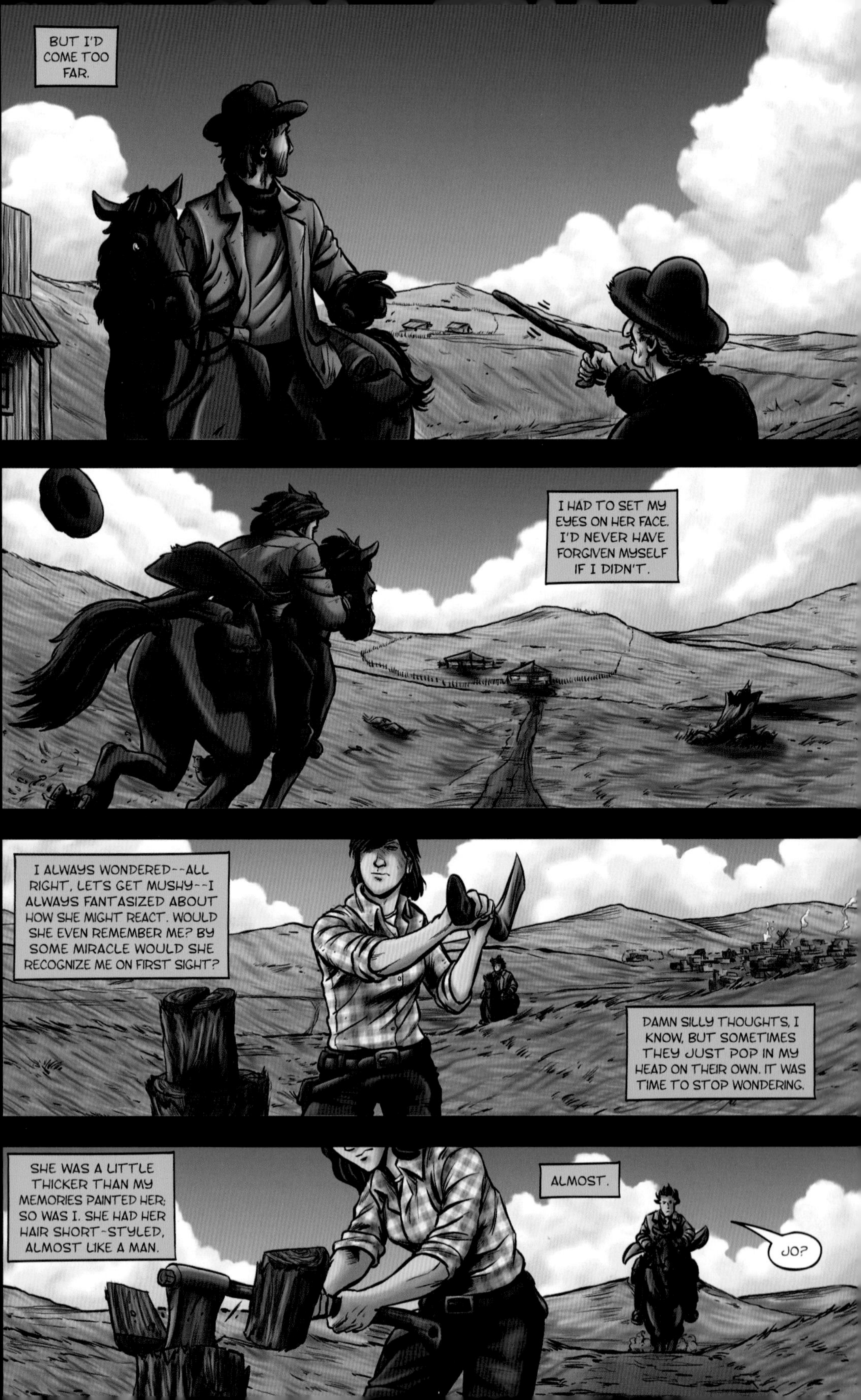
BUT I'D COME TOO FAR.
I HAD TO SET MY EYES ON HER FACE. I'D NEVER HAVE FORGIVEN MYSELF IF I DIDN'T.
I ALWAYS WONDERED--ALL RIGHT, LETS GET MUSHY--I ALWAYS FANTASIZED ABOUT HOW SHE MIGHT REACT. WOULD SHE EVEN REMEMBER ME? BY SOME MIRACLE WOULD SHE RECOGNIZE ME ON FIRST SIGHT?
DAMN SILLY THOUGHTS, I KNOW, BUT SOMETIMES THEY JUST POP IN MY HEAD ON THEIR OWN. IT WAS TIME TO STOP WONDERING.
SHE WAS A LITTLE THICKER THAN MY MEMORIES PAINTED HER; SO WAS I. SHE HAD HER HAIR SHORT-STYLED, ALMOST LIKE A MAN.
ALMOST.
JO?

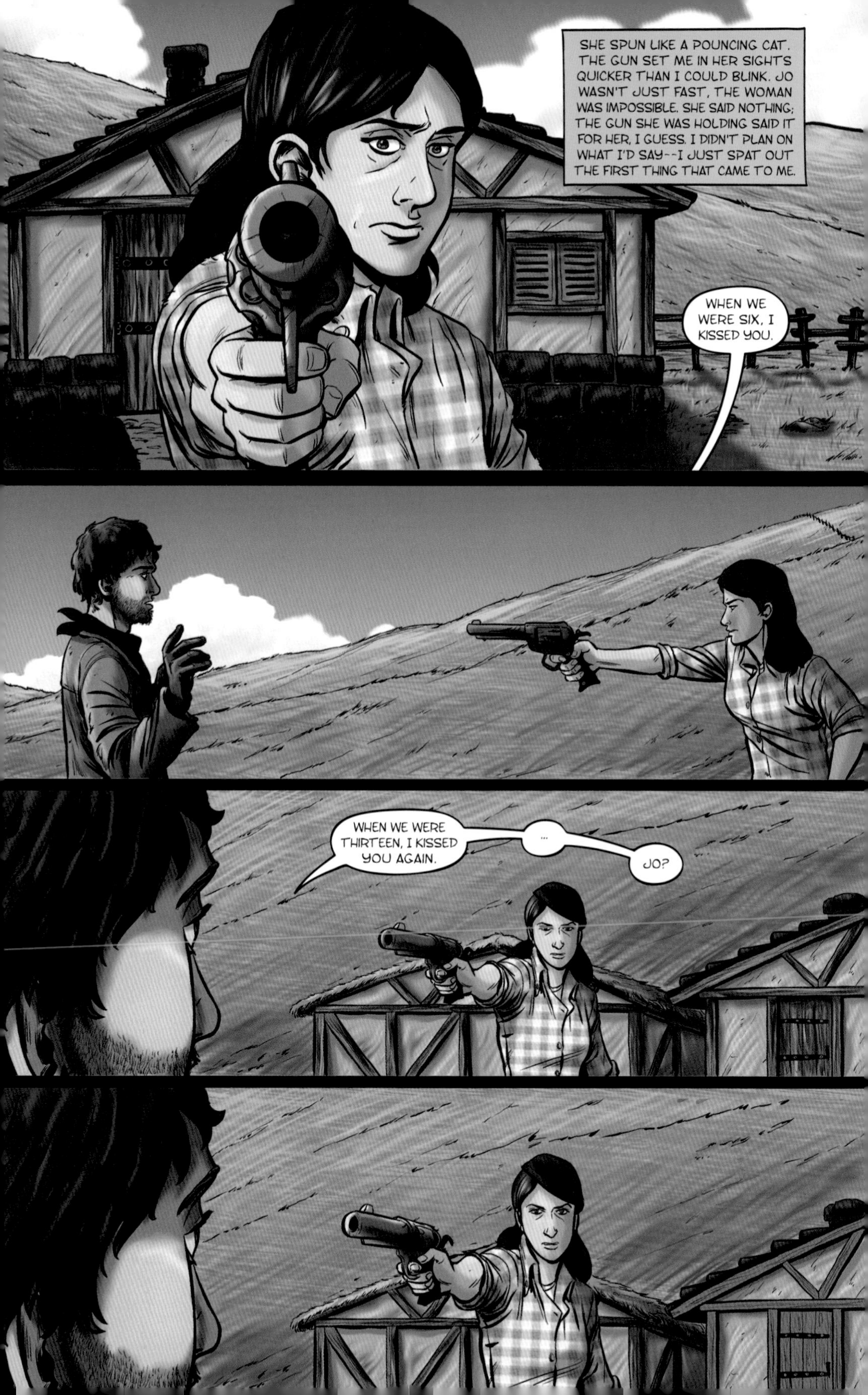
SHE SPUN LIKE A POUNCING CAT. THE GUN SET ME IN HER SIGHTS QUICKER THAN I COULD BLINK. JO WASN'T JUST FAST, THE WOMAN WAS IMPOSSIBLE. SHE SAID NOTHING; THE GUN SHE WAS HOLDING SAID IT FOR HER, I GUESS. I DIDN'T PLAN ON WHAT I'D SAY--I JUST SPAT OUT THE FIRST THING THAT CAME TO ME.
WHEN WE WERE SIX, I KISSED YOU.
WHEN WE WERE THIRTEEN, I KISSED YOU AGAIN.
...
JO?

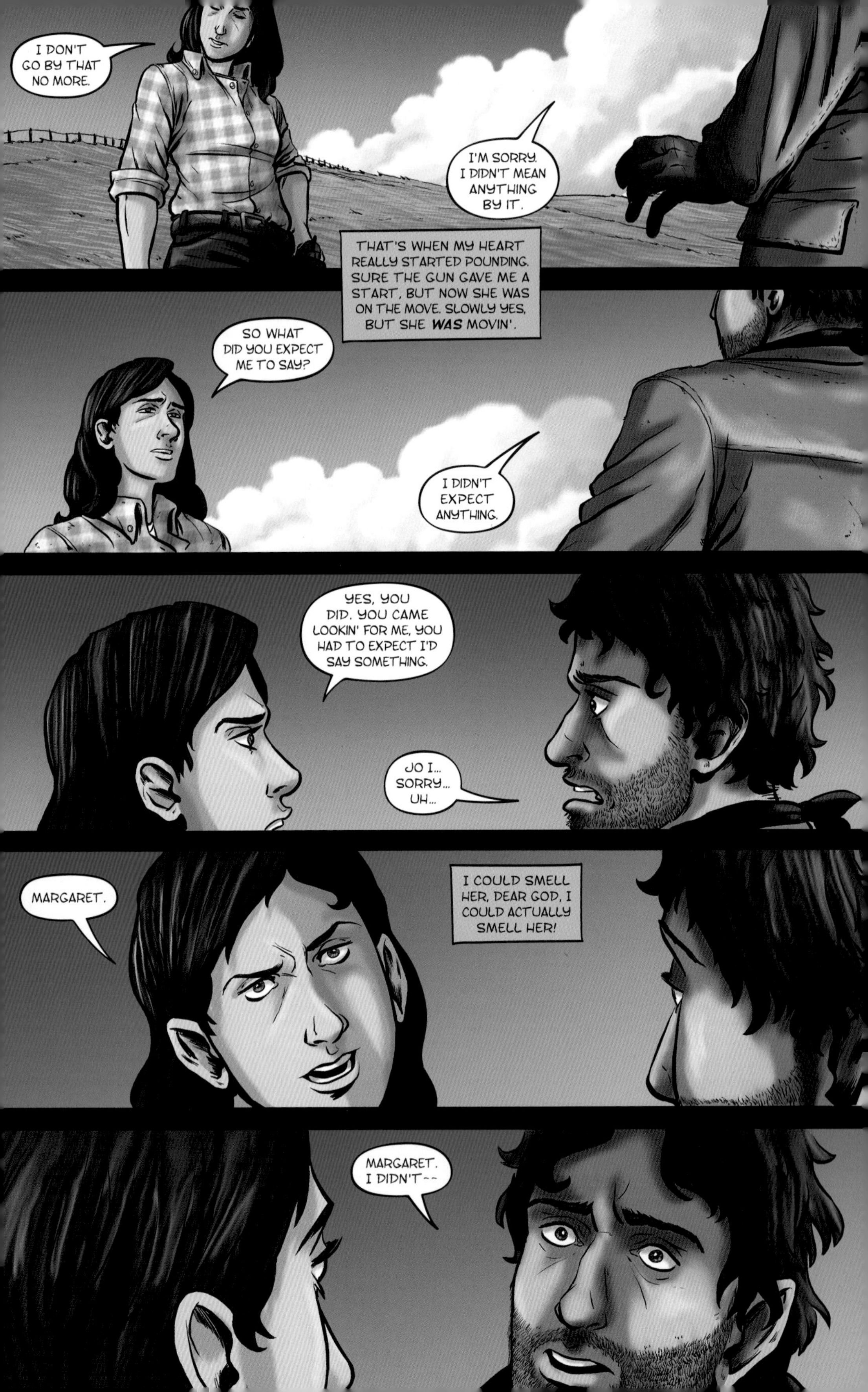
I DON'T GO BY THAT NO MORE.
I'M SORRY. I DIDN'T MEAN ANYTHING BY IT.
THAT'S WHEN MY HEART REALLY STARTED POUNDING. SURE THE GUN GAVE ME A START, BUT NOW SHE WAS ON THE MOVE. SLOWLY YES, BUT SHE **WAS** MOVIN'.
SO WHAT DID YOU EXPECT ME TO SAY?
I DIDN'T EXPECT ANYTHING.
YES, YOU DID. YOU CAME LOOKIN' FOR ME, YOU HAD TO EXPECT I'D SAY SOMETHING.
JO I... SORRY... UH...
MARGARET.
I COULD SMELL HER, DEAR GOD, I COULD ACTUALLY SMELL HER!
MARGARET. I DIDN'T--

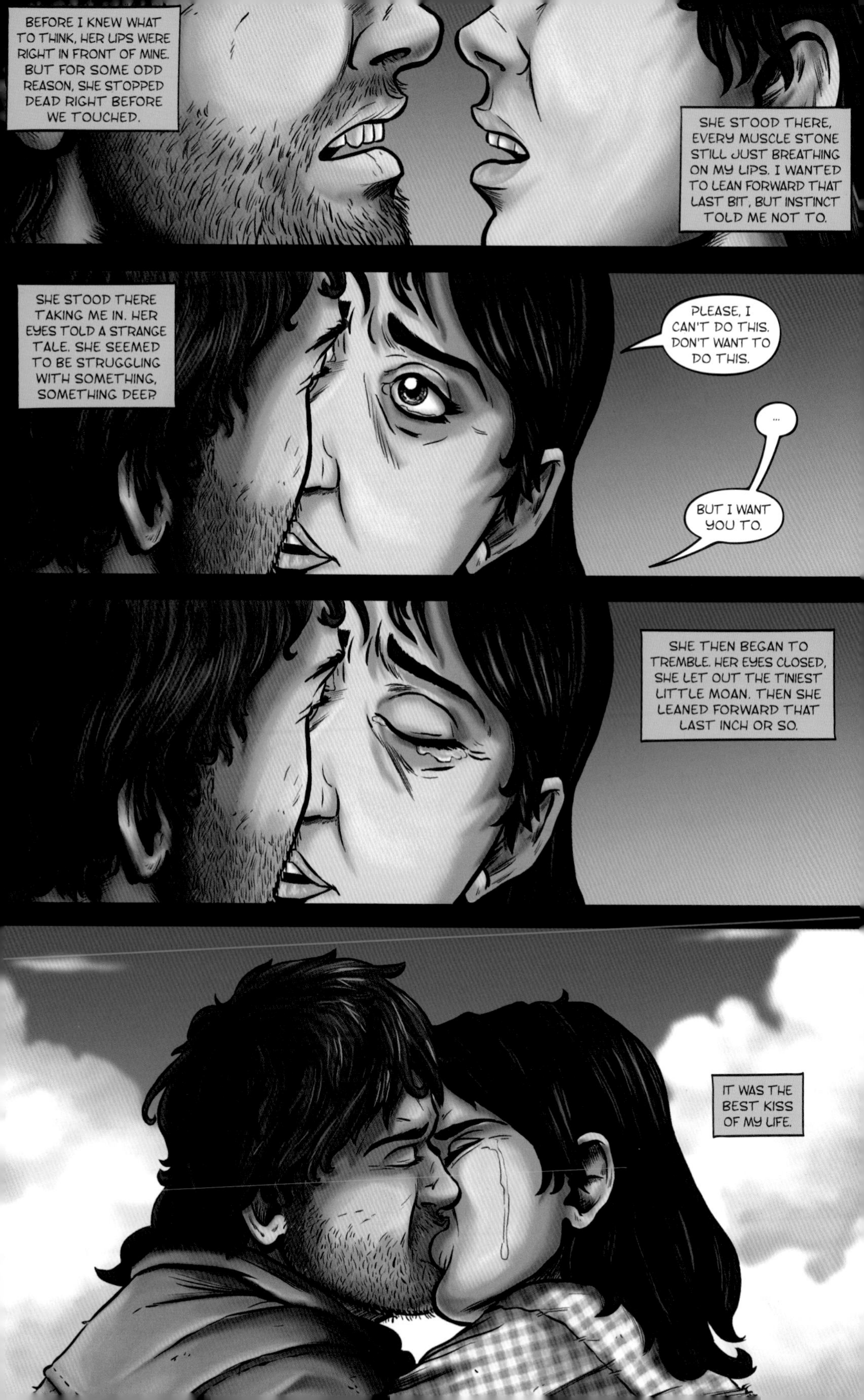
BEFORE I KNEW WHAT TO THINK, HER LIPS WERE RIGHT IN FRONT OF MINE. BUT FOR SOME ODD REASON, SHE STOPPED DEAD RIGHT BEFORE WE TOUCHED.
SHE STOOD THERE, EVERY MUSCLE STONE STILL JUST BREATHING ON MY LIPS. I WANTED TO LEAN FORWARD THAT LAST BIT, BUT INSTINCT TOLD ME NOT TO.
SHE STOOD THERE TAKING ME IN. HER EYES TOLD A STRANGE TALE. SHE SEEMED TO BE STRUGGLING WITH SOMETHING, SOMETHING DEEP.
PLEASE, I CAN'T DO THIS. DON'T WANT TO DO THIS.
...
BUT I WANT YOU TO.
SHE THEN BEGAN TO TREMBLE. HER EYES CLOSED, SHE LET OUT THE TINIEST LITTLE MOAN. THEN SHE LEANED FORWARD THAT LAST INCH OR SO.
IT WAS THE BEST KISS OF MY LIFE.

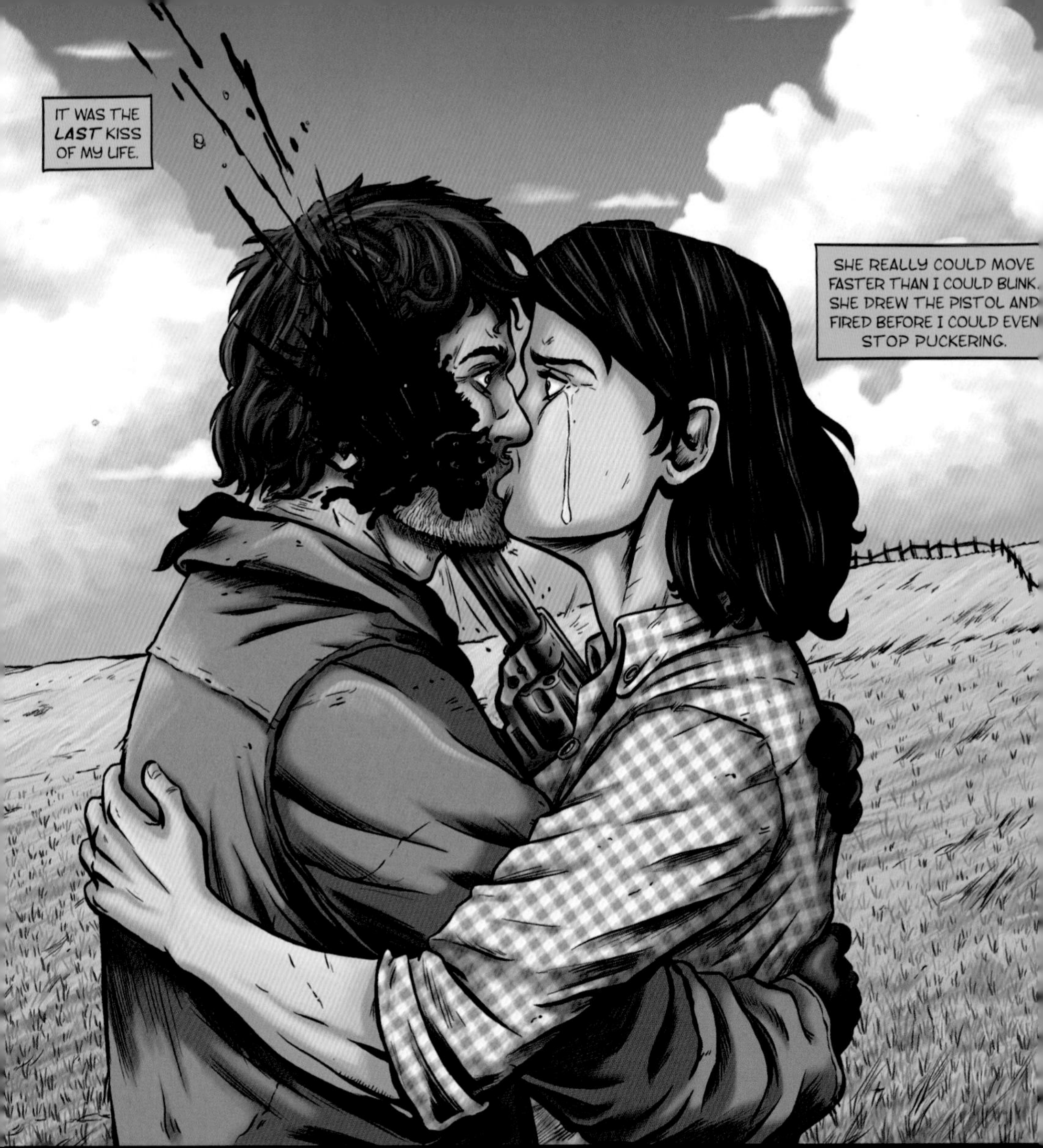
IT WAS THE LAST KISS OF MY LIFE.
SHE REALLY COULD MOVE FASTER THAN I COULD BLINK. SHE DREW THE PISTOL AND FIRED BEFORE I COULD EVEN STOP PUCKERING.

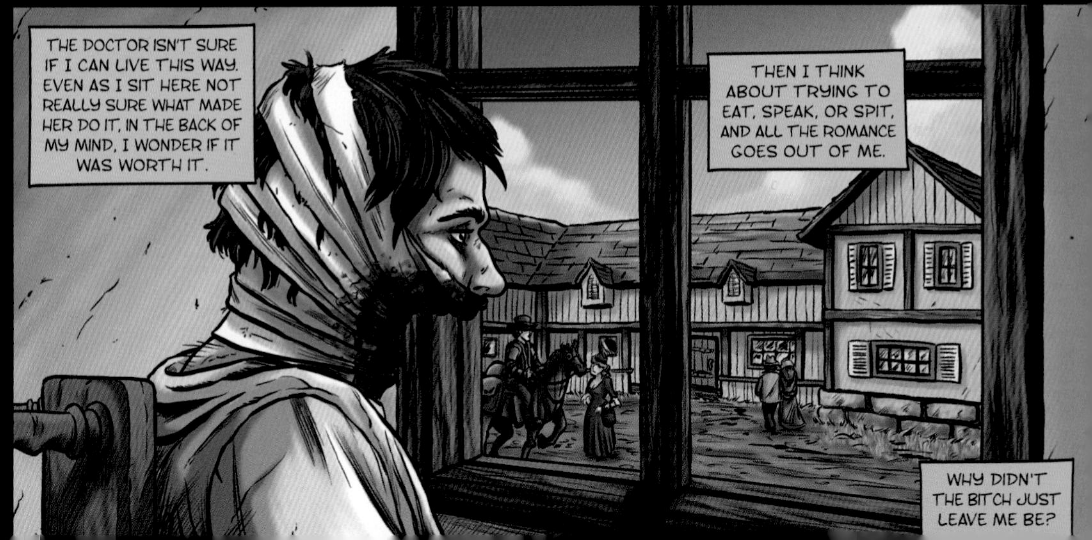
THE DOCTOR ISN'T SURE IF I CAN LIVE THIS WAY. EVEN AS I SIT HERE NOT REALLY SURE WHAT MADE HER DO IT, IN THE BACK OF MY MIND, I WONDER IF IT WAS WORTH IT.
THEN I THINK ABOUT TRYING TO EAT, SPEAK, OR SPIT, AND ALL THE ROMANCE GOES OUT OF ME.
WHY DIDN'T THE BITCH JUST LEAVE ME BE?

working on christmas

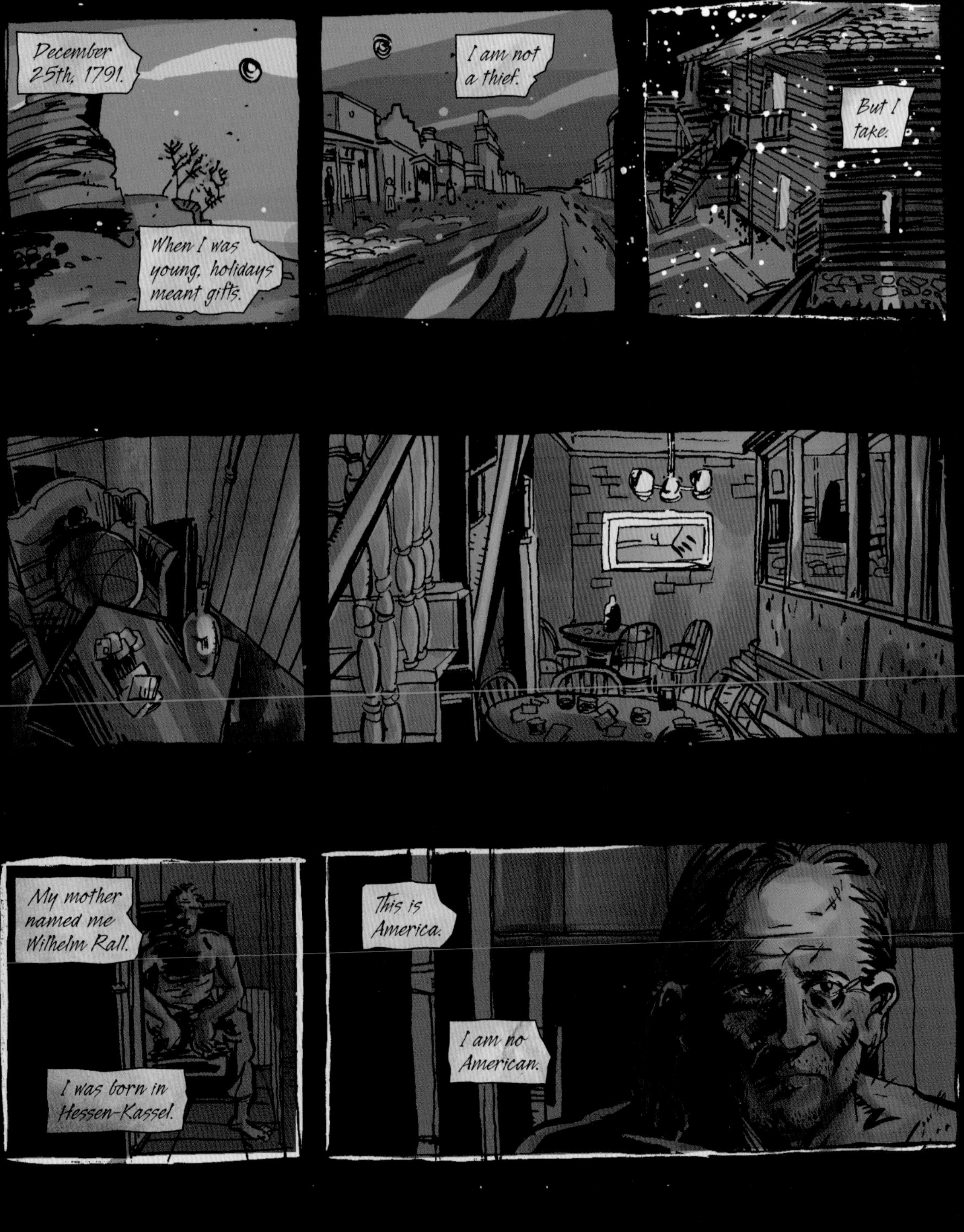
December 25th, 1791.
When I was young, holidays meant gifts.
I am not a thief.
But I take.
My mother named me Wilhelm Rall.
I was born in Hessen-Kassel.
This is America.
I am no American.

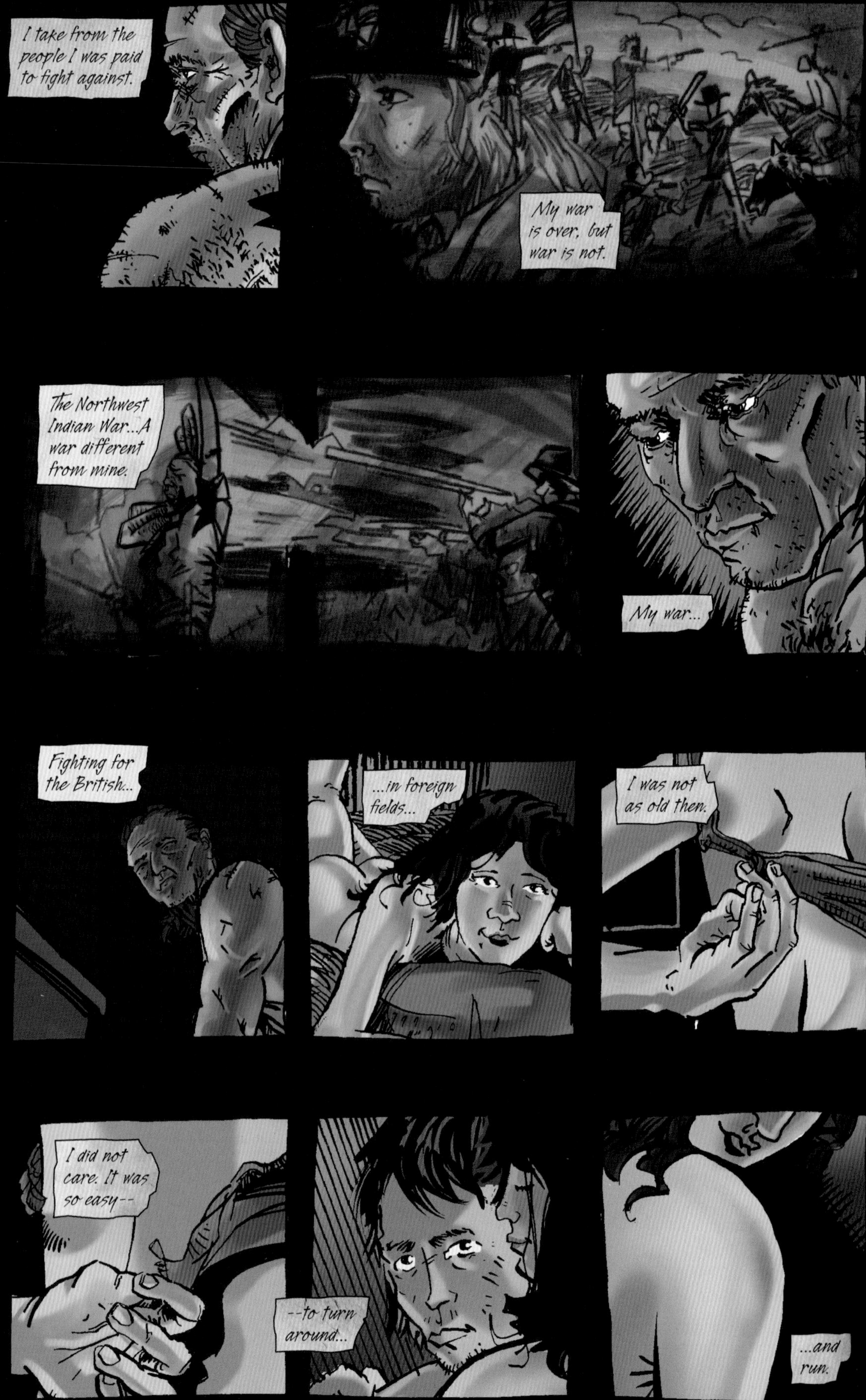
I take from the people I was paid to fight against.
My war is over, but war is not.
The Northwest Indian War...A war different from mine.
My war...
Fighting for the British...
...in foreign fields...
I was not as old then.
I did not care. It was so easy--
--to turn around...
...and run.

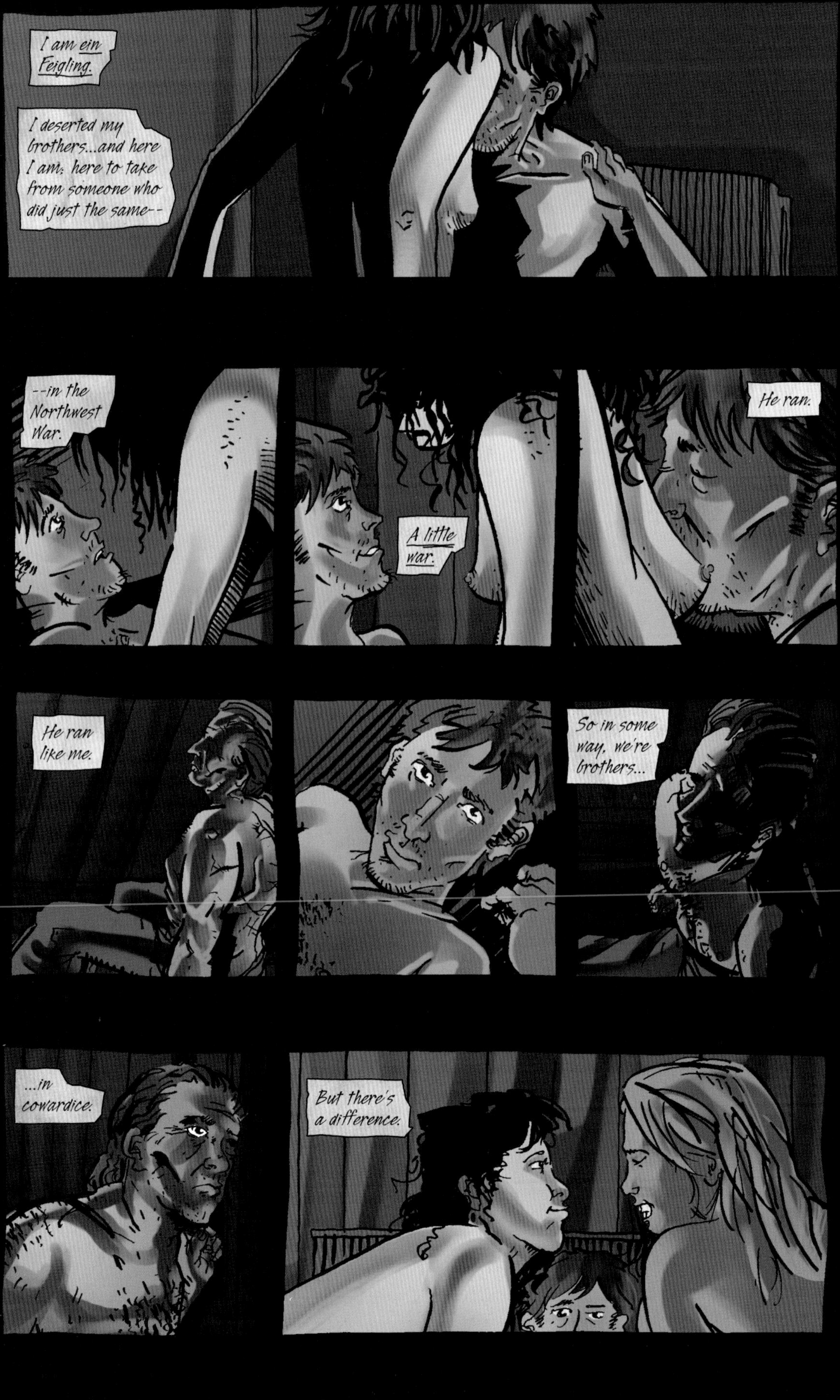
I am ein Feigling.
I deserted my brothers...and here I am: here to take from someone who did just the same--
--in the Northwest War.
A little war.
He ran.
He ran like me.
So in some way, we're brothers...
...in cowardice.
But there's a difference.

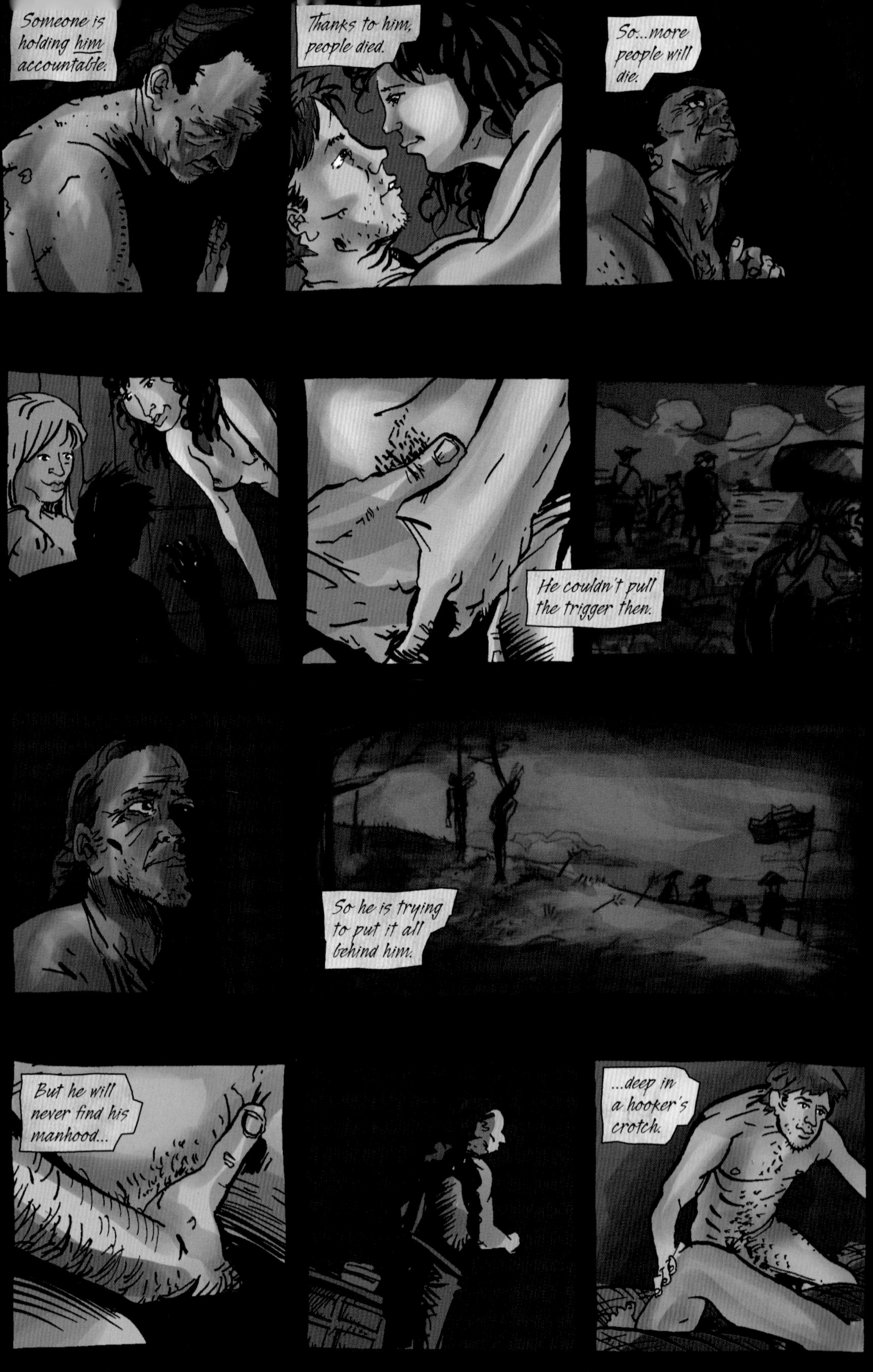
Someone is holding him accountable.
Thanks to him, people died.
So...more people will die.
He couldn't pull the trigger then.
So he is trying to put it all behind him.
But he will never find his manhood...
...deep in a hooker's crotch.

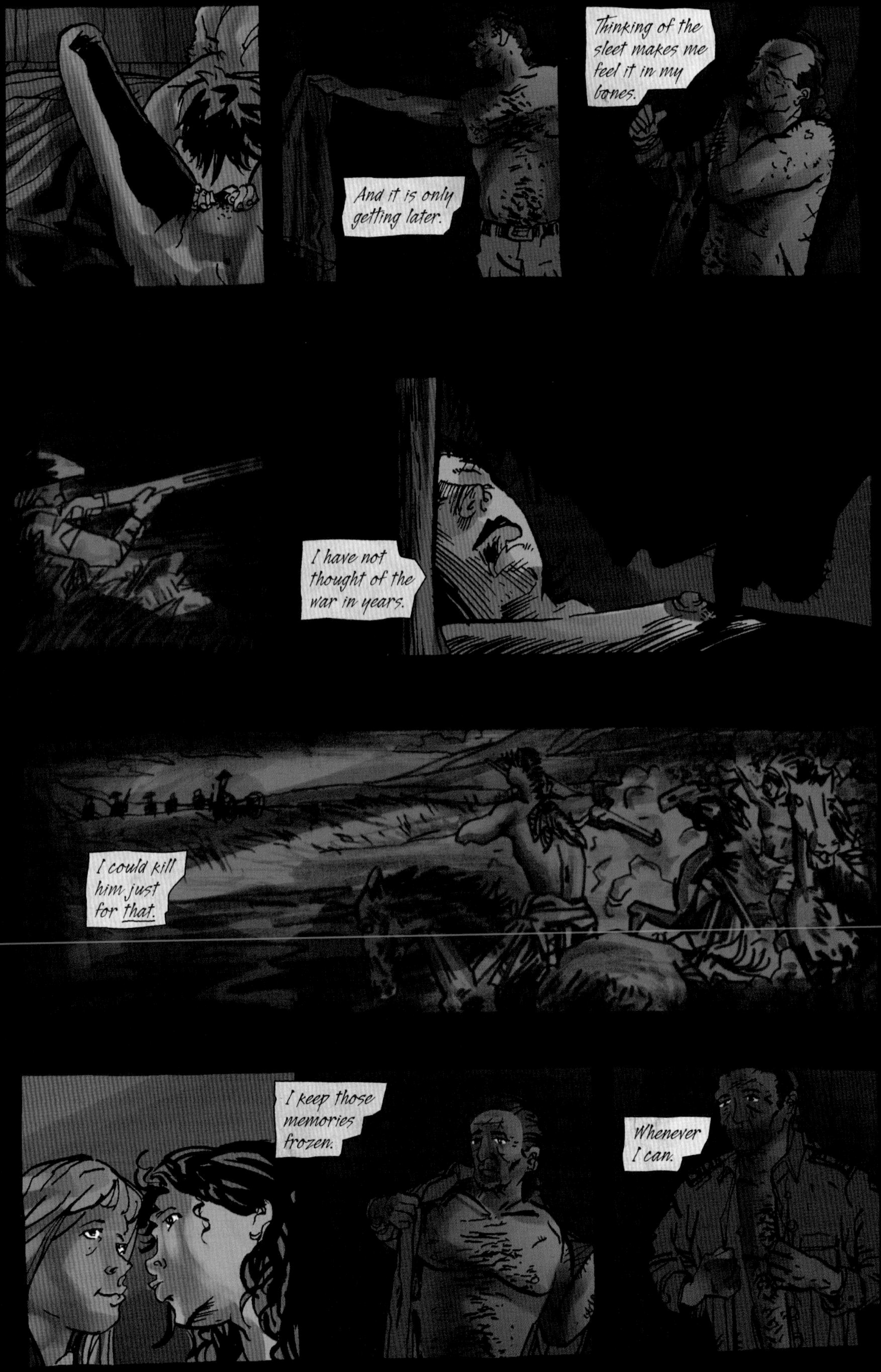
Thinking of the sleet makes me feel it in my bones.
And it is only getting later.
I have not thought of the war in years.
I could kill him just for that.
I keep those memories frozen.
Whenever I can.

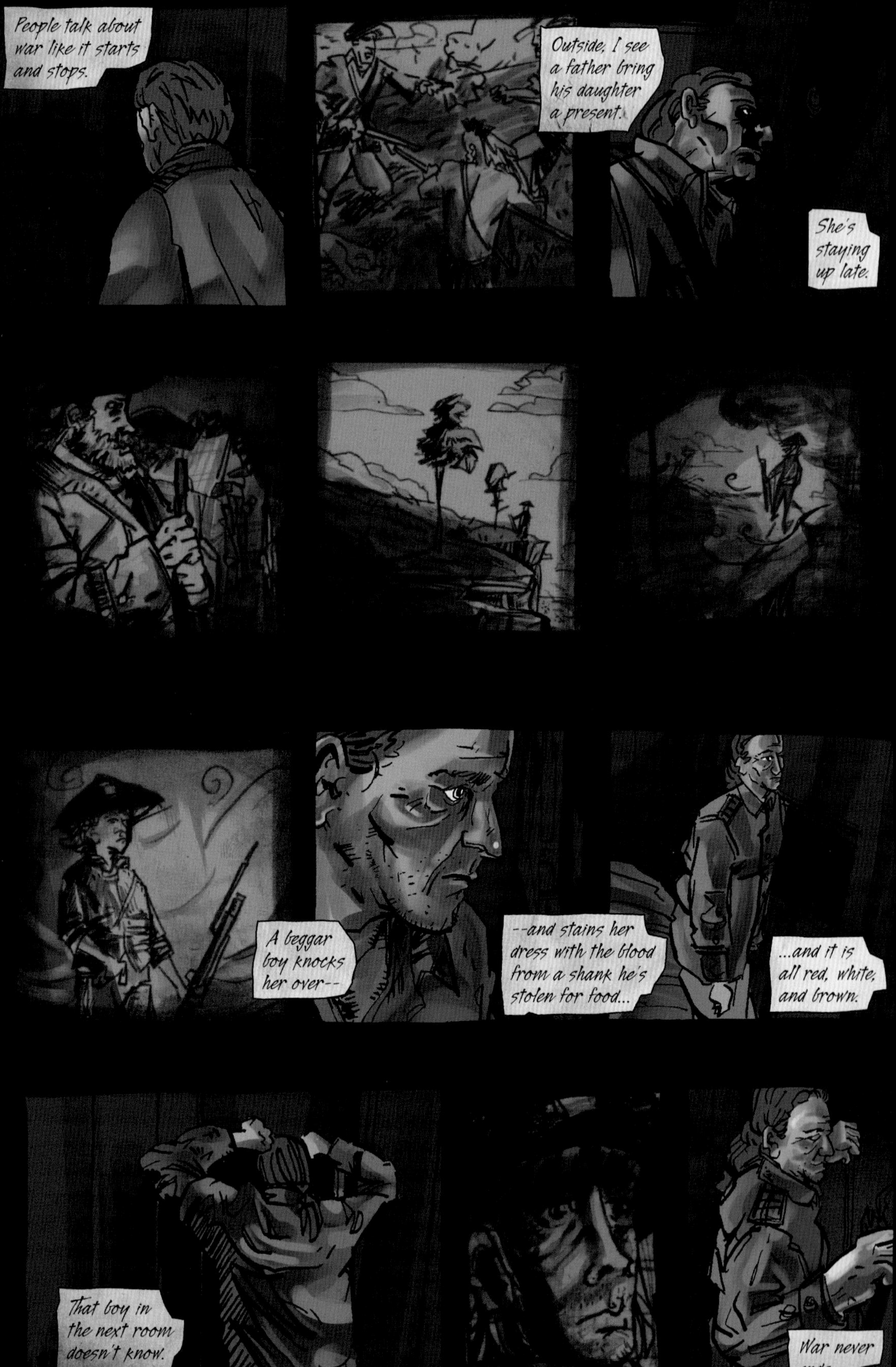
People talk about war like it starts and stops.
Outside, I see a father bring his daughter a present.
She's staying up late.
A beggar boy knocks her over--
--and stains her dress with the blood from a shank he's stolen for food...
...and it is all red, white, and brown.
That boy in the next room doesn't know.
War never ends.

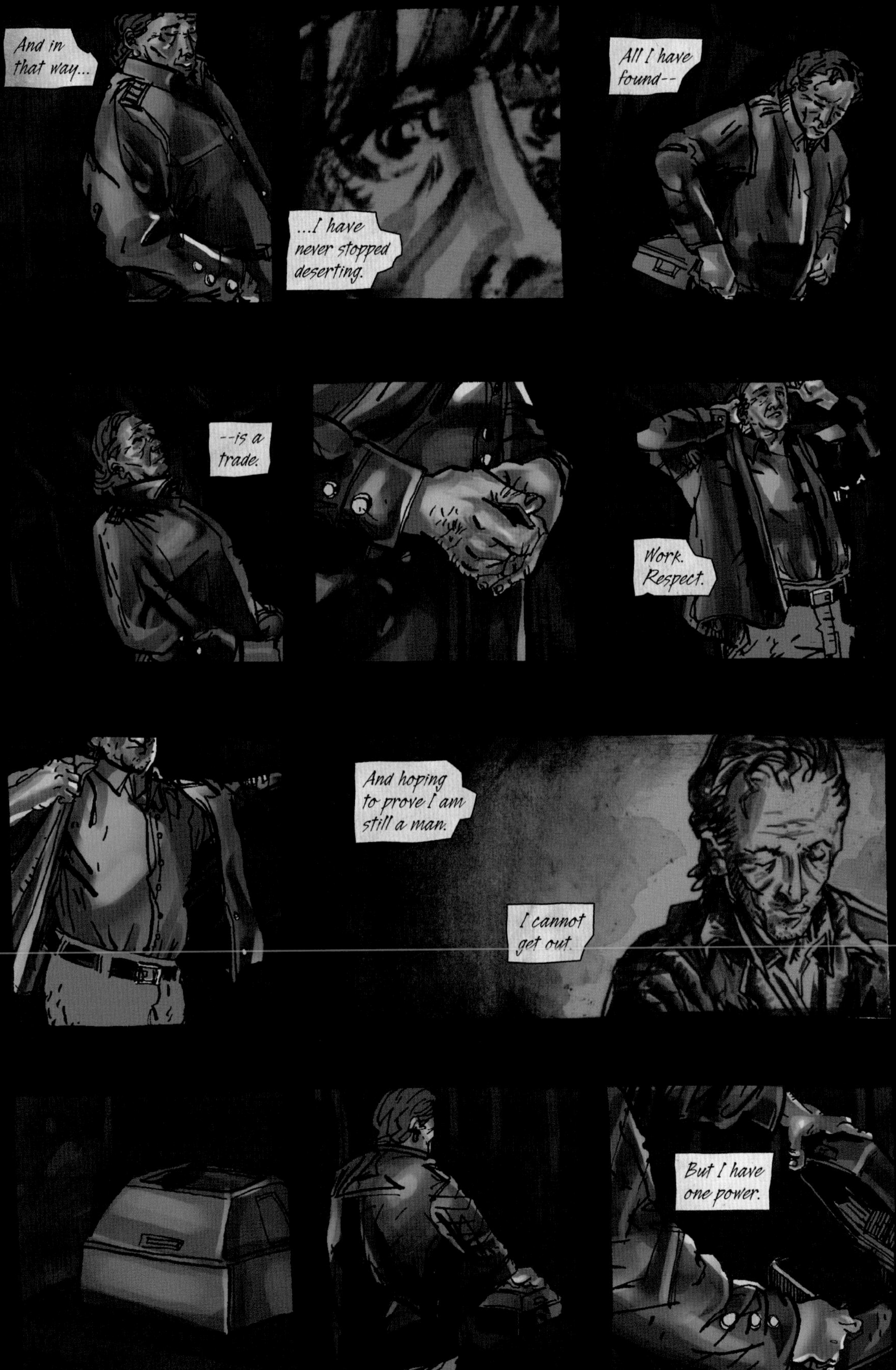
And in that way...
...I have never stopped deserting.
All I have found--
--is a trade.
Work. Respect.
And hoping to prove I am still a man.
I cannot get out.
But I have one power.

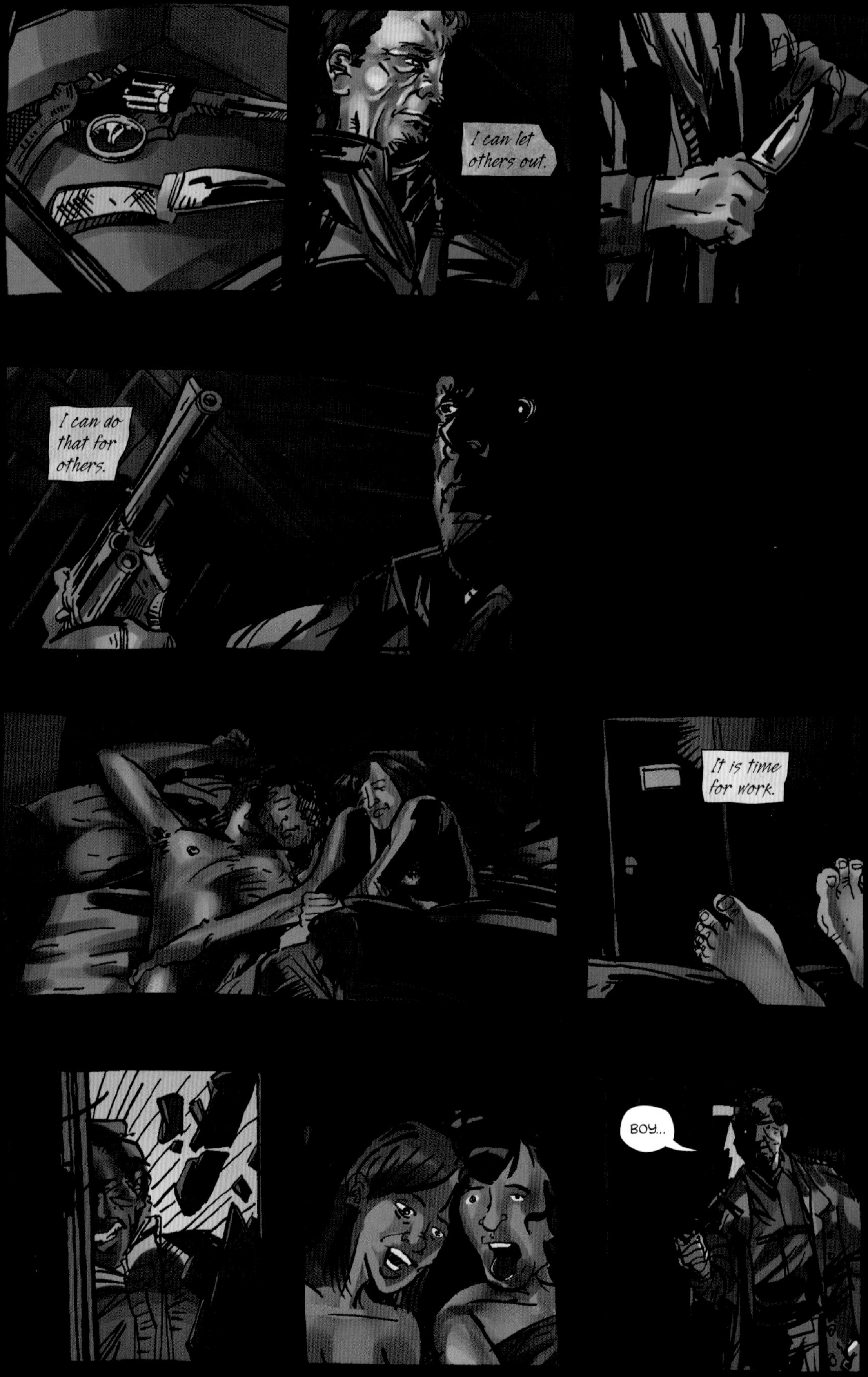
I can let others out.
I can do that for others.
It is time for work.
BOY...

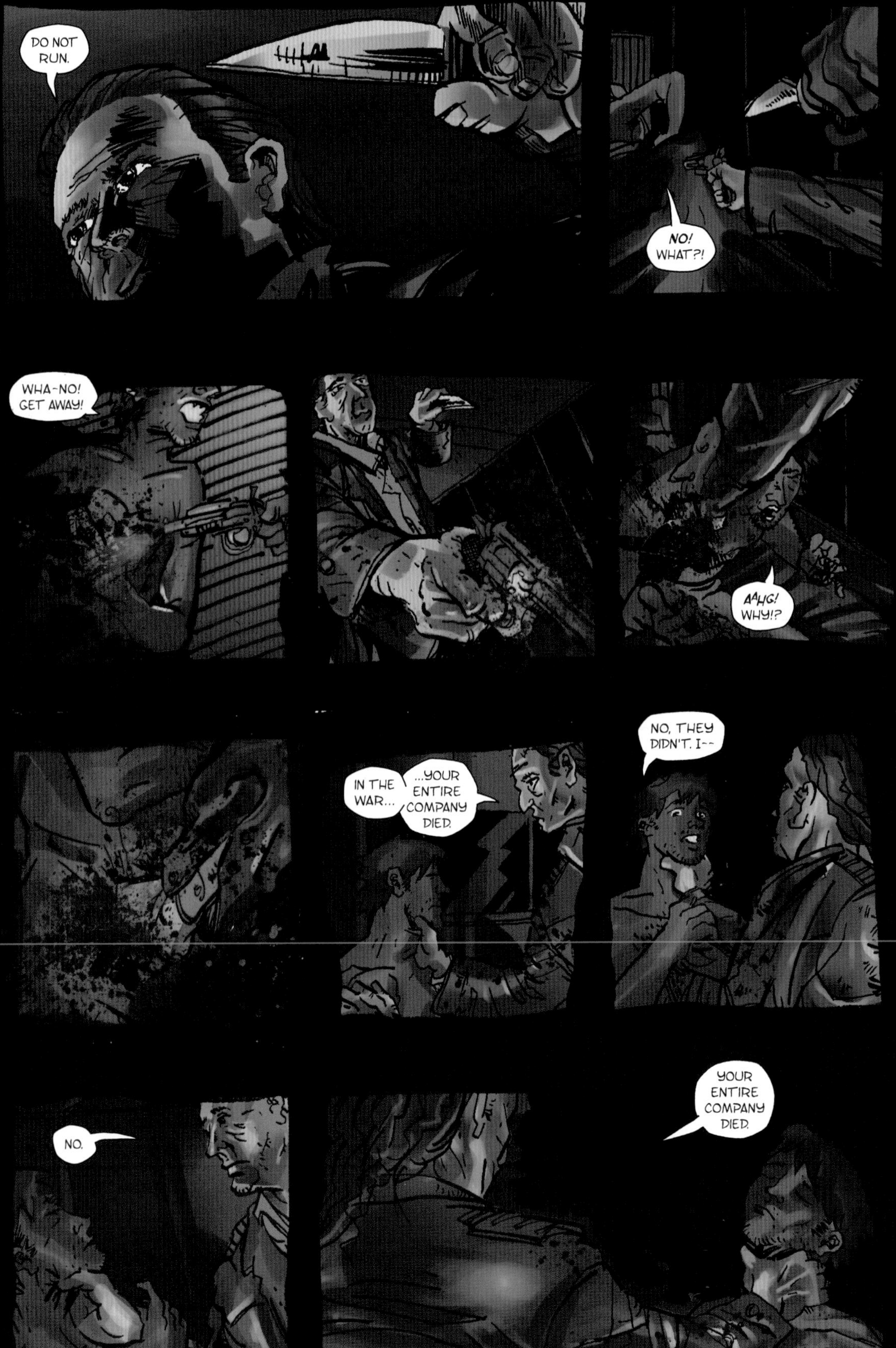
DO NOT RUN.
NO! WHAT?!
WHA-NO! GET AWAY!
AAHG! WHY!?
IN THE WAR...
...YOUR ENTIRE COMPANY DIED.
NO, THEY DIDN'T. I--
NO.
YOUR ENTIRE COMPANY DIED.

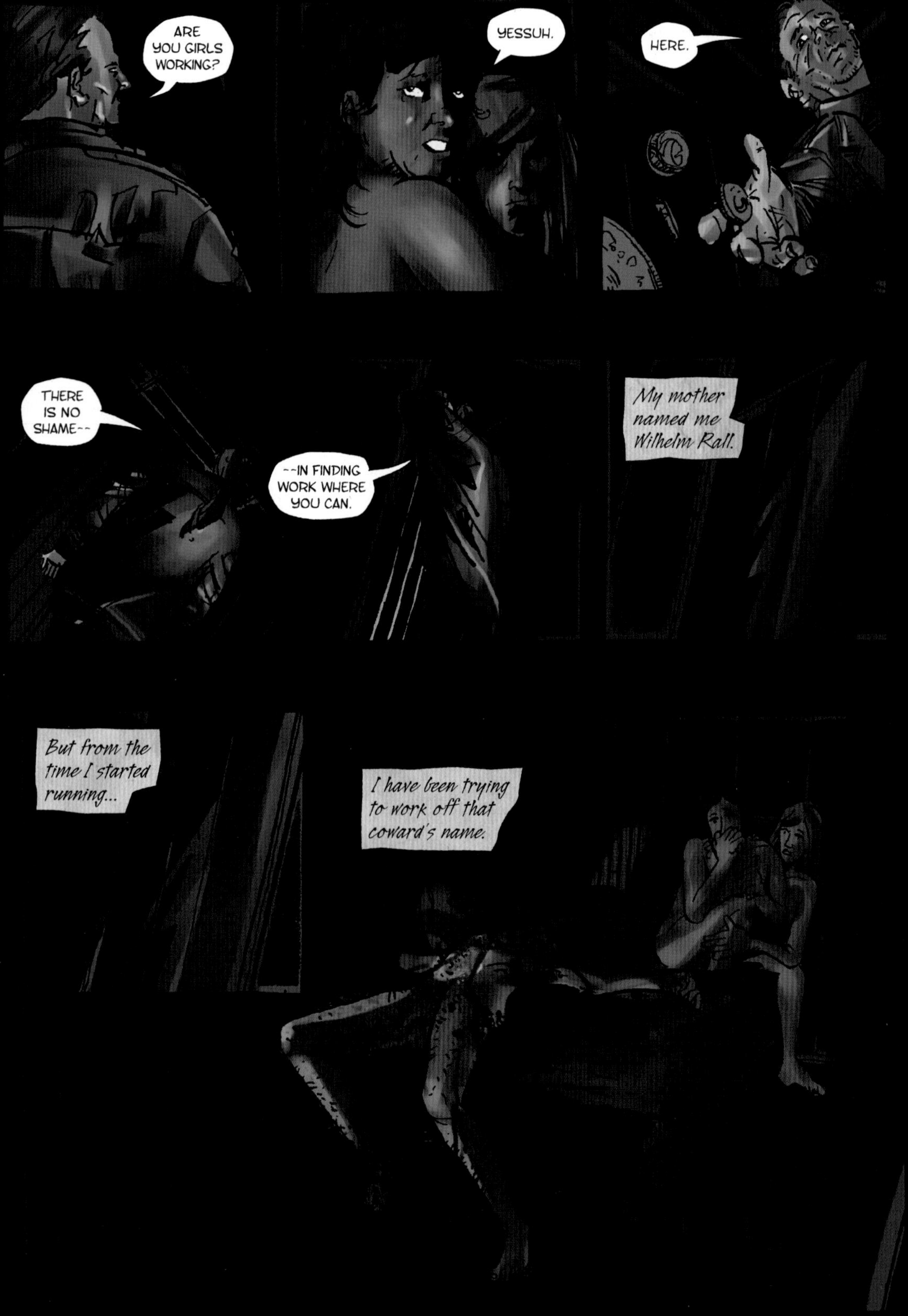
ARE YOU GIRLS WORKING?
YESSUH.
HERE.
THERE IS NO SHAME--
--IN FINDING WORK WHERE YOU CAN.
My mother named me Wilhelm Rall.
But from the time I started running...
I have been trying to work off that coward's name.

STORY: STEVE ORLANDO ART: TYLER NICCUM

COLORS: MATT RAZZANO

LETTERS: THOMAS MAUER

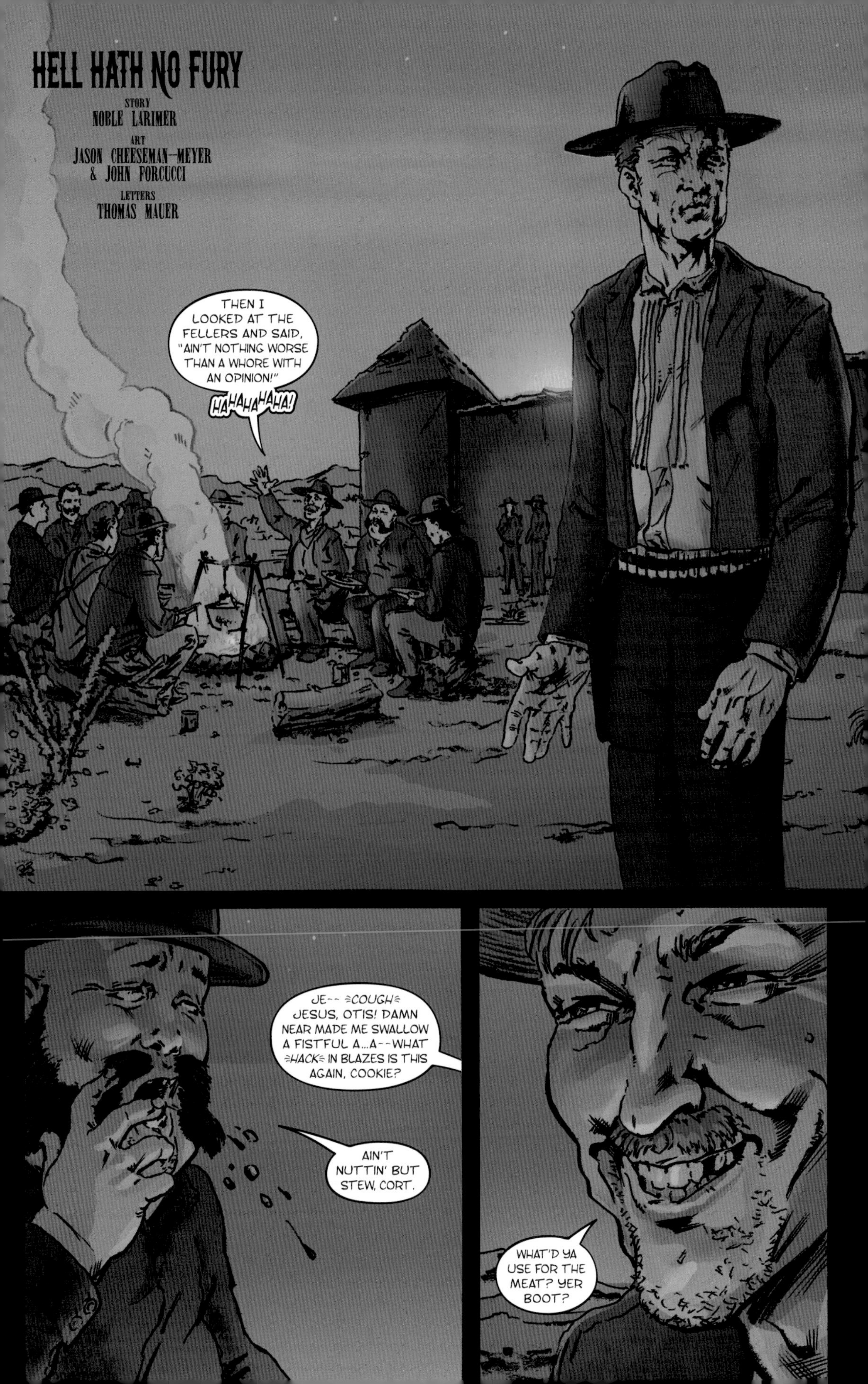
HELL HATH NO FURY
STORY
NOBLE LARIMER
ART
JASON CHEESEMAN-MEYER
& JOHN FORCUCCI
LETTERS
THOMAS MAUER
THEN I LOOKED AT THE FELLERS AND SAID, "AIN'T NOTHING WORSE THAN A WHORE WITH AN OPINION!"
HAHAHAHAHA!
JE-- ≈COUGH≈ JESUS, OTIS! DAMN NEAR MADE ME SWALLOW A FISTFUL A...A--WHAT ≈HACK≈ IN BLAZES IS THIS AGAIN, COOKIE?
AIN'T NUTTIN' BUT STEW, CORT.
WHAT'D YA USE FOR THE MEAT? YER BOOT?

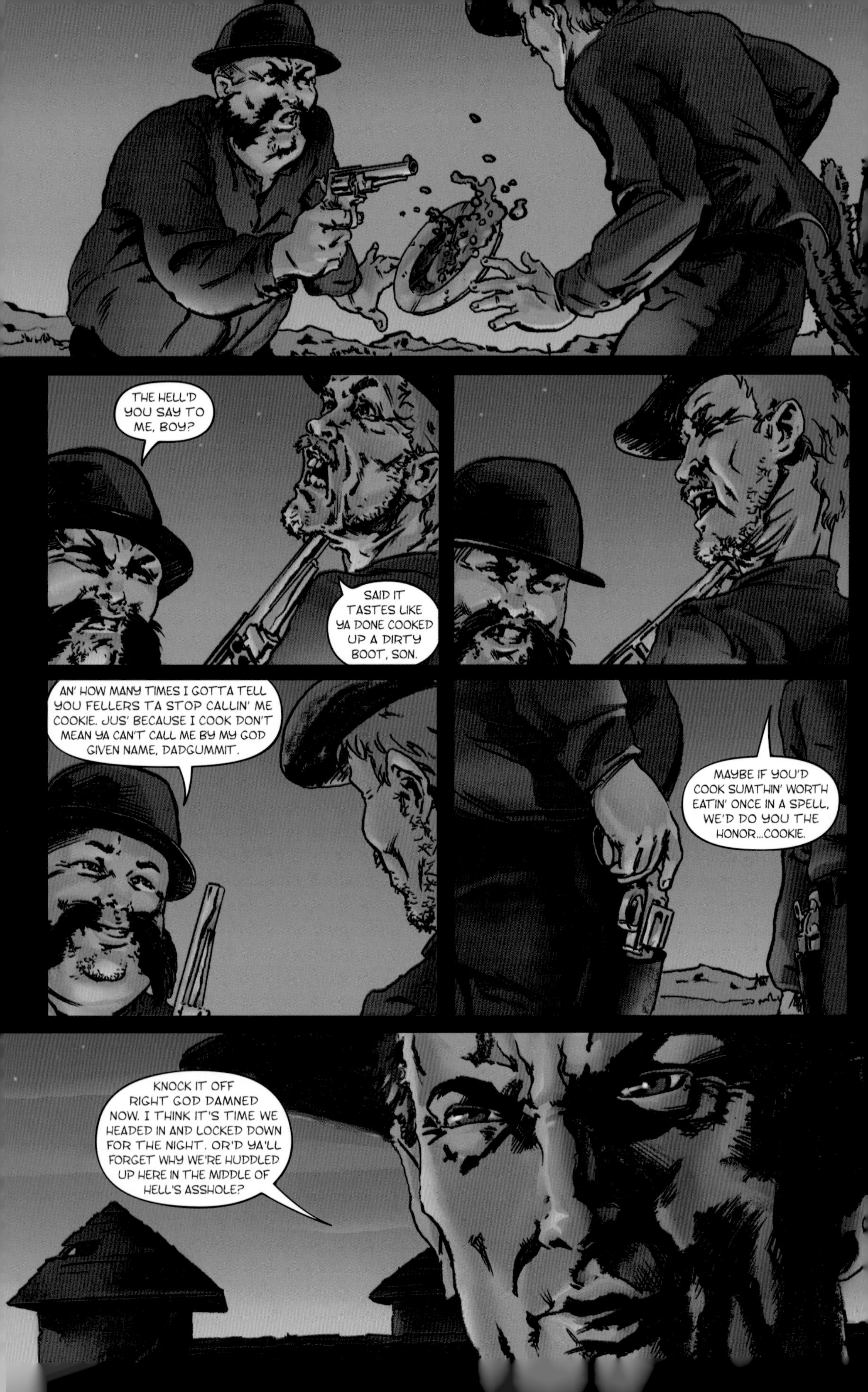
THE HELL'D YOU SAY TO ME, BOY?
SAID IT TASTES LIKE YA DONE COOKED UP A DIRTY BOOT, SON.
AN' HOW MANY TIMES I GOTTA TELL YOU FELLERS TA STOP CALLIN' ME COOKIE. JUS' BECAUSE I COOK DON'T MEAN YA CAN'T CALL ME BY MY GOD GIVEN NAME, DADGUMMIT.
MAYBE IF YOU'D COOK SUMTHIN' WORTH EATIN' ONCE IN A SPELL, WE'D DO YOU THE HONOR...COOKIE.
KNOCK IT OFF RIGHT GOD DAMNED NOW. I THINK IT'S TIME WE HEADED IN AND LOCKED DOWN FOR THE NIGHT. OR'D YA'LL FORGET WHY WE'RE HUDDLED UP HERE IN THE MIDDLE OF HELL'S ASSHOLE?

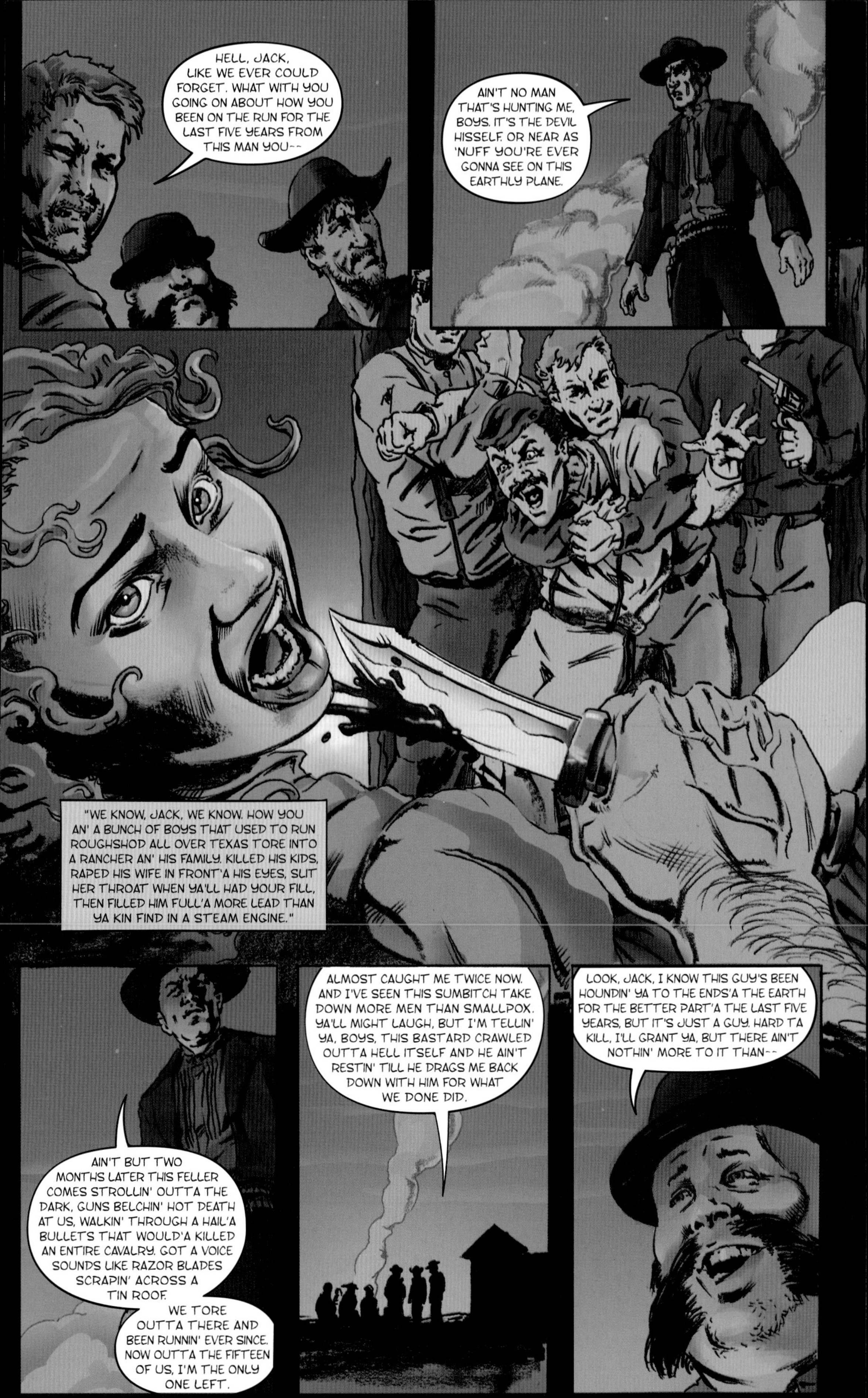
HELL, JACK, LIKE WE EVER COULD FORGET. WHAT WITH YOU GOING ON ABOUT HOW YOU BEEN ON THE RUN FOR THE LAST FIVE YEARS FROM THIS MAN YOU--
AIN'T NO MAN THAT'S HUNTING ME, BOYS. IT'S THE DEVIL HISSELF. OR NEAR AS 'NUFF YOU'RE EVER GONNA SEE ON THIS EARTHLY PLANE.
"WE KNOW, JACK, WE KNOW. HOW YOU AN' A BUNCH OF BOYS THAT USED TO RUN ROUGHSHOD ALL OVER TEXAS TORE INTO A RANCHER AN' HIS FAMILY. KILLED HIS KIDS, RAPED HIS WIFE IN FRONT'A HIS EYES, SLIT HER THROAT WHEN YA'LL HAD YOUR FILL, THEN FILLED HIM FULL'A MORE LEAD THAN YA KIN FIND IN A STEAM ENGINE."
AIN'T BUT TWO MONTHS LATER THIS FELLER COMES STROLLIN' OUTTA THE DARK, GUNS BELCHIN' HOT DEATH AT US, WALKIN' THROUGH A HAIL'A BULLETS THAT WOULD'A KILLED AN ENTIRE CAVALRY. GOT A VOICE SOUNDS LIKE RAZOR BLADES SCRAPIN' ACROSS A TIN ROOF.
WE TORE OUTTA THERE AND BEEN RUNNIN' EVER SINCE. NOW OUTTA THE FIFTEEN OF US, I'M THE ONLY ONE LEFT.
ALMOST CAUGHT ME TWICE NOW. AND I'VE SEEN THIS SUMBITCH TAKE DOWN MORE MEN THAN SMALLPOX. YA'LL MIGHT LAUGH, BUT I'M TELLIN' YA, BOYS, THIS BASTARD CRAWLED OUTTA HELL ITSELF AND HE AIN'T RESTIN' TILL HE DRAGS ME BACK DOWN WITH HIM FOR WHAT WE DONE DID.
LOOK, JACK, I KNOW THIS GUY'S BEEN HOUNDIN' YA TO THE ENDS'A THE EARTH FOR THE BETTER PART'A THE LAST FIVE YEARS, BUT IT'S JUST A GUY. HARD TA KILL, I'LL GRANT YA, BUT THERE AIN'T NOTHIN' MORE TO IT THAN--

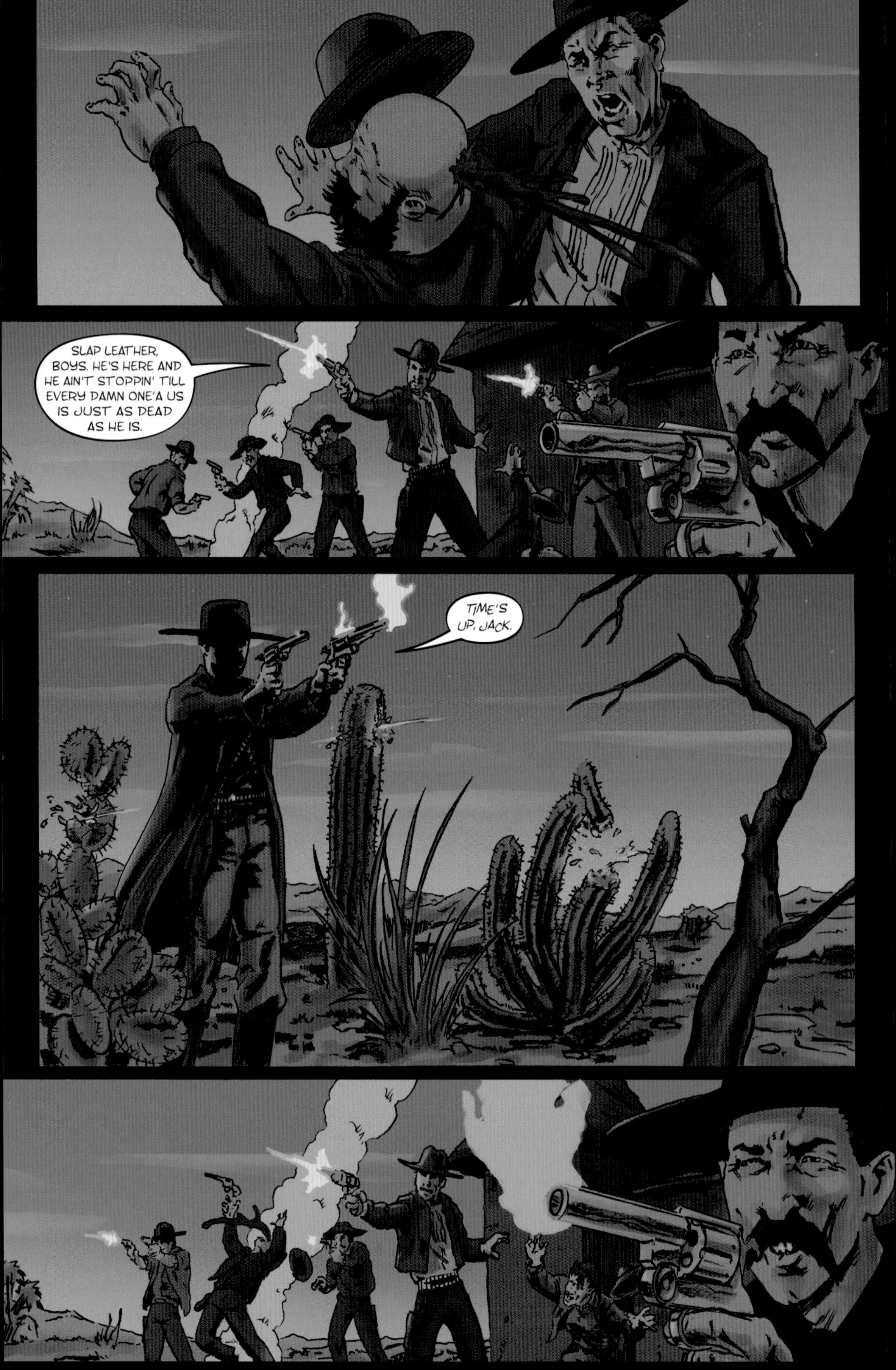
SLAP LEATHER, BOYS. HE'S HERE AND HE AIN'T STOPPIN' TILL EVERY DAMN ONE'A US IS JUST AS DEAD AS HE IS.
TIME'S UP, JACK.

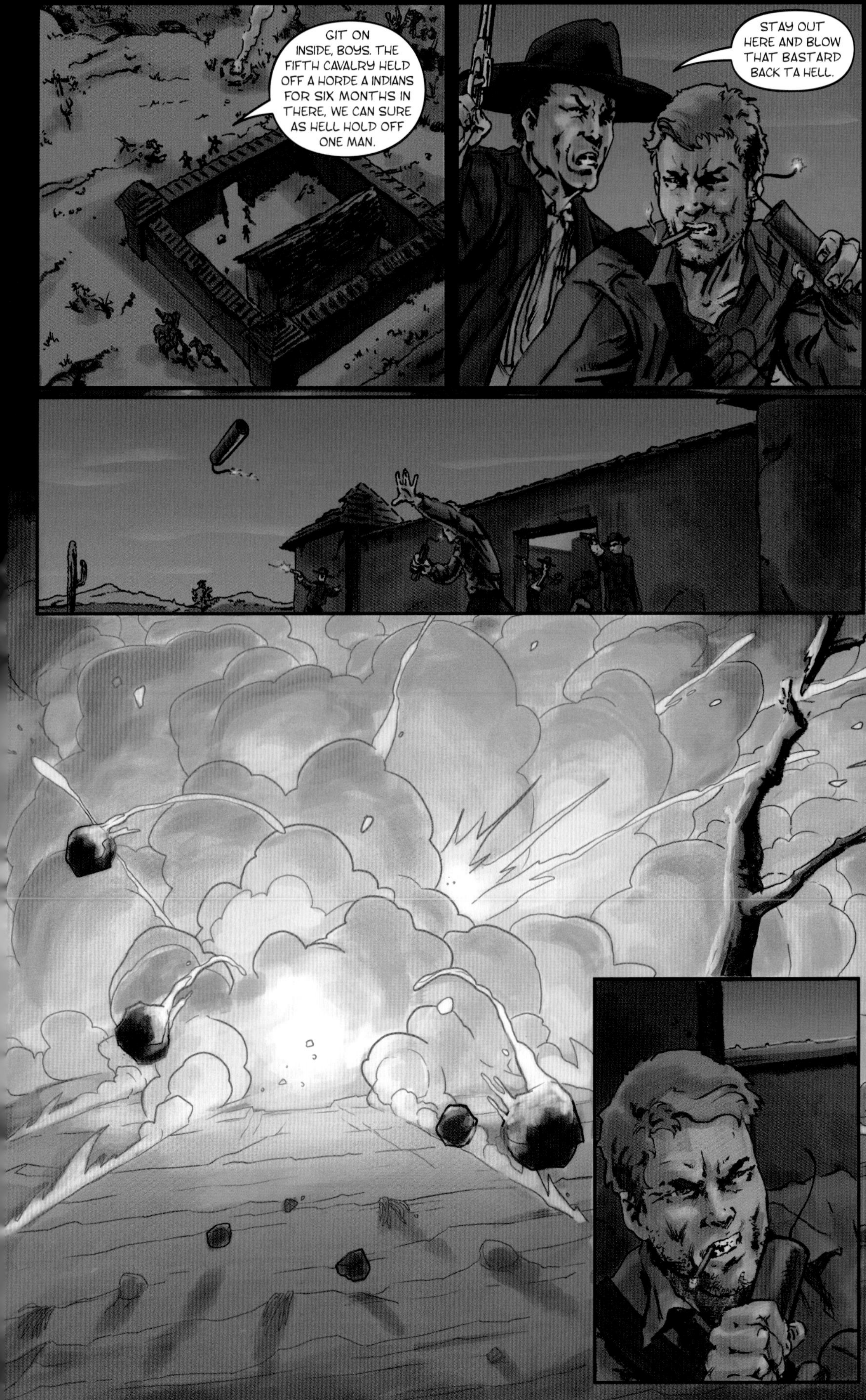
GIT ON INSIDE, BOYS. THE FIFTH CAVALRY HELD OFF A HORDE A INDIANS FOR SIX MONTHS IN THERE, WE CAN SURE AS HELL HOLD OFF ONE MAN.
STAY OUT HERE AND BLOW THAT BASTARD BACK TA HELL.

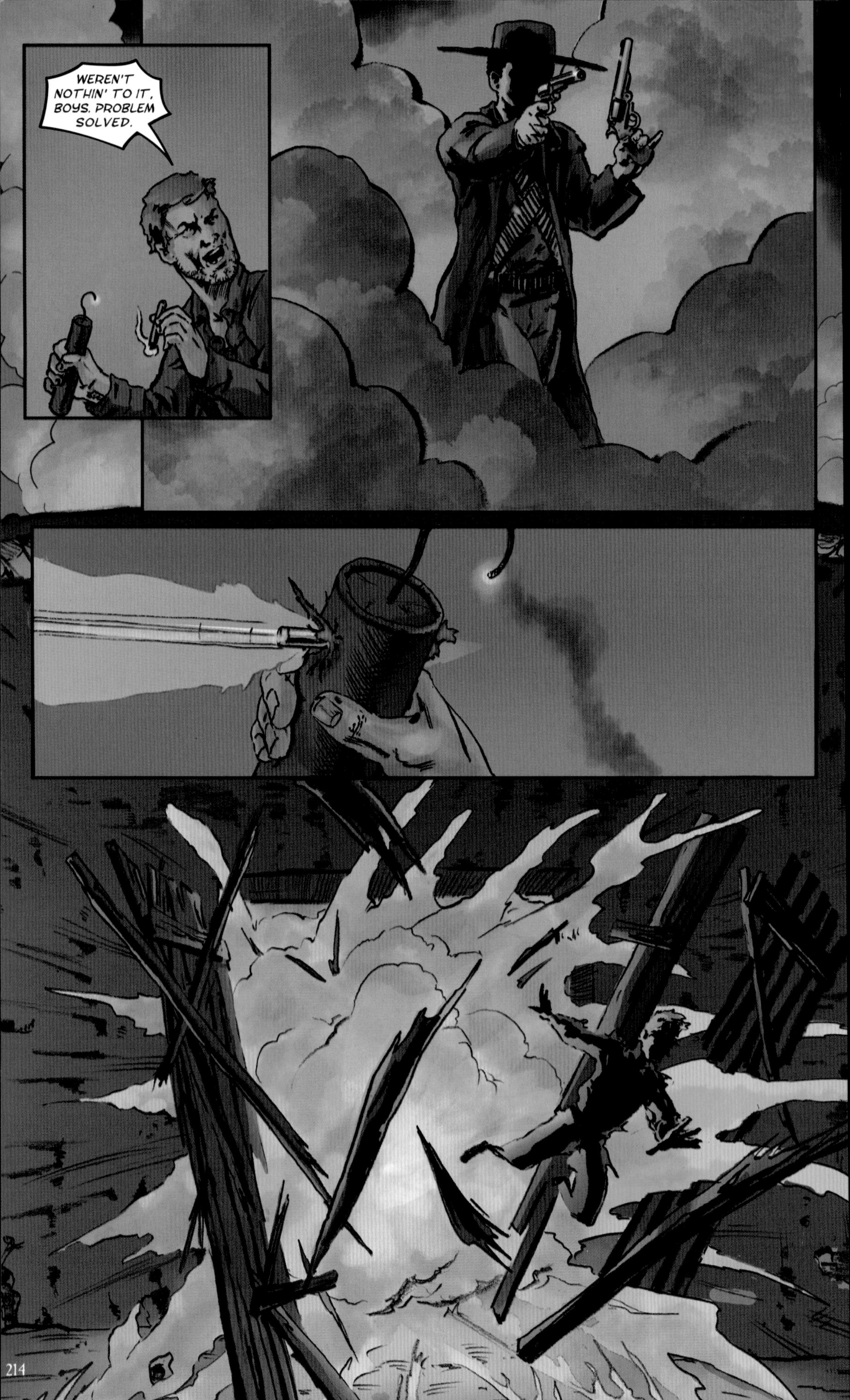
WEREN'T NOTHIN' TO IT, BOYS. PROBLEM SOLVED.

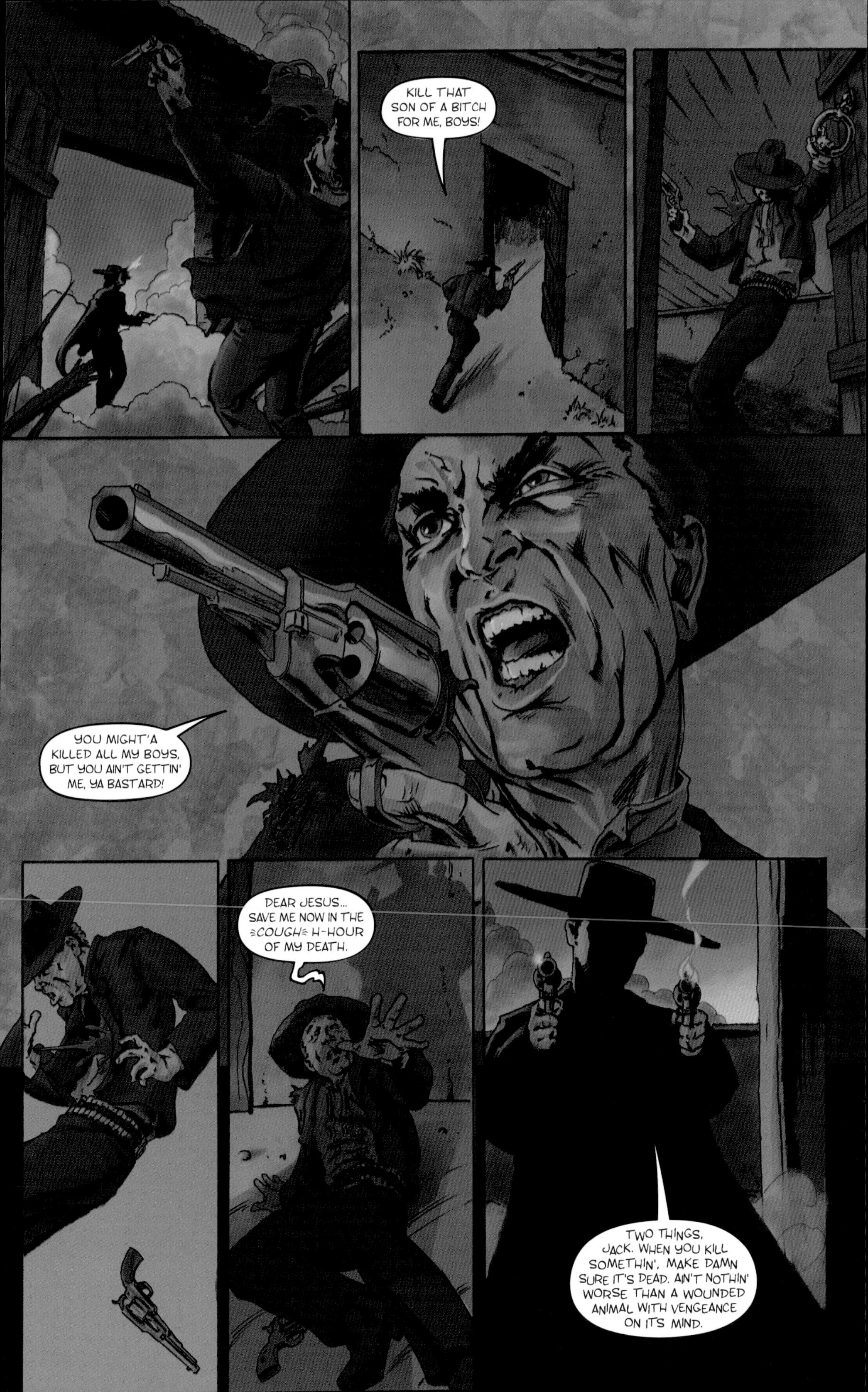
KILL THAT SON OF A BITCH FOR ME, BOYS!
YOU MIGHT'A KILLED ALL MY BOYS, BUT YOU AIN'T GETTIN' ME, YA BASTARD!
DEAR JESUS... SAVE ME NOW IN THE =COUGH= H-HOUR OF MY DEATH.
TWO THINGS, JACK. WHEN YOU KILL SOMETHIN', MAKE DAMN SURE IT'S DEAD. AIN'T NOTHIN' WORSE THAN A WOUNDED ANIMAL WITH VENGEANCE ON ITS MIND.

AND...HELL HATH NO FURY LIKE A WOMAN SCORNED.

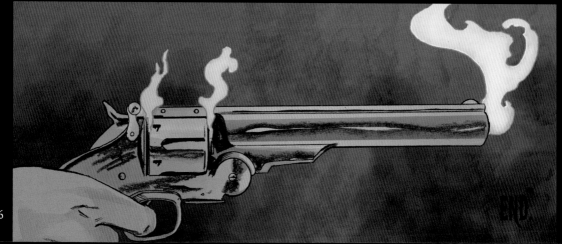

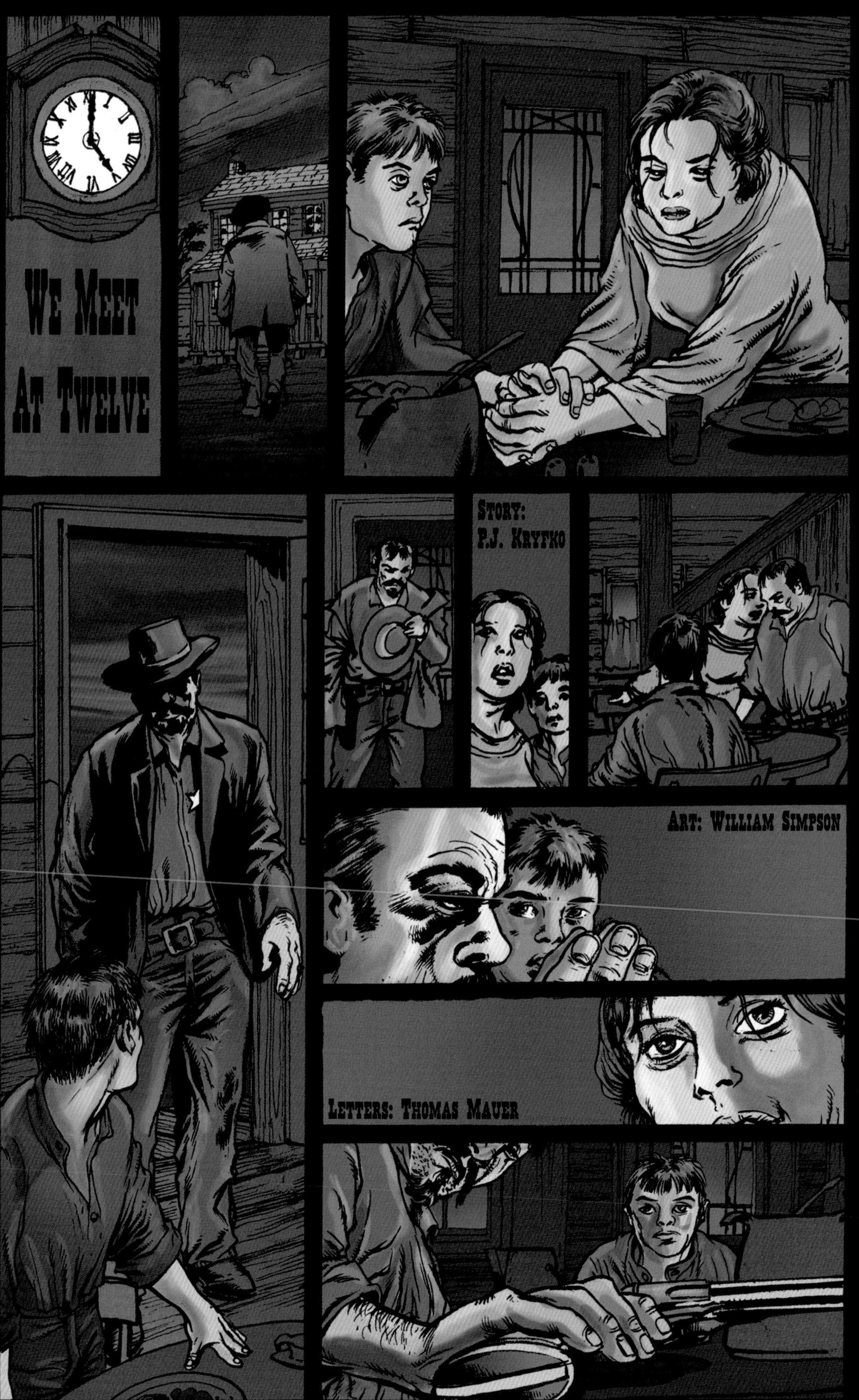
We Meet
At Twelve
Story:
P.J. Kryfko
Art: William Simpson
Letters: Thomas Mauer

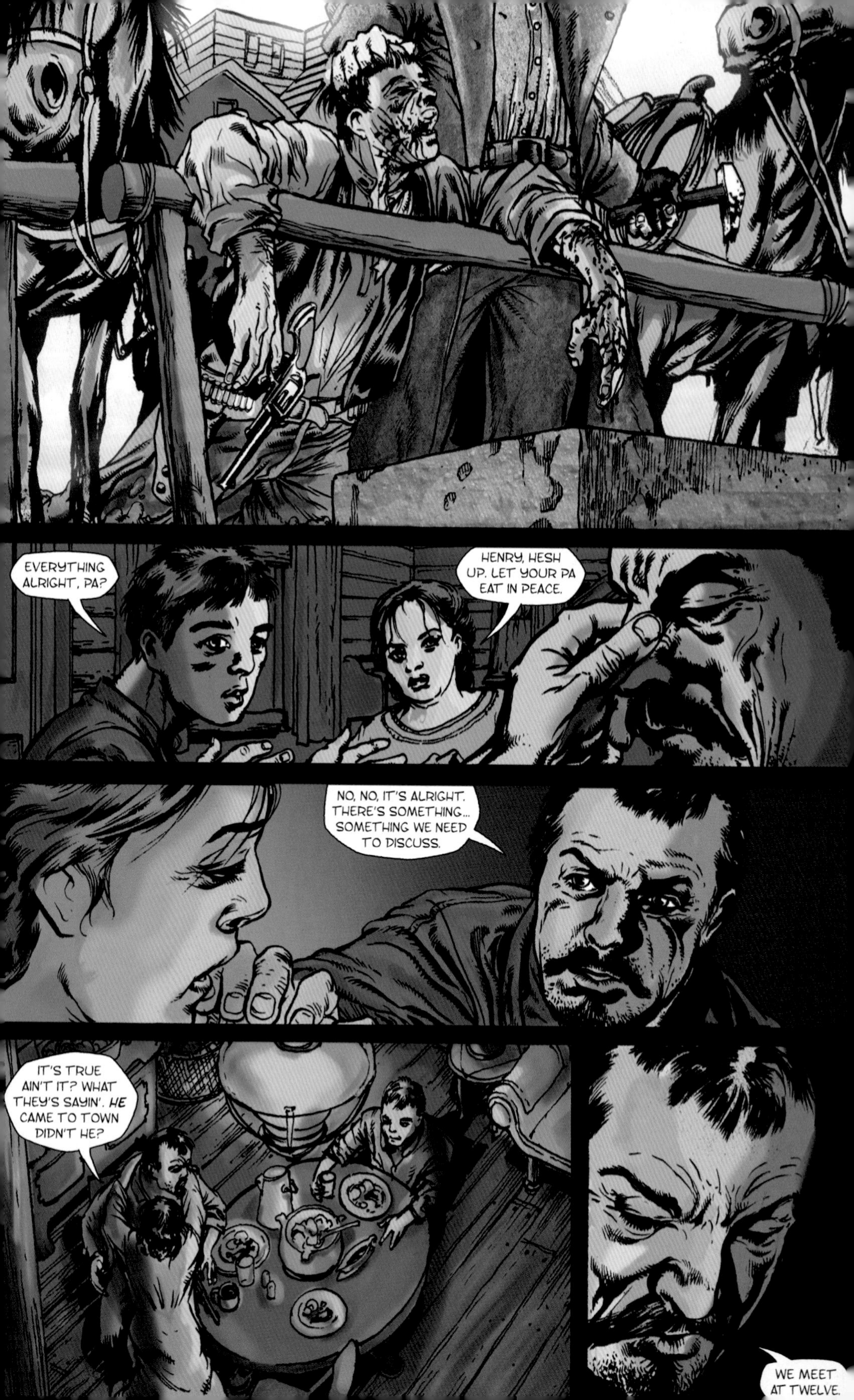
EVERYTHING ALRIGHT, PA?
HENRY, HESH UP. LET YOUR PA EAT IN PEACE.
NO, NO, IT'S ALRIGHT. THERE'S SOMETHING... SOMETHING WE NEED TO DISCUSS.
IT'S TRUE AIN'T IT? WHAT THEY'S SAYIN'. *HE* CAME TO TOWN DIDN'T HE?
WE MEET AT TWELVE.

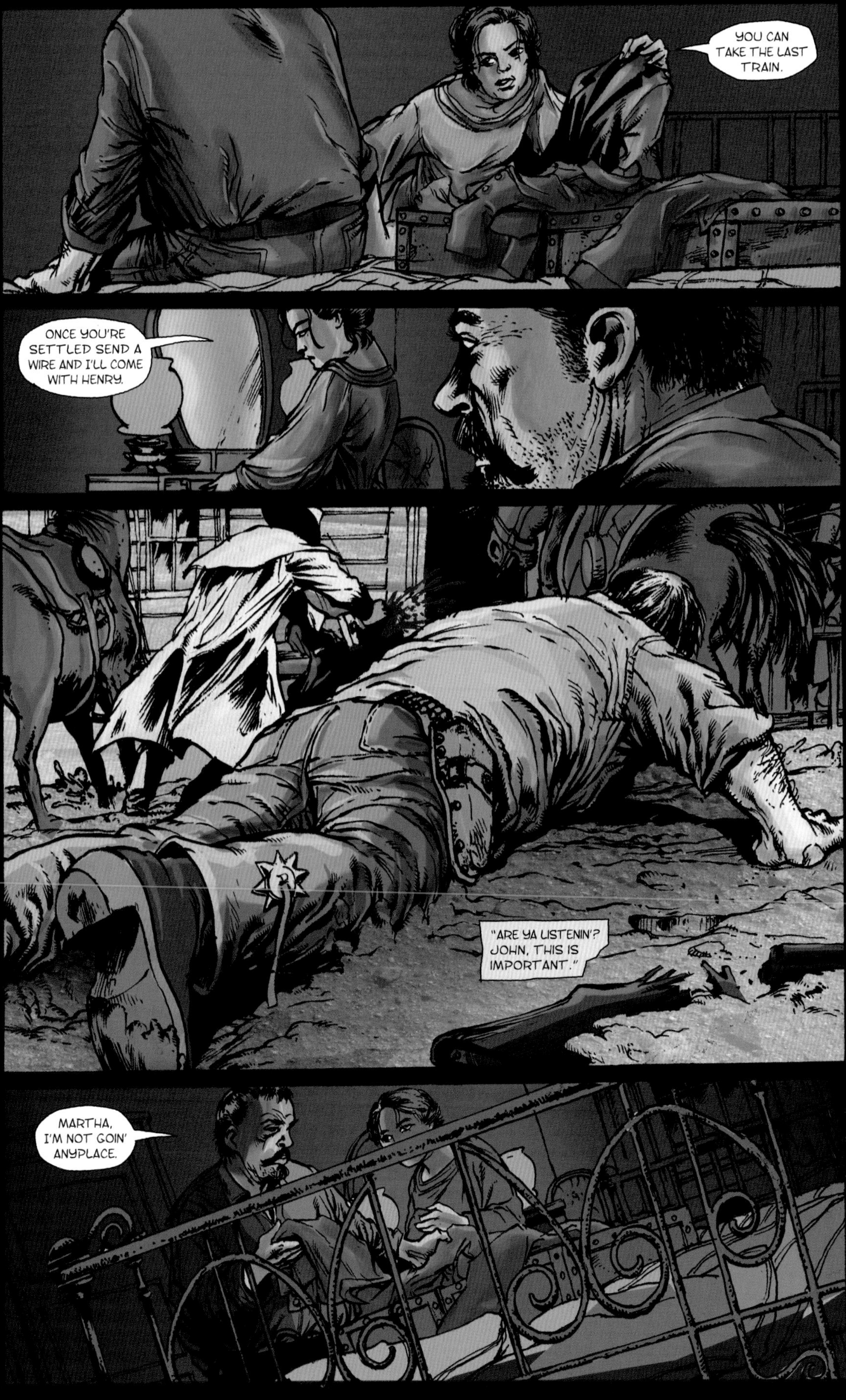
YOU CAN TAKE THE LAST TRAIN.
ONCE YOU'RE SETTLED SEND A WIRE AND I'LL COME WITH HENRY.
"ARE YA LISTENIN'? JOHN, THIS IS IMPORTANT."
MARTHA, I'M NOT GOIN' ANYPLACE.

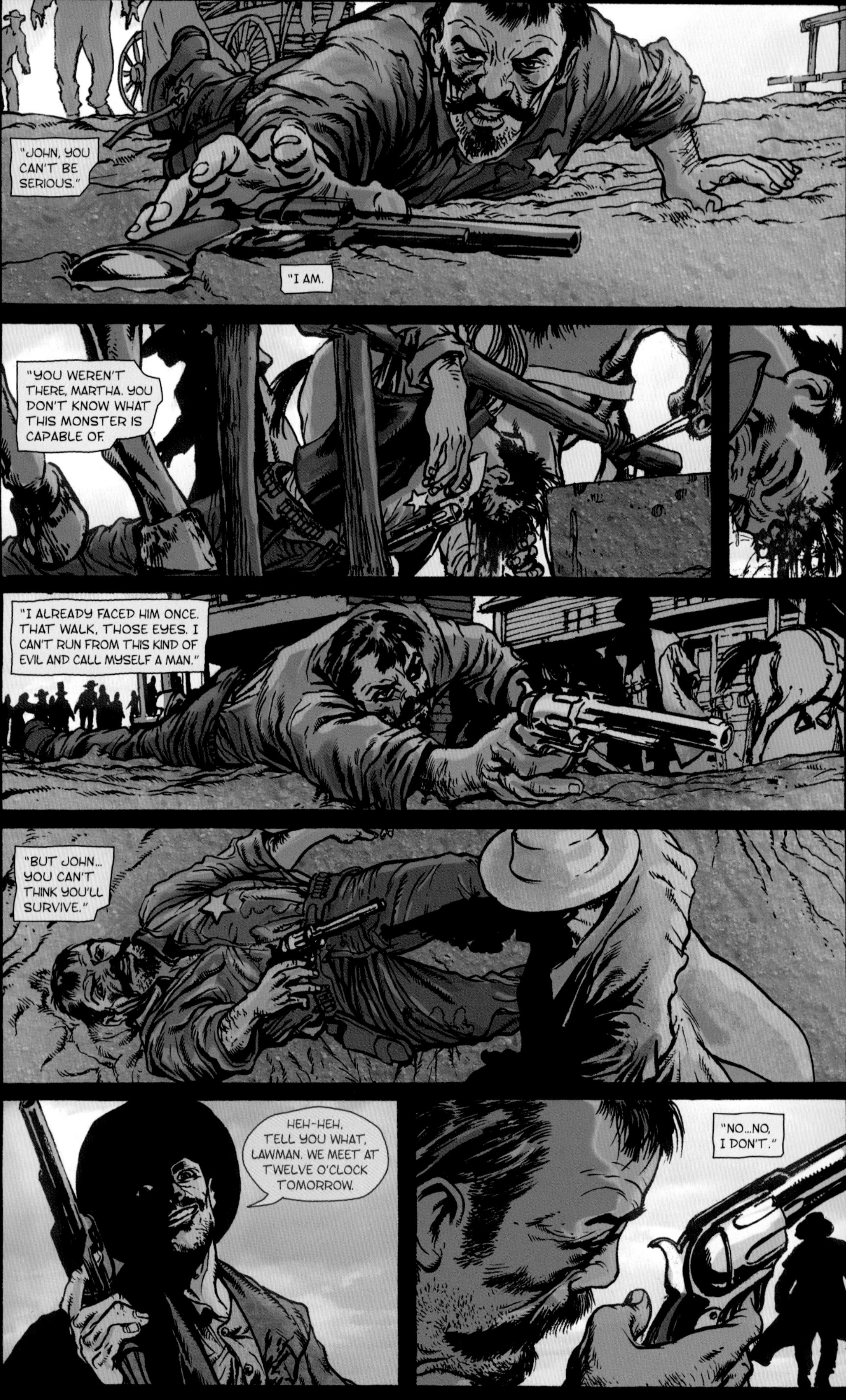
"JOHN, YOU CAN'T BE SERIOUS."
"I AM.
"YOU WEREN'T THERE, MARTHA. YOU DON'T KNOW WHAT THIS MONSTER IS CAPABLE OF.
"I ALREADY FACED HIM ONCE. THAT WALK, THOSE EYES. I CAN'T RUN FROM THIS KIND OF EVIL AND CALL MYSELF A MAN."
"BUT JOHN... YOU CAN'T THINK YOU'LL SURVIVE."
HEH-HEH, TELL YOU WHAT, LAWMAN. WE MEET AT TWELVE O'CLOCK TOMORROW.
"NO...NO, I DON'T."

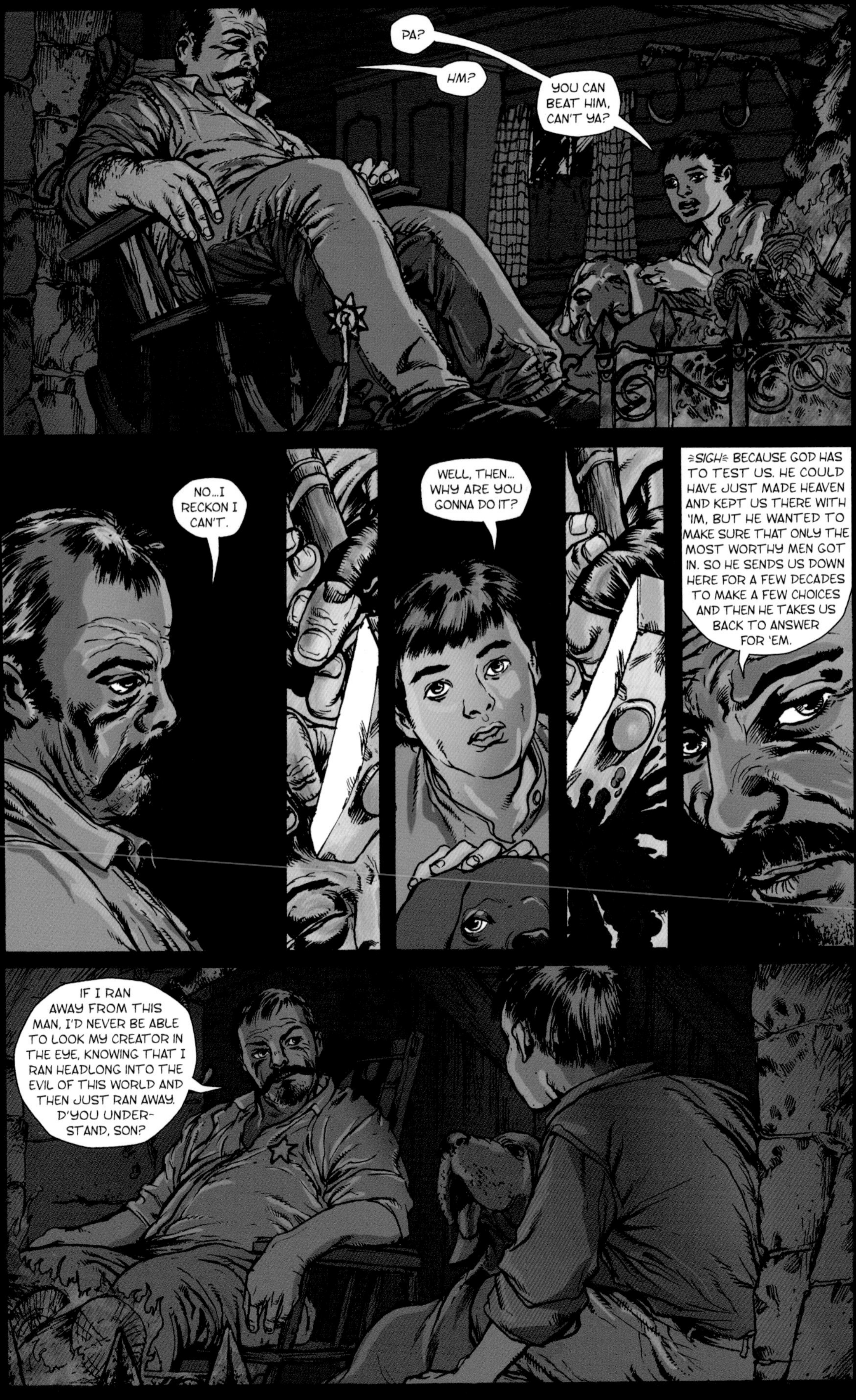
PA?
HM?
YOU CAN BEAT HIM, CAN'T YA?
NO...I RECKON I CAN'T.
WELL, THEN... WHY ARE YOU GONNA DO IT?
≈SIGH≈ BECAUSE GOD HAS TO TEST US. HE COULD HAVE JUST MADE HEAVEN AND KEPT US THERE WITH 'IM, BUT HE WANTED TO MAKE SURE THAT ONLY THE MOST WORTHY MEN GOT IN. SO HE SENDS US DOWN HERE FOR A FEW DECADES TO MAKE A FEW CHOICES AND THEN HE TAKES US BACK TO ANSWER FOR 'EM.
IF I RAN AWAY FROM THIS MAN, I'D NEVER BE ABLE TO LOOK MY CREATOR IN THE EYE, KNOWING THAT I RAN HEADLONG INTO THE EVIL OF THIS WORLD AND THEN JUST RAN AWAY. D'YOU UNDERSTAND, SON?

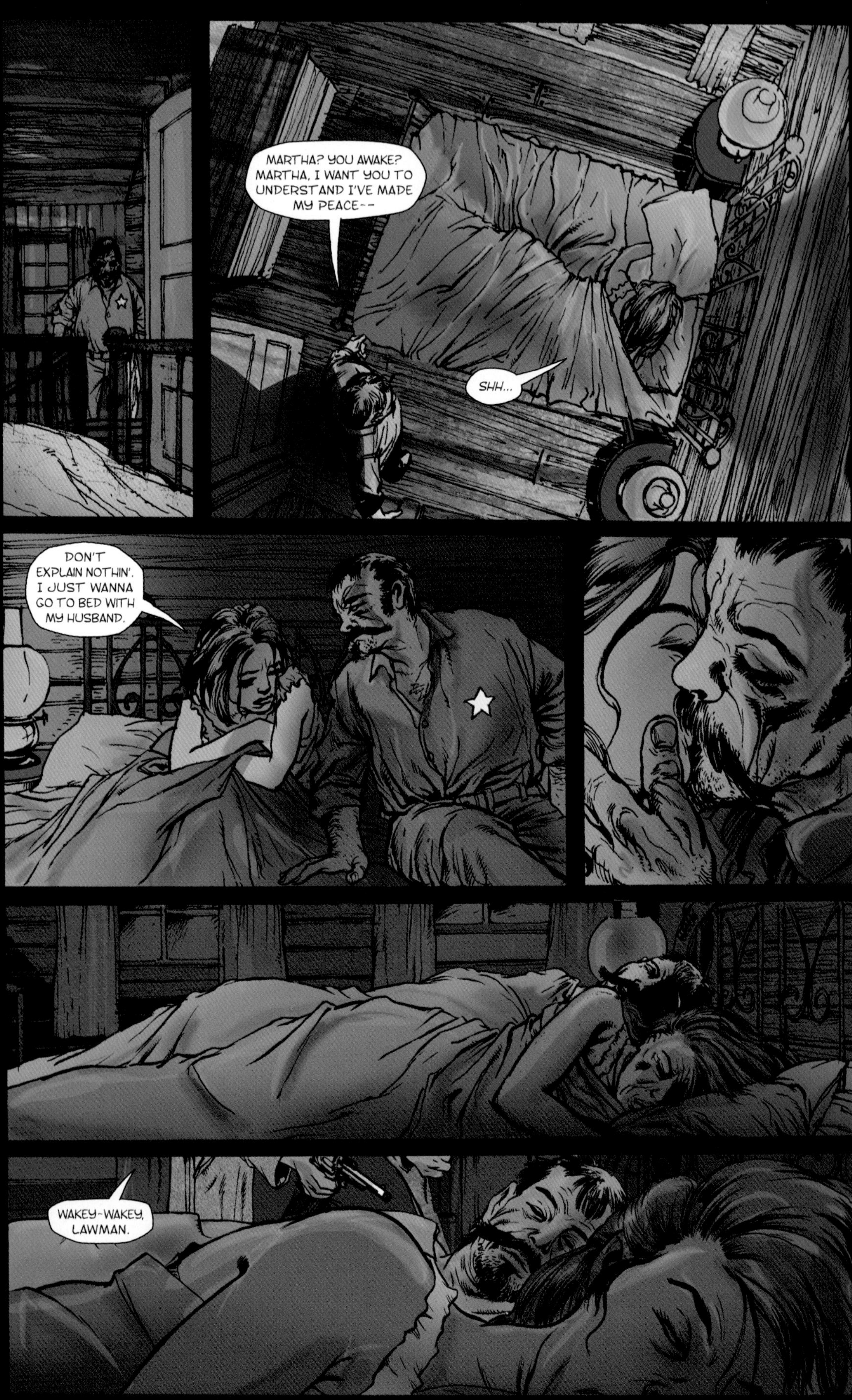
MARTHA? YOU AWAKE? MARTHA, I WANT YOU TO UNDERSTAND I'VE MADE MY PEACE--
SHH...
DON'T EXPLAIN NOTHIN'. I JUST WANNA GO TO BED WITH MY HUSBAND.
WAKEY-WAKEY, LAWMAN.

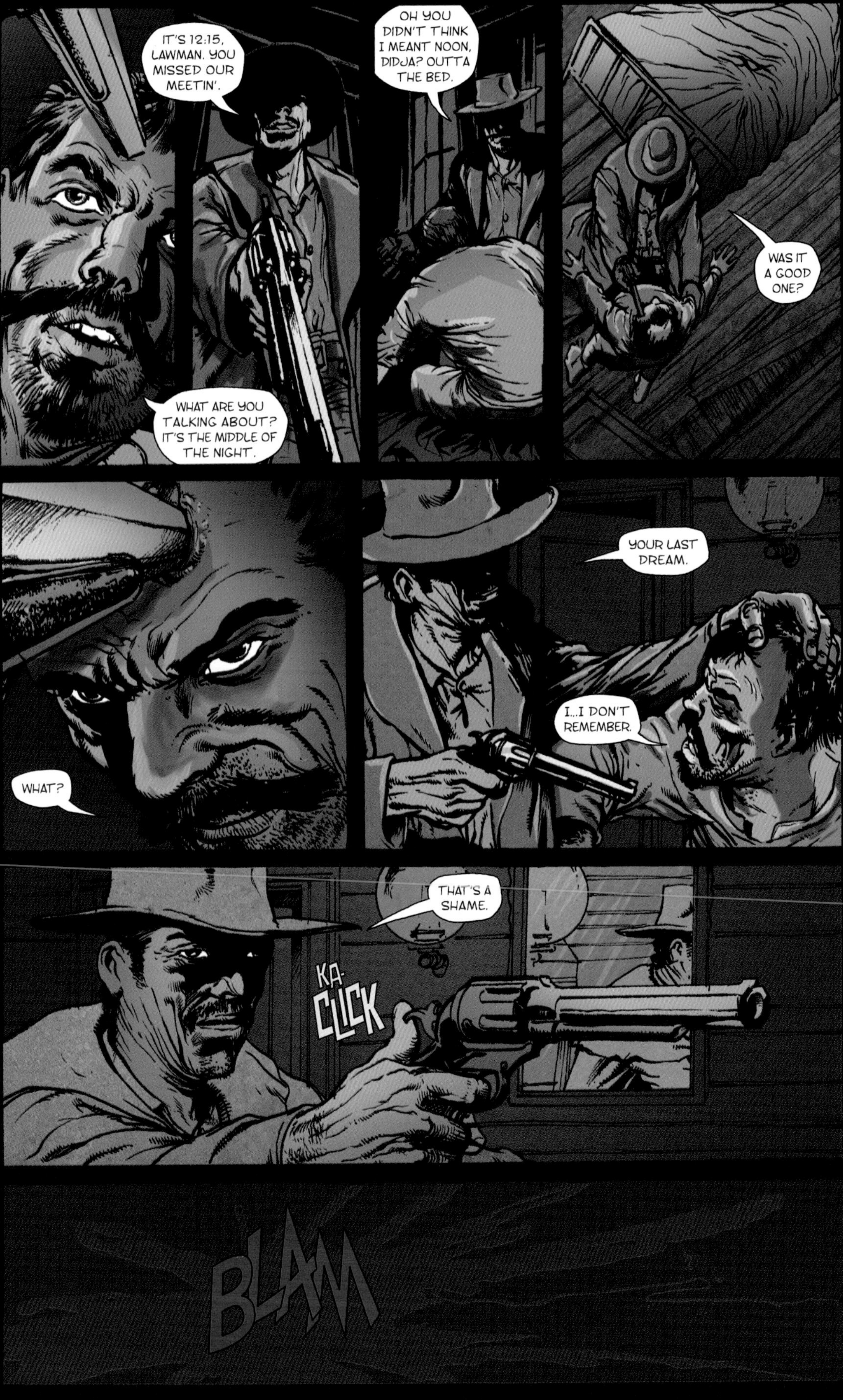
IT'S 12:15, LAWMAN. YOU MISSED OUR MEETIN'.
WHAT ARE YOU TALKING ABOUT? IT'S THE MIDDLE OF THE NIGHT.
OH YOU DIDN'T THINK I MEANT NOON, DIDJA? OUTTA THE BED.
WAS IT A GOOD ONE?
WHAT?
YOUR LAST DREAM.
I...I DON'T REMEMBER.
THAT'S A SHAME.
KA-CLICK
BLAM

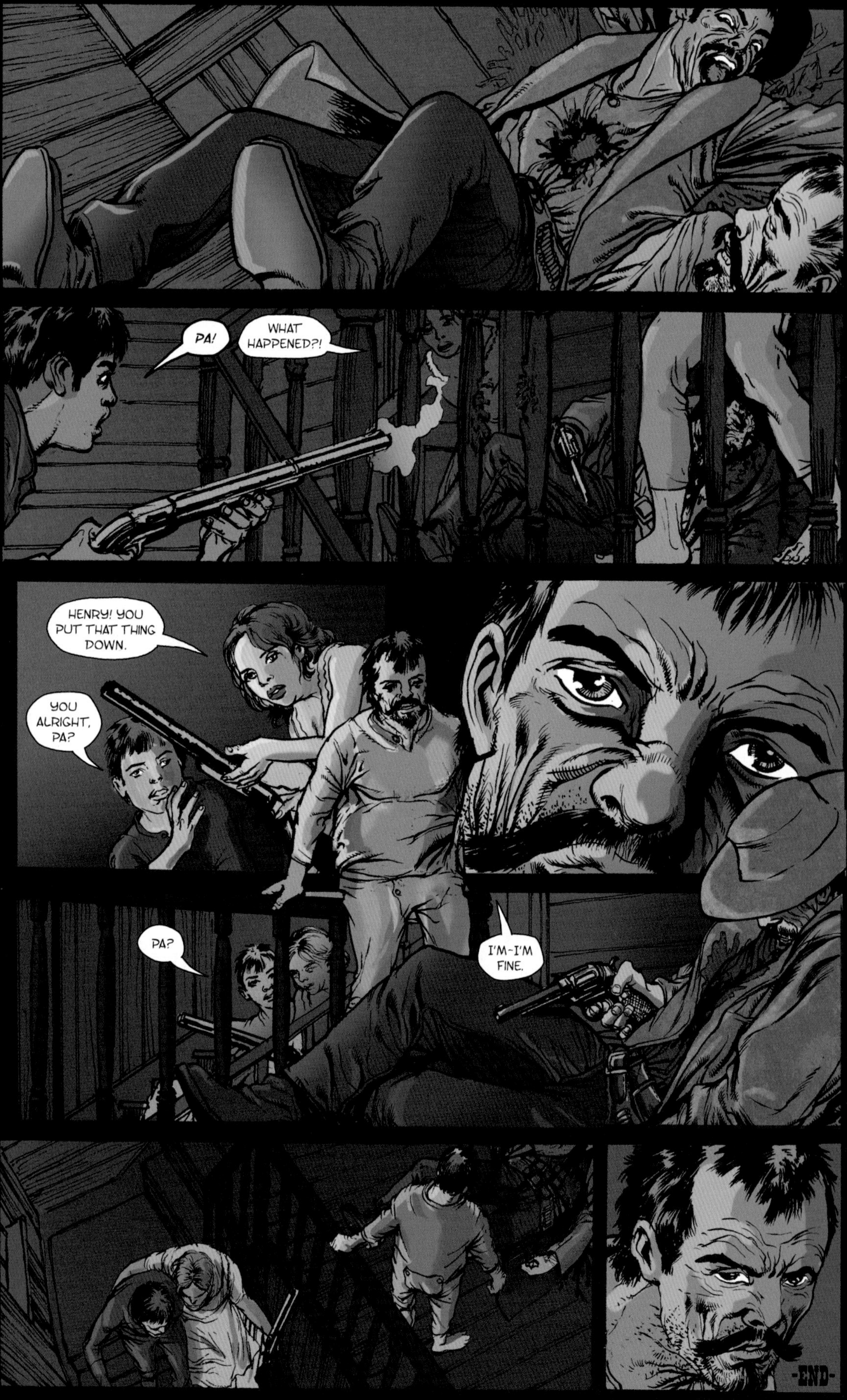
PA!
WHAT HAPPENED?!
HENRY! YOU PUT THAT THING DOWN.
YOU ALRIGHT, PA?
PA?
I'M-I'M FINE.
-END-

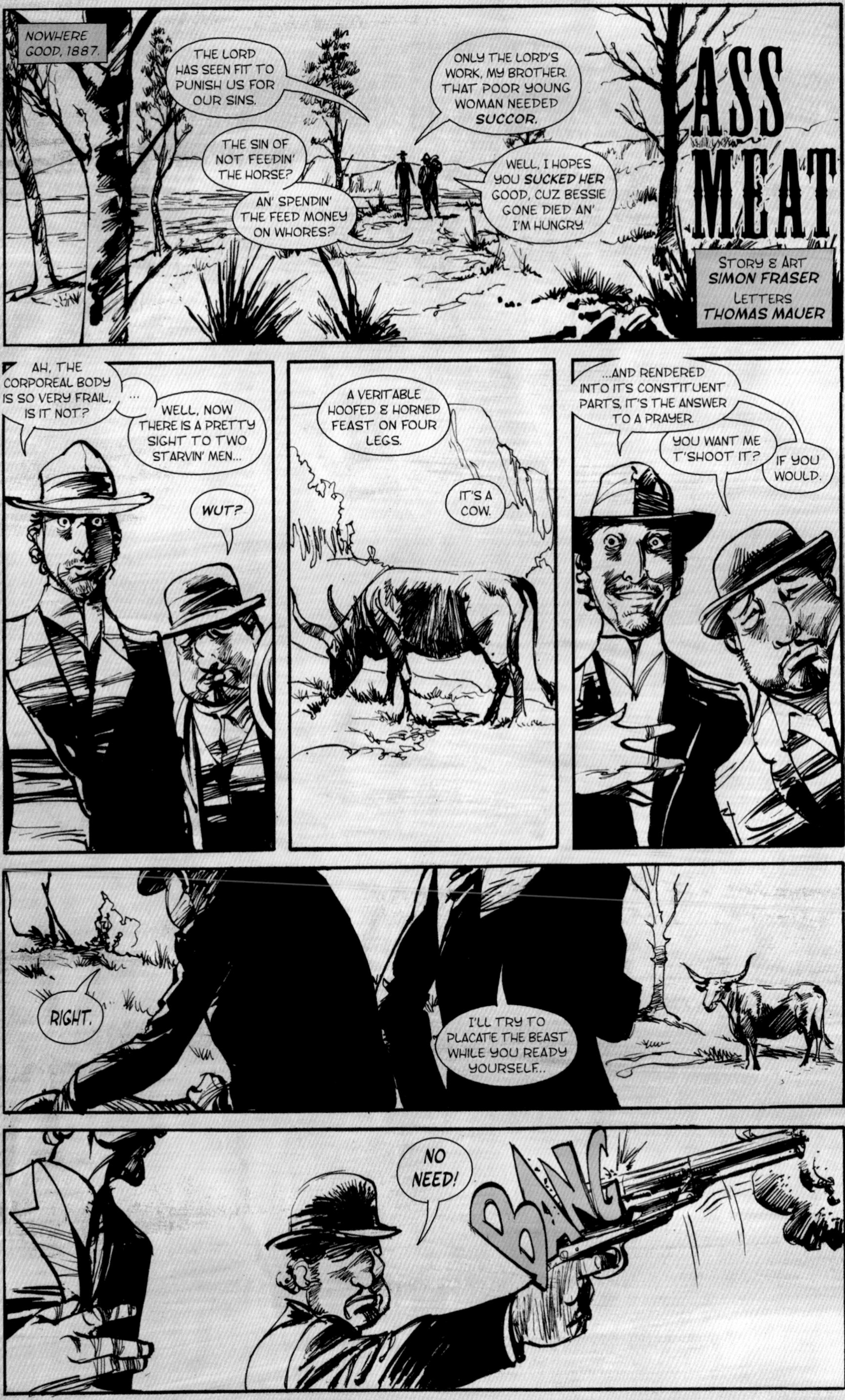
NOWHERE GOOD, 1887.
THE LORD HAS SEEN FIT TO PUNISH US FOR OUR SINS.
ONLY THE LORD'S WORK, MY BROTHER. THAT POOR YOUNG WOMAN NEEDED SUCCOR.
THE SIN OF NOT FEEDIN' THE HORSE?
AN' SPENDIN' THE FEED MONEY ON WHORES?
WELL, I HOPES YOU SUCKED HER GOOD, CUZ BESSIE GONE DIED AN' I'M HUNGRY.
ASS MEAT
STORY & ART SIMON FRASER
LETTERS THOMAS MAUER
AH, THE CORPOREAL BODY IS SO VERY FRAIL, IS IT NOT?
...
WELL, NOW THERE IS A PRETTY SIGHT TO TWO STARVIN' MEN...
WUT?
A VERITABLE HOOFED & HORNED FEAST ON FOUR LEGS.
IT'S A COW.
...AND RENDERED INTO IT'S CONSTITUENT PARTS, IT'S THE ANSWER TO A PRAYER.
YOU WANT ME T'SHOOT IT?
IF YOU WOULD.
RIGHT.
I'LL TRY TO PLACATE THE BEAST WHILE YOU READY YOURSELF...
NO NEED!
BANG

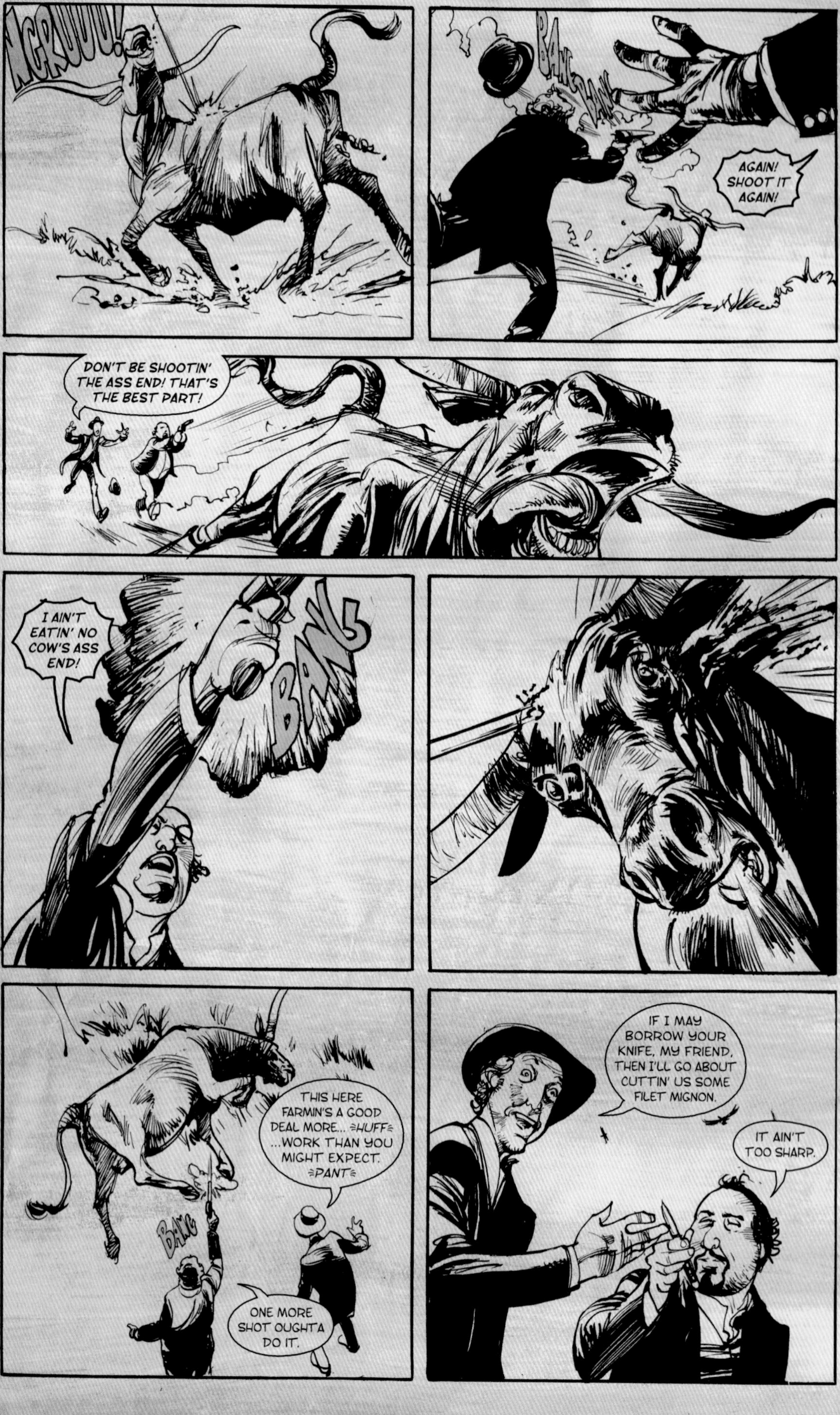
NGRUUU!
BANG BANG
AGAIN! SHOOT IT AGAIN!
DON'T BE SHOOTIN' THE ASS END! THAT'S THE BEST PART!
I AIN'T EATIN' NO COW'S ASS END!
BANG
THIS HERE FARMIN'S A GOOD DEAL MORE... HUFF ...WORK THAN YOU MIGHT EXPECT. PANT
BANG
ONE MORE SHOT OUGHTA DO IT.
IF I MAY BORROW YOUR KNIFE, MY FRIEND, THEN I'LL GO ABOUT CUTTIN' US SOME FILET MIGNON.
IT AIN'T TOO SHARP.

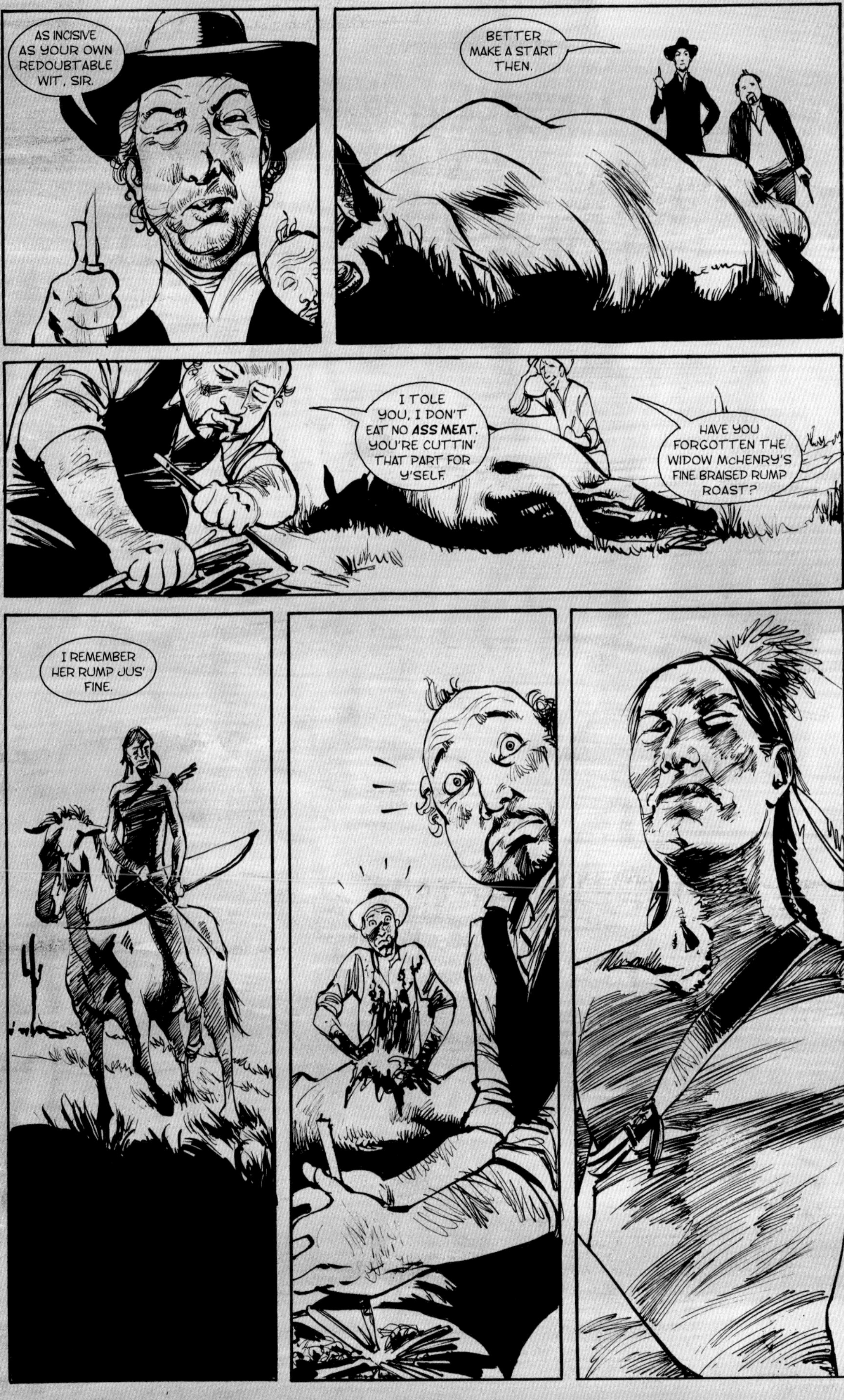
AS INCISIVE AS YOUR OWN REDOUBTABLE WIT, SIR.
BETTER MAKE A START THEN.
I TOLE YOU, I DON'T EAT NO **ASS MEAT**. YOU'RE CUTTIN' THAT PART FOR Y'SELF.
HAVE YOU FORGOTTEN THE WIDOW McHENRY'S FINE BRAISED RUMP ROAST?
I REMEMBER HER RUMP JUS' FINE.

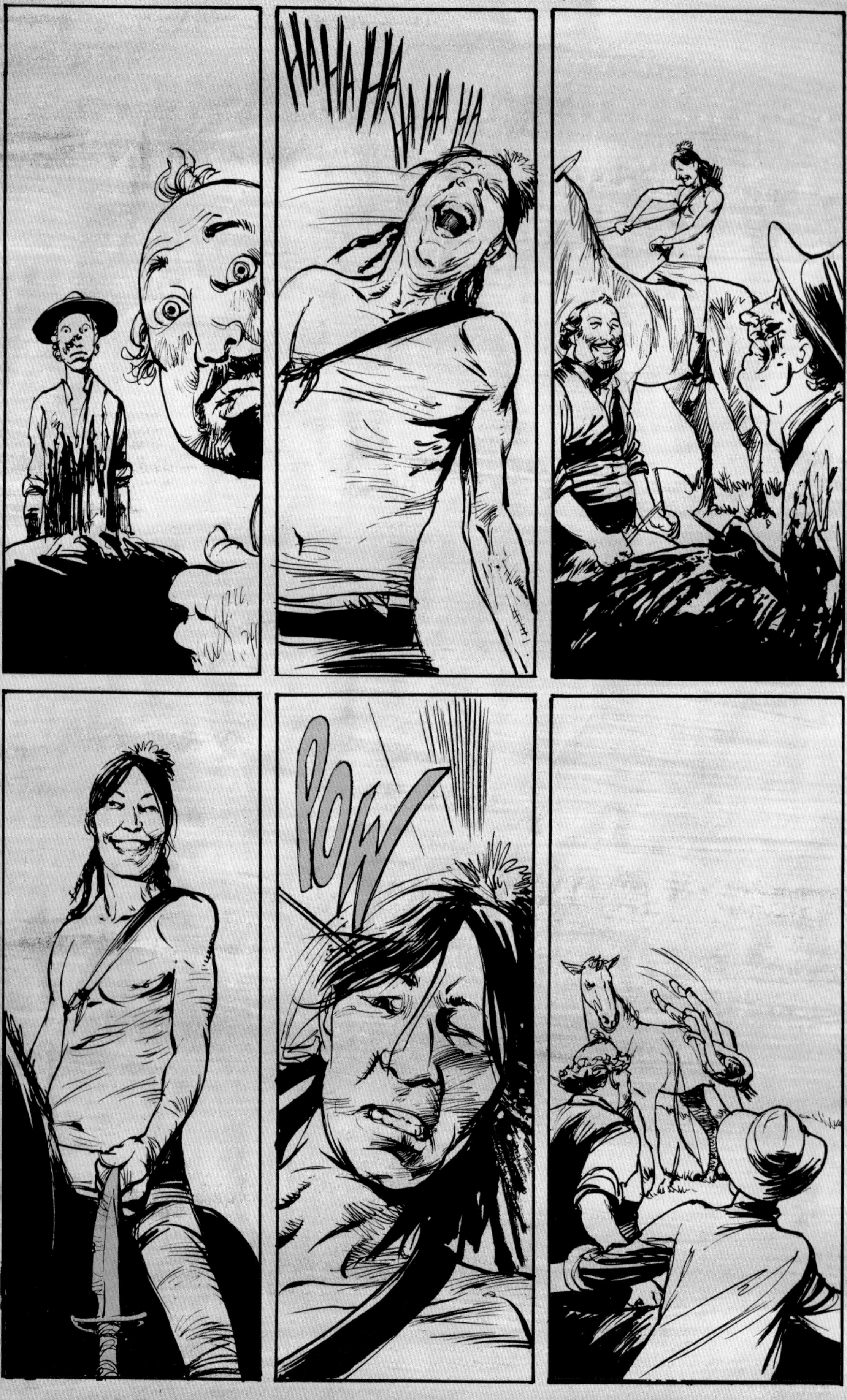
HA HA HA HA HA HA HA
POW

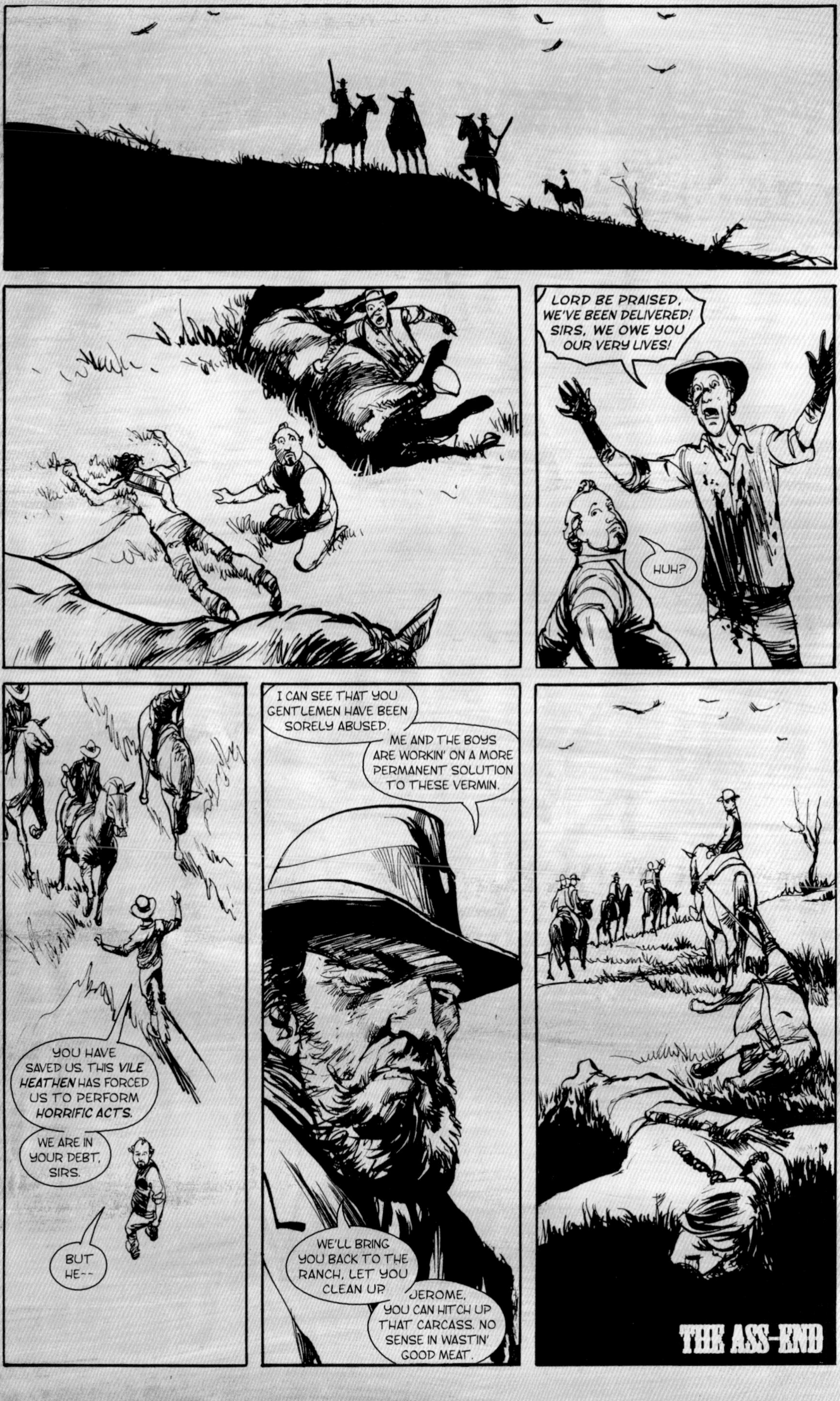
LORD BE PRAISED, WE'VE BEEN DELIVERED! SIRS, WE OWE YOU OUR VERY LIVES!
HUH?
YOU HAVE SAVED US. THIS VILE HEATHEN HAS FORCED US TO PERFORM HORRIFIC ACTS.
WE ARE IN YOUR DEBT, SIRS.
BUT HE--
I CAN SEE THAT YOU GENTLEMEN HAVE BEEN SORELY ABUSED.
ME AND THE BOYS ARE WORKIN' ON A MORE PERMANENT SOLUTION TO THESE VERMIN.
WE'LL BRING YOU BACK TO THE RANCH, LET YOU CLEAN UP.
JEROME, YOU CAN HITCH UP THAT CARCASS. NO SENSE IN WASTIN' GOOD MEAT.
THE ASS-END

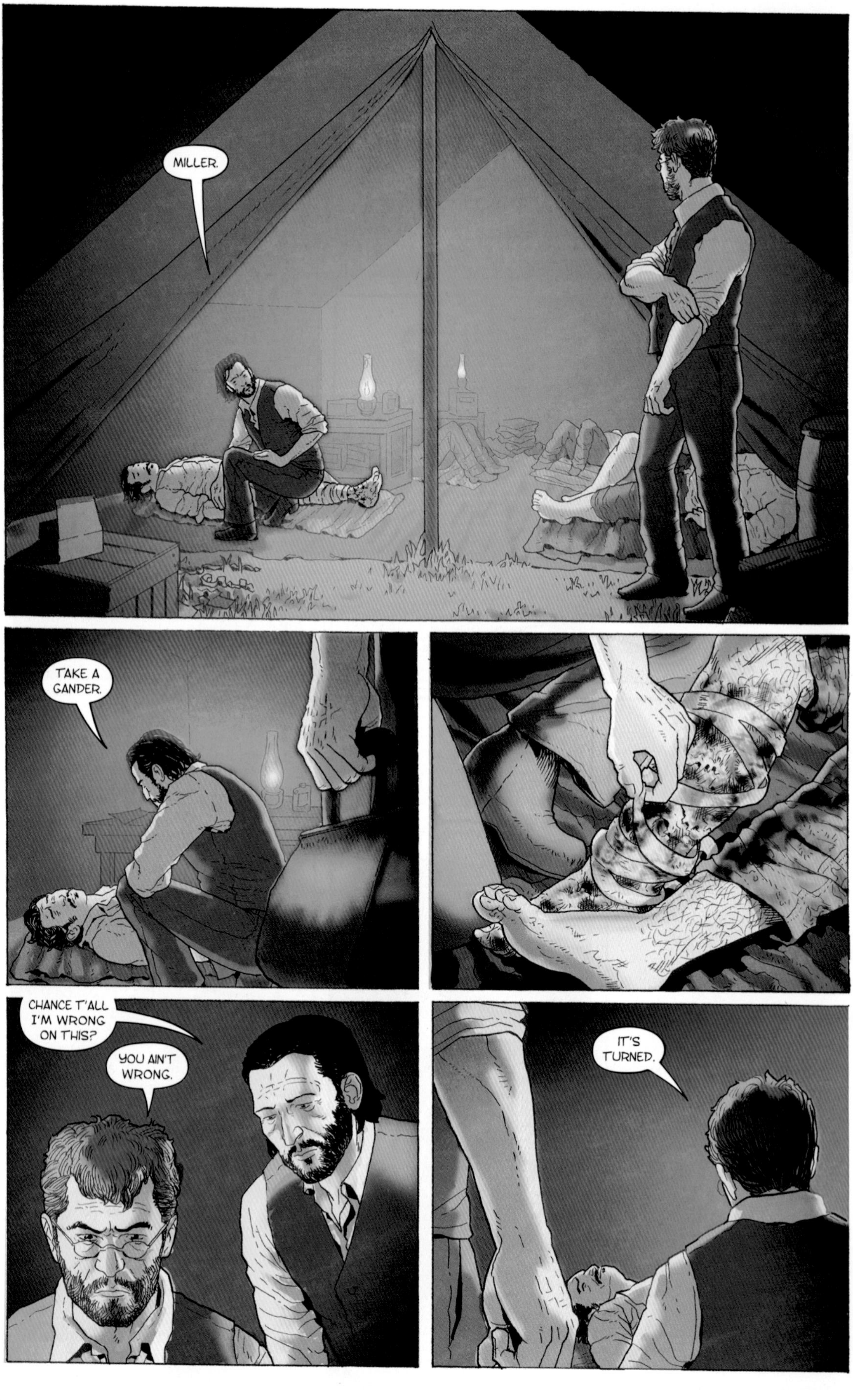
MILLER.
TAKE A GANDER.
CHANCE T'ALL I'M WRONG ON THIS?
YOU AIN'T WRONG.
IT'S TURNED.

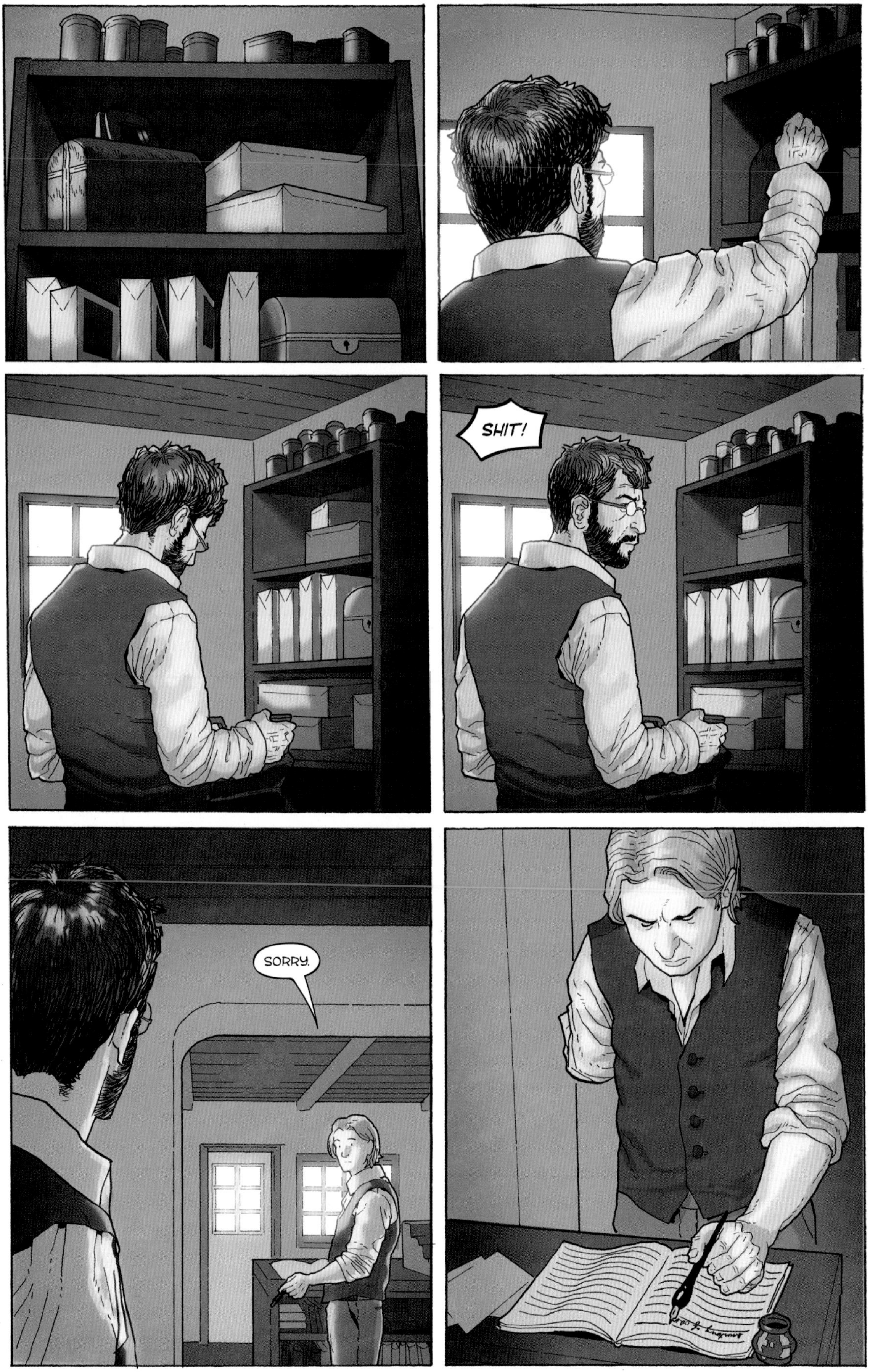
SHIT!
SORRY.

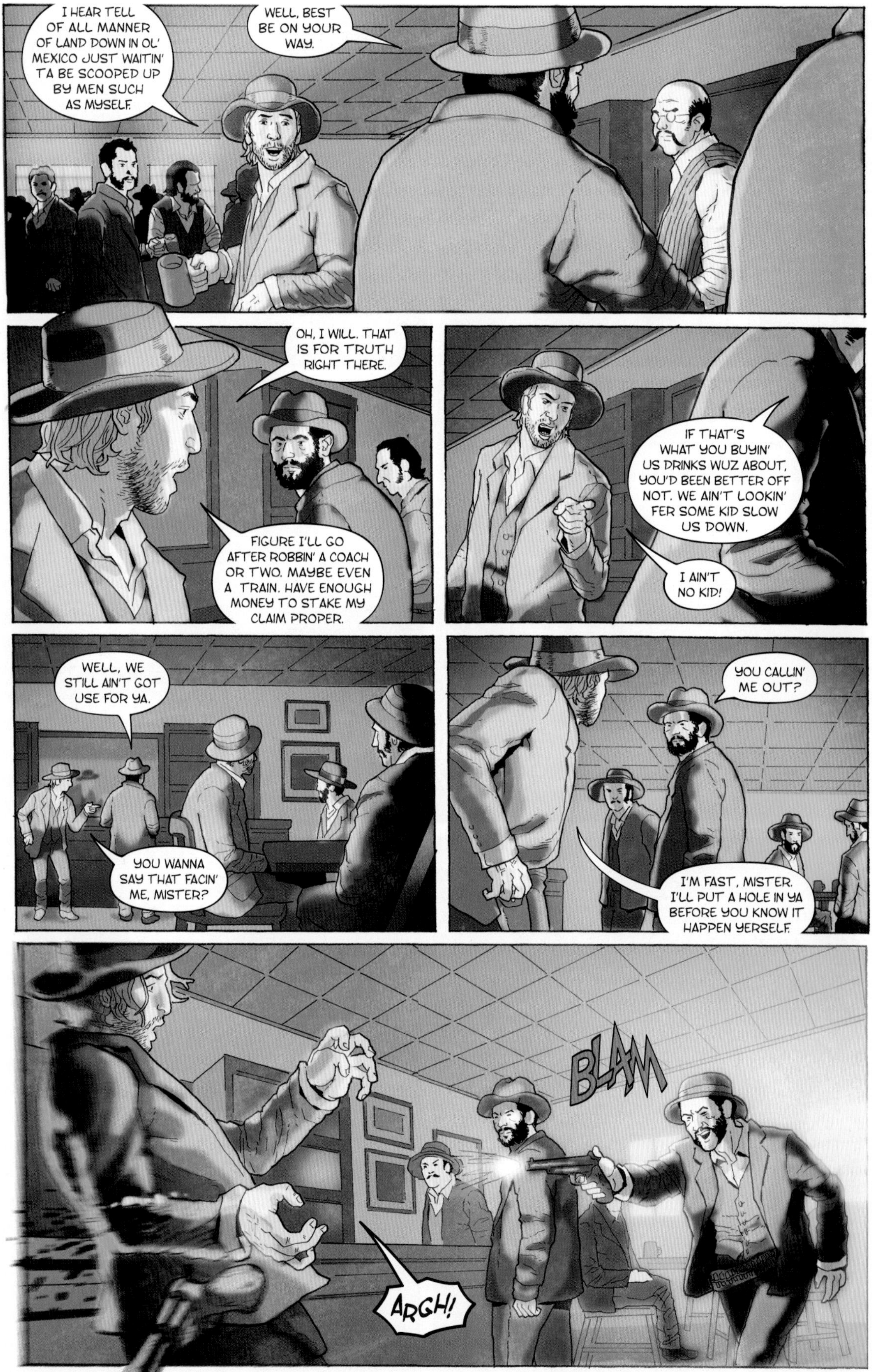
I HEAR TELL OF ALL MANNER OF LAND DOWN IN OL' MEXICO JUST WAITIN' TA BE SCOOPED UP BY MEN SUCH AS MYSELF.
WELL, BEST BE ON YOUR WAY.
OH, I WILL. THAT IS FOR TRUTH RIGHT THERE.
FIGURE I'LL GO AFTER ROBBIN' A COACH OR TWO. MAYBE EVEN A TRAIN. HAVE ENOUGH MONEY TO STAKE MY CLAIM PROPER.
IF THAT'S WHAT YOU BUYIN' US DRINKS WUZ ABOUT, YOU'D BEEN BETTER OFF NOT. WE AIN'T LOOKIN' FER SOME KID SLOW US DOWN.
I AIN'T NO KID!
WELL, WE STILL AIN'T GOT USE FOR YA.
YOU WANNA SAY THAT FACIN' ME, MISTER?
YOU CALLIN' ME OUT?
I'M FAST, MISTER. I'LL PUT A HOLE IN YA BEFORE YOU KNOW IT HAPPEN YERSELF.
BLAM
ARGH!

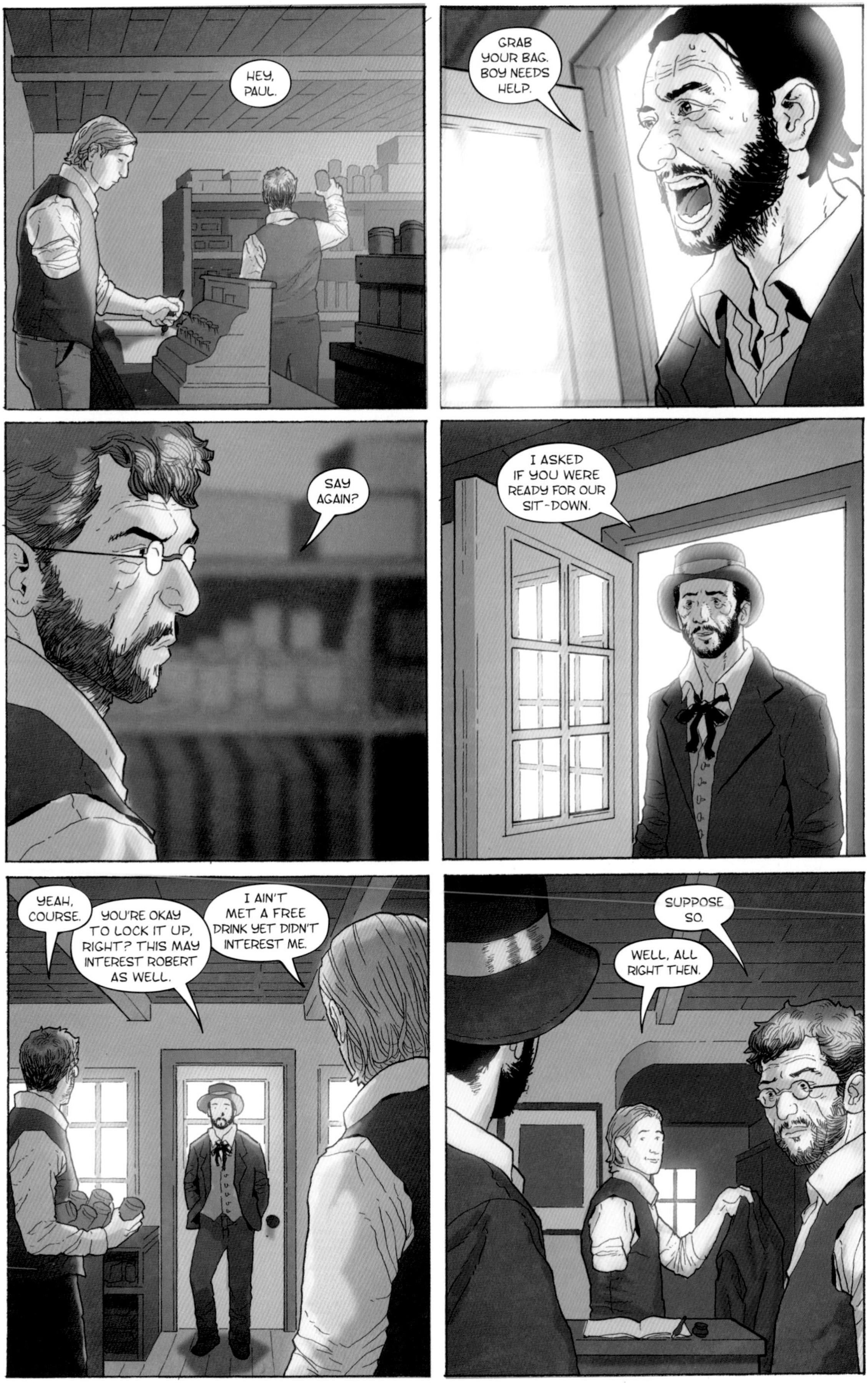
HEY, PAUL.
GRAB YOUR BAG. BOY NEEDS HELP.
SAY AGAIN?
I ASKED IF YOU WERE READY FOR OUR SIT-DOWN.
YEAH, COURSE.
YOU'RE OKAY TO LOCK IT UP, RIGHT? THIS MAY INTEREST ROBERT AS WELL.
I AIN'T MET A FREE DRINK YET DIDN'T INTEREST ME.
SUPPOSE SO.
WELL, ALL RIGHT THEN.

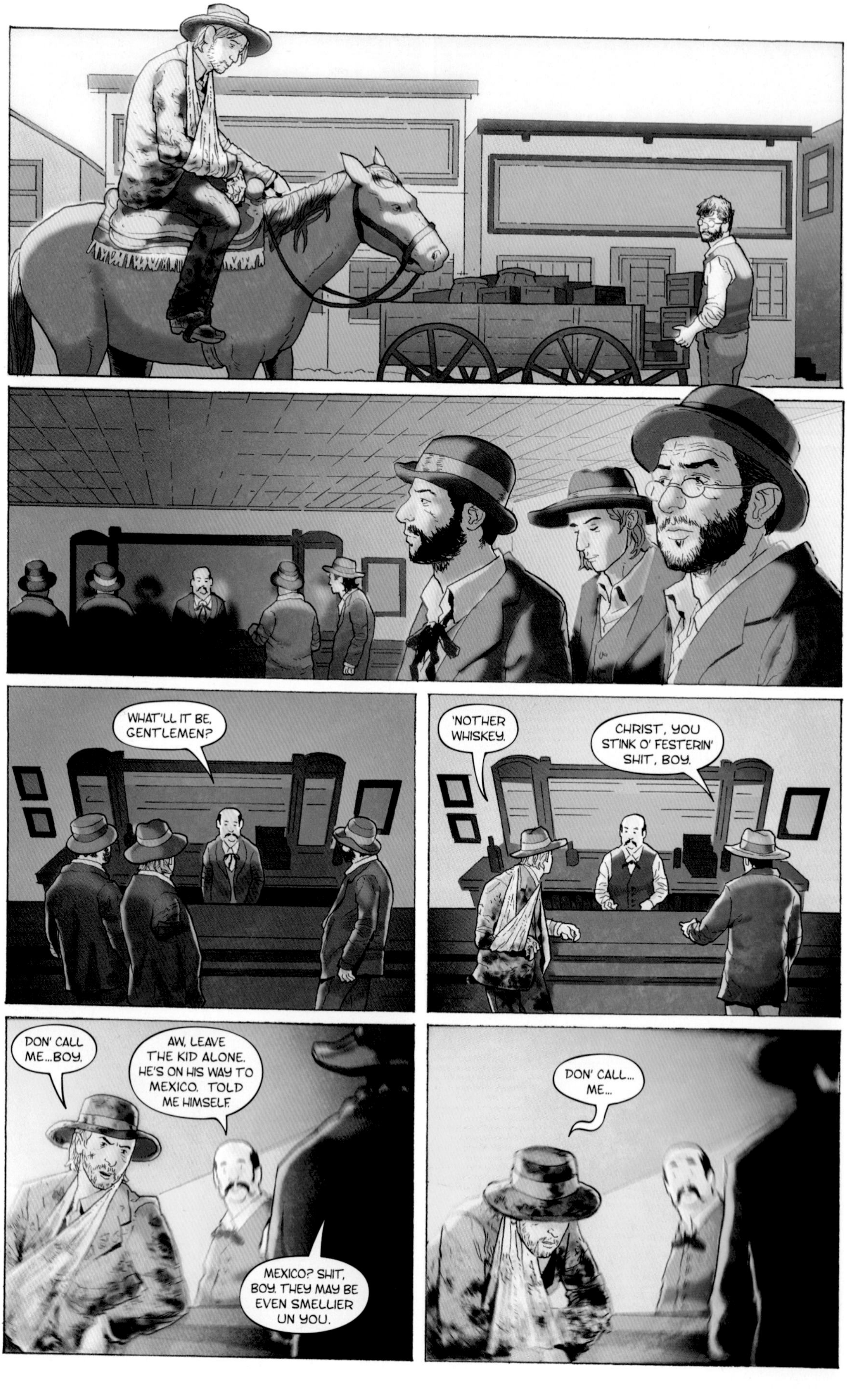
WHAT'LL IT BE, GENTLEMEN?
'NOTHER WHISKEY.
CHRIST, YOU STINK O' FESTERIN' SHIT, BOY.
DON' CALL ME...BOY.
AW, LEAVE THE KID ALONE. HE'S ON HIS WAY TO MEXICO. TOLD ME HIMSELF.
MEXICO? SHIT, BOY. THEY MAY BE EVEN SMELLIER UN YOU.
DON' CALL... ME...

THERE YOU GO.

OBLIGED.

YOU HEARD 'BOUT DOC LEWIS, I TRUST.

YEAH.

ROBERT?

HE'S GOIN' OFF TO LIVE WITH HIS DAUGHTER NOW THAT HE HUSBAND'S PASSED.

THAT IS WHAT I HEARD.

TOWN NEEDS A DOCTOR, PAUL.

BEST GET TO LOOKIN' THEN.

IS IT THE STORE? ROBERT SEEMS CAPABLE ENOUGH NOW.

WE CAN EVEN GIVE HIM HELP IF NEED BE.

WHAT?

THE BOY COLLAPSED IN THE SALOON. DOC AIN'T 'ROUND TO HELP 'EM.

WANT 'EM ON THE TABLE?

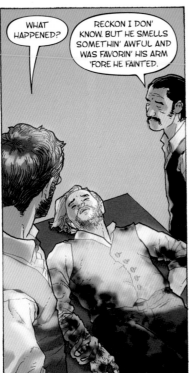

WHAT HAPPENED?

RECKON I DON' KNOW. BUT HE SMELLS SOMETHIN' AWFUL AND WAS FAVORIN' HIS ARM 'FORE HE FAINTED.

OH, HELL. BOY AIN'T CHANGED THIS RECENT, IF 'T ALL.

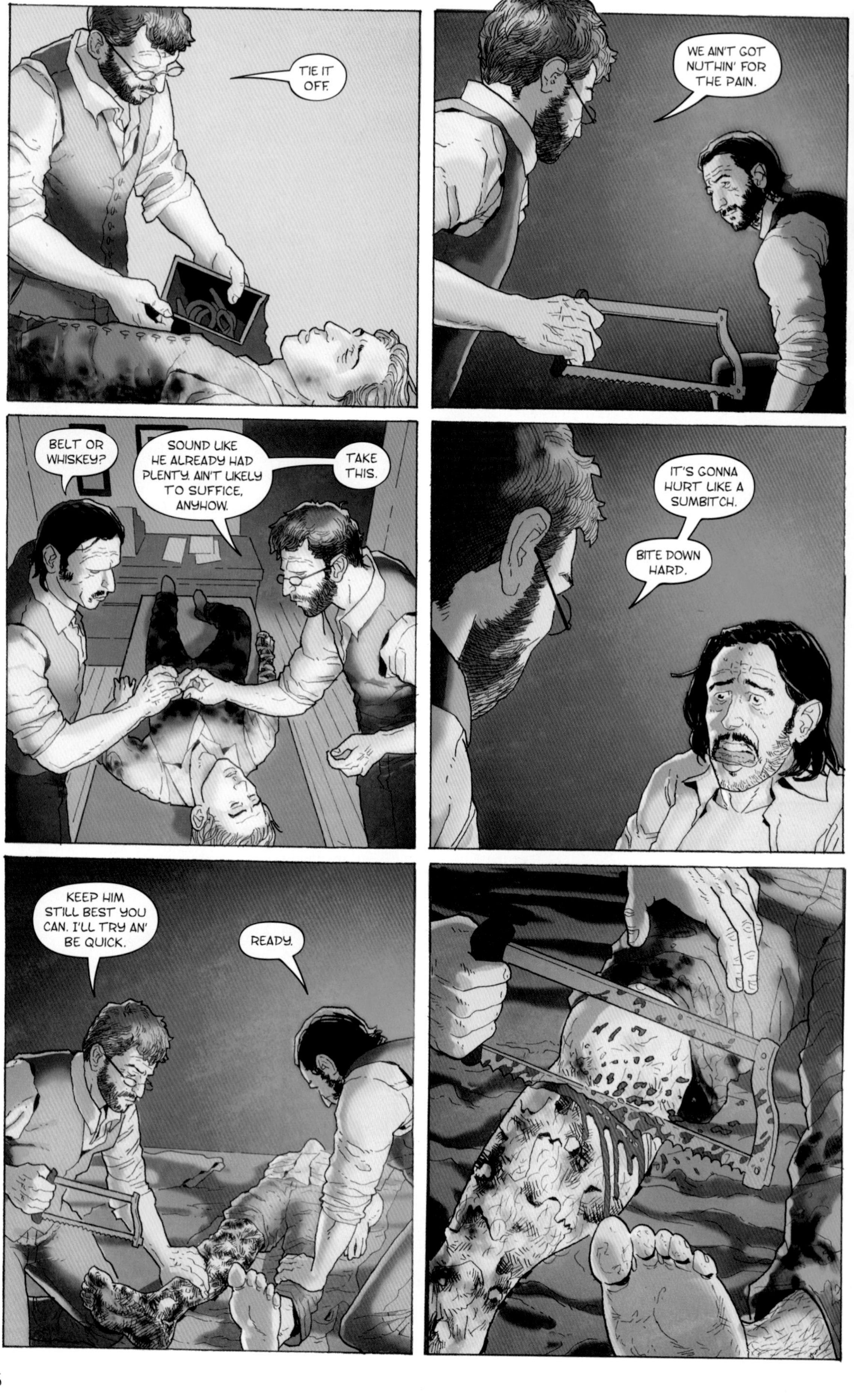
TIE IT OFF.
WE AIN'T GOT NUTHIN' FOR THE PAIN.
BELT OR WHISKEY?
SOUND LIKE HE ALREADY HAD PLENTY. AIN'T LIKELY TO SUFFICE, ANYHOW.
TAKE THIS.
IT'S GONNA HURT LIKE A SUMBITCH.
BITE DOWN HARD.
KEEP HIM STILL BEST YOU CAN. I'LL TRY AN' BE QUICK.
READY.

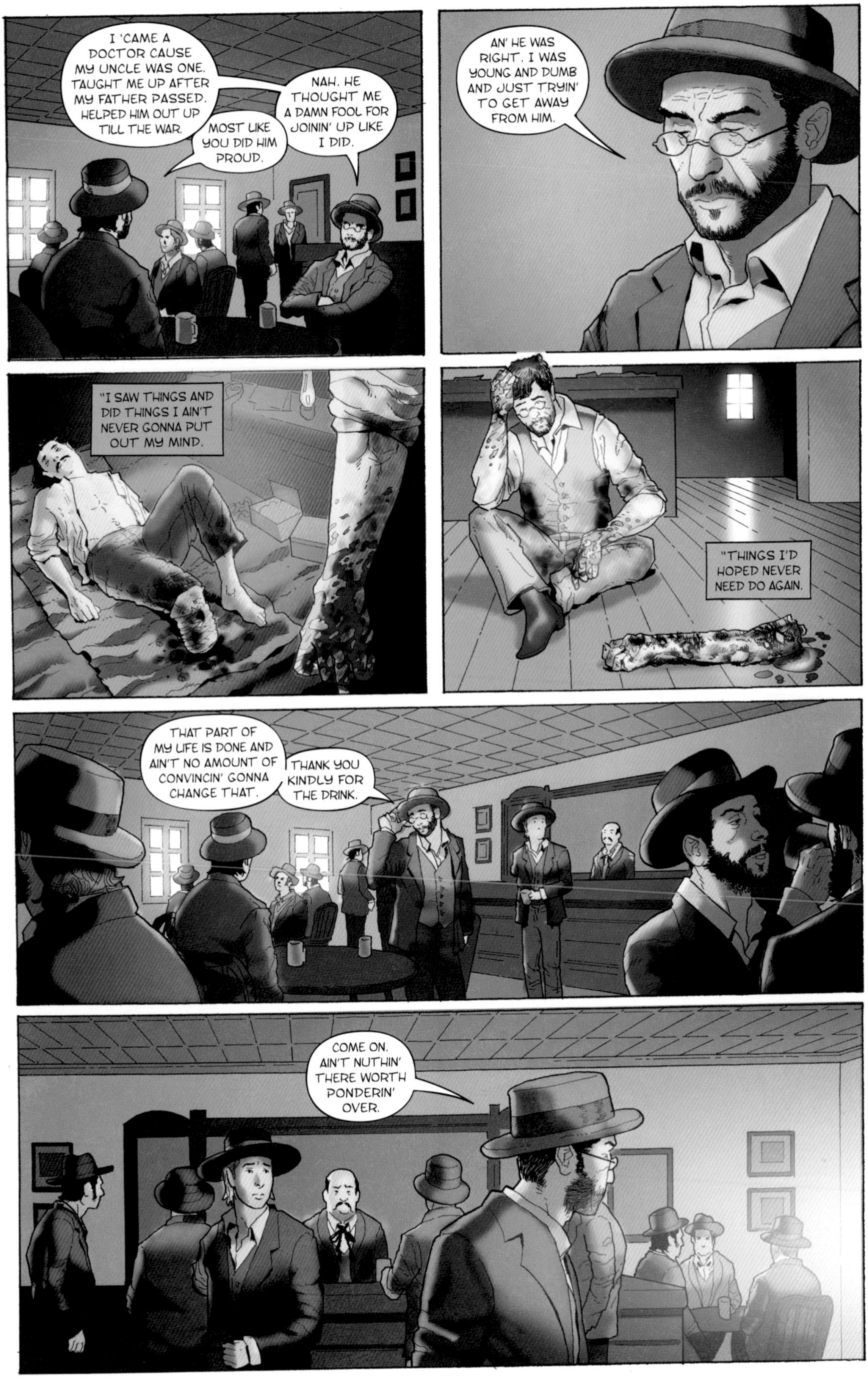

I 'CAME A DOCTOR CAUSE MY UNCLE WAS ONE. TAUGHT ME UP AFTER MY FATHER PASSED. HELPED HIM OUT UP TILL THE WAR.
MOST LIKE YOU DID HIM PROUD.
NAH. HE THOUGHT ME A DAMN FOOL FOR JOININ' UP LIKE I DID.
AN' HE WAS RIGHT. I WAS YOUNG AND DUMB AND JUST TRYIN' TO GET AWAY FROM HIM.
"I SAW THINGS AND DID THINGS I AIN'T NEVER GONNA PUT OUT MY MIND.
"THINGS I'D HOPED NEVER NEED DO AGAIN.
THAT PART OF MY LIFE IS DONE AND AIN'T NO AMOUNT OF CONVINCIN' GONNA CHANGE THAT.
THANK YOU KINDLY FOR THE DRINK.
COME ON. AIN'T NUTHIN' THERE WORTH PONDERIN' OVER.

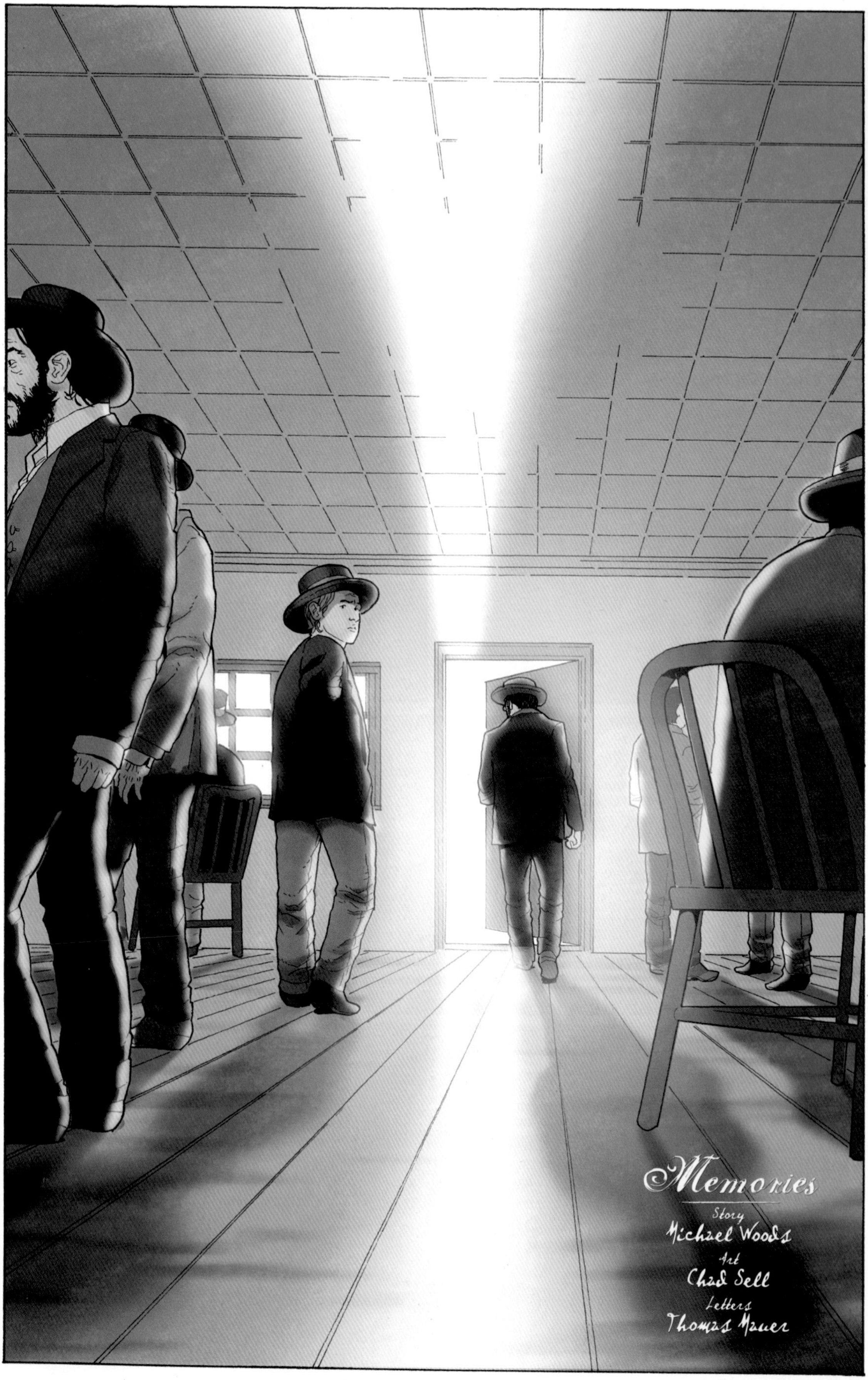
Memories
Story
Michael Woods
Art
Chad Sell
Letters
Thomas Mauer

In the next volume of Outlaw Territory:

BEHIND EVERY GUN
THE BALLAD OF J. GIRAUD
THE BROTHERS MacKENZIE
COLD BLOOD
DEAD MAN'S HAND
DEATH OF AN OUTLAW
THE FACE ON THE POSTER
FOREVER IS A LONG TIME
FRONTIER CONSUMPTION
LULLABYE
THE MAKING OF A LEGEND
REDEEMER
RUSTLING UP BUSINESS
SANTA FE
SAY YOU'RE DEAD
THE STRONGBOX
THEY'LL BURY YOU WHERE YOU STAND!
WHERE THE WHITE MAN CANNOT FOLLOW
THE WHORES OF TRINIDAD NEED WITNESSING TO
WILD ONE

(and more)